Intermediate Microeconomics

Intermediate Microeconomics
Price Theory and Applications

Robert B. Ekelund, Jr.
Auburn University

Richard Ault
Auburn University

D. C. Heath and Company
Lexington, Massachusetts   Toronto

Address editorial correspondence to:

D. C. Heath and Company
125 Spring Street
Lexington, MA 02173

Acquisitions Editor:	James Miller
Developmental Editor:	Pat Wakeley
Production Editor:	Bryan Woodhouse
Designer:	Kenneth Hollman
Photo Researcher:	Billie Porter
Production Coordinator:	Richard Tonachel
Permissions Editor:	Margaret Roll

Published simultaneously in Canada.

Printed in the United States of America.

International Standard Book Number: 0-669-28914-0

Library of Congress Catalog Number: 94-70647

10 9 8 7 6 5 4 3 2 1

For my students, by whom I have been taught

R. B. E.

For Emily, Rosebud, and my parents

R. A.

Preface

There is no reason that economics cannot be "fun" as well as useful. Too often, textbooks at this level are written in a dispassionate style and present technique without good examples—or *any* examples. Over many years of teaching microeconomics, we have discovered that the important thing in an intermediate textbook is the quality and readability of exposition, explanations, and examples. This approach, rather than a sterile presentation of theory, is the best way to reach students. Although microeconomic theory is basically the same in all books on the subject, *Intermediate Microeconomics: Price Theory and Applications* is different: intuition and applications, rather than mere technique, characterize our text. It offers a lavish use of interesting and appealing applications, issues, and social problems amenable to economic analysis. We wrote it for junior and senior students and for MBA or law school classes in microeconomics, and we believe that it provides relevant material that will capture student interest.

Organization

The book is divided into six Parts, and the presentation of basic price theory follows traditional lines. The introductory Part I presents the elements of theory, the importance of institutions, and property rights (Chapter 1) and a review of demand-and-supply theory (Chapter 2). Part II develops the elements of consumer choice, demand, and elasticity (Chapters 3 and 4), followed by a special chapter (Chapter 5) filled with applications relating to consumer behavior. Part III treats traditional production and distribution theory (Chapters 6 and 7). Competitive and imperfectly competitive market structures, including an introduction to game theory, make up the bulk of Part IV (Chapters 8–11). Once again, an applications chapter—this time dealing with industry structure—concludes the formal discussion of market theory. Part V (Chapters 12 and 13) examines input markets of all types, with a focus on labor markets. Issues relating to welfare, market failure, externalities, and public goods are treated in Part VI (Chapters 14 and 15). International trade and exchange are the focus of the concluding chapter (Chapter 16), although throughout the text we have included as much material as possible with an international flavor. Altogether, we have followed a fairly traditional sequence of microeconomic topics, but instructors who wish to emphasize particular areas (such as externalities or market failure) may do so without much loss of continuity.

Features

Several different kinds of features help to weave together the two kinds of material:

Text and Highlights. Economic interpretations and applications of theory appear in both the text proper and special boxed features called Highlights. Illustrations in the book are short and completely integrated with the text material. Examples range from minimum wage, immigration policy, and education-system "vouchers" (Chapter 5), team production (Chapter 6), political entry control (Chapter 9), and advertising (Chapter 11) to franchising (Chapter 12), transfer pricing (Chapter 12), and wage discrimination (Chapter 13). Highlights—up to four per chapter—illustrate theoretical material with important and relevant "real world" issues and introduce interesting new ideas that cannot be easily placed elsewhere. A small sample of these Highlights includes

- "The Impact of More Law Enforcement on the Drug Problem in America" (Chapter 2)
- "Choice, Marriage, and the Evolving American Family: Economics Meets Sociology" (Chapter 3)
- "Elasticity, Brand Allegiance, and Substitutes: Nicotine Patches and Health Foods" (Chapter 4)
- "The Culinary Arts: Production in the Kitchen" (Chapter 6)
- "Parking Spaces on Campus: The Allocative Function of Competition" (Chapter 8)
- "How Local Monopoly is 'Made': The Case of Cable Television" (Chapter 9)
- "Welfare, 'Workfare,' and the Labor-Leisure Tradeoff" (Chapter 12)
- "Salary Compression and the Issue of Age Discrimination" (Chapter 13)
- "Markets and Special Interests: In-Kind Payoffs and the Lobbying of State Politicians" (Chapter 14)
- "Will an Ivory Ban Save the African Elephant?" (Chapter 15)

Global Emphasis. This text significantly emphasizes the interface between microeconomic theory and the global marketplace. These very important and current topics are included in both text discussion (Chapter 16 is devoted completely to microeconomics and international trade) and text applications. See, for example, the Highlights entitled

- "Supply and Demand in the Sports-Car Market: Will the German Porsche Survive?" (Chapter 2)
- "Pay a Trifle for a Truffle: Calculating Elasticity in Dollars ($) and French Francs (FFr)" (Chapter 4)
- "First-Degree Price Discrimination: Kidney Transplants in Europe and India" (Chapter 9)
- "The Impact of Imports on Domestic-Market Competition" (Chapter 11)
- "Inventories and the Price of Space in Japan" (Chapter 13)
- "Taxes on Foreign Goods and Economic Welfare" (Chapter 14)

Emphasis on Law and Economics. Besides providing material on international matters, this textbook develops a clear, if brief, presentation of the roles played by property rights, laws, and regulation in modern price theory. Chapter 1, which introduces microeconomic theory, emphasizes the importance of the legal and institutional setting of economic systems, and a number of Highlights continue this theme throughout the book. Examples include

- "Law and Economics: Lose But Don't Lend Your American Express Card" (Chapter 1)
- "Jurors: The Last (?) American Conscripts" (Chapter 7)
- "Law, Economics, and Incentives: Legal Restrictions on Competitive Markets" (Chapter 8)
- "President Clinton and the Beekeepers: Imaginary Externalities" (Chapter 15)

Pedagogy and Student Self-Help. Each chapter opens with a general statement of the chapter's objectives and ends with a review of its main points. Each chapter also contains at least two sample questions and answers. These are followed by Questions for Review and Discussion—primarily relating to the technical material of the chapter—and Problems for Analysis, which challenge students to apply what they have learned. Each chapter provides twenty to thirty questions and problems; answers to about half of them are in the back of the text.

Supplements

Several excellent supplements, written especially for this text, are available:

John Keith Watson, University of Southwestern Louisiana, has written a *Study Guide* that will both assist and challenge the student. For each text chapter, the *Study Guide* provides a brief summary, study goals, a wealth of completion exercises, a checklist of key formulas, multiple-choice and essay questions, and analytical problems that develop the student's ability to work with graphs. The wide variety of question formats will encourage every student to master the basic concepts of microeconomics. Complete answers are provided.

The *Instructor's Guide and Test Item File* has been prepared by Franklin G. Mixon, University of Southern Mississippi. A full summary at the beginning of each chapter will help the instructor who wants a quick review of the material. Next come the answers to text questions and problems that are not answered at the end of the text. Each chapter concludes with approximately fifty multiple-choice questions suitable for examinations. Many of these require graphical analysis. Some (those indicated with asterisks) are picked up from the *Study Guide*.

The *Computerized Testing Program,* which reproduces the multiple-choice questions from the *Instructor's Guide,* allows instructors to create quizzes and exams tailored to their students' needs. The testing program's User's Guide explains how to select test items, how to modify those already on disk, and how to add items. It also explains how to request a random selection of items and how to print a test or the entire test bank. The *Computerized Testing Program* is available in MS-DOS and Macintosh versions.

Acknowledgments

This text was made possible by the help and cooperation of many people. Foremost, our thanks go to Professor Edward O. Price III of Oklahoma State University, whose assistance was tantamount to that of a co-author. His contribution to every chapter of the text, particularly to those on production theory, improved the book immensely, and many of the best examples came from him. We also acknowledge our former professors in microeconomics: Bill Breit, Trinity University; the late Charles E. Ferguson, Texas A & M University; Ed Olsen, University of Virginia; James P. Payne, Louisiana State University; Tom Saving, Texas A & M University; Bernard Sliger, Florida State University; and Bill Stober, University of Kentucky. Bob Tollison, George Mason University, has been a constant source of examples and ideas in microeconomic theory. We are also grateful to colleagues and friends at Auburn University who read parts of the manuscript: Andy Barnett, Randy Beard, Richard Beil, Bob Hebert, John Jackson, Dave Kaserman, Richard Saba, Henry Thompson, and Mark Thornton. We thank our present and former graduate assistants for their careful help. In particular, we thank George Ford, Federal Communications Commission; Paula Gant, Auburn University; Rand Ressler, University of Southwestern Louisiana; and above all Audrey B. Davidson, University of Louisville, who put portions of our manuscript through a trial run.

The following former students—many of them now professors themselves—challenged us, forcing us to state our arguments more clearly: Don Boudreaux, Clemson University; Mark Crain, George Mason University; Elynor Davis, Georgia Southern University; David Gay, University of Arkansas; Don Hooks, University of Alabama; John McCauley, University of Maine; Bobby McCormick, Clemson University; Franklin G. Mixon, University of Southern Mississippi; Margaret O'Donnell, University of Southwestern Louisiana; and David Saurman, San Jose State University. Cathy Kruse, a veteran of many projects, made our job much easier.

We thank the following reviewers, whose candid and perceptive comments helped make this a better book: Klaus G. Becker, Texas Tech University; David W. Boyd, Denison University; James Cobbe, Florida State University; Donald J. Cocheba, Central Washington University; Cliff P. Dobitz, North Dakota State University; Harry Ellis, Jr., University of North Texas; Keith Evans, California State University—Northridge; Paul G. Farnham, Georgia State University; Robert Fisher, California State University—Chico; Darrell Glenn, Providence College; Frederick Goddard, University of Florida; Mehdi Haririan, Bloomsburg University; Craig R. MacPhee, University of Nebraska—Lincoln; James Marchand, Westminster College; Jon R. Miller, University of Idaho; Julianne Nelson, New York University, Leonard N. Stern School of Business; Cliff Nowell, Weber State University; William F. Stine, Clarion University of Pennsylvania; Colin Wright, Claremont McKenna College.

Finally, thanks to developmental editor Pat Wakeley for much useful advice and to production editor Bryan Woodhouse for conscientious management of the project.

R. B. E.
R. W. A.

Contents in Brief

Contents

Intermediate Microeconomics

Introduction to
Microeconomic Theory

1

1

Exchange and Property:
An Introduction to Microeconomics

Svetlana, a Soviet housewife, had been standing in line since 6:30 A.M. outside a downtown Moscow market, waiting for bread and sausages. By 10 o'clock the November chill had begun to subside, but she had at least three more hours to wait. At 1:30, the door of the market opened and the manager poked his head out. No meats available but a little bread today! In disgust, nearly half of the 400 shoppers rushed away to lines at other markets, hoping to acquire products that they could use or sell on the black market. The store "manager," himself a black marketeer, signaled others to return later to pay outrageous prices for the minuscule amount of poor-quality meat that *was in fact* available. Svetlana stayed on — perhaps today she could at least get bread for her family's evening meal. Although such shortages were a major feature of life for the ordinary citizen, consumer durables such as automobiles, refrigerators, washing machines, and stoves were practically nonexistent except for the favored few of the Communist party bureaucracy. Such scenes, a daily part of life in the Soviet Union prior to 1990, were played out by countless Soviet citizens for the seven decades of communist rule.

The cataclysmic events in Eastern Europe and in the Soviet Union between 1989 and 1991 — when one communist regime after another fell to decentralized democratic processes — were among the most staggering world events of modern times. Was the Soviet Union truly an "evil empire," as depicted by President Ronald Reagan? Did the system collapse *because* it was "evil"? Did the desire for free and democratic leadership overwhelm the philosophical basis of communism? Was the refusal of the Soviet people to accept the rigors of communism simply a character defect that led to the destruction of the system? The most plausible answer is none of these. The end of communism almost worldwide was due to a complex combination of forces. New leadership in the Soviet Union is certainly a partial explanation, as is the emphasis on the production of war goods at the expense of consumer goods. But the *form* of the Soviet economic system was also a clear factor in the collapse of communism. It was the widespread inability of many Svetlanas to get their sausages that brought the system down. The system could not produce and deliver goods and services to millions of Soviet and Eastern European citizens with any degree of regularity and certainty. It collapsed for philosophical, cultural, and political reasons, to be sure, but also because it failed to use markets for efficient production, distribution, and exchange of goods and services.[1]

Microeconomics contributes to an explanation of the failure of economic systems such as that of the Soviet Union. It also tells the story of why a broad use of markets to produce, distribute, and exchange goods will beat a system of central planning in terms of improving average living standards. The long and often-painful transition to new institutions under which markets may flourish has begun in the old communist world. Microeconomic theory holds a key to understanding this transition and what might be expected from reliance on markets to "deliver the goods." Legal and institutional factors determine economic outcomes, including economic efficiency and wealth distribution. But the *questions* to be answered by any economic system — in effect, the problems any economic system is expected to solve in a world of ubiquitous scarcity — are exactly the same. We must consider these questions before tackling the nature of the institutions that underlie all economies and all forms of specialization and exchange.

Economic Problems and Economic Efficiency in a World of Scarcity

There are certain basic choices that every society must make; it must:

1. decide what mix of products and services are to be produced and how much of each to produce;
2. determine methods of production;
3. decide how the goods and services produced will be distributed among its members.

Economic efficiency in production — getting the maximum output of goods and services — is imperative since we live in a world where resources are scarce. Because of this **scarcity,** no nation or society is capable of producing

---

1. An Austrian economist, Ludwig von Mises (1881–1973), predicted the fall of communism *on grounds of economic functioning* in 1922. In his paper "Economic Calculation in the Socialist Commonwealth," Mises argued that money prices determined by supply and demand were necessary for rational economic calculation. His main point was that no economy could approach high levels of efficiency and development without a price system and free markets to guide resources into their most highly valued use.

goods and services in quantities sufficient to meet the desires of all its citizens. In this crucial context, it is also important to remember that *all* production and consumption carry an **opportunity cost** with them. The opportunity cost is the value of the most highly valued alternative that must be given up in order to produce or consume any good or service (see Highlight 1.1).

Highlight 1.1   *Time Is Money: Opportunity and Full Costs of Producing, Acquiring, and Consuming Goods*

Svetlana

The French have it right. Time *is* money. Time is a resource that constrains all human activities. From Svetlana standing in the queue at the Moscow market, to the production of new Saturn automobiles, to the vacation you take at the beach, to your consumption of a symphony, rock concert, or pizza for lunch, time is a scarce resource. Twenty-four hours, no more, no less, is allocated to production and consumption activities every day. You must "spend" your allocation, and however you spend your time, an opportunity cost is involved.

The decision by General Motors to produce a new product, the Saturn, entailed the use of an enormous quantity of physical resources. A major cost was the time spent by GM executives planning and executing the design and construction of the new plant and the new products. Even when existing salaried employees were used, the time they spent on the Saturn project prevented them from being productive on other GM projects. This loss of output was one of the major costs of the Saturn project to GM. In addition, the hundreds of millions of dollars that the production of the first Saturn automobile required were invested years before one nickel was returned in sales. Had this money not been spent on the Saturn project, it could have earned millions of dollars in interest. That forgone interest represents the time value of the money invested.

Opportunity cost applies to acquiring and consuming goods as well. The example of the Moscow housewife is apt in this regard. Line standing *always* bears an opportunity cost that is part of the full cost or price of acquiring goods or services. That cost is the opportunity cost of time spent in the process of acquiring those goods or services. Economists often approximate that value by an individual's wage rate in market work. If Svetlana could have earned 10 rubles an hour as a seamstress, the full price of the bread for her would be its nominal price plus 10 rubles times the number of hours spent in line. If Svetlana did not engage in market work, the implicit value of her time would have been its productivity in washing clothes, tending her small garden, or in walking, reading Tolstoy, or any other activity that brought her pleasure. *Opportunity cost does not have to be measured by a wage rate.*

Shortages created the long lines and high time costs at this Moscow meat market.

Finally, we all spend time consuming goods and services. Whether we choose fast food or a leisurely sit-down lunch, part of the cost of consumption is the time opportunity cost of eating it. Generally, as our incomes increase due to a higher hourly wage rate, we will choose patterns of consumption that economize on time as a scarce and fixed resource.[a] The rapid growth of fast foods, microwaves, and frozen dinners (along with a multitude of other products and activities) may be explained in this manner.

[a] Note, however, that a lengthier meal with increased enjoyment or fellowship may be more valuable and produce more satisfaction to some individuals. Those who get a lot of pleasure from shopping ("Shop till you drop" or "When the going gets tough the tough go shopping"!) may prefer leisurely shopping trips. The economist argues only that the net value of time must be considered.

In the face of scarce resources and unlimited wants, opportunity cost is an extremely important issue. There, the failure to solve any of the three basic economic problems efficiently lowers living standards for at least some members of society. Ultimately, economic efficiency is determined by the legal system and other institutions of a society, particularly those dealing with property, contract, and enforcement.

Production and Efficiency

Literally millions of different types of goods and services get produced each year in every country, including our own. Of all the different combinations of these goods and services that we are capable of producing, it is likely impossible to determine the one combination that best provides maximum satisfaction to our citizens. Because of opportunity costs, it is imperative that we avoid the serious error of producing a bundle that is inappropriate. If too many of our resources are devoted to agricultural pursuits, we may find overcrowded housing, even rampant homelessness, at the same time that crops lie unsold and rotting in the field. Similarly, if we fail to account for demographic changes in our society, we might find ourselves with excess capacity in our universities but with overcrowded hospitals and nursing homes.

Methods of Production The production of any good or service requires the use of productive inputs, and no country has sufficient resources to produce unlimited quantities of all goods and services. As more resources are used to produce one good — cars, for example — fewer are available to produce other goods, such as tractors. This is another example of opportunity cost: the production of any one good has a cost in terms of reduced production of other goods. By focusing on this cost, we can gain insight into the importance of economic efficiency in production.

Suppose that the decision has been made to produce 100,000 bushels of wheat. We need not be agricultural experts to understand that there are likely to be a number of different ways to produce this quantity of wheat. The more land we use, the less fertilizer we spread; the more fertile the land we use, the less farm equipment we need; the more farm equipment we use, the less farm labor we require. There are hundreds of ways to produce the quantity of wheat in question. Which is most efficient? It is the method that uses the bundle of inputs that is least valuable in producing other goods. Every method of producing the wheat has a cost; the most efficient method is the one with the lowest opportunity cost.

Economic efficiency is quite different from other technical definitions of efficiency. For example, some people extol the efficiency of U.S. agriculture by comparing our output per worker with that of other countries. On this basis we *do* look quite good, but when we consider output per unit of fertilizer used or output per unit of fuel used, we get a different picture. There is no universally most efficient way of producing things. In countries in which labor is relatively abundant and good land is relatively scarce (for example, Japan), it is efficient to use a lot of labor and very little land in agriculture; the reverse is

true in countries with less labor relative to arable land (for example, certain African nations or Australia). The farming techniques used in the United States are very different from those used in India, but both countries tend to use the technique that is most economically most efficient, given its resources.

Efficiency in Exchange When we consider the practical consequences of an inefficient distribution of goods and services, we see that it is of little use for a society to produce the correct mix of goods and services if it is unable to distribute them efficiently. To understand why, consider the effect of redistributing the goods that are already being produced and sold. For example, suppose that you go to the grocery store and buy $80 worth of groceries. However, when you drive to the front of the store to pick up your bags, the store employee mistakenly gives you someone else's groceries. When you get home and discover the mistake, you are almost certain to be disappointed. Instead of the bottle of red wine you had purchased to go with your steak, you find two bottles of diet root beer; in place of the potatoes, shrimp, and apples you had purchased, you find baby food and laundry detergent. Just as the reallocation of groceries disappoints you, it is likely as well to disappoint the person who receives your groceries. Your bottle of red wine may be small consolation to the parent who has to deal with children demanding their root beer.

Although a certain number of shoppers would benefit from this redistribution, the typical shopper would end up worse off. Because the value of a particular item differs among consumers, much of a good's value is destroyed if it is taken from a person who places a high value on the item and is redistributed to someone who places a much lower value on it. Therefore, it is imperative that goods be allocated to those who value them the most.

This example is not meant to imply that in centrally planned economies goods are arbitrarily distributed among individuals. Even in such economies, consumers have some say in their selection of goods. One way that they express their preferences is by deciding which lines to stand in. However, because centralized economic planners are reluctant to allow market prices to be used to allocate goods among consumers and because consumers are poorly informed about the availability of goods, inefficient distribution is inevitable.

In free-market economies, consumers are informed by advertising about the availability of goods. Also, to keep the good will of customers, business firms find it necessary to maintain adequate inventories of goods. Buyers therefore know in advance of their shopping what goods are available. In contrast, the Svetlanas in the Soviet Union had no way of knowing in advance what goods (if any) they could buy. As a consequence, they ended up buying bread when they wanted meat or size 10 shoes when they wore size 8.

Whenever goods are inefficiently distributed, it is possible to redistribute them (to make trades) such that all parties benefit. For example, on the same day that Svetlana goes out to buy meat and returns with bread, her neighbor Raisha might have succeeded in purchasing an unusually large quantity of sausage. In this case, an exchange of some of Svetlana's bread for some of Raisha's sausage would benefit both parties (see Highlight 1.2). However, in the old Soviet Union such exchanges were made difficult by laws that prevented private markets (called "black markets") from operating. Such laws prevented the achievement of **efficiency in exchange.** Efficiency in exchange, which is sometimes called *allocative efficiency,* is obtained when goods are distributed in such a way that any further exchanges, including exchanges involving cash, would harm at least one of the parties involved.

⚹ Highlight 1.2   *The Use of Markets to Allocate Faculty Offices: The Example of Arizona State University*

One task that is performed in every department in every university is the assignment of faculty offices. Although relatively little thought is given to this allocation, it involves decisions of some importance. All faculty members do not place the same value on having a comfortable or attractive office. Also, many faculty prefer an office near colleagues with whom they work or are particularly friendly and far away from certain colleagues with whom they do not get along. Therefore, allocation schemes that ignore faculty preferences fail to produce an efficient allocation. Despite this flaw, office assignments are almost always based on rank and/or seniority.

An article by William Boyes and Stephen Happel[a], economists at Arizona State University, examines different allocation schemes that were used when the College of Business moved to a new six-story building in 1983. That move caused entire departments to be relocated, and necessitated a completely new assignment of office space. Because the offices in the new building were not homogeneous (only half the offices had windows), office assignments did make a difference.

According to Boyes and Happel, different departments adopted different solutions to the allocation problem. The management department allocated its offices entirely on the basis of seniority — the person with the greatest number of years of service at ASU got the first choice, and so on. The marketing department and the accounting department did the same. This is not to say that the seniority system was universally defended within these departments. Many professors, particularly younger ones, felt that offices should be allocated on the basis of how much they were used, implying that at least some senior professors were seldom on campus and therefore had little "need" for a nice office.

The chairman of the finance department decided to avoid these criticisms, so he posted a sign-up sheet by his office door. Professors were then allowed to select offices in the order in which their names appeared on the sheet. This allocation scheme also received criticism on the basis that it unfairly rewarded professors who were inclined to roam the halls (and thus discover the sign-up sheet first).

The statistics department decided to avoid all these complaints by assigning offices randomly. They met and rolled dice to determine the order in

---

[a] William J. Boyes and Stephen K. Happel, "Auctions as an Allocation Mechanism in Academia: The Case of Faculty Offices," *Journal of Economic Perspectives* 3, 3 (Summer 1989): 37–40.

which they would select offices. However, many of the professors with pleasant offices in the old building fared poorly in this allocation scheme and objected loudly. The department head caved in, withdrew the initial office assignments, and reassigned space on the basis of seniority.

Boyes, the economics department chairman, asked for ideas from his faculty. Among the suggested criteria were seniority, age, height, research productivity, and weight in making the assignments. One person even suggested that they have a departmental "Wrestlemania," which essentially meant resorting to brute force to determine office space! Instead, the chairman created a market for offices. Faculty were given a period of time in which to submit sealed bids for offices. The policy was to allow the highest bidder to go first, the second highest bidder to select second, and so on. The proceeds of the office auction were to go to a fund for graduate student support.

When the bids were opened, the highest bid was for $500, and the second highest bid was for $250. Everyone who submitted a bid over $75 was able to obtain an office with a view; those who bid less ended up with an interior office.

According to Boyes, the only major complaint came from the winner, who was unhappy about paying twice what was necessary to secure the right to choose first. The others appeared pleased with the results — those who were willing to pay to get choice offices got them, and the remaining faculty were content with interior offices.

Based on this experience, the market allocation scheme was clearly superior to the alternatives used by the other departments. However, there remains considerable opposition to the use of markets. When word was leaked to the press that office space had been "sold," members of the public and university administrators expressed outrage. Had the proceeds not gone to a scholarship fund, the opponents likely would not have tolerated the free-market solution.

The Arizona State experience suggests that administrators should consider applying market solutions to allocation problems. For example, rooms in dormitories and in fraternity and sorority houses have to be allocated in some fashion. It might be possible to conduct a room auction in which bids are submitted for the right to select first. The proceeds could be donated to charity, added to a social fund, or be used to compensate "losers" in the room auction. In offices in which workers have to coordinate their vacations, an auction could be held to determine who gets first choice. People who jointly own vacation homes also could use an auction to determine which weeks go to whom. In the absence of an auction, every member of the group might well insist on enjoying the cottage on the Fourth of July. With an auction, each member has a financial incentive to avoid use during the most popular time periods. In this way, the use of markets brings cooperation to the group — not conflict.

Efficiency and Economic Organization

Factors such as the endowment of natural resources do, of course, play a role in determining the economic performance of nations. However, over the long haul, the economic success of any country depends crucially on its ability to produce an appropriate mix of goods, to produce those goods efficiently, and to distribute those goods in a sensible and efficient fashion. The purpose of studying microeconomics is to gain an understanding of how a market economy handles each of these problems. Indirectly, that understanding explains why economic problems were not solved successfully in countries, such as the former Soviet Union, in which markets were not allowed to function.

When we consider the operation of large economies like those of the United States, Japan, Poland, or Russia, we can see how overwhelmingly complex it is to solve basic economic problems. Given the millions of decisions that must be made and the informational demands of decision makers, it is clear that *perfect* economic efficiency is unattainable for *any* kind of society. However, some practical "working" systems are clearly more efficient than others. To attain efficiency, decision makers must have the *incentive* to make correct economic decisions. In addition, they must have the *information* they need to make these basic decisions. The critical factors underlying the solution to economic problems and the determinants of efficient solutions to the problem of scarcity are institutions, particularly legal institutions.

The Legal and Institutional Setting of Economic Systems

Economic efficiency — producing goods at lowest cost and exchanging goods so as to maximize the advantage of all traders — can be discussed only under some given set of institutions. Likewise, the three basic questions that every society must answer (What to produce? How to produce? For whom to produce?) are answerable only under the legal rules that determine rights, ownership, and obligations. But the forms of legal institutions regarding contracts, property rights, and their enforcement are central to the attainment of high or low economic efficiency. They guide production, exchange, and consumption in all economies.

Property Rights and Contracts

We exchange property every day. Billions of exchanges — contracts between exchanging parties — take place in the U.S. alone. Explicitly or implicitly, we make a contract when we supply labor. On the New York Stock Exchange, an average of 200 million trades take place daily. Svetlana made a contract when she bought bread. Our purchase of cat food at the supermarket is as much a contract as the agreement by a New Jersey electrical utility to buy a five-year supply of coal from a Montana mine. Throughout the world, in stock and commodity markets, bazaars, and resource markets, literally trillions of contracts are made every day. Property, a bundle of rights, is transferred through contracts in all cases.

The ability of individuals to make these exchanges rests on the system of property rights that has been established. Some societies feature **private property rights,** by which individuals and business firms have the right to own and transfer most goods or services. Other societies place a greater emphasis on **common or public property rights** by having property controlled communally or by the government.

Rights and Efficiency: The Tragedy of the Commons

The classic tale illustrating the economic efficiency of private versus public property rights is that of the so-called tragedy of common property. During the Middle Ages (between the tenth and fifteenth centuries) and at other times in history, much land was owned by monarchs and their local vassals. Some of the land was designated "commons" (as in the Boston Common or, implicitly, in the lobster fishery of the northeastern Atlantic coast) and was open to use by anyone. Clearly some of the land was better suited for tillage — for growing crops — and some was more suited for pasturage — for grazing cattle or sheep.

When the meadow in question is communally owned, no one can exclude others from its use. All members of the community regard the use of the land as "free" and of zero opportunity cost. A rush will be on to exploit the resource, because the price of using it is zero. Maximum demand (at a zero price) may lead to overgrazing and the ultimate destruction of the soil. This socially perverse incentive to overgraze or overuse communal resources is called the "tragedy" of common property.[2] The tragedy occurs when the failure to assign property rights to valued resources of any kind leads to the destruction or misuse of the resource. The tragedy exists today in the problems generated by common property resources such as fisheries and endangered species (see Highlight 1.3).

---

2. The tragedy of the commons may have been of critical importance in determining relative growth rates of countries. Given their resource endowments, for example, why did countries like England or the Netherlands grow relatively faster in terms of output than did others such as Spain or France? Property-rights assignments may help explain differences. See Douglas North and R. P. Thomas, *The Rise of the Western World,* (Cambridge, 1973), or in the case of Spain, Robert B. Ekelund, Jr., Donald R. Street, and Robert D. Tollison, "Rent Seeking and Property Rights Assignments as a Process: The Mesta Cartel of Medieval-Mercantile Spain" (unpublished manuscript, 1993).

Highlight 1.3   *Biology, Anthropology, and Property Rights: Economics and Extinctions*

In these days of increasing environmental concerns, economists have become very familiar with problems created by common property and the "tragedy of the commons." In economics there is an extensive body of research and literature, based on self-interested human behavior, that explains the common-property-rights basis for acid rain, overfishing, water pollution, and global warming. These problems may arise whenever property rights are undefined or poorly defined and wherever individual costs or benefits for some activity differ from the society's costs and benefits.

For example, fishermen in the Gulf of Mexico do not set out to destroy or endanger fish or turtle populations. But because property rights are not specifically defined, each individual fisherman has little incentive to conserve. Property is acquired on a "first-come, first-served" basis, and the actions of many individual fishermen have, in many cases, seriously reduced present and future catches, which imposes costs on society. However, the cost to each individual of overfishing is essentially zero. If one reduces his catch today, another is likely to increase his tomorrow. Therefore, individual efforts to conserve are fruitless.

Biologists and anthropologists have discovered numerous, "primitive" environmental problems that were caused by a failure to establish private property rights. The disappearance of the North American Anasazi Indians from Chaco Canyon in New Mexico apparently resulted from the systematic deforestation of the areas surrounding it (they failed to conserve or replant trees). The moa, a flightless bird that laid large nutritious eggs, disappeared from New Zealand for the same reason. The wooly mammoth and countless other species were "overkilled"[a] and became extinct.

Solutions for these problems today depend, in part, on a case-study approach to past problems and on the scientific understanding of biological characteristics of populations in the case of reproducible plants and animals. But solutions also depend on the ability of political or legal processes to devise efficient and effective approaches. Taxes, subsidies, production quotas, positive incentives, and rules and regulations of all types have been tried with varying degrees of success.

Most economists advocate legal assignment of property rights where possible. The owner of moas would have had an incentive to preserve stocks for reproduction, whereas no one conserves when it is personally costly and of low benefit to do so. The same is true of gorillas, redwood trees, deer, and oysters. For obvious reasons, no one worries much about the extinction of dairy cattle

---

[a] See Jared Diamond, "The American Blitzkrieg: A Mammoth Undertaking," *Discover* (June 1987), and "The Golden Age that Never Was," *Discover* (December 1988).

Private property rights and the ability to enforce those rights means that sheep, in contrast to common-property resources (such as, say, sandhill cranes, which belong to the public at large) will be preserved and conserved.

Privatization

because legal rights to them are clearly defined. Economist Frederick Bell, for example, studied the varying rights and restrictions assigned to lobster fishermen in different states along the Atlantic Coast.[b] He concluded that those states in which lobster fishing was most productive (in terms of catch and regeneration of the resource) were states that placed limits and territorial restrictions on lobster fishermen. (This definition of rights might be termed "privatization."[c]) Looser definitions of rights were less productive, and no definition of rights (open season on lobstering all year) was the least productive in terms of catch and yield.

[b] See Frederick W. Bell, "Technological Externalities and Common Property Resources: An Empirical Study of the U.S. Northern Lobster Fishery," *Journal of Political Economy* (January–February, 1972): 148–58.

[c] The term *privatization* is also used to refer to the return of certain functions of governments, especially local governments, to private enterprise. Thus the city of Stockdale, Arizona, is said to privatize garbage collection when it turns over exclusive municipal rights to supply services to competing waste-collection companies, who charge users of their services directly. The "right" reverts to private industry.

Although an exact definition of property rights is not possible in all cases (for example, a three-mile x three-mile, policed fishing area for Joe or Sally), a holistic approach is called for in important cases such as acid rain, global warming, and elephant extinction. Such an approach must enlist the combined talents of biologists, paleontologists, anthropologists, legal experts, political scientists, and economists.

Now consider what would happen if someone actually owned and had control over a particular meadow that was best suited for tillage. Private property rights would replace communal rights. Because the owner can now exclude nonpayers or nonrenters of the land, a positive price will be charged to those who would use the land for grazing sheep. That price (or rent) will be equal to the opportunity cost of using the land in its next best alternative — raising crops. Potential renters of the land as pasture would not pay such a rent, because the land has a lower value as pastureland. The land would therefore be placed in its best use. The assignment of private property rights means that property will be used efficiently — that is, in its highest-valued use.

This example may at first seem to have little relevance to the modern world, but it is central in understanding how economies reach economic efficiency. In the United States and in other "capitalistic" nations, property is, for the most part, privately owned. This means that individuals are free to select their occupation, enter into contracts, and purchase or sell whatever goods or services they desire in a price system in which prices reflect opportunity cost. If they operate a business at a profit, the profit is theirs to keep; if they incur a loss, the money comes from their pockets or from their creditors. In such a system, the rule of law is primary and the role of government is limited.

Property rights also existed in the Soviet Union prior to its dissolution. Property, after all, is always under *someone's* control. But *private* property rights were severely limited; rights over property were placed largely in the hands of the secretary general of the Communist party. Within this nexus, the leader of the party dispensed with rights as *he* saw fit, rewarding party loyals and bureaucrats with largesse and punishing dissidents. The common people (such as Svetlana) had few property rights beyond the barest private control over their own labor. When one can own nothing, including land, house, tools, or anything of substance, one cannot contract to transfer anything.[3] Thus market-style contracting was minimal and economic efficiency was dismal.

Although communal property hinders economic efficiency, there are many countries in the world with even less efficient systems of property rights. Some

3. See George Melloan, "Coase Was Clear: Laws Can Cure or Kill," *Wall Street Journal,* October 21, 1991, p. A19, for further discussion of this point.

societies have experienced such a breakdown in respect for the law that property rights effectively do not exist. Theft and pillaging become common, and property falls into the hands of those who are most willing and able to use force. Property rights virtually cease to exist.

In such a society, most property loses all its value, because the costs of guarding a piece of property are too great. A family that "owns" a cow will choose to kill the cow and quickly eat it before the animal or the meat is stolen. The incentive to produce goods or services is essentially nonexistent. Why spend time producing something when the finished good is almost certain to be stolen?

One has only to look at the current situation in Somalia to see the connection between property rights and economic efficiency. The government of that country collapsed around 1990 and was replaced by competing factions headed by "warlords." The warlords and their followers were well-armed and perfectly willing to seize whatever they wanted. As a consequence, individuals in the country ceased to have property rights. Within a short period of time, hunger and starvation became a fact of life in Somalia. Drought was a contributing factor, but even in parts of the country in which rainfall was normal, agricultural production fell precipitously. The reason was that farmers simply had no incentive to produce food that would only be stolen by the warlords. When international relief agencies finally came to the aid of Somalia, the warlords stole the supplies sent to the country. The situation appeared so hopeless that the United States sent troops to the country late in 1992, first to provide protection for the relief agencies and then to help reestablish a government that could protect property rights.

Rational Decision Making

Decisions, whether made by factory managers in the Soviet Union, warlords in Somalia, or by households or business owners in free-market societies, are all *rational*. By rational, we mean that the decision maker attempts to maximize net benefits. In order to maximize net benefits, all decision makers pursue activities until the marginal benefits no longer exceed the marginal costs — **marginal decision making.**

For example, a consumer decides how many baseball tickets to purchase by comparing the marginal benefit he receives from the tickets (the extra satisfaction from viewing an additional game) with the marginal cost of the tickets (the price of $13). (To keep things simple, we will ignore the time costs of the games.) A fan who chooses to buy tickets to ten games per year reveals that the marginal benefit of each of the ten games is $13 or more. In deciding not to buy a ticket to an eleventh game, the fan reveals that the marginal benefit of that game is less than $13. Similarly, the manager of a grocery store decides how many cashiers to employ in the check-out line by comparing the marginal benefit with the marginal cost for each successive employee. Additional workers are worth employing if, by reducing customer waiting time, they increase sales sufficiently to produce owner benefits that exceed the costs of their salaries and fringe benefits.

In examining economic behavior in the former Soviet Union, we make exactly the same assumption about individual choice. Svetlana's decision about how long she is willing to stand in the bread line is also a marginal decision, as is a Soviet manager's decision about how many check-out clerks to hire.

Why do "rational" decisions lead to inefficiency in Soviet-type economies but to efficiency in market economies? The answer is that the costs and benefits faced by decision makers under central planning fail to reflect economic reality. The bread that Svetlana waits in line to buy is priced well below its production costs. Because of its artificially low price, Svetlana has an incentive to attempt to consume "too much" bread. Similarly, the Soviet manager is not paid from profits made by his enterprise, so he has no incentive to economize in hiring employees.

Of course, although there are undoubtedly times when decision makers fail to act rationally, economists tend to ignore such behavior. When engaging in economic analysis, we always consider how a "rational" individual will act in a given situation. Economists expect individuals to act rationally most of the time and place their bets on such behavior. Whereas other disciplines consider a myriad of factors (tradition, power, status, and so on) that influence individual choice, economics focuses on costs and benefits on the margin. Other factors are viewed as relevant only to the extent that they affect perceptions of benefits and costs.

Rules and Rule Changes: Incentives Matter for Economic Efficiency

Property-rights assignment and freedom to contract directly determine economic efficiency. Microeconomics, the primary focus of this book, always takes such institutions as the backdrop to market functioning. But property-rights assignments to achieve efficient, low-cost exchange are, in particular cases, extraordinarily tricky. Although the evolution of private property rights in Western nations has *generally* proceeded along the lines of economic efficiency, the goal of efficiency has remained quite elusive. Consider how market functioning and the concept of efficiency — the very heart of microeconomics as expressed in this book — are inextricably bound with law, the assignment of property rights, and liability.

Economic Efficiency and Rights Assignment

Any rights assignment carries with it an incentive structure that will produce more or less efficiency. Suppose that Dot, a student, owns a bicycle. This means that she has complete and exclusive property rights over the bicycle in terms of use. Naturally, Dot must take precautions, such as locking the bike to a stand, storing it in a secure garage, registering it with her local police department or with the university police. Suppose that, despite such precautions, someone steals Dot's bike. Does she still own rights to that bicycle? Should she, for the sake of economic efficiency, still own rights to it? Read on.

Now, suppose that Yvonne, also a student, does not own a bicycle but is interested in buying a used one. Still another student at the university, Fred, is known to sell used bikes from time to time. Yvonne goes to him and he offers to supply her with a slightly used but freshly painted Schwinn for $200. He assures her that his bicycle operation is strictly legal — that is, that he can legally transfer this property. Yvonne immediately enters into a contract with Fred to buy the bike. Later in the week, the university police confiscate the bike and return it to Dot. Fred, Yvonne discovers, has withdrawn from school and is nowhere to be found. Who owns the bike: Dot, the original owner, or Yvonne, the good-faith purchaser?

We are immediately tempted to say that Yvonne (who *does* have recourse against fraudulent Fred) must give up the bike, which should be returned to its "rightful" owner Dot. In virtually all American legal jurisdictions, the law would mandate this result, but under most European law, the good-faith purchaser (Yvonne) would acquire property rights. In terms of economic efficiency, however, either result might be the desired one in a particular situation. Any rights assignment (to Dot or to Yvonne, in our case) carries with it **incentives.** In the case at hand, incentives exist, both for Dot to protect her property and for Yvonne to verify her ownership. There is a cost, however, to both parties. For Dot, there is the cost of protecting the bicycle against theft. There are the money costs of locks, registration fees, having her social security number embossed on the bike, and so on. Add to these the opportunity cost of her time in always locking the bike to a post or tree, contacting the police, or putting the bike away in her garage.

Yvonne also must spend resources in terms of money and time to verify that Fred has legal title to the bicycle. She must obtain assurances from Fred and from the police that the bicycle is not stolen property. The cost of verifying Fred's ownership and legal authority to transfer the property may be substantial.

For economists, the key issue is efficiency, which in this case means property-rights assignment to reach the lowest sum of costs across parties to the exchange. If Dot's costs of protection are lowest, the law should be written so that the good-faith purchaser (Yvonne) acquires title against Dot. If Yvonne's costs are lower, the owner should retain title against the good-faith purchaser (Yvonne). Here the law must apportion or weigh the risk that a good-faith purchaser (Yvonne) will acquire stolen property. That risk will either fall on the initial owner or the good-faith purchaser.[4] Note that the economic solution

4. See Robert Cooter and Thomas Ulen, *Law and Economics* (Glenview, IL: Scott, Foresman, 1988), pp. 152–53, from which this example is extracted.

does not bring in normative concepts of justice, feelings, or rights. Dot may be a millionaire and Yvonne a poor struggling student. These factors would be irrelevant in the narrower sense of economic efficiency. Economic efficiency would require different assignments of property rights in each case, although the law and practice goes far in the direction of efficiency[5] (see Highlight 1.4). The essential point is that the legal system — especially those parts of it dealing with property and the conveyance of property through contracts — assists individuals in conducting private relationships. All such assignments and legal rules respecting contracts will carry economic incentives with them that will either promote or thwart efficiency.[6] Administrative reform and legislative rule changes may also affect economic efficiency and social goals (see Highlight 1.5).

Highlight 1.4   *Law and Economics: Lose but Don't Lend Your American Express Card*

Occasionally we confront liability laws that, at first blush, do not make a lot of sense. Take credit cards. So many people, including students, use them often. Should you have to convince a clerk of the "validity" of your card — that you have sufficient credit to cover a purchase? Or should the company be responsible for verifying your credit status? Should your liability be different when (1) you lose your credit card or (2) you lend your card to a friend who runs up your charge to the absolute limit without your permission? Different incentives and costs are attached to each system.[a]

The law in fact is the following: by law, you are liable for only $50 if you lose your card or if it is stolen. (In fact, you can avoid even this liability if you notify the card company promptly.) However, if you lend your card to a friend to charge a $25 meal and she charges $1,000 on the card, you are liable for it all.

There is sound economic logic behind this rule. In situation 1, the unauthorized use of the card gives financial institutions a powerful incentive to

---

5. Devices have, of course, emerged that help minimize the costs of property protection and of verification in exchange transactions, especially for valuable items. Automobile and home transactions must be registered and recorded. In some communities police keep records of property of lesser value, such as TVs, VCRs, and bicycles. Some police departments provide low-cost services for verification of property as well.

6. Torts, yet another branch of law, deals with the apportionment of losses between potential injurers (say, drug companies) and potential victims (in this case, potential users of a dangerous drug) where the *ex ante* transactions, or bargaining costs between the parties to the exchange, are prohibitively high. There has been a big push on the part of politicians to restrict economic and punitive damages in such cases, but there may be little economic justification for such limits in terms of economic incentives: see Mark F. Grady, "Torts: The Best Defense Against Regulation," *Wall Street Journal,* September 3, 1992, p. A11.

develop new technology for verifying credit. Because they are in the best (that is, the *lowest-cost*) position to do so, liability should be placed on them for such unauthorized use of your card. However, in situation 2, *you* are in the low-cost position to monitor the truthfulness and behavior of a friend or an employee (in the case of a business).

Such legal rules are set to maximize economic gain for all market participants, cardholders, merchants, and banks that issue cards. They do so by establishing appropriate incentives to reduce the costs of exchanging goods and services.

[a] This example is adapted from Robert Cooter and Thomas Ulen, *Law and Economics* (Glenview, IL: Scott, Foresman, 1988), p. 153.

Highlight 1.5 *British Transportation of Prisoners to Australia*

Legislation and bureaucratic administration of rules and regulation in addition to the law may be used to channel incentives and interests in order to achieve economic and/or social ends. This principle was first noted by the nineteenth-century British philosopher Jeremy Bentham (1748–1832) and his reformist secretary Edwin Chadwick (1800–1890). In their zest to bridge the gap between economic incentives on the one hand, and desirable social outcomes on the other, they proposed the following principle: administrative rules should be made to bring about an "artificial" identity of private and public interests.[a] It was a device, in effect, to make contracts more perfect in terms of incentives and outcomes. A historical example serves to bring home this important idea of incentive manipulation.

Chadwick, who was at one point a bureaucrat in charge of improving sanitation, devised a plan for reducing the mortality of British criminals transported to Australia. Chadwick noted that the British government paid a flat fee to a ship's captain for each convict who boarded from a British port. The captains quickly discovered that they could maximize their profits by packing on as many prisoners as could be carried without endangering the ship and by minimizing expenditures on prisoner food, drink, and hygiene en route to the colony. The survival rate stood at 40 percent under this incentive system. Humanitarians were outraged at the state of affairs. After a quick assessment of the program, Chadwick changed the payment system so that the ship's captain received a fee for each *live* convict that *disembarked* in Australia. Soon, the

[a] Here we skirt the important debate between incentives created by an evolving legal system and those affected by the (arguably more capricious and uncertain) legislative or administrative system.

survival rate increased to $98\frac{1}{2}$ percent. The rule change gave ships' captains incentives to protect the health of the convicts. A rearrangement of incentives created an "artificial" identity between the public interest (that is, the health and safety of the prisoners) and the private interests (that is, the profit of the shipper).[b]

[b] See Edwin Chadwick, "Opening Address," *Journal of the Royal Statistical Society of London* 25 (1862): p. 12. This and a number of other examples are discussed in Robert B. Ekelund, Jr., and Robert F. Hebert, *A History of Economic Theory and Method*, 3rd ed. (New York: McGraw-Hill, 1990), pp. 214–223.

Common Property and Incentives

Failure to use an extensive system of private property led to reduced output and ultimately to economic chaos in the Soviet Union. This failure produced an incentive structure in which economic efficiency was impossible.

Even in societies such as the United States, in which private property is extensively used, common-property problems and perverse incentives can emerge. Earlier (in Highlight 1.3) we noted that the disappearance of the wooly mammoth, the decimation of the bison, and the vanishing of Indian populations from specific locales in the American Southwest were caused by overexploitation of a common property resource. The debate of the early 1990s over the Pacific Northwest's spotted owl is an example. That particular owl is endangered due to extensive logging in its habitat. However, a direct assignment of property rights might solve the problem in an economically efficient manner. This would involve assigning a *particular* individual or group rights over *particular* owls and permitting legal enforcement of these rights.

In a fully analogous argument, efficient use of public parklands may be achieved by making the parks private property and leaving the actual use to the discretion of the highest bidder. Those valuing owls or wilderness (the Sierra Club, the Audubon Society, and so on) would be free to bid for *private* property rights just as could ranchers and loggers. Economic efficiency would be obtained when the land was allocated to its highest-valued use, which may mean destruction of wilderness or the disappearance of owls. But economic efficiency is not the only relevant issue. Goals other than economic efficiency — ecological preservation, justice, beauty, harmony with nature, the pleasure of future generations — are also important. Individuals often appeal to political regulation and legislative solution, and they show little concern for an efficient use of resources. Here, economics can spell out only some of the costs and benefits of private- versus common-property utilization.

Free markets provide economically efficient incentives and information through a price system in the vast majority of cases. In some instances, the market even evolves to address problems posed by common property. In the 1980s, citizens became concerned over the decimation of the Pacific dolphin by tuna boats from the U.S., Japan, and other countries. At first, no tunafish company would dare implement the costly procedures necessary to exclude dolphins from becoming entangled in the fishing nets for fear of putting themselves out of business. However, growing awareness of the plight of the dolphin in the United States, along with boycotts of dolphin-killing tuna suppliers, was the key to saving the dolphin. A major seller of tuna soon began to advertise that its tuna was caught without killing dolphins. Soon Starkist, Chicken-of-the-Sea, and Bumble Bee were all forced (through competition) into adopting similar procedures to protect the dolphin. These beneficial results will obviously not occur in every case, but the market system may, in some instances, successfully address the social and economic problems created by common-property resources.

Microeconomics and the Case for Laissez-Faire

The economic case for minimal government and for the primacy of the rule of law and private property rights is grounded in incentives and outcomes. The former Soviet Union failed on most counts to deliver goods, because markets as we know them could not thrive under a common property structure. To be sure, some small amounts of property were privately owned and some market activity (mainly in illegal black markets) did take place. The failure of incentives to produce economic efficiency was inevitable because of the absence of the clear delineation of decentralized property rights. Masses of freely negotiated contracts, which is the stuff of markets and of demand and supply, were legally impossible in the Soviet system. Despite a thriving underground economy and black markets, shortages remained a dominant feature of the Soviet economy.

The case for laissez-faire thus hinges critically on the primacy of law, on private property, and on the incentives that are created in such a system. Adam Smith (1723–1790), the father of economics who wrote the *Wealth of Nations,* believed in a natural identity of interests. Practically, this means that the pursuit of private gain in a decentralized system of property rights will maximize the public interest. Economic efficiency tends to flow from private property and enforceable contracts to transfer property. Perfect economic efficiency, however, is an unattainable goal for many of the reasons given in this chapter. Incorrect assignment of rights (the Dot-and-Yvonne example) may prevent low-cost and efficient solutions in a variety of cases. Failure to achieve efficiency may be the result of an inability to define clear property rights to some resource (fishing grounds, oil reserves under the ocean). Further, the failure to achieve economic efficiency by assignment of property rights may reflect society's evaluation of other goals as more important than economic ones.

The narrow case for laissez-faire, for private property, for minimized public control over resources, for the primacy of law over discretionary power, is simply that markets, which are the product of laissez-faire, are more efficient at alleviating scarcity than any other system yet observed. The incentive structure that results when we are able to direct our own labor and other resources to produce, exchange, and consume what we want is one that minimizes the universal problem of scarcity. Microeconomics is the study of how markets achieve that end and of how human satisfactions are maximized in the process.

Many critics argue that economists place inordinate emphasis on achieving economic efficiency and that this single-mindedness causes them to ignore other important goals of society. In their defense, the reason for the emphasis on efficiency is that economists are concerned about the economic well-being of members of society. They, perhaps more than others, realize that improving economic efficiency can mean raising average living standards.

This is not to suggest that other goals are of no importance. Indeed, few people are convinced that a policy is desirable simply because it is economically efficient. Before they are willing to advocate a policy, most observers also want to know something about the policy's **equity,** its fairness. They need additional information about who gains and who loses. The mere fact that the gains are larger than the losses is not a decisive factor.

Thus, although economists are trained to determine what policies, institutions, and laws are economically efficient, they cannot tell us which ones are desirable. Making this determination entails value judgments about the tradeoffs that have to be made between economic efficiency and other important objectives. Economists have no particular expertise in evaluating such tradeoffs.

This explains why economists tend to agree about some issues but to disagree about others. When it comes to **positive propositions,** where one predicts the economic consequences of some change, economists reach a reasonably high degree of agreement because their conclusion can be tested logically or by collecting data. When it comes to **normative propositions,** which deal with statements about a policy's desirability, economists often fail to reach a consensus. This is due primarily to differences in their value judgments.

There is a good reason for why most economists are so attracted to the standard of economic efficiency. If an inefficient policy is replaced by an efficient one, it is possible, in principle, to redistribute the net gains in such a way that *all* parties are made better off. Economists therefore have trouble accepting inefficient policies even when their implementation generates benefits for certain intended groups.

Microeconomics is, in the broadest sense, a study of how markets work to "deliver the goods" and to maximize the satisfactions of a society within the constraints of limited resources. Societies that utilize markets will not necessarily become more "perfect" societies. Perfection is a normative concept and will naturally vary in the eye of the beholder. Further, use of markets does not suggest that such a system *always* and *everywhere* produces economic efficiency. We have already seen that common-property problems in both ancient and contemporary societies may prevent markets from establishing efficient production and exchange in some cases.

Free markets, however, tend to underlie a philosophical predilection for free expression and free thought in both economics and politics. Free and creative thought, after all, is what powers entrepreneurship. Microeconomics, as a study of how markets function to provide goods and services to consumers, is not only concerned with efficiency; it is biased toward intellectual freedom as well.

Key Terms

economic efficiency in production	scarcity
opportunity cost	efficiency in exchange
private property rights	common or public property rights
incentives	marginal decision making
equity	positive propositions
normative propositions	

Sample Questions

Question

The allocation of scarce resources is often a difficult problem for administrators. Parking on college campuses is viewed by many students, staff, and faculty members as a scarce resource. How could college administrators use markets to allocate parking spaces efficiently?

Answer

Administrators could use markets to allocate parking spaces in the same manner that the economics department at Arizona State University allocated offices. The administration could develop a market for parking spaces in which, during a specified time period, potential occupants parking spaces in the various lots could submit sealed bids. The highest bidder would select his or her space in the specified lot first, followed by the next highest bidder, and so on. The proceeds from the auction could be used to fund the construction of additional parking facilities. By setting up an auction system, those who valued spaces in particular lots would have the highest willingness to pay for the space.

Question

Edwin Chadwick explained over a century ago that an artificial identity of interests often leads to improved social and economic welfare. Explain what

Chadwick meant by the "artificial identity of interests" and describe how this principle can be applied.

Answer

The artificial identity of interests maintains that legislation and administrative rules can be implemented so as to align private and public interests to arrive at a socially desirable outcome. For example, Chadwick applied this principle when he changed the payment system for the transport of prisoners. Rather than receiving payment before embarking, the captain would receive payment for each live prisoner delivered to the destination. Thus the private interests of the captains were aligned with the public conscience of the humanitarians, who had complained about the high prisoner mortality rate.

Question

Economists maintain that the common-pool problem leads to the misuse or overuse of resources. What is the source of this problem? Explain.

Answer

The common-pool problem arises as a result of the lack of private property rights. Where no property rights exist for a resource, the resource is perceived as free and its use is heavily exploited. Overuse and general misuse of the resource are common outcomes, and as a result, the resource is not used efficiently in its highest-valued use.

Questions for Review and Discussion

*1. What fundamental problem in the former Soviet Union prevented consumers from being able to purchase the goods and services they desired?

2. Some people argue that the reason central planners in the former Soviet Union failed to attain the best product mix for society was that the government became corrupt and the planners stopped trying to serve the public. Do you think that honest economic planners could have succeeded?

*3. The opportunity cost of spending time at one activity is defined as the value of the *highest-valued* alternative, not as the value of *any* alternative. Is this an important distinction? Explain.

*4. Discount stores are generally viewed as inexpensive places to shop. However, the check-out lines at discount stores are generally longer than those at other stores. Taking this difference into account, is it necessarily true that it is cheaper to shop where prices are lowest?

5. How does the economic view of efficiency differ from the technical view?

6. Why is the existence of private-property rights as opposed to common-property rights important in an economy?

*7. Some dormitories and student apartments have four or five "private" bedrooms around a shared living and cooking area. Do the problems that arise among roommates about use of the shared area have anything in common with the "tragedy of the commons" problem? Explain.

8. The lack of ownership in Soviet-style economies leads to the absence of a profit motive in industry. What are some of the consequences for investment and production when there is no profit motive?

9. What is efficiency in exchange, and why was it less likely to occur in the old Soviet Union than in the United States?

*10. Do you use marginal analysis in deciding how much time to spend studying for an exam? in deciding how much education to attain? In what way?

*11. Do you think that criminals are rational — in the sense of considering marginal costs and marginal benefits — when deciding whom to rob? If so, does this suggest a strategy that you might adopt to reduce your chances of being robbed?

12. In most states, farmers are liable for damages if their livestock wander onto highways and are struck by vehicles. In some Western states, however, the motorist is liable for the damages resulting from that type of accident. Which of the two ways of assigning liability do you think is more efficient? Explain.

*13. Police officers' and school teachers' salaries are determined primarily on the basis of years of service. Do you think that this payment system provides proper incentives? If not, can you think of any changes that would improve the incentive structure?

Problems for Analysis

*1. Using marginal analysis, analyze and discuss the following slogans:
   a. "Drive 55, Save Lives!"
   b. "A Job Worth Doing Is Worth Doing Well."

2. John, a busy college student, uses the automatic teller machine instead of going into his bank to cash a check, although the ATM method costs $2 per transaction and check cashing at the bank is "free."
   a. Is John irrational? What are his motivations?
   b. Is check cashing at the bank "free"?

*3. June, a department store manager, is concerned about shoplifting in her store. Would she be rational to hire enough detectives to totally eliminate shoplifting?

4. The Kemps Ridley sea turtle, found in the Gulf of Mexico, is an endangered species. It has been decimated due to extensive fishing in the Gulf.
   a. Why is the turtle on the endangered species list?
   b. What might be done to save the turtle? Be specific.
   c. How many turtles do you think should be saved? Explain.

5. "It is not true that markets did not exist in the former Soviet Union. On the contrary, it was possible in the 'black' (illegal) markets to buy almost anything you wanted. These markets were not unlike the illegal drug market in the United States." Comment.

6. Suppose that the United States decided to lease all federal prisons to private enterprise with stipulations as to treatment, quality of food, and so on, in the lease. Imagine further that (after a period of time) it was discovered that a very high rate of prisoners were dying under the conditions established by the private management. How might incentives be altered to produce fewer deaths? (*Hint:* see Highlight 1.5.).

2

Demand and Supply

Prices play a crucial role in solving all basic economic problems. Problems encountered in real-world situations (including some market dislocations in the former Soviet Union) are less severe when markets are used as signals to suppliers and demanders of goods.

The very foundations of market study are the twin concepts of demand and supply. A careful understanding of these simple theories will permit you to analyze real-world problems.[1] In doing so, however, keep in mind one basic premise of economics: decision makers are assumed to behave rationally and thus to act predictably in market dealings.

The goal of this chapter is to establish a framework for analyzing problems by explaining basic theories and by applying them to a variety of real-world situations. Specifically, this chapter

- presents demand and supply curves as examples of rational behavior on the part of buyers and sellers.
- explains in theory and with practical examples how market prices are determined through the interaction of demand and supply.
- illustrates and explains the market impact of taxes and subsidies.
- analyzes the imposition of price ceilings and price floors.
- extends the simple theories to show how demand-and-supply interactions determine prices when production processes yield more than one good or service.
- develops a theory of relative prices that will enable us to understand how different markets are interrelated.

---

1. You may already be familiar with some of the basic concepts of market theory discussed in this chapter. Other theories (such as the supply of multiple products and the theory of relative prices) will likely be new, however, and a review of the basics will prove very useful.

Markets and Price Takers

A primary function of microeconomic analysis is to focus on the operation of particular markets in which buyers and sellers of goods or services interact by making purchases and sales. Some markets may be local or regional; others are national or international in scope. Market size depends on which sellers are convenient to buyers and which buyers are accessible to sellers. For example, one could consider a local market for gasoline consisting of buyers and sellers in a particular city. This market delineation makes sense, because most buyers may find it costly (inconvenient) to purchase elsewhere. At the other extreme, stock markets and commodities markets are truly international, because buyers and sellers from around the world can easily carry out transactions. Competition is assumed to exist in any market in which individual buyers and sellers have little control over price.

An individual demand curve for anything — fast-food lunches, cellular phones, housing — shows how many units of a good a buyer will choose to buy at each possible price. But demand curves make good sense only in cases in which the individual buyer has no control over the price at which he or she buys goods and services. Such buyers are referred to as **price takers**. For example, it would be silly (irrational) for you to buy a compact disk at $15 if you believe that you can easily bargain the price down to $10. However, you may be eager to buy at $15 if your alternative is to go without. Therefore, whenever we construct a demand curve, we assume price-taking behavior. The demand curve shows how many units the buyer in question will buy at each possible price, assuming that the alternative is to buy none at all.

In constructing supply curves we similarly assume price-taking behavior. Let's say that you are in the business of washing cars. If the price offered to you were $25 per car, your response as to the number of cars you would wash should depend on how many car washes you would be able to sell at prices above $25. If you could keep busy washing other cars at $35 per car, your response to the $25 offer would be zero cars. It is only if you assume that you are *unable* to sell at a price above $25 that you can reasonably determine what quantity to offer for sale at that price.

In surveying real-world markets, we find relatively few in which individual buyers and sellers have *no* control over their price. Owners of apartment units, grocery stores, gasoline stations, and convenience stores, for example, all have some control over the prices they charge. If sales of gasoline at a gas station currently amount to 2,000 gallons per day at a price of $1.30, the station could undoubtedly sell *some* gasoline at a slightly higher price, such as $1.40. Therefore, this seller of gasoline (and the other types of sellers listed above) is not literally a price-taker.

Competition and competitive markets are defined as those in which many small buyers and sellers are "too small" to influence price. This being the case, should demand and supply be used to examine markets whose participants are not literally price takers? Our answer is yes. Demand and supply have proven to be quite useful tools in explaining behavior in markets in which some participants have *some* control over *some* prices, although the tools lose their power as buyers and/or sellers gain greater control over price. We therefore encourage their general use even in markets that are not "perfectly competitive," as long as they are not completely controlled by buyers or sellers. Even though the owner of the apartment complex has some control over the rent he charges, the use of demand and supply to analyze the rental-housing market enables us to understand why rents are at their current level and what forces are likely to cause them to rise or fall.

This is not to say that we will choose to examine every market in terms of demand and supply curves. In some markets, certain buyers or sellers have great control over the prevailing price. In later chapters, we will develop alternative models to understand behavior in markets of those types.

Individual Demand Curves

An **individual demand curve** shows how much of a good a particular individual will choose to buy at each possible price, other things remaining unchanged. For a price-taking buyer, deciding how many units to buy is a straightforward application of marginal analysis. If, for example, we are considering Sam's demand for pizza, at a given price of $10 per pizza, then the cost of each pizza to Sam *on the margin* is the price, $10. The optimizing choice for Sam is to continue to buy pizzas until the **marginal benefit** to him no longer exceeds $10. If only the first 4 pizzas that Sam consumes per week yield marginal benefits of $10 or more, then he will elect to purchase 4 per week at that price. Assuming that the marginal benefit of an additional pizza is less than the price of $10, Sam will be better off buying 4 than he would be buying 5 per week. At a price of $10, 4 is the optimal quantity for Sam to buy per week.

To construct a complete demand curve for Sam, we must repeat the above process for each possible price. At a price of $5 per pizza, Sam would obviously be willing to buy *at least* 4 pizzas per week, because each of the 4 yields marginal benefits that exceed the new marginal cost of $5. Whether Sam would be willing to buy *more* than 4 units depends on his marginal benefits from additional pizzas. Assuming that the fifth pizza per week yields benefits of $7, and the sixth yields benefits of $4, Sam would elect to buy 5 at a price of $5. This is the optimal quantity to buy at that price. Because each of the first 5 pizzas produces benefits in excess of the marginal cost, each purchase improves Sam's well-being. For each pizza the marginal benefits exceed the marginal cost. However, Sam's decision to buy a sixth pizza would be counter to his interest because its marginal cost ($5) exceeds the marginal benefit ($4). If he elected to buy 6 pizzas per week, he would be worse off than if he purchased 5 and used the last $5 to buy something else. It would be irrational for Sam to buy the sixth pizza at any price above $4.

Under the assumption that Sam acts rationally in deciding how many pizzas to buy, his demand curve will be identical to his marginal-benefit curve. Suppose that Sam is able to determine the total dollar benefit to him of being able to consume various quantities of pizza per week, and that these values are presented in the first two columns of Table 2.1. On the basis of this information, it is straightforward to compute (in the third column) the marginal benefit, expressed in dollars, of *each* pizza from Sam's *total* benefit (in the second column), which increases as he consumes successive pizzas. Each entry in the third column shows how much Sam's total dollar benefit from consuming the given number of pizzas per week exceeds his dollar benefit from consuming one less pizza. For example, the marginal benefit from the second pizza is $16, because the total benefit from 2 pizzas per week ($36) exceeds the total benefit of 1 pizza ($20) by $16.

This particular marginal benefit curve, depicted in Figure 2.1, shows the best quantity for Sam to consume at each possible price. Therefore, this curve is both Sam's marginal-benefit curve and his demand curve.

The numbers presented in Table 2.1 follow a pattern. Up to a point, consumers prefer more to less, so Sam's total benefits increase as the quantity increases until the tenth pizza is consumed. At this point Sam is satiated with pizza in the given time period (a week), and additional pizza would cause his total benefits to fall. We have chosen to omit such quantities from the table below because Sam would never purchase pizza in such quantities below,

Table 2.1 Sam's Demand and Marginal Benefit Curve for Pizza
Sam will buy pizza up to the point at which his marginal benefit equals the price of pizzas. At a price of $10, for example, Sam will buy only 4 pizzas.

Pizzas Per Week	Total Dollar Benefit	Marginal Dollar Benefit
0	$ 0	—
1	20	$20
2	36	16
3	49	13
4	60	11
5	67	7
6	71	4
7	74	3
8	76	2
9	77	1
10	77	0

Figure 2.1 An Individual's Demand Curve

This step-function demand shows Sam's marginal-benefit schedule for pizzas. If Sam acts rationally, his demand for pizza will be identical to his marginal-benefit schedule.

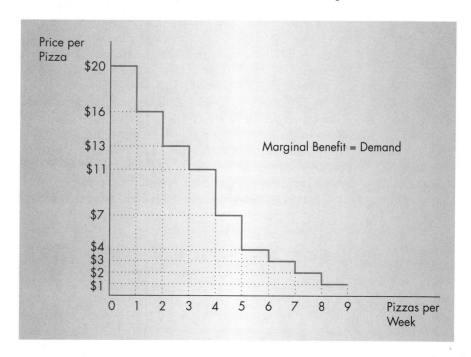

given that pizza sells for a positive price. Table 2.1 shows not only that Sam's total benefit increases as the quantity consumed increases, but it also shows that his *total benefit increases at a decreasing rate* —that is, the increments in total value decline as the quantity increases. The first pizza adds $20 to Sam's total benefit, the second pizza adds only $16, and the third pizza only $13. To say that the total benefit increases at a decreasing rate is equivalent to saying that the marginal benefit declines as larger quantities are consumed. We therefore see that declining marginal benefits imply traditional demand curves that are negatively sloped. Because successive pizzas are less valuable on the margin, Sam will choose to buy additional pizzas only at successively lower prices. Although the rate at which marginal benefits decline will vary among consumers, it is reasonable to assume that this is a general fact of life. We refer to it as **diminishing marginal utility.** In the next chapter, we will discuss the relationship between utility and demand curves more thoroughly.

Market Demand Curves

Although sellers may have some interest in individual demand curves, they are generally more interested in how many units buyers *as a group* are willing to

buy at a given price. Just as an individual demand curve shows desired purchases by a given buyer, a **market demand curve** shows desired purchases by
all the buyers in a market as a group.

To construct a market demand curve, we start with an individual demand
curve for each potential buyer of the good. We obtain this in precisely the way
that we determined Sam's demand curve for pizza. Because different individuals are likely to value pizza differently, we have no reason to believe that all
buyers will have the same total-benefit and marginal-benefit curves. However,
we have a strong reason to believe that every buyer, like Sam above, will find
that his or her marginal benefit declines as the number of pizzas consumed in
any time period increases. For example, we might imagine three potential buyers of pizza (A, B, and C) whose respective marginal-benefit curves for pizza
are represented by MB_A, MB_B, and MB_C respectively in Figure 2.2. Assuming
that the price of one pizza is $8 and that each of the three buyers obeys the
rule of rational life, buyer A would elect to purchase 3 pizzas, B would buy
7 pizzas, and C would buy 10 pizzas. To obtain the market demand curve for

Figure 2.2 The Derivation of a Market Demand Curve
The curves labeled MB_A, MB_B, and MB_C show the marginal benefit schedules for three
individual buyers of pizza. The market demand curve is obtained by adding the individual marginal benefit curves horizontally.

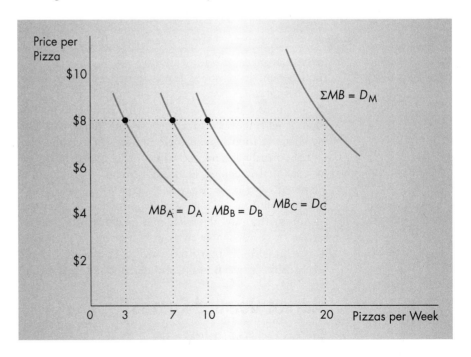

these three buyers, we add the individual demand curves horizontally. At a price of $8, all the buyers in the market as a group will elect to buy a total of 20 pizzas. The market demand curve, labeled D_M in Figure 2.2, is obtained by summing the individual demand curves in exactly that fashion for each possible price of pizza. Because the individual demand curves slope downward, the market demand curve must also slope downward.

You might reasonably ask why the individual demand curves in Figure 2.2 are smooth lines, in contrast to the step-function demand depicted in Figure 2.1. The answer is that in Figure 2.1 we considered only the purchase of discrete quantities of pizza. For Sam to elect to buy 2 whole pizzas per week instead of only 1, the price would have to fall from $20 down to $16; we ignored the possibility of Sam buying fractional pizzas. If we consider this possibility, we can see that as the price of a pizza falls from $20 down to $16, the quantity that Sam would elect to buy per week would *gradually* increase from 1 whole pizza to 2 whole pizzas. For example, at a price of $18 per pizza, it would not be sensible for Sam to buy 2 pizzas per week, because the second pizza has a marginal benefit of only $16. However, the first half of that second pizza might be worth an additional $9 to him, and the second half worth an additional $7. In this case, he would be willing to buy 1.5 pizzas at a price of $18 per pizza — not just one pizza as depicted in Figure 2.1. From this point on, the demand and supply curves in this text will in general be depicted as smooth lines, not steps, to allow for the purchase of fractional units.

You may also wonder how the quality of a good or product relates to demand. In constructing a demand curve, we consider a *given* quality of the good — in our example we assumed that Sam consumed a given quality of pizza. To improve quality is to produce a product that yields higher marginal benefits at each price. Marginal benefit and demand curves would thus lie to the right of those considered in Figures 2.1 and 2.2. Unexpected forces can always have an impact on the quality of products. The powerful earthquake that hit the San Francisco area in the fall of 1989, for example, interrupted the live broadcast of the World Series baseball game in progress there. Devastating loss of life was accompanied by high economic damages. One of those losses was the condemnation and subsequent removal of the Embarcadero freeway that rimmed the waterfront around San Francisco bay and limited some apartment views of the Bay Bridge and other sights. (The freeway became a casualty, because a similarly constructed freeway in Oakland had collapsed during the quake.)

But it is an ill wind that brings no one benefit. Those lucky San Francisco residents whose apartment and condo views were obscured by the freeway received a windfall. The "quality" of those dwellings improved relative to possible substitutes and demand for them increased, causing their price to rise. In other words, the effect of this one-time increase in the value of apartments and homes in the area was increased demand, because more buyers found these places attractive. The value of these properties went up by 20 to 50 percent!

Factors that Cause the Market Demand Curve to Shift

Because the market demand curve is obtained by horizontally summing individual demand curves, the *market* demand can change only if the *individual* demand curves change or if the number of potential buyers changes. Clearly, if new buyers enter the market, their demands must also be included to obtain the market demand. Therefore, one factor affecting market demand is a change in the number of buyers.

In addition, any change that alters the marginal-benefit curve for individual buyers will also alter market demand. The following four factors are most likely to cause a **shift in demand**:

• changes in the tastes or preferences of individual buyers
• changes in the incomes of individual buyers
• changes in the prices of related goods
• changes in information or expectations

Each of these factors is sufficiently important to warrant an explanation. Clearly, the marginal benefit you receive from a good depends crucially on your tastes and preferences. If a buyer's tastes change in favor of a particular good, the marginal benefit will increase, causing the buyer to be willing to purchase greater quantities of the good at each possible price than previously.

Similarly, changes in income affect the marginal benefit of the good in question to the extent that they make substitute goods more or less affordable. For example, an increase in income that makes a car more affordable may reduce the marginal benefit of tickets on a commuter bus, thereby reducing the number of such tickets a typical consumer would be willing to buy at any price. Note that we are *not* assuming that a change in income affects preferences. We are, rather, supposing that the buyer has a fixed preference for transportation to work that is independent of his or her income. However, given that preference, the buyer's marginal benefit from a commuter ticket is lower when the buyer owns a car that provides an alternative way of getting to work. Therefore, the increase in income that leads to the purchase of a car indirectly leads to a decrease in the demand for commuter tickets.

On the other hand, increases in income enable buyers to purchase more goods and services overall. The increase in specialty stores and catalogs, as well as a rising number of ethnic restaurants, are examples of the effect larger incomes can have on the demand for goods and services. Many minority groups overlooked by retailers in the past are now gaining attention because they comprise large demand groups that can provide increased revenues for attentive retailers. Today we see a large number of ethnic food stores, shops that cater to the demands of African-Americans, Hispanics, and Asians, and restaurants that specialize in Indian, Japanese, or Thai cuisine.[2] The availability

2. See Laurie M. Grossman, "After Demographic Shift, Atlanta Mall Restyles Itself as Black

of these new products and services means that the goods a consumer must forgo to buy a particular good will have less value to the consumer, thus leading to an increased demand for the good in question. Therefore, changes in income can affect demand in different ways for different goods and different consumers. In some cases, an increase in income will lead to a decrease in the demand for a given good, but the reverse relation will hold in other cases. When higher income leads to an increase in the demand for given goods, such as steak or lobster, those are said to be **normal goods. Inferior goods,** on the other hand, such as beans and commuter tickets, are defined as those for which demand *decreases* as income increases.

In considering the importance of the price of related goods on a consumer's marginal-benefit curve for a particular good, let's look at two types of related goods. First, there are **substitute goods** — products whose attributes are similar but not identical. For example, most brands of soft drinks are substitutes for each other. As the price of alternative brands decreases, the marginal benefit of a buyer's favorite brand decreases because the user can switch to a substitute brand, pay less, and enjoy the same satisfaction. Substitutes in the soft-drink market are increasingly available with the development of private-label, soft-drink brands. Wal-Mart now sells "Sam's Choice" colas in regular, diet, and caffeine-free varieties. These colas are sold at lower prices than Coke and Pepsi, and the high quality of the private-label colas makes the differences virtually indistinguishable in taste tests. As a result of these and other low-priced alternatives in the soft drink market, consumers are substituting away from Coke and Pepsi with increasing frequency. The reverse is true when the price of substitute goods increases.

Changes in the price of **complementary goods** — those used *in conjunction* with the good in question — also affect the marginal benefits from the good in question. One example of complementary goods is downhill skiing equipment and ski-lift passes. Both are required in order to ski. However, the marginal benefit of ski equipment depends crucially on the price of lift passes. The higher the price of the lift pass, the lower the marginal benefit of rental equipment: if a day of skiing is worth $50 and the lift pass costs $40, then the equipment is worth only $10. However, as the price of the lift pass falls, the marginal benefit of ski equipment rises, and with it the demand.

Changes in information or expectations concerning a product will also shift the demand curve. Often, altered information affects expectations, which in turn changes demand. Consider the threatened trade war between France and the United States in the fall of 1992. The French government wanted to maintain subsidies on certain French-grown grains, which kept prices artificially low. The practice disadvantaged American farmers in export markets (subsidies are discussed later in this chapter). In retaliation, the U.S.

Shopping Center," *Wall Street Journal,* 26 February, 1992, pp. B1, B7; and Yumiko Ono, "Japan's Fast-Food Companies Cook Up Local Platters to Tempt Local Palates," *Wall Street Journal,* May 29, 1992, pp. B1, B16.

government proposed a 300 percent increase in the tariff on imported French white wines, with vague suggestions that new and higher tariffs would be imposed on other French wines (and other goods) as well. The proposed new U.S. tariffs would not take place until a "cooling off" period had passed — with enough time to settle the trade issue. The particular issue was settled before the target date, but in the meantime U.S. wine sellers reported record sales of French wines to buyers in anticipation of the tariff increase. The dramatic increase in demand was the result of new information to wine consumers; information coupled with expectations shifted wine demand curves sharply to the right.

In summary, four factors affect individual demand curves: (1) tastes and preferences, (2) income, (3) the prices of related goods, and (4) information and expectations. Therefore, the position of the market demand curve depends on each of these four factors plus the number of potential buyers in the market. So long as these five factors remain unchanged, we can reasonably expect the market demand curve to remain in its initial position. A market demand curve shows how many units of some good or service buyers as a group will be willing to buy at each possible price, given the number of buyers in the market, the tastes and preferences of the individual buyers, the incomes of those buyers, the prices of goods that are related to the good in question, and the information and expectations people hold about the good. So long as these five factors hold constant, lower prices will lead to larger purchases, because each individual consumer receives decreasing marginal benefits from consuming successive units of the good or service in question. The **law of demand** means precisely that: "The lower the price, the greater the quantity demanded, other things remaining unchanged." Here, the other things that are held constant are the five factors that affect the market demand curve.

Changes in Demand Versus Changes in Quantity Demanded

A discussion of those factors held constant along a demand curve suggests the important distinction between a *change in demand* and a **change in the quantity demanded.** When we talk about the latter, we are considering different points along a given demand curve. In other words, we are holding tastes and preferences, income, price of related goods, expectations, and the number of potential buyers constant, and we are changing only the price of the good in question. Because marginal-benefit curves slope downward, we can be certain that demand curves slope downward — lower prices lead to increases in the quantity demanded, and higher prices lead to decreases in the quantity demanded.

In contrast, when we refer to a "change in demand" (as opposed to a "change in the quantity demanded"), we are referring to a shift in the *entire demand curve*. An increase in demand means a shift to the right of the demand curve, from D_1 to D_2 in Figure 2.3. A decrease in demand means a shift to the left of the entire curve.

Figure 2.3 A Shift (Increase in Demand)

The shift to the right in the demand curve from D_1 to D_2 shows an increase in demand. For such a shift to occur, there must be a change in the number of potential buyers (an increase), a change in tastes in favor of the good, an increase in the price of a substitute, a decrease in the price of a complementary good, changed expectations about the good, or a change in buyers' incomes that makes them more willing to buy the good.

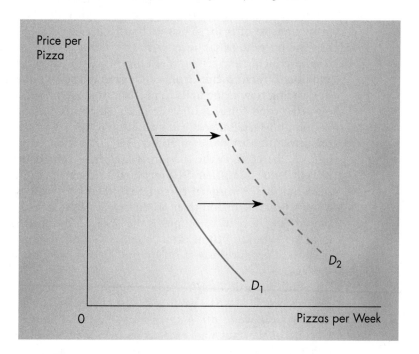

What could cause demand to change? There are many potential causes, but the one thing that cannot *possibly* lead to a change in the demand curve is a change in price! Why? Because a given demand curve, by definition, shows how buyers respond to price changes. Because it shows precisely what buyers will choose to do at every possible price, changes in price cannot possibly affect the position of the curve. What then could cause a change in demand? The five factors that determine the position of the market demand curve are changes in

- tastes and preferences,
- income,
- prices of related goods,
- information or expectations,
- the number of potential buyers.

This distinction between a change in demand and a change in the quantity demanded is probably not new to you. Nevertheless, it is very easy to fall into the trap of confusing the two concepts, because it sounds logical to say that "a fall in the price will cause demand to rise." However, such a mistake leads directly to conclusions that are nonsense.

Individual and Market Supply Curves

Individual supply curves show how many units a price-taking seller would be willing to sell at each possible price. For an individual seller, deciding how many units to offer for sale at each price is again a problem of marginal analysis. The price he or she receives for each unit represents the marginal revenue from producing and selling that unit. More formally, **marginal revenue** is the addition to total revenue from producing and selling one more unit of a good. In deciding how many units to produce at some price (say $10), the price-taking seller need consider only the marginal cost of producing various quantities of output. **Marginal cost** is the addition to total cost resulting from producing one more unit of the commodity. The optimizing decision is to produce as long as the cost on the margin is less than $10. If the producer finds that marginal cost is less than $10 for the first 5 units per time period, but that the sixth unit has a marginal cost of $12, then he or she is better off producing 5 units per time period than producing either 4 or 6. The decision to expand output from 5 units to 6 units is the decision to incur $12 in additional costs in order to enjoy $10 in extra revenues — an "irrational" decision because it makes the producer worse off by the $2 that marginal costs exceed marginal benefits.

Similarly, a decision to reduce output from 5 units per time period to 4 reduces benefits by $10 while reducing costs by less than $10. This also makes the producer worse off — in this case by the amount by which the marginal revenue of the fifth unit exceeds its marginal cost. The decision to produce either more or less than 5 units harms the producer, so the optimal output is clearly 5 units at that particular price of $10. To complete the entire supply curve, the same decision process must be applied to all possible prices. For example, at a price of $12.50 per unit, output should be expanded—at least to 6 units. Whether a seventh and additional units should be produced at that price depends, of course, on whether the marginal cost is below or above the price.

So long as an individual producer acts rationally in deciding how many units to supply at each price, that producer's supply curve will be identical to the curve showing the marginal cost of producing all possible quantities of output. If we assume that a producer of some good — say, pizzas — can determine the total cost of producing various quantities of pizza per time period, then it is easy to determine that producer's supply curve. Assuming that the first two columns in Table 2.2 show the total cost of producing various quantities of pizza, then the **marginal cost** (the change in total cost caused by each unit increase in output) is presented in the third column. In this table we

Table 2.2 The Producer's Marginal Cost and Supply Curve

The producer's marginal cost curve is the change in total cost as output of pizzas increases one unit at a time. The marginal-cost curve and the supply curve are identical.

Pizzas Per Week	Total Cost	Marginal Cost
0	$0	—
1	4	$4
2	9	5
3	15	6
4	23	8
5	33	10
6	45	12
7	60	15
8	90	30
9	140	50
10	240	100

can see that the marginal cost of the first unit is $4, because the cost of producing 1 unit per time period ($4) exceeds the cost of producing zero units by $4. Similarly, the marginal cost of the second unit is $5 ($9 − $4), and the marginal cost of the third unit is $6. Assuming this marginal cost schedule, a rational producer would be unwilling to sell pizzas at any price below $4. At prices from $4 up to $5, he or she would elect to supply 1 unit; at prices from $5 to $6, 2 units; and so on. This marginal cost or supply curve is depicted in Figure 2.4.

It is important to see that the quantities indicated by that cost curve represent "optimizing," or profit-maximizing, quantities at each possible price. For example, the supply curve shows that at a price of $11, the supplier would choose to sell 5 units because the profits associated with 5 units exceeds the profits associated with any other quantity. If the sixth unit were produced, costs would rise by $12, but revenues would rise by only $11, causing profits to fall by a dollar. Similarly, the decision to reduce output below 5 units would also reduce profits. Each unit reduction would cause revenues to fall by $11, but costs would fall by less, because the marginal costs are less than $11.

To say that each point on a supply curve represents profit maximization for the producer in question does not, however, imply that producers make the same profit at each price. As prices rise, profits also rise. Nonetheless, each point represents the most profitable level of output at each respective price.

The hypothetical total cost schedule in Table 2.2 depicts a situation in which, as output increases, total cost *increases at an increasing rate*. Because it increases at an increasing rate, the marginal cost increases as output increases. The marginal cost of the second unit exceeds the marginal cost of the first, the

Figure 2.4 An Individual Supply Curve

This step curve shows the marginal cost of producing various quantities of pizza per week. Assuming that the producer correctly uses marginal analysis to decide how many units to produce at each price, the supply curve will be the same as marginal cost.

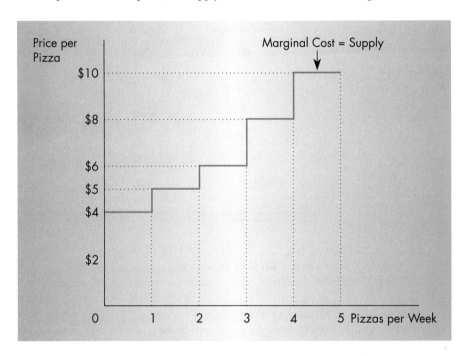

marginal cost of the third exceeds the marginal cost of the second, and so on. This being the case, the supply curve slopes upward.[3]

The supply curve in Figure 2.4 shows desired sales at each price by one particular seller. However, price-taking markets consist of a number of sellers. In determining the market price of any good, we are interested in the **market supply curve,** not the supply curve of any particular firm. The method for obtaining a market supply curve from firm supply curves is identical to the method we used earlier to obtain a market demand curve from individual demand curves. From the suppliers of the good in question we can obtain firm supply curves (marginal-cost curves) and add them horizontally to obtain the market supply curve. A market supply curve like the one shown in Figure 2.5

3. If we were certain that total costs always increase at an increasing rate — that marginal costs increase — then we would be willing to state a "law of supply" that corresponds to the "law of demand" — namely, the higher the price, the greater the quantity supplied. However, as we will see in later chapters, total costs do not always increase at an increasing rate. For this reason, we will avoid referring to a "law of supply." However, for the time being, we will focus only on examples in which individual supply curves slope upward.

Figure 2.5 Deriving A Market Supply Curve

Here S_1 and S_2 are supply curves for two firms. Assuming that the market consists of only these two firms, the market supply is obtained by horizontally summing the firm supply curves. At a price of $10, the total quantity supplied is 32 units — 14 by the first firm and 18 by the second. At a price of $16, the total quantity supplied rises to 45 pizzas — 20 supplied by the first firm and 25 by the second.

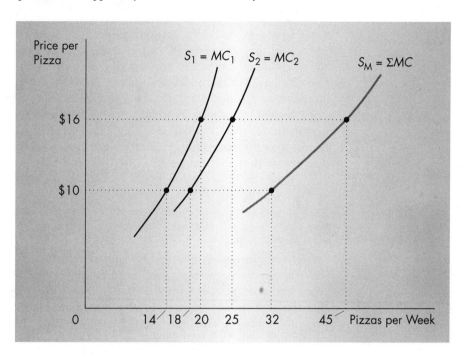

shows the number of units that all sellers as a group will choose to supply at each possible price. Because individual firm supply curves generally slope upward — that is, larger quantities are supplied at higher prices — the market supply curve will also, in general, be positively sloped.

Factors that Cause the Supply Curve to Shift

Given that the market supply curve is obtained by horizontally summing the marginal cost curves of individual producers, *shifts in market supply curves* can be caused either by a change in the number of firms in the market or by a change in the marginal-cost curve of the existing firms. If the number of firms in a market increases, then the supply curves of the additional firms must be added to the initial market supply curve, causing it to increase — shift to the right. Similarly, a decrease in the number of firms in the market will lead to a decrease in supply — a leftward shift in the entire supply curve.

Anything that affects the marginal cost curves of individual firms will also cause the market supply curve to shift. Factors that are most likely to cause such a **shift in supply** are these:

- changes in the technology used to produce the good in question
- changes in the price of the inputs used to produce the good
- changes in information or expectations concerning the good

To produce additional output, larger quantities of inputs are necessary. Therefore, the marginal cost of the extra output depends on (1) how much additional input is required to produce the extra output and (2) the price that must be paid for the additional inputs. The level of technology determines how much extra input is necessary to produce additional units of output. An improvement in technology usually makes it possible to use smaller quantities of additional inputs to produce an extra unit of output. Therefore, an improvement in technology causes the marginal cost to decrease and the supply curve to shift to the right.

Changes in the price of inputs also affect marginal costs. If the price of inputs rises, the cost of the additional inputs used to produce additional output also rises. This leads to an increase in marginal costs and a decrease in supply. The supply will increase if the price of inputs falls, causing a reduction in the marginal costs of production.

Finally, changes in information or expectations concerning the good will shift the supply curve rightward or leftward. Anticipations of a shortage in some vital resource may, for example, diminish the present supply of goods that use that input. (Note that such information will also affect demand.) News that a famous artist has a fatal disease will affect the present supply of her work on the market. Willingness to sell the artist's work will be dampened, causing the present supply to fall. (Note, again, that demand will also be affected.) The impact of news about probable future events will, to use another example, affect current stock prices. In all cases, the economist must carefully assess the direction and magnitude of the effect of changes in information and expectations on the supply curve.

Changes in Supply Versus Changes in Quantity Supplied

It is important to make a clear distinction between a *change in supply* on one hand and a **change in quantity supplied** on the other. When economists refer to a change in supply, they mean a shift in the entire supply schedule, or curve. A shift in the entire supply curve can be caused only by a change in

- the number of sellers in the market,
- the technology used to produce the good in question,
- the price of the inputs used to produce that good, or
- information and expectations.

Increases in supply, represented by shifts to the right of the entire supply curve, can be caused by

- increases in the number of sellers,
- technological improvements,
- reductions in input prices, or
- improved information or expectations.

Opposite changes in any of these four factors will lead to a decrease in supply, represented by a shift to the left of the entire curve.

When economists refer to a change in the quantity supplied, they mean a movement along a given supply curve as a consequence of a change in price. As the price of the good in question increases — as we move up along the supply curve — the quantity supplied increases. Decreases in price lead to decreases in the quantity supplied.

Although the above distinction seems straightforward, it is very easy to confuse a change in supply with a change in the quantity supplied. To avoid this confusion, remember this fact: the one thing that is certain *not* to affect the supply curve is a change in price.

Market Equilibrium

In the previous sections we described how to obtain a market demand curve and a market supply curve for any market in which both buyers and sellers are price takers. Using the demand and supply curves together, we can then see how market forces establish the prevailing price and quantities exchanged. In Figure 2.6, D_M is the market demand for pizzas and S_M is the market supply. There is no reason to believe that any market participant knows the position of either the demand curve or the supply curve. Figuring out what the demand or supply curve looks like would be difficult or impossible to do, and besides, no one has much incentive to do so. Despite the fact that, before the market opens, no single person knows the **equilibrium price** — the price at which quantity demanded and quantity supplied are equal — market forces will tend to drive the price to that level.

Should the existing price be above the (unknown) equilibrium price (above P_E in Figure 2.6) some potential sellers will find that they are unable to sell as many pizzas as they wish because the number of pizzas that buyers as a group choose to buy is less than the number that sellers wish to sell. To secure additional buyers, sellers will find it in their interest to lower their asking price. Doing this will force other sellers in turn to lower their prices in order to retain buyers. In this fashion, in any market in which the price is temporarily above the equilibrium level, market forces will tend to drive the price downward until the equilibrium is reached.

Figure 2.6 Market Equilibrium

The interaction of market demand (D_M) and market supply (S_M) determine the equilibrium price (P_E) and the equilibrium quantity (Q_E).

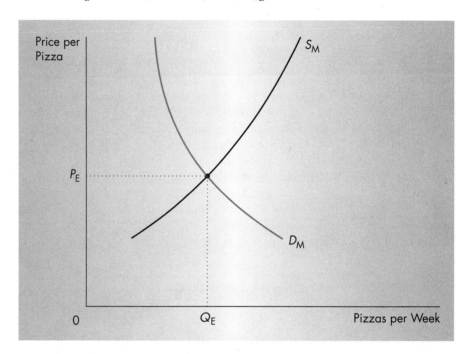

Similarly, the market price may temporarily be below the equilibrium. In that case, the quantity offered for sale by sellers is less than the quantity that buyers prefer to purchase. Sellers find that they are constantly running out of pizzas, so they have an incentive to raise the price and produce more. In this fashion, the price will be driven upward, sellers will be induced to offer larger quantities for sale, and buyers will respond to the higher price by electing to buy less. This process will continue until the price rises to P_E.

The **equilibrium price,** P_E, and **equilibrium quantity,** Q_E, may be presented in equivalent, but more precise, algebraic terms. Demand, supply, and equilibrium price may all be expressed in the shorthand of simple algebra. For example, we could express demand, supply, and equilibrium as

$$P = 100 - 2Q_D \text{ (the demand equation)}$$
$$P = 25 + 3Q_S \text{ (the supply equation)}$$
$$Q_D = Q_S = Q_E \text{ (the equilibrium equation)}$$

The demand and supply equations, thus expressed, are simply straight lines that may be plotted as the curves in Figure 2.6. The negatively sloped demand equation (with a slope of –2) is constructed by drawing a straight line from $100 on the vertical axis and 50 units on the horizontal axis. The supply curve is similarly drawn, first by assuming that Q_S is zero (giving a point of $25 on the vertical axis) and then by assuming price to be zero, giving an intercept of –8.33 on the horizontal axis. (The slope of the supply curve is +3.)[4] These two straight lines intersect (as they do in Figure 2.6) at an equilibrium price. That equilibrium price is found where the demand and supply curves intersect, or where

$$100 - 2Q = 25 + 3Q$$

If the equality is solved for equilibrium Q, that quantity is determined to be 15 units of product. If the equilibrium quantity is substituted into *either* the demand or supply equations, equilibrium price is determined to be $70 per unit.

This approach to equilibrium quantity and price using supply and demand is exactly equivalent to the numerical and conceptual treatment given earlier. The algebraic treatment basically adds nothing to that discussion and our presentation does not make extensive use of it. However, the potential is improved for quantifying the effects of changes in demand or supply (such as taxes or subsidies on sellers or consumers). See footnotes 6, 7, and 8 in this chapter, for examples.

No matter how demand and supply are depicted, neither buyers nor sellers view the equilibrium price as ideal. Sellers would obviously like to sell *more* than Q_E, the **equilibrium quantity**, and at higher prices, and buyers would like to be able to buy more than Q_E at lower prices. However, the ability of either buyers or sellers to control the price is generally possible only when a government grants legal restrictions to favored groups. Many groups of suppliers or demanders attempt to gain such restrictions through the legislative process (see Highlight 2.1).[5] However, in this chapter we are assuming competitive conditions *without* any legal restrictions that benefit suppliers. At the equilibrium price of P_E the sellers collectively find that Q_E is the best level of output for them to produce. A decision to produce either more or less than Q_E on the part of sellers would be irrational because that is the optimal or profit-maximizing quantity for them to supply at that price.

4. Economists often present demand and supply equations in terms of *quantity* rather than *price,* as in the text. Thus the demand and supply equations are often given in *inverse form* as $Q_D = 50 - .5P$ and $Q_S = .333P - 8.33$. But this is exactly backward from the manner in which mathematicians operate. One potential confusion that results from the economists' use of the inverse form of the equations is that the slopes of the demand and supply curves are *not* −.5 and .333, but −2 and +3 respectively (as shown in the text). The tradition of economists — presenting demand and supply in inverse form — persists.

5. We will see in more detail in Chapter 5 that many groups have incentives to restrict competition and that they will do so if they are able.

Highlight 2.1   *American Nannies Try for International Controls in Child-care Market*

Chrysler, General Motors, and U.S. textile workers aren't the only companies or groups complaining about "unfair competition" from imports these days. American nanny agencies — specializing in the training and placement of in-home child-care workers — are demanding that Congress impose a "level playing field." Specifically, the Network of American Nanny Agencies (NANA) is asking that the au pair program, which brings in foreign child-care workers, be regulated in conjunction with cultural exchange and educational programs of the federal government.[a]

NANA is claiming unfair competition. The au pair workers are recruited by eight authorized private agencies that are permitted to bring as many as 22,700 European women into the United States for one-year duties and education. About 8,000 actually enter the U.S. work force each year. The au pairs typically put in 45 hours per week in light housekeeping and babysitting in return for room and board and $100 (per week) in spending money. Nannies, in contrast, earn between $175 and $400 per week plus room and board. U.S. nanny agencies — generally small firms — place about 150,000 nannies per year. A number of smaller agencies place only 100 nannies each year.

The for-profit au pair agencies (authorized by the nonprofit Scholarship Foundation) advertise in foreign countries for participants. One of them, the American Institute for Foreign Study, charges each employing family $3,450 for placement, an amount that includes evaluation, transportation, training, health insurance, and so on. These agencies are also paid an undisclosed amount to administer the au pair program.

We can analyze the market for in-home child care in terms of supply and demand. Consider Figure 2.7, which depicts the annual estimated market for in-home nannies of average quality in the United States. The figure shows two supply curves plotted against a stationary demand curve. The average equilibrium wage rate for nannies *without* the au pair program, shown as W_1 in the figure, is produced by the interaction of the demand curve and the supply curve S_1. At point E_1 the quantity demanded of nannies is exactly equal to the quantity supplied. Nannies — or rather nanny-placement agencies — claim that the existence of the au pair program increases the supply of in-home child care workers to curve S_2. That increased supply reduces the nanny wage rate from W_1 to W_2. More child-care workers are employed with the inclusion of au pairs, but nannies' wages are lower. In March 1992 seven Boston-area nanny agencies argued that the impact of the au pair program was as shown in Figure 2.7.

In response to these allegations of unfair competition, the organizers

[a] Material for this discussion is drawn from Brent Bowers, "Nanny Agencies Say Threat from 'Au Pairs' Isn't Kid Stuff," *Wall Street Journal*, May 28, 1992, pp. B1, B2.

Figure 2.7 The Market Effects of a Supply Restriction

If au pairs can be kept out of the market, the market equilibrium will be at E_1, with nannies earning a wage of W_1. Otherwise, the equilibrium will be at E_2 and nannies will earn less.

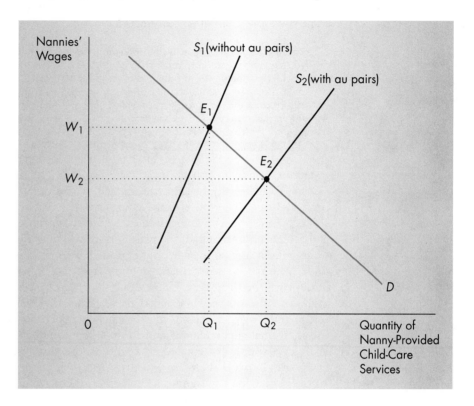

of exchange activities argue that too few au pairs come in each year to significantly affect nannies' wage rates. Further, they argue that the au pair program is part of a true cultural exchange with the far broader aim of introducing young foreigners to American values and culture.

Nanny agencies counter that au pairs are exploited workers brought in "on the cheap" and that they are virtually unregulated. A spokesperson from the U.S. Information Agency (which currently administers the program) does note that a "45-hour work week" seems excessive and that the USIA has initiated legislation to transfer the program to the U.S. Immigration and Naturalization Service (ostensibly to regulate it more closely).

Rules, regulations, and institutional changes will always influence economic returns to specific groups of labor.[b] Often, as in the case of the au pair program, other goals (such as cultural exchange) are pursued along with economic objectives. There are also distributional considerations — that is, which families will get the services of high-priced nannies, which will use au pairs, and which will do without any hired child care? The answers, in our society as in most others, are determined by political as well as market forces. Any limitations or wage regulations on au pair workers will affect the employers of these workers, the returns to nonregulated nannies, and the au pair placements as well. It is often difficult to disentangle the market aspects of some situations from other features.

[b] The nanny market has been further influenced by the Immigration Act of 1990, which favored (legal) immigration of those with high levels of education and skills and halved the number of visas for unskilled immigrants (to 10,000). That law has created a booming market in the underground (and illegal) supply of nannies from abroad to meet the huge demand for child-care workers by middle- and upper-income households, where women are working in the professions and elsewhere. See Nicola Clark, "A Nannies' Advocate Argues Their Case," *Wall Street Journal,* January 26, 1993, p. A14.

Correspondingly, buyers as a group find that Q_E units is the "best" quantity for them to buy because the choice of any other quantity would be an irrational one. Therefore, once equilibrium is reached, neither buyers nor sellers have any incentive to try to exchange either more or less. So long as D_M and S_M remain unchanged, the market price will tend to remain at P_E, with Q_E units bought and sold each time period. However, should any of the factors underlying the market demand or the market supply change, the initial equilibrium will be disturbed. If, for example, the price of mozzarella cheese (an ingredient used in making pizza) rises, each individual seller of pizza would find that the marginal cost is higher, causing a decrease (leftward shift) in both the individual supply curves and the market supply curve. In Figure 2.8 the change in supply is depicted as a shift in the supply curve from S_M to S_M'. Individual producers may not perceive this increase in chees e prices as having any significant impact on the pizza market. However, at the initial equilibrium price of P_E, the number of pizzas that the sellers as a group prefer to sell (Q_1) is less than Q_E, the number that buyers prefer to buy. What was formerly an equilibrium price is now a price that is below equilibrium. The price will therefore rise to the new equilibrium level, P_E'. To ensure the proper use of economic terminology, review the following sequence of events. The increase in the price of an input (mozzarella) used to produce pizza has led to a *reduction in the supply of pizza,* represented by a shift to the left in the entire supply curve, which causes the price to rise from P_E to P_E' and leads to a *decrease in the quantity demanded,* from Q_E to Q_E'.

Using the same logic, we could examine the consequence of a decrease in the price of mozzarella cheese. This change would reduce the marginal cost of producing pizza to individual sellers of pizza, causing their individual supply curves and the market supply curve to increase (shift to the right). The increase in supply will lead to a reduction in the equilibrium price and to an increase in the quantity demanded.

A change in any of the factors underlying the market supply curve (the price of inputs, the level of technology, the price of related goods, and the

Figure 2.8　The Effects of a Rise in Input Prices

An increase in the price of an input used to produce pizza causes the marginal cost of each producer to rise. This in turn leads to a decrease in the market supply from S_M to S'_M.

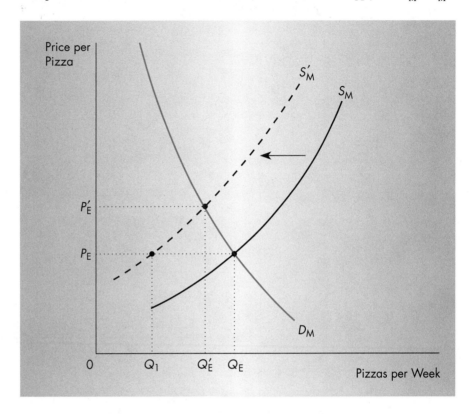

number of sellers) will lead to either an increase or a decrease in the market supply and therefore to either an increase or a decrease in the quantity demanded. Further, a change in any of the factors underlying the market demand curve (the number of buyers, the tastes and preferences of the buyers, their incomes, the price of related goods, and information and expectations) will lead to either an increase or a decrease in the market demand, to an increase or a decrease in the equilibrium price, and to a decrease or an increase in the quantity supplied. For example, suppose new health reports convince buyers that pizza consumption is more detrimental than was previously believed. This information will affect buyers' preferences and lead to a decrease in the market demand for pizza. In Figure 2.9, this decrease is depicted as a leftward shift in the market demand curve, from D_M to D'_M. Assuming that the market is initially in equilibrium at a price of P_E, the decrease in demand will mean that sellers will still be willing to sell Q_E units at that price, but buyers

Figure 2.9 The Effects of a Change in Tastes and Preferences

A reduction in consumers' preference for pizza will cause a decrease in demand from D_M to D_M'. The equilibrium price will fall from P_E to P_E', and the equilibrium quantity will fall from Q_E to Q_E'.

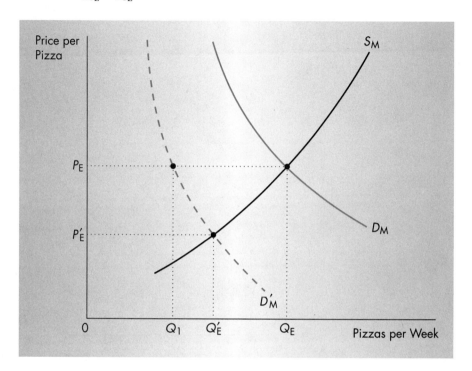

will be willing to buy only Q_1 units. The surplus of pizzas at the initial price will cause the price to fall to the new equilibrium, P_E'.

A change in any of the other factors that underlie the supply curve will also lead to either an increase or a decrease in supply. The change in supply will disturb the initial equilibrium, so that the initial price will be either one at which there is a *surplus* of pizza (the quantity supplied will exceed the quantity demanded) or one at which there is a *shortage* of pizza (the quantity demanded will exceed the quantity supplied).

Applying the demand and supply model is sometimes complicated by real-world events such as international currency problems, recessions, or special market problems (see Highlight 2.2). But the underlying principles generally remain the same: always look for the underlying factors that change market supply and market demand — costs, prices of related goods, number of buyers and sellers, incomes, information and expectations, and tastes and preferences.

Highlight 2.2 *Supply and Demand in the Sports-Car Market: Will the German Porsche Survive?*

For almost 50 years, since its inception, the German automaker Porsche has produced some of the fastest and most beautiful and desirable sports cars in the world. Young Americans of several generations have dreamed of owning one, and more than a few have bought them. For many years Americans were huge supporters of Porsche, purchasing fully one-third of Porsche's annual output. (Californians buy more than half the Porsches sold in America.)

The sports-car market in general, and Porsche in particular, has recently fallen on hard times. Prices have certainly not fallen for the prized automobiles. In 1984 the price range for Porsches was between $21,440 and $44,000, but by 1991 the *lowest* priced model sold for $44,000 and the highest priced (regular production) Porsche went for $95,000. At these prices, it is no wonder that so few of our friends drive them.

The Porsche company's strategy in the 1980s was to upgrade the car's exclusive image by directing its sales effort and price structure to the highest end of the luxury car market. What is disturbing to the Porsche company in the early 1990s is that the attempt has been a failure. Sales of Porsche automobiles in the United States fell by 50 percent between 1990 and 1991 (to only 4,388 units). Moreover, 1991 sales were only about 15 percent of the 1986 level (30,471 units). These price and output data are simulated in Figure 2.10. We may think of the mid-1980s Porsche price and output combination as P_0Q_0 (at point E_0) and the early 1990s situation as depicted at E_1 (price-output combination P_1Q_1).

The simple tools of demand and supply can help us understand what has happened in this particular market. However, shifts in both supply and demand make matters more complex. Specifically we must recognize how the relative amount of supply and demand shifts will affect equilibrium price and quantity. A decrease in supply by itself causes a quantity decrease and a price increase. A decrease in demand by itself causes a quantity decrease and a price decrease. Simultaneous leftward shifts will therefore cause a predictable decrease in quantity, but the equilibrium change in price will be determined by the relative size of the shift in demand and supply. The Porsche market is a case in point.

First, consider tastes and preferences. If anything, Porsche has a brand image, or "cachet," so many young Americans are ambitious to own one. Some have suggested that, in the 1990s, the image of driving a Porsche is somewhat less desirable. This proposition is doubtful, and reliance on a "suggestion" of this kind would be most unwise. Consider some other factors relating to demand and supply:

First, competition among sports cars available to Americans has improved

Figure 2.10 The American Market for German Porsches

The dollar's fall on foreign-exchange markets increases the marginal cost (measured in U.S. dollars) of selling Porsches in the United States and the supply of Porsches declines. The United States recession reduces the incomes of Porsche buyers, causing a decrease in the demand for Porsches in the United States. The simultaneous decreases in supply and demand reduce the number of Porsches sold in the United States, and as the graph shows, the price of Porsches rises.

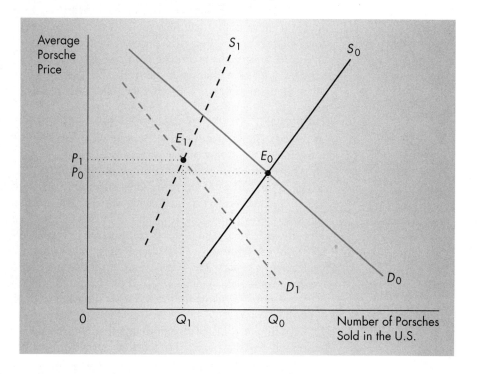

markedly. Japan, especially, has provided ample competition in the luxury-car market. New sports cars, such as the Mazda RX7 and the Nissan 300ZX, vie for the American consumer's dollar against the (generally) higher priced German Porsches. The price and availability of related goods, in other words, has changed, reducing the demand for Porsches. Moreover, the 1990–1992 U.S. recession reduced incomes, including those of the white-collar professionals most apt to purchase Porsches, also suggesting a reduction in demand. In 1990, a new federal excise tax was imposed on luxury automobiles, so that consumers had to pay 10 percent in taxes for every dollar in excess of $30,000 spent on cars. This means that a car with a $40,000 sticker price would actually cost the buyer $41,000, with $1,000 going to pay the federal tax. These factors, more than simply a "taste change," explain the leftward shift or reduction in demand for Porsches shown in Figure 2.10. Taken by themselves, these factors have a price-decreasing impact in the market. But other supply-driven factors must also be considered.

A somewhat obvious and simple explanation exists for the leftward shift in the supply curve shown in Figure 2.10. The U.S. dollar has been falling in value relative to the German mark since the mid-1980s. This means that the dollar-denominated supply of Porsches has shifted leftward, as shown. At every quantity of Porsches sold in the United States, the company's supply price has increased. Taken alone, the supply curve decrease would increase price. The result has in fact been an overall *increase* in the equilibrium price accompanying a reduction in the equilibrium quantity of Porsches sold in the United States. We may think of such an equilibrium as point E_1 in Figure 2.10.

Although the luxury-car market, including that for Porsche sports cars, has apparently been quite sensitive to recession and economic downturns, Americans have not seen the end of these beautiful machines. The company is fighting back by offering a new 968 model (to sell at $39,850 before taxes) and promising a whole range of new Porches by 1995. Many of them will be "popularly" priced. It is unlikely, moreover, that well-heeled Americans will end their love affair with the car. Of the (approximately) 560,000 Porsches in existence in 1992, more than 260,000 are in America.

[a] See Krystal Miller and Terence Roth, "Porsche, a Favorite in Times of Plenty, Struggles to Survive in a More Frugal Era," *Wall Street Journal*, January 27, 1992, pp. B1, B5.

It is important, further, to recognize that market equilibrium is intimately related to the allocative mechanisms of markets. An understanding of the interplay between demand and supply enables us to see how the market works as an efficient rationing device. Anyone with the desire *and* the ability to buy goods and services gets them. Those whose effective demand (desire and ability to pay) is less than the equilibrium price are eliminated from the market. Likewise, suppliers who are unable to supply goods and services because of high costs are effectively eliminated from the market. Only those suppliers whose costs are below the equilibrium price allocate resources to production. In this manner, markets — the products of demand and supply — allocate resources to their highest valued uses through price signals to buyers and sellers.

This demand-supply framework is the means by which economists examine most real-world markets. In certain markets in which individual buyers or sellers are able to exercise great control over price, this framework of analysis is not useful. Nonetheless, your ability to engage in economic analysis is to a large degree contingent on your mastery of demand and supply. Even in markets in which individual participants are not really price takers, this supply-demand model can prove very useful in understanding how prices are established.

Taxes and Subsidies

Market demand and market supply curves indicate the relationship between price and quantity, holding all other factors that influence the decision to buy or sell constant. For demand, these factors include income, prices of other goods, buyers' tastes, and the number of buyers; for supply, resource prices, technology, and the number of sellers determine the position of the curve. These are not, by any stretch of the imagination, the only *ceteris paribus* factors that affect market behavior.

Another important factor that is held constant is taxes and subsidies, each of which affects the prices paid by buyers and received by sellers. For analytical purposes we define a **tax** as any payment — cash or in-kind — made to some governmental authority, including local, state, and federal governments. This definition encompasses the usual array of taxes: personal and corporate income taxes, social security contributions, general sales taxes, property taxes, and the maze of excise taxes on specific goods and services. It also includes all fees collected by public agencies and the value of resources, goods, or services that are commandeered by legislative authority. The former would include such items as park fees, airport landing charges, and water, sewer, and trash-collection assessments. The latter includes the land that developers are sometimes required to set aside as green areas and the labor of those (such as Swiss and Israeli citizens) subject to compulsory military and/or public service.

A **subsidy** is similarly defined as any benefit — cash or in-kind — received *from* government; subsidies likewise come in many guises. Many college students benefit from government support of colleges and universities. Small businesses and selected homeowners get low-interest loans. Nearly everyone benefits from indirect subsidies in the form of tax deductions for home-mortgage interest payments, charitable contributions, and medical and business expenses. Many households and businesses further benefit from goods and services provided at no or low cost by government-supported research in the basic and applied sciences. Job-training programs are an example of in-kind subsidy programs.

The Economic Impact of Taxes

According to Benjamin Franklin, nothing is certain but death and taxes. The vast majority of market activity generates a tax liability as a result of the exchange. The simple act of buying and driving a car puts one firmly in the clutches of the tax collector. You may pay a sales tax on the purchase price of your car, another tax to license it for street use, and yet another every time you have it inspected. You are taxed every time you fill the tank with gas and every time you drive on a toll highway. You even pay taxes when you talk on your cellular phone or pick up an order of fries at the drive-thru. How do these

Figure 2.11 The Market Effects of a Tax

A tax on gasoline retailers reduces the retail supply of gasoline, increases the price of gasoline, and reduces the quantity of gasoline consumed. The price, however, does not rise by the full amount of the tax: part of the tax is paid by buyers, the remainder by sellers.

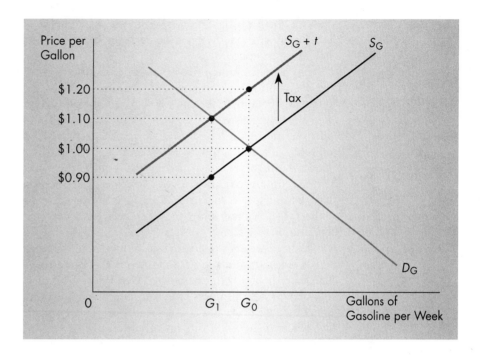

taxes influence their respective markets? Supply-and-demand analysis can be used to determine the market effects of a tax. We will use a tax on gasoline to illustrate these effects.

The retail market for gasoline can be illustrated using the supply-and-demand model of this Chapter. The large numbers of buyers (drivers) and sellers (service stations) of gasoline leave little room for any one driver or service station owner to influence the price of gasoline. The supply and demand for gasoline would, *ceteris paribus*,[6] establish an equilibrium price, as illustrated in Figure 2.11. The intersection of the demand curve (D_G) and supply curve (S_G) sets the price of gasoline at $1 per gallon with G_0 gallons of gasoline consumed each week.

Suppose the government decides to expand the highway system and to finance the new construction with a 20-cents-per-gallon tax on gasoline, to be

---

6. *Ceteris paribus* is Latin for "other things being constant."

collected from gasoline retailers.[7] The imposition of a gasoline tax alters the market equilibrium by changing one of the elements held constant. Service-station operators will add the tax to the pump price, whatever it may be. If the price were $1, the pumps would be reset at $1.20; if the price were $0.90, the pumps would be reset at $1.10. In terms of supply and demand, the tax is added to the supply curve, shifting it vertically by the amount of the tax to $S_G + t$ (where t is the amount of the tax) in Figure 2.11. This leftward shift of the supply curve indicates a decrease in supply; at any given price, a smaller quantity is supplied.

Simply raising the price of gasoline by 20 cents to $1.20 does not produce a new equilibrium, because the quantity supplied at this price exceeds the quantity demanded. A new market equilibrium occurs at the intersection of D_G (the original demand curve) and the new supply curve, $S_G + T$. The tax on gasoline raises the equilibrium price of gasoline to $1.10 and reduces the quantity of gasoline used per week to G_1 gallons. Thus drivers pay more for gasoline and use less than they did before the tax was imposed. How do drivers conserve on their use of gasoline? They plan better in order to elimi-nate extra trips to the store, they car-pool or use public transportation, they walk or bicycle, and sometimes they even purchase more fuel-efficient vehicles. One ultimate effect of the tax, then, is that the increased cost of operating a car induces drivers to find alternative modes of transportation.

What is true of the gasoline tax in this example is true of all taxes. A tax will raise the market price of the taxed item and reduce the quantity traded in the market as consumers switch to alternatives. Taxes on wage earnings (per-sonal income taxes and social security) raise the price of labor but reduce the net return-to-work effort, and the number of hours worked may decline as workers substitute leisure time for labor time. All taxes affect behavior. Taxes on restaurant meals raise the price of eating out and consumers respond by eating out less. Tuition increases at state-supported colleges reduce enrollment as some students seek alternative forms of higher education.

Supply-and-demand analysis of taxes entails an important lesson for government budget directors. Suppose the legislature decides to eliminate a $300 billion budget deficit with a special tax on gasoline. Where 150 billion gallons of gasoline are consumed, a $2 per gallon tax would theoretically bal-ance the budget. Budget directors, however, must take all the market effects of the tax into account when they develop economic forecasts. The revenue gen-erated by the tax will be the amount of the tax multiplied by the quantity exchanged after the tax. Using the pre-tax equilibrium quantity to forecast tax receipts will overestimate future tax collections. The $2 per gallon tax will *not* generate $300 billion — consumers will not consume the same amount of gasoline when the price of a gallon nearly triples. The tax will generate less

---

7. This specific result (equal tax burdens) is a consequence of the specific positions and shapes of the supply and demand curves as drawn in Figure 2.11. The factors that determine the relative tax burdens will be discussed in Chapter 6.

revenue than might otherwise be expected, because taxes reduce the level of market activity.

Who actually *pays* the tax? The question of **tax incidence** investigates the impact of a tax to determine who (buyers or sellers) bears the burden. We can derive the incidence of the gasoline tax discussed above by closely examining Figure 2.11. The station operators' initial response to the tax, increasing the pump price by the amount of the tax, did not move the market to a new equilibrium. A price of $1.20 (the original price plus the tax) is above the intersection of the demand curve and the after-tax supply curve. The price had to fall to $1.10 to generate a new equilibrium. The burden of the tax then is determined by comparing the before- and after-tax equilibrium prices.

The incidence of the tax depicted in Figure 2.11 falls equally on the buyers and the sellers.[8] The buyers' price rises from $1.00 to $1.10 per gallon, a $.10 increase. At the same time, the gasoline retailers experience a $.10 reduction in the price they receive for each gallon sold. Buyers are now paying $1.10, but $.20 of that amount goes to the government, leaving $.90 for the service station. This is $.10 less than the retailer received prior to the tax. The burden of this $.20 tax is divided evenly between the buyers and the sellers. In general, the incidence of a tax is on both the buyers and the sellers. A tax forces a rise in the market price of the taxed item. The price increase will usually be less than the amount of the tax, indicating that part of the tax is paid by the buyer and part by the seller. This is why there is usually a consensus opposing taxes: they affect all market participants in the same way. More will be said about taxes in future chapters, but we now turn our attention to the question of government subsidies.

---

8. The market effects and incidence a tax can be illustrated algebraically. Suppose, as in the text, that (1) market demand is described by the equation $P = 100 - 2Q$ and (2) market supply is described by the equation $P = 25 + 3Q$. The pre-tax equilibrium will be the point at which the curves intersect, or where

$$100 - 2Q = 25 + 3Q$$

Solving the above equality for Q, we find that the equilibrium quantity is 15 units of the good. Substituting the equilibrium quantity into either the demand or supply equations gives us the equilibrium price of $70.

Now assume that the government levies a $5 per unit tax on the sellers. The tax must be deducted from the price received by the seller, so the supply equation becomes $P - 5 = 25 + 3Q$. Rearranging this equation so that price is isolated gives us the after-tax supply curve $P = 30 + 3Q$. The after-tax equilibrium will be at the intersection of the demand and after-tax supply curves, or where

$$100 - 2Q = 30 + 3Q$$

Solving for Q, we find that the equilibrium quantity has fallen to 14 units of the good. Substituting into the demand equation, we find that buyers are now paying $72 per unit of the good, of which $5 goes to government and $67 goes to the seller. The tax reduces the equilibrium quantity, raises the price paid by buyers, and reduces the price received by sellers. The price paid by buyers rises by $2 — the burden of the $5 tax borne by consumers. The price received by sellers falls by $3 — the burden of the $5 tax borne by producers.

Subsidies

Subsidies may not seem as numerous or pervasive as taxes; however, this may be more perception than fact. Most people use a very narrow definition of government subsidies — cash payments from government. Actually, there are relatively few government programs that involve a direct cash payment to consumers or producers, but subsidies can be defined to include *any* benefit granted by government. Nearly everyone, consumers and producers, benefits in some way. Subsidies range from public funding of basic and applied research and the deductibility of mortgage interest payments to public funding of education and subsidies to the agricultural sector of the economy. Subsidies, obviously, do not create the controversy that taxes generate. Whereas ballot initiatives to limit government's ability to tax abound, no one has ever sought to limit government's ability to grant subsidies.

Figure 2.12 The Market Effects of a Subsidy

Government subsidies of colleges and universities increase the supply of higher education. The subsidy reduces the price of a college degree and increases the number of college students. Students and their families benefit from lower tuition and greater educational opportunities, while colleges enroll more students at a higher net price. The net price received by the colleges is the sum of tuition rates and the subsidy.

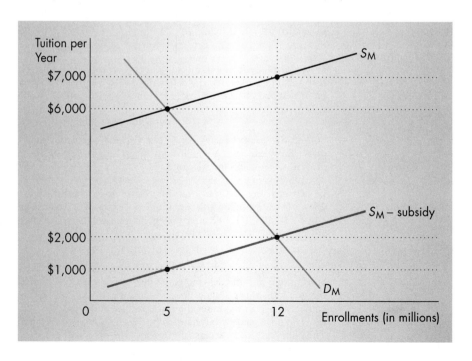

The Market Effects of a Subsidy In terms of the government's impact on economic agents, a subsidy is the opposite of a tax; that's why economists sometimes refer to subsidies as **negative taxes.** If we view subsidies in this way, it follows that we can analyze the market effects of a subsidy in essentially the same way as for a tax. The only difference is that the market impact of a subsidy is the reverse of the impact of a tax. A tax will decrease supply; a subsidy will increase supply.

Suppose that all colleges and universities were private schools with students (and their families) bearing the entire cost of a college education. The initial market equilibrium might look something like Figure 2.12, where D_M and S_M are the initial market demand and supply curves for a college education. The market would be in equilibrium with 5 million students enrolled and tuition at $6,000 per year. If the government were to provide a subsidy of $5,000 per year per student, the subsidy would shift the supply curve downward by the amount of the subsidy, or to S_M – $5,000. Although the marginal costs of providing a college education would remain the same, the college would be able to cover those costs by collecting $5,000 less from each student. If enrollments were to remain constant, tuition would fall to $1,000 per year. The lower tuition, however, would increase the quantity of higher education demanded. Enrollments would increase and tuition would rise until a new market equilibrium was reached. The post-subsidy equilibrium will occur at the point at which tuition is $2,000 and college enrollment has risen to 12 million students. The subsidy lowers the market price and raises the equilibrium quantity.

This quantity-raising effect of a subsidy has important budgetary considerations. If enrollment had remained at 5 million students, the subsidy would have cost the taxpayers $25 billion per year. But by lowering the market price of a college degree, the increase in the quantity demanded increased the costs of the subsidy proportionately (to $60 billion). Because a subsidy lowers the market price and increases the equilibrium quantity, the total cost to taxpayers of providing the subsidy also increases. Given that subsidies are a part of the burden that falls on taxpayers, why hasn't an antisubsidy movement joined the ubiquitous antitax movements? Part of the answer lies in who benefits from the subsidy.

The Beneficiaries of a Subsidy Who benefits from a subsidy? The simple answer is whoever cashes the government's check. Our example began with the colleges receiving tuition of $6,000 per student, so the colleges are the direct beneficiaries of this hypothetical program. The subsidy lowers tuition from $6,000 to $2,000, but the $5,000 per student payment increases the total receipts per student to $7,000. The suppliers thus benefit from a higher net price for their product. This higher net price translates into even higher total revenues when we consider the quantity effect. The pre-subsidy equilibrium has colleges earning $30 billion per year (5 million students at $6,000 per student). In the postsubsidy equilibrium, colleges generate $24 million in tuition revenues (12 million students at $2,000 per year) *plus* $60 billion in government subsidies, for total receipts of $84 billion. Clearly, the subsidy increases the amount of money going to producers of the subsidized good or service.

The colleges (producers) are not the only beneficiaries of the subsidy, however. Everyone involved on the supply side of the market benefits as well. University employees (faculty, staff, and administration) all benefit as employment and wages rise to meet the expanded student population. Those who sell the materials and supplies used in the production of a college education also gain from the expansion of economic activity. For instance, textbook publishers (and authors) experience a gain as more students buy more books. In short, everyone connected with the industry benefits from the subsidy.

The last, and certainly not least, of the beneficiaries are the students themselves and their families. Subsidizing the schools reduces the tuition costs of a college education. In our example, tuition falls from $6,000 to $2,000. This is a $4,000-per-year savings to the 5 million who would have enrolled anyway. The lower tuition also opens the door to 7 million other students who would not have gone to college otherwise. The demand side of the market benefits from the subsidy even though the money goes directly to the suppliers. Consumers benefit from both lower market prices and higher quantities of goods exchanged.[9]

Taxes and subsidies are also similar in that they both have an impact on market prices. The change in market prices may well be an unintended by-product of tax and expenditure policy. There are programs, however,

---

9. The impact of a subsidy can also be illustrated with some simple algebra. Suppose that we are dealing with the same market curves as in footnote 7 examining the impact of a tax. The market demand is described by the equation $P = 100 - 2Q$, and the market supply is described by the equation $P = 25 + 3Q$. The pre-tax equilibrium is the point at which the quantity is 15 and the price is $70.

Now assume that the government provides a $5 per unit subsidy to the sellers for each unit sold. The subsidy is added to the price received by the seller, so the supply equation becomes $P + 5 = 25 + 3Q$. Rearranging this equation to isolate price gives us the after-subsidy supply curve

$$P = 20 + 3Q$$

The after-tax equilibrium will be at the intersection of the demand and after-tax supply curves, or where

$$100 - 2Q = 20 + 3Q$$

Solving for Q, we find that the equilibrium quantity has risen to 16 units of the good. Substituting into the demand equation, we find that buyers are now paying $68 per unit of the good. Sellers, on the other hand, are receiving $73 per unit — the $68 amount paid by the consumer plus the $5 received from government. The subsidy increases the equilibrium quantity, reduces the price paid by buyers, and increases the price received by sellers. The price paid by buyers falls by $2 — the share of the $5 subsidy received by consumers. The price received by sellers rises by $3 — the share of the $5 subsidy received by producers.

whose intent is to alter market prices. One way in which the government intentionally alters market prices is by imposing price controls.

Price Controls

In many societies certain prices are established by law rather than by the interaction of supply and demand. In the United States the prices of many goods and services are subject to government control. For example, in many cities rent-control laws hold rents below their equilibrium levels. Simultaneously, minimum-wage laws hold wages above their equilibrium levels. Rent-control and minimum-wage laws are examples of price controls. **Price controls** are imposed when government decision makers determine that a market price is somehow unacceptable (for example, the price is unfair, unreasonable, exploitative, and/or irresponsible). The market response to price controls differs according to whether the controlled price is above or below the market equilibrium price.

Price Ceilings

A **price ceiling** is a maximum price that sellers can legally accept (and buyers can legally pay) for a product. Price ceilings are imposed when governments determine that a market price is "too high." Virtually all consumer goods were under price ceilings during World War II, when the diversion of resources to the production of military goods made civilian goods unusually scarce. Contemporary American examples of price ceilings include rent controls and usury laws, which set limits on the interest rates that lenders may charge. As noted in Chapter 1, the former Soviet Union held food prices below equilibrium levels to reduce the financial burden of food purchases. Although price ceilings are very popular among those who expect to benefit from the lower price, they are not always the boon that consumers expect. An analysis of price ceilings using supply and demand reveals some of the market distortions they cause.

Consider the price ceiling in Figure 2.13, which shows hypothetical supply and demand for medical malpractice insurance in Wisconsin. The initial market demand and supply for the insurance are shown as D and S, respectively. At a market price of $9,000 per year, a market equilibrium is reached with a quantity of Q_E policies bought and sold. Assume that the number of medical malpractice suits skyrockets in the state, matching legal activities that have had an impact on insurance rates all over the country.

As liability awards begin to rise in increasing numbers of lawsuits, the cost of coverage for individual doctors begins to rise, too. These events have the impact of shifting the supply curve for medical insurance leftward, as in Figure 2.13. Rising costs cause the insurance companies to appeal to the state board

Figure 2.13 A Price Ceiling on Medical Insurance

A regulated maximum price of $9,000 per year on medical insurance will, if the supply curve has shifted leftward to S', create an excess demand for insurance of AF. A supply curve of S'' will mean that *no* insurance will be purchased at the regular rate of $9,000.

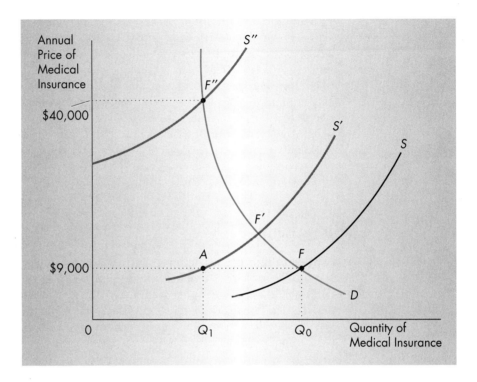

to increase the premiums the companies can legally charge. Suppose the board denies the appeal for higher rates and instead imposes a maximum rate (ceiling) of $9,000 per year. If the cost increase shifts the supply curve from S to S' (in Figure 2.13), an excess demand of A_F or $Q_1 Q_E$ would develop. At that price, Q_E policies would be demanded, but only Q_1 would be supplied per year. Many physicians in the state would have their malpractice insurance cancelled.

If the market for medical insurance were unregulated, a rise in price could be expected (to point F' in Figure 2.13). Physicians — who must have insurance in order to avoid the personal bankruptcy that a successful suit against them would bring — tend to be very unresponsive to changes in the price of insurance. This resistance explains the nearly vertical demand curve in the figure. Because such insurance is essential to doing business, the unavailability of insurance at $9,000 per year discourages some physicians from continuing to practice. This result is a decrease in the number of specialists — obstetricians in particular — in the state. This is shown by the total quantity of OQ_1 insurance bought by practicing physicians with the price ceiling in effect. (Moreover, those doctors who continue to practice without insurance are often poorer-quality physicians.)

In the extreme, rising damage awards against physicians may reduce the supply curve for insurance all the way to S'' in Figure 2.13. The market equilibrium would take place at point F'' at a price of $40,000. With a legal price ceiling of $9,000, *no* medical insurance would be sold. In addition to the direct effect of lowering prices to some buyers, price ceilings also have the indirect effect of reducing the availability of the good — creating a **shortage.** The good could in fact disappear from the market altogether. These side effects are often unanticipated and unintended by those who enact and administer price ceilings.[10]

Price Floors

In addition to imposing price ceilings in some markets, the government — through the political process — imposes price floors in others. A **price floor** is a minimum price legislatively imposed at some level above the equilibrium price. An above-equilibrium price is required by someone in the public sector who believes that the market price is "too low." Clearly, price floors are designed to benefit the seller of the commodity. Some of the most contentious problems in trade relations among individual members of the European Community and between the EC and the United States relates to agricultural floors. Farmers, the designated beneficiaries of price floors, understandably do not want to give up their subsidies in order to provide a level playing field in trade relations between, say, France and Germany or between the European Community and the United States or Japan. This means that different levels of subsidies to farmers in different countries or regions can put countries at "unfair" advantages in export markets.

How do these price floors work? Imagine a market for some U.S. agricultural product — wheat, avocadoes, peanuts, oranges, milk, or any of a hundred other products would do. We take milk as our example. Figure 2.14 illustrates (with hypothetical numbers) the operation of price supports on such a market. Assume that the equilibrium price received by dairy farmers is initially P_0 and

---

10. The market effects of a price ceiling can be demonstrated with some simple algebra. Assume that market demand is described by the formula $P = 500 - 10Q$. Also suppose that the equation for the supply curve is $P = 100 + 10Q$. In the absence of price controls, this market achieves equilibrium at a price of $300 and quantity of 20.

Now suppose that the legislature sets a price ceiling of $200. By the equation for the demand curve, consumers will want to purchase 30 units of the good when the price is $200. Conversely, producers will be willing to sell, by the equation for the supply curve, only 10 units of the good when the price is $200. A $200 price ceiling causes a shortage of 20 units of the good.

Figure 2.14 The Effects of Milk Price Supports

The price floor creates a surplus of milk produced in the market in the amount of *GH*. Either the excess supply must be stored or the U.S. Department of Agriculture must develop policies to reduce dairy-milk production.

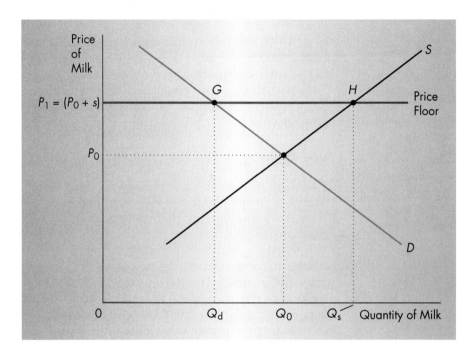

that the equilibrium or unregulated market quantity is Q_E. By pressuring the federal government through the political process, dairy farmers succeed in obtaining price supports for their output. Further assume that the price floor is, as shown in Figure 2.14, placed *above* the equilibrium price. At price P_1 (the support price), the government promises to give farmers a subsidy equal to the difference between the market price and the support price.

The guaranteed price is in effect the price P_1 — the market price (P_0) and the subsidy (S), or $P_1 = P_0 + S$. At price P_1, however, the quantity supplied of milk is Q_S but quantity demanded is Q_D. A **surplus** is created by the subsidy in the amount G_H. Clearly the government has a problem: it must either pay subsidies on the quantity produced of Q_S or pursue policies to reduce the amount of the surplus. In terms of agricultural commodities, this means crop-production or herd-size restrictions. Past and present failures to restrict supply have led to "surplus products" storage problems. Ever-increasing inventories of products pile up in warehouses. Each year's surplus is added to previously accumulated inventories, and the cost of carrying the expanding inventory of unsold goods rises. The buyer-of-last-resort is usually the government, which means that taxpayers end up paying for the surplus.[11]

The American economy is well supplied with examples of regulated prices, both above and below equilibrium prices. Many, including minimum-wage laws, rent controls, and controls in markets for particular goods, will be discussed throughout this textbook. Attempts to place controls in markets seldom work in the sense that they have costly and (often) unpredictable effects.

Demand and Multiple Products from One Supply Source

Agricultural C

Simple demand-and-supply theory, covered thus far in the chapter, applies to an incredibly large number of goods and services. There are, however, important classes of cases in which simple supply-and-demand theory must be modified. One such case involves instances of a single production process yielding more than one good or service. The classic examples come from agriculture. The production of steers, for example, enables the production of both edible beef and hides for leather.[12] Sheep production creates both edible lamb and wool. Certain chemical production or extraction processes (for example, gas and coke) produce multiple usable materials. Many of these necessarily involve the production of unwanted smoke or pollution as additional by-products.

Joint-Supply Theory

The problem for these types of goods is fundamentally that cost can be determined for the **jointly supplied good** (a steer or a sheep, for example) but *not for the separate commodities that are sold from producing it.* Consider the classic

---

11. The market effects of a price floor can also be demonstrated with simple algebra. Start with the same market as in the price ceiling example (footnote 9) where market demand is $P = 500 - 10Q$ and market supply is $P = 100 + 10Q$. The uncontrolled market equilibrium is still at a price of $300 and a quantity of 20.

Now suppose the legislature sets a price floor of $400. By the equation for the demand curve, the quantity demanded at a price of $400 is 10 units of the good. Conversely, producers will be willing to sell, by the equation for the supply curve, only 30 units of the good when the price is set at $400. The $400 price ceiling causes a 20-unit surplus of the good to develop.

12. This classic case was analyzed as early as 1848 by classical economist and philosopher John Stuart Mill (1806–1873). Mill called the example a "peculiar case of value" but, as we will see, its applicability is far wider than Mill thought or understood. Alfred Marshall (1842–1924), Cambridge economist and modern founder of organized microeconomic theory, added the graphics of the joint supply case to Mill's discussion. See Marshall's *Principles of Economics,* Chapter 6, Book V, (London: Macmillan, 1920 [originally published in 1890]).

case of beef and hides.[13] The rancher who raises steers incurs resource costs to do so — feed, land, water, labor, and so on. When steers are processed, assume that at least two products are of value — beef for consumption and hides for sale to shoe manufacturers. How do we determine the individual supply curves for beef and hides? Likewise, how do we allocate the costs of producing steers between the two commodities produced?

The answer, not a surprising one, is that there is no scientific way of partitioning or allocating the steer costs between the two commodities. There *is*, however, a clever (if arbitrary) way to allocate these costs with only *one* quantity of steers produced. After all, it would be impossible to produce one quantity of steers for beef and another for hides, because the attempt would always result in over- or under-production of one of the goods. Costs are allocated so that the *sum* of the revenue from the equilibrium prices of the two goods equals the supply price (the average production cost) of steers. Before turning to a formal graphical model of this case, consider several facts and assumptions that apply to such cases.

Although it is not necessary that the proportions of hides and beef to steers be fixed, the problem is simplified if they are. In practical terms this means that the ratio of the square feet of hides obtained from steers and the number of pounds of beef obtained from steers are constant. Each steer not only produces beef and hides but also produces them in fixed proportions.

An obvious but critical distinction about this case must also be noted. In all of the markets considered so far in this chapter, consumption is "competing." If you and I are both at a grocery store at the same time and are considering the demand and supply of bananas, your consumption competes with mine. If you buy more bananas, fewer are available for me. In the case of beef and hides, the consumption is not competing but is complementary in nature. True, if we are both buying beef or both buying hides, the more of either that you get, the less for me. But if I am buying beef and you are buying hides, the *more* beef I buy, the *more* hides are available to you. This essential characteristic, which applies only to jointly supplied goods, is often called **noncompeting,** or **complementary, consumption.**[14]

In the case described in Figure 2.2 of this chapter, individual demand curves for pizza were added horizontally to get a market demand curve for pizza. Likewise, we would add each individual's demand curve to get the

---

13. Steers may yield many other products besides beef and hides, such as tallow or horns. Beef may be further decomposed into sirloin steaks, hamburger, and so on. Chickens, likewise, may be thought of as producing many products — wings, thighs, legs, breasts, feet (popular in Asian cuisine), and so on. We can easily analyze these situations within the framework of multiple products and joint supply.

14. In Chapter 15, we will see that "different products" are not required in order to obtain this characteristic. A "nontransferrable" characteristic is all that is necessary in the public goods case.

Figure 2.15 Demands for Jointly Supplied Goods

Because the supplies of beef and hides are complementary rather than competing, the demands for beef and hides must be added vertically to obtain the (total) demand for steers. The optimal quantity of steers is found at point *E*, the intersection of steer demand and steer supply. In equilibrium (at *E*), supply equals the demand for steers.

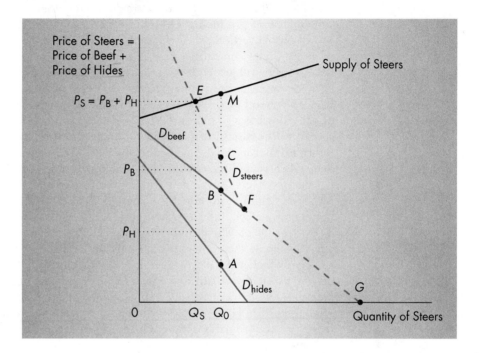

market demand curves for both beef and hides in Figure 2.15. But in order to obtain the equilibrium quantity of beef and hides produced, we must equate the demand for and the supply of steers. However, we can obtain the demand for steers only by adding *vertically* the respective market demands for beef and hides. Obviously, a demand for a quantity of beef implies a demand for steers and a demand for hides implies a demand for steers. The total demand for steers is derived, therefore, by adding the demand for beef and the demand for hides.

Graphical Analysis

Consider Figure 2.15 at a quantity Q_0 of steers produced. The demand for steers is constructed as just discussed. The total demand for steers at that quantity is the vertical sum of the demand for hides and the demand for beef, or $Q_0A + Q_0B = Q_0C$, which is the demand for steers. Clearly, however, the supply of steers will not equal the demand for steers at that quantity. The revenue from producing steers, on average, will only be $Q_0 C$, whereas the supply cost of producing that quantity will be $Q_0 M$. The only point at which supply will equal the demand for steers is at point E, which corresponds to quantity Q_S. In order to cover the supply costs of producing that number of units, price P_B will be charged for units of beef and price P_H will be charged for hides. When these two prices are added together, they will just equal the supply cost of producing Q_S units of steers. Note that the price of steers shown on the vertical axis is the simple *sum* of the price of hides and the price of beef. (Under competitive conditions the price or average revenue from producing steers will just equal average cost in equilibrium.)

One important test for whether joint supply exists in the production and sale of any good is to ask this question: Will an increase in the demand for one of the goods (say, hides), reduce the equilibrium price of the other good (beef)? In the case shown in Figure 2.15, the answer is clearly yes! Think of a rightward shift in the demand curve for hides. The vertical addition of this new demand curve and the (stable) demand curve for beef would increase the total demand for steers. At the new equilibrium to the right of point E, the demand for steers would again equal the supply of steers. A line drawn down to the horizontal axis will intersect the individual demand curves for beef and hides. The price of beef will fall and the price of hides will rise.

This simple theory has an amazingly wide range of applicability. Examples, some of which we will consider in this book, may be drawn from areas as diverse as electrical utilities and telephone services, public goods such as national defense, even the seasonal supply of hotel and motel rooms (see Highlight 2.3). The examples of multiple production are many, but the basic theory is extraordinarily simple. Once mastered, the theory may be applied to numerous cases.

Highlight 2.3   *Florida Vacations, Seasonal Rates, and the Theory of Multiple Products*

The north coast of Florida is an increasingly popular spot for seashore and winter vacations. The emerald-colored water, sandy white beaches, and fabulous recreational facilities, including world-class golf courses and year-round art and food festivals, attract visitors all year long. Relatively high mean winter temperatures are especially appealing to Canadians and northeasterners who crave an escape from the cold weather. In spite of the brisk winter demand, summer vacation demand dominates (is greater than) demand in all other seasons. The "discovery" of this relatively new vacation haven has been heavily encouraged in the press and on television in the United States and in Europe.

Clearly, the expense you will incur to visit north Florida will depend on the season of the year you choose. In particular, the rental rates on vacation and recreational properties vary widely from season to season. The rate

Table 2.3 Rental Rates at The Tradewinds Condos, 1991–92

Rates vary with the season of the year at most vacation sites. Seasonal demands are noncompeting in nature and competitive pricing requires different prices for different seasons.

	Daily*	Weekly	Monthly
Spring Rates (Effective April 1 – Memorial Day Weekend)			
1 Bedroom/1 Bath	$75	$400	
2 Bedrooms/2 Baths	85	450	
Summer Rates (Memorial Day Weekend – Labor Day Weekend)			
1 Bedroom/1 Bath	$85	$500	
2 Bedrooms/2 Baths	95	600	
Fall/Winter Rates (After Labor Day Weekend – March 31)			
1 Bedroom/1 Bath	$65	$350	$500
2 Bedrooms/2 Baths	75	400	600

*Daily rates based on three-day minimum stay.

schedule for one and two bedroom condominiums at the Tradewinds complex in Destin, Florida — typical of those along the coast — is presented in Table 2.3. As you can see, expenses for a Florida visit vary widely. Even more important, from the perspective of economic theory, is that the hotel-motel business in this and in all other vacation areas involves the pricing of multiple products. Common sense tells us that it would not (ordinarily) be possible to build one quantity of hotel or motel rooms for summer and another quantity for winter in Destin, Cancun, the French Riviera, or anywhere else. A quantity of rooms is built and is available during *all* seasons of the year.

The theory of demand for multiple products from a single supply source gives us guidance in analyzing the situation. The condo-rental situation is a perfect analogy to the case of beef and hides discussed earlier, except that the multiple commodities (the actual accommodations from season to season) are physically identical (unlike hamburger, sirloin, and leather). What, then, makes the analogy to the beef-and-hides case correct? It is that hotel rooms in July *do not compete* with hotel rooms in April or December. If the Tradewinds or any other supplier built more one- or two-bedroom units for the summer traffic, they would have to try to fill them in the winter as well. Therefore, the addition of two-bedroom units for summer visitors to Florida necessarily involves the additional supply of two-bedroom units for spring and winter visitors as well. This feature of noncompeting consumption is the essence of the multiple-product, joint-supply case. In effect, the commodity "rooms in winter" is different than "rooms in summer."

Off-season and on-season rate differentials in vacation resorts and elsewhere are an economic pricing policy designed to keep hotel, motel, and rental units filled.

The solution is exactly the same as that shown in Figure 2.15. In Figure 2.16, the demands for a specific commodity — two-bedroom, two-bath condos on a *weekly* rental — are shown for all four seasons of the year. Because you and I would be competitors in any given season, say spring, the summation to get the spring demand would be horizontal. But if you visit in winter and I visit in spring, our demands would be complementary (noncompeting) and the two curves would be, as they are in Figure 2.16, added vertically.

If the costs of supplying condos are assumed constant, as they are in Figure 2.16, the equilibrium quantity of two-bedroom/two-bath condos to build for the entire year's vacation rental demand is Q_0, where total demand and supply intersect at point E. The solution demands that different prices be charged depending on the strength of demand in the various periods. In summer, the season of highest demand, a price of $600 per week is charged; in fall and winter, the rates fall by $200 to $400 per week (to point A in Figure 2.16).

A number of aspects of the solution are interesting. If demand in any one season — say, spring — were to increase (perhaps by college students discovering this new spring-break destination), the entire demand curve would shift rightward. In the case shown in Figure 2.16, the result would be reduced rates

Figure 2.16 Seasonal Demands and Jointly Supplied Vacation Condos
The seasonal demands for vacation condos must be added vertically in order to obtain the total demand for the commodity. The optimal solution is to price the *same* condos differently in different seasons of the year.

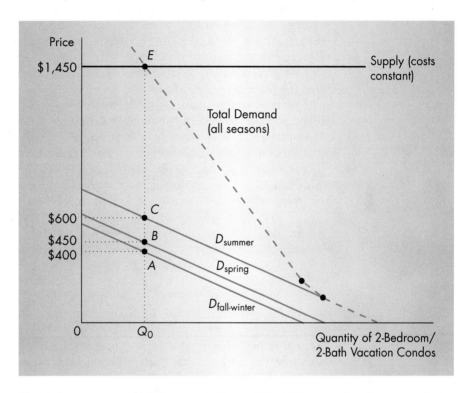

for both summer and fall-winter visitors. Why? The supply of more units in spring necessarily means an increased supply of the units in both winter and summer. Given that these particular demands do not change, an increased supply of rooms would have this effect.

The Theory of Relative Prices

In our development of demand and supply, we have expressed the price of the various goods in terms of dollars — that is, we have considered the **nominal price** of the goods in question. However, in considering the importance of changes in price on economic choice, it is at times useful to consider changes in **relative prices,** not just changes in nominal prices. By changes in relative prices we mean how the price of a good changes relative to the prices of other goods.

Often, changes in taxes or shipping costs cause equal nominal changes in the prices of different goods. For example, if the cost of shipping a bottle of wine rises by $1, this will tend to cause the price of all wines after shipment to rise by about $1. However, this equal nominal change in the price of all types of wine will have the effect of altering the relative price of wines: a bottle of wine that initially sold for $4 will now sell for $5, one that sold for $16 will now sell for $17. However, the price of the more expensive wine will have fallen relative to the price of the cheaper wine, even though the nominal price of both wines changes by the same amount. Initially, the expensive wine was four times the price of the other; now it is 3.4 times as expensive. Because shipping costs tend to change relative prices, these costs can be used to explain the common phenomenon of "shipping the best goods out," which applies to Maine lobsters, French wine, and German automobiles, among other items.

Economic theory does in fact supply a rationale for "shipping the best apples (autos, cognac, oranges, or whatever) out."[15] Consider Table 2.4, which considers a simple example of the relative price effect of shipping high- and low-grade whiskey from Ireland to Boston. The absolute (simple money) price of low-grade whiskey in Ireland is, after exchange rates are calculated, $10 per liter, and the cost of high-grade is $20 for the same quantity. Clearly the ratio of high to low price in Ireland is 2:1. High-grade is exactly twice as expensive as low-quality whiskey.

Assume that when Irish whiskey is exported to Boston, the transport cost, invariant as to quality, is $10 (per liter). Clearly, the transport charge makes the relative price in Boston different than the relative price in Dublin. Specifically, the price ratio of high- to low-grade whiskey in Boston is 3:2. This means that high-quality Irish whiskey is only 1.5 times as expensive as low-quality in Boston, whereas it is twice as expensive in Dublin. Bostonians rationally decide to purchase whiskey on the basis of the relative price, and they therefore buy a higher proportion of high-grade whiskey than do Dubliners.

The Irish may, on this basis, rightfully claim that whiskey manufacturers are in fact "shipping the best Irish out." This will be the case whenever a fixed cost (in this case money transport costs of $10 per liter) is added to the absolute money prices of closely substitutable goods or services. *Relative prices will always be altered in favor of the absolutely more expensive good.* This case gives rise to a number of interesting and important applications, including prohibitions and blockades of all kinds (see Highlight 2.4).

---

15. This principle is often dubbed the "Alchian and Allen Effect," after two economists who emphasized it in their economics textbook some years ago. See Armen A. Alchian and William R. Allen, *University Economics* (Belmont, CA: Wadsworth, 1972). For an elaboration of the principle, the interested reader should also consult Thomas E. Borcherding and Eugene Silberberg, "Shipping the Good Apples Out: The Alchian and Allen Theorem Reconsidered," *Journal of Political Economy* (February 1978): 131–38.

Table 2.4 **The Relative Price of Whiskey in Dublin and Boston**
In terms of relative price, high-quality whiskey is cheaper in Boston than in Dublin. The price of high-quality whiskey is twice that of low-quality liquor in Dublin, but only one and one-half times as expensive in Boston.

	Money Price in Dublin	Transport Cost	Money Price in Boston
Low-Grade (liter)	$10	$10	$20
High-Grade (liter)	20	10	30

Highlight 2.4 *The Impact of More Law Enforcement on the Drug Problem in America*

Drug consumption, legal and illegal, has become a formidable individual and societal problem in recent years. "Get tough" laws, such as the $1.7 billion antidrug bill that passed Congress in 1986, have poured millions of tax dollars into enforcement. The problem is multidimensional, but the economic tools described in this chapter can provide insight into several aspects of the drug issue. Whatever else they may be, drug sales are economic transactions.

Perhaps the most interesting issue relating to economics and drugs is the impact of law enforcement on drug potency and health risks.[a] In the text discussion of relative price effects (and Irish whiskey), we argued that the relative prices of low-grade and high-grade whiskey will differ between Dublin and Boston. The reason: a *constant* transport cost. A similar result arises whenever a constant cost is added to the price of closely substitutable goods, including high-potency and low-potency drugs.

In the case of illicit drugs, the full price that anyone pays is the nominal price of the drug (either high potency or low potency) plus the risk of arrest. Assuming that drug enforcement is constant across the board, with no distinction between high-potency drugs and low-potency drugs, drug enforcement efforts impose a uniform risk cost on buyers of all drugs. With little drug enforcement, a potential drug buyer might face a $20 nominal price for a given quantity of a low-potency drug and a $40 nominal price for the same quantity of a high-potency drug. With little risk of arrest, the full price of the high-potency drug is essentially twice that of the low-potency drug.

[a] See Mark Thornton, *The Economics of Prohibition* (Salt Lake City: University of Utah Press, 1991), from which the argument in this section is developed.

The net effect of efforts by law-enforcement agencies to reduce the flow of drugs into the United States has been to increase the average potency of the drugs being smuggled; because the risks are essentially the same — and the profits much higher — on high-potency drugs, dealers (rationally, economically speaking) opt to handle them rather than low-potency varieties.

However, as enforcement efforts increase and the risk of arrest rises to all drug buyers, the *relative* price of high-potency drugs falls; the greater the enforcement effort, the lower the relative price of high-potency drugs. Increased enforcement will tend to reduce total drug consumption (users will substitute legal drugs and nondrug goods for illegal drugs), but its effect on relative prices will induce many buyers to switch from low-potency drugs to ones of a higher potency. Suppliers, who also face a risk cost, will be more inclined to import and market drugs of higher potency, and the "bad" drugs will tend to displace the less potent ones.

The psychoactive ingredient in marijuana is tetrahydrocannabinol, or THC. The level of THC in marijuana has been rising steadily over time. During the decade ending in 1984, according to a potency monitoring project at the University of Mississippi's School of Pharmacy, the average potency of marijuana confiscated in the United States increased more than eightfold from its 1973 level.[b] Over the same period, the federal law enforcement budget (in terms of constant 1972 dollars) rose from less than $200 million per year to more than half a billion dollars, indicating rising risk to marijuana and other drug users. Penalties vary little with respect to the *kinds* of marijuana used or sold, so the risk of arrest and punishment, as viewed by marijuana demanders and suppliers, is constant with respect to potency.

The data regarding potency of marijuana and marijuana products over the period 1973–1984 produce a startling conclusion. The *relative price* of hashish (a potent form of marijuana) fell from 14.8:1 in 1973–1977 to only 3.1:1 in 1979–1983. Economic theory contends that these relative price changes are the result of dramatically rising investment in law enforcement activities. In the late eighties, due to similar effects, cocaine use replaced marijuana use, and "crack," a powerful and concentrated form of cocaine, was substituted for ordinary cocaine (and sold in single doses for less than $5).[c] Why? Dealers' penalties for selling them are similar, making the higher-priced and more profitable substance a more attractive product to sell.

In the mid-1980s, data on hospital emergency room drug episodes and medical examiners' reports from the National Institute on Drug Abuse added support to the view that higher-potency drugs were being consumed, with significantly greater health problems resulting.[d]

The nightmare did not end with crack cocaine. As we entered the 1990s, the producers, smugglers, dealers, and consumers of illegal drugs began to switch from cocaine to heroin. The traditional suppliers in Burma, Afghanistan, and Mexico have been joined by China, Africa, the Far East, and South America. Growers and producers in South America are converting from cocaine to heroin, which is ten times more profitable. Increases in the international production of illicit heroin, record-size seizures of heroin, increases in emergency-room visits, and overdoses from heroin all indicate that heroin is

---

[b] Potency Monitoring Project, Research Institute of Pharmaceutical Sciences, School of Pharmacy, University of Mississippi, Quarterly Report, Nos. 7 and 17, 1983 and 1986.

[c] The new cocaine form was a far cry from the low-potency cocaine product sold by the Coca-Cola Company prior to narcotics prohibition.

[d] U.S. Department of Health and Human Services, National Institute on Drug Abuse, *Annual Data from the Drug Abuse Warning Network (DAWN)* (Washington, DC: U.S. Government Printing Office, 1985).

now displacing cocaine just as cocaine once displaced marijuana. Mark A. R. Kleiman, an adviser to the Office of National Drug Control Policy, said in April 1992 that heroin use in the United States has reached a "pre-epidemic stage" and that it could overtake cocaine in a couple of years.[e]

The view that marijuana use leads to heroin addiction is based on the notion that the product and the producer can control the consumer. It is certainly correct that experience with "addictive" products such as drugs do affect consumption. But recent research also indicates that consumers are "rational" in the economic sense that even heroin addicts will reduce quantity consumed in the short run if prices rise. More important, consumers are rational when faced with tougher drug-law enforcement. They switch to higher-potency varieties and ultimately convert to higher-potency products. Although little scientific evidence supports the notion that marijuana use leads directly to heroin addiction, the economic theory of relative prices would predict that the market will evolve from marijuana to heroin in the face of tougher law enforcement.

[e] "Study Says U.S. Fails to See Heroin Problem," *New York Times,* April 19, 1992, p. 24. Also see Joseph B. Treaster, "Hospital Data Show Increase in Drug Abuse," *New York Times*, June 14, 1992, p. 7, and Robert D. McFadden, "Colombia's Drug Lords Add New Product: Heroin for U.S.," *New York Times*, January 14, 1992, p. 1.

Market Solutions to the Three Basic Economic Problems

In Chapter 1, we discussed the three basic problems that every economy has to resolve:

1. It must use its scarce resources to produce the correct mix of products, avoiding overproduction of some goods and underproduction of others.
2. It must see that the goods that get produced are distributed efficiently among consumers.
3. It must assure that the goods it does produce are produced in an efficient fashion.

Having developed a demand-supply model of price determination, we can now turn to these three problems and see how market-determined prices provide a solution to each of them.

To see how the product mix is determined in a market economy, it is useful to refer back to Figure 2.8. The graph shows that, given the initial demand curve (D_M), the quantity of pizzas that gets produced under a market system will be Q_E units per week. We can also see that Q_E is a very sensible level of output to produce. Beyond a doubt, buyers want more than Q_E units. By examining D_M, we see that additional units beyond Q_E yield benefits to buyers. However, the value of the additional units is less than the P_E. The supply curve shows that additional pizzas beyond Q_E could be produced, but the cost on the margin would exceed P_E dollars. Therefore, the additional pizzas cost more than they are worth to buyers, meaning that it would be inefficient to produce them. We can also see in Figure 2.8 that a reduction in output will release some inputs to produce other goods. Because the value of these units exceeds the costs, it is more efficient to use resources to produce these pizzas than to put them to alternative uses.

Figure 2.8 is useful not only for explaining the equilibrium quantity but also for showing which goods are produced and which ones are not. Given the initial demand curve (D_M), pizzas will be produced because the price is sufficiently high to make production worthwhile to sellers. Even if the demand falls to D'_M, pizzas will continue to be produced in a quantity equal to Q'_E rather than Q_E. However, should demand fall to the point that no buyer is willing to pay as much as P_0 for a pizza, pizza production will cease in this particular market. In a similar fashion, changes that increase the cost and reduce the supply sufficiently can also cause production of a product to cease. Look again at Figure 2.7: the shift in the supply from S_M to S'_M was caused by an increase in the price of an input used to produce pizzas. Had the price of the input risen so much that no producer could produce pizzas at a cost of less than P_1 dollars, no producer would find it advantageous to sell pizzas, so production would cease. It is not hard to find historical examples of goods that are no longer produced because of decreases in demand, decreases in supply, or a combination of both. It was not too many years ago that the sale of record players was a big business. Nearly every college student owned one, and hundreds of thousands were sold annually. However, the development first of inexpensive, high-quality tape decks and then of compact disk players greatly reduced the demand for record players. As a consequence, what was once a big industry no longer exists.

Demand and supply curves also show how goods get distributed in a free-market system. In Figure 2.8, assuming that demand is represented by D_M, the Q_E pizzas that are produced get distributed to those buyers who are willing and able to pay a price of at least P_E dollars. Other buyers may want the pizzas, but they choose not to buy them because their effective demands (willingness plus ability to pay) are less than P_E dollars. Again, this market solution is an efficient one in that it distributes the goods to the buyers who have the most effective demands for them. The less able and/or less interested consumers are deterred from consuming goods by a price that they view as too high.

To see how private firms decide which techniques to use for producing goods and services, we need to consider markets for the inputs used to produce the final goods. Just as it is useful to consider the demand and supply of pizza, it is also useful to think of a market comprised of buyers and sellers of specific inputs used to produce pizzas. One such market might be for laborers, another for equipment like pizza ovens, another for ingredients such as sauces and spices. In order to make a profit, producers have to carefully economize on expensive inputs and to use greater quantities of the less expensive inputs.

Perhaps the clearest examples of such substitution between inputs is found in agriculture. In the United States, certain inputs used in agriculture are cheap by international standards — fertilizer and modern equipment, for example. On the other hand, labor in this country is expensive compared to other countries. Therefore, a U.S. corn producer will find it to his advantage to produce using relatively large quantities of fertilizer and farm equipment but relatively little labor. In contrast, a producer in India, Mexico, or Brazil will find it economical to produce the same corn with less fertilizer and much less equipment but with much more labor.

In India, Mexico, Brazil, or Kenya, where labor is abundant, the market system encourages producers to utilize much more labor while economizing on scarce equipment and fertilizer. A U.S. producer is similarly motivated to use the inputs that are abundant, fertilizer and equipment, while economizing on labor. In societies in which markets for inputs are not permitted to operate, it has proven impossible to get producers to make the "how" decision with any reasonable level of efficiency. Their economic system is simply unable to provide producers with either the information or the motivation to economize on scarce inputs.

Summary

The incentives of rational and self-interested demanders and suppliers — buyers and sellers — of goods and services have been the subjects of this chapter. We have described and illustrated the factors underlying both demand and supply. In our discussion, we have

- developed a theory of demand and supply as the logical outcome of rational behavior on the part of buyers and sellers.
- shown how prices are determined within these theories in a variety of theoretical and real-world examples.
- analyzed some of the effects of taxes and subsidies on consumers and producers of goods and services.
- demonstrated the effects of price regulation above (price floors) and below (price ceilings) equilibrium market price.
- developed important extensions of demand-and-supply theory to include cases in which multiple products are supplied within a single production process and in which buyers and sellers are guided by relative, rather than absolute, prices.
- shown, more broadly, how a price system provides informational and other signals to all market participants so that their actions answer the fundamental economic questions faced by all societies.

Key Terms

price takers	marginal benefit
individual demand curve	diminishing marginal utility
market demand curve	shift in demand
inferior goods	normal goods
substitute goods	complementary goods
law of demand	change in quantity demanded
individual supply curve	marginal revenue
marginal cost	market supply curve
shift in supply	change in quantity supplied
equilibrium price	equilibrium quantity
tax	subsidy
tax incidence	negative tax
price controls	price ceilings
shortage	price floors
surplus	jointly supplied goods
noncompeting consumption	nominal price
relative price	

Sample Questions

Question

The situation for restaurant owners in New York City prior to the Democratic National Convention in 1992 was bleak indeed. *The New York Times* nevertheless reported that, in December 1992, both less and more expensive restaurants were doing a booming business. Earlier in the year and prior to the convention, the *Times* reports, only 6 to 10 diners appeared each night at the Grill Room of the Four Seasons, a landmark New York eatery. By December, the Grill Room was attracting 140 guests per night and virtually all Manhattan restaurants were experiencing similar prosperity. What happened? Diners left in droves with cutbacks in the publishing, retailing, advertising, and finance industries during the recession of 1991–1992. For the Democratic convention, city officials urged the restaurants to offer a fixed price *(prix fixe)* lunch for $19.92 (a price that was four or five times lower than the standard luncheon price at the fanciest establishments). The low price proved so popular that most of the restaurants kept the low price and even added low *prix fixe* dinners as well (at $24.92). (See Florence Fabricant, "After Harsh Lesson, Restaurant Business Surges in New York," *New York Times*, December 10, 1992, p. B16, for further details.)

a. Graphically analyze the initial situation facing the New York restaurants before the recession. Analyze the situation prior to the special price offered for the Democratic National Convention but *after* the 1991–1992 layoffs. (*Hint:* Put "Number of Meals Served" on the horizontal axis and assume that all meals are of the same quality.)
b. Show graphically the impact of the reduction in meal price during and after the convention.
c. Was a change in the demand curve or a change in quantity demanded the "cause" of the new equilibrium?
d. Why did restaurant managers take so long to lower prices?

Answer

a. The initial equilibrium is shown in the figure at point E. The typical restaurant served a quantity Q_0 of meals at price P_0. After the recession and job losses in New York City, incomes fell. Because income is one of the determinants of demand, the demand curve for restaurant meals fell to D' when income fell. However, despite the demand decrease, prices were "sticky" at P_0, creating an "excess" supply of EF (or Q_0Q_1).
b. The introduction of the specially priced meals during the Democratic National Convention brought restaurant managers to a price (P_1) that equated supply and demand. Restaurants began to fill up as demand and supply again reached equilibrium at E'. The new quantity of meals served is Q_2 at price P_1.

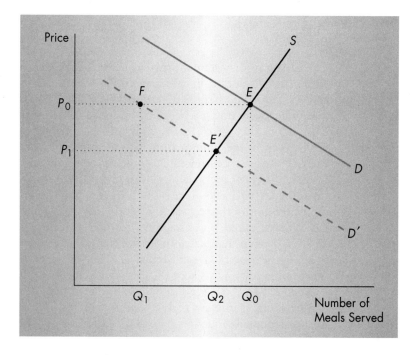

c. Demand for meals decreased because of the decrease in New Yorkers' income. This was a demand change rather than a change in quantity demanded (along a given demand curve).

d. Restaurateurs were slow to recognize a significant and prolonged decrease in demand. It is important to recognize that adjustments to demand and/or supply changes do not occur instantaneously. In the interim between recognizing the demand reduction and lowering the price, the price P_0 acted as a kind of "price control" or "temporary price floor" (see discussion of price controls in this chapter). The excess supply of meal capacity showed up in the inability to fill seats at lunch and dinner.

Question

Economists were not surprised by the amount of time that Soviet consumers spent standing in line for food and other consumer goods and services. In general, price ceilings created the long lines.

a. How did price ceilings create the lines for goods and services?

b. How were goods rationed in the former Soviet Union in the light of the price ceilings? Was the ruble price the full "price" paid for goods and services?

Answer

a. Price controls at below-equilibrium levels created an excess demand for goods and services. This meant that, at the regulated price, quantity demanded exceeded quantity supplied (see, for example, Figure 2.13 and the accompanying discussion in this chapter).

b. Goods were rationed in the Soviet Union in a number of ways, principally by providing items on a first-come, first-served basis. Hence the long lines of consumers. The excess demand gave Soviet planners an opportunity to allocate the scarce goods on a number of nonprice bases, including membership in the Communist party, favoritism, fraud, and side-payments to officials. The full price of the goods (including waiting time and other factors) was greater than the ruble price.

Questions for Review and Discussion

*1. What is the difference between an individual demand curve and a market demand curve? How is a market demand curve for a single commodity constructed?

2. Why will a technological improvement usually decrease the marginal cost of producing a good?

3. Explain what would happen to your demand for steak and your demand for Spam if you receive a raise at work. Provide graphs to illustrate your answer.

*4. What is the consequence of an increase in the price of flour in the market for pizzas?

*5. If price falls below the equilibrium level, what happens to the relationship between quantity demanded and quantity supplied? How is equilibrium restored? Provide both verbal and graphical components in your answer.

6. Using demand-curve analysis, show and explain how an increase in the price of beef affects the demand curve for chicken.

7. If neither perfect competition nor price takers are realistic assumptions, why do we use demand-and-supply analysis?

*8. Does simple demand-and-supply analysis help us explain why, for example, barbers or carpenters would lobby the city to invoke tougher standards on entrants into these fields? (*Hint:* Think of the restrictions demanded by nannies in Highlight 2.1.)

*9. Explain how the concept of demand relates to marginal benefit and the concept of supply to marginal cost.

10. Explain why higher-quality goods tend to be consumed in greater quantities in locations other than where they are produced.

*11. If the price of tennis rackets rises, what will happen to the demand for tennis balls?

12. Special weekend rates at leading hotels are increasingly common. Why are deals offered on weekend stays but not during the week?

*13. Explain the consequences of an increase in across-the-board drug enforcement with respect to relative price and the use of low- and high-potency drugs.

14. What is the effect of a decrease in the price of steel on the supply of automobiles? What happens to the supply curve in the market for automobiles?

Problems for Analysis

*1. Demand and supply may be expressed in terms of simple algebra, as noted throughout the chapter. Ordinarily they are given in inverse form, with quantity as the dependent variable:

$$Q_D = A - BP$$
$$Q_S = MP - N$$

and, for equilibrium, quantity supplied must equal quantity demanded:

$$Q_D = Q_S$$

Here, A, B, M, and N are all positive constants.

a. Solve the simple system for equilibrium price. (*Hint:* Use the equilibrium equation and solve for price in terms of the constants.)
b. Solve the demand-and-supply system for equilibrium quantity. (*Hint:* Substitute the equilibrium price into either the demand or supply equation.)
c. What is the slope and intercept of the demand curve?
d. What is the slope and intercept of the supply curve?

2. Suppose that numbers (estimated from some real-world demand and supply for fine wine) replace the constants (A, B, M, N) in the equations of question 1. Let the demand and supply system now be

$$Q_D = 100 - P$$
$$Q_S = P - 10$$

a. Calculate the equilibrium price of wine sold over some period of time.
b. Calculate the equilibrium quantity of wine traded.

3. Taxes and subsidies to both buyers (demanders) and sellers (suppliers) may also be analyzed using simple algebraic systems. A tax on sellers or a subsidy to buyers will always be *subtracted* from price in the supply or demand equation, whereas a tax on demanders or a subsidy to sellers is always *added* to price in the demand or supply equation. Take, for example, a tax on the seller in question 1. The initial supply curve $Q_S = MP - N$ would, after the tax, become $Q_S = M(P - t) - N$, where t is the unit amount of the tax.

a. Using the initial demand and supply curves of question 2, impose a tax of $20 per bottle on sellers of wine. Recalculate the equilibrium price.
b. Recalculate the equilibrium quantity of fine wine sold.
c. What does the taxing authority (government) take in as revenues? (*Hint:* That amount is the per-unit amount of the tax multiplied by the quantity of wine sold *after* the imposition of the tax.)
d. Recalculate parts a, b, and c when a tax of $20 per bottle is imposed on demanders. Compare the solutions.

4. The sale and consumption of marijuana is illegal in most parts of the United States. Is the black market (or illegal) price for marijuana higher, lower, or the same as it would be if marijuana were legalized? Be sure to include the probable effects on both supply and demand functions. Discuss fully as many possible alternatives as you can think of.

a. How do you think government regulations and taxes would affect the price-quantity outcome?
b. Given that organized crime is responsible for most drug traffic, who do you think would be most opposed to legalization? Why?

*5. Suppose that you are a supplier-processor firm supplying a commodity — turkeys — to the retail market. Further, assume that (a) the supplier-processor and retail markets are competitive; (b) the turkeys that all firms supply are exactly the same; and (c) turkey is supplied to the market in fixed proportions in four forms — turkey legs, turkey breasts, all other turkey parts besides breasts and legs, and whole turkeys. Assume that the strongest demand at the initial supply-demand equilibrium quantity is for whole turkeys and that there are positive prices for all of the forms of turkey sold in the initial equilibrium. Assume (as we did for the condos in Highlight 2.3) that turkeys are supplied at a constant supply price. Finally, all costs of cutting up, grinding, packaging, and so on are assumed to be zero.

   a. Develop a graph showing the supplier-processor's demand for turkeys. (*Hint:* Assume that whole turkeys compete with cut-up turkeys but that turkey legs and turkey breasts are complementary and noncompeting.)

   b. What impact will a health fad that increases the demand for turkey breasts have (1) on the price and quantity of turkeys produced? (2) on the price of turkey legs? (3) on the price of whole turkeys?

6. Each season of the year gives transport rental companies (such as U-Haul) serious location problems. Trailers pile up at southern locations in winter, at northeastern locations in summer. Assume that the transport rental business is competitive, that average costs of operations rise with rental quantities, that there are only two transport seasons, summer and winter, and that trailers only move north-south and south-north. Graph and analyze a pricing model that gives the firm a guide to efficient stocks of trailers in any given season. How would the trailer firm decide on new investments in trailers?

7. It is common to group some taxes under the simple title of "sin taxes." These are taxes on goods and services that can be harmful to the consumer. Tobacco, alcohol, and gambling are the usual objects of sin taxation. What are the market effects of such taxes? How might consumers be helped by the imposition of sin taxes?

8. The 1986 Tax Reform Act passed by Congress included a special 10 percent tax on luxury items — expensive cars, jewelry, fur coats, and yachts. What was the effect of this tax on the markets for luxury items? The sellers of luxury items complained about having to bear the burden of this tax. Show that, under normal market circumstances, the tax would be borne by both the buyers and the sellers.

9. Suppose that the market demand for a good is described by the equation $P = 1000 - 10Q$ and that the supply is defined by the equation $P = 10 + 5Q$. What is the equilibrium price and quantity? What happens to the equilibrium price and quantity when the government imposes a $100-per-unit tax on sellers? What portions of the tax are paid by the buyers and sellers, respectively?

10. Suppose that the market demand for a good is described by the equation

$P = 400 - 20Q$ and that the supply is defined by the equation $P + 5Q$. What is the equilibrium price and quantity? What happens to the equilibrium price and quantity when the government provides sellers with a $100-per-unit subsidy? What portions of the subsidy go to the buyers and sellers, respectively?

11. The deductibility of home mortgage interest is, in effect, a subsidy to home owners. Their taxes are reduced by a fraction of the mortgage interest that they pay. What impact does this tax break have on the market for owner-occupied housing? What would happen in the rental housing market if tenants could deduct their rent from their taxable income?

12. Used tires present a difficult disposal problem because they are not biodegradable. Tires tend to be piled into mountains of rubber that are both health and fire hazards. An innovative approach to this problem is to tax new tires and use the tax proceeds to pay a subsidy for each tire that is recycled. What would be the effects of this subsidy on the tire-recycling market?

13. Suppose that instead of a subsidy, the used-tire market described in problem 12 were subject to a price ceiling set at $60. What would be the effects of this price ceiling? What side effects might you expect to develop in the market?

14. Usury laws are fairly common in most countries. What happens to the operation of credit markets when the equilibrium interest rate is above the legal limit? Be sure to include the direct and indirect effects of this price ceiling.

15. The teenage unemployment rate is relatively high. Do minimum-wage laws (assume them to be above equilibrium) have anything to do with this unemployment problem? Explain.

Theory of Consumer Behavior

C H A P T E R

3

Consumer Choice

Consumers the world over make trillions of choices each week. Svetlana chooses bread and sausages in Moscow, Sam buys dry cleaning services and frozen pizza in New York, and Yeung-Nan buys rice wine and a silk shirt in Beijing. On and on, day after day, we function as "choice machines." Without deliberately stopping to consider our choices, we most often behave in a consistent and predictable manner.

Our demand for goods and services, explained in Chapter 2, is a key dimension of consumer behavior. Demand — perhaps the single most important concept in microeconomics — expresses our willingness to buy certain items at various prices at some period in time. But what lies *behind* this willingness called demand? It is the **utility** that we obtain from those goods and services and the process of choosing from among the massive array of possibilities that confront us daily. When you have mastered this chapter, you should understand

- how marginal analysis applies to the problem of consumer choice as consumers maximize utility given a limited amount to spend,
- the notion of utility and its expression in what are called indifference curves — curves that show one's willingness to give up units of one good in order to obtain additional units of a second good,
- the budget line or constraint, which depicts the limits confronting a consumer who must choose between one good and another,
- how indifference curves and budget lines are combined to illustrate and explain how the consumer maximizes utility through optimizing purchases of goods,
- the effects of taste and price changes on consumer behavior.

Throughout, we highlight the *rationality* of consumers in their selection of goods and services. The economic theory of consumer choice will lead us full circle to a theory of how and why consumers demand all things that yield value and utility.

The Nature of Utility

A formidable problem that economists must address is the fact that utility is not directly observable, nor is it even measurable in the ordinary sense of the word. Therefore, when we refer to a "utility-maximizing individual," we have no direct way of showing that any specific behavior maximizes utility. For this reason, the economic analysis of individual consumers is more difficult than, say, the economic analysis of certain aspects of the behavior of business firms. Business firms use various inputs to produce *observable* levels of output. In contrast, consumers use goods to produce levels of utility that we cannot see.

Diminishing Marginal Utility

There was a time when many economists believed that utility could be measured in the same way that height or distance can be measured. They viewed utility as something that could be measured in a *cardinal* fashion. By a cardinal measure, we mean a measure that assigns numerical values whose difference is

"It's been fun, Dave, but I think we're entering the diminished marginal utility phase of our relationship."

numerically significant. For example, distance is a cardinal measure. If we observe that from Shanghai to Buenos Aires is 12,000 miles and from Manila to Oslo is 6,000 miles, then we can say that the distance between Shanghai and Buenos Aires is twice the distance between Manila and Oslo.

A **cardinal utility** measure would assign a numerical measure of utility to each possible level of consumption of a particular good. For example, Table 3.1 shows the total utility that an individual receives from various quantities of food. For that individual, an increase in food consumption from 1 unit per day to 2 units per day increases the utility level from 20 units to 32 units. Increasing consumption from 2 units to 3 units increases utility from 32 units to 40 units. Because the increase in utility from the third unit is less than the increase from the second unit, this particular example depicts **diminishing marginal utility** — the extra utility provided by additional units decreases as additional units are consumed.

Numerical examples of cardinal utility measures help to demonstrate utility-maximizing behavior. For example, consider the individual who receives satisfaction from the consumption of food as depicted in Table 3.1 and who also receives utility from the consumption of wine. Further, assume that the person's levels of utility from the consumption of various quantities of wine are as depicted in Table 3.2.

As was the case in with food, Table 3.2 shows this person's diminishing marginal utility for wine — each additional unit of wine adds less to total utility. The marginal utility declines from 14 units for the first wine to 10 units for the second, 6 for the third, and so on for successive increases in the quantity of wine.

If wine and food were free, maximizing utility would be extremely simple: this consumer would simply consume at least 6 units of food and 5 units of wine per day. Doing so would be perfectly rational behavior. Because food is

Table 3.1 An Example of Cardinal Utility
The marginal utility of food is the addition to total utility that comes about because of unit additions of food per day.

Quantity of Food per Day	Total Utility	Marginal Utility
0	0	—
1	20	20
2	32	12
3	40	8
4	44	4
5	46	2
6	47	1
7	47	0

"free," the cost on the margin is zero. Utility-maximizing behavior means continuing to consume until benefits on the margin no longer exceed costs. In this case, food should be consumed until the marginal benefits are zero, or after the sixth unit.

By similar reasoning, this individual should consume 5 units of wine per day if the price of wine is zero. However, the issue becomes more complicated when the two goods sell for positive prices and when the buyer has limited income. For example, we could assume that the price of food is $2 per unit, the price of wine is $1 per unit, and the income of the consumer only $6 per day. In this case, the consumer could buy 3 units of food per day or 6 units of wine per day, or some combination of the two.

Utility-Maximizing Combinations

One approach to selecting the utility-maximizing combination of food and wine is the mathematical equivalent of brute force: compute the total level of utility associated with each affordable combination of food and wine and then select the combination that yields the highest utility. Table 3.3 summarizes these choices.

Of the four possibilities, combination C, which consists of 2 units of food and 2 of wine, yields the highest level of satisfaction. A brute force approach is entirely manageable when the number of options is quite limited as in this case of only four alternatives. However, as income level increases, the number of choices also increases, making brute force a cumbersome and time-consuming solution.

In general, it is much simpler to view this problem as an optimizing problem, in which we equate the marginal benefits and marginal costs to find the

Table 3.2 A Second Example of Cardinal Utility
As units of wine are added to a person's consumption, total utility rises but marginal utility declines.

Quantity of Wine per Day	Total Utility	Marginal Utility
0	0	—
1	14	14
2	24	10
3	30	6
4	33	3
5	34	1
6	34	0

solution. Starting at combination A, we can calculate the marginal costs and benefits of purchasing additional units of food. The decision to use $2 to buy the first unit of food requires that wine consumption be reduced by 2 units from 6 to 4. The consumer gains the marginal utility associated with the first unit of food (20 units) while losing the marginal utility associated with the fifth and sixth units of wine (1 unit). Clearly the marginal benefits exceed the marginal costs, so it makes sense to purchase and consume at least 1 unit of food. By the same reasoning, the purchase of the second unit of food yields 12 units of utility (the total utility associated with 2 foods is 12 units higher than the utility associated with 1 food) at a cost of 9 units of utility. Again, the decision to increase food consumption is a rational one, because the marginal benefits exceed the marginal costs.

To purchase more than 2 units of food, however, would not be rational given the $2 price of food and the $1 price of wine. Although the consumer desires the third unit of food (it yields 8 additional units of utility), a decision to purchase it would not be rational, because it would come at a cost of the 24 units of utility provided by the remaining 2 units of wine. The application of marginal analysis to utility maximization leads to the selection of combination C, the combination that yields the highest total utility. The use of marginal analysis is equivalent to the use of brute-force methods in terms of making the best choice. However, marginal analysis is much simpler — particularly when the range of choices is extensive.

The application of marginal analysis to consumer choice has a number of variations. A fruitful one examines the change in utility per dollar spent on each good. Table 3.4 reproduces the numbers from Tables 3.1 and 3.2 for the marginal utilities of consuming alternative quantities of food (MU_F) and wine (MU_W); the table also shows the marginal utility per dollar spent on food (MU_F/P_F) and wine (MU_W/P_W), respectively. The rational consumer allocates her income ($6 per day) incrementally and purchases first the good that entails the greatest marginal benefit per dollar. The consumer would thus begin the

Table 3.3 The Utility-Maximizing Combination of Food and Wine
The rational consumer will attempt to maximize total utility from consuming two goods, food and wine.

Combination	Units of Food	Units of Wine	Utility from Food	Utility from Wine	Total Utility
A	0	6	0	34	34
B	1	4	20	33	53
C	2	2	32	24	57
D	3	0	40	0	40

Table 3.4 A Second Approach to Utility Maximization
The rational consumer maximizes total utility by equalizing the
marginal utility per dollar spent on each of the goods.

Quantity	MU_F	MU_W	MU_F/P_F	MU_W/P_W
1	20	14	10	14
2	12	10	6	10
3	8	6	4	6
4	4	3	2	3
5	2	1	1	1
6	1	0	0.5	0
7	0	0		

process by buying a unit of wine, because the first unit of wine has the highest
marginal utility per dollar. Next she would purchase a first unit of food and a
second unit of wine, because both entail equal marginal utilities per dollar.
This selection process continues until her budget is exhausted — that is, based
on the numbers in Table 3.4, until she has purchased 2 units of food and 3
units of wine. Note that this is the same solution to the consumer-choice
problem as determined by Table 3.3. Utility is maximized at the point at
which MU_F/P_F equals MU_W/P_W.

Consumers routinely choose on the basis of *marginal utility*, and this
rationale for consumer choice explains numerous events and means of
exchange. Why, for example, are we able to take as many newspapers as we
wish when we buy from a paper vending machine but only get one cola from a
soft-drink machine? The answer is that the marginal utility of today's newspapers to us is generally exhausted after just one paper, but we can save cans of
cola for later.[1] The marginal utility of a second newspaper is nearly zero,
whereas the marginal utility of a second soft drink is not. Vending machine
companies can therefore reliably assume that newspaper buyers will take only
one paper.

It is important to recognize that it is in the interests of sellers of all goods
and services to develop rules and devices that take into account utility-maximizing behavior by consumers. In other words, the concept of diminishing
marginal utility shapes the behavior of proprietors as well as consumers. For
example, many newsstands and bookstores keep magazines such as *Playboy* and
Playgirl behind the counter. The proprietor obviously wants to sell these magazines, so why hide them from consumers? The answer is simple: to prevent
customers from ogling the pictures. After a sneak preview, the marginal utility

1. This example of marginal utility originated in Marshall Jevons (alias economists William
Breit and Kenneth Elzinga), *The Fatal Equilibrium* (Cambridge, MA: MIT Press, 1985),
pp. 113–114. This murder mystery, solved by an economist sleuth, is highly recommended
for educational and entertainment purposes.

yielded from buying the magazine is lower than it would be if no prepurchase peek were allowed. Preventing customers from flipping through the pages of such magazines results in a higher marginal utility at purchase time; this, in turn, increases the sales of such magazines.[2]

In contrast, proprietors encourage customers to leaf through the pages of such magazines as *Science Digest* or *National Review*. By doing so, customers get a glimpse of what topics are discussed and what authors contributed. This information enhances the marginal utility of the magazine for many consumers and results in greater sales. The marketplace is full of many, many different kinds of such "sales" devices (for an example, see Highlight 3.1).

Highlight 3.1   *Diminishing Marginal Utility and the Origin and Purpose of Menus*

Individuals make all kinds of choices. Consumers will demand, *and suppliers have profit incentives to supply,* choices in forms that increase total utility. Often, goods and services are offered in packages, sequences, and presentations that do not readily appear to have anything to do with utility. To complicate the problem, many of us make the common mistake of misidentifying the period over which goods or services are related to units of consumption. How often have we bragged, "I could never get enough popcorn (caviar, Porsches, vacations, potatoes, and so on)." We recognize such statements as gross exaggerations when we understand the law of diminishing marginal utility and the role of clever entrepreneurs in molding goods and their presentation to maximize our utility.

Consider the typical restaurant menu. The idea of a menu is said to have originated in 1541, during the reign of Henry VIII, at a banquet party given by a world-class gastronome, the duke of Brunswick. According to one account, one of the duke's guests observed His Grace occasionally consulting a piece of paper during the banquet[a]. Unbearably curious, the guest finally made bold to ask the duke what he was doing. The duke replied that he was consulting a list of dishes to be served so that he could decide which pleased him most in order to save his appetite for them. The idea gained in popularity with elaborate and decorated menus becoming the order of the day at elegant royal dinner parties.[b]

---

2. Clearly, there are other means of preventing previews (e.g., shrink-wrapping) and other reasons for restricting viewership (e.g., limiting access to adults). Even so, alternative methods and complementary goals do not diminish the usefulness of the marginal-utility approach to explain the phenomena.

[a] *Gourmet's Menu Cookbook,* (New York: Gourmet Books, 1963), p. 9.

[b] *Gourmet* incorrectly observes, however, that "It is doubtful ... that menus ever found their way to the tables of Henry VIII. There was no necessity for that trencherman to save his

Although they only occasionally appear at dinner parties, the practice of using menus survives mainly at restaurants, where they are either posted or presented individually to customers. However they are used, one function of menus is to serve as a device that limits diminishing marginal utility and increases the total utility of *any given meal*.[c] The typical menu is divided into appetizers, soups, salads, entrees (often subdivided into more specific categories of meat, seafood, pasta, and the like), and desserts. Like the duke of Brunswick, we pick and choose the kind and variety of foods we eat so that excesses among the early courses do not diminish the marginal utility of later courses and so that the total utility of the whole meal is as great as possible. A huge quantity of onion soup will ordinarily provide less total utility than a cup of soup combined with a small salad and a modest entree.

Many variations and extensions of the menu exist. In some French and American restaurants (Emerils in New Orleans, for instance), a *de gustation* menu is offered. This menu typically offers very small quantities of many dishes to thrill the palate of diners seeking higher total and less diminishing marginal utility. Cafeterias post the entire menu at the beginning of the queue and (for reasons related to diminishing marginal utility) usually present desserts early in the line. To say that "you haven't saved room for dessert" usually refers less to the capacity of your stomach than to the total utility-maximizing choices made after the range of offerings on a menu. How many times have we "regretted" total consumption levels at a *menuless* meal when our favorite dessert arrives; its identity previously unannounced.

Menus are devices that provide information to consumers about the availability of specific items. But a menu also enables an individual diner to plan his or her meal so as to maximize total utility from eating at any particular time. It also reminds us that the expression "variety is the spice of life" applies to temporarily postpone diminishing marginal utility.

appetite for the dishes he liked best. Apparently he liked and ate everything" (p. 9). Given the discussion of diminishing marginal utility in this chapter, we should recognize that even Henry had to "save his appetite" by *combining* foods at any *particular* meal. Even if he liked all foods "equally well" through time, it is doubtful that he ate an entire suckling pig rather than a portion of pork with some kidney pie at one sitting. Diminishing marginal utility tells us why.

[c] Another important function of menus is to convey information regarding the prices of each offering. The prices *do* affect the choice process, but our concern here is with other dimensions of the diner's choice.

Although numerical examples like those shown in Tables 3.1 through 3.4 have an intuitive appeal, modern economists do not believe that consumers are able to measure their utility in a cardinal way. Instead, they view consumers as being able to measure only **ordinal utility** — ranking alternatives in order of preference but making no attempt to quantify differences in utility between different bundles of goods. An ordinal measure of utility might rank 4 units of food above 3, 3 units above 2, and so on, but it would not quantify the differences in utility associated with 4 over 3 or 2. When we view utility as ordinal, we are not able to say anything about the size of marginal utility. If you prefer 4 units of food to 3 and 3 units to 2, you can be certain that the third and fourth units yield positive marginal utility. However, you are not able to compare the marginal utility of the fourth unit of food with the marginal utility of the third.

Indifference Curves

Even though ordinal measures of utility provide less information than do cardinal measures, ordinal measures are all that we need in order to develop the indifference curves on which we will rely to explain consumer choice. An **indifference curve** is simply a curve that traces out different combinations of goods yielding the same level of utility to a particular consumer. The curve thereby shows different combinations among which the consumer is indifferent.

For graphical ease, we can imagine a consumer who selects different combinations of two goods, perhaps food and wine, which are measured on the horizontal and vertical axes, respectively. Starting with some arbitrarily selected combination of the two goods, say bundle *A* in Figure 3.1, we can proceed to identify other bundles that yield the same utility. Assuming that both food and wine are desired by the consumer in question, points other than *A* that yield the same level of total satisfaction as *A* must lie either to the northwest or to the southeast of *A*. The reason for this is that if the consumer were to continue consuming 12 units of wine and at the same time increase his quantity of food, moving horizontally to the right of point *A*, his total utility would rise. Therefore, combinations of the two goods represented by points like *B* in Figure 3.1 must be preferable to the combination of goods represented by point *A*. Any new equivalent combination that contains more food than combination *A* must necessarily contain less wine. The new point therefore cannot lie directly to the east of point *A;* it must lie to the southeast.

To identify such a point, we can start at point *B* and then reduce the quantity of wine, moving directly south. As we do so, utility falls until we ultimately find a point, like *C*, that is equivalent to point *A* in the sense that it yields the same total utility. A close examination of the movement from *A* to *C* provides a clear distinction between cardinal and ordinal measures of utility. Viewing utility as cardinally measurable, we would say that the movement from point *A* to point *B* increases total utility by a certain quantity. The movement from *B* to *C* reduces total utility by a certain quantity. If the utility at *C* is identical to that at *A*, then the marginal utility of the tenth, eleventh, and twelfth units of wine combined must exactly equal the marginal utility from the fourth unit of food.

Figure 3.1 The Derivation of an Indifference Curve

A consumer is able to choose in rational fashion by selecting combinations of wine and food that leave her equally as well off (*A* or *C*) or better off (point *B*). Points that leave her as well off (but no better off) are on a single indifference curve.

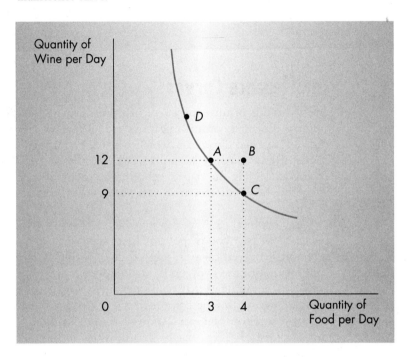

In contrast, viewing utility as measurable only in ordinal terms, all we can say is that combination *B* ranks higher than combination *A*, combination *B* ranks higher than combination *C*, and combination *C* ranks equal to combination *A*. It is important to recognize that we are able to identify points among which a consumer is indifferent without relying on a cardinal measure of utility.

Using the procedure described above, we can identify additional points that lie on the same indifference curve. For example, we could start at point *A* and then increase the quantity of wine. The new consumption point would lie directly above point *A* and would be preferable to it. From that point we could reduce the quantity of food moving to the northwest of point *A* until we reach some point, like *D*, that is equivalent to *A*. All equivalent points will lie to the northwest or the southeast of point *A*, which means that our indifference curves are negatively sloped.

The indifference curve we derived in Figure 3.1 passed through an arbitrarily selected point *A*. Using similar logic, we could select any other point, say point *B* in Figure 3.1, and derive another indifference curve that connects combinations of the two goods yielding a total utility equal to that of combination *B*.

Consumer-Preference Assumptions

In order to make generalizations about the shapes of indifference curves and their relationships to each other, we need to make three assumptions about consumer preferences:

1. We assume that a consumer *can and does rank all combinations of goods.* This means that she can compare any two combinations of goods and determine either that (a) she prefers the first to the second, (b) she prefers the second to the first, or (c) she is indifferent between the two bundles. Because the consumer is able to make one of these three judgments regarding the relative merits of any two combinations of goods, her preferences are a **complete ranking**.

2. We assume that *the consumer's ranking of combinations of goods is a* **transitive ranking** — that is, it is consistent. For example, if a consumer prefers combination *E* to combination *F* and combination *F* to combination *G*, then consistency requires that he also prefers combination *E* to combination *G*.

3. We assume that *if one combination of goods differs from another combination by containing more of at least one good while providing no less of any good, then the first combination is preferred to its alternative.* This assumption is often referred to as the "more-is-preferred-to-less" assumption. Unlike the first two assumptions, which we will always maintain, there will be times when we elect to drop this third assumption. For example, we might want to use indifference curves to examine an individual's behavior when that person is confronted with an *economic bad,* an item for which less is preferred to more. That person has the opportunity to obtain a higher-paying job by working under more dangerous conditions. In this case, less danger is preferred to more. However, our general assumption will be that the items included in the bundle of goods being evaluated are economic goods. Therefore, the "more-is-preferred-to-less" assumption will hold.

On the basis of these underlying assumptions, we can reach two conclusions about indifference curves. First, *indifference curves must be negatively sloped.* Assuming that both items making up the bundle are goods, an increase in one good will raise total utility. Therefore, to keep total utility constant along an indifference curve, an increase in the quantity of one of the goods must be offset by a decrease in the quantity of the other.

Indifference curves that are not negatively sloped are inconsistent with the "more-is-preferred-to-less" assumption. For example, a horizontal indifference curve would imply that additional units of the good measured on the horizontal axis have no impact on total utility. Given the quantity of the good measured on the vertical axis, utility is the same regardless of how many units of the other good the consumer acquires. This implies that the item measured on

Figure 3.2 Why Indifference Curves Do Not Intersect

Intersecting indifference curves are a contradiction. The consumer would have to be simultaneously indifferent between 4 food/8 wine (point *A*) and 3 food/12 wine (point *B*) and between 4 food/8 wine (point *A*) and 2 food/10 wine (point *C*). This is logically impossible.

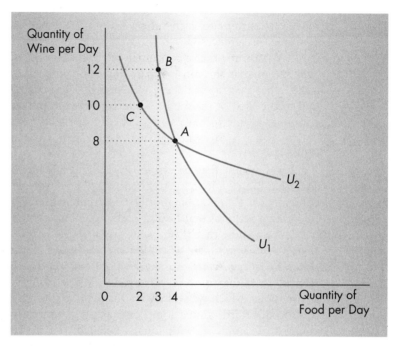

the horizontal axis has no value, so more is *not* preferred to less. Similarly, an indifference curve drawn as a vertical line implies that the item on the vertical axis has no value — that it is not an economic good.

The remaining alternative to a negatively sloped indifference curve is a positively sloped one. Such an indifference curve would imply that two combinations are equally preferable, even though one contains greater quantities of both the goods involved. Such an indifference curve is clearly inconsistent with the "more-is-preferred-to-less" assumption. It implies that one of the two items is a "bad." Therefore, the loss of utility associated with larger quantities of the bad must be offset by larger quantities of an economic good.

The second important conclusion we can draw about indifference curves from the basic assumptions described earlier is that *no two indifference curves can intersect.* In Figure 3.2, two intersecting indifference curves are drawn. As you can see, U_1 shows a combination of points, including points *A* and *B*, that lie on a single indifference curve. To include those two points on one indifference curve means that for the consumer in question, *A* is equal to *B*. Figure 3.2 also shows a second indifference curve, U_2, which intersects U_1 at point *A*

Figure 3.3 Convex and Concave Indifference Curves

The convex indifference curve in panel (a) implies that the more food the individual consumes, the more willing she is to substitute food for wine. The concave indifference curve in panel (b) indicates that the more food she consumes, the less willing she is to substitute food for wine.

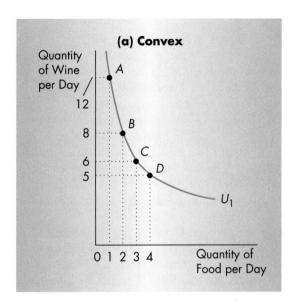

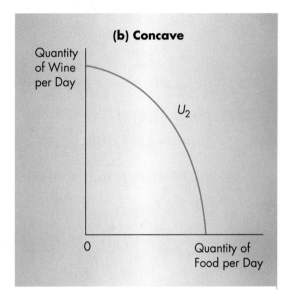

and includes point *C*. Because *A* and *C* lie on the same indifference curve, the consumer is indifferent between *A* and *C*. Both *C* and *B* then are ranked equal to *A*, so the transitivity assumption requires that *C* be ranked equal to *B*. But *C* and *B* cannot be equal. Point *B* contains more of both food and wine than does *C*, so it is preferable to *C*. Therefore, it is impossible to construct intersecting indifference curves without violating our basic assumptions about preferences.

One additional characteristic of indifference curves is important in the economic view of consumer choice: *indifference curves are convex to the origin*. In other words, indifference curves become flatter as we move down along them. As an example, see the convex indifference curve depicted in Figure 3.3a.

Logic requires that indifference curves are generally convex. Think for a minute about the slope of an indifference curve, in particular, the indifference curve labeled U_1 in Figure 3.3a. Point *A* on that curve consists of 12 units of wine and 1 unit of food. A second point, *B*, represents 8 units of wine and 2 units of food. In changing from bundle *A* to bundle *B*, the consumer gives up 4 units of wine for 1 additional unit of food. Because *A* and *B* lie on the same indifference curve, starting at point *A* the individual in question is willing to give up 4 units of wine for 1 more food. The slope of the indifference curve between points *A* and *B* is –4. We can interpret this slope as showing the consumer's willingness to give up units of the good on the *y* axis (wine) for the good on the *x* axis (food); a slope of –4 means that the consumer is willing to give up 4 of good Y for 1 of good X.

The Marginal Rate of Substitution

The indifference curve depicted in Figure 3.3a is convex to the origin; we observe that it gets flatter as we move down along it. Therefore, the slope between points *B* and *C* is lower (in absolute value) than the slope between points *A* and *B*. Specifically, the slope between *B* and *C* is –2. That equals the number of units of good Y the consumer is willing to give up for an additional unit of X, given that he initially has 8 units of Y (wine) and 2 units of X (food).

The slope of the indifference curve, called the **marginal rate of substitution**, shows one's willingness to give up units of the good measured on the vertical axis for an additional unit of the good measured on the horizontal axis. To say that indifference curves are convex to the origin is to say that the marginal rate of substitution diminishes as we move down along an indifference curve.

Now consider the concave indifference curve labeled U_2 in Figure 3.3b; you can see that as we move down and along U_2, the slope increases in absolute value. A concave indifference curve therefore implies an increasing marginal rate of substitution. To argue that indifference curves are concave is to argue that individuals become more and more willing to give up units of Y for additional units of X as they increase their consumption of X. Common sense dictates that the reverse is true. Starting at some point like point *A* on U_1, at which the consumer has a lot of wine and very little food, his willingness to sacrifice wine for additional food (his marginal rate of substitution) is likely to be quite high. However, as the consumer substitutes food for wine moving down along his indifference curve, it is likely that his marginal rate of substitution will diminish. For this reason, economists assume that diminishing marginal rates of substitution are the norm.

While we are on the topic of marginal rates of substitution (MRS), let's examine how this concept relates to marginal analysis. If we consider a consumer who initially has some specific bundle of goods, then the slope of the indifference curve passing through that point shows his MRS, the highest number of units of good Y (wine in Figure 3.3a) he is willing to give up for an additional unit of good X (food). We can therefore interpret the MRS as showing the marginal benefit to him of consuming one more unit of X, with the marginal benefit measured in units of Y.[3] Later in this chapter we will

---

3. The marginal rate of substitution can be related to the concept of marginal utility discussed earlier. The loss of utility from having less of a good Y is equal to the change in the quantity of good Y consumed (ΔY) times the marginal utility of Y (MU_Y). The gain in utility from having more of another good X is equal to the change in the quantity of the good

discuss the notion of a budget line and see that the slope of a budget line shows the marginal cost of an additional X in terms of Y. Combining indifference curves and budget lines will therefore prove to be a fruitful way of seeing how to apply rationality and maximizing behavior to consumer decisions.

Consumer preferences are usually illustrated as in Figure 3.4, which depicts a typical **indifference map**, a set of indifference curves. Each curve represents a different level of utility from consuming two goods, X and Y.

Figure 3.4 A Typical Indifference Map

The indifference map is typical in that the four indifference curves are negatively sloped, convex, and do not intersect.

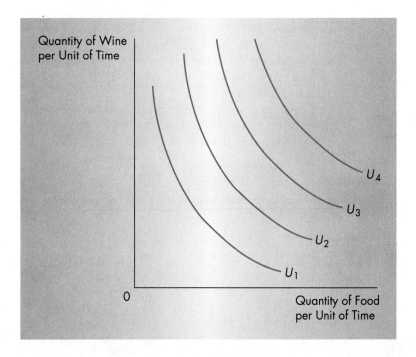

consumed (ΔX) times the marginal utility of X (MU_X). Because total utility is constant along an indifference curve, the two changes must have equal impacts on the consumer's total utility and we can write

$$(\Delta Y)\,(MU_Y) = (\Delta X)\,(MU_X)$$

Rearranging the terms we find that

$$\Delta Y / \Delta X = MU_X / MU_Y$$

where $\Delta Y / \Delta X$ is the slope of the indifference curve. The marginal rate of substitution equals the ratio of the marginal utilities. The *MRS* declines because the marginal utility of X declines, and the marginal utility of Y increases as the consumer moves down along the indifference curve.

Moreover, each curve displays the characteristics typical of indifference curves: each of the four indifference curves is negatively sloped; each displays diminishing MRS, and none of the indifference curves intersect.

Indifference Curves and Consumer Tastes

The previous section demonstrated individual indifference curves and an indifference map for a particular consumer. That discussion may have led you to think that a particular indifference curve or map applies to all consumers, but that is not the case. Instead, each consumer has a unique indifference map that reflects his or her own individual *tastes and preferences*. By tastes and preferences, we mean the willingness to give up one good in exchange for more of another good. In terms of an indifference curve, the stronger someone's preferences for good X relative to good Y, the more willing that consumer is to give up Y for X, and therefore the steeper will be that person's indifference curves. On the other hand, a person who has relatively strong tastes for Y will be relatively unwilling to give up Y for X. That person's indifference curves will therefore be relatively flat.

Figure 3.5 shows indifference maps for two individuals, Tim and Gwen. Gwen's indifference map shows that her preferences are strong for wine relative to food. In contrast, Tim's preferences lean more toward food and less

Figure 3.5 Indifference Maps for Individuals with Difference Tastes

Tastes and preferences are revealed in the *shape* of the indifference curves. Gwen has a preference for wine vis-à-vis food and Tim for food vis-à-vis wine.

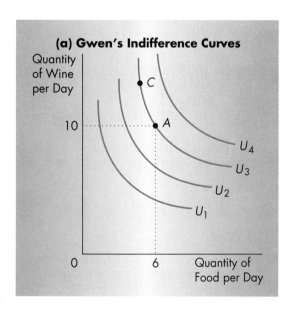

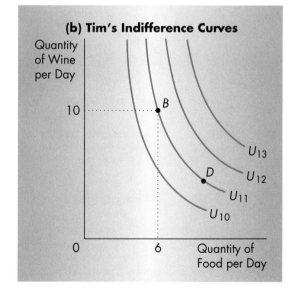

toward wine. In general, strong preferences for the good on the horizontal axis imply high marginal rates of substitution. For example, we can compare point A on Gwen's indifference curve U_3 with point B on Tim's indifference curve U_{12}. The two points each represent the same bundle of goods — 10 units of wine and 6 units of food. At that combination of wine and food, Tim has a higher MRS — his indifference curve is steeper at point B than is Gwen's at point A. However, we must not conclude that the person with the stronger preference for good X will always have a larger MRS. If we compare Gwen's MRS at point C with Tim's at point D, Gwen's is clearly larger. This just shows that although Gwen has weaker preferences for food, she may be more willing to give up wine for food when she has a lot of wine and a little food than Tim is when he has a lot of food and a little wine. Both individuals have diminishing MRS; if we move far enough down Tim's indifference curves, his MRS may be smaller than Gwen's at some point far up along one of her indifference curves.

Indifference Maps for Goods Viewed as Substitutes or Complements

Tastes and preferences determine not only the general slope of indifference curves, but also their general shape. A consumer can regard any pair of goods as perfect substitutes, close substitutes, strong complements, or perfect complements. If two goods are perfect substitutes, the consumer will give up one for the other in a fixed ratio. For example, if Tim views Coca-Cola and Pepsi as perfect substitutes, he would always be willing to give up at most one Pepsi for an additional Coke, regardless of the number of Pepsis and Cokes he is currently consuming. His indifference curve will be a straight line, and his marginal rate of substitution will be constant (see Figure 3.6a).

If the two goods are viewed as close substitutes, then the indifference curves will flatten slightly as we move down along them (see Figure 3.6b). The good on the x axis is viewed as being somewhat different from that on the y axis, so the marginal rate of substitution will fall slowly as more of X and less of Y is consumed.

Complementary goods are goods that are used in conjunction with one another. For example, left-handed gloves and right-handed gloves are nearly perfect complements. If you had four of each, then you would be unwilling to give up any left-handed gloves for additional right-handed gloves. Similarly, you would not be willing to give up right-handed ones for left-handed ones. In fact, your utility would be determined entirely by the smaller of the number of left-handed and right-handed gloves. Figure 3.7a shows an indifference map for perfect complements.

Close complements are goods that are used together but not necessarily in fixed proportions. For example, hours of time on a tennis court and tennis

Figure 3.6 Indifference Maps for Perfect and Close Substitutes

Panel (a) shows an indifference map for a consumer who views Pepsi and Coke as *perfect* substitutes. Panel (b) is an indifference map for a consumer who views the two goods as *close* substitutes.

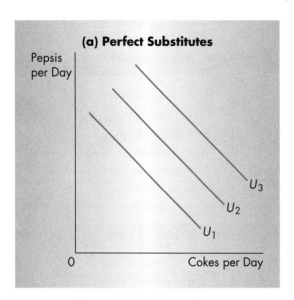
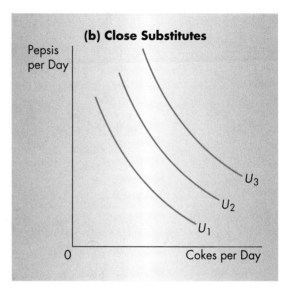

Figure 3.7 Indifference Maps for Perfect and Close Complements

Perfect complements are two goods used in fixed proportions with each other (left- and right-handed gloves). Near complements are goods used together but not necessarily in fixed proportions.

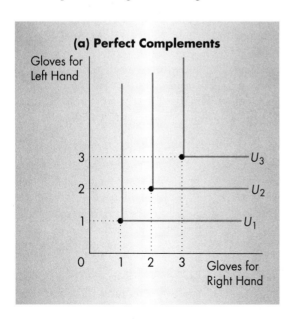
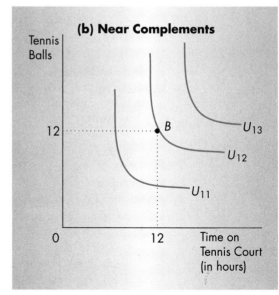

balls might be considered close complements. For the sake of argument, let's suppose that a tennis ball lasts for one hour of play with little deterioration in quality. Beyond an hour of use, the ball quickly loses its bounce and further play loses much of its appeal. Therefore, a player has little reason to change balls more often than once an hour and a fairly strong incentive to change them on the hour. (The indifference map for this case is depicted in Figure 3.7b.) Suppose that Gwen initially has 12 tennis balls and has reserved 12 hours of playing time, placing her at point B on indifference curve U_{12}. For her to give up tennis balls in exchange for additional playing time would mean using each tennis ball for more than one hour and reducing the quality of the play. However, because additional play has some benefit, she would have some willingness to make this tradeoff. The marginal rate of substitution would not be zero, as was the case for perfect complements, but it would be quite low. Likewise, Gwen would be willing to give up some playing time for additional tennis balls. However, additional tennis balls would have only slight value, and a large number of them would be required to compensate for the loss of playing time. At points on the indifference curve above point B, the MRS would be very high.

Indifference Maps for Economic Bads and Economic Neuters

Up to this point, we have drawn indifference curves between two economic goods and maintained the assumption that "more is preferred to less." However, as indicated earlier, we sometimes use indifference curves to examine consumer choice involving items that are *not* economic goods. Specifically, certain items may be viewed as economic "bads" in that less is preferred to more — that is, the item reduces total utility or entails what is called **disutility**. Other items may be viewed as "economic neuters": the consumer is indifferent about quantity, and thus the item neither contributes to nor detracts from total utility.

The indifference map in Figure 3.8a is drawn assuming that the good on the vertical axis is an economic good and that the good on the horizontal axis is an economic bad. Note two important differences between this case and the standard case:

1. *The individual's indifference curves are positively sloped.* The reason for this is that because good X is an economic bad, increases in the quantity of X reduce total utility. Therefore, any increase in the quantity of X must be offset with an *increase* in the quantity of Y to keep total utility constant. For example, starting at point A on U_2, a 1-unit increase in the quantity of X to 4 units would reduce the consumer's total utility. To identify a second point on U_2, the quantity of Y must be increased enough to offset the disutility associated with the fourth unit of X. This particular indifference curve shows that it takes 4 additional units of Y to compensate for the 1 additional unit of X.

Figure 3.8 Indifference Maps for Economic Bads and Economic Neuters
An indifference map between an economic good and an economic bad (for example, pollution) is positively sloped as in panel (a). An economic neuter is shown in flat indifference curves as in panel (b).

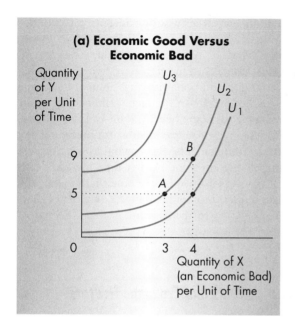

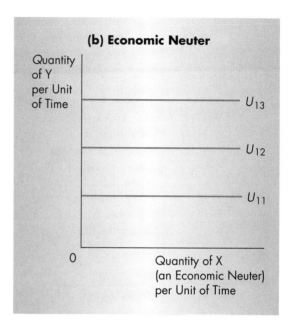

2. *The indifference curves in Figure 3.8a become steeper as the quantity of X is increased.* The logic behind this is that the marginal value of additional units of Y falls as the quantity of Y rises. Because each successive unit of Y adds less to utility, larger amounts of Y are required to offset units of X as the number of units of Y increases.

Figure 3.8b shows a representative indifference map in which the good on the horizontal axis is an economic neuter. The consumer is indifferent about the quantity of X he receives, so the indifference curves are horizontal. Changing the quantity of X does not affect total utility, because there is no utility or disutility associated with the consumption of X. Suppose Loretta enjoys the ballet but is totally indifferent toward opera. Loretta's indifference map would look like Figure 3.8b. Additional ballet tickets (good Y) would increase Loretta's utility, whereas additional opera tickets (good X) would leave her neither better nor worse off. The consumer's level of utility is determined solely by the quantity of good Y.

In this section, we have discussed indifference maps for substitutes, for complements, and for items described as economic bads and economic neuters. Despite the convenience of these classifications, it is important to note that there is nothing inherent in particular goods that automatically places them in certain categories. Tennis balls can be an economic good to one consumer and an economic neuter to another. One consumer may view Coke and Pepsi to be perfect substitutes; another may view them as not even close substitutes. All the classifications we have discussed reflect the tastes and preferences that differentiate consumers, not the goods themselves.

Concluding Note on Indifference Maps

Indifference maps provide a simple graphical means of showing how consumers rank various combinations of goods. They also provide an effective framework for discussing the objective of a consumer. Economists assume that consumers are rational, and it follows that consumers make choices to maximize their utility. In terms of indifference maps, the objective of each consumer is to attain the highest possible indifference curve. However, consumers are not able to consume every combination of goods. The goods generally have to be paid for, so consumers' choices are limited to what they can afford given their income and the prices they must pay for the goods they consume. In order to use indifference maps to explain consumer choice, we need to distinguish the combinations of goods that are affordable to the consumer from those that are not affordable. For this we need a budget line.

Budget Lines

During a given period of time, a typical consumer has a fixed income, which he uses to purchase various goods. For simplicity, imagine one consumer who has a fixed income of $100 per day to spend either on food or on wine or on some combination of the two. Further assume that the consumer finds the price of food (P_F) is $4 and the price of wine (P_W) is $2. His objective is to spend his income rationally — to obtain the maximum possible level of utility. It would be fairly easy to list all the combinations of food and wine that are affordable. He could spend all $100 on wine and obtain 50 units, or he could spend his entire income on food by purchasing 25 units, or he could spend a portion of his income on wine and a portion on food.

A graph can depict very simply the various combinations of wine and food that he could afford: in Figure 3.9, the straight line connecting points *A* and *E* shows all such combinations. At point *A* the person buys 50 units of wine and no food; at $2 each, the 50 units of wine would exhaust his entire budget of $100, making it impossible for him to buy any food. At the other extreme, the consumer could select point *E*, at which he buys 25 units of food and no wine; again, this is a combination of the two goods that would exhaust the entire budget. Between these two extremes there are other points, such as *B*, *C*, and *D*, which show the consumer purchasing some of both goods. At point *B* the

Figure 3.9 A Budget Line

A budget line reveals all of the possible combinations of two goods that a consumer could obtain with a given income and at given prices for the two goods.

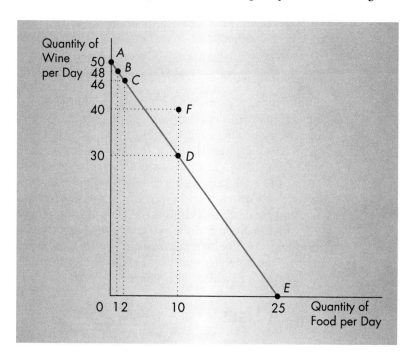

consumer is buying 48 units of wine, which exhausts $96 of his budget. The remaining $4 is sufficient to buy one unit of food. At point C, he buys 2 fewer units of wine. With the $4 he saves, he is able to increase his consumption of food from 1 unit to 2 units.

The line connecting points A and E is called a budget line. A **budget line** connects all the possible combinations of two goods that a consumer can afford, expending all of a given income and with given prices of the two goods. Each point on this particular budget line shows a combination of goods that costs exactly $100. Points located to the northeast of the budget line may be attractive to the consumer, but they are not affordable. For example, point F lies beyond the budget line; it represents the purchase of 40 units of wine and 10 units of food, which would require a total outlay of $120. Points to the southwest of the budget line represent combinations of wine and food that fail to exhaust the entire budget. We can therefore think of the budget line as separating affordable combinations of the two goods from nonaffordable combinations — affordable combinations lie on or inside the budget line; non-affordable combinations lie beyond the budget line.

Changes in the Budget Line

The specific budget line depicted in Figure 3.9 holds for the income and prices assumed in that case. Obviously, a change in income, in the price of wine, or in the price of food would lead to a new budget line. In order to see how each of these possible changes would affect the budget line, it is helpful to express the budget line in equation form. The budget line shows various combinations of food (Q_{FOOD}, which is measured on the horizontal axis) and wine (Q_{WINE}, which is measured on the vertical axis) that exhaust the budget (M). If P_F and P_W represent the prices of food and wine, then $P_F Q_{FOOD}$ is the number of dollars spent on food and $P_W Q_{WINE}$ is the number of dollars spent on wine. Assuming that the entire budget is spent, then

$$M = P_F Q_{FOOD} + P_W Q_{WINE} \tag{1}$$

Dividing both sides of equation (1) by P_W yields

$$M/P_W = (P_F/P_W)Q_{FOOD} + Q_{WINE} \tag{2}$$

Rearranging the terms we get

$$Q_{WINE} = M/P_W - (P_F/P_W)Q_{FOOD} \tag{3}$$

If we consider Q_{FOOD} and Q_{WINE} as variables and M, P_F, and P_W to be constants, then it is clear that equation (3) is simply the formula for a straight line on which (M/P_W) is the vertical intercept and $(-P_F/P_W)$ is the slope. Returning to the previous numerical example in which $M = \$100$, $P_F = \$4$, and $P_W = \$2$, the vertical intercept is $\$100/\$2 = 50$ and the slope is $-\$4/\$2 = -2$. The budget line depicted in Figure 3.9 has that intercept and that slope.

Equation 3 is a general expression for a budget line for food and wine purchases.[4] We can see that, holding prices constant, an increase in income (M) leads to a new budget line with a larger intercept but with the same slope. It causes the original budget line to shift outward in a parallel fashion. Similarly, a decrease in income leads to a parallel shift inward in the budget line. Figure 3.10 displays such shifts in the budget line caused by changes in M.

Equation 3 also shows us precisely how changes in prices affect the budget line. For example, an increase in P_F causes the slope to rise in absolute value,

---

4. The equation for the budget line can be generalized to reflect any two goods, X and Y, whose prices are P_X and P_Y. The budget relation becomes $M = P_X X + P_Y Y$, which yields the budget line equation

$$Y = M/P_Y - (P_X/P_Y)X$$

Figure 3.10 The Effect of Income Changes on the Budget Line
Assuming prices held constant, an increase in income shifts the budget line
rightward. A decrease in income shifts the budget line leftward.

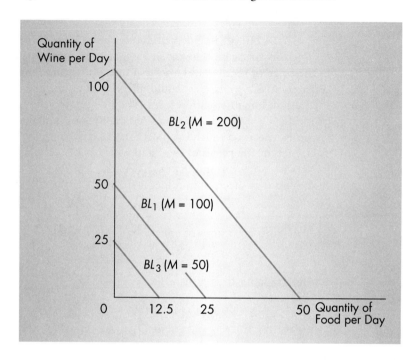

leading to a budget line that is steeper but that has the same vertical intercept.
A reduction in P_F leads to a budget line that is flatter but that has the same
vertical intercept. Figure 3.11 shows the effect of both raising P_X to \$8 and
lowering P_X to \$1. This economic experiment showing the effects of price
changes must be understood as an experiment on the *individual*. It is of
critical importance to understand the differences in budget-line shifts for an
individual consumer versus those for consumers in general.

In equation 3 we saw that budget lines have a slope equaling $-P_F/P_W$. The
economic interpretation of that slope is quite important. In the case in which
P_F = \$4 and P_W = \$2, the slope is −2: the consumer *must* give up 2 units of
wine (or the good on the vertical axis) in order to buy 1 more unit of food (or
the good on the horizontal axis). When the price of food is twice the price of
wine, the consumer must reduce his consumption of wine by 2 units in order
to free up enough income to afford 1 more unit of food. We can therefore
think of the slope of the budget line as the marginal cost of an additional unit
of the good measured horizontally in terms of units of the good measured vertically. If P_F rises to \$8, the slope of the budget line will become −4, and each
additional unit of food will require the sacrifice of 4 units of wine.

Figure 3.11 The Effect of Price Changes on the Budget Line
A change in the price of food rotates the budget line around a point on the vertical (wine) axis.

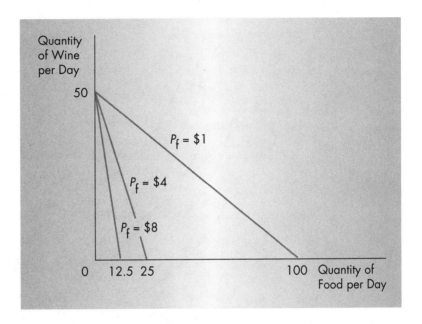

Optimizing Behavior: Budget Lines and Indifference Curves

Earlier in this chapter we developed indifference maps, and we have just developed the budget line. If you examine the relevant graphs, you will observe that they measure the quantity of one good on one axis and the quantity of the other good on the other axis. Therefore, there is nothing to prevent us from drawing a budget line and an indifference map on a single graph. Let's return to our continuing example, the consumer whose preferences for wine and food are reflected in the indifference map in Figure 3.12. Let's further assume that this person has an income of $100, the price of wine is $2, and the price of food is $4. The budget line connecting points A and E show the different combinations of the two goods that the consumer can afford, and her objective is to attain the highest level of utility possible — to get to the highest possible indifference curve. Of all the affordable combinations available, combination D is the one that lies on the highest attainable indifference curve, U_3. Many points on the graph are preferred to point D; point F on U_5 is one of them. However, that combination of food and wine is not within her budget.

Figure 3.12 The Use of a Budget Line and an Indifference Curve to Show Optimizing Behavior

The consumer achieves utility maximization at point *D*, where the highest attainable indifference curve is tangent to the budget line. The consumer would prefer points such as *F*, but they are not attainable.

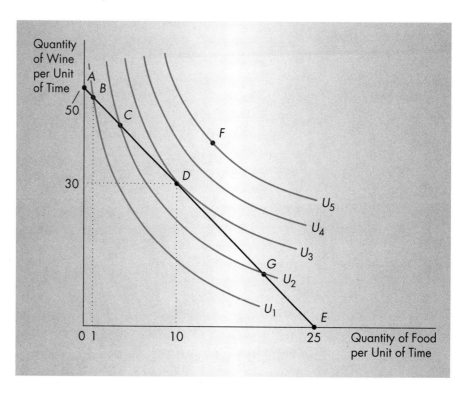

To select point *D* and buy 10 units of food and 30 units of wine per time period is the best this consumer can do, given her income and the prices she must pay. It would be irrational for her to select any point other than *D* given her circumstances.

It might seem strange to refer to point *D* as the "best" quantity of food to buy without referring to marginal costs and benefits. Can we be sure that buying 10 units of food in this case equates the marginal benefit with the marginal cost of food? The answer is yes, and to see why, we need to think about the slope of the budget line and the slope of indifference curves. Suppose that this consumer changed her behavior by selecting point *B* and bought only 1 unit of food each time period. If we focus our attention on point *B*, we see that indifference curve U_1 crosses the budget line at that point. At *B*, the indifference curve is steeper than the budget line. We know that the slope of the budget line $(-P_F/P_W)$ is -2, so the slope of the indifference curve must be a larger negative number. To be specific, let's assume that the slope of U_1 at point *B* is

–8. This means that at point *B*, this individual is willing to give up 8 additional units of wine for 1 additional unit of food. The marginal benefit of additional food is 8 units of wine. However, the marginal cost of an additional unit of food is given by the slope of the budget line, –2. At point *B* the marginal benefit of an additional unit of food is greater than the marginal cost, so more food should be consumed. In Figure 3.12 you can see that as the consumer increases her food consumption and moves down her budget line from point *B* to some point like *C*, she ends up on a higher indifference curve.

   This example shows that at any consumption point at which the indifference curve is steeper than the budget line, the marginal benefits of food exceed the marginal costs, so more food should be purchased. It is also the case that at any consumption point at which the indifference curve is flatter than the budget line, such as point *G*, the marginal cost of food exceeds the marginal benefit, and less food should be purchased. (To make certain that you are following this reasoning, think carefully about why the selection of combination *G* violates maximizing behavior.) The individual's optimal consumption point

Figure 3.13 The Effect of a Change in Income on a Consumer's Choice

An increase in income expands consumption possibilities available to the consumer. To maximize utility, the consumer will advance from point *D* on indifference curve U_3 to point *J* on indifference curve U_5.

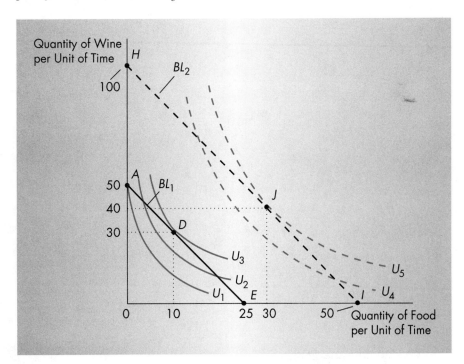

occurs where the budget line and indifference curve have the same slope — in this case at point *D*, where the budget line is tangent to the indifference curve.

Optimizing consumer behavior occurs at the point at which an indifference curve is tangent to the budget line. The equality of slopes at a tangency indicates that the marginal rate of substitution (the slope of the indifference curve) equals the price ratio (the slope of the budget line). The marginal rate of substitution measures the consumer's willingness to substitute one good for another. The price ratio indicates the consumer's ability, through the market, to substitute between goods. The consumer will have reached an optimum (maximized) utility when the willingness and ability to substitute are equal.

You can also use budget lines and indifference maps to show how changes in incomes or prices affect consumer behavior. For example, suppose that our consumer receives an increase in income from $100 to $200 per time period. Figure 3.13 illustrates this as an outward shift in the budget line. The new budget line, BL_2, connects points *H* and *I*. With the increased budget the consumer finds that the new optimizing point is *J*, at which she purchases 40 units of wine and 30 units of food. Given the tastes and preferences represented by the indifference map shown in Figure 3.13, this increase in income leads to a 10-unit increase in wine consumption and a 20-unit increase in food

Figure 3.14 The Effect of a Change in Price on a Consumer's Behavior
A reduction in the price of food permits the consumer to increase her utility by purchasing more food (and more wine as well).

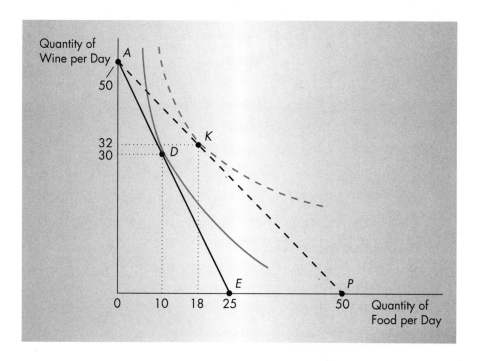

consumption. The effects of a decrease in income could similarly be shown by shifting the budget line inward and determining the new optimizing point. As an exercise, try to work through such a shift.

Budget lines and indifference curves also illustrate how consumers react to changes in price. If we return to our basic example in which M = $100, P_x = $4, and P_y = $2, we can see how a change in the price of X (food) affects consumer behavior. If, for example, the price of food fell from $4 to $2, the budget line would rotate from AE to AP in Figure 3.14. The new optimizing point would be K, at which the consumer buys 18 units of food and 32 units of wine. The $2 reduction in the price of food causes this consumer to increase food consumption from 10 to 18 units. For a consumer with different tastes, the effect of this price change would of course be different.

In addition to analyzing the impact of changes in price or income, the budget-line/indifference-curve apparatus can also be used to examine changes in tastes. For example, in the wine/food example a consumer might discover that wine consumption has some beneficial health effects of which he was previously unaware. Knowing this, he would be less likely to give up wine for

Figure 3.15 The Effect of a Change in Tastes on a Consumer's Behavior
A change in consumer tastes affects the whole indifference map of the consumer and changes the equilibrium level of his or her consumption.

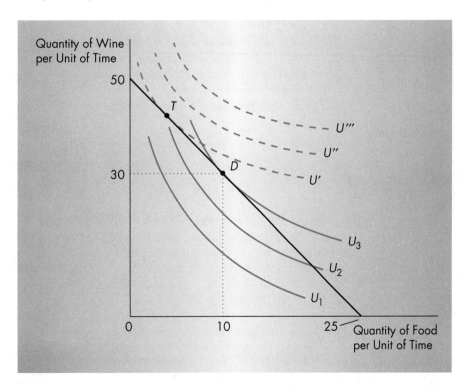

food, and his indifference curves would become flatter. Such a change in tastes is depicted in Figure 3.15, in which the indifference curves labeled U_1, U_2, and U_3 are replaced with a new indifference map whose indifference curves are labeled U', U'', and U'''.[5] The new optimizing point is point T.

A More General Model of Budget Lines and Indifference Curves

The budget-line/indifference-curve model developed in this chapter has been limited to examples in which the consumer chooses between two particular goods. The reason for this simplification is that the two-goods case is easiest to show with a graph. The problem with a two-good model obviously is that it is far removed from the real-world decisions that typical consumers must make. Typical consumer choice consists of selecting quantities of one good when there are not two but literally thousands of alternative goods available. It is possible to expand the model to three goods using three-dimensional graphs; however, the marginal costs of doing so are greater than the marginal benefits. Three-dimensional graphs are much more complicated than two-dimensional graphs, and a three-good model has relatively few advantages over a two-good model.

Fortunately, there is a way to make the model more general without adding to its complexity. The strategy is to identify the one good to which we want to pay particular attention and to lump all other alternatives together as a composite good. We can then measure the quantity of good X on the horizontal axis and the number of dollars spent on other goods (non-X) on the vertical axis. (See Highlight 3.2 to appreciate the usefulness of the composite-good convention.)

Highlight 3.2   *Micro Versus Macro Budget Lines: The Politicians' Free Lunch of Pork Pie*

One of the most common mistakes when dealing with budget lines is to confuse the principles underlying individual versus group experiments. Consider first an individual experiment such as the one described in the text. If the composite good measured on the vertical axis represents "all other goods" and the good measured on the horizontal represents housing, a lower price of housing rotates the budget line in a counterclockwise direction. Such a rotation is

---

5. Because the dashed indifference curves (U', U'', and U''') replace the original indifference curves (U_1, U_2, and U_3), it does not matter that some indifference curves *seem* to intersect. The dashed curves exist only when the solid curves do not exist.

shown in Figure 3.16a, where the budget line rotates rightward from a point labeled Q_{AOG} on the vertical axis. The *cause* of the rightward rotation, of course, is a *decrease* in the price of housing (holding the nominal income of the consumer unchanged). The set of opportunities for the individual is enhanced from $OQ_{AOG}A$ to a new and enhanced set of consumption opportunities, $OQ_{AOG}B$. The shaded area of Figure 3.16a indicates the increased consumption opportunities. Practically, the consumer may increase his or her purchases of housing, of all other goods, or of both housing and all other goods.

Note, however, the assumption hidden within this experiment. If the consumer buys more housing (an expected result) and more of all other goods (possible within the expanded opportunities available), resources must clearly be available to support the new level of consumption. The hidden assumption is that these resources are in fact available at zero costs to all other consumers. Resources are, in effect, shifted around to produce Sue's new consumption set *without reducing consumption opportunities to Sam, Keith, Joan, or anyone else.*

In the microeconomics of consumer choice, this assumption is defensible. A small amount of increased consumption of housing (and perhaps other goods as well) does not appreciably deplete resources available to produce other goods for other people. Because we assume that each consumer is exceedingly insignificant (with respect to quantities purchased) relative to the total market for any good, that assumption is justified.

Many politicians, however, would like us to believe that the same argument applies for the entire economy. In their zest to enhance their reelection prospects, they promise goods and services and all manner of public projects to particular constituents and special-interest groups. This is accomplished by opportunistic behavior of all sorts, including log rolling and vote trading. The result is a budget filled with "pork." The public is led to believe that the shaded area of Figure 3.16a expands magically *for society as a whole.*

Those who understand budget lines and the differences between microeconomics and macroeconomics know that this cannot be the case. Figures 3.16b and 3.16c, which show the market effects of a program to reduce the price of housing, help to illustrate these differences. The price of housing is brought down by increasing the supply of housing, as in Figure 3.16b. This increase in housing supply requires a diversion of resources from other uses and reduces the supply of other goods. This in turn leads to an increase in the price of other goods, as shown in Figure 3.16c. Figure 3.16d presents the net effect of these changes on each consumer.

Any legislated increase in the supply of housing (or any other good or service that uses resources) will require a rotation of the budget line, but not at point Q_{AOG} as in Figure 3.16a. Rather, the rotation will take place around some point such as J in Figure 3.16d. Why? Because the increased resources to produce more housing or more nuclear missiles or infrastructure *must come from somewhere.* If society is operating close to its production-possibilities frontier (close to its "budget line"), those resources *must* be reallocated from other

Figure 3.16 Micro versus Macro Budget Lines: The Politician's Free Lunch

In analyzing a single consumer's budget line, it is appropriate to show greater consumption possibilities with a decrease in the price of housing, as in panel (a). The lower price of housing comes about via an increase in the supply of housing, as shown in panel (b). The increased supply of housing comes at the expense of the supply of other goods and the prices of other goods rise, as in panel (c). Panel (d) shows the net result: instead of rotating about point H, the budget line rotates about point J.

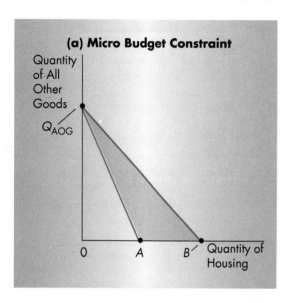

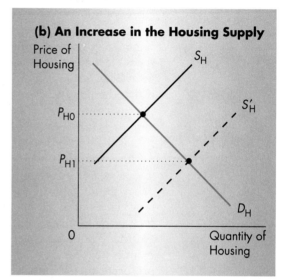

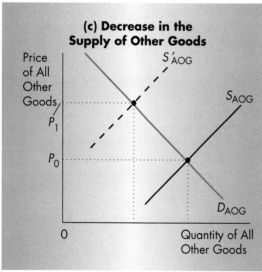

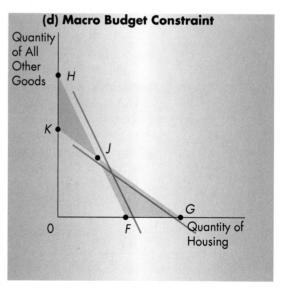

outputs and the prices of other goods will rise. The shift from "all other goods" to housing must means that each consumer and society will experience a reduction in the availability of all those other goods (area *HKJ* in Figure 3.16d) as they receive more housing (area *JFG* in Figure 3.16d). In the real world, such reallocations are brought about through increases in the price of all other goods — within the price system — or more directly by taxation of incomes or consumption to pay for the increased housing.

Highly disaggregate microeconomic experiments in consumer behavior in effect suspend the rule that "there is no such thing as a free lunch" in order to understand individual behavior. In the aggregate, however, there really is no free lunch, politicians' promises and inferences notwithstanding.

The budget line therefore has a vertical intercept equal to income *(M)*, and a slope of $-P_X$. Figure 3.17 depicts consumer choice, measuring the composite good on the vertical axis. The optimal point, point *D*, shows the consumer buying 10 units of X at $4 each and spending $60 on other goods.

Figure 3.17 A Budget Line and Indifference Map with a Composite Good

A composite good ("all other goods") may replace any one good.

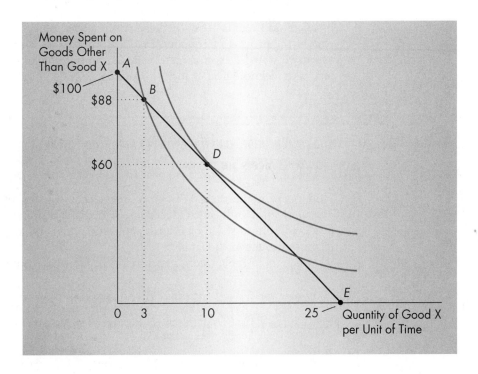

We have every reason to believe that the indifference map relating the quantity of good X to a composite good will have the same characteristics as an indifference map relating the quantity of X to the quantity of one particular good. Both the indifference curves will be negatively sloped and nonintersecting and will display diminishing MRS. The MRS, however, has a slightly different interpretation here. Specifically, it shows the maximum number of dollars that the consumer is willing to give up for an additional unit of good X. Because the slope of the budget line shows the number of dollars that you have to give up for an additional unit of X, you can again use indifference curves and budget lines to show at what point your marginal benefits from additional units of the good in question equal your marginal costs.

In Figure 3.17, at any point on the budget line other than *D*, the slope of the indifference curve is not equal to the slope of the budget line. For example, at point *B* the number of dollars you are willing to give up for an additional X is greater than the number of dollars you must pay for an additional unit of X. It is rational to increase consumption of X until marginal benefits no longer exceed marginal costs. You should therefore increase your consumption of X to 10 units, where the indifference curve is tangent to the budget line. There, the marginal benefits are equal to marginal costs. Because the composite-good model has several advantages and no real disadvantages, it is the model generally used in the remainder of this text.

It is important to see that choice theory is "alive" in its ability to explain utility-maximizing behavior through time. Institutions and rule changes, social practices and habits — even these cultural phenomena may be identified as part of the process of equating marginal benefits and marginal costs. A more expansive view of economizing yields an important harvest in explaining the results of technological change (for example, see Highlight 3.3).

Highlight 3.3   *Choice, Marriage, and the Evolving American Family: Economics Meets Sociology*

How broad is the theory of choice discussed in this chapter? It is capable of explaining not only static decisions of single consumers but, according to modern economists, far broader applications dealing with the evolution of institutions such as the family.[a]

Changes in the modern structure of the family are not a myth. In America,

[a] See, for example, Gary S. Becker, *A Treatise on the Family* (Cambridge: Harvard University Press, 1991), and Richard A. Posner, *Sex and Reason* (Cambridge: Harvard University Press, 1992), as prime examples of the interface between economics and numerous facets of traditional sociology. For his work in this area Becker was awarded the Nobel Prize in economics in 1992.

according to the 1990 census, Cleaver-style families — husband works, wife tends children and hearth — are a clear minority. Currently, only about one-fourth of families fit this description. Between 1960 and 1990 the percentage of households that were headed by a married couple fell from 78 percent to 55 percent, and the number of female-headed households more than doubled.

Many reasons have been advanced to explain these phenomena (changes in the welfare structure, and so on). Economic sociologists, however, look elsewhere to explain changes in family-household structure since the 1950s and the dramatic alteration in the proportion of women in the civilian work force — from about 30 percent in 1960 to almost 50 percent in 1992.

The essence of the economic explanation is that families equate marginal costs and marginal benefits just as individuals do. Whatever the many reasons people marry, economic advantage and security have been central to the marriage contract throughout human history. Just as specialization and trade form the basis for economic growth and progress in production and exchange, they also establish a solid foundation for the family. A key point is that the payoff to participants was and is greatest when family members have widely disparate talents and skills. Chief among these is childbearing and child rearing. Marriage as a historical institution arose due to female vulnerability during pregnancy and child development. The price of marriage (in terms of what the individual gives up) was low vis-à-vis the alternative (that is, single parenting). A woman's role, far from being subsidiary in the joint venture, was primary in family organization, progeneration, and education. Such familial relations were efficient and maximized individual and social welfare throughout the centuries that they were in effect.

Twentieth-century technology has rapidly turned this timeworn socioeconomic organization on its head by changing relative prices. Although various forms of birth control have existed in all ages, only since the 1950s have women been able to control the timing and incidence of reproduction with high and increasing degrees of certainty. The far-reaching implications of The Pill are profound for numerous social and economic institutions, including the traditional concept of family. Although biological specialization will certainly exist into the foreseeable future, the educational and workplace equality of women, made possible by pill technology, means that alternative and perhaps "looser" ties in the traditional household structure must emerge. Each partner is becoming more alike in market skills and, in effect, has less to trade. The increasing lack of specialization makes formal and traditional marriage less attractive by changing the costs and benefits of such unions. More education and higher income potential for women means that childbearing and rearing are more costly in terms of opportunities forgone. Higher divorce rates, lower birth rates, later marriages, single-parent households, and many variants of "families" may all be examined with respect to cost, choice, and relative prices. Technology cannot be disinvented; therefore, expect the process to continue.

Love and relationships constituting family are, we would argue, not in

Economic incentives in the evolving American family have led to
many changes in traditional family specialization. Here a father
walks his young son to school in New York City.

jeopardy. But even though love is here to stay, traditional marriage contracts
will ultimately change to match ongoing and evolving behavioral practice.
Further, the legal system is responding to the changes. Spousal equivalency
contracts, recognition of palimony, and expansion of health and other
insurance to declared unions are only three innovations that are receiving
consideration at law. Although the final outcome is hard to predict, the
traditional marriage contract and the traditional definition of family will likely
survive, but only as one of a variety of alternatives.

A still picture of the world does carry the suggestion that the laws and
institutions of any one time determine behavior. The broader truth is,

arguably, exactly the reverse: legal, family, marital, and household institutions are themselves the product of behavior over a longer period. That behavior is, in turn, a direct product of the relative costs and benefits to individuals of particular forms of behavior (constituting institutions). These changing costs and opportunities are ultimately caused by the most important of all forces — technology. Technology is the dynamic force that, as it unfolds, molds and shapes institutions. It does this through the processes of choice described in this chapter.

Other constraints may arise in time along with the relative price of certain types of behavior. These "prices" are not necessarily expressed in terms of money; they are just as relevant and important when expressed as the real costs to individuals of certain types of behavior. These broader notions of economizing, as is evident in Highlight 3.3, are just as much a part of the explanatory power of consumer (or family) choice as is the formal derivation of demand curves, the subject of Chapter 4.

Summary

In this chapter, we developed a graphical model to illustrate optimizing behavior by consumers. This basic model will be used in Chapter 4 to formally derive individual demand curves so as to emphasize the utility-maximizing nature of consumer choice.

In order to develop that graphical model we

- defined the notion of utility and explained cardinal and ordinal measures of utility,
- developed indifference curves based solely on ordinal utility,
- explained the characteristics of indifference curves and indifference maps,
- introduced budget lines to show the choices available to a consumer,
- applied budget lines and indifference maps to determine utility-maximizing behavior.

Key Terms

utility	cardinal utility
diminishing marginal utility	ordinal utility
indifference curve	complete ranking
transitive ranking	marginal rate of substitution
indifference map	disutility
budget line	

Sample Questions

Question

Pizza is sold in a variety of ways — by the slice, by the pie, and all you can eat. Why are you more likely to overeat at all-you-can-eat buffets than when you purchase pizza by the pie? Why are you more likely to overeat pizza purchased by the pie than by the slice?

Answer

You are most likely to overeat at an all-you-can-eat buffet because the marginal cost of consuming additional pizza is zero. Once you have paid to go through the line, additional trips to the buffet table are essentially costless. Being a rational consumer, you consume up to the point at which the marginal benefit equals the marginal cost. If the marginal cost is zero, you eat pizza until the marginal utility of pizza (at the one sitting) is zero. When purchased by the pie, the marginal cost of an additional slice is zero until the entire pizza is consumed, at which point the marginal cost is the price of another pizza. People tend to overeat if the pizza is larger than needed to reach the desired level of satiation. When purchased by the slice, the marginal cost of an additional slice is the price per slice. You then apply marginal analysis to each piece of pizza.

Question

Most consumers purchase only a small fraction of the goods and services available in a modern economy. Use the concepts of "economic bads" and "economic neuters" to explain this observation.

Answer

The role (or lack thereof) that economic bads and neuters play in consumer behavior can be revealed by referring back to Figure 3.8 and imagining a budget line on the indifference maps for economic bads and neuters. With upward-sloping indifference curves as in Figure 3.8a, the consumer maximizes utility at the point at which the budget line intersects the vertical axis. This vertical intercept lies on the highest indifference curve that the consumer can reach with his or her budget. At this point, the quantity of the economic bad (something the consumer detests) consumed is zero. You get the same result, an equilibrium on the vertical axis, when the indifference curves are horizontal. This does not mean that every unpurchased item is a bad or a neuter. Many items that would yield positive marginal utility to a consumer are never purchased because the price of the good is too high relative to the marginal utility. At some point in your life, you might be able to afford a BMW. However, it's a safe bet that you will not buy one. That does not mean that (to you) a BMW is a bad or a neuter.

Questions for Review and Discussion

1. What, specifically, is the difference between cardinal and ordinal utility? Does one give us more information than the other? Is one more "scientific" than the other? Explain.
2. Explain the derivation of an indifference curve.
3. What is the implication of *intersecting* indifference curves? Does a contradiction result? Show this graphically and explain.
4. What is meant by a complete ranking of preferences?
*5. What is the marginal rate of substitution and what is its relation to the convexity of indifference curves?
6. Draw an indifference map that illustrates perfect substitutes and one that illustrates perfect complements.
*7. Explain what happens to the slope of the indifference curve when a good is an economic bad.
8. What is a budget line? What does a point beyond the budget line represent?
*9. Derive the equation of a straight line from the equation of a budget line. Indicate the slope and intercept.
10. What is the difference in the effect of a change in income and a change in price on the budget line?
*11. What can be inferred about purchases from a situation in which the budget line is steeper than the indifference curve?
12. Using indifference curve analysis with a budget constraint, illustrate utility maximization for a consumer.
13. If a consumer's tastes change toward preferring less wine to food, what happens to that consumer's indifference curves?
*14. When the budget line/indifference curve model is generalized to incorporate a composite good, what is the interpretation of the marginal rate of substitution?
*15. Suppose three consumers purchase food and wine. If the price of food decreases, what happens to the budget line? Will each of the three consumers change food consumption by the same amount? Explain.

Problems For Analysis

1. Modern economists argue that tastes (preference functions or the indifference curves of this chapter) are relatively stable for individuals and households. This means that our behavior is conditioned mainly by relative price and income changes. If this is true, how would you explain the following two events, both hypothetical:
   a. The Iraqis obtain and deploy *intercontinental* ballistic rockets capable of striking the United States. Americans take more vacations and buy fewer new homes. How would you explain the change?

b. You win the New York lottery and are guaranteed $5 million a year for the rest of your life. Your behavior will change. How might the change be explained?

2. Seismologists warn us that few buildings, freeways, or other structures could currently survive an earthquake ranked 8+ on the Richter scale of earthquake severity. The probability of earthquakes of this size is fairly low, however. Does it make economic sense to build structures in northern California and in Missouri (with the New Madrid fault) to withstand such cataclysmic jolts? Explain. (*Hint:* Think of costs and benefits.)

3. Throughout history, wartime has produced alterations in behavior. Rampant savagery, increased prostitution, higher degrees of "religious behavior," brave and valorous acts, and so on, have always gone hand in hand with wars. Does the economist have anything to say concerning such behavior? Do tastes change? Do constraints change? Explain.

*4. Actress/singer Madonna published a book of controversial photos entitled *Sex* in October 1992. With bookstores rushing to cash in, more than 1 million of the volumes were printed. The volumes came shrink-wrapped in polyester and merchants required that the book be sold unopened. Using the theory of marginal utility, explain this policy.

5. Price gouging typically occurs after natural disasters. Why are people willing to pay many times the usual price for items such as lumber, roofing materials, bottled water, and so on, after a hurricane?

6. Many bad habits entail what we may call "near complements." Many smokers, for example, find that their smoking is linked with other goods — coffee, meals, alcohol. What does this imply for those who attempt to give up their bad habits?

7. In Figure 3.17, consider some point directly above D that consists of 10 units of X and $120 to spend on goods other than X. Call that point G. If you were to draw an indifference curve through point G, would the slope at point G be equal to the slope of the lower indifference curve at point D? Why or why not?

*8. Again, consider Figure 3.17: a consumer initially faces budget line AE and selects point D. Suppose that the price of X rises and the consumer's income increases enough to enable her to continue to purchase bundle D. Will she do so?

9. If your income and the prices of all goods doubled, how would your consumption pattern be affected?

10. The French consume much more wine per capita than do Americans. One explanation is that their tastes are different. Can you think of an alternative explanation?

11. Suppose that you are paying for your own education and that your college tuition is $200 per credit hour. At that price you generally take 15 hours per semester at a cost of $3,000. Now suppose your college changes to a policy of charging $3,000 per semester, regardless of the number of hours taken. Will this alter your budget line? Will it affect your course-load choices?

4

Individual Demand and Elasticity

Individual demand curves, their basis in utility, and aspects of their construction were discussed in earlier chapters. Demand, as an expression of utility-maximizing behavior, is fundamental to all of microeconomics and to the policy issues — health care, the stock market, and markets of all kinds — that it touches. The illustration of utility-maximizing behavior with budget lines and indifference maps is only part of the story. An understanding of that behavior is the key to microeconomic theory. In the present chapter we extend our understanding of how individuals react to changes in price and in other economic variables. Specifically, we

- illustrate how demand curves can be derived with the use of budget lines and indifference curves.
- use the budget line/indifference curve model to illustrate both price elasticity and income elasticity.
- reassess the determinants of elasticity and illustrate the concept with real-world examples.
- use indifference curves to explain the important concept of consumer surplus.

Derivation of an Individual Demand Curve

A demand curve shows the number of units of a particular good or service that a particular consumer would choose to buy at each possible price. The purpose of a demand curve is to show how a consumer will respond to changes in price. In constructing a demand curve, we must therefore allow the price of the good in question to vary while holding constant all other variables that are likely to have an important impact on the decision to buy. These other variables generally include the consumer's income, his or her tastes and preferences, and the prices of other goods. Specifically, if we want to derive the demand curve for some hypothetical good X, we can consider a consumer who must choose between good X and good Y under the following conditions:

the price of Y is held constant at, say, $10; the consumer's income is held constant at, say, $200 per time period; and the price of good X is allowed to vary. To hold the buyer's tastes and preferences constant, we consider a given **indifference map** such as that depicted in Figure 4.1. With a fixed income ($200) and a fixed price of $10 for other goods (good Y in this example), the consumer will face a different **budget line** for each possible P_X. However, each of the budget lines will have a vertical intercept equal to 20, because income is held constant at $200 and P_Y is held constant at $10. Figure 4.1 shows three representative budget lines, which correspond to $P_X = \$10$, $P_X = \$5$, and $P_X = \$2$. To illustrate what quantities of X this consumer will elect to buy at each of the three prices, we must superimpose the consumer's indifference map on the budget lines. This is done in Figure 4.1. The figure shows that the buyer in question faces BL_1 if the price of X is $10. Faced with that budget line, the buyer selects a combination of goods X and Y which is represented by point A. He buys Q_A units of good X. Then Q_A units is the quantity of X that maximizes the consumer's utility at that price — it places the consumer on the highest possible indifference curve, given his budget line. The consumer in question can afford more than Q_A units of X, because he has sufficient income to buy 20 units per time period at a price of $10 each. However, the decision to buy more than Q_A units would move the consumer to a point on BL_1 below point A, which would put him on an indifference curve that yields less utility than U_A.

In Figure 4.1 we can also see that if P_x is equal to $5, the consumer selects point B on BL_2. At a price of $2, the consumer selects point C on BL_3. This means that when the price of X is $10, the buyer selects 9 units ($Q_a = 9$); when the price is $5, he selects 16 units ($Q_b = 16$); and when the price of X is $2, he selects 28 units ($Q_c = 28$). To plot a demand curve, we need to graph Q_a, Q_b, and Q_c with their respective prices. This is shown in Figure 4.2. To determine what quantities would be demanded at prices other than $10, $5, and $2, we simply construct the budget line that corresponds to each possible P_x and determine which Q_x would be optimal at that price.[1]

In considering the particular demand curve depicted in Figure 4.2, it is important to understand that it was derived from the specific indifference map depicted in Figure 4.1. If the buyer's tastes were different, the optimal point along each of the three budget lines would in all likelihood have been different as well. For example, consider tastes and preferences, which are represented by

---

1. It is important to note that you cannot obtain a demand curve simply by drawing a line through points A, B, and C in Figure 4.2. Such a line is called a **price-consumption curve**, but it is not a demand curve. A price-consumption curve shows the different combinations of goods Y and X that the consumer in question selects at different prices of X. However, it clearly is not a demand curve, because it does not plot the optimal quantity of good X against the price of X. The price-consumption curve is fully discussed later in this chapter (see Figure 4.10 and accompanying discussion).

Figure 4.1 The Individual's Choice Pattern

As the price of good X falls, the individual chooses quantities of X that correspond to points *A*, *B*, and *C*.

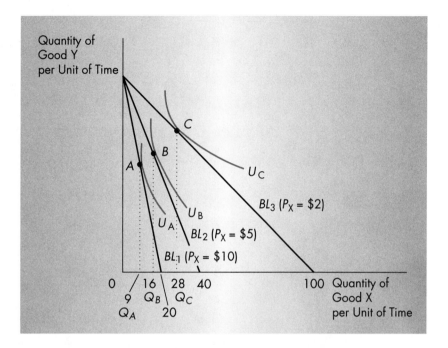

indifference curves much steeper than those depicted in Figure 4.1. Figure 4.3 shows such an indifference map, along with three budget lines identical to those discussed above. In Figure 4.3, points *A'*, *B'*, and *C'* are the optimizing points on the three budget lines. However, at each price the optimal quantities of X are greater than previously. At a price of $10, the new buyer selects 14 units of X instead of 9 units. Similarly, at a price of $5, the optimal quantity of X is now 32 units; at a price of $2, the optimal quantity is 58 units. Figure 4.4 depicts both of these demand curves; the demand curve associated with the original indifference map is labeled D_1 and the demand curve associated with the new indifference map is labeled D_2.

Both demand curves depicted in Figure 4.4 are "typical" in that they slope downward — along each of the curves, the consumer in question responds to a lower P_x by buying larger quantities of X.

It is useful to examine closely how a change in the price of X affects the incentive to buy X. When the price of X falls, say, from $10 to $5 as in the previous example, there are two distinct effects on the consumer. First is the **substitution effect**. The slope of any budget line shows how many units of

Figure 4.2 The Individual's Demand Curve
The figure illustrates a demand curve for X, which plots the price of X against the quantities demanded of X from indifference maps and budget lines (Figure 4.1).

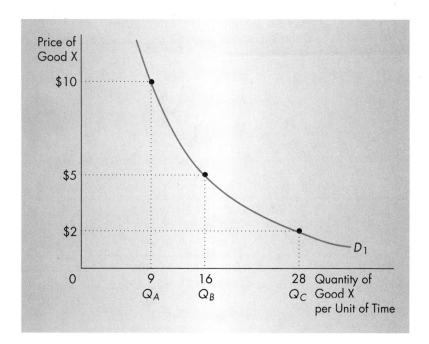

good Y the consumer must give up in order to obtain an additional unit of X. On BL_1 in Figure 4.3, the consumer must give up one unit of Y for each additional unit of X. When P_x falls to $5, the consumer only has to give up one-half a unit of Y for each unit of X. Because the reduction in the price of X (holding the price of Y constant) *reduces* the amount of Y that must be given up for additional units of X, the consumer will be induced to substitute away from Y in favor of buying more of X. If we look only at the substitution effect, a reduction in the price of a particular good will always lead to an increase in the quantity demanded. Therefore, the substitution effect is always negative — decreases in price lead to increases in the quantity demanded, whereas increases in price lead to decreases in the quantity demanded. If the substitution effect were the only influence on the consumer, demand curves would of necessity slope downward.

However, the reduction in the price of X has a second, more subtle impact on the consumer. This is called the **income effect**. If we hold the consumer's dollar income constant at, say, $200 and reduce the price of X, we have increased the consumer's real buying power — his real income. The consumer is richer when the price of X is $5 than when it is $10. Therefore, we also have

Figure 4.3 How Tastes and Preferences Alter the Individual's Choices

With tastes and preferences that differ from those shown in Figure 4.1, the individual would purchase different quantities of X than shown in the demand curve in Figure 4.2.

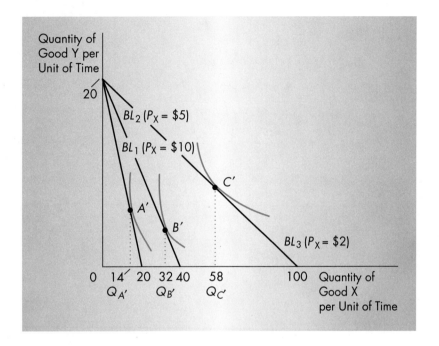

to consider how this change in **real income** will affect the consumer's choice of good X. The income effect shows the consumer's response to a change in real income. However, the income effect differs from the substitution effect in that its sign is ambiguous. An increase in income can lead a consumer to buy either larger quantities of X or smaller quantities of X, depending on the consumer's tastes and preferences for X.

To give an example, we could consider Joe College, a struggling student who constantly battles to stretch his meager income to his next payday or to the arrival of the next check from home.[2] How, then, might an increase in Joe's income affect his purchases of various goods? That impact would vary from good to good. For example, it is quite likely that an increase in his income would lead to an increase in his purchases of orange juice. If so, the

---

2. Note that *expectations* of receiving income from home might cause Joe to act *as if* his income had increased. Such behavior could be potentially embarrassing if the expectation is not realized.

Figure 4.4 Demand Curves Based on Different Tastes and Preferences

The indifference maps and their shape determine the position of the demand curves in the figure.

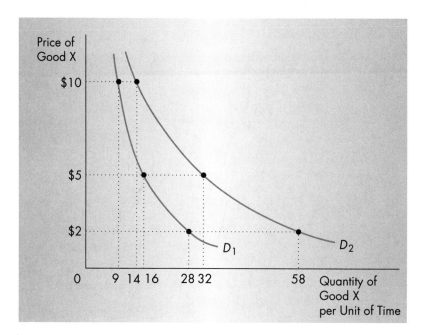

income effect for orange juice is positive — an increase in income leads to an increase in the amount of orange juice purchased. A decrease in income would lead to a decrease in orange juice purchases.

However, Joe is likely to consume other goods for which the income effect would be negative. For example, in a typical month Joe might consume four boxes of generic macaroni and cheese. The fact that he buys this product does not imply that he necessarily *likes* generic macaroni and cheese very much. It only implies that he occasionally finds it a good choice, given his impoverished circumstances. What would happen if his income rose? It is likely that he would buy less generic macaroni and cheese and instead switch to more expensive food items that he likes better.

How Income and Substitution Effects Are Separated

Now consider Joe's demand curve for generic macaroni and cheese. His demand curve shows the combined income and substitution effects of price changes. To be specific, suppose that at a price of $0.79, Joe buys 4 boxes per month. If the price fell to $0.49, the substitution effect would lead Joe to increase his consumption of macaroni and cheese; but the income effect would cause him to decrease his consumption. Whether his consumption would rise or fall depends on which of the two effects is stronger. If the substitution effect is greater than the income effect, as we expect in virtually all cases, a reduction in the price will lead to an increase in the consumption of macaroni and cheese — Joe's demand curve will slope downward.

In the case of orange juice, there is no ambiguity about Joe's response to a price reduction — Joe's demand for orange juice must slope downward. This is so because increases in real income led Joe to increase his orange-juice consumption. Therefore, a reduction in the price of orange juice generates a substitution effect and an income effect that operate in the same direction — both lead to an increase in the consumption of orange juice at a lower price. Therefore, the demand curve for orange juice must slope downward regardless of whether the income effect is greater or smaller than the substitution effect.

Up to this point, when we have used budget lines and indifference curves to show a consumer's response to a price change, we have illustrated the combined substitution and income effects. For example, in Figure 4.1, P_x is initially reduced from \$10 to \$5, which causes the relevant budget line to shift from BL_1 to BL_2. In response, the consumer moves from point A to point B by increasing his consumption of good X from 9 to 16 units. However, BL_2 differs from BL_1 in that it reflects a lower relative price of X and an increased real income. The movement from A to B therefore shows the combined income and substitution effects of this price change.

To separate the two effects, we can illustrate the **rotation in the budget line** from its initial position BL_1 to its new position BL_3 as the combination of two distinct changes — one that shows the income effect, the other the substitution effect. In Figure 4.5, assume that the consumer's income is \$200 and that P_y = \$10 and P_x = \$10. The budget line is therefore BL_1, where point A is the optimizing point. Now consider a reduction in P_x to \$5, rotating the budget line to BL_3. Compared to BL_1, BL_3 reflects a lower relative price of X and a higher real income. If we want to hold real income constant and show only the change in relative price, it is necessary to construct an additional budget line, the slope of which is the same as BL_3 but which holds the consumer's real income at its initial level. In principle, we need to reduce the consumer's **dollar (or nominal) income** sufficiently to offset the increase in real income that is caused by the reduction in the price of good X.

To determine how large a reduction in dollar income is necessary to keep real income constant, we must decide what we mean by holding real income constant. One reasonable view of real income is to treat changes in real income as equivalent to changes in utility. In this view, any **shift in the budget line** that enables a consumer to attain a higher indifference curve represents an increase in real income. In Figure 4.5, if we are to hold the consumer's real income constant while reducing the price of X to \$5, we must reduce his dollar income sufficiently to prevent him from attaining a level of utility greater than U_A. This is done by shifting BL_3 downward in a parallel fashion until it is just tangent to U_A. The budget line labeled BL_2 shows this shift.

Figure 4.5 Income and Substitution Effects of a Price Change

A price change will always have both income and substitution effects. The substitution effect is *always* in the opposite direction of the price change.

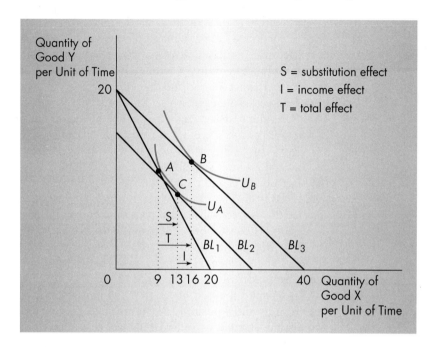

We can now view the rotation in the budget line from BL_1 to BL_3 in two component parts — the change from BL_1 to BL_2 and the change from BL_2 to BL_3. Note that BL_2 differs from BL_1 in that its slope represents a lower price of X. However, because point A (the optimal point on BL_1) and point C (the optimal point on BL_2) lie on the same indifference curve, the two budget lines reflect a fixed level of real income. Therefore, the change in the budget line from BL_1 to BL_2 and the resulting movement from A to C depict the substitution effect. If we reduce the price of X from \$10 to \$5 and hold real income constant, this consumer will increase his consumption of X to 13 units from 9 units. In a second step, we can then restore the consumer's dollar income to its initial level. This will cause the budget line to shift outward, in a parallel fashion, from BL_2 to BL_3. These two budget lines have the same slope, but BL_3 represents an increase in real income. Faced with BL_3 instead of BL_2, the consumer in question will select point B instead of point C. The movement from C to B represents the pure income effect.

In this fashion we have broken the total effect of the price reduction (the movement from A to B) into its two component parts. The first is the substitution effect, which is represented by the movement from A to C. The second, the income effect, is shown as the movement from *C* to *B*. In this particular case the income effect reinforces the substitution effect. Both induce the consumer to increase his or her consumption of X in response to the reduction in price. In this price range the demand curve for X slopes downward — the consumer prefers to buy 9 units at a price of $10 and 16 units at a price of $5, other things remaining the same.

Normal and Inferior Goods

In order for the income effect to reinforce the substitution effect, an increase in income must lead to an increase in consumption of the good in question. If a price reduction is considered, the change in price induces substitution toward the good. Because the price reduction causes real income to rise, in order for the income effect to reinforce the substitution effect the increase in income must also cause consumption to rise. A good for which an increase in income leads to an increase in consumption is called a **normal good**. Therefore, normal goods have income effects that reinforce substitution effects.

Figure 4.6 An Inferior Good
When price falls for an inferior good, the income effect is in the opposite direction from the substitution effect.

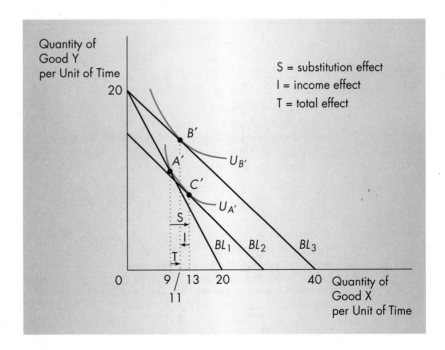

For the indifference map depicted in Figure 4.5, the income effect reinforces the substitution effect; however, this need not always be the case. In Figure 4.6 we depict the same price change for X, but in this case an increase in real income leads to a reduction in the consumption of X. The three budget lines BL_1, BL_2, and BL_3 correspond to the budget lines in Figure 4.5. The total effect of the reduction in the price of X is depicted as the movement from A' on BL_1 to B' on BL_3. The substitution effect is the movement from A' on BL_1 to C' on BL_2. This shows the effect of a reduction in P_x, holding real income constant. The income effect is shown as the movement from C' on BL_2 to B' on BL_3. Here the increase in income causes consumption of X to *fall* from 13 units to 11 units. Although the income effect in this case works in the opposite direction from the substitution effect (the substitution effect induces the consumer to substitute toward *more* X, whereas the income effect causes a shift in consumption *away* from X), the substitution effect (an increase in X of 4 units) is larger than the income effect (a decrease of 2 units). Therefore, the indifference map depicted in Figure 4.6 implies a demand curve for X which is also negatively sloped in the $5-to-$10 price range. As the price falls from $10 to $5, the quantity of X demanded increases from 9 units to 11 units.

Goods whose income effect works in the opposite direction of the substitution effect are called **inferior goods**. For such goods, increases (decreases) in income must lead to decreases (increases) in consumption. There is therefore an inverse or negative relationship between income and consumption for inferior goods. The income effect for an inferior good fails to reinforce the substitution effect of a price change — a rise in price *reduces* consumption, a fall *increases* it.

In Figure 4.6 we could have illustrated a different indifference map such that the tangency point along BL_3 occurred at some point to the left of point B'. In fact, it is even possible that the tangency point lies to the left of point A' on the original budget line. For this to occur, the income effect must operate in the opposite direction of the substitution effect and be larger in magnitude. The combined income and substitution effects in such a case would lead to lower consumption of X at the lower price — the demand for X would be positively sloped. Goods of this type are called **Giffen goods**.[3]

---

3. Although Giffen goods are a theoretical possibility, there is little convincing evidence of their existence, especially for market demand curves in developed nations. Further, it is hard to imagine goods that have such large and perverse income effects in countries such as the United States. For most goods we consume, even large changes in price lead to relatively small changes in real income. It is therefore extremely unlikely that the income effects can bring about changes in consumption that more than offset the substitution effects. For these reasons, we will ignore Giffen goods in the remainder of this text. They are a theoretical curiosity, but they have no practical relevance.

The Impact of Full Price on Consumer Choice

We must also remember that our behavior in purchasing goods and in the patterns by which we consume goods and services through time depends on the full price of any good or service in question. This means that we must add the value of our search time to the nominal or money price of the full array of goods and services available to us for our consumption. A trip to your mailbox will probably reveal an increase in the number of catalogs sent to your home or apartment. Further, a flip through the TV or cable channels in many locations will turn up more than one home shopping station. Why? Because consumers place different values on their time, depending on such factors as their level of education, employment, and salary. As a result, consumers face different relative prices and full prices as the value of their time varies. There is less time for traditional shopping at a low full cost with the increasing number of women in the work force and more individuals working 50 or 60 hours per week.

Because of increases in the full cost of purchasing goods and services, alternative means of shopping have increased, either through mail-order (or 800-number) catalog shopping or by dialing a number from your TV screen when you use a shopping channel. These substitutes to traditional shopping provide consumers who have higher time costs with an opportunity to buy goods at (often) higher *nominal* prices but at a lower full price (when the value of their time is considered); see Highlight 4.1.

Highlight 4.1 **Time, Full Price, and the Problem of Identifying Normal and Inferior Goods**

Conceptually, the important economic characteristics of "normality" and "inferiority" are easy to identify. If consumption rises when income rises, the good or service is normal. If consumption falls when income rises, the good or service is inferior. As noted in the text, moreover, the character of goods may change at different income levels for the same person. An increase in a college student's income by 10 percent may increase her consumption of hamburger or chicken. Later, when she is earning an executive's salary, a 10 percent increase in income may lead to increased consumption of filet mignon and duck and *reduced* consumption of hamburger and chicken.

Sometimes, however, the accurate identification of normal and inferior goods is complex. Consider a simple example. Joan, an executive in Chicago, plans a holiday trip home to San Francisco. Jason, a clerk also living in Chicago but a native San Franciscan, also plans a holiday homecoming. Two means of transportation are available to Joan and Jason — bus and air. The one-way busfare is $120 and the one-way airfare is $550. Joan (who earns about $40 per hour) flies, and Jason (who earns $12 per hour) takes the bus. Can we conclude on the basis of such evidence that bus rides are an inferior

Table 4.1 Full Price of Bus and Air Tickets to Joan and Jason
In order to accurately determine the relevant relative prices of a trip, the opportunity cost of time must be added to the nominal ticket price.

	Joan		Jason	
	Bus	*Air*	*Bus*	*Air*
Ticket	$120	$550	$120	$550
Time and Other Costs	1200	160	360	48
TOTAL	$1320	$710	$480	$598

good and that plane rides are a normal good? The answer is no. To answer this question for Joan and Jason, we would have to change their respective incomes and then see how their choices between the two alternatives were affected.

This example indicates that different choices may appear to be the consequence of differences in income when in fact they are at least partly caused by differences in full prices. To see why, assume that the bus trip takes 30 hours and the air trip only 4 hours. Further, assume that the wage rates earned by Joan and Jason accurately reflect the opportunity cost of their time. Table 4.1 shows the full price of the trip by air and by bus to each of them.

Any possible inferences concerning the "normality" or "inferiority" of the two goods would be spurious. Because we always behave on the basis of the relative full price to us, Joan would substitute the relatively cheaper air trip for the relatively more expensive (higher full-priced) bus trip. Jason, on the other hand, would substitute bus trips for air trips on the same basis. They could be making these selections on the basis of *relative full prices,* not income.

On the basis of the evidence given, it is possible that air trips may be either normal or inferior to *either* Joan or Jason. Normality or inferiority is a characteristic of the indifference curves facing Joan or Jason, *not* of the goods themselves. That characteristic may be revealed only by studying consumption patterns as income changes.

Price Elasticity of Demand

In addition to illustrating income and substitution effects, budget lines and indifference curves can also be used to illustrate the important concept of **price elasticity**. The discussion in the previous section suggests that, neglecting

Giffen goods, individual demand curves slope downward. When we incorporate both the income and substitution effects, a reduction in the price of any good will lead to an increase in the quantity demanded. However, in many cases it is insufficient just to "know" that lower prices lead to demand for larger quantities. It is also important to be be able to determine the *extent* to which a change in the price of a particular good or service will affect the quantity demanded of that good or service. (This is sometimes called own-price elasticity in contrast to cross-price elasticity calculated on the basis of a change in the price of some *other* good.) In measuring the responsiveness of a consumer or of a group of consumers to a change in price, economists rely on the concept of price elasticity of demand. The price elasticity e_D is defined as

$$e_D = -\frac{\% \text{ change in quantity demanded}}{\% \text{ change in price}} \qquad (4.1)$$

Note the negative sign; the reason for it is that, holding incomes, the prices of other goods, and tastes and preferences constant, we are reasonably certain that an increase in price of a good will lead to a decrease in the quantity demanded. Similarly, we know that a decrease in price will lead to an increase in the quantity demanded. Therefore, the numerator and the denominator in our expression for price elasticity will always have opposite signs. Without a negative sign in front, our measures of price elasticity would always be negative numbers. Because we are more accustomed to dealing with positive numbers, it is simply more convenient to define price elasticity in such a way that we always end up with a positive number. Insertion of the negative sign simply converts a negative number to a positive number of equal magnitude.

Also note that *percentages* are always used to make the elasticity calculation. By reducing both the numerator and the denominator of the elasticity expression to percentages, the value of e_D is *independent* of the units of measurement used in the calculation. For example, in talking about the amount of gasoline demanded at various prices, we can measure gasoline in terms of quarts, liters, or gallons and the resulting elasticity calculations will be the same. Thus if a 10 percent change in price leads to a greater-than-10 percent change in quantity demanded, demand is said to be price *elastic,* regardless of the units in which gasoline is measured. If the same percentage change in price causes a less-than-10 percent change in quantity demanded, demand is said to be price **inelastic**. An equal change — a 10 percent change in price matched by a 10 percent change in quantity demanded — means that demand is of *unit* elasticity.

In calculating the percentage changes in both price and quantity that appear in equation 4.1, we must take care to do so in a consistent fashion. For example, if the price of some good were to fall from \$100 to \$60, we might be tempted to describe this as a 40 percent reduction in price, because the fall in price (\$40) is 40 percent of the initial \$100 price. If the price were then to rise back to $100, we might be inclined to describe this as a 66.66 percent rise in price — the $40 increase is two-thirds of $60. However, it seems strange to say that the price falls by 40 percent and then rises by 66.66 percent and ends up right where it started.

The problem with this method of calculating percentage changes is that it selects the denominator in an inconsistent fashion — in the first calculation we selected the higher of the two prices; in the second calculation we selected the lower of the two. For consistency, it is more logical to use the average of the two prices in the denominator. Instead of using $100 in one case and $60 in the other, use the average, $80, in both cases.

With this procedure, a price reduction from $100 to $60 would be calculated as a 50 percent reduction in price, because

$$\% \text{ change in price} = \frac{\text{change in price}}{\text{average price}}$$

$$= \frac{-\$40}{((\$100 + \$60)/2)}$$

$$= \frac{-\$40}{\$80}$$

$$= -0.50 = -50\%$$

In calculating the percentage change in quantity, the same procedure is to be used. Therefore

$$e_D = -\frac{\% \text{ change in quantity demanded}}{\% \text{ change in price}}$$

$$= -\frac{\dfrac{\text{change in quantity demanded}}{\text{average quantity}}}{\dfrac{\text{change in price}}{\text{average price}}} \tag{4.2}$$

To see how this applies in some particular case, consider Joe College's demand for tennis balls. Suppose that if the price of tennis balls is $3 per can, Joe would buy 20 cans per year; if the price rose to $5 per can, he would reduce his quantity demanded to 10 cans per year. To calculate the price elasticity of Joe's demand for tennis balls in the $3-to-$5 price range, we need only substitute these numbers into equation (4.2):

$$e_D = -\frac{(10 - 20/((10 + 20)/2)}{(\$5 - \$3)/(\$5 + \$3)/2)} = -\frac{-10/15}{\$2/\$4}$$

$$= -\frac{-0.6666}{0.50} = 1.333$$

How should we interpret this measure of elasticity of 1.333? In this particular case, the price increased by 50 percent, and this led to a 66.66 percent reduction in the quantity demanded. Therefore, the percentage change in quantity demanded was 1.333 times as large as the percentage change in price. This implies that in this price range, each 1-percentage-point increase in price led to a 1.333-percentage-point decrease in quantity demanded.

Here the price elasticity *exceeds* 1.0. However, in many cases the price elasticity will be *less* than 1.0. For example, Figure 4.5 illustrated an indifference map showing an individual who responded to a reduction in the price of X from $10 to $5 by increasing his quantity demanded from 9 units to 16 units. If we use the foregoing procedure to calculate the percentage changes in price and quantity, we find that the price fell by 66.66 percent, and the quantity demanded increased by 56 percent. The price elasticity of demand in that price range is 0.84. The percentage change in quantity was only 84 percent of the percentage change in price.

As we go from cases in which consumers are very unresponsive to changes in price, to cases in which they are extremely responsive, we will find that price elasticity ranges from zero to infinity. In cases in which the price elasticity of demand is less than 1.0, we say that demand is **inelastic** with respect to price. This does not mean that buyers are completely insensitive to changes in price; it only means that to achieve a given percentage change in quantity demanded, the price has to change by a larger percentage.

When the price elasticity of demand is greater than 1.0, demand is **elastic** with respect to price, meaning that a given percentage change in price will bring about an even larger percentage change in the quantity demanded. Should the price elasticity equal 1.0, demand is said to be **unit elastic** — each percentage point change in price leads to an equal percentage change in the quantity demanded, but in the opposite direction. A 10 percent increase in price would lead to a 10 percent decrease in the quantity demanded; a 6 percent decrease in price would lead to a 6 percent increase in the quantity demanded.

We can easily determine whether demand is elastic or inelastic in any particular price range by observing the slope of the price-consumption line described earlier. In Figure 4.7 there are three budget lines indicating prices of X of $10, $5, and $2, respectively. The optimal points on the three budget lines are points A, B, and C, respectively. The line connecting the three optimal points is called the **price-consumption line**. We can see that from point A to point B, the price-consumption line slopes downward; from point B to point C it slopes upward. A price-consumption curve shows the combination of goods (in this case X and "all other goods") that the consumer selects at different prices of X. (The price-consumption curve is not to be confused with a demand curve, which plots quantity demanded of one good, X, against the prices of X.) But what information does this provide us about the price elasticity of demand? Well, if we stop to think about it, points A and B each show the

Figure 4.7 The Price-Consumption Curve

A price-consumption curve shows the relationship between the price of a good and the consumer's purchases of it. Both income and substitution effects are included in the consumption of points *A*, *B*, and *C* shown in the figure.

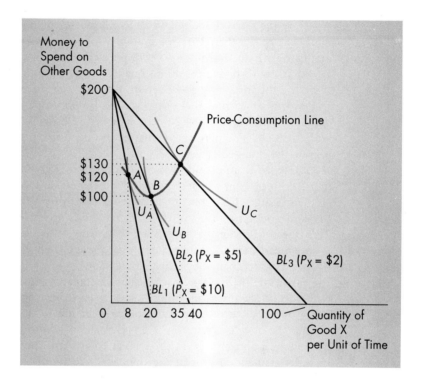

number of dollars spent on goods other than X and the number of units of X that are bought. As the price of X falls from $10 to $5, we see that the number of dollars spent on goods other than X falls — point *B* lies below point *A*. If the consumer in question has a fixed income of $200 and spends fewer dollars on other goods, then he must be spending more dollars on good X at the lower price. In order for dollar spending to increase when the price decreases, the quantity purchased must increase by enough to more than offset the price reduction. In other words, if the price falls by some percentage, then the quantity must rise by a larger percentage in order for dollar spending to rise. If the percentage change in quantity is greater than the percentage change in price, demand is elastic. Therefore the negatively sloped price-consumption line between points *A* and *B* means that in the price range of $10 to $5, demand for X is elastic with respect to price.

To confirm this, we can calculate the price elasticity in that price range. As the price falls from $10 to $5, the quantity demanded rises from 8 units of X to 20 units, which is an 85.7 percent increase in the quantity demanded. The price reduction from $10 to $5 is a 66.66 percent reduction, so the percentage change in quantity demanded is greater than the percentage change in price. The demand is elastic in this price range. With elastic demand, the decrease in price has caused dollar spending on good X to rise from $80 (8 × $10) when the price was $10 to $100 (20 × $5) when the price is $5. With elastic demand, if the price moves in one direction, dollar spending moves in the other direction.

In Figure 4.7 the price consumption curve is positively sloped between points *B* and *C*. Therefore, as the price of X falls from $5 to $2, the number of dollars spent on goods other than X increases (from $100 to $130), which means that the number of dollars spent on good X decreases from $100 to $70. For this to have happened, this price reduction must have caused the quantity demanded to increase by a smaller percentage than the percentage decrease in price. We can confirm this by computing the percentage changes. The increase in the quantity demanded from 20 units to 35 units represents an increase of about 54.5 percent. The price reduction from $5 to $2 is a 120 percent reduction in price. Clearly, the percentage change in quantity is less than the percentage change in price, so the demand is inelastic in this price range. In the case of inelastic demand, we see that dollar spending moves in the same direction as the price — if the price falls, dollar spending decreases, and if the price rises, dollar spending also increases.

Using Demand Curves to Determine Elasticity

One way to determine price elasticity between two prices is to examine the slope of the price-consumption line. However, there are also geometric techniques by which the price elasticity can be determined directly from the demand curve. Up to this point, in measuring price elasticity we have considered fairly large price changes and then calculated the elasticity between two distinct points on the demand curve. For that reason, our previous method of measuring elasticity has measured the **arc elasticity** — the elasticity over some range on the demand curve. It is also possible to calculate **point elasticity** — the elasticity at some specific point on the demand curve. Previously, in equation 4.2, we expressed price elasticity as

$$e_D = -\frac{\dfrac{\text{change in quantity demanded}}{\text{average quantity}}}{\dfrac{\text{change in price}}{\text{average price}}}$$

where the average price and quantity took into account two distinct points on a demand curve. Because we were calculating an arc elasticity, we had to use the average of the beginning and ending prices and quantities. In calculating a point elasticity, we consider only a single point on the demand curve. We can therefore think of that point as the beginning and ending point, so the average price is just the price at that point, and the average quantity is simply the quantity at that point. Equation 4.2 can be modified as

$$e_D = - \frac{\dfrac{\text{change in quantity demanded}}{\text{quantity}}}{\dfrac{\text{change in price}}{\text{price}}} \qquad (4.3)$$

We can rearrange these terms so that

$$e_D = - \frac{\text{change in quantity demanded}}{\text{quantity}} \times \frac{\text{price}}{\text{change in price}}$$
$$= - \frac{\text{change in quantity demanded}}{\text{change in price}} \times \frac{\text{price}}{\text{quantity}} \qquad (4.4)$$

To give meaning to equation (4.4), consider the linear demand curve depicted in Figure 4.8. We can select any point on that demand curve and

Figure 4.8 Demand and Elasticity

Along the linear demand curve in the figure, slope is constant, but elasticity varies.

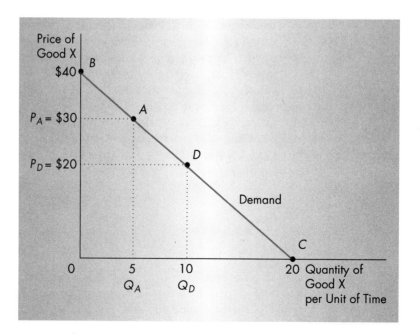

determine the elasticity at that point in terms of the foregoing expression. For example, consider point A, where the price is P_A and the quantity demanded is Q_A. In equation (4.4), the second term on the right side is simply the price divided by the quantity or P_A/Q_A. The first term on the right, change in quantity/change in price is simply the inverse of the slope of the demand curve. Because the demand curve depicted in Figure 4.8 is linear, the slope is the same at every point. The slope of the demand curve can be expressed a number of ways, but one is the distance BP_A divided by the distance $P_A A$. The inverse of the slope is $P_A A/BP_A$, and the elasticity is $-(P_A A/BP_A)(OP_A/OQ_A)$. Because $P_A A = OQ_A$, $e_D = OP_A/BP_A$. By similar triangles we can demonstrate that $AC/AB = OP_A/BP_A$. Therefore, the price elasticity at point A equals AC/AB. To generalize, *for a linear demand curve, the price elasticity at any point is equal to the portion of the demand curve below that point divided by the portion above that point.* In Figure 4.8, the distance AC is clearly greater than the distance AB, so demand is elastic at point A. To be specific, the elasticity at that point is 3.0, because three-quarters of the demand curve lies below point A and one-quarter lies above that point. If we were to move down to point D, the elasticity would be DC/DB, or 1.0. A linear demand curve is therefore unitarily elastic at its midpoint. If we select any point on the demand curve below point D, the segment below that point will be less than the segment above, so demand will be inelastic.

We can therefore make the following generalization; for any linear demand curve, demand is elastic at prices above the midpoint, inelastic at any price below the midpoint, and unit elastic at the midpoint. The top half of a linear demand curve is elastic; the bottom half is inelastic.

It may seem counterintuitive that the elasticity changes along a linear demand curve. However, if we focus on equation 4.4, we see that the first expression on the right-hand side is constant along the linear demand curve. However, the second expression falls continuously as we move down along a demand curve to lower prices and higher quantities demanded.

It is important to note that the conclusions above hold only for straight-line demand curves. For nonlinear demand curves, it is not possible to make generalizations concerning changes in the elasticity as we move along a demand curve. Nonetheless, there is a handy graphical method for determining the elasticity at any point along a nonlinear demand curve. Figure 4.9 shows a nonlinear demand curve. If we want to know the elasticity at any point on that demand curve such as point A, we draw a straight line tangent to the demand curve at that point. The elasticity at point A is the portion of that tangent line that lies below the point divided by the portion that lies above that point. The elasticity at point A is AB/AC. Similarly, the elasticity at point D is DF/DE. However, we cannot make any generalization comparing the elasticity at points A and D. For nonlinear demand curves, price elasticity may increase, decrease, or stay the same as we move to points further down the demand curve.

Figure 4.9 A Nonlinear Demand Curve

The slope of a nonlinear demand curve is found by taking its tangent at any point along it. Elasticity is the portion of the tangent line that lies below the point divided by the portion that lies above the point.

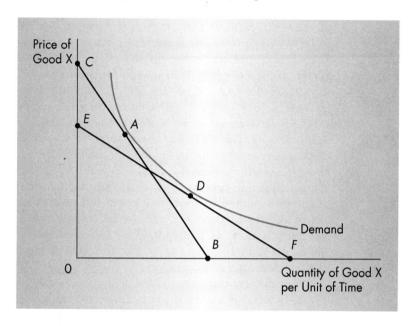

Elasticity and Total Expenditure

From the law of demand we know that, other things remaining unchanged, lower prices will lead to larger quantities demanded and higher prices to lower quantities demanded. However, decision makers may be more interested in the effect of a price change on dollar revenues than on the number of units sold. For example, if the college or university that you attend is typical, your tuition has been increased in the last year or so. A rudimentary knowledge of economics would enable those in charge of setting tuition rates to know that an increase in tuition will lead to a reduction in the number of students who choose to enroll. However, faced with a financial crunch, those decision makers may be more concerned about the number of dollars they receive from tuition than about the level of student enrollment. Although it is clear that a higher tuition will lead to a lower enrollment, it is not clear what its effect will be on the total dollar expenditure by those students who enroll. With a smaller number of students each paying a higher tuition, total expenditure may increase, decrease, or stay the same, depending on the size of the tuition increase and the size of the resulting decrease in enrollment. If a certain percentage increase in tuition leads to a smaller percentage reduction in enroll-ment, the total expenditure will increase. However, if the resulting reduction in enrollment is larger in percentage terms than the tuition increase, then total expenditure will fall.

If we know the price elasticity of demand for the good or service in ques-tion, then we can tell what effect a given price change will have on total expenditure. Suppose that the change in tuition we are contemplating is a 10 percent increase. If demand is elastic with respect to price, the 10 percent tuition increase will cause enrollment to fall by more than 10 percent, so total expenditures on tuition by students (or total tuition receipts by the university) will decline. On the other hand, if demand is inelastic, the 10 percent tuition increase will lead to a drop in enrollment of less than 10 percent and the receipts of the university will increase. In the case of unitary elastic demand, the drop in enrollment will just offset the increase in tuition, and the univer-sity's receipts will remain unchanged.

This relationship between price elasticity and total expenditure can be seen in Figure 4.10. The left panel, Figure 4.10a, shows a linear demand curve, for which the top half is elastic and the bottom half is inelastic. At a price of $10,

Figure 4.10 Elasticity and Total Expenditure
As total expenditure rises with price declines, the demand curve is elastic. It is unitary when total expenditure is at a maximum, and inelastic when total expenditures fall as price falls.

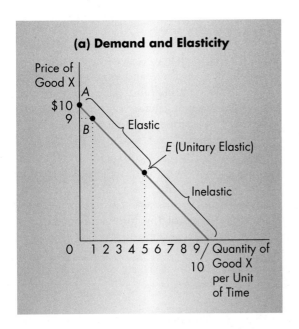

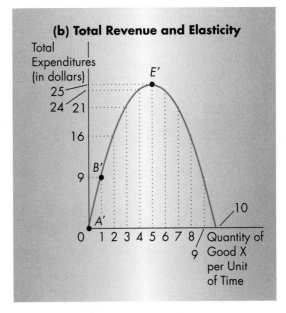

the quantity demanded is zero, so total expenditure at this price is also zero. Point A' in Figure 4.10b corresponds to point A in Figure 4.10a. If we then consider a lower price, $9, the quantity demanded rises to 1 unit, generating $9 in total expenditure. Because demand is elastic in this price range, the percentage increase in quantity demanded is larger than the percentage decrease in price. This explains the increase in total expenditures from $0 to $9.

Successive reductions in price from $9 down to $5 continue to lead to increases in total expenditures. Each $1 price reduction leads to a 1-unit increase in quantity demanded. However, at higher prices, the 1-unit increase in quantity demanded represents a larger percentage increase than the $1 reduction in price. Figure 4.10b shows that total expenditure rises as the quantity sold increases in the elastic range of the demand curve. However, as the price is reduced below $5, we move into the inelastic portion of the demand curve, and total expenditure falls as larger quantities are sold. Six units can be sold at a price of $4, yielding $24 in total expenditures; 7 units can be sold at a price of $3 each to yield $21 in total revenue. Figure 4.10b shows this clearly — lower prices lead to reductions in total expenditures when demand is inelastic. These hypothetical relationships are shown in an actual elasticity calculation in Highlight 4.2.

Highlight 4.2   *Pay a Trifle for a Truffle: Calculating Elasticity in Dollars ($) and French Francs (FFr)*

When scarcity is mentioned, we tend to think of such natural resources as diamonds, platinum, and gold. But some things that we eat — especially items concerned with gourmet dining — are just as scarce and expensive. Russian caviar (Beluga) and saffron (a spice grown in India and elsewhere) are two cases in point. In some dishes, such as French bouillabaisse (a fish-and-shellfish soup) and Spanish paella (rice, chicken, and seafood), there are no good substitutes for saffron, for example. Another item of great scarcity is the Périgord truffle — a type of mushroom found only in the Périgord region of France. Long prized by gourmets for firmness and strong fragrance, truffles are still harvested (actually sniffed out) by pigs and dogs in chalky earth around oak, hazel, and juniper trees. Some are grown on "truffle farms" where young oak, beech, or hazel trees are infected with spores of the fungus. The result is extremely unpredictable, however, and success is never assured.[a]

Now comes a "crisis" (of plenty) in the truffle market. Unusually favorable weather in 1992 resulted in a surge in the harvest of *Tuber melanosporum,* the

[a] Data and other material for this discussion are taken from "A Trifle for a Truffle," *The Economist,* January 23, 1993, p. 67.

Périgord truffle. The harvest was 16,000 kg, up from the 8,000 kg collected the previous year. Moreover, the price of the delicacy fell from the 1991 price of FFr 3,500 per kilogram to FFr 2,000. Assuming that the demand for Périgord truffles remained constant between 1991 and 1992 and all of the harvest is consumed (demanded) in both years, we may put the elasticity analysis of this chapter to work with some actual calculations.

If we use the rules of thumb regarding the price elasticity of demand to determine whether the demand for Périgord truffles is elastic or inelastic, what initial conclusions can we reach? Clearly, the demand for these particular mushrooms should be relatively elastic, because there are many other varieties of mushrooms available from around the world. That, moreover, is exactly what we find: The 8,000 kg increase in quantity represents a 66.66 percent change in quantity demanded. Further, the FFr 1,500 decrease in the French-franc price represents a 55.55 percent change. Because elasticity is measured as the ratio of the percentage changes in quantity to price, the elasticity coefficient is 1.2, indicating that demand is elastic.

Suppose, now, that we calculate the elasticity coefficient in terms of U.S. dollars (assuming a rate of FFr 5.45 to $1) and in pounds (1 kg = 2.2045 lb). Is elasticity independent of the units of measurement? Converting the data, we find that

1991 production of truffles = 176,368 lbs.

1992 production of truffles = 352,736 lbs.

1991 price = $642.20/kg = $291.30/lb.

1992 price = $366.97/kg = $166.46/lb.

Clearly, the elasticity coefficient is independent of the units of measurement, because 1992 production of truffles is 66.66 percent greater than that in 1991, and the 1992 price in dollars shows a 55.55 percent decrease from 1991.

A check of the expected relationship among price changes, elasticity, and total revenue to ascertain whether the demand is elastic, inelastic, or of unit elasticity gives the same result. Total truffle sales for 1991 equaled FFr 28 million and for 1992, FFr 32 million. The lower price was more than offset by the increase in quantity, indicating that demand for truffles is elastic (see Figure 4.10 and discussion in this chapter for the graphics of this relationship).

In any real-world elasticity calculation, a number of factors must be assumed constant, as emphasized in the text. In calculating truffle price elasticity, for example, it is necessary to assume that truffle demand is constant, because elasticity is measured along or at a point on a demand curve. If demand for truffles had changed — perhaps because of an increase in income of truffle buyers or a change in the price of a substitute mushroom — part of the price change would have been attributable to the change in demand.

The foregoing discussion may seem to suggest that the best price to select is the price at which the demand elasticity is unitary, because that is the price that maximizes total revenue. However, for reasons discussed in considerably more detail in later chapters, this is not generally a correct conclusion if the seller has some control over price. In the usual case, it is better for the seller to select some price in the elastic portion of the demand curve. To see why, first consider some price below the point of unitary elasticity. For example, in the situation depicted in Figure 4.10, consider a price of $4. Lowering the price below $5 would cause total revenue to the seller to fall. In addition, the cost to the seller of producing 6 units will exceed the costs of producing only 5. Therefore, the decision to move down into the inelastic portion of the demand curve is the decision to simultaneously reduce total revenue and increase total cost. Such a decision can only lead to reduced profits.

What would be the consequences of raising the price above $5 and moving into the elastic portion of the demand curve? One consequence is that total revenues would fall. However, there is an advantage to selling less output — production costs can also be reduced. Therefore, if higher prices and lower levels of output cause costs to fall by more than revenues fall, the seller can increase its profits by raising the price and moving to a point in the elastic portion of the demand curve.

Determinants of Demand Elasticity

There are three fundamental determinants of price elasticity of the demand curve: the price and availability of substitute products or services, the relative importance of the item in the budget of the consumer, and the time period over which the price change is in effect.

Elasticity and Product Substitution. Far and away the most important determinant of price elasticity is the ability of consumers to substitute another product for the one they are buying. This proposition is intuitively obvious — we make substitutions every day. As the price of one type of pizza rises in a college town (or university area), customers flock to other types. While food is a commodity that is (ultimately) necessary for life, pizza does not have to be a part of it. If the price of all types of pizzas rises precipitously because of the shortage of some ingredient, we would simply switch to other types of food. All producers of goods and services want to secure our allegiance to some particular item through advertising and the "branding" of products, but when substitutes are available, these sellers are limited in the price they can extract from consumers. Other things being equal, the larger the number of these substitutes and the lower their prices, the higher the price elasticity of demand for the good in question.

Note that demand elasticity will vary, depending on the "inclusiveness" of the class of good we are considering. Consider beef and beef products. The demand for beef will always be *less* elastic than the demand for hamburger meat or T-bone steaks, because different beef products will substitute for one another (to some degree) in consumption. If the price of hamburger or T-bone rises, meat consumers will switch to other beef products. Therefore, the price elasticity for any one of the components of "beef" will be greater than the price elasticity for beef itself. Carry this idea further. The demand for *meat* will be less elastic than the demand for beef. This is true because beef is only one component of the demand for meat. As the price of beef falls, consumers will switch to substitutes like pork, lamb, or poultry. And the analogy goes even further. If the price of meat rises, we will clearly substitute other products yielding "nutrients necessary for life" into our consumption. Vegetables, legumes, dairy products, and other items can be substituted for meat. The general rule: *the broader the product or service group, the lower the price elasticity of demand for the item in question because of less substitutability between broad product groups.*

In order to understand this concept, consider a real-world example. We tend to think of certain brands as possessing enormous consumer allegiance. Coca-Cola (and more recently Pepsi) are international icons as brand names. Does this mean that they have total control of the soft-drink market between them? Not at all. In the broader category "drinks," both Coke and Pepsi must compete with other soft drinks, beer, wine, juice drinks, milk, bottled water, and a host of other products. The ability to price six-packs of Coke or Pepsi depends on the relative substitutability. More critically, these soft-drink giants must contend with other brands (RC cola, Seven-Up, and so on) and with private-label colas. Until recently, the quality (and therefore the substitutability) of these private brands was viewed as poor, giving Coke and Pepsi more power to charge premium prices. In recent years, however, the emergence of the private brands of Wegmans Food Markets (W POP), Wal-Mart (Sam's American Choice), and the soft-drink product developments of A&P and Kmart have the giants worried. By 1991, according to *Beverage Digest,* the private-label share of supermarket soft-drink sales was a full 8 percent of the market, up from 7.2 percent in 1990.[4] Although the upsurge may, in part, be explained by the recession of 1991–1992, the products' tastes have improved. Moreover, they are pushed by increasingly powerful retailers. In terms of elasticity, this means that the demand for both Coca-Cola and Pepsi products has become (and is becoming) more price elastic.

Although the soft-drink market involves two "giants" competing against a larger number of smaller competitors, the case reveals another aspect of elasticity and its relationship to markets. In general, the larger and better the number of substitutes in any given market, the more competitive it is. For further illustrations of substitutability and elasticity see Highlight 4.3.

4. Data reported in Michael J. McCarthy, "Soft Drink Giants Sit Up and Take Notice as Sales of Store Brands Show More Fizz," *Wall Street Journal,* March 6, 1992, p. B1.

Highlight 4.3   *Elasticity, Brand Allegiance, and Substitutes: Nicotine Patches and Health Foods*

Elasticity, as you have undoubtedly (if unconsciously) realized, is a two-way street. To say that you would "rather fight than switch," as a famous cigarette commercial had it, suggests a lot about consumers' attitudes; but it conveys information to sellers as well. Any seller would like his or her consumers to prefer to fight than to switch brands. Thus the demand curve is not only a revelation of the consumer's wants and desires, it is a principal subject of sellers' attention, because the demand curve determines total sales and (through sales and costs) profits to a firm.

Sellers are not solely interested in increasing the demand for their products; they also want to reduce its price elasticity. Successful producers and sellers accomplish this feat in many ways. Advertising to get brand-name identity and allegiance is one way. Selling the product in more convenient packaging or locations is another. Many producers and sellers offer alternative qualities and amounts of information about products and services. Inventing, offering, and selling entirely new products is yet another means of influencing demanders.

Any product group contains a range of substitutes, so sellers continuously attempt to increase the demand for their products. There is much uncertainty about what will "sell" in real-world markets, and the static theory of elasticity described in this chapter is only a still picture of what is a dynamic process. Consider the following real-world examples of how sellers attempt to shape demand and demand elasticity for the products they sell.

Smoking cessation has become important in U.S. society in view of the much-publicized health problems associated with the activity in recent years. Not only is smoking itself alleged to be an "addictive" behavior; the attempt to kick the habit appears to be a "habit" as well. Smokers who want to quit but have been unsuccessful will keep trying. They have used hypnotism, acupuncture, aversion therapy (akin to mild shock treatment), group therapy, and nicotine gum. Many of these "therapies" are available only under a doctor's care or with a medical prescription.

Recently, a new product entered the market that will soon be a $1 billion-a-year business. The development of the nicotine patch and its quick success demonstrate that smokers will try almost anything (and pay up to $120 per month) to give up smoking. Individuals have adopted the product (which must be prescribed by a physician) with little information as to short- and long-term effects. The important point in the present discussion concerns elasticity, product development, and entry. Consider Figure 4.11, which gives a static picture of the market in early 1993. The three demand curves represent, from left to right, the individual demand for a particular patch product (Nicoderm, Prostep, or Habitrol), the demand for all nicotine patches, and the

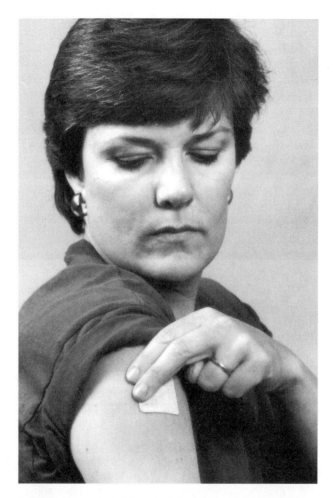

The transdermal nicotine patch is only one of a variety of smoking-cessation products. The more substitutes there are for any particular product, the higher the elasticity of demand.

total demand for all smoking-cessation products. At some hypothetical price P_0, elasticities will decrease as the product identified becomes *more* inclusive. Thus the demand for any one of the products (Nicoderm, for example) will be more elastic than the demand for patches in general, but the demand for patches in general will be of greater elasticity than the demand for all smoking-cessation products. Substitution explains this relationship. The shifting profitability of each of these products is explained by "marketing wars" to make the demand for each brand of smoking-cessation product less elastic. This

Figure 4.11 The More Inclusive the Product Group, the Lower the Elasticity
Demand elasticity at some particular price is higher for Habitrol than for all nicotine patches and higher for the latter than for all smoking-cessation products.

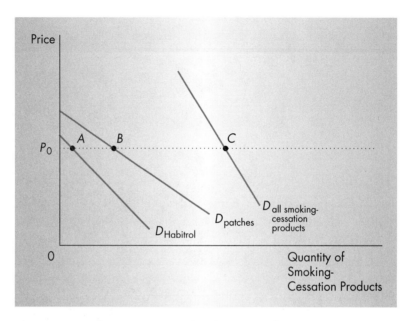

advertising-marketing war cost the three manufacturers of patches (considered alone) $100 million in 1992.[a] Initially, patch manufacturers ran into shortages because they miscalculated product demand. But attempts to speed up and enlarge production may also be risky. Health problems associated with patches are a potential negative side effect, as are the relatively low success rates for those who attempt to quit by using this method. Shifting demands and elasticities are expected over the longer run.

Virtually all markets function dynamically as sellers attempt to alter demand and to change its elasticity. The seemingly never-ending competition in the "healthy" frozen foods, low-calories, and "fat-free" markets are further examples. Healthy Choice products are popping up everywhere. Campbell's sells "healthier" soups. Competitors in the frozen-food market include Weight Watchers, Lean Cuisine, Budget Gourmet Light, Ultra Slim Fast, and Right Course. Even bread and fig newtons come in low-fat or nonfat varieties. Athletes are used in increasing numbers to tout these and other products.[b] No

[a] Kathleen Deveny, "Heated, if Smokeless, Competition Rages Among Makers of Nicotine Skin Patches," *Wall Street Journal,* March 4, 1992, p. B1.

[b] Robert Slager, "Commercial Success: Advertisers Vie to Find Athletes With the Right Stuff," *San Francisco Examiner,* July 26, 1992, pp. E1, E4.

product is immune from the emergence of new competing products and strategies. The relationships among elasticity, consumer demand, and substitution is an ongoing and familiar process in the real world of markets.

Importance in Budget and the Time Factor. A second, but less important, determinant of the price elasticity of demand for a particular product or service elasticity is the "importance of being unimportant." Other things being equal, the smaller the proportion of your budget that some good or service takes, the lower the price elasticity of demand. Two goods from the food group, salt and sugar, immediately come to mind. Both of these items are relatively inelastic in most consumers' budgets because they tend to be a small proportion of expenditures. This does not mean, of course, that the availability and price of substitutes play no role. If the price of salt and sugar rose dramatically, consumers would in fact switch to substitutes. All manner of substitutes — citrus juice and citrus products, artificial salt, sugar substitutes of all kinds — are available (mainly for "health" reasons). These substitutes limit the ability of salt and sugar sellers to set prices. There are, of course, many producers and sellers of both salt and sugar, which means that the markets tend to be competitive in any case.

We must remember that "size in budget" is only one factor in determining elasticity. Both size in budget and substitutability must be gauged. Consider the water we purchase for household use. Water bills, usually from municipal sellers, are ordinarily a small portion of our total monthly expenditures. Other things being equal, we would expect low elasticity for water. A national drought (similar to the one in California in the late 1980s and early 1990s) might change the portion of water in the average budget if the price of water rises sharply. Does this mean that water demands will become more elastic? The answer for most consumers is no! Substitutes are important in assessing elasticity, and (for most individuals) there are few good substitutes for municipal water available. We *could* dig a well outside our apartment building or home, but at great cost. We *could* carry water home from a river or the grocery store for bathing, drinking, and so on, but this would also be costly (do not forget that the possibility of sickness from "bad water" or the time and transportation costs must be added to the nominal price to get the full price of the water). The demand elasticity would be low for these reasons even if water becomes a large portion of the consumer's budget.

A final determinant of elasticity is the time period over which a price change is in effect. This factor suggests that the longer a price change is in effect, the more elastic the demand for a good or service. Actually, the time effect is related to our ability to substitute goods and services and our information about them.

Suppose that we use a commuter railway or subway to get to school or work every day and that the rate doubles or triples unexpectedly. How do we react? At first we knuckle under and pay the increased fare, perhaps because we are unaware of substitutes. We will not, however, be the only ones affected. Others will also want to substitute alternative forms of transport to work or school. Car pools, buses, bicycles, or other forms of transportation will become viable over time, and the demand elasticity for travel on the commuter railway or subway will become more elastic.[5] (Note that the same argument holds for both price increases and price declines.)

Information accessibility and technology are also a factor in assessing elasticity. As "big city" newspapers become instantly available on computer, advertisements for all goods and services will also become available. This means that, when shopping for photographic or stereo equipment, for instance, we will easily be able to compare prices in distant cities like Chicago and Houston. If we wish to purchase a particular camera or part, we can buy at the lowest price (adjusted for shipping, of course). The ready availability of price information will tend to reduce the time costs of exchange and increase elasticity.

Other Elasticities

Any elasticity measure quantifies the response of one variable to a change in a second variable, holding other variables constant. Therefore, the number of different elasticities that could be defined and, perhaps, computed is endless. However, in the field of consumer behavior there are two elasticities in addition to price elasticity in which economists have particular interests. The two are the **income elasticity**, which measures the effect of changes in income on demand, and the **cross-price elasticity**, which measures the impact of changes in the price of one good on the demand for a second good.

In our previous discussion of the income effect, we indirectly addressed the issue of income elasticity. In depicting the pure income effect for a particular good, we changed the consumer's nominal income while holding his preferences, the price of that good, and the prices of other goods constant. In doing so, we saw that for normal goods, increases in income led to increases in consumption. For inferior goods, there is an inverse relationship between income and consumption.

Figure 4.12 shows three budget lines reflecting a fixed price of good X and increasing levels of nominal income. Given the preferences reflected by the

---

5. Note that (over the long run) technology also alleviates such problems. Widespread use of modern computers and information transfer and retrieval have created many work-at-home jobs in cities (such as New York and Los Angeles) where urban transport is a high-cost activity. Some employees only actually "come in" to work in the city two days a week, work at home the rest of the time, and communicate their work via computer or fax machine. Technology, in this sense, has increased the elasticity of demand for subway or commuter railway travel.

Figure 4.12 The Income-Consumption Line

The income-consumption line (traced out as points *A*, *B*, and *C*) shows how consumption of *X* and all other goods changes as income rises or falls.

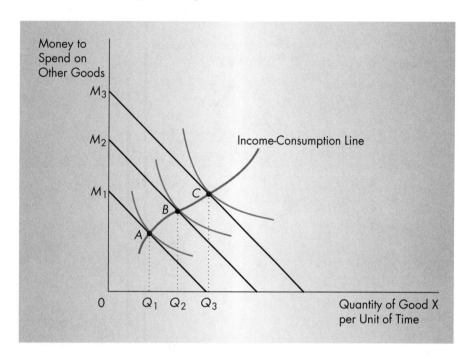

indifference map drawn there, the consumer in question increases his consumption of X from Q_1 to Q_2 to Q_3 units as his income is increased from M_1 to M_2 to M_3 dollars. The income elasticity (e_M) is defined as

$$e_M = \frac{\text{\% change in quantity demanded}}{\text{\% change in income}}$$

$$= \frac{(Q_2 - Q_1)/((Q_1 + Q_2)/2)}{(M_2 - M_1)/((M_1 + M_2)/2)}$$

(4.5)

If we calculate the income elasticity between points *A* and *B* or *B* and *C*, we will find that the income elasticity is positive — both consumption of X and income increase between those two pairs of points. Therefore, we see that a normal good is a good whose income elasticity is positive. Note also that if we draw an **income-consumption line** in Figure 4.12, a line connecting each of the optimal points on the budget lines, it is positively sloped. If we construct an income-consumption line for an inferior good, it will have a negative slope.

Figure 4.13 The Income-Consumption Line for an Inferior Good
The income-consumption line for an inferior good (X in the figure) is negatively sloped.

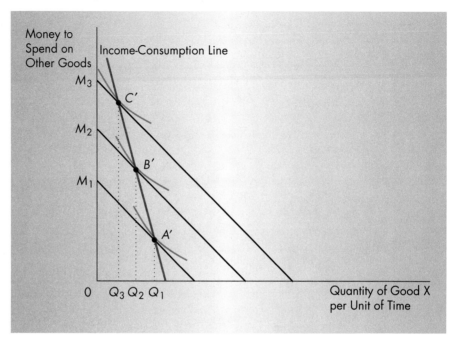

This is shown in Figure 4.13. In the figure, increases in income lead to decreases in the optimal quantity of X. If we use equation (4.5) to compute the income elasticity between points A' and B', for example, we will find that the income elasticity is negative. Therefore, we define an inferior good as a good for which the income elasticity is negative.

Although it is common practice to refer to goods as being normal or inferior, in fact these adjectives really pertain to the indifference map of the consumer in question. A good may be a normal good for one consumer and an inferior good for another consumer. Further, a given consumer may find that a specific good is a normal good in some income ranges but that it is an inferior good in other income ranges. Figure 4.14 depicts such a good. As the buyer's income rises from M_1 to M_2, his consumption of X rises from Q_1 to Q_2 units. In this income range X is a normal good to the consumer in question. However, as income rises from M_2 to M_3, X becomes an inferior good, because the level of consumption is lower at the higher income level.

There can be many examples of goods like the one depicted in Figure 4.14. For example, we could return to the case of Joe College and examine the impact of changes in his income on his consumption of ground beef. When he

Figure 4.14 Normality or Inferiority Shown in the Indifference Map

A good may be normal over some income levels and inferior over others for the same consumer.

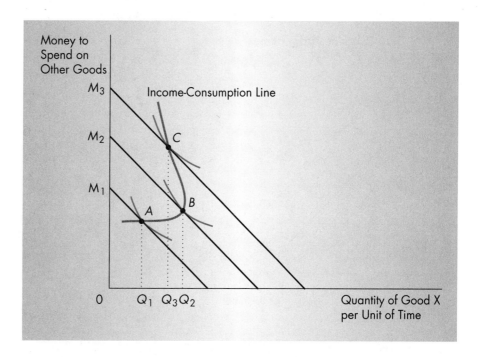

is poor (his income equals M_1), he buys relatively little ground beef. However, as his income rises to M_2, he buys less of goods like generic macaroni and cheese and more ground beef. However, at even higher income levels like M_3, he will reduce his consumption of ground beef and buy more of other things like steak or lobster.

There is one final point that needs to be made about income elasticity: the income elasticity shows the direction and extent by which a demand curve shifts in response to a change in income. The left panel of Figure 4.15 shows three budget lines corresponding to different income levels with the price of X fixed at $10. Points A, B, and C in the left panel, Figure 4.15a, show that the consumer in question will choose to increase the number of units of X he purchases from 8 to 15 to 20 units at income levels of M_1, M_2, and M_3, respectively, assuming a price of $10. Each point represents a single point on different demand curves which correspond to the three income levels. The three demand curves are depicted in Figure 4.15b. The increases in income from M_1 to M_2 to M_3 cause the demand to shift from D_1 to D_2 to D_3, respectively. Had the good in question been an inferior good, the demand curves corresponding to higher incomes would have been to the left of D_1.

Figure 4.15 Income Changes and Demand Curves

As income increases from M_1 to M_2 to M_3, the demand curve shifts rightward for *normal* goods. For inferior goods, the shift is in the opposite direction.

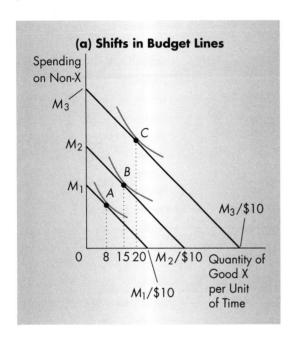

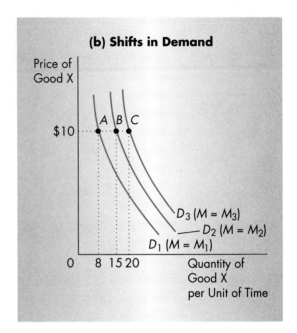

The final elasticity of interest for economic analysis is called **cross-elasticity**. Cross-elasticity measures the effect of a change in the price of one good Y on the demand for another good X. Specifically, e_{XY}, the cross-elasticity of demand, is defined as

$$e_{XY} = \frac{\text{\% change in the quantity demanded of X}}{\text{\% change in price of Y}} \tag{4.6}$$

Measures of cross-elasticity provide information about the relationship between two goods. Positive cross-elasticities imply that the two goods are substitutes. If this is the case, an increase in the price of one good Y leads buyers to substitute away from Y in favor of X. Examples of goods that are substitutes are two different brands of the same good, such as Coke and Pepsi. An increase in the price of Coke (good Y) will lead buyers to increase their consumption of Pepsi (good X).

Goods that have negative cross-elasticities are called complements. Complements are goods that are used together. For example, a rise in the price of personal computers will likely lead to a reduction in purchases of software packages used on PCs. When we first introduced the concept of a demand curve, we argued that one factor that could cause the demand for a good to shift was a change in the price of a "related" good. By a related good, we meant a good that serves either as a substitute for or as a complement to the good in question. Now we see that if the price of a substitute good rises, demand for the good in question will rise; if the price of a substitute good falls, demand for the good in question will fall. If the price of a complementary good rises, demand for the good in question falls; and if the price of a complementary good falls, the demand for the good in question rises.

Consumer Surplus

At the beginning of this chapter we used budget lines and indifference curves to derive a demand curve. One of the things that we observed was that as P_X fell and the budget line rotated outward, the consumer was able to attain higher indifference curves. This implies that the lower the price of "X," the better off are buyers of "X." These gains are called **consumer surplus**. There are two approaches to measuring consumer surplus; one is in reference to demand curves, and the other uses budget lines and indifference curves.

To see how to use demand curves to measure consumer surplus, let's consider Joe College's roommate, Pete. Pete is a video junky who likes all movies. Currently he is able to rent videos at a price of $2 each, and in a typical week he rents 10. At that price, he spends $20 per week on videos. This is money that he could spend on other things, but he chooses not to. The fact that he gives up the opportunity to enjoy $20 worth of other goods in order to rent videos means that he values the 10 videos at more than $20. His consumer surplus from videos is the difference between what he has to pay for the videos, $20, and the maximum amount he would have been willing to pay. Consumer surplus derives from the marginal utility that Pete receives from videos — a concept discussed in Chapter 3.

To determine the maximum amount he would have been willing to pay, it is useful to think of his demand curve. We can start by imagining a price so high that even Pete would be unwilling to rent videos. We could then imagine successively lower prices until we get down to a price of $2, at which Pete elects to rent 10. Suppose that even Pete is unwilling to rent any videos at a price above $11. However, assume that at that price he would be willing to rent one per week. Further, assume that each time the price falls by $1, Pete is willing to increase the number of videos he rents by one. In other words, the value he places on one video per week is $11, the additional value he places on a second video is $10, the additional value of a third is $9, and so on. Under these circumstances, Pete's demand for videos is depicted in Figure 4.16.

The total value that Pete receives is equal to the sum of the marginal values for each video rented. The 10 videos therefore have a total value of $11 + $10 + $9 + $8 + $7 + $6 + $5 + $4 + $3 + $2 = $65. The total cost is $20,

Figure 4.16 Pete's Demand for Videos: Consumer Surplus
When price falls for videos by $1, Pete increases the number he rents by one a week. Pete receives a surplus when he pays less than he would be willing to pay for the videos.

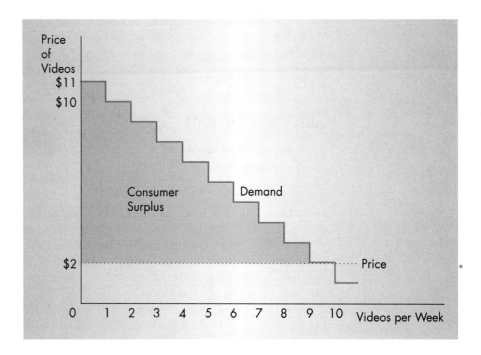

so the consumer surplus is $45. In terms of Figure 4.16, we can depict the consumer surplus as the shaded area that lies below the demand curve but above the price line. That area can be viewed as consisting of 9 rectangles whose areas are $9, $8, $7, and so on and whose sum is $45. Figure 4.17 shows that we can approximate a stepped demand curve like the one depicted in Figure 4.16 as a straight line. Note that the area below the linear demand curve but above the price line is identical to the area below the stepped demand curve but above the price line. Therefore, the area of triangle *ABC* in Figure 4.17 is the consumer surplus when the price is $2. If the price rose to $4, Pete would reduce his consumption to 8 units, and his consumer surplus would be the area below the demand curve but above a horizontal line at $4. Consumer surplus at this price would be $28.

In addition to using areas under demand curves to measure consumer surplus, we can also use budget lines and indifference curves. For the purpose of comparison, let's again consider the case of Pete who, with a given income, rents 10 videos per week when the price is $2. Figure 4.18 depicts his budget line with *C* as the optimizing point. In that figure, U_A is an indifference curve that passes through the vertical intercept of Pete's budget line. It therefore

Figure 4.17 A Linear Demand Curve and Consumer Surplus
A linear demand curve approximates the "stair-step" demand of Figure 4.16. Consumer surplus is therefore the area *ABC*.

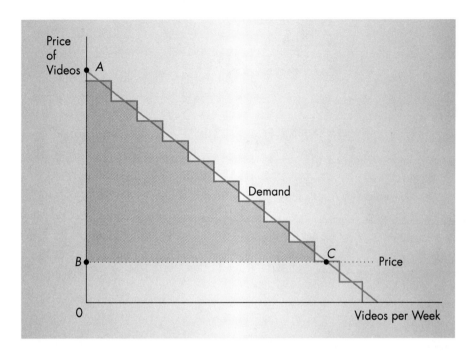

shows the various combinations of videos and dollars-to-spend-on-other-goods that enable Pete to be just as well off as he would be if he didn't rent videos but instead used all M_1 dollars to buy other goods. However, by renting 10 videos and selecting point *C*, Pete moves to a higher indifference curve — the one labeled U_C.

To compute Pete's consumer surplus, we need to determine how many dollars Pete would be willing to pay to move from U_A to U_C. The answer is the number of dollars represented by the distance from *B* to *C* in Figure 4.18. To see why, consider the movement from point *A* to point *C*; the distance from M_1 to M_2, shows the number of dollars ($20) that Pete has to give up to rent 10 videos. However, the distance from M_1 to M_3 shows the number of dollars that Pete would have been willing to pay to rent the 10 videos. Therefore, the difference between M_2 and M_3 (which is equal to the distance from *C* to *B*) shows how much Pete gains by renting 10 videos at the $2 price as opposed to paying the highest price he would have been willing to pay. It therefore provides an ideal measure of consumer surplus.

Can we be certain that our two measures of consumer surplus provide the same answer? Is the shaded area in Figure 4.17 exactly the same as the distance

Figure 4.18 Consumer Surplus and Indifference Curves

The distance $M_2 - M_3$ or CB in the figure is the amount of consumer surplus
Pete gets from renting 10 videos.

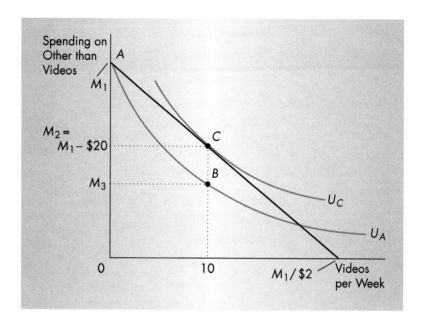

from C to B in Figure 4.18? The answer is "Not necessarily." The reason the
two measures may differ is that the demand-curve approach includes income
effects of price changes, whereas the indifference-curve approach excludes any
income effects. Only if the income effect of the price change is zero will the
two measures of consumer surplus coincide. However, for small price changes,
the difference between the two approaches is quite small. Therefore, the area
under the demand curve but above the price line provides a reasonably close
approximation of the true gains to the consumer.

The concept of consumer surplus has enjoyed widespread acceptance by
economists in policy applications (although the normative nature of the measure has been criticized). International trade is a prime, though controversial,
example. In trade deals, such as the North American Free Trade Agreement
(NAFTA) between the United States and Mexico passed in 1993, there will be
winners and losers. The gains to American and Mexican consumers and to
groups of laborers in both countries must be balanced by the losses to laborers
displaced in both countries by shifting trade patterns. The economist uses the
measure of consumer surplus to evaluate the gains and losses (see Chapter 16).
She is interested in whether the gains are sufficient to justify costs — that is,
whether there is a *net* welfare gain from enactment of the NAFTA policy.

Many other kinds of policy assessments are made possible with the consumer-surplus measure.

Gains from Exchange

Compared to other groups, those who are trained in economics tend to be more inclined to defend the rights of individuals to trade with each other on an unrestricted basis. One reason for this is that economists generally view trade as mutually advantageous, whereas others are more inclined to view trade as coercive. Indifference maps provide an ideal way to present the economic argument in favor of free exchange. We can imagine two individuals, each with an initial endowment of two goods, perhaps football tickets and money. We can then examine the consequence of allowing them to trade with each other.

Fred's initial endowment is shown as E_F in Figure 4.19a. Jack's initial endowment is shown as E_J in Figure 4.19b. The endowments we have chosen are purely arbitrary, and our argument is in no way based on the endowments selected. Given the initial endowments, we can draw an indifference curve for each of the individuals through their respective endowment points. When we do so, there are two distinct possibilities: either the two indifference curves have the same slope at points E_F and E_J or they don't.

Figure 4.19 The Gains to Trade
Trade between two individuals will be mutually beneficial when evaluations of goods differ between individuals.

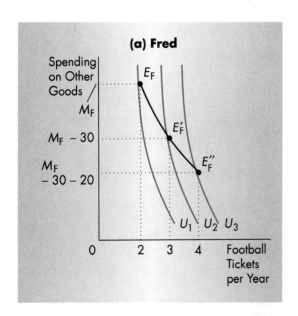

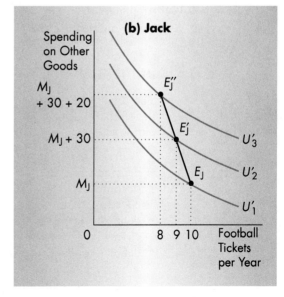

Let's suppose that the slopes differ at the endowment points. In particular, suppose that Fred's indifference curve has a slope of −50 and Jack's is −10. Fred would be willing to pay up to $50 for an additional ticket. Jack would be willing to sell one of his tickets at any price above $10. If we allow the two to bargain with each other, it is quite likely that they will reach some agreement whereby Fred will buy a ticket from Jack at some price between $10 and $50. Suppose that they agree on a price of $30. Fred will give up $30 for Jack's ticket, moving in a southeasterly direction to a new point E_F', which lies beyond the indifference curve that passes through his endowment point. This exchange will enable Fred to move to E_J', which also lies beyond his initial indifference curve. The exchange is mutually beneficial in that it enables each of the two parties to gain.

Because Fred now has more tickets and fewer dollars to spend on other goods, his indifference curve at E_F' is likely to be flatter than at his initial endowment point. With fewer tickets and more dollars to spend on other goods, Jack's indifference curve at E_J' is likely to be steeper than at his endowment point. If the slopes continue to differ, the two have an incentive to make an additional exchange, until they get to points like E_F'' and E_J'', where the slopes of their respective indifference curves are equal. Had the slopes of the respective indifference curves been the same at the initial endowment points, then Fred and Jack would have had no reason to trade initially.

Ticket sales of this type by Jack to Fred are often called "scalping." This practice, often condemned, is illegal in many areas. However, it is a practice which is mutually advantageous. Even though the price at which the tickets are "scalped" may exceed the face value, the exchange is mutually beneficial. Attempts to prevent voluntary exchanges prevent individuals from moving to higher indifference curves.

Summary

The theory of consumer behavior is the centerpiece of demand theory and, therefore, of all of microeconomic theory. In this chapter we have completed our development of the theory of consumer behavior. We have

- analyzed how budget lines and indifference curves can be used to derive demand curves.
- decomposed price changes to consumers into income and substitution effects.
- defined price elasticity of demand and discussed the determinants of price elasticity.
- defined goods and services as normal or inferior in relation to the way consumption changes as income changes.
- provided theoretical measures of various elasticities as well as consumer surplus, and measures to illustrate the gains from voluntary exchange.

Key Terms

indifference map	budget line
price-consumption curve	substitution effect
income effect	real income
rotation in the budget line	dollar (nominal) income
shift in the budget line	normal good
inferior good	Giffen good
price elasticity	inelastic demand
elastic demand	unitary elasticity
arc elasticity	point elasticity
income elasticity	cross-elasticity
income-consumption line	consumer surplus

Sample Questions

Question

Patterns of cigarette consumption in the United States are consistent with the following generalization: at low income levels, cigarettes are a normal good, but as income rises, cigarettes become an inferior good. If this generalization is true and if the same pattern holds in other countries, which countries do you think might prove to be major importers of American cigarettes in the future?

Answer

American tobacco companies should expect sales to grow fastest in countries in which incomes are relatively low (by American standards). For example, some countries in South America and Central America and many of the countries which were a part of the former Soviet Union should provide growing markets for U.S. firms. In contrast, many of the Western European countries (France, Italy, Germany, and so on) may prove to be markets in which sales actually decline in the future.

Question

Many individuals have health insurance with a copayment provision: the insurer pays a percentage of medical expenses and the insured person pays the rest. For example, Joe's insurance might pay 50 percent of the cost of Joe's prescription drugs, and Joe pays the remaining 50 percent. Does this type of insurance affect the price elasticity of Joe's demand for prescription drugs?

Answer

Co-insurance greatly reduces Joe's price elasticity. Specifically, it displaces his demand upward by doubling the price Joe is willing to pay for each unit of prescription drugs. For example, if we assume that, in the absence of insurance, Joe's demand is linear, with a vertical intercept of $50 and a horizontal intercept of 50 units, then with the insurance, his demand will be linear but with a vertical intercept of $100 and a horizontal intercept of 50 units. At every price above zero, his demand with the insurance is less elastic than his demand without the insurance.

Questions for Review and Discussion

1. What are the four most important variables that affect the derivation of a consumer's demand curve?

*2. What is a price-consumption curve and how is it constructed?

*3. Explain how a demand curve can be derived from an indifference map and budget line.

4. Why is the substitution effect always negative and what is its effect on the slope of the demand curve?

*5. If the price of steak decreases and the income effect is smaller than the substitution effect, what happens to the consumption of steak?

6. Which of the following goods are normal goods? Which are inferior goods?
   a. steak
   b. Yugos
   c. Porsches
   d. compact discs
   e. apartment rentals
   How do you know? (*Hint:* Read Highlight 4.1.)

7. Suppose that the price of sweaters increases from $25 to $40 and the quantity demanded falls from 3 to 1 sweater per year. What is the price elasticity of demand for sweaters using arc elasticity?

*8. Bryan's Discount Tapes lowered the price on its portable CD player from $65 per player to $55 per player. The following month, sales of the player increased from 320 units to 500 units. What was the price elasticity of demand?

9. When busfare in Dallas increased from $0.40 to $0.60, the number of riders decreased from 800 per week to 620 per week. What was price elasticity over the price range?

*10. What does a downward-sloping portion of the price-consumption curve indicate about price elasticity of demand?

11. Assuming a linear demand curve exists, how can the point price elasticity be determined graphically?

*12. Explain the relation between elasticity and total expenditure.

13. What are the relationships among a normal good, income elasticity, and the slope of the income-consumption curve?

*14. Show graphically a good X that becomes an inferior good and then a normal good as income increases.

15. Illustrate and explain in a general graphical model of demand how to determine consumer surplus.

*16. Why might measurements of consumer surplus vary, depending on whether the demand-curve or indifference-curve approach is used?

*17. How are the relative slopes of indifference curves of trading partners used to determine when trade will be beneficial?

18. How does the degree of substitutability affect the price elasticity of demand for a particular good?

19. What is the effect of technological advancement and increases in the availability of information on elasticity?

20. What does a positive cross-elasticity imply about the two goods in question?

Problems for Analysis

1. Dieters are becoming very disillusioned with "liquid meals," according to a report in the *Wall Street Journal* (November 13, 1992). A comparison between equal periods in 1991 and 1992 revealed that sales of products such as Ultra Slim-Fast, DynaTrim, and Carnation Slender were sharply declining. Sales of *all* liquid-diet products were down by $73.3 million in 1992, a reduction of 44 percent from the year before. Average price in supermarkets declined to $2.48 from $2.89 in 1991.
   a. Can you calculate demand elasticity from this data? If so, what is the value? If not, why not?
   b. Present a graphical analysis of the possibilities.

*2. The Good Friends Pet Store sells both parakeets and canaries. During April the price of each parakeet was $15. In May the price increased to $20. The store sold 23 canaries in April and 35 canaries in May. Calculate the cross-elasticity of demand. Are parakeets and canaries substitutes? What assumptions about demand curves for parakeets and canaries are you making?

3. Assume a set of parallel linear demand curves. Assume that a straight line from the origin of 45 degrees intersects them. Is price elasticity equal to, greater than, or less than 1 at the points of intersection? Explain.

4. "All Giffen goods are inferior goods, but not all inferior goods are inferior." Analyze this statement, using graphical analysis.

5. In general, there are definite relationships between the prices charged for new goods and the demands and demand elasticity of used goods of the same type. Take luxury car imports as an example. As the prices of new Mercedes, Lexus, and Porsches rise in the United States (possibly because of increases in the yen or German mark value of the dollar or a rise in import taxes), the demand for *used* models of the cars will be affected. This will be true of used cars in the same model years and in used cars of previous years.

    a. Using tools developed in this chapter, explain how the demand for used cars will be affected.

    b. Comment on the probable effects on the elasticity of demand for used cars *of the same make and model* of the same year and for similar used cars of earlier years.

6. If your weekly income changes from $200 to $300 per week and your quantity demanded for steak increases from 5 to 10 pounds, which is your income elasticity of demand for steak? Is steak a normal good in this example?

7. "Normality and/or inferiority for a good tells us the same thing as income elasticity for the good." Discuss.

8. "If the price elasticity of demand for Gillette Super Blue blades is –1.6, the slope of the demand curve for razor blades must be more than –1.6." Is the statement true? If so, why? If not, why not?

9. For Al, one good is inferior. If that is so, all other goods considered as a group must be normal to him. Explain.

10. We are all familiar with food-delivery services, especially when we are students. Most food-delivery business is concentrated in pizzas and (in urban areas, particularly) in Chinese and other Asian cuisines. Are there any economic reasons why we do not (ordinarily) observe delivery of fried chicken or hamburgers? How do we explain the difference?

11. Alice buys "housing" and "all other goods." A doubling of all prices she faces and of her income has no effect on the amounts of anything she consumes. True or false? Why?

*12. "The price of higher education has risen relative to other goods in the 1990s, but the quantity of higher education has also risen." Does this statement contradict the law of demand?

5

Consumer Behavior: Issues and Applications

Microeconomic theory illuminates practical real-world problems and at the same time is enriched by application to those problems. We now turn to a number of interesting examples that deal with consumers in actual markets. We confront markets not only as buyers of goods and services but as employers, workers, voters, taxpayers, or college roommates. In all cases we examine how individuals react, under constraints, to changes in relative prices (including wages, interest rates, and "implicit" prices, as in trading housekeeping chores).

Tools relating to consumer behavior — including demand and supply, elasticity and consumer surplus, indifference curves and budget lines — have all been highlighted in previous chapters. These tools of the trade will carry the reader to an understanding of a variety of problems and cases. In order to achieve this goal, we will devote this chapter to problems that concern consumer behavior and to the impact of markets on individuals. The chapter shows how to apply techniques of analysis to such problems as

- how the minimum wage and rent control distort markets and often have unintended consequences on quality for workers and renters.
- the impact of student loans on student behavior.
- how subsidies in kind differ from subsidies in money and how this difference relates to welfare recipients, conservation, and water-rationing schemes.
- how nonprice rationing schemes affect markets.
- schemes to improve public education, including voucher schemes.
- the impact of absolute prohibition on consumers and markets.

Price Regulations and Product Quality

In many markets, prices are established through the regulatory actions of the government. In some cases the regulations establish a price ceiling — a maximum price that suppliers are permitted to charge. In other cases they set price floors or minimum prices. Simple demand-and-supply analysis shows that effective price floors and ceilings create surpluses and shortages, respectively. However, when the regulated prices remain in effect for sufficiently long periods of time, they tend to lead to predictable changes in the quality of the good or service being sold. Rather than having prices adjust to equilibrate the market, quality adjustment plays this role.

Minimum-Wage Regulation: Price Floors

One example of an effective price floor is the minimum wage. Let's assume we are dealing with a local labor market for unskilled labor. The supply curve in that market consists of untrained or inexperienced workers with few labor skills. The demanders are individuals, government agencies, or business firms seeking workers to perform tasks for which little or no training is required. Figure 5.1 depicts such a market. In the absence of a minimum wage, the equilibrium wage rate in that locality would be $4.00 per hour. If the government enacted minimum-wage legislation requiring the payment of a higher hourly wage (such as $5.00 per hour), the immediate effect of the legislation would be to create a surplus. The number of workers employed would fall from Q_E to Q_D, while the number of potential workers seeking employment would rise to Q_S. An excess supply of *FA* would exist, as shown in Figure 5.1. However, it would be naive to believe that this market disequilibrium would persist indefinitely. Faced with a surplus of workers, employers would be able to pick and choose among job seekers. In fact, they would have an incentive to raise their employment standards and to require more of their workers. For example, after the minimum wage is imposed, they might begin to require a high-school diploma or previous work experience as a condition of employment, or they might institute an aptitude test. In general, they would come to expect and require a higher quality of worker.

As the quality of workers increased, both the demand and the supply would shift. Higher-quality workers would be worth more to employers, so the demand would increase. The higher standards would eliminate some potential workers from the market, causing the supply curve to shift to the left. The skills required for employment would rise until the new equilibrium wage equaled the minimum wage. Any wage can be the equilibrium wage if the required skills adjust sufficiently. If the minimum wage had been set at, say, $15 per hour, then a standard employment practice might be to require a college degree, even for the least demanding jobs.

Figure 5.1 Quality and Price Floors

Initially, the labor market is in equilibrium at a wage of $4.00 per hour and with Q_E workers *of a given quality* being employed. When the minimum wage is raised to $5.00 per hour, this initially leads to a labor surplus of $Q_S - Q_D$. Employers respond by requiring better skills as a condition of employment. As the quality improves, the demand increases to reflect the higher productivity. At the same time, the higher job qualification limit the supply. The market will ultimately clear at a price of $5.00 per hour, but the workers who obtain jobs must have more skills than previously. The number of workers employed (given the new quality standard) will likely fall, but the amount will be determined by the magnitude of the shifts in supply and demand.

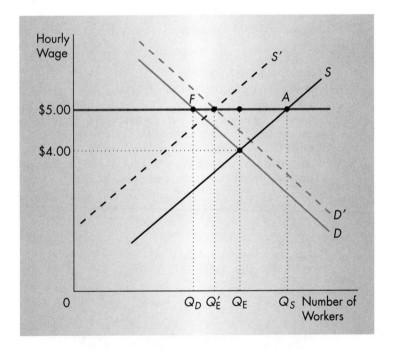

Note that the final equilibrium obtained in Figure 5.1 will be determined by the magnitude of the shifts in demand and supply. If higher standards eliminate workers from the market in large quantities (a shift to S' in Figure 5.1), the total number of workers could decline to Q_E'. Quality changes will ensure that a new equilibrium will be created, however.

Rent Controls: Price Ceilings

Price ceilings have just the opposite effect on quality. Several major cities in the United States and Canada (Los Angeles, New York, Washington, D.C.,

Vancouver, and Toronto, to name a few) currently have a program of rent control. The essence of rent-control programs is to hold the rental price of housing below the equilibrium level. Imagine how a rent-control program would work in your college town. Consider a typical two-bedroom apartment and suppose that the demand and supply for that type of apartment unit is depicted in Figure 5.2. The equilibrium rent is $650 per month in the figure. Suppose that the local city council then passes a law prohibiting rents in excess of $500 per month. At that price, the quantity demanded exceeds the quantity supplied by Q_D minus Q_S. It is important to note that prior to rent controls, landlords found it imperative to maintain the quality of their units at prevailing levels. At the market-clearing price of $650, there were just enough tenants to go around, so a landlord who allowed his units to become run-down by local standards would find it impossible to keep his units fully occupied unless the rent was reduced below $650. However, after rent controls are imposed, it

Figure 5.2 Quality and Price Ceilings

With the initial demand and supply curves D and S, the rent ceiling causes a shortage of $Q_D - Q_S$. Owners of rental units then have an incentive to allow the quality to decline. If this happens, the demand drops to reflect the lower value of the units to renters, and the supply increases to reflect the reduced costs to suppliers. Given enough time, the quality of the existing stock of housing will decline sufficiently to create a new equilibrium at the ceiling price of $500.

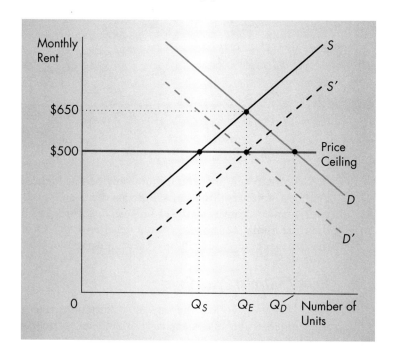

ceases to be necessary to maintain quality in order to prevent vacancies. At a price of $500, there are many prospective tenants seeking apartments. Therefore, landlords who allow their units to deteriorate can still obtain tenants. Over a longer time period, moreover, landlords have an *incentive* to allow deterioration — the costs of normal maintenance are high, and yet the unit can be rented at the same price ($500) whether or not it is well maintained. Therefore, we would expect a general decline in the level of maintenance under rent control. The "typical" apartment would no longer be as well maintained as previously. As a consequence of this decline in quality, demand will fall (the run-down apartments are worth less to tenants) and the supply will rise because it costs less to supply poorly maintained units. These shifts in supply and demand will ultimately bring the equilibrium price into line with the ceiling price of $500.

The extent to which this deterioration will occur depends on how low the ceiling price is set. The lower the ceiling price, the lower the equilibrium quality of rental housing.

In the case of rental housing, one additional type of quality adjustment is likely to take place. When rent controls are initially imposed, landlords find themselves able to exploit the shortage by picking and choosing among prospective tenants. Therefore, to the extent that the law allows, we would expect certain types of tenants to be excluded — tenants who have pets, tenants who have children, and tenants who are young and unmarried. No landlord wants to rent to four young beer-drinking undergraduates if other tenants are available. Under free-market conditions, many landlords accept such tenants because the alternative is vacant apartments. However, such tenants are likely to fare poorly under a program of rent control.

Direct Quality Restrictions

Product quality refers to any characteristic of a good or service that matters to consumers or producers. Quality can refer to purity, reliability, durability, ease of operation, built-in safety features, point-of-sale service, repair service, fit, or convenience. In the broadest terms, quality includes everything except the price and the quantity. Economics views quality like everything else: quality is scarce and consumers must choose how much quality they will purchase. Often these decisions are restricted by government regulations.

The quality of the products we purchase is subjected to a dizzying array of regulations. Every nation's public payroll includes officials whose job it is to monitor the content of the goods and services consumed by its citizens. In the United States this type of official can be found in the Consumer Product Safety Commission, the Environmental Protection Agency, the National Transportation Safety Board, the Food and Drug Administration, and other federal and state government agencies. Although quality controls may be instituted out of the best of intentions their impact may not always benefit the consumer; for an example, see Highlight 5.1.

Highlight 5.1   *Safety, Efficacy, and the Regulation of Medicines*

Health-care sectors are some of the most heavily regulated markets in many nations. Physicians and other health-care professionals are tested and licensed to ensure their competency. Hospitals, medical labs, and other health-care facilities are certified as well. Such regulation is intended to protect consumers from low-quality health care. The process by which public agencies approve new medical treatments is one of the most visible programs for enhancing product quality. In the United States the Food and Drug Administration (the FDA) is the agency responsible for approving drug treatments.

All drug-treatment regimens must go through an approval process before their use among the general population is allowed. The approval process has the twin goals of establishing the effectiveness of the proposed treatment and the safety of the treatment. The FDA is empowered to keep ineffective drugs off the market. The intent is to conserve health-care resources by eliminating treatments that have no medical benefits. The FDA is also charged with keeping dangerous drugs off the market in order to protect consumers. The safety and efficacy of drugs are established through medical experiments. A scientifically valid experiment is designed to determine whether the drug is (1) effective, and (2) safe for human use.

The very nature of medical experiments is extremely time consuming. It often takes time for experimenters to determine the appropriate dose of the test drug. Both the benefits of a treatment and the side effects of a drug may take even longer to manifest themselves. Therefore, the experiment must run long enough to allow detection of potentially harmful side effects. Once the experiment is complete and all the data have been collected, it takes the medical researcher some time to analyze the data. After all this has been done, the FDA will make a determination on the merits of the drug and either approve or disapprove the drug for widespread use. Although this process is extremely time consuming in and of itself, matters are made worse by a limited FDA staff. The FDA does not have enough employees to ensure prompt processing of all the applications it receives. Consequently, it can be many years between the discovery of a promising new treatment and FDA approval of the drug.

Health-care consumers enjoy the benefits of higher-quality medications. They can be reasonably confident that the drugs prescribed for them are effective and safe. As the text has discussed, the higher quality does entail a higher price. The FDA approval process increases the marginal costs of producing medicines, and this decreases the supplies of the products. The lengthy approval process entails another important cost: the testing process delays the introduction of medications that might benefit the very sufferers that the drug is designed to cure. A thorough economic analysis of the FDA's approval process must consider this implicit cost.

The AIDS epidemic has focused attention on the implicit costs of delay in the health-care market. AIDS patients do not have the time it normally takes for the FDA to approve new drugs. Activists have been pressuring the FDA to change its procedures to expedite wider access to promising new drugs. The changes do not shorten the approval process; new treatments must go through the same testing program. The changes liberalize access to the drugs on an experimental basis, and the FDA reserves the power to withdraw the drug if evidence of serious side effects or ineffectiveness arises.

These changes will alter the markets for AIDS treatments, but some other changes will have a broader impact. The FDA has recently entered into an agreement with drug companies to expedite the approval process by attacking an obvious deficiency at the FDA: the size of its staff. The drug companies will provide the resources for an expansion of the FDA staff. Under the new program, drug companies will pay the FDA $330 million in fees (over a five-year period).[a] The FDA will be able to hire 600 new employees to speed up its approval process and to reduce the backlog of drugs awaiting FDA approval. This program increases the marginal cost of producing drugs by having the drug companies pay for the approval process directly.

[a] "New Drug Plan Sparks Hope for Biotech," *The Wall Street Journal*, October 19, 1992, p. C1.

The market effects of quality controls can be illustrated by lawn-mower safety regulations. Lawn-mower use and misuse results in an estimated 50,000 trips to hospital emergency rooms annually.[1] The hazard comes mostly from the cutting blade's high rate of revolution. Regulations have required design changes (blade brakes, automatic cut-off switches, and warning labels) that have reduced, but not eliminated, the danger in using power lawn mowers.[2] These additional safety features increase the marginal cost of producing power lawn mowers, thereby decreasing the supply of this labor-saving product. The reduction in supply raises the equilibrium price of mowers and lowers the quantity of mowers traded in the market. Buyers get a better product, but they also pay a higher price for the safer lawn mowers.

While some consumers may be satisfied with this tradeoff between price and quality, others will not. Most consumers already know that it is hazardous to put hands and/or feet under a lawn mower. A warning label is of no value

1. U.S. Bureau of the Census, *Statistical Abstract of the United States: 1991*, 111th ed. (Washington, D.C., 1991).

2. Although it may be possible to make something foolproof, it is impossible to make anything damn foolproof. One enterprising gardener set out to prune a hedge by attempting to hold a lawn mower over the hedge.

to these consumers. Others are aware of the many dangers involved and will prevent accidents by taking the necessary precautions — such as stopping the engine when doing anything other than mowing, or not lifting a running mower off the ground. The automatic cut-offs and blade brakes that lawn-mower safety regulations require are of little or no value to these users. A side effect of quality controls is that some consumers pay for quality-enhancing features that do nothing to benefit them personally.

Student Loans and Student Vacations

Former Secretary of Education William Bennett created a furor among college students when he used a spring visit to Florida to criticize college loan programs. He claimed that loans were used by students to finance Florida vacations during spring break. At that time we asked our students what they used their student loans for, and nearly all of them insisted it was to pay tuition. According to them, they received a loan at the beginning of each semester and effectively turned their entire loan check over to the university.

However, their analysis of their own behavior appears to be in error. Even if it is literally true that they "used their loan check to pay tuition," it doesn't necessarily follow that Secretary Bennett's accusations were false. To examine the impact of a student-loan program on student behavior, it is useful to see how the receipt of a loan alters the budget line of a typical student and what effect this change in the budget line has on consumption behavior.

Let's suppose that a typical student who qualifies for student loans has an income (what she earns from working plus support she receives from home) totaling $10,000 per year. Let's also suppose that she attends a university where tuition is $200 per credit hour. (Naturally, tuition is not the *only* cost of attending college — but here we are simplifying.) This student would be confronted by the budget line labeled BL_1 in Figure 5.3. In the absence of student loans, she would select the bundle of goods on BL_1 that lies on the highest indifference curve. For the preferences represented in Figure 5.3, this point is bundle A. She attends college on a part-time basis (15 hours per year) and spends $7,000 on other goods and services.

Now, let's suppose that this student qualifies for and obtains a $6,000 student loan. This is sufficient to pay for an additional 30 credit hours per year. If there were no conditions attached to receiving the loan, the loan would shift the budget line outward to BL_2. However, a condition is placed on the loan — that the borrower remain a full-time student, which might mean taking at least 20 hours per year. If so, receipt of the loan requires her to spend at least $4,000 per year on tuition and at most $12,000 on other goods. This restricts her to points at or below point B on BL_2. Which of these points she selects depends on her preferences.

Figure 5.3 Student Loans and Student Spending Patterns

By obtaining a loan of $6,000, a student is able to shift her current budget constraint from BL_1 to BL_2. To determine the impact of the loan on this student, we compare her spending at point C, the optimal point on BL_2, with her spending behavior at point A.

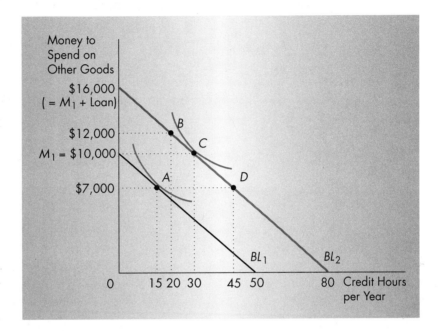

Suppose that she behaves like our students say they do — she takes her student loan ($6,000) and uses it all to pay for 30 hours of tuition per year. In other words, suppose that her preferences are those depicted in Figure 5.3 where point C is the optimal point. What impact does the loan have on her behavior? It induces her to select point C instead of point A. At point C she buys 15 additional hours of education and spends $3,000 additional dollars on other goods and services — including, perhaps, a Florida vacation. Even though she uses her entire student loan check to pay tuition, the effect of the loan is revealed by comparing her consumption choice with and without the loan. The loan frees up income to be spent on noneducation.

For the student in question to use the entire loan for additional education, she must select point D on the new budget line, where she spends $9,000 on education and the same amount on other goods ($7,000) as in the absence of the loan. She would select this point only if her income elasticity for other goods is zero.

This example is incomplete, however, in that it ignores the fact that loans must be repaid. To complete the analysis, we would have to look at the student later in life when loan repayments reduce spendable income by the

Figure 5.4 In-Kind Versus In-Cash Subsidies

An income subsidy program causes the entire budget line to shift outward from BL_1 to BL_2. An equally costly food subsidy program enables the same family to select points on BL_2 that lie below point C. To see how the two programs compare and what impact they have on consumer behavior, it is necessary to compare the new equilibrium points with point A.

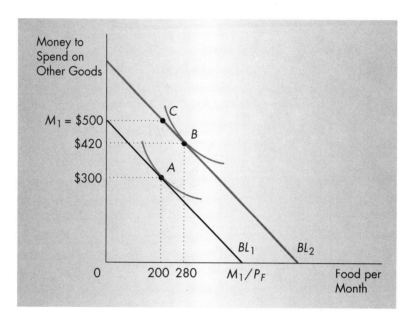

amount of the loan plus accumulated interest. The loan repayments would force her to spend less on goods like housing, cars, and, perhaps, Florida vacations.

The same framework can be used to analyze the impact of various government subsidy programs. A continuing debate in welfare policy concerns payment-in-kind versus payment-in-cash programs. Some policy makers argue that the poor should be given cash subsidies, which simply shift their budget lines outward and allow them to spend as they wish. Others argue that welfare recipients are not to be trusted with cash, because it may be spent on drugs or alcohol instead of on food for the family and medical care for the children.

To analyze the impact of these two programs, imagine a poor family whose monthly income is $500. Suppose that the price of food is $1, so the family is initially confronted with BL_1 in Figure 5.4. Given the tastes and preferences reflected in the indifference map in Figure 5.4, the family buys $200 worth of food and spends the remaining $300 on other goods and services. Suppose that a payment-in-cash subsidy program is then initiated, and that the family qualifies for a $200-per-month income supplement. This cash-subsidy program causes the budget line to shift outward to BL_2, and as a result the family selects point *B* instead of point *A*. Given their tastes and preferences, the family has elected to use the additional $200 in cash to buy 80 additional units of food each month and to buy an additional $120 worth of other goods.

What would happen if, instead, the family received a subsidy in kind rather than in cash? For comparability, suppose that in lieu of the cash, the family is given $200 worth of food coupons, which can be legally redeemed only for food items. The consequence of this subsidy program is to change the budget line in a slightly different way than the cash subsidy changed it. Assuming that the family does not sell the food coupons (which is illegal), the most they can spend on nonfood items is $500. However, if they spend $500 on nonfood, they can now consume 200 units of food. With no subsidy, they would have no money left to buy food had they spent $500 on other goods. Their new budget line differs from BL_1 in that for any dollar expenditure on nonfood, the family is able to consume 200 more units of food than it would have without a subsidy. The food-coupon program makes that portion of BL_2 from point *C* downward available to this family. For the preferences specified, the subsidy in kind has exactly the same impact on consumption as the cash subsidy.[3] The impact of the two programs will differ only if the optimal point on BL_2 lies above point *C*. Even if the family accepts $200 in food coupons and spends all 200 coupons on food, it is incorrect to view the program as increasing food consumption by 200 units. To determine the impact of the program, just compare point *B* with point *A*.

Taxes, Rebates, and Conservation

Periodically, public officials engage in attempts to get the public to conserve various resources. For example, in the 1970s, after the Organization of Petroleum Exporting Countries (OPEC) was formed, numerous energy-conservation schemes were proposed to reduce our dependence on imported oil. More recently, droughts both in California and in the Northeast have caused various localities to debate and enact a variety of plans designed to reduce water use. In parts of the country in which landfill capacity is being exhausted, attempts are being made to get the public to recycle and reduce the volume of trash sent to the landfills.

Each of these "crises" occurred when public officials were slow to allow prices to rise in the face of large increases in demand or reductions in supply. One example is the water crisis in California, where, in normal years, water flow from the reservoirs is more than adequate to meet demand, even at very low prices. Figure 5.5 represents a situation in which, during a year of normal

3. For families whose satisfaction is maximized at points above *C* along BL_2 in Figure 5.4, the government will create more satisfaction from a given in-cash rather than an in-kind subsidy.

Figure 5.5 Drought and the Market for Water
During years of drought when the supply of water falls to S_1, one way to
allocate the water is to increase the price to P_1. If the price is kept at P_0,
some inefficient method of rationing must be implemented.

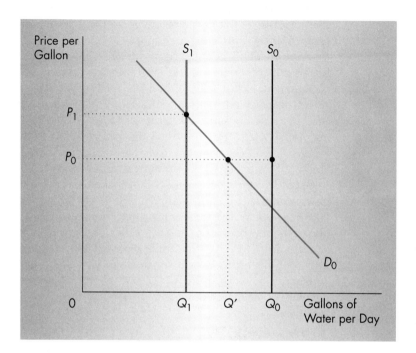

rainfall, a reservoir produces a water flow of Q_0 gallons per day. At a price of
P_0, demand fails to meet the reservoir's capacity, so during normal years a surplus of water exists. However, after several years of drought, the flow from the
reservoir drops to Q_1. At the initial price of P_0, a shortage of Q' minus Q_1
develops, and some method of water rationing must be implemented. Among
the methods used to ration water was a ban on certain uses of water. In some
areas, laws were passed making it illegal to wash cars; other areas prohibited or
greatly limited the use of water for lawn watering.

Water-rationing schemes of this type were not without their problems. In
many cases, they were difficult to enforce. In addition, there was great disagreement about which usages should be declared nonessential. Those who
liked gardening and who had invested heavily in landscaping were outraged by
laws that prohibited them from watering plants. Further, they could not
understand why lawn watering was forbidden when their neighbors were
allowed to use water to fill swimming pools. In addition, there was much hos-
tility between homeowners and farmers, who, in California, use about 85

percent of the water. Each group felt that the other should be the one who was forced to reduce water usage.

One obvious solution was to allow the price to rise to P_1. However, that solution received little support for at least two reasons: (1) Some public officials refused to believe that users could be induced to restrict water consumption by higher prices. They appeared to believe that demand for water is perfectly inelastic with respect to price. (2) More important, most of the politicians in the state were unwilling to risk angering voters by imposing new water fees. When the suggestion was made, a common rebuttal was that those on fixed incomes and the poor simply could not afford to pay much higher water bills.

However, there is a fairly simple solution by which prices can be raised to encourage conservation without imposing much of a financial burden on users. The way to do this is to impose a price increase (a tax) and then rebate the entire tax to users of water. Because the rebate is equal to the taxes collected, the tax-rebate program avoids imposing a large burden on water users.

On the surface, the tax-rebate program would apparently have no effect on consumption. Because you pay more for water but then get it all back, the effective price of water appears to be unchanged. However, the secret is to avoid basing any one consumer's rebate on his water consumption. One way of doing this is to take all the taxes collected and then divide them equally among all the users.

Let's consider a typical consumer of water. Suppose that the price of water is initially $1, and the consumer is constrained to BL_1 in Figure 5.6. That consumer selects point A and buys Q_A units of water. Then, suppose that the water authority imposes a $1-per-unit tax on water and rebates the proceeds evenly among all users. Ignoring the rebate for the time being, the tax would rotate the budget line to BL_2, causing the consumer to select point B and reduce his water consumption from Q_A units to Q_B units. Careful inspection of Figure 5.6 will indicate how many dollars the government receives in taxes from this consumer. Consider a vertical move upward from point B on BL_2 to point C on BL_1. At point B a consumer who buys Q_B units of water with the tax in effect has M_B dollars to spend on other goods. At point C, a consumer who buys the same quantity of water in the absence of the tax has M_C dollars to spend on other goods. Therefore, the difference between M_C and M_B is the additional cost of the water because of the tax, and it is equal to the tax revenue the government collects from this consumer. Because we've assumed that this consumer is average, M_C minus M_B (which equals the distance between points C and B) represents the average of the tax revenues from all of the customers. Let's call this average R. The total revenue collected from the tax will be $(R \times N)$, where N is the number of customers. If the extra revenue is divided evenly and then rebated to the customers, each customer will receive R dollars. This rebate will shift the budget line upward to BL_3. With an income of $(M + R)$, the consumer could select any point on BL_3. However, to keep the

Figure 5.6 Taxes, Tax Rebates, and Water Conservation

One way in which water conservation can be achieved without imposing a large tax burden on consumers is to raise the price of water by adding a tax that is then rebated to consumers. The combination of tax and rebate changes the typical consumer's budget line from BL_1 to BL_3, which causes the consumer to reduce his consumption from Q_A to Q_B.

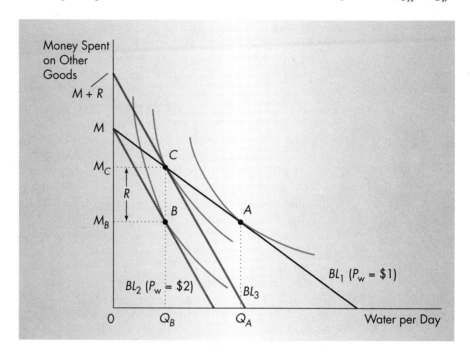

analysis simple, let's assume that point C is the optimal point on BL_3.[4] The tax-rebate plan therefore changes the budget line from BL_1 to BL_3 and causes the consumer to select point C instead of point A. After the tax and rebate, the average consumer is worse off; point C lies on a lower indifference curve than point A. However, the rebate takes much of the sting out of the tax. Without the rebate, the consumer would have selected point B on BL_2 and been forced to a much lower indifference curve.

4. This assumption implies that the income elasticity for water is zero in this price range. The reason we have made this assumption is that we are trying to describe a tax-rebate scheme that, for the average customer, will enable him to remain on the original budget line. However, we do not know how large that subsidy must be until we know how much water he elects to consume when the rebate is added to his income. If, after the rebate, he consumed more than Q_B units of water, he would be below his initial budget line. In that case, a rebate of more than $M_C - M_B$ dollars would be required to completely rebate the tax. Correspondingly, if the tangency point of BL_3 is above point C, the average consumer is above his initial budget line, which means that the government is paying more in rebates than it collects from the price tax.

Note also that the tax-rebate scheme keeps the *average* consumer on his original budget line, but it does not achieve this for all consumers. A consumer, for instance, may select an above-average quantity of water. Even when this consumer receives his rebate of R dollars, his tax payments will still exceed his rebate, and he will be forced to a point below his original budget line. In contrast, a consumer who consumes less than Q_B units will get a rebate that exceeds his taxes. It may then be tempting to try to devise a rebate program that assures that all consumers can return to their initial budget line by adjusting their rebate to equal their tax payments. However, such a program would be senseless. Each unit of water consumed would cost an additional $1 because of the tax, but its consumption would lead to a $1 increase in the rebate. Such a rebate scheme would have no effect on the budget line, so it would fail to provide any incentive to conserve.

In contrast, a program in which each consumer gets the same rebate encourages conservation. Unless the number of buyers is quite small, the amount of water a consumer buys will have little impact on his rebate; his consumption has very little impact on the average consumption. Therefore, his decision to consume more water forces him to pay more water taxes, but it does not generate an offsetting increase in his rebate. As we can see in Figure 5.6, it causes the budget line of the average consumer to change from BL_1 to BL_3 and leads the average consumer to select Q_B units instead of Q_A units. Further, it does so while keeping the cost to users small.[5] Although not exactly optimal for *each* consumer, such a plan may be politically feasible.

Nonprice Rationing, Gut Courses, and Immigration

Even in a society like the United States, in which the price system is used widely to allocate scarce goods and services, numerous other allocation schemes are also used. In certain instances, the refusal to use the price system stems from the belief that its use is immoral; in other cases, prices are not used because those in charge of allocation are prevented from profiting from the sale of the good or service in question. Whatever the reason, one can learn much about the price system by studying the outcomes of alternative rationing schemes.

Sailing Through College

If your university is typical, certain courses in the curriculum are generally viewed as jokes. These "gut" courses often feature a humorous professor who delights in pleasing his students. He does this by making minimal demands on his students and by rewarding them with amazingly high grades. Some students try to avoid such courses, but many seek them out. As a consequence,

---

5. Farmers with water rights have had some success in getting permission from government to sell water to urban dwellers.

the courses are often "impossible" to get into. Each semester hundreds more students attempt to enroll than the classroom can accommodate. The university must then find some way to allocate the scarce seats. To an economist, one easy way would be to impose a tuition surcharge on students who enroll in that particular course. Figure 5.7 shows the demand for that particular class. The demand curve depicted there shows how many students would be willing to enroll at each particular surcharge. Without a surcharge, 300 students would attempt to enroll in the class whose capacity is shown as 50 students. Assuming that the course capacity is not expanded, a tuition surcharge of $125 would be adequate to allocate the 50 seats to those students who are willing to pay the most. Other prospective students would have to find an alternative course.

This pricing solution is seldom used by universities, because it is widely perceived as unfair. Two students who have identical subjective evaluations of the course may have widely differing abilities to pay. There is, after all, an important difference between effective demand, based on income, and

Figure 5.7 Rationing Seats in Class

Certain university courses are consistently oversubscribed. For example, 300 students may attempt to register for a course when there are only 50 seats available. One way to determine who gets the seats is to impose a tuition surcharge of $125 on the course.

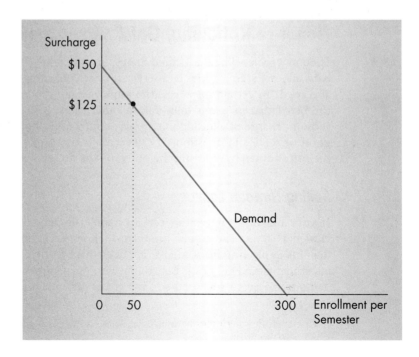

subjective values of goods and services. Instead of using effective demand for seats, therefore, universities rely on alternative allocation schemes that in turn are debated and criticized. In some universities, students are selected randomly; in others, students queue and spaces are given to these who are first in line. But in most universities, priority schemes are devised. Some universities give highest priority to students with the highest GPA, a few give highest priority to those with the lowest GPA; most universities give a preference to seniors over underclassmen and to scholarship athletes over nonathletes.

No matter which of the priority schemes is used, it is almost certain to be defended on the basis of "fairness." Universities that select students randomly defend this practice as the only fair system, and universities that give priority to seniors use the same justification. Although it is futile to attempt to resolve the debate over which system is most fair, it is not futile to examine the economic consequences of nonprice rationing schemes. There are two important objectives of any rationing scheme:

1. It must place the goods or services in the hands of those who place high values on them instead of those who place low values on them. To do otherwise is to dissipate much of the value of the scarce goods.
2. The allocation scheme must achieve the first objective in a low-cost manner.

Unfortunately, none of the nonprice allocation schemes succeed in meeting both objectives. Consider random distribution. In Figure 5.7 the 300 prospective students place values on the course ranging from $150 down to $0. If 50 students are selected randomly, they will occupy points all along the demand curve — not just the spots on the top end of the demand curve. Random selection may be "fair," but it does a miserable job of distributing the seats.

In contrast, a system of first-come-first-served is likely to do a reasonably good job of allocating the seats to those who value them the most. Students who place a low value on the class are unlikely to make a considerable effort in order to get into the class, so those who are most willing to stand in line will tend to be those who place the highest values on the class. However, first-come-first-served will fail as miserably in achieving the second objective as it succeeds in achieving the first. To return to Figure 5.7, one way of allocating the 50 seats would be to charge a money price of $125. In lieu of a dollar price, the seats could be sold to those who are willing to pay the highest amount of waiting time. Assuming that students value their time at about $10 per hour, there should be 50 students who would be willing to stand in line for at least 12.5 hours in order to obtain a position in the class. Therefore, if the seats were issued to the first 50 students in line at some fixed time, to be among the first 50 you would have to be there about 12.5 hours ahead of time. Instead of paying $125, each of the 50 students pays a price of about

$125 worth of his or her time. Much of the value of the spaces is wasted by having to stand in line.

What about the priority schemes of allocating the seats? Whichever of them is used, there is no assurance that the seats will go to those who value them the most. It is not obvious that seniors will value the seats more than freshmen or that those with high GPAs will value them more than other students. It is therefore not clear that the priority systems are superior to random allocation in allocating the seats to those who value them the most. These alternatives to the price system may be perceived as more equitable. However, this increase in equity comes at a high efficiency cost.

Economics and Immigration Policy

The problems faced by college administrators in deciding how to allocate spaces in popular courses are conceptually similar to those faced by

Figure 5.8 Immigration

Under current U.S. immigration policy, the number of immigrants that we admit from a country is typically less than the number of persons in that country who desire to move to the United States. As a consequence, some method has to be used to determine which aspiring immigrants are selected. One method would be to auction the right to be an immigrant. Given the demand shown in the figure, a price of $30,000 would be necessary to allocate the 10,000 slots.

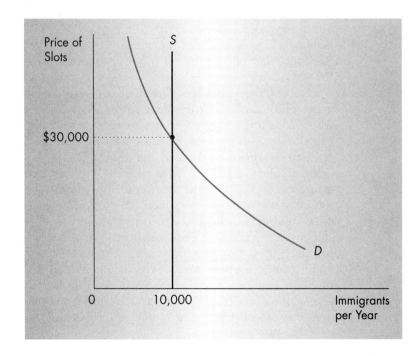

immigration authorities in deciding how to select potential immigrants. Historically, the policy of the United States has been to establish an overall number of immigrants to be accepted each year and then to divide the total into quotas for immigrants from various countries. Our purpose is not to debate the desirability of limiting the number of immigrants — it is to consider alternative ways to select the restricted number of immigrants from each country. The demand curve shown in Figure 5.8 is the demand for admission to the United States by immigrants from a particular country. Assuming that our policy is to admit 10,000 persons from that country per year, we can see that one way would be to sell the right to become an immigrant. Assuming the demand curve depicted in Figure 5.8, at a price of $30,000 there would be only 10,000 immigrants who would be willing to pay for entry into the United States.

As a matter of policy, the United States has never auctioned the right to become an immigrant. Historically, our policy has been to combine a priority system with a first-come-first-served policy. Potential immigrants were given a high priority for having members of their immediate family as citizens of the United States or for having skills deemed valuable in the U.S. labor market and for some other reasons. For each country, a part of the quota would be filled on this basis. The remaining positions were then filled from waiting lists. For certain countries this meant that immigrants remained on the waiting list for years, so that the average immigrant was very elderly.

Policy makers in Congress and in the immigration service were never very happy with the outcome of the priority/waiting list system. In the past few years they have implemented a new system in which immigrants are increasingly selected on a random basis. Although it is unclear what the "best" system is for selecting immigrants, it is clear that the different allocation schemes will bring to the United States quite different types of immigrants.

The Impact of Communal Living Arrangements on Consumer Behavior

One of the best and also one of the worst experiences of college students is dealing with roommates. Most students have serious roommate problems at least once during their college career. As you are well aware, a vast array of living arrangements are possible among roommates. Some roommates split the rent and otherwise live a separate existence. In other cases, roommates have elaborate schemes in which they share not only rent but also the expense of food, furniture, cable service and video rentals, and newspaper and magazine subscriptions. Things can get very complicated when there are more than two roommates and some share only rent while others share in varying degrees in other things.

Among the many sources of difficulty between roommates, one is inherent in the economic incentives that arise when expenses are shared. Imagine four classmates who rent a house together and begin the year with the following understanding: "Because we all have similar interests, like pretty much the same things, and have similar budgets, let's make things easy by splitting our bills for food, utilities, video rental, beer, and so on, evenly. Whenever you pay for any of those things, just initial the receipt, put it in the top drawer, and we'll divide things equally at the end of the month."

The intent of this agreement is that each roommate should use good judgment and buy as if he were paying for things himself. However, that often is not the way things turn out. Even though the four may in general like the same things, preferences are bound to vary. One roommate may insist on having lime popsicles in the freezer at all times, a second may insist on Mexican beer, and the third roommate might eat gourmet ice cream both for breakfast and as a midnight snack. The fourth roommate might be a movie junkie who constantly rents weird movies for himself and his roommates to enjoy. Therefore, everything that they agree to pay for equally is not likely to be consumed evenly; in essence each of the four roommates is getting the other three to share equally in the cost of something he likes to consume.

To see how this may affect behavior, consider Figure 5.9. Here, we have focused on the fourth roommate's decision to rent videos. Given his income and the price of videos, his budget line is BL_1. On that budget line he would select point A and rent Q_A videos per month. However, when he is able to get his roommates to share the rental cost of videos, he is likely to perceive his budget line as BL_2 which differs from BL_1 in that the new price of videos is $(1/N)(P_{video})$, where N is the number of roommates. If the price of videos is \$2, he will perceive the price to be \$0.50 because the price is split evenly among the four roommates. He will respond by renting Q_B videos per month and thinking that he will be able to spend M_B dollars on other goods. On the surface, having roommates appears to be a great deal — it seems to enable him to move from point A on indifference curve U_A to point B on a much higher indifference curve, U_B.

The other three roommates are affected in essentially the same way. Each of them perceives the price of their favorite good to have been reduced to one-fourth its initial level, and they too are induced to consume more ice cream, beer, and the like.

Of course, all of their perceptions are flawed. If we look at point B in Figure 5.9, we see that it lies beyond BL_1. For this roommate to be able to consume at point B, he would have to receive a subsidy of $(M_B - M_C)$ dollars from his roommates. However, in order to receive this video subsidy from the other roommates, this roommate has entered into an agreement to help subsidize in turn their consumption of beer, ice cream, and popsicles. Assuming that his roommates' expenditures on popsicles, ice cream, and beer are each equal to his expenditure on videos, his share of their purchases will amount to

Figure 5.9 Roommates and Cost Sharing

When an individual enters a communal arrangement in which costs are shared, it may appear to her that the sharing agreement enables her to obtain goods at a fraction of their price. However, instead of being able to move from point *A* on BL_1 to point *B* on BL_2, the individual ends up at point *C* on BL_3 when other members of the group behave in the same way.

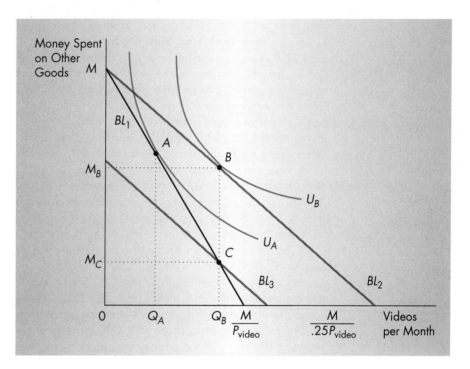

$(M_B - M_C)$ dollars. When this payment is taken into account, he will end up at point *C* on BL_3 instead of point *B* on BL_2. Instead of being better off as a consequence of having roommates, he ends up worse off. Each of the four roommates is induced to buy too much of the good in question because they can shift a portion of the cost on to their roommates. However, when they all behave this way, they end up worse off. Their consumption is distorted in such a way that they overconsume the shared goods and end up at nonoptimal points on their initial budget lines.

  If this analysis seems complicated, perhaps we can see what is happening in a simpler way. An individual can consume beyond his budget line only if someone is subsidizing him by paying a portion of his purchases. However, within the group of roommates, they cannot all be receiving subsidies — if one roommate is being subsidized by consuming *beyond* his initial budget line, at least one other roommate must be forced to some point *inside* his budget line. On average, the roommates are unable to consume beyond their initial budget line, BL_1. What the cost sharing does, however, is induce them to consume more of the subsidized good. As a consequence, they end up at some point like C on BL_1 where they are worse off than they were at point A.

This analysis perhaps explains a policy that we have all encountered in restaurants — the policy of "no separate checks for parties of eight or more." If one were to ask the management why they had the policy, they would probably say that it was to make things simpler for the waiters and waitresses. However, waiters and waitresses have told us that they dislike the policy because it reduces their tips. Perhaps the real explanation of the policy is that the owner realizes that, when separate checks are not provided, the diners respond by agreeing to split the bill equally. Once they have agreed to split the bill in this fashion, the cost on the margin of each item on the menu is reduced to $(1/N)$ times the menu price. As a consequence, the diners respond by increasing their consumption of the "subsidized" meals, thereby increasing the revenue and the profits of the restaurant.

The graphical model presented in Figure 5.9 may also help explain what often appears to be unusual spending patterns by state and local governments. At various times, federal programs make matching funds available to finance specific projects. For example, funds might be available for library construction, for the construction of a new court house, for a new water-treatment plant, or for new bridges and highways. When such funds are available, state and local officials often work hard to obtain them, even though the project may appear to be a low-priority item, given local conditions. However, if federal matching funds cover a sufficiently high proportion of the cost, nearly any project will be worthwhile. When the interstate highway system was constructed, the federal government provided 90 percent of the funds, with the state covering the rest. As a consequence, there were many states with excellent interstate highways where *state* highways were outdated and poorly maintained. State officials were probably acting rationally when they committed to interstate construction, but the resulting spending pattern was much different from what would have prevailed without the subsidies. Given the amount of money spent on highways, it would be much more sensible to reduce interstate spending and increase spending on other roads. State officials will not do this because they have to pay for state roads themselves.

Public Education and the Voucher System

Americans have recently become alarmed about the quality of our educational system. As a consequence, various proposals have been made to improve the quality of education. Although many of the proposals simply suggest ways to improve the current system (reduce class sizes, lengthen the school year, and so on), other suggestions would make fundamental changes in the way we finance education in this country. One proposal that has received considerable publicity and which has generated a lot of controversy is the voucher system.

Under a voucher system, parents in a particular community would be given an educational voucher. The voucher could be used either as an admission ticket for their child to the local public schools or as payment of at least some of the tuition at a private school of the parents' choice. For example, suppose that expenditure per student in a certain school district is $5,000. The parents of each school-age child would be given a $5,000 voucher. If they elected to enroll their child in public schools, they would surrender their voucher to local school authorities. However, if they choose a private school, they could use the voucher to pay $5,000 of their child's tuition, with the $5,000 being transferred out of the local school board's account and into the account of the private school.

Public Schools and Family Behavior

To see how this proposal would be likely to affect behavior, it is useful first to consider a world in which there are no educational subsidies. Then we can see how the public-school subsidy affects behavior and how a voucher system might change things.

One problem in developing an economic model of education is that it is extremely difficult to measure the output of an educational institution. It is easy enough to count graduates or to compute averages on standardized tests, but these are very imprecise measures of how much learning actually takes place. To overcome this difficulty, let's make the simplifying assumption that all educational institutions are equally efficient and that the amount of education they produce is in direct proportion to the amount of money they spend. Although one should not take this assumption very seriously, its adoption enables us to get a handle on the operation of various educational subsidy schemes. Specifically, it enables us to define units of education in terms of the cost of that education. Think of one unit of education as what a school can produce in a year at a cost of $1,000. With this assumption, we can measure the output of an educational institution in terms of its budget. Further, we can measure the amount of education any student receives in terms of the number of dollars spent on behalf of that student. School districts that spend $4,000 per student provide 4 units of education per student, while school districts spending $7,000 produce 7 units of education per student.

Given this assumption, it is simple to model the choice that would confront the parents of each child if there were no public schools and no educational subsidies. Because units of education cost $1,000 to produce, their price in the private marketplace would be about $1,000. A family with income of M_1 would face BL_1 in Figure 5.10. These parents would select a private school that provides 6 units of education and charges $6,000 in tuition for their child. The type of school to which a particular child was sent would

Figure 5.10 A Family that Consumes Less Education Given Free Public Education

"Free" public education is a strange type of subsidy in that it induces some families to purchase less education than they would in the absence of the subsidy. If a family is forced to buy educational services at market prices along BL_1, the family will select 6 units of education. However, if the same family is "given" 4 units of free education, it can move to a higher indifference curve by reducing its consumption of educational services from 6 units to 4 units.

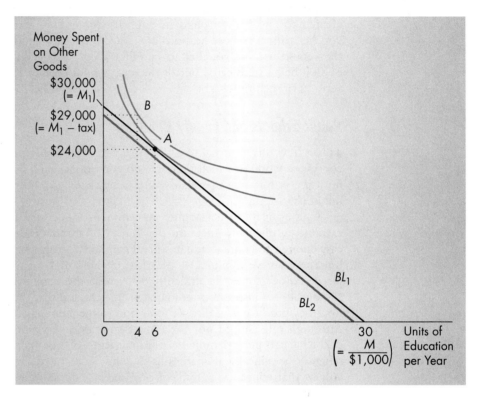

depend, of course, on the family's income and preferences. Children in families with high incomes and strong preferences for education would go to excellent schools, while children in some poor families whose parents place a low value on education would receive little, if any, education. The average quantity of education consumed might be 6 units, but there would be a large variation about the mean for different children. We must always remember that the effective demand for education (or any other good or service) is the product of *both* preferences and the income constraint.[6]

6. Effective demand in education is based on both preferences and incomes. We are all familiar with immigrant families who place high value on education and are willing to spend more on children's education than many richer families.

Now, consider how public schools affect choice. Under the public school system, education is financed through taxation, and public schools are tuition free. This affects the budget line of a typical family in two ways:

1. We have to account for additional taxes that the family might have to pay to finance public schools.
2. The family then has to compare the opportunities provided by the public schools with those provided by private schools.

How much any particular family will have to pay in taxes to finance the public education system will depend on three things — how much is spent per student in the public schools, how many students there are in the schools, and what type of taxes are collected to finance the public schools. Without extensive information it is impossible to say exactly how the taxes will affect any particular family's budget line. To give concreteness to the example, suppose that the school district decides to spend $4,000 per student (to provide 4 units of education), that there is one school-age student for every 4 families, and that the family depicted in Figure 5.10 pays an amount of taxes equal to the average family. This particular education system would cost $1,000 per family in taxes, which would shift the budget line down to BL_2 in Figure 5.10.

Now let's consider the choices available to this family. One option is to send its child to the public schools. If the family does so, it will have $29,000 (their after-tax income) to spend on other goods and be able to consume 4 units of education for its child. This will enable the family to select point *B* in Figure 5.10. What is these parents' alternative to selecting point *B*? Well, they can forgo the free public education and obtain education privately for their child by spending $1,000 per unit for privately provided education. To send their child to a private school is to select some point on BL_2. The choice between the "free" public school and the private school for this family will be determined by whether point *B* is preferred to each point on BL_2. If the indifference curve that passes through point *B* lies everywhere above BL_2, as it does in Figure 5.10, the family will be better off sending its child to the public school and spending $29,000 on goods other than education. However, for preferences that differ from those depicted in Figure 5.10, it would be possible that the indifference curve that passes through point *B* drops below BL_2. In that case, the family would be better off forgoing the tuition-free public school and sending its child to a private school that provides more than 4 units of education.

"Free" Education Versus Vouchers

It is interesting to note the effect of "free" public education on education consumption. For the family depicted in Figure 5.10, the provision of 4 units of "free" education leads to a 2-unit reduction in education consumption.

Instead of purchasing 6 units of education at point A on BL_1, the family sends its child to the public school, which provides 4 units of education.

Had that family's preferences been different such that the indifference curve that passes through point B drops below BL_2, the family would have selected some point on BL_2 that provides more than 4 units of education. However, assuming that education is a normal good, that point would consist of less than 6 units of education. We know this because the only difference between BL_1 and BL_2 is that income is $1,000 lower along BL_2. If education is a normal good, a reduction in income will lead to a reduction in consumption. The necessity of paying taxes to support the public schools will therefore reduce the education consumption by families who continue to send their child to private schools. This shows one of the ironies of our current system of public education.

Figure 5.11 Increased Consumption of Education

For many families, public education leads to increased consumption of education. The family depicted here would obtain 2 units of education in the absence of "free" public education and 4 units with public schools. However, one advantage of an educational voucher system is that it would enable this family to obtain more units of education without having to forgo the "free" units of education provided by public schools.

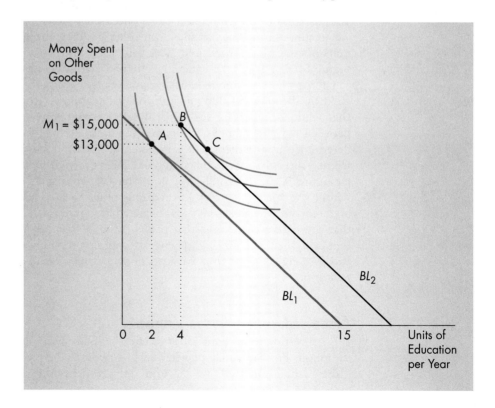

One should be careful to avoid jumping to the conclusion that the provision of tuition-free public education induces all families to reduce their educational consumption. Figure 5.11 shows the effect of public education on a typical poor family. In the absence of public schools, the family would buy 2 units of education and spend its remaining $13,000 on other goods. If the public schools in that community provide 4 units of education, the family would be able to select point *B*. Note that at point *B* the family consumes 4 units of education and slightly less than $15,000 on other goods to reflect the low school-tax burden. For families of this type, public education undoubtedly will lead to improved education.

To generalize, tuition-free public education causes families with low incomes and weak preferences for education to consume more education. For many families, the education their children receive in public schools is vastly superior to what they would receive if there were only private schools. However, certain families — primarily those with above-average incomes — consume less education as a consequence of "free" public schools.

How would things differ if a voucher plan was enacted? The major impact would be that it would enable families to consume more education than that provided by their local public schools without having to forgo 4 "free" units of education. They could keep their children in the public schools and continue to consume 4 units of education, or they could use their voucher at a private school that provided more than 4 units of education. The voucher system enables the family to select not only point *B* but all the other points on BL_2. For the family depicted in that graph, changing to a voucher system would induce it to select point *C* and consume substantially more education than is provided by the public school. Adopting the voucher system would lead many families to consume more education without inducing any families to consume less.

Some advocates of the voucher system would argue that the foregoing analysis ignores many of its important advantages. By eroding the monopoly that public schools currently have, vouchers would introduce an element of competition into the education industry. Schools would be forced to compete for students, and in doing so they would find new and innovative ways to provide education. These innovations would reduce the cost of providing education and lead families to further increase their consumption of education.

The Issue of "Fairness"

Critics of the voucher system raise a number of important objections that must be considered in any real-world attempt to implement the idea. They point out certain disadvantages associated with vouchers. First and foremost, critics argue that education could become much less equal under a voucher system. Emerging schools would be highly segregated, and the disparity between the education received by poor and rich children would be much greater than under our current system of public schools.

Families sending their children to emerging private schools would, in many cases, have to make additional out-of-pocket expenditures. Many low-income families would either choose not to make the additional expenditure or would be unable to do so. The diversion of public monies to private schools would further exacerbate the problems of public institutions and widen the disparity in the education received by poor and rich children.

Although a wide gulf in quality exists today between purely *public* schools in various communities (depending largely on tax receipts and income), critics of vouchers argue that society should maintain a purely public system. In this view, education is a "merit" good to which everyone has access as a matter of right. This "right" is financed out of taxes levied on *all* citizens, whether or not they have children. Voucher systems do not necessarily enhance this right, at least according to critics. Although these arguments relating to "fairness" in the system may have merit, the economist simply observes that such issues must be considered alongside the potential efficiency gains in the enhanced quality and choice offered by the use of vouchers.

Price Elasticity and the Cost of National Health Care

The past ten years has been a period of concern over the growing cost of health care in the United States. Spending on health care as a percentage of national income has risen rapidly to a level that may be the highest in the world. Despite this, by several standards, Americans fail to get high-quality health care.

Any number of proposals have been made to reform our system of health-care delivery and payment, but one that is receiving increased attention is a system of national health care. Under a comprehensive national health-care system, all health-care costs of all Americans would be paid by the government. National health care undoubtedly has certain advantages; with its adoption, no American would be denied health care because he was poor or uninsured. Further, no American family would be forced to dissipate its savings to pay for the cost of injury or illness.

However, the proposal has at least one major drawback — it will be expensive and necessitate substantial increases in taxes. Exactly how expensive the program would prove to be depends largely on how much health care Americans would use if it were "free." By free we mean that patients would not be charged for health care; its cost would be borne through some form of payroll taxes, with no linkage between the amount of health care a person uses and the taxes he or she has to pay.

Many critics of the proposed program contend that its adoption would lead to large increases in the consumption of health care, which would necessitate huge increases in payroll taxes. Figure 5.12 presents a model with which the effect of national health care on consumption can be examined. Let's imagine a person with an income of M_1 who initially pays for his own medical care. Although health care takes many different forms, let's focus our attention on the person's decision to visit a physician. Initially, let's suppose that it costs $40 to visit a typical doctor. This person faces BL_1, and he uses $(M_1 - M_A)$ dollars to pay for Q_A visits to a doctor per year. What would happen to this person's use of physician services if a comprehensive national health-care program were enacted? By "comprehensive" we mean a program in which the government pays all medical bills. His budget constraint would be altered in two ways: (1) His disposable income, which is initially M_1, would fall because of the increase in taxes to pay for national health care. (2) The price of visits to a physician would fall to zero. As a consequence, this consumer would face a budget line that is a horizontal line. The vertical intercept would be M_1 minus the health-care tax. If this person's health-care tax equaled his initial spending

Figure 5.12 National Health Care

One argument that is often made against national health care is that it would induce individuals to increase their consumption of medical care from Q_A units to Q_B. This analysis is misleading for two reasons. One is that it shows a typical consumer selecting point *B*, which lies beyond that person's budget line, which is impossible. Second, relatively few consumers face a budget line like BL_1, because so many of them are currently covered by insurance programs that provide medical care at a trivial cost on the margin.

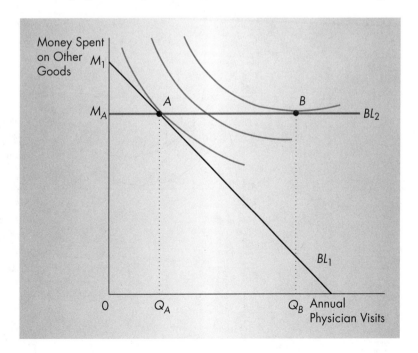

on medical care, then his new budget line would be BL_2, leading him to select Q_B visits to a physician per year.

Analysis like this is often used to imply that consumption of health care would rise so drastically under national health care that our current delivery system would be overwhelmed. In this view, huge waiting lines for health care would develop, and the cost of providing the service would prove to be overwhelming.

However, such analysis has several flaws. First of all, the typical consumer depicted in Figure 5.12 ends up at point B, which lies far beyond his initial budget line. For this to be the case, the cost of the health care he consumes must be greater than the taxes he pays. Therefore, BL_2 reflects a level of taxes that is inadequate to finance the system. With higher taxes, the budget line would be shifted downward, and the optimal point would reflect a quantity of physician services of less than Q_B.

Figure 5.13 Private Health Insurance

If the indifference map depicted here shows the preferences of a typical family, an insurance premium of $(M_1 - M_B)$ dollars would be required for a policy that provides comprehensive coverage. A family who buys such a policy would face BL_2 and select point B. Without insurance, the same family would select point A. The adoption of a national health-care system would have little effect on medical consumption by families who are currently insured.

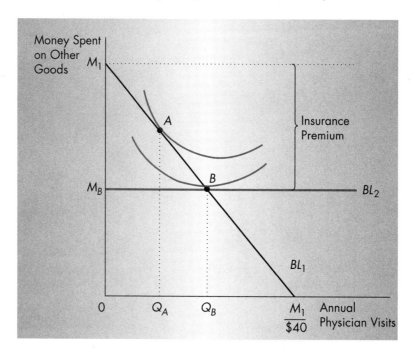

However, a more serious flaw in this analysis is that it depicts a typical consumer of physician services as one who initially pays for those services out of pocket. In fact, the vast majority of Americans are either covered by private medical insurance or Medicare or they qualify for Medicaid. For this majority, adopting a policy of national health care would have little impact on consumption.

To see why, consider a person who has medical insurance from a private company that, except for minor deductibles, completely covers his medical expenses. In Figure 5.13 his income is M_1, which would enable him to consume health care along BL_1 in the absence of insurance. However, his employer withholds $(M_1 - M_B)$ dollars to pay his insurance premiums. Note that the insurance premium is just enough to pay for Q_B visits to a physician at prevailing prices, so the insurance scheme is actuarially sound. Also note that the insurance coverage induces him to increase his use of physicians from Q_A to Q_B. Therefore, private insurance has essentially the same impact on consumption as does national health care. The analysis of those on Medicaid or Medicare is similar.

The important point is that many Americans currently face a price on medical care that is essentially zero. If the current system of financing health care is replaced by a system of national health care, the effect on health-care consumption by these Americans would be small. It is only the minority of Americans, currently not covered by private insurance or by Medicaid or Medicare, that would be greatly affected by the adoption of national health care.

A national health-care program would cost hundreds of billions of dollars, and substantial increases in payroll taxes would be required to generate the revenues. However, much of this increase would be offset by the elimination of payroll deductions, which currently are used to pay for private medical insurance.

Quantity Controls, Prohibitions, and Consumer Interests

Sometimes it is the equilibrium market quantity that governments attempt to manipulate. There are circumstances in which the public interest is promoted by an *increase* in output and others in which a *decrease* in output is beneficial. The justification for the quantity controls aside, the government can affect the quantity exchange in a market either directly or indirectly. Direct quantity controls specify some particular quantity to be produced and consumed. Examples of direct quantity controls include laws that (1) require drivers to carry auto insurance, (2) require immunization against childhood diseases, and (3) set limits on the number of shoes that may be imported. Indirect quantity controls manipulate supply and/or demand to affect the equilibrium market quantity. Among the many examples of indirect quantity controls are laws that require (1) newspaper publishers to use a minimum percentage of recycled paper products, (2) power companies to purchase a given amount of the coal that they use from in-state mines, or (3) owners to reduce the production from natural-gas wells to a fraction of their potential output. Note that quantity controls work both ways; they can either increase or decrease output. The extreme case of the latter occurs when the government resorts to outright prohibitions. The policy goal in this case is to eliminate production and/or consumption entirely. A politically extreme form of prohibition is the blockade or embargo such as that urged by the United States against Cuba or Iraq (see, for example, Highlight 5.2). But domestic prohibitions also have had an enormous impact on U.S. consumers.

Highlight 5.2   *Blockades, Embargoes, and the Rhett Butler Effect*

It's a minor scene in the classic film *Gone With the Wind*. Rhett gives Scarlett a present; a bonnet, the latest in European fashion, that he has smuggled through the Union blockade. Although Margaret Mitchell's *Gone With the Wind* is fiction, there is an element of truth behind the bonnet scene.[a] The Union blockade of Southern ports disrupted the normal flow of imports into the South. This disruption, however, was not evenly distributed across all goods. The supply of necessities was curtailed more than the supply of luxuries. Soldiers in the South went without food while wealthy ladies sported the latest fashions. Were the smugglers simply incompetent in failing to bring in necessities? An investigation of the market effects of blockades and embargoes will reveal that the blockade runners were definitely not incompetent; they were reacting rationally to economic constraints.

Blockades and embargoes are special cases of government attempts at prohibition. These two forms of prohibition entail a general ban on all international trade. Embargoes generally rely on legal constraints (denial of export licenses, the freezing of foreign assets, and so on) to isolate a country from international markets. Blockades go a step further by employing military force to assure compliance with the prohibition on trade. Although blockades and embargoes are designed to eliminate contact between a nation and international markets, they are rarely completely successful. Like any attempt at prohibition, illegal trading develops to get around the ban on trade. Smugglers and blockade runners find it profitable to violate the embargo and break through the blockade. The problem for such entrepreneurs is to determine the composition of their cargo. This decision is affected by what can be termed, in honor of the movie, the Rhett Butler effect.

[a] Much of the following is taken from R. B. Ekelund, Jr., and M. Thornton, "The Union Blockade and Demoralization of the South: Relative Prices in the Confederacy," *Social Science Quarterly* 73 (December 1992): 890–902.

Rhett Butler certainly "gave a damn" about his ill-gotten gains from running the Yankee blockade of the South during the Civil War.

The Rhett Butler effect is the rational response to a change in relative prices that occurs when blockades or embargoes are imposed. The change in relative prices comes about because of an increase in transportation costs. Smuggling and blockade running involve costs that are unique to entrepreneurs who will be imprisoned and have their cargo and ships confiscated if they are captured. The costs of these eventualities will be added to the cost of the goods being carried by the shippers. The nature of shipping is such that the shipping costs are a function of the bulk, weight, or volume of the good being transported rather than the value of the good. Two commodities of equal bulk, weight, and volume will incur equal shipping costs, regardless of their value. The costs of smuggling a pound of gold will be equal to those for smuggling a pound of lead.

Consider the entrepreneur contemplating a run through the Union blockade who must choose between cargoes of ladies' evening gowns and military uniforms. Assuming that the same number of apparel items can be carried in both cases, the blockade increases the per-unit shipping costs by an equal amount, say $10. If the price of evening gowns was $200 before the blockade, it will rise to $210 with the blockade. If the price of uniforms was $20 prior to the blockade, the postblockade price will rise to $30. Note what the blockade does to the relative prices of gowns and uniforms. Prior to the blockade, gowns were ten times as expensive as uniforms. With the blockade, gowns are only seven times as expensive as uniforms. The blockade has reduced the price of evening gowns relative to the price of uniforms.

The blockade alters the composition of imported goods in favor of luxury items, which tend to have high value-to-bulk ratios. The lower relative prices of these items stimulate consumption of these items, and black-market entrepreneurs respond to consumer demands. The Southern blockade runners were not incompetent; they were simply reacting to market conditions. The trade in luxury items was relatively more profitable. Although this example is historically based, the Rhett Butler effect will be observed in the modern world.

Blockades and embargoes, especially the latter, are often-used foreign-policy tools. As of this writing, the U.S. government has ongoing embargoes on trade with Cuba, Iraq, and the former Yugoslavian state of Serbia. These measures are intended to influence the policies of the governments involved by imposing economic hardships. Although the embargoes go a long way in reducing the quantity of American goods exported to these countries, it is doubtful that American goods are unavailable. The Rhett Butler effect tells us that we would find a preponderance of luxuries among the American goods being smuggled into these countries. The embargoes also seek to eliminate trade going the other way; that is, it is illegal to import goods from Cuba, Iraq, and Serbia. Again, the Rhett Butler effect tells us that we would expect to find Cuban, Iraqi, and Serbian luxury items taking precedence in the smuggling of goods from these countries. It will be hard to find an American cigar smoker who has not had a Cuban cigar.

There are activities and products whose effects are deemed, at one time or another, so harmful that they are simply banned. The Eighteenth Amendment to the U.S. Constitution prohibited the production and consumption of alcoholic beverages. Today most countries prohibit the trade in substances whose only or major attractions are their intoxicating effects. All efforts to prohibit a product or activity do so by criminalizing the good or service. Producers and consumers are subject to legal sanctions if caught and convicted of participating in the proscribed market. The immediate effect of criminalization is to eliminate the legal market for the good.

Producers and consumers of proscribed goods are denied access to the usual market settings. As was discussed in Chapter 1, the legal system is an important adjunct to market activity. Legal institutions set the rules of the game as far as trade is concerned. Of particular importance are contract law and its rules governing the transfer of property rights. The law of contract encourages economic activity by protecting the interests of buyers and sellers. Although buyers and sellers could protect their own interests, contract law does so at a lower cost and thus encourages market activity. The protection of contract law that is enforced through the courts is extended only to those activities that are sanctioned by government. Any trade in a proscribed good that might take place must do so through illegal or black markets.

Black markets operate on the same basic principles as legal markets: a demand (the black-market demand) and a supply (the black-market supply) interact to determine the black-market equilibrium. The demand for a good in a black market is likely to be less than the demand that would arise in a legal market for the good. Although the forbidden nature of the prohibited item might lure some consumers into the market, the possible criminal sanctions scare away other consumers and the demand for the good decreases. The passage of the Eighteenth Amendment might have tempted some teetotalers into trying "demon rum," but it also discouraged those who imbibed only casually and occasionally. Prohibition also closes off the usual, legal market distribution channels. Sellers become harder to find because they cannot advertise their product or location. Transactions must take place surreptitiously in back-alley speak-easies to avoid detection. Buyers will also have to worry about the quality of the produce (getting wood rather than grain alcohol) because the normal consumer-protection laws no longer apply. In general, buyers will find that the transactions costs of purchasing the forbidden produce have risen, causing a further decrease in demand. The effects of the Eighteenth Amendment on the demand for rum is illustrated in Figure 5.14. The curve labeled D_0 is the market demand that would prevail if rum consumption were legal. The black-market demand is at D_1, which represents a decrease from D_0.

Prohibition also decreases the supply of the proscribed good or service. Criminalization reduces the number of sellers by driving legitimate businesses out of the market. Prohibition raises the marginal costs of producing and selling the good, amplifying the decrease in supply. The Eighteenth Amendment drove the production of rum underground. Clandestine operations are generally smaller and entail higher production costs. Rum that was formerly imported from Jamaica now must be smuggled across the border, because legitimate transportation networks cannot be used for fear of being detected and having one's product confiscated. This raises the shipping costs of the illegally imported rum. Additionally, rum producers and sellers face the costs of criminal prosecution and attempts to avoid prosecution. The cost of paying off public officials, attorneys' fees, court costs, and court-imposed fines and prison sentences must be added to the black-market operations. All in all, the supply of rum will fall (shift leftward) as a result of prohibition. This decrease in supply is illustrated in Figure 5.14 as the movement of the supply curve from the legitimate supply, S_0, to S_1, the black-market supply.

Figure 5.14 The Eighteenth Amendment and the Market for Rum

Prohibition reduced both the supply and demand for rum. The combined effects of the two shifts in the market curves are to decrease the quantity of rum consumed. Where the decrease in the supply of rum is relatively larger than the decrease in demand, the equilibrium price of rum will rise.

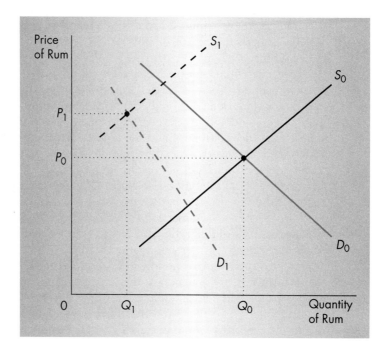

Prohibition causes simultaneous decreases in the supply and demand for rum. A decrease in demand, if supply remains constant, puts downward pressure on both price and quantity. A decrease in supply, demand being constant, puts downward pressure on quantity but upward pressure on price. Because both changes have similar effects on quantity, we can conclude that prohibition will reduce the amount of rum consumed, as illustrated in Figure 5.14. The main goal of prohibition, however, the elimination of alcohol consumption, is achieved if and only if the government is able to reduce demand and supply to the extent that the demand lies everywhere below the supply.

Prohibition's effect on the price of rum depends on how far the curves shift relative to one another. The simultaneous decreases in both supply and demand have opposite effects on the equilibrium price. Figure 5.14 was drawn to illustrate what often happens in black markets. The decrease in supply is large relative to the decrease in demand, resulting in higher prices in the black market.

Although prohibition may derive from the noblest of intentions, it seldom accomplishes its goals. At best, prohibition reduces consumption while raising the price of the proscribed good. If the goal is simply to restrict consumption, the government has less draconian measures, such as taxes, for restricting the quantity traded in the market.

Summary

The world of every individual is filled with surroundings, events, and institutions that can be usefully analyzed with the simple theory of consumer behavior and simple demand and supply. This chapter discusses only a sampling of a very wide array of applications. You can undoubtedly think of many more. This chapter

- discussed the effects of price regulation and direct restrictions on product quality.
- analyzed the impact of student loans on student behavior and choice.
- showed how prices can be manipulated to encourage conservation when resources become especially scarce.
- presented an analysis of nonprice rationing, which includes applications to "gut" courses and immigration.
- applied the tools of demand and supply and consumer behavior to a wide variety of issues including school choice, health care, and drug and alcohol prohibitions.

Sample Questions

Question

In our discussion of a voucher system, we have assumed that a student has to choose between a public school and a private school. Suppose, instead, that it is possible to obtain education from both. Specifically, assume that the student can attend public school and then obtain additional units of education from private tutors or by attending a private school in the evening at a price of $1,000 per unit of education. How would this option affect the budget line?

Answer

In terms of Figure 5.10, this would enable the family to select any point on a budget line that starts at point B and is parallel to BL_1.

Question

Ticket "scalping" is sometimes viewed as a terrible problem, and great pains are taken to stop the practice. For example, Garth Brooks has started an active campaign against organized scalping of tickets to his concerts. Any number of complex schemes have been designed and implemented to prevent fans from standing in line for many hours and to prevent the resale of concert tickets once they are issued. For example, for some concerts, randomly numbered tickets are issued to fans. The lucky fans who get low numbers are then able to buy tickets the day of the concert without having to spend hours in line.

If you view long lines and resale as a problem, can you think of any other type of solution?

Answer

This can be viewed as a pricing problem. Fans are willing to stand in line for long periods of time when tickets are sold at prices below the market-clearing level. Resale occurs when the tickets are issued in such a way that some people who place relatively low values on tickets obtain them, whereas others who value the tickets more highly fail to get a ticket. If the tickets are priced at a market-clearing level (say $50), everyone who values a ticket at $50 or more will obtain a ticket. Fans who fail to buy a ticket will be those who value the ticket at less than $50. The opportunity to scalp tickets will be nonexistent.

Questions for Review and Discussion

1. How do the immediate and long-term effects of minimum-wage legislation in the labor market differ?
2. What happens to the demand and supply of apartments when rent control remains in effect for a long time period?
*3. Suppose that the government regulates the prices of oranges and grapefruit below their equilibrium levels. Who (if anyone) will benefit from this regulation?
*4. Explain the rationale behind a taxation program that provides equal rebates to consumers.
5. What are the most important objectives of a rationing scheme? Does nonprice rationing meet these objectives?
6. What nonprice rationing scheme most closely reaches the goal of allocating the good to its highest valued use? What is the drawback of this scheme?
7. Suppose you are living with two roommates. What are the consequences of sharing all household expenses in three equal shares?
*8. Who is most likely to be best served the current framework of subsidized public education? Does your answer depend on family tastes for education?
9. How would the introduction of a voucher system affect families who have their children in private schools?
10. If the proposed system of national health care is instituted, will it really provide "free" health care to citizens? If not, how will it be financed and how will the appropriate "price" be determined?
11. Was Secretary of Education William Bennett correct when he criticized student-loan programs, claiming that loans financed vacations rather than

tuition for college students? Explain the effect on students' budget lines and on their behavior.

12. What is the most efficient way to allocate seats in a university class that is "always filled?"

Problems for Analysis

*1. Public schools differ with regard to "quality" — the number of units of educational services they supply to students. Can you use budget lines and indifference curves to explain why many families move (often at great cost) because of differences in the quality of public school systems?

2. Is there an optimal amount of safety for any product? Is the optimal amount identical to the maximum possible amount? Do you think that government regulatory agencies come close to optimal safety levels in their regulations?

3. Should those who receive food coupons be permitted to sell them?

*4. At many universities, the practice of ticketing students for parking violations becomes a subject of controversy. Students often argue that the university intentionally limits student parking in order to "profit" from the student fines. One solution would be for the university to refund all the money they collect from fines — perhaps by dividing the total equally among students. If this policy were enacted, would students have any incentive to avoid parking tickets? Would illegal parking by students increase?

5. Some countries try to limit emigration. Would a policy of auctioning the right to be an emigrant have some desirable consequences similar to those associated with auctioning the right to become an immigrant?

6. It is illegal to practice medicine without a license. Assuming that licensing improves the quality of physicians, is licensing a good deal to consumers of health care?

7. Safety records can be improved either by reducing the number of "accidents" or by reducing the injuries caused by each action. Is it possible that safety regulations designed to *reduce* the severity of injuries may have the effect of *increasing* the number of accidents?

The Theory of the Firm

CHAPTER 6

The Firm and the Theory of Production

Part II of this text dealt almost exclusively with consumer behavior. The analysis was greatly simplified by, in effect, ignoring the actions of sellers. The seller's role in consumer demand theory is essentially passive. From the perspective of the buyers, sellers produce and sell whatever quantity buyers wish to purchase, with the price being left unexplained. In Chapter 3, a utility-maximizing consumer had to choose between food and wine when the prices of food and wine were given. Individual demand curves were derived in Chapter 4 by positing alternative prices for a good and observing what happened to the utility-maximizing quantity of the good. Prices were altered repeatedly without reference to the impact of the price changes on sellers.

This chapter moves the sellers to center stage by investigating the firm and the production process. Although these topics are important in and of themselves, the theories of production and cost (the subject of Chapter 7) lay the foundation for understanding alternative models of buyer/seller interaction, the subject of Part IV of this text. The objectives of this chapter are straightforward; we seek to provide a basis for understanding

- the nature and motivations of producers and sellers,
- the relationships between inputs and outputs as embodied in production functions,
- production relations and choices when one or more inputs are fixed,
- production relations and choices when all inputs are variable,
- the relationship between the short-run and long-run options faced by the firm.

The Firm and Its Objectives: Analogies to Consumer Behavior

Central to explaining the behavior of those on the supply side of the market is the concept of the firm. In the most general terms, a **firm** is an economic

217

institution that specializes in **production**, the process of transforming resources (inputs) into products (outputs). A wide range of organizations fall under this broad definition of the firm. Government agencies, public enterprises, social clubs, religious organizations, and charities all transform inputs into outputs. Although it is useful (and often enlightening) to view organizations like the defense department, publicly owned and operated utilities, the Benevolent and Paternal Order of Elks, the Catholic Church, and the Red Cross as firms, that is not our concern here. Because the focus of this text is on the market, we are most concerned with the most common form that the firm takes in a market economy: a privately owned and operated business.

The Nature of the Firm

Privately owned and operated businesses dominate the supply side of markets. Although they may differ in the form of ownership (corporations, partnerships, and so on) and size (from Ford Motor Company to the local newsstand), the rationale for the existence of a firm is the same, regardless of the specific characteristics of the firm. Business firms exist because they are, as Ronald Coase (the 1991 Nobel laureate in economics) pointed out, the least-cost means of organizing production.[1] A firm is able to produce a given quantity of output at a lower cost (or a greater output at the same cost) than alternative means of organizing production. The firm accomplishes this by taking advantage of team production methods and by avoiding some of the transactions costs of organizing resources.

Transactions Costs. There are a number of ways to organize production. Suppose Fred wants a new home. One way for Fred to get a new home is to build it himself, presuming that Fred has all the necessary knowledge and skills to build a house. Another of Fred's options is to go through the market and to oversee the construction himself. There are, however, costs associated with using the market. These **transactions costs** include all the expenses and resources consumed to finalize the transaction. Transactions costs typically include the cost of

- obtaining the relevant information,
- searching for the best price or product,
- negotiating the terms of the transaction.

The transactions costs of building a house will be substantial. Fred will have to determine what resources he will need to build his house, identify appropriate suppliers, negotiate contracts with each of the suppliers, and see that the contracts are fulfilled. Fred will have to arrange the delivery of the materials (such as lumber, concrete, pipe, insulation, nails, wire, brick, glass,

1. See Ronald Coase, "The Nature of the Firm," *Economica*, 1937.

etc.) and hire and oversee architects, carpenters, bricklayers, electricians, and other crafts and trades. Clearly, this can be a daunting task.

If Fred does what the majority of new home buyers do, he will contract with a firm that specializes in home construction. Fred will probably find that he can buy a house from a builder (or a firm that specializes in building houses) at a lower cost than he could achieve himself. A builder, or any firm, can produce at a lower cost than an individual by avoiding some of the transactions costs of market activity. A firm establishes relationships with resource suppliers and thereby avoids the costs of searching for and negotiating with numerous suppliers in the market. The existing relationships between the firm and its suppliers free all from the need to negotiate contracts for each unit of the good that buyers might want to purchase. In all likelihood, the builder that sells Fred his new house will have some working agreement with a building-materials supplier and work crews to handle all the different stages of the construction process, from pouring the foundation to doing the final touch-up on the interior. The builder can construct homes at a lower cost, because she need not be engaged in continuous negotiations to continue construction.

Firms' agreements with their resource suppliers have a feature that further reduces the costs of production. The agreements generally define who is responsible for decision making within the firms. The operation of any business is a complex task with a multitude of decisions to be made. Although it would be possible to debate and negotiate each and every question, such a decision-making process would be time consuming and costly. The firm avoids these costs by assigning decision-making authority. Whereas the builder will be responsible for deciding where the walls go, it will be the framers who decide how the walls are nailed together. Internally, the firm operates on a command rather than a negotiated (or possibly democratic) basis.

Team Production. The firm's reliance on a command system for making decisions is closely related to another advantage of the firm. The command system is ideally suited to regulating team production. **Team production** involves the cooperation of individual resource suppliers in the production of a good or service. Individuals specialize in different tasks, and the resulting division of labor increases team and firm output. A thousand people working together to assemble automobiles will be able to produce more than a thousand people working independently. The fruits of the team effort are then distributed among the team members. An individual's reward for participating in team production is some fraction of the increase in output. Because team production relies on the effort expended by each team member, an individual's contribution to the process is not readily discernible. This feature of team production creates a perverse incentive.

Maximum team output requires maximum effort from each team member. The individual who provides less than maximum work effort, what economists call **shirking**, captures all of the benefits of shirking — a less taxing workday.

If the individual's share of team output is fixed, the costs of shirking, a reduction in team output, is distributed among all team members. In this situation, we should expect to observe shirking by rational workers. The individual benefits of shirking will exceed the individual costs, and individuals will have an incentive to reduce their work effort. Suppose that your economics professor decided to make your next exam a team effort. All students would receive the class average for the exam, rather than their individual score. How much time would *you* spend studying for the next exam under this grading scheme?[2] Because both you and your classmates would have an incentive to shirk, the advantages of team production would not be realized. Fortunately, firms are generally able to deter shirking. If those responsible for overseeing production (foremen or managers) are able to identify the shirkers, shirking can be reduced by punishing the offenders. The shirker's share of team output can be reduced, or shirkers can be kicked off the team. The overseers can provide incentives for maximum effort by rewarding those who provide superior work effort. Workers benefit from this system, because the output from team production is greater than the output from individual production. The command system benefits each member of the team by reducing shirking, increasing team output, and increasing each member's share of the output. The firm's ability to effectively use team production methods gives it an advantage over other means of organizing production.

Team Production and the Legal Forms of Business. The legal form that a business takes may be determined by the nature of the team production process. Businesses can take one of three basic legal forms: proprietorship, partnership, or corporation. A **proprietorship** is a firm that is owned and operated by an individual. A **partnership** is owned and operated by two or more individuals. Ownership in a **corporation** is represented by the firm's stock, and the stockholders hire managers to operate the firm.

The sole proprietorship is the optimal form of enterprise when there are relatively few team members and the team requires relatively little capital to accomplish its tasks. It is no coincidence that most newsstands are proprietorships. The limited requirements in terms of space (a few hundred square feet) and inventory (the magazines and newspapers) enable individuals to finance (from their personal wealth) the operations of the firm. A small team (one salesperson) also permits effective managerial control by a single owner. However, there is a limit to what one individual can afford and manage, and proprietorships reflect this in their propensity to be small organizations.

The partnership is particularly well suited for those team production

2. This is a special case of a more general economic phenomenon called the free-rider problem. The **free-rider problem** develops whenever an individual can avoid the costs of an activity without sacrificing the benefits of the activity. Chapter 15 provides a thorough examination of the free-rider problem.

processes in which shirking is difficult to detect. Law and accounting firms tend to be organized as partnerships because of this problem. Is an employee thinking about the results of an audit, or is he daydreaming? Is the employee on the phone to obtain new business, or is he talking to a friend? If shirking is difficult to detect, those who are responsible for monitoring shirkers will be unable to do so. Shirking will become the norm and team output will decline significantly. The incentive to shirk can be reduced by making the team member a partner in the enterprise. As partners, individuals have an economic stake in the performance of the firm. A partner bears the costs of shirking (lower profits), and the incentives to shirk are reduced.

The corporate form of business is particularly well suited for enterprises with large teams and large capital requirements, such as automobile or computer manufacturing. For legal purposes the corporation is treated as a separate entity with the right to own property and incur liabilities. One consequence of this separate legal existence is that it shields the owners from personal liability for any debts of the firm. Ownership of the corporation is represented in homogeneous units called the firm's stock. The sale of stock is an important means of raising funds to finance large-scale operations. Investors are willing to purchase corporate stock because

- their potential losses are limited to the price they paid for the stock,
- the ownership of stock is transferable, making it easy for investors to adjust their portfolios,
- the divisibility of corporate equity puts the price of stock within the means of many more investors.

Firm Objectives

As specialists in production, the directors or managers of firms

- determine what product to produce,
- decide how much to produce,
- find the "best" means of producing the product,
- acquire the necessary resources,
- oversee the resources as they are transformed into output, and
- sell the output to consumers.

The motive behind their decision to undertake such complicated and often risky tasks is quite simple: profits.

Profit Maximization.   At the core of the theory of the firm is the notion that firms are profit maximizers. Firm motivation follows directly from the notion of rational economic behavior introduced in Chapter 1. Although it is convenient to speak of the firm in the abstract, firm behavior is the result of human actions. Because rational self-interest provides a good basis for understanding

"You know what I think, folks? Improving technology isn't important. Increased profits aren't important. What's important is to be warm, decent human beings."

human behavior, rational self-interest will also provide the foundation for understanding *firm* behavior. Firm decision makers undertake production for the sake of profit, not out of some other desire, such as to promote the public interest. Moreover, because rational self-interest also entails the notion of maximizing net benefits, the firm seeks to maximize its profits.

The notion that firms always *succeed* in maximizing profits is easy to refute. Given the uncertainties and complexities of business life, it is impossible for firms to come up with strategies that earn them the greatest possible profit in all situations.[3] However, it is realistic to assume that firms *attempt* to maximize profits. The theory developed from the profit-maximization assumption allows us to predict firm behavior in many different situations. It is important to remember that accurate prediction, and not realism of assumption, is the goal of economic theory.

Alternative Views of Firm Objectives. The notion that firms are motivated by profits assumes that the people who manage the firm are motivated by profits. If there

3. For a discussion of the impossibility of profit maximization see A. Alchian, "Uncertainty, Evolution, and Economic Theory," *Journal of Political Economy*, 1950.

is no direct relationship between firm profits and managerial compensation, rational self-interest will take the firm in other directions. If managerial compensation is related to the level of sales, a sales-maximization assumption will be more appropriate. If employee compensation is unrelated or weakly related to some economic measure of firm performance, the firm might pursue any number of objectives.

In firms in which economic performance is not the objective, managers may attempt to maximize their individual utility by devoting firm resources to luxurious offices, country club memberships, and/or chauffeured company limousines. If profits are not the goal of the firm, the decision makers, being rational in an economic sense, will seek to maximize something else. This helps explain the prevalence of profit-sharing plans, employee stock ownership plans, and other business practices that tie compensation to profits.

The theory of the firm at the intermediate level deals with profit-seeking firms. Profits are the difference between a firm's revenues and its costs. Revenues are determined by the demand for the product. Costs are defined by the relationships between the inputs and the output. The remainder of this chapter is devoted to this relationship between inputs and outputs, a relationship that is summarized by the production function.

The Theory of Production

The primary function of a firm is to transform resources into finished products. A bakery combines flour, sugar, fruit, ovens, energy, and the talents of its employees, and the result is some sweet confection. The manner in which the finished product is obtained is determined by the prices and quantities of resources, the qualities of the resources, and technology. For simplicity we speak of four categories of resources:

1. *labor,* which includes nearly all forms of human power
2. *capital,* which encompasses resources such as plant and equipment that must be produced
3. *land,* which is defined to include all natural resources
4. *entrepreneurship,* a specialized form of labor that identifies profitable opportunities and bears the risk of failure or garners the fruits of success inherent in pursuing profits

Resources are always combined using some level of technology. **Technology** includes all knowledge regarding the utilization of resources. The essence of production is the bringing together of resources, using existing technology, to create goods and services.

Production Functions

The relationship between inputs and outputs is summarized by the **production function**.[4] The production function describes a subset of the alternative levels of output that can be obtained from a subset of the alternative combinations of inputs, given the available technology. The only output levels and associated input combinations included in the production function are those that are technologically efficient.

Efficiency in Production. The production function incorporates only efficient production alternatives. **Technological efficiency** is achieved when the greatest output is received from each input combination. Note that this type of efficiency looks only at quantities: the quantities of inputs are compared with the quantity of output. Technological efficiency ignores the expenses incurred when inputs are used in production.[5]

Technological efficiency is a consequence of rational behavior. The rational producer is a profit maximizer. Profits cannot be maximized unless the firm is using its resources efficiently in the technical sense. For a given level of resources, the firm cannot have maximum profits unless it is getting maximum output.

X-inefficiency exists whenever a producer obtains less than maximum output from a given quantity of resources.[6] This type of inefficiency is likely to arise whenever firms pursue goals other than profit maximization. If managers are maximizing their utility, the firm is likely to be x-inefficient. If management spends too much time on the golf course (via country club memberships purchased with company funds) and too little time monitoring shirkers, team output will fall. The firm will not be achieving maximum output from the resources that it employs.[7]

Production Notation. The production function concept can be summarized in equation form:

$$Q(Q_1, Q_2, \ldots, Q_M) = f(I_1, I_2, \ldots, I_N)$$

---

4. Production functions are the producer's counterpart to the consumer's utility function. In a sense, utility functions are production functions: they show how consumer goods are combined to produce consumer satisfaction. Although similar, utility functions and production functions differ in an important mathematical characteristic. Production functions are cardinal functions, whereas utility functions are ordinal. The values indicated by a cardinal function indicate magnitudes in an absolute sense; that is, 200 miles is twice as far as 100 miles. The values indicated by an ordinal function indicate rank or order; that is, 30 degrees Celsius is warmer than 20 degrees.

5. The next chapter integrates the costs of production into the production relations.

6. A discussion of the concept of X-inefficiency can be found in H. Leibenstein, "Allocative Efficiency and X-Efficiency," *American Economic Review,* 1966.

7. This example also shows that those who monitor shirkers have an incentive to shirk as well. This is to be expected, because shirking is rational economic behavior.

which is read as follows: the rate of output (Q) is a function (f) of the amount of inputs (I) that are used. This form of the production function is a generalized form. Neither the number of inputs nor the number of outputs is explicitly stated. The generalized function allows for N different inputs (denoted by the subscripts to the I's) and M different outputs (denoted by the subscripts to the Q's). This indeterminacy in the number of inputs and outputs reflects real-world experience. Few, if any, production processes involve one input and one output.

The necessity of taking multiple inputs and outputs into account is illustrated by considering the automobile industry. The production of automobiles requires many different types of labor, a multitude of different tools and machinery, and various raw and processed materials. The number of different types of inputs would surely reach into the thousands. The world's major automakers also produce multiple products, from subcompacts to luxury sports sedans to a wide variety of trucks. The explicit recognition of multiple outputs is a reminder that production may entail by-products (both desirable and undesirable) and variable output quality. The Q in the generalized production equation might represent the output of automobiles, where quality can be varied during the production process. Clearly, real-world production processes are extremely complex operations.

The Production Process Simplified. This text reduces the theory of production to the essentials that are necessary to understand a firm's behavior. This is achieved by assuming that production involves two homogeneous inputs, labor (L) and capital (K), and a homogeneous output (Q). In this abstract case, the production function can be written

$$Q = f(L, K)$$

where the $f(\ )$ represents the quantitative relationship between combinations of labor and capital and the level of output. The convenience of mathematical notation notwithstanding, there are other, very useful ways of representing a production function.

Input-Output Tables. Production functions can be presented in tabular form through an input-output table. An **input-output table** lists the quantity produced when selected combinations of the inputs are employed. Table 6.1 is an input-output table for a *hypothetical* production function. The rows of the table list different quantities of capital, and columns represent different quantities of labor. The cell at the intersection of a row and a column indicates the output that would result from the technologically efficient combination of the quantities of labor and capital represented by the column and row, respectively. For example, 4 units of labor and 3 units of capital will produce 19 units of output in our hypothetical production function. You should note that certain characteristics of this hypothetical example may or may not hold for real-world

Table 6.1 A Hypothetical Production Function
The table below, a tabular representation of a production function,
shows the maximum output that can be obtained from alternative
combinations of labor and capital.

L K	1	2	3	4	5	6	7	8
1	1	3	6	10	15	19	22	24
2	3	6	10	15	19	22	24	25
3	6	10	15	19	22	24	25	25
4	10	15	19	22	24	25	25	24
5	15	19	22	24	25	25	24	22

production functions. In particular, Table 6.1 shows cases in which output falls
as additional labor and capital are used. If the additional inputs can be freely
dispensed with, such reductions in output can be avoided.

The Production Surface. The information contained in Table 6.1 can be depicted
graphically as in Figure 6.1. Because there are three variables (labor, capital,
and output), the graphical form of the production function will be three-
dimensional. Such a graphical representation is called a *production surface.* The
height of the surface indicates the level of output, and the location in the horizontal plane represents a labor/capital combination. For example, the combination of 1 unit of capital and 5 units of labor produces 15 units of output.

Although the production surface illustrates the most basic production
problem, choosing among alternative combinations of inputs to obtain output,
it is rarely used in production theory. Few of us have enough artistic talent to
draw three-dimensional figures that are easy to interpret. Moreover, a problem
with three variables is more difficult to solve than a problem with two variables. Production theory takes this into account and simplifies the problem by
holding one of the three production variables constant while letting the other
two vary. This leaves two sets of two-variable problems: (1) hold output constant and vary the two inputs, and (2) hold one input constant and investigate
the relationship between output and the quantities of the other input.

Two Classes of Production Problems

The two basic sets of production problems are classified as long-run and short-
run production problems. The **long run** is defined as a period of time during
which all inputs are variable. The long-run production problem is to find the
optimum combination of inputs for each level of output. The **short run** is
defined as a period of time during which at least one input is fixed. In the
short run, the problem is to find the optimum quantity of a variable input to

Figure 6.1 The Production Surface

A production surface is a three-dimensional representation of a production function. The level of output is measured vertically and input usage is measured in the horizontal plane.

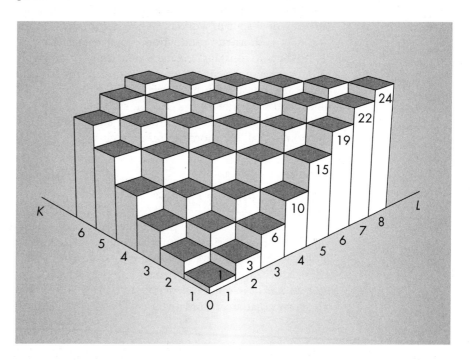

use with the fixed quantity of the other input. In terms of our production function, $Q = f(K,L)$, the long run involves holding Q constant (at least temporarily) while we vary K and L. The short run holds K constant while allowing L and Q to vary.

It is important to note that the terms *long run* and *short run* refer to operational time, not calendar time. We don't measure economic time in terms of weeks, months, or years. We measure economic time in terms of a decision maker's ability to make and implement a decision. In production, the difference between the long run and the short run hinges on the manager's ability to alter the firm's use of an input. The amount of capital employed by the firm is held constant in the short run but is variable in the long run. The amount of calendar time associated with the two runs depends on the type of capital involved. The long run in the pizza-delivery market tends to be quite short. The capital used to deliver pizzas — cars and trucks — can be purchased and put into service rapidly. On the other hand, the long run in the power industry tends to be very long. It can take a decade to plan, build, and bring a power plant on line. Although the long runs in these two industries are quite different, the analysis of each will be equivalent.

Production Choices in the Short Run

Short-run production theory examines the relationship between inputs and outputs when some of the inputs are fixed. The Sony Corporation is implementing a short-run decision when it increases television production by hiring an additional shift of workers. When the production function is of the form $Q = f(K,L)$, a short-run production choice entails changes in Q with variations in L, holding K constant. Fixing the quantity of capital and varying the amount of labor is equivalent to moving along a row in Table 6.1. Although such tables do indicate the basic relationships, the theory of production is usually illustrated in graphic form. Taking the data from a row in Table 6.1 and displaying it graphically, along with some modifications, produces what economists call the short-run product curves.

Short-Run Product Curves

Short-run product curves depict the geometric relationship between output and the use of a variable input. The plural is used because there are three economically relevant ways to measure output. The product curves reflect output measured in total, average, and marginal terms. Although these measures of output are developed independently, there are certain relationships between the curves that are informative.

Table 6.2 Hypothetical Short-Run Production Table
The table lists the short-run production relationships: the total product of labor, average product, or output per worker, and marginal product, the additional output from adding additional workers to the production process.

Labor Input	Total Product	Average Product	Marginal Product
1	6	6	—
2	10	5	4
3	15	5	5
4	19	4.75	4
5	22	4.5	3
6	24	4	2
7	25	3.56	1
8	25	3.13	0

Figure 6.2 The Total-Product Curve

The total-product curve shows the level of output (Q) obtained from employing varying quantities of labor (L) with a fixed amount of capital.

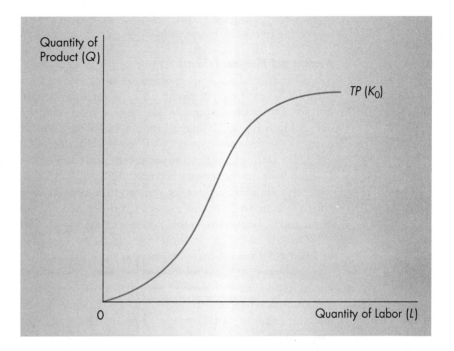

Total Product. The level of output that is associated with alternative amounts of labor, holding capital constant, is called the **total product** (*TP*) of labor. A total-product relationship can be derived from the hypothetical data of Table 6.1. Fixing the amount of capital at 3 units, the relationship between labor and output is found in the center row of Table 6.1. These data are rearranged to form the first two columns of Table 6.2, where alternative amounts of labor and the resulting output are displayed.

Thus far, our examples of production relationships have been confined to discrete intervals (that is, only whole numbers were considered). The theory of production generally assumes that all variables are infinitely divisible and that production functions are smooth and continuous. Smoothing the production relationships illustrated in the first two columns of Table 6.2 and graphing the data generates the total-product curve depicted in Figure 6.2. This is equivalent to taking a vertical slice (one that runs parallel to the labor axis) out of a production surface.

The total-product (*TP*) curve in Figure 6.2 is drawn as it usually appears in the theory of production. The *TP* curve initially rises at an increasing rate, goes through an area in which it increases at a decreasing rate, and reaches a maximum. Although the specific shape and position of the total-product curve are contrived, they are contrived to agree with what has been observed in the real-world. Real-world experience indicates that the rate of change in output follows the pattern described. This pattern is an important consideration in one of the two remaining product curves.

Average and Marginal Products. Table 6.2 includes two additional measures of output in the short run: average product and marginal product. **Average product** (AP) is output per unit of the variable input. It is found by dividing output (Q) by the amount of the variable input employed (L), or $AP = Q/L$. The column labeled Average Product in Table 6.2 is derived by dividing each entry in the second column by the entry in the first column. **Marginal product** (MP) is the change in output resulting from a one-unit change in the variable input or, in mathematical terms, $MP = \Delta Q/\Delta L$. Each entry in column 4 is equal to the difference between the entry in column 2 and the entry in the row above in column 2. In this example, it is not necessary to divide by the change in the input, because the table posits unit changes in the input.

The rate of change in short-run output because of a change in the amount of labor employed is measured by the marginal product of labor. Initially, the marginal product of labor is low, because there are not enough workers to effectively utilize the fixed capital. Consider a pizza-delivery outlet in which the amount of capital (building, ovens, delivery vehicles, and so on) is fixed and the number of workers is variable. The first worker would have a low marginal product, because she would not be able to get many pizzas delivered. The lone employee would have to take orders and make, bake, cut, box, and deliver the pizzas. However, if two workers are employed, the marginal product of labor will be higher. Two workers can divide up the tasks and get proportionately more pizzas delivered. As workers are added, the marginal product will rise to a peak. The number of workers will reach a point at which the "team" meshes well with the fixed capital. This might occur when the pizza-delivery business has one person taking orders, three more making pizzas in assembly-line fashion, another baking, cutting, and boxing the pizzas, and one driver for each delivery vehicle. At this point, the marginal product of labor is at a maximum. Beyond this point, additional workers result in a *declining* marginal product. Additional delivery personnel will have a low marginal product, because there are no more vehicles and the only way they can deliver pizza is on foot. Additional workers employed inside the outlet will tend to get in each other's way, reducing the marginal productivity of the labor force. The establishment can even get to a point at which additional workers have a negative marginal product. The pizza outlet can get so crowded that output declines with extra workers.

The Principle of Diminishing Marginal Returns. The total product curve takes its shape from the initial rise and subsequent fall in the marginal product of labor. The tendency of marginal products to decline is so widespread that this empirical tendency is given a name: the principle of diminishing marginal returns. The principle of **diminishing marginal returns** states that as additional units of a variable input are combined with a fixed input, the marginal product of the variable input will ultimately begin to fall. This property of short-run production relationships seems to be everywhere. A home gardener may find that he can increase the yield he gets from his ten tomato plants by applying fertilizer, by watering, or by using his labor time to remove harmful insects from his tomato plants. However, for each of these activities, the marginal product (the increase in tomato production) will eventually decline. Similarly, a student who spends time proofing a term paper may be able to find and correct 20 errors in the first hour he spends going over the paper. Should he spend a second hour, it is almost certain that the number of additional errors detected will be less than 20.

Any car dealer knows that the number of cars he can sell depends in part on the number of salespeople he employs. But once again, the marginal product (the increase in cars sold) will eventually diminish as additional salespeople are employed. Because this relationship seems to be universal, it is central to our explanation of short-run firm behavior.

The relationship between marginal and total product is illustrated in Figure 6.3. When the total product is increasing at an increasing rate (when the total-product curve is getting steeper), the marginal product is increasing. This occurs over the range from 0 to L in Figure 6.3. When the total product increases at a decreasing rate (when the total-product curve gets flatter), the marginal-product curve decreases. This occurs in the range from L_1 to L_2. At L_2, the total-product curve is at its maximum, and the marginal product is zero. Beyond L_2, total product falls and the marginal product is negative.

Short-Run Production Relationships

Short-run production choices will be influenced by the relationships among the total, marginal, and average products. There are precise mathematical and geometric relationships among the short-run product curves. The geometric properties of short-run production relationships are illustrated in Figure 6.4. Marginal product is the rate of change in total product, which is measured by the slope of the total-product curve. Geometrically, we measure the slope of a curve with the slope of the line tangent to the curve. Starting at the origin, the slopes of the lines tangent to the total-product curve increase up to point B, indicating that the marginal product is rising. From point B to point D, the tangent lines decrease in slope, indicating a declining marginal product. If marginal product is rising up to point B and falling thereafter, marginal product must reach a maximum at point B when L_2 workers are employed. At point D the tangent line is horizontal; that is, it has a slope of zero. This is the point at which the marginal product is zero and total product is at its maximum.

Figure 6.3 Marginal and Total Products

The shape of the marginal-product curve in panel b depends on the shape of the total-product curve in panel a. Between 0 and L_1 units of labor, the total product is increasing at an increasing rate, and the marginal product rises to its maximum level. From L_1 to L_2, total product gets flatter and the marginal product falls. At L_2 the total product is at its maximum level and the marginal product is zero.

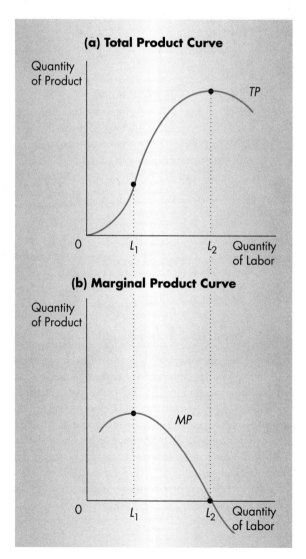

Figure 6.4 The Geometry of the Short-Run Product Curves

The slopes of the lines tangent to the *TP* curve in panel (a) are the *MP* curve shown in panel (b). The slopes of the lines from the origin to points on the *TP* curve in panel (a) form the *AP* curve in panel (b). The line tangent to the *TP* curve at point *C* also passes through the origin, indicating that the marginal and average product are equal when L_3 workers are employed.

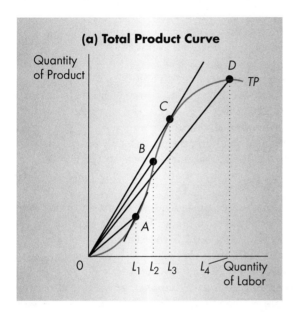

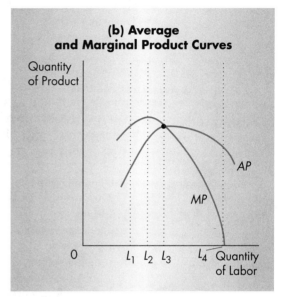

To understand the relationship between total product and average product, it is important to clarify the definition of the average product: $AP = Q/L$. Average product is output (the height of the total-product curve above the horizontal axis) divided by the quantity of labor (the horizontal distance from the origin to the quantity of labor used to produce the output). Graphically, the average product is the (vertical) rise of the total-product curve divided by the corresponding (horizontal) increases in L, with both values starting from the origin. This ratio equals the slope of the straight line from the origin to a point on the total-product curve. The average product at point *B* in Figure 6.4 is the slope of the line from the origin to point *B*. The average-product curve can be determined graphically by calculating the slope of each line emanating from the origin and going to the total-product curve, and then plotting the slope against labor. The average-product curve labeled *AP* in panel (b) of Figure 6.4 is derived in this manner.

There is an unusual convergence at point *C* in Figure 6.4. The line tangent to the total-product curve at point *C* also passes through the origin. At L_3 units of labor, the average and marginal products are equal. The line from the origin to point *C* is also the steepest of all lines that pass through the origin and intersect the total-product curve. This means that the average product is at a maximum at L_3, where it is intersected by the marginal-product curve.

There is another class of short-run production relationships that bears on the short-run production problem.

Average product

- rises when marginal product is greater than average product,
- falls when marginal product is less than average product, and
- is at a maximum when marginal product equals average product.

These relationships are true by virtue of the definitions of total, average, and marginal variables. The marginal is the value of an additional unit of a variable. If the marginal is greater than the average, the marginal is adding proportionately more to the total and is driving the average up. If the marginal is less than the average, the marginal is adding proportionately less to the total and is dragging the average down. If the marginal is equal to the average, the marginal is adding a proportionately equal amount to the total, and the average remains the same.

The relationship between your scores on individual exams and your average on exams (the usual basis for the course grade) is a good example of the average/marginal relationship. If your score on the second exam is greater than your score on the first, your average score will rise. If your score on the third exam is less than the average on the first two exams, your average will fall. If your score on a fourth exam just equals your average on the first three, your average will remain the same. The effect of each marginal exam on your course average depends on whether the marginal score is higher or lower than the previous average.

Short-Run Production: Three Stages of Production

Short-run product curves provide some insight into the short-run production decisions that firms must make. To use the curves for this purpose, it helps to divide the production relations into *three stages of production*. Figure 6.5 illustrates these three stages. Stage I is where the average product is rising. The firm is in stage I of production if it employs between zero and L_3 workers. In stage II, average product is falling and marginal product is greater than zero. This stage prevails over quantities of labor between L_3 and L_4. Stage III, in which the marginal product is negative, involves quantities of labor greater than L_4.

We identify these three stages of production in order to examine the rationality of producing in each of the stages. Profit maximization occurs somewhere within stage II. Operating in stage III is irrational from an economic perspective, because the marginal product of labor is negative. A firm operating in stage III incurs the costs of employing additional workers while output falls because of the negative marginal product. Suppose that an owner of a

Figure 6.5 The Stages of Production
In the short run, production will occur in stage II, where the average product is falling and marginal product is positive. When production occurs in stage I, profits will increase when more labor is employed. In stage III, profits will increase when less labor is employed.

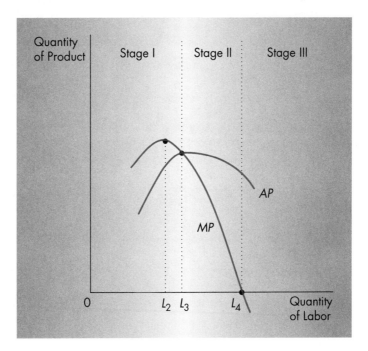

tavern hires an additional bartender to work two 8-hour shifts on weekends. If the additional bartender is paid $5 per hour, the tavern's labor costs rise by $80. Much to the tavern owner's surprise, the number of drinks sold on the average weekend falls. The extra bartender adds to congestion behind the bar and reduces the number of drinks that can be served. The loss to the tavern owner is twofold: the wages of the additional bartender and the lost sales. Increasing the costs while reducing output always reduces profits. The owner/manager cannot maximize profits if the marginal product of a resource is negative. However, certain resources may have a positive marginal product while appearing not to (see Highlight 6.1).

Highlight 6.1   *Leaning on Shovels: Doing More by Doing Nothing?*

The stereotypical road construction crew generally includes a number of workers whose primary function seems to be leaning on shovels. Many a frustrated motorist, caught in a traffic jam created by some road project, has concluded

Here workmen repair a concrete highway surface. Sometimes, idleness on the part of some workers may actually contribute to the total product.

that the project could be finished and traffic returned to normal much sooner if everyone worked rather than stood around. The frustrated motorist might attribute the worker's inactivity to laziness. The economist views the idle worker from a different perspective.

The "judgmental" motorist is overlooking the "idle" worker's role in the construction crew. The people with shovels are all part of a team whose objective is to move dirt, sand, or gravel. In additional to the people leaning on shovels, the team includes heavy-equipment operators who handle the bulk of the material to be moved with bulldozers, backhoes, and road graders. The heavy-equipment operators and their tools are unable to move 100 percent of the material that is in the way. The light-equipment (shovel) operators are crucial adjuncts to the heavy-equipment operators, because they are responsible for moving what the big equipment cannot reach.

Given the capacity of heavy equipment to move material, the key to timely completion of the project is to reduce the amount of time that this equipment is idle. Construction companies do this by having enough shovels and laborers to quickly move the material that the heavy equipment cannot reach. If the number of workers with shovels were reduced to eliminate "loafing," the heavy equipment would sit idle more frequently and the job would take longer to finish. The workers leaning on their shovels are increasing the output of the team. They are doing more by doing nothing while the heavy equipment operators work.

The foregoing presupposes that the construction company is managed by profit seekers. Some road projects are undertaken by public employees; governments everywhere have departments or agencies that build or repair roads and highways. Public road crews operate under very different constraints from their private counterparts. Public employees are forbidden from profiting from their operations. Public officials have been imprisoned for making money from road projects under their control. Where the profit motive is absent, the incentive to avoid wasting resources is diminished. The inefficient civil servant is not responsible for any cost overruns. This may lead to the inefficient use of resources in public road projects.

When a road project is undertaken by public contractors, the workers leaning on shovels may still be hastening the completion of the project. The "idle" workers may simply understand the concept of marginal product. If there are so many workers that the marginal product of labor is negative, those who are idle are actually increasing output. Their idleness prevents them from getting in the way of other workers and slowing completion of the project.

The irrationality of operating under stage I is somewhat more difficult to explain. Stage I production exists when average product is rising. Assuming constant input and output prices, profits will increase by expanding input usage when the average product of the input is rising. Suppose that the manager of a video rental store can hire workers at $5 per hour, regardless of how many people are hired. The constant wage rate means that labor costs will be proportional to the number of employees. A 5 percent increase in the number of workers will increase costs by 5 percent. If video rental rates are constant at $3 per day, the store's revenues will be proportional to the number of tapes rented. A 10 percent increase in the number of rentals will increase revenues by 10 percent. Suppose that the manager discovers that the average product of his staff is rising. Adding another employee increases the output per worker. In this case, a 5 percent increase in the number of employees might increase the number of rentals by 10 percent. The manager would increase profits by increasing the number of employees. A 5 percent increase in staff increases output and revenues by 10 percent, whereas labor costs increase by only 5 percent. Increasing the use of an input whose average product is rising will always increase profits, so a profit-seeking firm will never produce in stage I.

Because operating in either stage I or stage III is irrational, it follows that the profit-maximizing firm will operate somewhere in stage II. The optimal use of a variable input will depend on a number of variables in addition to the short-run production relationships. The solution to the firm's short-run input decision depends on the prices of the firm's inputs and output. The short-run production relationships, when combined with input prices, determine the short-run costs of the firm. Short-run costs and revenues determine short-run profits. The specific solution to the short-run production problem must be deferred until we have had a chance to consider the costs of production, the subject of Chapter 7, and the relationship between output and revenue, which will be considered in Chapters 9 through 11.

Production Choices in the Long Run

The long run is defined as the period during which all inputs are variable. Consideration of long-run production decisions requires a return to the three-dimensional production surface and the problems of three-dimensional graphics discussed previously. The production surface, when smoothed and drawn in three dimensions, will look somewhat like a hill. We can avoid three-dimensional graphics by employing the same technique that cartographers use to indicate altitude on maps: draw lines composed of points of equal altitude. The graphical device that uses this technique to illustrate the consequences of long-run production choices is called an isoquant map.

Isoquants: Long-Run Production Choices Illustrated

Isoquants are curves that represent all combinations of the two inputs, labor and capital, that can be used to produce a given level of output. As such, isoquants define the possible tradeoffs between inputs, holding output constant. This is the essence of the long-run production problem. The isoquant defines the choices that the firm faces regarding alternative ways of producing a given level of output. The problem is then to choose the appropriate method. General Motors is addressing a long-run problem when it closes certain plants and automates other plants. Air Canada makes a long-run decision when it orders new jets for its fleet and makes scheduling changes to reflect the expanded capacity. These solutions and others to the long-run production problem can be explained in terms of isoquants.

An isoquant is found by taking a horizontal slice of a production surface. The points of equal output are then projected down into the (L,K) plane. Drawing an isoquant is similar to slicing an orange and tracing the perimeter of the orange slice on a piece of paper. Taking a few representative slices out of

Figure 6.6 The Isoquant Map

Isoquants show all combinations of two inputs that produce given levels of output. Output increases as production moves to isoquants that are further from the origin.

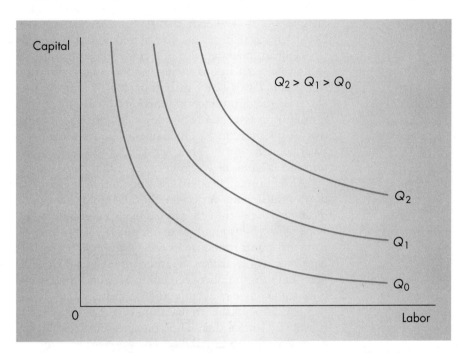

the production surface and projecting them into the (L,K) plane produces an isoquant map like that illustrated in Figure 6.6.[8]

Properties of Isoquants. An isoquant map illustrates graphically the relationships between two inputs and output. The nature of the relationships are defined by the geometric characteristics of the isoquant map. Figure 6.6 depicts a representative sample of three isoquants that are derived from one production surface. Each of the isoquants is for a specific level of output (Q_0, Q_1, Q_2). The three isoquants illustrated are not the only ones that could have been drawn. We can derive an isoquant for every level of output. Therefore, there will be an isoquant going through every point in the (L,K) space, because every combination of labor and capital will produce a specific level of output.

8. Figure 6.6 bears a striking resemblance to the indifference curves introduced in Chapter 4. Artistically, the only difference is in the labeling; in general look the graphs are identical. Moreover, the two graphs serve the same basic function: illustrating alternative means to achieve some objective. An indifference curve shows the combinations of two goods that yield the same level of utility. An isoquant shows the combinations of two inputs that yield a given level of output.

Another property of the isoquant map is that, in general, the farther an isoquant is from the origin, the greater the level of output associated with the isoquant. Moving to the northeast from the origin involves greater quantities of both inputs. Using greater quantities of both inputs will generally lead to greater output. The dairy that buys more milking machinery and milk cows is likely to increase its production of milk.[9]

Isoquant maps are also drawn so that isoquants do not intersect. An intersection between isoquants implies that one combination of labor and capital will produce two levels of output.[10] This is inconsistent with a fundamental characteristic of production functions discussed previously. A production function encompasses the technologically efficient combinations of resources — that is, the maximum output obtainable from each combination of resources. Each combination of labor and capital will lead to one point on the production surface, and the level of output at that point will be unique.

An important property of isoquants relates to their slope: isoquants are downward sloping. A decrease in the employment of one input must be offset by an increase in the other to maintain a constant level of output. The negative slope of isoquants indicates that inputs are substitutes in production. The company that wants to reduce its fuel consumption may substitute energy-conserving products (insulation, weatherstripping, and the like). The extent to which firms can substitute between inputs is defined by the change in the slope of the isoquant as one moves along the isoquant.

The shape of the isoquant indicates the degree to which one input can be substituted for another. The isoquants illustrated in Figure 6.7 represent polar cases of input substitutability. The isoquant in panel (a) is a straight line. This is the case when inputs are **perfect substitutes**. The firm can always substitute a given quantity of labor for each unit of capital and maintain the level of output. Isoquants can also form right angles, as illustrated in panel (b). In this case, production occurs under what are called **fixed proportions**. Increasing one input, holding the amount of the other input constant, leaves output unchanged. The inputs are **perfect complements** because they must be used in specific ratios to produce a commodity.

Between the extremes of straight-line and right-angle isoquants are those illustrated in Figure 6.7: isoquants that are convex to the origin. This shape indicates that inputs are imperfect substitutes in production. The firm is able to substitute one input for another, but its ability to substitute *between*

---

9. It is possible for an increase in the use of all resources to result in lower output. This range of the production function is usually ignored, because it is irrational for the firm to operate under these conditions. Employing more resources to obtain less output would necessarily result in lower profits.

10. The intersection of two isoquants means that the labor-capital combination defined by the point of intersection is on two different isoquants. Each isoquant corresponds to a different level of output.

Figure 6.7　Linear Isoquants
The isoquant in panel (a) represents inputs that are perfect substitutes. The rate at which labor can be substituted for capital is constant. The isoquant in panel (b) represents perfect complements. The inputs must be combined in fixed proportions to produce the product.

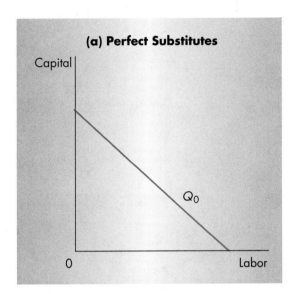

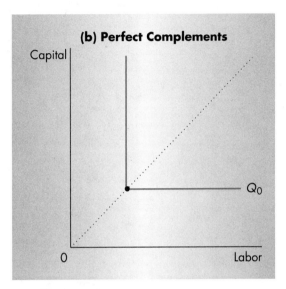

inputs is limited. As the firm alters the combinations of inputs, its ability to substitute among inputs is defined by the slope of the isoquant.

The Marginal Rate of Technical Substitution.　The slope of an isoquant is called the **marginal rate of technical substitution**, or simply the *MRTS*. The $MRTS_{LK}$ shows the rate at which the firm may substitute one input, *L*, for another, *K*, while holding output constant. The *MRTS* is instrumental in determining the optimal combination of resources that solves the long-run problem. The mechanics of this decision, like the mechanics of the short-run input decision, are deferred because it necessarily involves costs, the subject of the next chapter. This chapter is concerned with the production choices faced by the firm.

Calculating the $MRTS_{LK}$ is illustrated in Figure 6.8. The slope of the isoquant is the vertical change (ΔK) divided by the horizontal change (ΔL). The movement from point *A* to point *B* in Figure 6.8 is a vertical change of –4, a decrease in the amount of capital used in production, and a horizontal change of +1, an increase in the amount of labor. The firm substitutes 1 unit of labor for 4 units of capital and, because the movement is along an isoquant, leaves output unchanged. The slope of the line between points *A* and *B* is the $MRTS_{LK}$, and in this case it is equal to –4. Note that the *MRTS* is negative: substitution necessarily involves an increase in one input and a decrease in another.

Figure 6.8 The Marginal Rate of Technical Substitution
The *MRTS* is the slope of the isoquant. The slope between points *A* and *B* is –4. The
producer may substitute one unit of labor for 4 units of capital and maintain output at 200.

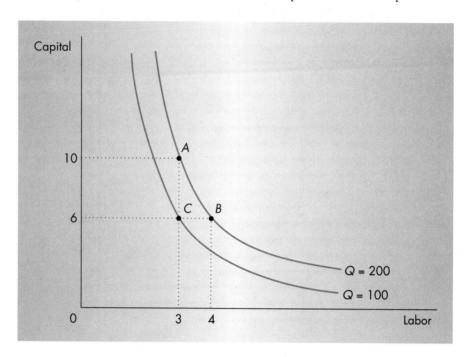

The *MRTS* is usually defined as the slope of an isoquant at a point on the
isoquant. When movement along a curve involves infinitesimally small
changes, the slope of the line tangent to the curve measures the slope of the
curve at the point of tangency. We interpret the slope of a line tangent at a
point on the isoquant as the *MRTS* at that point.

The Diminishing MRTS. Figure 6.9 illustrates three such measures of the *MRTS*. As
a producer moves down an isoquant, the $MRTS_{LK}$ decreases, and it becomes
increasingly more difficult to substitute labor for capital. The diminishing
MRTS implies that successive (and equal) reductions in the amount of capital
employed will require larger and larger increases in the amount of labor
employed to maintain output at a given level. A falling *MRTS* underlies the
shape of isoquants depicted in Figures 6.6, 6.8, and 6.9. The isoquants depicted in these (and following) figures are convex to the origin. A curve that has a
decreasing slope will appear to bow inward toward the origin. This feature of
isoquants is so pervasive that it has been labeled the law of **diminishing
marginal rates of technical substitution,** and it arises in most productive
endeavors, even in activities such as baseball. An important part of the game is

pitching. Pitchers use different types of pitches (fastballs, curveballs, knuckle-balls, spitballs) as inputs to record (produce) outs and limit their opponents' ability to score (that is, produce) runs. Figure 6.9 can be used to illustrate the pitcher's production problem if we view "outs" as the output and let K and L stand for fastballs and curveballs, respectively. The pitcher who throws mostly fastballs will have to throw quite a few to record a given number of outs. Knowing that a fastball is likely, batters will adjust their swing to get a hit. The pitcher that throws a few more curveballs (and fewer fastballs) will fool more batters into striking out. A few curveballs will substitute for many fastballs (that is, the $MRTS$ is relatively high). As curveballs come to dominate the mix of pitches, fewer batters will be fooled and it takes relatively more curveballs to substitute for a given number of fastballs; the $MRTS$ declines.

The declining $MRTS$ can be explained by referring back to Figure 6.8. Between points A and B on the isoquant, there is no change in output. Moreover, the movement from A to B can be split into two components: a decrease in the amount of capital, holding labor constant initially, and an increase in the amount of labor, holding capital constant at its new, lower

Figure 6.9 The Diminishing *MRTS*

The slopes of lines tangent to the isoquant indicate the $MRTS$. The $MRTS$ declines as production moves down and along the isoquant. The decreasing $MRTS$ accounts for the isoquant being convex to the origin; that is, it bows outward.

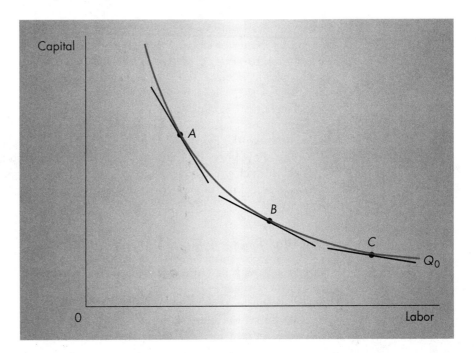

level. The decrease in capital, with labor constant, moves the firm to point C, which is on a lower isoquant. The decrease in output caused by the reduction in the use of capital (ΔQ_K) is equal to the change in capital (ΔK) times the marginal product of capital (MP_K), or $\Delta Q_K = MP_K \Delta K$. The increase in labor, holding capital constant at its new level, moves production from point C to point B. The increase in output caused by this increase in labor (ΔQ_L) is equal to the change in labor (ΔL) multiplied by the marginal product of labor (MP_L), or $\Delta Q_L = MP_L \Delta L$. Because the two changes involve a movement along the isoquant, the two changes in output (ΔQ_K and ΔQ_L) must be equal, or $\Delta Q_K = \Delta Q_L$. It was previously noted that each change in output equals the change in the amount of the input multiplied by the marginal product of the input. Therefore, because $\Delta Q_K = \Delta Q_L$, then

$$MP_K \Delta K = MP_L \Delta L$$

Rearranging the terms in this equation, we get

$$\frac{\Delta K}{\Delta L} = \frac{MP_L}{MP_K}$$

where $\Delta K / \Delta L$ is the definition of the $MRTS_{LK}$. The marginal rate of technical substitution is, by the above equation, equal to the ratio of the marginal product of labor to the marginal product of capital.

The $MRTS$ diminishes because the marginal products of the inputs change as the quantities of each input employed change. Increasing the quantity of labor employed reduces (by the principle of diminishing marginal returns) the marginal product of labor. This leads to a decrease in the $MRTS$ by reducing the numerator in the MP_L / MP_K ratio. Reducing the amount of capital employed will increase the marginal product of capital. This causes a further reduction in the $MRTS$ by increasing the denominator in the $MRTS$ expression. The same reasoning applies to the pitch selection problem discussed earlier. When mostly fastballs are being thrown, the marginal product of a fastball is low, whereas the marginal product of a curveball is high. Changing the mix to include more curveballs and fewer fastballs reduces the marginal productivity of the former while increasing the marginal productivity of the latter. The $MRTS$ is high along the upper part of the isoquant and falls as you move along the isoquant.

Long-Run Production and Returns to Scale

An isoquant map describes the effects of changing the quantities of resources used in the production of goods and services. An increase in all resources will move the firm to a higher isoquant and generate greater output. A decrease in resource utilization reduces output by pushing the firm to a lower isoquant. Although it is useful to know the direction of the change in output, knowledge regarding the relative magnitude of the change in output will be especially useful. The relative magnitude of a change in output is determined by a characteristic of production functions called returns to scale.

Returns to scale measures the change in output relative to a proportionate change in all inputs. If the change in all inputs is not proportional, the returns-to-scale concept is not applicable. **Increasing returns to scale** exist if a given percentage change in all inputs changes output by a greater percentage. If an equal percentage change in all inputs results in a proportionate change in output, then **constant returns to scale** are present. A production function that exhibits **decreasing returns to scale** will show less-than-proportionate changes in output for a given change in inputs. The concept of returns to scale is illustrated in Figure 6.10. Movement from point A to point B represents a doubling of both inputs (a proportionate change in all inputs). If there are increasing returns to scale, Q_2 will be more than twice Q_1. If there are decreasing returns to scale, Q_2 will be something less than two times Q_1. With constant returns to scale, Q_2 will be exactly two times Q_1. Doubling the quantity of resources devoted to the production of soybeans will more than double,

Figure 6.10 Returns to Scale

A proportionate increase in inputs (doubling both L and K) will increase output. Constant returns to scale exist if output doubles: $Q_2 = 2Q_1$. Increasing returns exist if output more than doubles: $Q_2 > 2Q_1$. Decreasing returns exist if output less than doubles: $Q_2 < 2Q_1$.

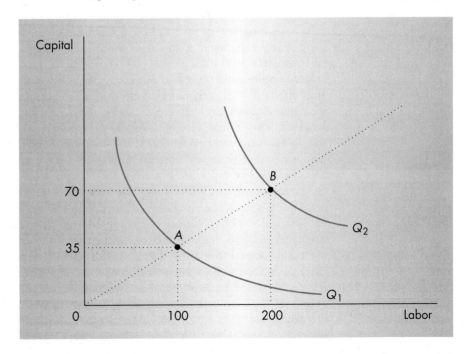

less than double, or exactly double the quantity of soybeans produced as the production of soybeans reflects increasing, decreasing, or constant returns to scale.

There is a tendency to confuse the concepts of returns to scale and diminishing marginal returns because of the similarity in terminology. Although the terminology is similar, the concepts are very different. Diminishing marginal returns is a short-run characteristic of the production function. It applies as one input is varied while another is fixed. Returns to scale is a long-run characteristic of the production function. Returns to scale apply only when all inputs are varied proportionately. This can occur only in the long run. The notion of returns to scale as it pertains to cooking is examined in Highlight 6.2.

Highlight 6.2   *The Culinary Arts: Production in the Kitchen*

You don't need to spend much time in the kitchen to learn that meal preparation is the very embodiment of the production process. Every recipe, from the instructions on a box of boil-in-a-bag vegetables to the directions for making a bernaise sauce, is a production function. Recipes (or package instructions) tell the cook how to combine ingredients, labor, kitchen appliances, and kitchen implements to produce a particular culinary product. Although this may be obvious to even the most inexperienced cooks, what may be surprising is the number of concepts from the theory of production that apply to the kitchen.

One conceptual problem in the application of the theory of production to the culinary experience is to define the isoquant. An isoquant will exist for a particular quantity of a dish, say, sautéed shellfish over linguine. The flavor of sautéed shellfish over linguine will vary perceptibly with even the slightest variation in seasoning, preparation, or freshness. The gourmet will consider dishes with the slightest taste difference to be different products. There are those, however, who would allow much greater variation in taste without deeming the dishes as different products. At the bottom of the food chain are those for whom flavor is relatively unimportant — all they care about is portion size. These eat-to-live types are irrelevant for our purposes, because by definition they are unconcerned with recipes. Our analysis is intended for the gourmet.

The nature of the isoquant will vary with the definition of a dish, which itself depends on how finicky one is regarding flavor. The gourmet deals with isoquants that are single points in input space. Any variation, however slight, from the recipe results in a different dish. Gourmands, who tend to be less exacting in their judgments, will view isoquants as lines that form right angles. Ideally, the ingredients should be combined in specific ratios, which form the corner of the isoquant (see Figure 6.7b), as defined by the recipe. Slightly increasing the quantity of one ingredient or another will produce the same quantity of the same basic dish. Adding a little more garlic to your shellfish

Recipes direct a meal-production function in which labor, ingredients, appliances, and implements are all inputs.

sauté does not change the portions. Although there is some variability in ingredients, there are limits to how far you can diverge from the recipe. One inattentive chef had the misfortune of misreading a cake recipe and used 3 cups of cooking oil rather than the $\frac{1}{3}$ of a cup called for in the recipe. The "product" remained in semi-liquid form, even after 4 hours of baking. The "cake" and cakepan were buried in a solemn ceremony at sunrise.

Anyone who has spent much time reading cookbooks has a perfect understanding of the concept of substitutes in production. Many recipes have notations identifying acceptable substitutions. Often these substitutions fulfill the notion of perfect substitutes, in which the isoquants will be straight lines. One is allowed to substitute one ingredient for another at a constant rate. Current concerns regarding cholesterol, weight, and other health matters have led those who promote nutritional correctness to develop substitutes for offending ingredients — for example, artificial sweeteners for sugar and canola oil for lard.

Examples of imperfect substitutes (convex isoquants) can also be found in the kitchen. This phenomenon arises when you consider the time it takes to prepare meals. Food preparation involves many different activities: chopping, measuring, stirring, basting, broiling, baking, and more. Many times there are nonlinear tradeoffs among these activities. Chinese cuisine involves very little cooking time (you can stir-fry in minutes) but much time cutting and chopping. Barbeque, on the other hand, entails very little chopping/cutting, but proper cooking entails hours. One's handiness with a knife defines the tradeoff between cutting/chopping time and cooking time, and diminishing returns in cutting and chopping result in a diminishing rate at which one may substitute time at the chopping block for time at the cooktop.

Finally, the kitchen can provide some interesting examples of returns to scale. Most recipes exhibit constant returns to scale; a doubling of ingredients (inputs) doubles the number of servings (output) without changing the taste. Chinese cooking is an exception to constant returns to scale in cooking. Aficionados of Chinese cuisine maintain that the scale cannot be changed without altering the flavor of the dish. If you want to double the number of servings, you have to cook the dish twice.

Technological Change and the Isoquant Map

The characteristics of an isoquant map derive from the underlying production function. The production function shows the maximum output that can be produced from alternative combinations of inputs, given the current technology. A change in technology will result in a change in the output that can be produced by any given combination of inputs. Specifically, each combination of inputs will produce a greater quantity of output when an improvement in technology occurs. This change in output exhibits itself in movements of the isoquants and a change in the isoquant map. The specific form of these graphical movements depends on the nature of the technological change. Any change will be one of three types: **neutral technological change, labor-saving technology**, or **capital-saving technology**.[11] Each affects the isoquants in a different way.

11. The phrases *labor-using* and *capital-using* are synonymous with the phrases *capital-saving* and *labor-saving*, respectively. A technological change that conserves on the use of one resource necessarily increases the use of the other.

Figure 6.11 Neutral Technological Change

Neutral technological change increases the output of each combination of inputs without changing the slope of the isoquant. The MRTS for each input combination remains the same.

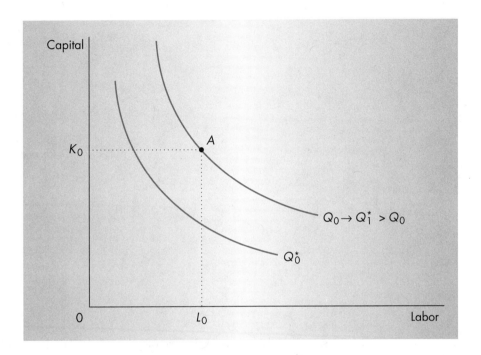

Neutral Technological Change. Technological change is neutral when it leaves the marginal rates of technical substitution unchanged. The effects of neutral technological change are illustrated in Figure 6.11. The isoquant for a given level of output Q_0 shifts inward to isoquant Q_0^* while the space occupied by the original isoquant is occupied by a new isoquant, Q_1^* representing a greater level of output. The neutrality of the technological change is evident in the constant *MRTS* for any input combination. The slope of the isoquant at point *A* is unchanged even though output at point *A* is increased.

Biased Technological Change. Biased technological change alters the marginal rates of technical substitution associated with each input combination. The possibilities are limited because the *MRTS* (the slope of the isoquant) can either increase or decrease. Technological change that increases the slope of the isoquant is said to be capital saving where capital is measured on the vertical axis as in Figure 6.12a. A change in technology that reduces the slope of the isoquant is said to be labor saving and is illustrated in Figure 6.12b. Because

Figure 6.12 Biased Technological Change

Capital-saving technological change increases the slope of the isoquant as shown in panel (a). The change facilitates the substitution of labor for capital. Labor-saving technological change decreases the slope of the isoquants as shown in panel (b). The change facilitates the substitution of capital for labor.

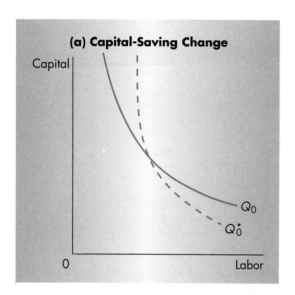
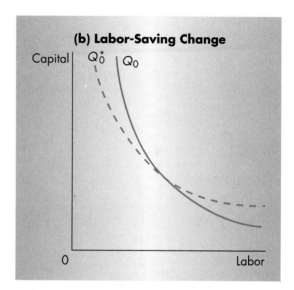

$MRTS_{LK} = MP_L / MP_K$, a change in the $MRTS$ occurs through an increase or decrease in the relative marginal productivity of labor. An isoquant gets steeper when the relative marginal productivity of labor increases. This induces the substitution of labor for capital, and the technological change is said to be capital saving. Conversely, a lower $MRTS$ implies a relatively lower marginal productivity of labor and the substitution of capital for labor. A flatter isoquant is indicative of labor-saving technological change.

Long-Run Production Choices

Although the determination of the optimal combination of inputs is being deferred to the next chapter, the isoquant map does allow the determination of an area in which a profit-maximizing firm will operate. The rational firm will operate somewhere between the curves labeled R_1 and R_2 in Figure 6.13.

Ridge Lines. The curves labeled R_1 and R_2 are ridge lines. **Ridge lines** mark the boundary between rational production choices and irrational production choices. The ridge lines are the locus (collection) of all points at which isoquants begin to exhibit a positive slope. Point A in Figure 6.13 is the point at which the isoquant becomes vertical and then bends backward. At point A, the

Figure 6.13 Long-Run Production Choices

The ridge lines R_1 and R_2 separate rational production choices from irrational choices. Production outside the ridge lines is irrational, because movements along the isoquants require more of both inputs to keep output constant. The producer would be spending more to keep output constant. One of the marginal products will be negative when production occurs outside the ridge lines.

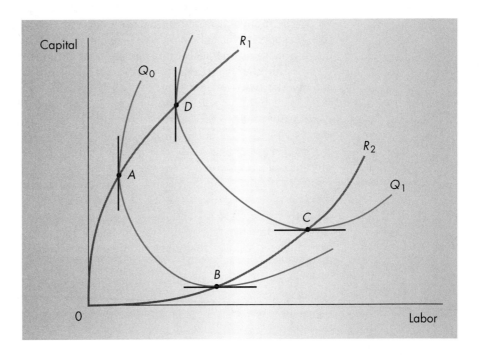

marginal product of capital is zero. The decision to use larger amounts of capital would be irrational, because the marginal product would be negative. At point *B* the isoquant is horizontal and the marginal product of labor is zero. It would be irrational for a firm to use any combination of inputs on isoquant Q_0 that lies to the right of point *B*. To do so would entail the use of labor for which the marginal product is negative. Of all the possible combinations of inputs that can be used to produce Q_0 units of output, only the choices that lie between points *A* and *B* are sensible ones.

In Figure 6.13 the ridge lines R_1 and R_2 connect points at which different isoquants become vertical and horizontal. The isoquants illustrated in graphs prior to Figure 6.13 have intentionally omitted the positively sloped portions of the isoquants. This omission is justified on the grounds that it is irrational to operate at a point on an isoquant where it is upward sloping. See Highlight 6.3 for an example of irrational use of study time.

Highlight 6.3   *Academic Performance, Economically Considered*

Academic performance can be analyzed using the production principles presented in this chapter. Each student combines inputs to produce an output. The output can be one's score on an exam, one's grade in a course, or one's GPA. The inputs into this production process are labor (study time), materials (books, paper, pens, and so on), and capital. The capital used in academic production may include such things as personal computers (the usual notion of capital) but always includes human capital. Human capital is the knowledge and abilities that students bring to class or college. Although academic performance can be discussed in production terminology, this does not mean that the principles of production theory necessarily apply to study. This application was tested with some interesting results.

Data were collected by one of the text's authors for three consecutive offerings of an economics course for MBA students. The data included the results of the first exam and factors that might have some bearing on each student's performance on exams. The three classes were taught by one instructor using the same textbook and the same grading scheme. Each of the exams was curved so that the second-highest grade was equal to 100 percent. The data were analyzed using statistical techniques to isolate the influence of each factor on academic performance.

The list of factors that had no bearing on exam scores is of interest. The age, sex, and marital status of the students were unrelated to performance on the exam. The student's undergraduate college (business, engineering, and so on) and previous coursework in economics were also unrelated to exam scores. This was as it should be. The course, for beginning MBA students, was designed to familiarize them with the basics of economic analysis. There were no economics prerequisites, and fairness dictates that no one be penalized for lack of experience with economics. The most striking insignificant factor was the hours studied on the day before the exam. Those who tried to cram had nothing to show for their efforts.

The factors that had some bearing on test performance were (1) previous coursework in mathematics, (2) the students' general academic abilities, and (3) the amount of time devoted to studying the course material.

The grades on the first exam were positively related to the number of math courses on the students' transcripts. The course had a calculus prerequisite because it was a calculus-based introduction to microeconomic analysis. The first week of class was devoted to a review of calculus, mathematical techniques were used extensively throughout the first five weeks, and the first exams all had strong quantitative components. A strong math background gave students an advantage on the first test. An important economic result was that the variable (previous math courses) was subject to the law of diminishing returns.

Students optimize some output (a GPA or a grade in a single class) by combining inputs (such as time, capital, and human capital). The labor-time component — hours spent studying — is a critical element in the production process.

Additional math coursework increased the grade, but the incremental effect fell as the number of math courses rose.

The measure of general academic abilities was also subject to positive but diminishing marginal returns. The students' academic abilities were measured by combining their undergraduate GPA with their score on a standardized test. This measure of academic ability was constructed to give equal weight to past academic success and the standardized test. The statistical analysis of the data concluded that those with a higher score on this measure of academic ability earned high scores on the first test.

The analysis of the labor component of the grade-production process produced the most surprising results. These results confirm the wisdom of a rule of thumb (whose origins are unknown) that is widely quoted in academic circles. Undergraduate courses are said to require two hours of outside work for each hour spent in the classroom, whereas graduate courses require three hours of outside work for each class hour. This rule of thumb indicates that 45 hours of study would be required for the first exam in this class. The exam was in graduate classes that met three hours per week, and the material was presented over five weeks. The data show that the closer one got to the "recommended" 45 hours of study, the higher one's grade. On average, those who studied more than 45 hours had a lower score on the exam, indicating a negative marginal product of study time.

The Feasible Production Set. The feasible production set is the space between the ridge lines. The profit-maximizing firm will select an input combination somewhere in this space. The irrationality of operating outside the ridge lines is revealed by considering the implications of an upward-sloping isoquant. An upward-sloping isoquant requires an increase in both inputs to maintain the same level of output. Increasing both inputs to maintain a constant level of output implies that at least one of the inputs has a negative marginal product. Above ridge line R_1, the marginal product of capital is negative. Moving vertically from point A in Figure 6.13 increases the use of capital, holds the amount of labor constant, and moves the firm to a lower isoquant. The increase in capital reduces output; that is, the marginal product of capital is negative. Similarly, the area below ridge line R_2 involves combinations of labor and capital for which the marginal product of labor is negative. Moving horizontally from point B in Figure 6.13 reduces output by moving the firm to a lower isoquant. Because the cause of this movement is an increase in the amount of labor employed, the marginal product of labor is negative. It is clearly irrational to operate where the marginal product of an input is negative. The firm incurs higher costs to achieve a lower output. Profit maximization therefore requires production on the downward-sloping portion of an isoquant.

Summary

The economic well-being of any society depends crucially on that society's success in transforming inputs into outputs. There are many different ways of organizing this production process. However, in free-market societies, most production is carried out by private, for-profit business firms. The remarkable ability of these firms to exploit the advantages of team production and to deter shirking enables them to achieve a high level of efficiency, and this is a major factor in explaining the relative success of free-market economies.

In this chapter we have examined how business firms make production decisions. In doing this, we have

- introduced the notion of a production function,
- explained the short-run options of a firm in terms of total-, average-, and marginal-product curves,
- developed isoquant maps to illustrate a firm's production options in the long run,
- used isoquant maps to make the important distinction between diminishing marginal returns and diminishing returns to scale,
- examined technological change in the context of isoquant maps.

Key Terms

firm

transactions costs

shirking

proprietorship

corporation

production function

X-inefficiency

short run

diminishing marginal returns

perfect substitutes in production

perfect complements in production

diminishing marginal rate of
    technical substitution

ridge lines

production

team production

free-rider problem

partnership

technology

technological efficiency

long run

total, average, and marginal product

isoquants

fixed proportions in production

marginal rate of technical
    substitution

increasing, constant, and decreasing
    returns to scale

neutral, labor-saving, and capital-
    saving technological change

Sample Questions

Question

If a firm is producing outside the region bounded by ridge lines, in which stage of production is the firm producing? Would a firm want to produce here? Explain.

Answer

A firm producing outside the ridge lines is producing in stage III of production. When production takes place on the positive-sloped portion of an isoquant (outside the ridge lines), increasing quantities of both inputs are required to maintain the level of output, indicating that a negative marginal product of an input is negative and a firm would benefit from using less of this input. Production outside the ridge lines in stage III is irrational, because the marginal product of an input is negative, and profitability would increase by decreasing the use of this input.

Question

Explain the derivation of the marginal- and average-product curves. Are these curves ever equal?

Answer

The marginal-product curve is derived from the slope of the total-product curve. To graph the marginal-product curve, the slope of lines tangent to the total-product curve determines the shape of the marginal-product curve. The average-product curve is derived somewhat similarly. The slope of straight lines from the origin to points on the total-product curve can be plotted against labor to develop the average-product curve. The two curves intersect, indicating that they are equal, at the point at which a line from the origin to the total-product curve is also tangent to the curve. This point of equality occurs where the average-product curve is at a maximum and the marginal-product curve is declining.

Questions for Review and Discussion

*1. A firm that employs team production stands to gain from this organization, but there are also potential costs. Identify and explain the costs and benefits of team production.

2. What are the differences between proprietorships, partnerships, and corporations?

*3. When problems with shirking arise, which legal form of business is best suited to reduce the incentive to shirk, and how is this accomplished?

4. Define the production function. Why are levels of output below the maximum level excluded from the production function?

5. There are several ways to depict a production function. Identify each representation that is discussed in this chapter.

6. What information is conveyed by the height and location of a production surface?

*7. Define the total product of labor. What are the different ranges that the total-product curve passes through?

8. What is the law of diminishing marginal returns? How do diminishing returns affect a baseball game?

9. Graph the marginal- and total-product curves and explain the relationship between the two curves.

10. Illustrate and explain the relationship between the average- and marginal-product curves.

*11. Why will a profit-maximizing firm avoid producing in stage III?

12. Discuss the five properties of isoquants.

*13. Suppose that 5 units of capital and 3 units of labor are initially used in production. Now suppose that the input combination is changed so that 2 units of capital and 8 units of labor are used to produce the same level of output. Calculate the marginal rate of technical substitution. What information does this number convey to you?

*14. What are returns to scale? Identify the different classifications of returns to scale, and explain how this concept differs from diminishing marginal returns.

Problems for Analysis

1. Do you think that the amount of shirking by workers is in any way connected with the size of the firm that employs the workers? Explain.

*2. All business firms have an interest in quality control. A part of quality control is inspecting output. Do you think that large firms have to deal with shirking (sloppy inspection) by individual inspectors? If so, do you know of any techniques the firms use to deal with this problem?

*3. In the past fifteen or so years there has been an increase in the frequency of "hostile takeovers," in which one corporation acquires a controlling interest in the stock of another corporation against the will of its management. Do you think that there is any connection between the success a firm has in maximizing its profits and the likelihood that it will become involved in a hostile takeover?

4. Suppose that as a producer you are able to obtain as much as you want of a certain input without having to pay for it. Assuming that you have a fixed amount of another input, how much of the "free" input would you use? (Frame your answer in terms of the marginal product of the free input.) Does your answer above say anything about the best quantity to use if you have to pay for that input?

5. Suppose that your roommate spends hours studying for an exam and then says to you that "diminishing returns have set in, so any further study will only hurt my grade." Do you agree with him? Should he quit studying just because "diminishing returns have set in"?

6. In our discussion of production in the short run, we stressed the principle of diminishing marginal returns. In our discussion of production in the long run, we stressed the notion of a diminishing marginal rate of technical substitution. How does diminishing *MRTS* differ from diminishing marginal returns?

7. A notion of efficiency that is frequently embraced by engineers (but seldom by economists) is the notion of maximizing output per unit of some particular input. This is equivalent to producing a given level of output using the smallest possible amount of a particular input. Use an isoquant to illustrate the production technique that would maximize output per unit of labor. What technique would maximize output per unit of capital?

7

The Costs of Production

Scarcely a day goes by that one doesn't see a newspaper article or television news segment dealing with costs. Someone, somewhere, is always trying to cut costs. The corporate reorganizations that occurred during the early 1990s were instigated by a desire to reduce operating costs. Some college students felt the cost cutter's axe as colleges and universities eliminated degree programs and academic departments to reduce operating costs. The North American Free Trade Agreement has caused concerns in parts of Canada, Mexico, and the United States over the possibility of plant relocations to reduce production costs. Costs seem to be on everyone's mind.

This chapter completes the process begun in the previous chapter, which lays the foundation for Part IV of this text. Chapter 6 discussed the nature of the firm, its motivations, and the theory of production. There was, however, a significant gap in the chapter: firm behavior was described as profit maximizing, but there was no direct link between production and profits. The linkage that is needed lies in the costs of production. The objectives of this chapter are to provide an understanding of

- the economic view of costs and profits.
- long-run production decisions and the costs generated by these decisions.
- short-run production decisions and the costs generated by these decisions.
- the relationship between short- and long-run costs.
- the factors causing changes in costs.

Costs and Profits from an Economic Perspective

Costs and profits are a potential source of confusion for students of economics. As will be explained in Chapter 8, there are circumstances in which a firm continues to operate with zero profits. Many people question the notion of a zero-profit equilibrium, because it is obvious to them that firms must make some profit to stay in business. This apparent contradiction arises because economists use definitions for the terms *costs* and *profits* that differ from those commonly used by the public. Although there are important reasons for these differences, this is little consolation to those who are confused by using every-day notions of costs and profits to interpret economic analysis.

The Economist's View of Cost

A primary concern of economics is decision making, and the economist's definition of cost reflects this concern. To an economist, the **economic cost** of an activity is the value, in the next-best use, of the resources committed to the activity. When the activity is the production of goods and services, the costs are the value, in the next-best use, of the resources expended in production. The emphasis is on the "next-best use." The terms *alternative cost* and *opportunity cost*, used interchangeably with economic cost, highlight this aspect of the economic view of cost. The cost of a college education includes the value of the next-best use of the time that is forgone by students while they are in school. A full understanding of economic costs comes from breaking them into its two components: explicit costs and implicit costs.

In order to produce goods or services, it is necessary to use inputs. Many of the inputs used by a business firm are owned by someone else. Examples include raw materials purchased from suppliers, working capital borrowed from a bank, or labor services provided by employees. These inputs are purchased or rented in markets, and the market price of these inputs is their **explicit cost**. The explicit cost is simply what the user has to pay for these inputs.

However, businesses also use their own inputs to produce output. Even though these inputs are not paid for directly, there is a cost associated with their use. This is an **implicit cost**, equal to the highest-valued alternative use of these inputs.

For example, a restaurateur might own his own building, work as a chef and an accountant in his own establishment, and perhaps grow some of the herbs and vegetables that he uses in his restaurant. By doing so, he forgoes the rent that could have been earned on the building, the income he could have earned by working elsewhere as a chef or an accountant, and revenue he could have generated by selling his produce. Even though he does not pay directly for these inputs, there is a very real cost associated with their use. From an economic perspective, the cost of producing anything includes both the explicit costs (the market costs) and the implicit costs. In contrast, noneconomists tend to consider only explicit costs.

The economist's view of cost is firmly rooted in the present. It is based solely on current alternatives and ignores past decisions and actions. What one paid for a resource, the **historical cost**, is irrelevant to economic costs. At one time the price of silver rose to $50 per ounce. Not much later the price had fallen to around $5 per ounce. Many jewelers bought silver at the high price and had inventories of silver when the price fell. The economic cost of using the inventory was $5 (the current market price), not $50 (the purchase price) per ounce. Economic costs are always calculated on the basis of current market values and not historical values. (An example of economic costs, taken from our judicial system is consider in Highlight 7.1.)

Highlight 7.1   *Jurors: The Last (?) American Conscripts*

The conscription of soldiers has a long and continuing history. Every major conflict has been fought with draftees, and many countries continue to have some form of mandatory military service. Since the U.S. adoption of the all-volunteer military, the justice system's method of selecting jurors is the last American example of conscript labor. A conscript is someone who is forced, by law and the threat of punishment, to provide labor services. Although conscripts are usually compensated for their services — jurors are paid a nominal sum — this compensation usually falls short of the costs of jury duty. If juror stipends exceeded the costs of jury duty, people would volunteer their services and no conscription would be necessary.

Jurors are just one of many inputs in the process that produces justice. Other necessary inputs include judges, attorneys, court reporters, and courtrooms. Jurors are different in that they are resource suppliers who are not paid their opportunity costs.[a] The other inputs take part in the process voluntarily, implying that their compensation (monetary or nonmonetary) is at least equal to the value of their next-best alternative.

The conscription of labor does not reduce the costs of producing any product, whether it is justice or national defense. Conscription simply shifts the costs of production from one group to another. The economic costs of jury duty are the alternative value of the jurors' time. Under an all-volunteer jury system, these costs would be explicit. An all-volunteer jury system would attract jurors by bidding them away from other activities. Under the conscript system, only a portion of the costs are explicit — namely, the jury fees. The remainder is paid, implicitly, by those called to jury duty. The conscription of jurors shifts some of the costs of the judicial system from taxpayers to conscripts. An all-volunteer jury would make all costs explicit. The nation's citizenry and taxpayers would know the exact cost of their system of justice. It is difficult to make informed decisions when some of the costs of the decision are hidden, as they are in the jury conscript system.[b]

The question mark in the title of this Highlight implies that jury duty may not be the last bastion of public servitude. There have been a number of proposals for some form of compulsory public service by the youth of America.

---

[a] Jurors are not the only participants who are not paid. The defendant is not paid, nor are witnesses who are required to testify.

[b] D. L. Martin attempts to estimate the full costs of the jury system in "The Economic of Jury Conscription," *Journal of Political Economy*, 1972.

Conscripted jurors are generally not paid the opportunity cost of their service. An all-volunteer jury would make all costs explicit.

One proposal makes some form of public service, either military or civilian, a prerequisite for college aid programs. Another would make it necessary for college admission, and yet another would make it universal. One rationale for these programs is to develop a stronger sense of citizenship among young Americans. The advocates of public service fail to note that the programs also represent a tax on younger Americans and lower taxes for the benefit of older Americans.

Profit from an Economic Perspective

Profit is the difference between revenues and costs; even economists, who seem to have a perverse desire to create their own definitions, define profits in this way. The uniqueness of the economic view of profit derives from the economic view of cost. The economic interpretation of profit is the difference between the revenues generated by selling the output and the *economic* costs of producing the output. The economic costs include both explicit costs and implicit costs. In contrast, noneconomists limit their concept of costs to explicit costs. Therefore, in calculating profits they subtract only the explicit costs from the revenues. The full ramifications of the concept cannot be embraced without understanding a special type of economic cost that economists refer to as normal profit.

Normal Profits.   The **normal profits** of an enterprise are the returns that the owners could have earned in their next-best investment opportunity. Because these profits represent a forgone opportunity, they are a cost of operating the enterprise. The normal profit is an economic cost because it represents forgone earnings, but it is still a net return (profit, in everyday terminology) to the owner. To avoid terminological confusion, purists sometimes refer to normal profits as the opportunity cost of capital.

Economic Profits.   When economists speak of profit, they are referring to **economic profits**, a return in excess of all economic costs. Because economic costs include the opportunity cost of capital (the normal profit), a firm that is earning an economic profit is providing its owners/investors with a return in excess of what they can earn elsewhere. By their very nature, economic profits are critical to the operation of a market system. Economic profits are the lure that attracts investors and allocates resources to their highest-valued use.

   The remainder of this chapter is devoted to the derivation of cost functions. Cost functions define the relationships between output and the costs of production. The basis for these relationships is the production function of the previous chapter. After explaining the relationship between long-run and short-run cost functions, the chapter concludes with a brief examination of the factors that cause changes in cost functions.

Long-Run Costs of Production

The long run is a time period of sufficient length to permit any decision concerning production to be made and carried out. The long run exists when the firm is able to adjust the quantity of each resource that it uses in the production process. As the previous section explained, the use of resources always entails costs. The long-run costs of production originate in the production choices that are made in the long run.

Production Choices in the Long Run

Long-run production decisions simultaneously take into account the relationship between input usage and output, and the relationship between input usage and costs. This decision process can be simplified by assuming that a single output is produced using two inputs, labor and capital. The quantities of output, labor, and capital will be abbreviated Q, L, and K, respectively. Our

Prices of labor (= w)
capital (= r)

analysis is further simplified by assuming that all costs are explicit and that labor and capital are purchased at fixed prices. The prices of labor and capital will be indicated by *w* and *r*, respectively. Given these assumptions and abbreviations, our study of the firm's production choices begins with the production function.

The Isoquant Map Revisited. The long-run production options are revealed by the isoquant map illustrated in Figure 7.1 and developed in Chapter 6. The isoquant map is a two-dimensional representation of the three-dimensional production surface defined by the production function $Q = f(L,K)$. Each isoquant indicates all combinations of L and K that produce a given quantity of output. The negative slope of the isoquants reflects the possibility of substituting one input for another while keeping output constant. The decreasing slope of the isoquant implies a limited ability to substitute between inputs. Additionally, isoquants that are farther from the origin represent greater quantities of output. The isoquant map points out the production consequences of any input choice. The information conveyed by the isoquant map is denominated in

Figure 7.1 The Isoquant Map
The isoquant map is composed of representative isoquants. Each isoquant shows the combinations of two inputs required to produce a particular level of output.

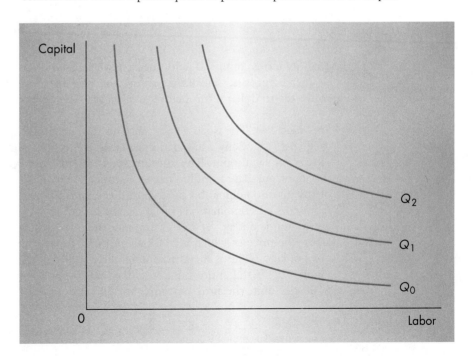

Figure 7.2 The Isocost Curve

The isocost curve C_0 shows all combinations of L and K that can be purchased for a total expenditure of $1,000 when the prices of labor and capital are $50 and $100, respectively.

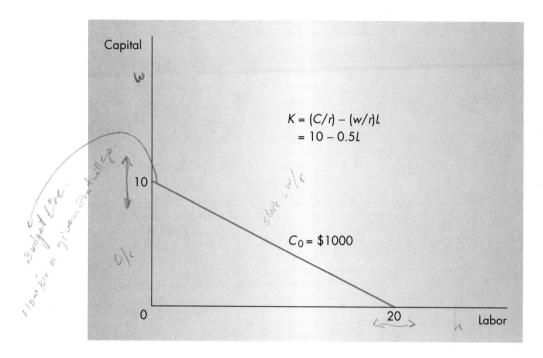

quantity terms, but production decisions are based on monetary considerations — that is, profits. The information conveyed by the isoquant map must be converted to dollar terms before our analysis can proceed.

The Isocost Line. The isocost line translates resource usage into dollar terms. The total cost (C) of any combination of labor and capital is the sum of the expenditures on each input. The amount spent on an input will be the quantity of the input purchased, multiplied by its price. Thus, in equation form, the cost of any given combination of labor and capital is $C = wL + rK$. An **isocost line** represents all combinations of labor and capital that can be purchased with a given money outlay.[1] If a given expenditure, say $1,000, is devoted entirely to labor, the price of which is $50 per unit, the firm will be able to purchase 20 units of labor. This is the horizontal intercept of the isocost curve illustrated in Figure 7.2. If the entire budget is devoted to purchasing capital at a price of $100 per unit, the firm can purchase 10 units of capital. This is the vertical

---

1. The isocost line is the producer's version of the consumer's budget line. Both show how far a given dollar amount will go.

intercept of the isocost line in Figure 7.2. The firm is able to purchase any combination of labor and capital along the straight line between these two points with no change in total costs.[2]

The slope (a vertical change divided by a horizontal change) of the isocost line indicates the rate at which labor can be substituted for capital, holding costs constant. Between the endpoints of the isocost line in Figure 7.2, the vertical change is minus 10 — the firm goes from purchasing 10 units of capital to using no capital. Between these same two points, the horizontal change is 20 — the firm goes from using no labor to purchasing 20 units of labor. The slope of the isocost is the ratio of these changes –10/20, or –0.5. The slope of the isocost, the rate at which the firm can substitute one input for another, is equal to the price of the input measured on the horizontal axis divided by the price of the input measured on the vertical axis. In Figure 7.2 that is W/r or 50/100. If accountants earn $30,000 and computers cost $5,000, an accounting firm can substitute at the ratio of $30,000/$5,000 or 6 computers for 1 accountant.

The isoquant map and isocost line provide the tools to analyze the long-run production decision. This decision, reflecting profit-maximizing behavior, can be formulated in two seemingly different (but, as we shall see, identical) ways. The production decision will minimize the cost of producing a given level of output or maximize output for a given total cost. To maximize profits, the firm must produce its output at the lowest possible cost, or, equivalently, the firm must produce the maximum output, given the costs it is incurring.

Output Maximization. Profits are maximized if and only if resources are used efficiently. One way of viewing optimal resource utilization considers the level of output. Resources are being used optimally if the firm obtains the greatest output for a given expenditure. Figure 7.3 summarizes this cost-constrained output-maximization problem.

Isocost line C_1 in Figure 7.3 indicates all combinations of labor and capital that can be purchased at a total cost of $2,000, when labor and capital are each priced at $100 per unit. Isoquants Q_0, Q_1, and Q_2 indicate the combinations of labor and capital required to produce 100, 150, and 200 pocket calculators, respectively. Given the $2,000 cost constraint, the firm is unable to produce 200 calculators, because every point on Q_2 is beyond isocost line C_1. The firm is able to produce 100 calculators using either of the capital-labor combinations indicated by points A or B. Either combination (A or B) is feasible, because both are on C_1 and can be purchased for $2,000. Neither A nor B represents a solution to the output-maximization problem. Starting from

---

2. The equation for an isoquant can be derived from the cost equation: $C = wL + rK$. Subtracting wL from both sides of the equation yields $C - wL = rK$. Dividing both sides by r yields $K = [C/r] - [w/r]L$. Here C/r is the vertical intercept of this line, whereas the slope is $-w/r$.

Figure 7.3 Maximizing Output for a Given Cost

When the prices of labor and capital are both $100 and costs cannot exceed $2,000, the manufacturer can produce a maximum of 150 calculators. The optimal combination of inputs is where the isoquant Q_1 is tangential to the isocost C_1. Any other input combination along C_1 results in lower output; that is, production occurs on an isoquant that is closer to the origin.

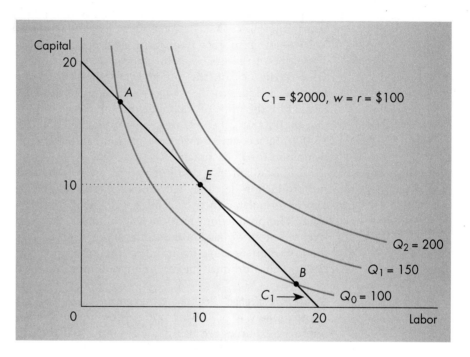

either point and moving along C_1 toward point E will increase output. Calculator production reaches a maximum (given the $2,000 budget) of 150 units at point E. Output, given costs of $2,000, is maximized by selecting the combination of labor and capital (10 units of each) at which the isoquant is tangential to the isocost line. Every other affordable (in terms of the budget constraint) combination of labor and capital lies on a lower isoquant.

Cost Minimization. An identical solution is reached viewing the long-run production decision as a cost-minimization problem. It is essential to find the combination of labor and capital that produces a given quantity of output at the lowest cost. The solution to this process requires a mechanism to identify the level of cost associated with each combination of capital and labor. Isocost lines provide this mechanism.

Introduction to Microeconomic Theory

Figure 7.4 Minimizing Costs of Producing a Given Output

C_0, C_1, and C_2 are isocost curves showing combinations of L and K that can be purchased at a total cost of \$1,500, \$2,000, and \$2,500, respectively. The production of 150 calculators is accomplished at least cost by using 10 units each of capital and labor. Any other combination of L and K that produces 150 calculators — that is, lies on isoquant Q_1 — will entail a higher total cost. The total costs of producing a particular level of output are minimized at a tangency between an isocost and an isoquant.

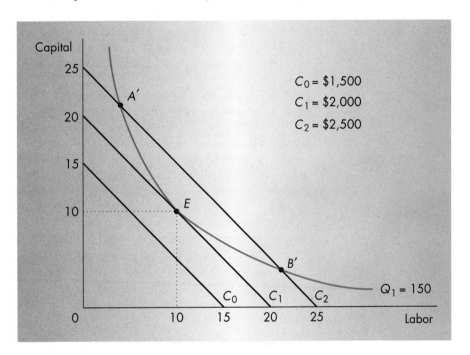

Different levels of costs will generate different isocost lines. Figure 7.4 illustrates three alternative isocost lines. The endpoint of each isocost line is the level of cost (\$1,500, \$2,000, and \$2,500 for curves C_0, C_1, and C_2, respectively) divided by the respective input prices. With constant input prices, the endpoints move further from the origin (from 15 to 20 to 25) as the level of cost rises. The farther the isocost line is from the origin, the higher the level of cost. The slope of any isocost line equals the ratio of the input prices. Constant input prices also mean that isocost lines for different levels of cost will have equal slopes and will be parallel to one another.

Minimizing the costs of producing a given level of output entails finding the capital-labor combination that generates the desired level of output on the isocost line that is closest to the origin. This process is illustrated in Figure 7.4. Suppose that the calculator company wants to produce 150 calculators. This output can be achieved by using any capital-labor combination along the isoquant Q_1. Two such combinations are indicated by points A' and B', both of which are on isocost line C_2. Using either of these input combinations will cost the firm $2,500. The firm can reduce the costs of producing 150 calculators by moving along the isoquant from either point (A or B) toward point E. Costs fall because all points along isoquant Q_1 and between points A' and B' are inside isocost line C_2. This movement along the isoquant reduces costs until point E is reached. Every point on Q_1 other than E is on an isocost line that is beyond C_1. If the firm reduces costs to $1,500 by moving to C_0, it will not be able to produce 150 calculators. The combination of capital and labor denoted by point E (10 units each) is that which minimizes the costs of producing 150 calculators. Note that the isoquant is tangential to the isocost line for cost minimization.

Long-Run Firm Equilibrium. The **optimal input combination** is found at the point at which an isocost line is tangent to an isoquant. As the previous two sections showed, the tangency is where costs of producing a given output are minimized and where the output is maximized, given the costs. The two approaches to the long-run production problem lead to identical solutions, the long-run equilibrium illustrated in Figure 7.5. The techniques used to find the solution to the long-run production problem reflect an underlying economic logic that is not readily apparent. Further study of the equilibrium point is necessary to reveal this economic reasoning.

A given output is produced using the combination of labor and capital at which an isocost is tangential to an isoquant, or at (L^*, K^*) in Figure 7.5. At the tangency, the slopes of the two curves are equal. Earlier in this chapter we saw that the slope of the isocost is equal to the input price ratio, (w/r). In Chapter 6 we saw that the slope of the isoquant equals the marginal rate of technical substitution ($MRTS$), which itself is equal to the ratio of the marginal products of the inputs, (MP_L/MP_K). The equality of the slopes allows us to write

$$MRTS_{LK} = \frac{w}{r} = \frac{MP_L}{MP_K} \qquad (7.1)$$

These equalities reveal the economic logic behind the tangency solution to the long-run production problem.

The firm optimizes resource use by equating the input price ratio to the marginal rate of technical substitution. The input price ratio indicates the rate at which the firm can substitute labor for capital, holding costs constant. The $MRTS_{LK}$ indicates the rate at which the firm can substitute labor for capital, holding output constant. If these two rates of substitution are not equal, the firm can profit from changing its input mix. Suppose that the $MRTS$ of computers for accountants is 4, whereas the price ratio of computers to accountants is 2. The $MRTS$ indicates that 1 computer can be substituted for 4 accountants and output (audits completed) will remain constant. The input price ratio, on the other hand, indicates that 1 computer costs the same as 2

Figure 7.5 Optimal Input Combinations

The solution to the long-run production problem is at the point where an isocost is tangent to an isoquant, or at a point like *E* in the figure. Points *L** and *K** are the least-cost means of producing *Q** and generate the greatest output for an expenditure of *C**.

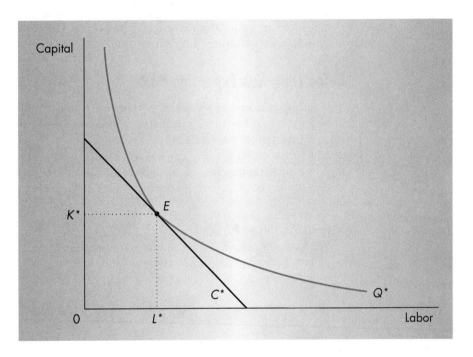

accountants. If the firm makes the substitution of 1 computer for 4 accountants, output stays the same but the firm saves the cost of 2 accountants. Profitable substitutions will persist until the *MRTS* equals the input price ratio.

Rearranging the terms in the foregoing equation, we get

$$\frac{MP_L}{w} = \frac{MP_K}{r} \tag{7.2}$$

which allows a slightly different interpretation of the long-run input decision. Each side of this equation is the marginal product of an input per dollar spent on the input. If the marginal products per dollar are not equal, the firm can profit from changing its input mix. If the additional number of audits completed per dollar spent on accountants is greater than the additional number of audits completed per dollar spent on computers, output can be increased, with no increase in cost, by reallocating a dollar from the computer budget to hiring additional accountants. The decline in output from using fewer computers is more than offset by the increase in output from using more accountants.

Profits are increased by reallocating expenditures whenever the ratios of marginal product to input price are not equal.

Up until now, our discussion of the long-run production problem has been confined to particular isoquants or isocost curves. The level of output and the costs of producing that output affect the firm's profits and are a major element in managerial decision making. The next section investigates the optimal input mix for alternative levels of output. This is one more step on our roundabout path to the firm's long-run cost functions.

The Long-Run Expansion Path

It has been noted previously that there is an isoquant for each level of output and an isocost for each level of cost. Moreover, every isoquant will have an isocost line tangent to it. The points of tangency show the combinations of inputs that minimize the costs of production for alternative levels of output. Three such tangencies (*A*, *B*, and *C*) are illustrated in Figure 7.6. The locus (collection) of all points of tangency between isoquants and isocost lines forms

Figure 7.6 The Long-Run Expansion Path

The long-run expansion path shows the optimal input combination for every level of output. Each point on the *LREP* curve is a point of tangency between an isoquant and an isocost line.

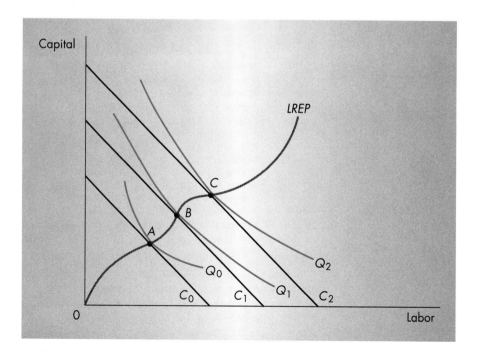

the **long-run expansion path**. An example of a long-run expansion path is the curve labeled *LREP* in Figure 7.6. Each point on *LREP* is a tangency between an isoquant and an isocost line and represents the input mix necessary to minimize the long-run costs of producing a given level of output.

The expansion path shows the optimal combination of inputs for every possible level of output for a firm. As such, it is a map to the firm's input usage in the long run. The expansion path indicates how employment of labor and capital will expand (contract) as output increases (decreases). Once the firm determines the profit-maximizing level of output, the expansion path shows how the output will be produced in the long run. As such, the long-run expansion path is the bridge between the long-run theory of production and the long-run costs of production. Although the expansion path is drawn in terms of input quantities, each point on the expansion path is associated with a unique level of output and a unique level of cost. The costs are the minimum costs of producing output when the firm is able to vary all inputs.

Long-Run Cost Curves

The expansion path is the foundation of the long-run cost functions. The *long-run cost functions* and their graphical counterparts, *long-run cost curves*, describe the relationship between output and cost when all inputs are variable. There are three long-run cost relations: long-run total cost (*LRTC*), long-run average cost (*LAC*), and long-run marginal cost (*LMC*). These long-run cost relations, derived from the expansion path, reflect the assumptions underlying that path. Specifically, these curves describe the relationship between costs and output for a given level of technology and input prices.

Long-Run Total Cost. **Long-run total cost** is the relationship between total cost and output when all inputs are variable. It is derived directly from the long-run expansion path. Each point on the long-run expansion path corresponds to a tangency between an isoquant (which indicates a unique quantity of output) and an isocost line (which indicates a unique total cost). These tangencies have the additional property that the total cost of producing each output is the minimum for that quantity. Two representative points are noted in Figure 7.7a. The minimum cost of producing Q_0 is C_0, and the minimum cost of producing Q_1 is C_1. The long-run total-cost curve is the collection of all cost/output combinations defined by the long-run expansion path and plotted on a graph measuring cost vertically and output horizontally. Each point on the expansion path produces a point on the long-run total-cost curve. The two points (A and B) in panel (a) become the two points (A' and B') on the long-run-total cost curve (*LRTC*) in panel (b). Note that the *LRTC* curve passes through the origin. In the long run, the firm is able to vary all inputs. Its cost of producing no output is therefore zero dollars.

Figure 7.7 Long-Run Total Cost

Panel (a) illustrates a long-run expansion path with points A and B defining the minimum costs C_0 and C_1 of producing output Q_0 and Q_1. Panel (b) illustrates the long-run total-cost curve that is derived from the expansion path in panel (a). Points A and B in panel (a) become points A' and B' in panel (b). Each point on the *LREP* curve translates to a point on the *LRTC* curve.

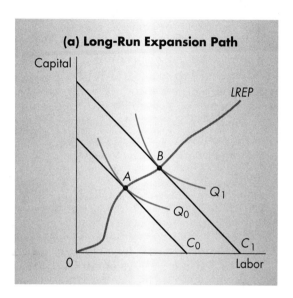
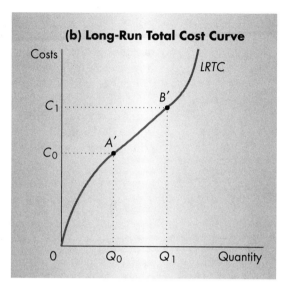

Long-Run Average and Marginal Costs. Although total cost is useful, particularly to calculate profits, it is seldom used in economic analysis. The cost measures most often used are average and marginal costs. **Long-run average cost** (*LAC*) is long-run total cost divided by output (*LRTC/Q*) or costs per unit. **Long-run marginal cost** (*LMC*) is the change in long-run total cost per unit change in output ($\Delta LRTC/\Delta Q$). Your previous experience with economics should tell you that long-run marginal cost will have particular importance, because decisions are made at the margin.

    A representative set of long-run cost curves is illustrated in Figure 7.8. The long-run total-cost curve in panel (a) is drawn so that long-run total costs initially increase at a decreasing rate (from the origin to output Q_1) and then increase at an increasing rate thereafter. The changing slope of the *LRTC* curve in panel (a) has specific implications for the shapes of the long-run average and long-run marginal curves depicted in panel (b). Because marginal cost indicates the change in total cost, marginal cost will be falling when the total is increasing at a decreasing rate and rising when the total increases at an increasing rate. The long-run marginal-cost curve falls between the origin and Q_1 and rises thereafter, reaching a minimum at Q_1. When marginal costs are below average costs, the per-unit costs of production will be falling. The less-than-proportionate increase in costs (with respect to the change in output)

Figure 7.8 Long-Run Cost Curves

The long-run total-cost curve in panel (a) is the source of the *LAC* and *LMC* curves in panel (b). Long-run average costs are long-run total costs divided by output. Long-run marginal costs are the change in long-run total costs. The *LAC* and *LMC* curves exhibit the necessary relationships between average and marginal variables.

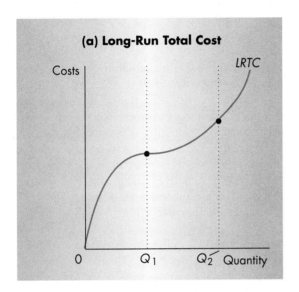

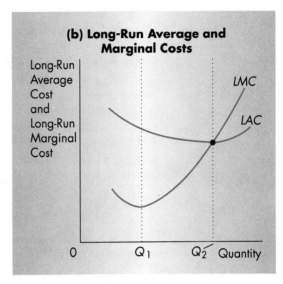

pulls the average down. Eventually, production will reach a point at which increasing marginal costs equal and then exceed the average costs. This will cause per-unit costs to begin rising. The less-than-proportionate increase in output (with respect to the change in costs) pulls the average up. When long-run total costs appear as they do in Figure 7.8a, long-run average costs will initially fall, reach a minimum, and then rise. An important feature of Figure 7.8b is that long-run marginal and long-run average costs do not reach their respective minima at the same level of output.

Figure 7.8 embodies the fundamental relationships between averages and marginals discussed in Chapter 6. When the marginal is less than the average, the average is falling. This is evident at quantities between zero and Q_2, where long-run marginal cost is less than long-run average cost and the *LAC* curve is downward sloping. Quantities greater than Q_2 involve a rising average where the marginal is greater than the average. At Q_2, long-run marginal cost equals long-run average cost, and the *LAC* curve is at its minimum.

The cost curves of Figure 7.8 are representative of the cost curves that will be used extensively in later chapters. The particular shapes that these curves take are not the only ones that are possible. The shape exhibited by specific cost curves reflects underlying production relationships embodied in the production function. These underlying production relationships and the long-run cost curves they give rise to are our next subject.

Characteristics of Long-Run Cost Functions

The shape of a long-run cost function derives from the production function that generates the long-run expansion path. Production functions exhibit a number of characteristics that are particularly relevant to economic analysis. Among these are economies of scale, returns to scale, economies of scope, and minimum efficient scale.

Economies of Scale. An important feature of long-run cost curves is the slope of the long-run average-cost curve. A downward-sloping *LAC* curve indicates **economies of scale**. The production process is such that long-run average costs decrease as the scale of production, or output, increases. Large operations may be able to take advantage of mass-production techniques that reduce the per-unit costs of production. Assembly lines are costly to set up but allow increases in output with relatively little additional costs. Large-scale production tends to keep very specialized (and very productive) equipment and workers busy, allowing for more than proportionate increases in output. The *LAC* curve in Figure 7.9a illustrates scale economies occurring over all quantities of output.

Some production processes cannot be adapted to mass-production techniques and/or highly specialized inputs. A good or service that requires an individual's skills or talents (giving a legal or medical opinion, for instance), is difficult to mass-produce. An increase in production in this situation can lead to higher per-unit costs. A rising *LAC* curve is indicative of **diseconomies of scale**. The *LAC* curve in Figure 7.9b exhibits diseconomies of scale for all quantities.

Economies and diseconomies of scale are not an either/or proposition. The *LAC* in Figure 7.9c exhibits economies of scale when output is less than Q^* and diseconomies of scale for outputs greater than Q^*. This is the characteristic U-shape of the curves in Figure 7.8. The *LAC* curve in Figure 7.9d exhibits neither economies nor diseconomies of scale, with long-run average costs being constant. One might want to equate the shape of the *LAC* curve in Figure 7.9d with constant returns to scale. We must, however, take care to differentiate between scale economies and returns to scale.

Returns to Scale Revisited. Returns to scale were defined (in Chapter 6) as the change in output resulting from proportionate changes in all inputs. As such, this concept looks only at quantities and ignores costs. Although we can solve for the change in unit costs in the face of returns to scale, the answer may be meaningless in view of long-run average costs. Long-run average-cost curves are based on cost-minimizing input use, whereas returns to scale require proportionate changes in all inputs. If proportionate changes in inputs keep the firm on the long-run expansion path, returns to scale will tell us what is happening to long-run average costs. If a proportionate change in inputs

Figure 7.9 Returns to Scale

The figure illustrates four possible *LAC* curves. The declining long-run average costs of panel (a) arise from economies of scale. The rising *LAC* curve in panel (b) is the result of diseconomies of scale. Initial scale economies followed by diseconomies account for the U-shaped *LAC* curve in panel (c). The horizontal *LAC* in panel (d) indicates the absence of scale effects.

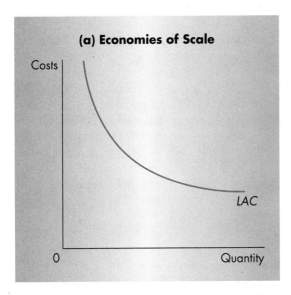

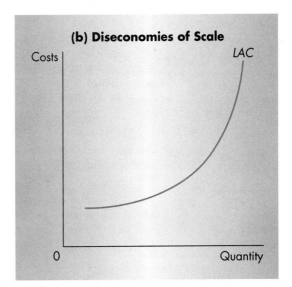

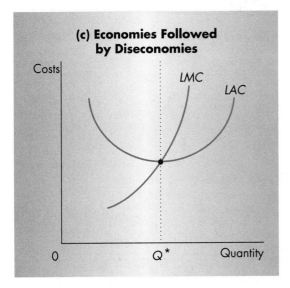

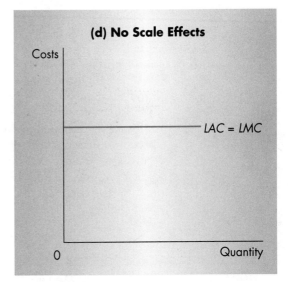

moves production off the expansion path, the firm will be using incorrect combinations of inputs and will be off its long-run total-cost curve. Because the long-run total-cost curve shows the minimum costs of producing each level of output, the proportionate input changes result in higher-than-necessary costs per unit of output. Any information that we may glean regarding the relative changes in output and costs is meaningless.

Minimum Efficient Scale.   **Minimum efficient scale** (*MES*) refers to the quantity at which long-run average costs reach their lowest level. In Figure 7.9c the *MES* is Q^*. The *MES* is important because it plays a role in determining the number of firms that will exist in the market (a prime consideration in Part IV of this text). The *MES* indicates the minimum output necessary to reduce unit costs to their lowest level. If the *MES* is small relative to the market, the market will be able to support many firms. This situation is common in many retail markets in which economies of scale are limited. A low *MES* is associated with small and numerous retailers. If the *MES* is large relative to the market, only a few firms will populate the industry. Manufacturing is subject to significant scale economies and tends to have relatively large *MES*'s. This explains, in part, why there are just a few large automakers.

Economies of Scope.   The cost curves developed above assumed a single output. Real-world markets are populated by firms producing and selling multiple products. One factor contributing to the production of multiple outputs is **economies of scope**, cost savings that result from producing a number of products. The costs of producing one good may be reduced by producing other goods. A fabricator of steel transmission towers for power companies may reduce its costs of producing towers by producing other products that are also fabricated from steel.

Increasing the range of products does not always lead to cost reductions. Production may also be subject to *diseconomies of scope*, in which costs *rise* with diversification of the firm's product line. One source of diseconomies of scope is found in the limited ability of managers to control operations. Firms can become so large and their operations so diverse that it is impossible for individuals or small groups of individuals to effectively control the operation. When firms encounter diseconomies of scope, one option is to reorganize and reduce the scope of its operations, an option taken by IBM in the early 1990s (see Highlight 7.2).

Highlight 7.2   *The "New and Improved" IBM[a]*

The IBM story hinges on long-run cost concepts. Prior to 1980, the firm was known for its mainframe computers, a market it continues to dominate. Part of

IBM's dominance in the mainframe market can be traced to scale economies and a relatively high minimum efficient scale in the production of mainframe computers. IBM's output of large, complex mainframe computers was sufficient to take advantage of scale economies, and the relatively low unit costs gave IBM a competitive edge in the market. Moreover, the relatively high *MES* prevented other mainframe manufacturers from entering and competing effectively.

The 1980s saw the introduction of personal computers and the opening of new computer markets. IBM expanded its product line to include these markets; economies of scope reduced costs; and profits peaked at $6.5 billion in 1984. Central to this success was IBM's memory-chip operations. Although IBM is one of the largest producers of memory chips, it only accounts for a small share of the memory-chip market. IBM, using its voluminous chip production in its own manufacturing operations, reaped the resultant economies of scope, becoming what some called "Battleship IBM."

The 1990s have been unkind to the IBM dreadnought. The firm grew into an organization that many felt was hindered by inertia and inflexibility brought on by its sheer size. In essence, IBM's operations entered the range in which diseconomies of scope dominated production. IBM's solution was a simple one: it reorganized itself into smaller, quasi-independent operating units, each specializing in a single product line. The loose confederation of subsidiaries is designed to stimulate the efficiency of the individual operating units and increase combined profits.

Although it will take time to determine the success of IBM's strategy, the strategy itself has a long history of success. General Motors underwent a similar reorganization years ago when it created its current divisions (Chevrolet, Oldsmobile, and so on). The strategy wasn't new with GM. Similar reorganizations were undertaken by DuPont and even the Catholic church. In the Middle Ages, the church went through a decentralization that some economists believe was designed to increase the efficiency of its operations.

[a] The information contained in this application was taken from J. Markoff, "I.B.M. Announces Sweeping Shift in Its Structure," *The New York Times* 141, no. 48,797 (Nov. 27, 1991), p. A1.

The cost curves that we have developed represent the consequences of production decisions when all inputs are variable. These long-run curves are usually referred to as **planning curves**, because they correspond to a time horizon that goes beyond the day-to-day operations of firms. In making day-to-day decisions, firms are constrained to fixed quantities of some inputs. Decisions that are constrained in this way fall within the province of short-run costs of production.

Short-Run Costs of Production

The day-to-day production decisions that firms must make to operate involve a number of factors beyond their control. A notable constraint is the plant and equipment, or capital, that the firm uses in its operations. The inability to alter the amount of capital employed is, as was noted in Chapter 6, the distinguishing feature of what we call the short run. The short-run production problem is to find the optimal quantity of the variable input(s) to produce various levels of output.

Production Choices in the Short Run

Short-run costs arise from short-run production decisions. Following the convention used in Chapter 6, short-run production decisions encompass a variable amount of labor employed in conjunction with a fixed amount of capital. The use of both entails costs, and these costs are related to output through the short-run production relations depicted in the total-product curve. This curve relates output to the use of labor, given some amount of capital. Because the amount of capital is fixed, the firm chooses the quantity of labor necessary to produce the desired level of output.[3]

Short-Run Cost Curves

In the short run it is necessary to differentiate between fixed and variable costs. Consider the costs faced by the owner of a day-care center. The owners must pay the fixed costs of maintaining and insuring the center that do not vary with the number of children enrolled. They also face the variable costs of supplies and teacher salaries, both of which vary with the number of children. In our simplified, two-input model, fixed costs are those costs associated with capital, and variable costs are those associated with the employment of labor.

Variable Costs. In the simplified, two-input model, **variable costs** (*VC*) arise from the employment of labor. Total variable costs will, in this case, equal the price of labor times the quantity of labor, or $VC = wL$. These costs are related to output, because each quantity of labor produces a given output. Table 7.1 displays this relationship among labor, output, and variable costs.

Table 7.1 is an adaptation of Table 6.2, with the variable-cost column added by multiplying the quantity of labor by the price of labor (w is set equal to $5 for this example). Note that the variable costs of producing no output

---

3. This is in contrast to the necessity of finding the optimal capital-labor combination that we faced in the long run. The derivation of long-run costs required the development of the long-run expansion path to relate inputs to outputs before we could find the relationship between output and cost.

Table 7.1 Short-Run Variable Costs

Labor (L)	Total Product (Q)	Variable Cost (w x L)
0	0	$ 0
1	6	5
2	10	10
3	15	15
4	19	20
5	22	25
6	24	30
7	25	35
8	25	40

are zero. The firm is able to avoid paying any variable costs by not hiring any labor (L = 0 when Q = 0). Although the information in Table 7.1 can be graphed to obtain the variable-cost curve, it is also possible to obtain the variable-cost curve directly from the total-product curve.

The total-product curve graphs Q against L. Multiplying the L-axis of the total-product curve by the price of labor (w) transforms the horizontal (L) axis into variable cost. If the graph is then rotated so that the Q-axis becomes the horizontal axis and the (newly obtained) VC-axis becomes the vertical axis, we get the variable-cost curve. This procedure is illustrated in Figure 7.10; the total-product curve is illustrated in panel (a), and total variable costs are illustrated in panel (b). Close inspection of panel (b) will reveal that the VC curve is the mirror image of the TP curve in panel (a). The mirror image is created when the axes are switched.

The shape of the total-product curve dictates the shape of the variable cost curve, because the two are mirror images. As was discussed in Chapter 6, diminishing returns dictate the shape of the total-product curve. When the marginal product is rising, total product is rising at an *increasing* rate and variable costs will be increasing at a *decreasing* rate. When the marginal product is falling, the total product is increasing but at a *decreasing* rate, and variable cost is increasing at an *increasing* rate. The relationship between output and cost is defined by the underlying relation between the inputs and output.

Average variable costs (AVC) are per-unit variable costs, or AVC = VC/Q. By the same basic logic as was used regarding long-run average cost, the general shape of the average-variable-cost curve can be inferred by examining the slope of the variable-cost curve. Although this method gives the general shape of the AVC curve, its precise shape and position can be found by examining one of the short-run production relationships: the average product.

Figure 7.10 Variable Cost and Average Variable Cost

The total product curve is illustrated in panel (a). Multiplying the horizontal axis of panel (a) by the price of labor and then switching the axes produces the variable cost (*VC*) curve in panel (b). The *VC* curve is the mirror image of the *TP* curve. Panel (c) replicates the average product (*AP*) curve of Chapter 6. Inverting the *AP* curve and multiplying by the price of labor produces the *AVC* curve in panel (d).

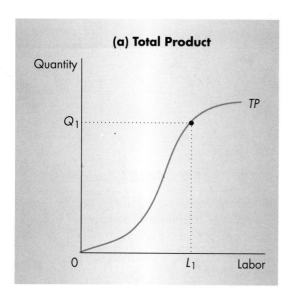

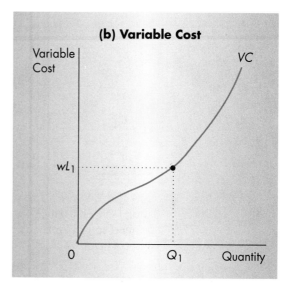

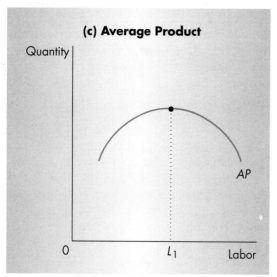

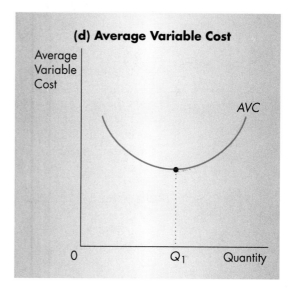

The relationship between average product and average variable cost is revealed by examining the definitions of *AVC*, *VC*, and *AP*. Some algebraic manipulation of these definitions yields the equation

$$AVC = w\left(\frac{1}{AP}\right) \tag{7.3}$$

that is, average variable cost is the inverse of the average product multiplied by the price of labor.[4] This fact is revealed by inspecting Figure 7.10c and d, which illustrate average-product and average-variable-cost curves, respectively. The *AVC* curve is simply the *AP* curve turned upside down and shifted by a multiple equal to the wage rate. Average variable costs will be falling (rising) when the average product is rising (falling). Additionally, the *AVC* curve attains its minimum when the *AP* curve reaches its maximum. These relationships should have some intuitive appeal. The labor cost per unit of output (the *AVC*) will be inversely related to the output per unit of labor (the *AP*). If output per worker is rising, hiring more workers will increase output more than proportionately, whereas costs will increase proportionately, causing a decline in cost per unit of output.

Fixed Costs. Fixed costs are the easiest to understand and illustrate. Because the amount of capital employed is fixed, the costs of using capital are fixed and do not vary with output. **Fixed costs** (*FC*) are calculated as the (fixed) quantity of capital (K_0) multiplied by the price of capital (r), or $FC = rK_0$. Graphing fixed costs as a function of output generates a line horizontal at rK_0, as illustrated in Figure 7.11a. The average-fixed-cost curve is illustrated in Figure 7.11b. **Average fixed costs** (*AFC*) are fixed costs per unit of output, or $AFC = FC/Q$. In calculating the average fixed costs for increasing outputs, repeatedly dividing a constant numerator by an increasing denominator yields a continually declining number. Fixed costs of $1 million leave a car company with average fixed costs of $1 million when 1 car is built and $1 when a million cars are produced. The *AFC* curve will be downward sloping throughout.

4. The definitions are, in mathematical form:

$$AVC = \frac{VC}{Q}, \quad VC = wL, \text{ and } AP = \frac{Q}{L}$$

Substituting *wL* for *VC* in the equation for *AVC* yields

$$AVC = \frac{wL}{Q}$$

Noting that $L/Q = 1/AP$ (the inverse of *AP*), we can substitute for L/Q and find that

$$AVC = \frac{w}{AP}$$

Figure 7.11 Fixed Cost and Average Fixed Cost

Fixed costs do not vary with output as indicated by the horizontal *FC* curve in panel (a). In panel (b), *AFC* falls continuously as the (constant) fixed cost is divided by ever-increasing quantities.

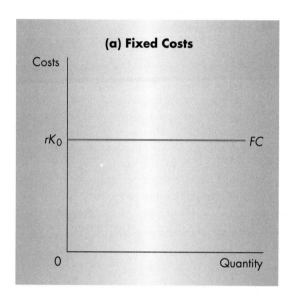

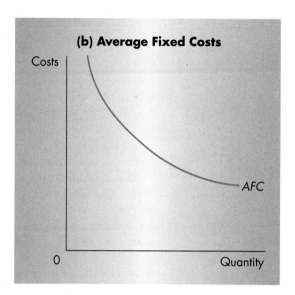

Total Costs. Short-run total costs *(SRTC)* are the sum of fixed and variable costs, or $SRTC = FC + VC$. The *SRTC* curve is found by summing the *FC* and *VC* curves vertically. Because fixed costs are constant, the vertical summation is equivalent to shifting the *VC* curve upward by the amount of fixed costs and relabeling it as *SRTC*. This process is illustrated in Figure 7.12a. There are three important characteristics of this graph:

1. The vertical distance between the *SRTC* and *VC* curves is constant (reflecting the fixed cost).
2. Short-run total costs equal fixed costs when output is zero. This occurs because variable costs are zero when output is zero.
3. The shape of the *SRTC* curve is identical to that of the *VC* curve. Diminishing returns affect both total and variable cost in precisely the same way.

The average-total-cost curve is illustrated (along with average variable and average fixed costs) in Figure 7.12b. The **average total costs** *(ATC)*, defined as the total costs per unit of output, are calculated by the equation $ATC = TC/Q$. Because total costs are the sum of fixed and variable costs, average total cost will be equal to the sum of average fixed and average variable costs. The *ATC* curve in Figure 7.12b is the vertical sum of the *AFC* and *AVC* curves.

Figure 7.12 Total Cost and Average Total Cost

Total cost, in the short run, is the sum of fixed and variable costs. The *SRTC* curve in panel (a) is the vertical sum of the *FC* and *VC* curves. Average total cost is total cost divided by quantity or the sum of average variable and average fixed costs. The *ATC* curve in panel (b) is the vertical sum of the *AVC* and *AFC* curves.

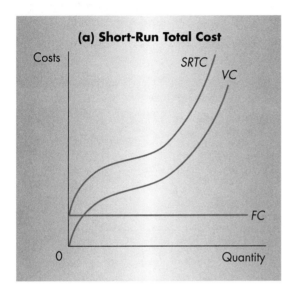

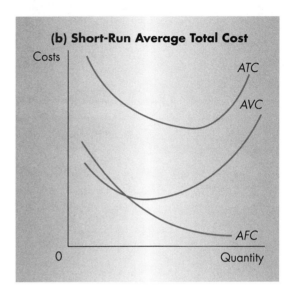

Marginal Cost. **Marginal cost** (*MC*) is the change in total cost (Δ*SRTC*) per unit change in output (Δ*Q*), or *MC* = Δ*SRTC*/Δ*Q*. Because total cost is composed of variable and fixed costs, any change in total cost must arise from a change in the variable cost (because fixed costs do not change). Algebraically we can write $SMC = \Delta TC/\Delta Q = \Delta VC/\Delta Q$. If data were available showing the total costs of producing every level of output, marginal cost could be found by taking the difference in the total-cost figures for consecutive units of output. If the total costs of producing 7 units of output are $169 and 8 units cost $173, the marginal cost of the eighth unit is $4, or $173 − $169. Although we may derive a marginal-cost curve in this fashion, a quicker method is to consider the relationship between marginal costs and the marginal product.

The relationship between marginal product and marginal cost is illustrated in Figure 7.13. Panel (a) reproduces the marginal- and average-product curves of the previous chapter, and panel (b) shows the marginal-cost and average-variable-cost curves that come from the curves in panel (a). The relationship between marginal product and marginal cost is identical (for mathematical reasons) to that between average product and average variable cost. Marginal cost

Figure 7.13 Marginal Cost
Average and marginal product curves are illustrated in panel (a). Inverting the product curves produces the *AVC* and *MC* curves in panel (b). Because *MP* = *AP* at the maximum of *AP*, *MC* = *AVC* at the minimum of *AVC*.

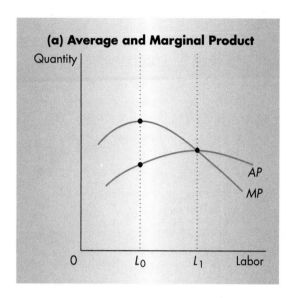

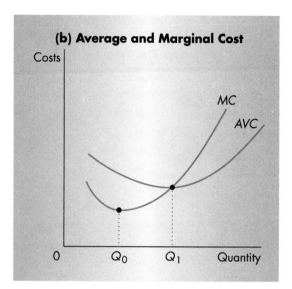

is the inverse of marginal product multiplied by the price of labor, or

$$MC = w\left(\frac{1}{MP}\right)$$

In other words, the *MC* curve in panel (b) is the *MP* curve from panel (a) turned upside down and shifted by a factor equal to the wage rate.[5] This inversion process carries with it a number of basic relationships. Inverting the *MP* curve means that the *MC* curve will reach its minimum where the *MP* curve attains its maximum. This is at quantity Q_0 in panel (b). Moreover, where marginal product is falling (rising), marginal cost will be rising (falling). Finally, because marginal product equals average product at the latter's maximum, marginal cost will equal average variable cost at the minimum of average variable cost. Both of these equalities occur at quantity Q_1 in Figure 7.13.

5. By definition, $MC = \Delta TC/\Delta Q$. The change in total cost occurs in variable cost; therefore, we can write $\Delta TC = \Delta VC$. The change in variable cost arises from a change in the amount of labor employed. Thus we can write $\Delta VC = w\Delta L$. Substituting this last expression for ΔTC in the equation for marginal cost yields $MC = w\Delta L/\Delta Q$. Noting that $MP = \Delta Q/\Delta L$ and that $1/MP = \Delta L/\Delta Q$, we can write $MC = w(1/MP)$.

Figure 7.14 Short-Run Costs United

The *AVC, ATC,* and *MC* curves contain sufficient information to determine any short-run cost. The marginal, average variable, or average total cost of any quantity can be read directly. The *AFC* can be found by taking the vertical difference between the *ATC* and *AVC* at any quantity. Total, variable, and fixed costs can be found by multiplying quantity by the *ATC, AVC,* and *AFC,* respectively.

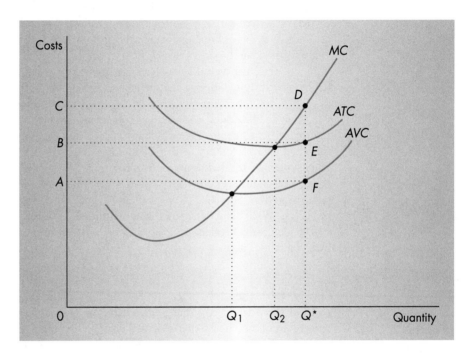

Short-Run Cost Curves United. The mechanics of working with short-run costs are complicated by the number of short-run cost relationships. In the short run we have fixed costs, variable costs, total costs, average fixed costs, average variable costs, average total costs, and marginal costs. All of these cost functions have their uses, yet just three of them will be sufficient to answer any question regarding short-run costs. All of the information contained in the seven short-run cost functions can be obtained from the *ATC, AVC,* and *MC* curves. The means of divising the necessary information is illustrated in Figure 7.14.

The cost curves in Figure 7.14 can be used to determine the average total, average variable, or marginal cost associated with any level of output.[6] The average variable costs of producing Q^* is the vertical distance between the horizontal axis and point *F* or, equivalently, the distance 0*A*. Average total

---

6. Output Q^* is used to illustrate this process, but the same methods apply to any Q.

costs are the distance between E and the horizontal axis, which equals the distance $0B$. The marginal costs of Q^* are equal to the distance between D and Q^* or the $0C$ difference. Although not illustrated explicitly, average fixed costs of Q^* can be found by taking the difference between the ATC and AVC curves, or the distance between points A and B.

Total costs, variable costs, and fixed costs are found by multiplying the respective averages by the quantity. Note that the averages are measured vertically, whereas the quantities are measured horizontally. Graphically, the product of a vertical distance and a horizontal distance is the area of the rectangle formed by the two sides. If we denote rectangles by the points that form their corners, the variable cost of producing Q^* is equal to the area of the $0AFQ^*$ rectangle. Short-run total costs of producing Q^* equal the area of $0BEQ^*$. Finally, because $0Q^*$ equals AF, fixed costs equal the area of $ABEF$.

Figure 7.14 added the average-total-cost curve to the curves illustrated in Figure 7.13b to create a graph that will be used repeatedly in the next part of this text. The placement of the ATC requires some care, because marginal cost equals average total cost at the minimum of average total cost. The relationship between an average variable and a marginal variable prevails in all circumstances. Where the MC curve is below the ATC curve, the ATC curve will be falling. Where the MC curve is above the ATC curve, the ATC curve will be rising. Average total cost will achieve a minimum when the average and marginal are equal.

Plant Capacity. The U-shape of the MC and AVC curves, caused by first increasing and then decreasing marginal returns to a variable input, carries over into the ATC curve. The U-shape of this curve means that there will be some output at which the average costs of production are at a minimum. This output is referred to as the firm's **plant capacity**. Plant capacity, the short-run equivalent of long-run minimum efficient scale, is an important topic in Part IV of this text.

The Relationship Between Short-Run Costs and Long-Run Costs

Thus far we have treated short-run and long-run costs as if they were unrelated. Although they are used separately and for different purposes, it is important to recognize the link between these cost concepts. The link between short-run and long-run costs is found in their common basis, the theory of production. The relationship between them is revealed by contrasting long-run and short-run production decisions.

Long-Run Versus Short-Run Production Choices

Figure 7.15 explains the relationship between long-run and short-run production choices. In the long run, the firm operates on the long-run expansion path, denoted *LREP* in Figure 7.15. A firm wishing to increase production from Q_0 to Q_1, for example, will move from A to B along the *LREP* curve. The firm uses input combination (L_0, K_0) to produce Q_0 and combination (L_1, K_1) to produce Q_1. In the short run, production choices are constrained by the amount of capital. A firm that is initially at point A in Figure 7.15 will, in the short run, be restricted to the labor-capital combinations along the line horizontal at K_0. This line is called a **short-run expansion path** and is labeled $SREP_0$. It is necessary to append a subscript to the label of the curve because it is but one of the many possible short-run expansion paths. There will be a short-run expansion path for each quantity of capital that can be used in production. Each short-run expansion path will be a line horizontal at the

Figure 7.15 Long-Run and Short-Run Production Choices

The figure contrasts output expansion in the long run and the short run. Output is increased from Q_0 to Q_1 in the long run by moving along the long-run expansion path to point B. Output is increased from Q_0 to Q_1 in the short run by moving along the short-run expansion path to point B'. The costs of producing Q_1 are greater in the short run, C_1', than in the long run, C_1.

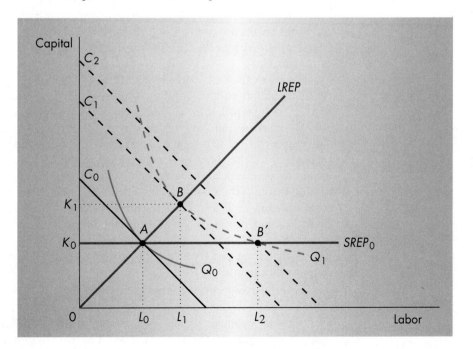

appropriate level of capital. Moreover, each short-run expansion path will intersect the long-run expansion path, because each level of capital will be the optimal amount needed to produce some level of output.

$SREP_0$ is the only short-run expansion path illustrated in Figure 7.15, because it is sufficient to illustrate how a short-run production choice differs from the long-run option. $SREP_0$ shows how the firm expands (or contracts) when capital is fixed at K_0. We can expand output to quantity Q_1, holding capital constant at K_0, by moving from point A to point B' and increasing the amount of labor from L_0 to L_2. Note the difference between the short- and long-run use of resources to accomplish identical changes in output (Q_0 to Q_1). In the short run, input use changes from (L_0,K_0) to (L_2,K_0), and in the long run, it goes to (L_1,K_1). This difference in input use leads to long- and short-run cost differentials.

Long-Run Versus Short-Run Total Costs

Figure 7.15 contains the elements necessary to illustrate the difference between long-run and short-run total costs. Long-run total costs are derived from the long-run expansion path; each point on the *LREP* curve is tied to a point on the *LRTC* curve. Similarly, short-run total costs can be derived from the short-run expansion path. The short-run expansion path reveals (via the isoquants it intersects) the output from different quantities of labor, holding capital constant. Each of these labor-capital combinations entails a total cost. Matching output with the total cost of producing the output generates a short-run total-cost curve. The relationship between long-run and short-run costs can be discovered by closer examination of the respective expansion paths.

The two expansion paths in Figure 7.15 have one point (A) in common. At that point the input combinations are identical, and the respective total costs must be equal. This is illustrated in Figure 7.16, where the $SRTC_0$ and *LRTC* curves are equal at point A. At any other output in Figure 7.15, there is a divergence of the two total costs. We can expand production to Q_1 by going to point B' in the short run and point B in the long run. The total costs of using any combination of labor and capital are indicated by the isocost curve passing through the combination. The costs of being at B are C_1, whereas the costs of being at B' are C_2. The short-run costs of producing Q_1 are greater than the long-run costs. Plotting these output-cost combinations generates points B and B' in Figure 7.16 where, for output Q_1, short-run costs are greater than long-run costs. What is true of output Q_1 is true for every level of output other than Q_0.

With the exception of the point at which the expansion paths intersect, the short-run costs will be above long-run costs. The *LRTC* curve shows the minimum cost of producing each level of output. This minimum is obtained by varying all inputs to the desired level. The firm is not able to vary inputs

Figure 7.16 Long-Run and Short-Run Total Costs

A short-run total-cost curve will be tangential to each point on the long-run total-cost curve. The tangency occurs because short-run total costs equal long-run total costs at one level of output, but they are higher at all other levels of output.

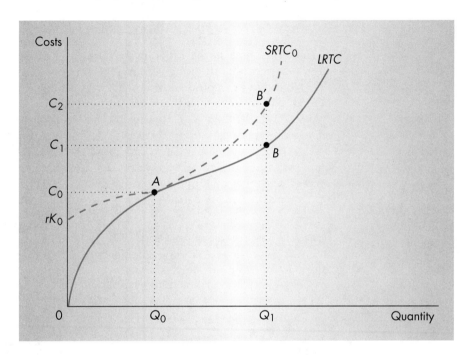

optimally in the short run because it cannot change its use of capital. Changing output in the short run entails, from the long-run perspective, an inefficient use of resources and, consequently, higher costs. An obvious example of this is what occurs when the firm decides to produce no output. In the short run, fixed costs (rK_0) must be paid, even if nothing is produced. In the long run, the firm is able to avoid all costs when production is halted. This is illustrated in Figure 7.16, where the $LRTC$ curve starts at the origin, whereas the $SRTC_0$ curve starts at rK_0. From this beginning, the $SRTC_0$ curve is above the $LRTC$ curve for all outputs with the exception of output Q_0, where the two are equal. This relationship between the short-run and long-run total-cost curves requires the short-run curve to be tangent (from above) to the long-run total-cost curve at output Q_0.

Each point on the $LRTC$ curve corresponds to a point on the $LREP$ curve; each point on the $LREP$ curve is associated with a different amount of capital; each level of capital has a short-run expansion path associated with it, and, a short-run total-cost curve exists for each short-run expansion path. The implication of all these interconnected points is that each point on the $LRTC$ curve will have a different $SRTC$ curve tangential at that point. This fact made it necessary to append a subscript to the abbreviation for short-run total cost. Each point on the *LRTC* represents production with a different amount of capital. Fixing each of those levels of capital pushes the producer into the short run and generates a different short-run total-cost curve.

Average Costs: Long-Run Versus Short-Run

Taking each point on the *LRTC* curve in Figure 7.16 and calculating the average costs produces the long-run average-cost curve, labeled *LAC* in Figure 7.17. Repeating this process using the points on the short-run total-cost curve in Figure 7.16 generates the short-run average-cost curve labeled ATC_0 in Figure 7.17. Dividing totals by quantity to determine the averages does not change the basic relationships between the short-run and long-run cost curves. The ATC_0 curve is tangential to and above the *LAC* curve, just as the $SRTC_0$ curve was tangential to and above the *LRTC* curve in Figure 7.16. Short-run average costs will be above long-run average costs for every quantity except one, where the two are equal.

Figure 7.17 Long-Run and Short-Run Average and Marginal Costs

The *LAC* curve has an *ATC* curve tangential to it at each of its points. The *LAC* curve is the envelope of points on *ATC* curves representing the least per-unit cost for each level of output. All average and marginal curves reflect the usual relationship between average and marginal variables.

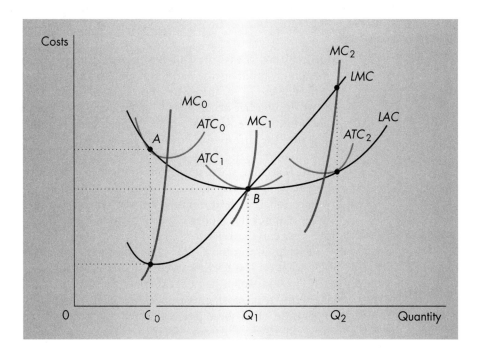

ATC_0 is but one of many ATC curves that exist. Every point of the LAC curve will have an ATC curve tangential to it at that point: ATC_1 and ATC_2 are representative of this phenomenon. The ATC_1 and ATC_2 are derived from different short-run total-cost curves, each of which uses the level of capital defined by the long-run expansion path for Q_1 and Q_2, respectively. The points of tangency between the short-run and long-run average-cost curves are occurring where short-run expansion paths intersect the long-run expansion path, which is where $SRTC$ curves are tangent to the $LRTC$ curve. The long-run average-cost curve is often called the **envelope curve**, because it can be viewed as the collection of these tangency points. Each of these points represents the consequence of using the least-cost means of producing each level of output.

Marginal Costs: Long-Run Versus Short-Run

The foregoing analysis has ignored the marginal cost curves included in Figure 7.17. Every average-cost curve has an accompanying marginal-cost curve. The LMC curve in Figure 7.17 indicates the change in long-run total cost for a change in output. The LMC curve conforms to the usual average/marginal relations. The LMC curve (1) is below the LAC curve when the LAC is downward sloping, (2) is above the LAC curve when the LAC curve is upward sloping, and (3) intersects the LAC curve where the LAC curve is at its minimum.

Similarly, every short-run average-cost curve will have a companion marginal-cost curve. Each of the ATC curves has a MC curve that fulfills the three parts of the relationship between averages and marginals. The MC curves in Figure 7.17 must also conform to the relationships between short-run and long-run costs. The LAC/ATC tangencies occur where $SRTC$ curves are tangent to the $LRTC$ curve. The tangencies of the total-cost curves involve equal slopes, where the slopes measure the respective marginal costs. Thus the relationships between short-run and long-run cost place a fourth requirement on the placement of the MC curves: short-run marginal cost equals long-run marginal cost where short-run average cost equals long-run average cost. Note that this condition (as well as the requirements of the average/marginal relationship) is met by each of the SMC curves illustrated in Figure 7.17.[7]

Short-Run and Long-Run Costs: Reprise

Close inspection of Figure 7.17 reveals an unusual convergence at point *B*. Four curves (LAC, LMC, ATC_1, and MC_1) pass through this point. Point *B* is at the output (Q_1), where production exhausts economies of scale and

---

7. Note that each of the short-run marginal-cost curves are steeper than the long-run marginal-cost curve where the two intersect. The change in total cost for any change in output will be larger in the short run than in the long run, because inputs cannot be varied optimally in the short run. The long-run adjustment will entail lower marginal costs.

diseconomies of scale begin, leaving long-run average costs at a minimum. Because the average is at a minimum, the marginal must be equal to the average at this point, and the *LMC* curve also passes through point *B*. The convergence of a third curve at point *B* follows from the relationship between short-run and long-run average costs. Each point on the *LAC* curve has an *ATC* curve tangential to it and ATC_1 is the short-run average curve that is tangential to the *LAC* curve at *B*. Because *B* is the minimum of long-run average costs, *B* must also be the minimum of ATC_1.[8] If *B* is the minimum of ATC_1, then the curve that is marginal to ATC_1, MC_1, must also pass through point *B*. Four curves converge at the point at which long-run average costs are at their minimum. The relevance of this characteristic of cost functions will be revealed in Chapter 8, where competitive markets are considered.

Changes in Cost Curves

The development of cost curves requires holding everything except output and the level of resource use constant. A change in any other factor that affects the costs of production will result in a movement of the cost curves, because a cost curve shows the relationship between output and costs, *ceteris paribus*. An increase in costs is depicted as an upward movement of the cost curves, whereas a decrease would be illustrated with a downward shift of the curves. The prime suspects behind such shifts in the cost curves are changes in technology, input prices, taxes, and regulations. Although this is not an exhaustive list of factors that cause movements of the cost curve, they are representative of the class of phenomena that cause such changes.

Technology affects costs through the isoquants map. Technological change increases the output associated with any input combination. Increasing the output when everything else is constant (especially the quantity of resources used) shifts the cost curves downward. Recent reductions in the costs of producing PCs arose from technological advances (more powerful computer chips, and so on).

Input prices, regulation, and taxes affect costs via the isocost line. A change in any of these factors will change the costs associated with each combination of inputs and shift the cost curves appropriately. Falling gasoline, diesel, and jet fuel prices reduce the costs of transporting people and products.

---

8. None of the other *LAC/ATC* tangencies have this property. For outputs less than Q_1, the *LAC/ATC* tangency occurs where the *LAC* curve is downward sloping. The *ATC* curve must also be downward sloping, because a tangency requires an equality of the slopes. If short-run average costs are declining (the curve is downward sloping), they cannot have reached their minimum. For quantities less than Q_1, the *LAC/ATC* tangency occurs before the minimum of the *ATC* curve. Similar reasoning leads to the conclusion that, for quantities greater than Q_1, the *LAC/ATC* tangency occurs after the *ATC* curve has reached its minimum.

The costs of producing electricity rise by the expense of installing smoke-stack scrubbers required by the Clean Air Act. Finally, taxes on diesel fuel increase the costs of operating a trucking company. Technology, input prices, regulation, and taxes affect more than the position of the cost curves. Highlight 7.3 shows how changes in input prices affect the relative quantities of the resources that are employed.

Chapters 6 and 7 have been rather tedious, but necessary, excursions in economic theory. Theories about production and the costs of production are abstract models that strive to provide insight into these vital aspects of economic activity. Although you may or may not find them interesting as purely intellectual exercises, they are crucial to understanding the subject matter of Part IV. The next part of the text investigates the economic consequences of alternative market structures.

Highlight 7.3 *Production, Costs, and the Minimum Wage*

Minimum-wage legislation is a consistent source of controversy. Proponents of an increase in the minimum wage stress the need to increase the incomes of those at the bottom of the pay scale. Opponents focus on the unemployment created by minimum-wage laws. Another concern is the impact that such laws have on the costs of production. The minimum-wage controversy is an ideal opportunity to apply the techniques developed in this chapter.

Periodically, legislation is enacted that increases the minimum wage. One consequence of this legislation is that the price of unskilled workers (those whose wage is affected by the minimum wage) rises relative to the price of skilled workers, whose wage is not directly affected by the legislation. This change in relative prices is illustrated in Figure 7.18. There, the production choice is shown to be between skilled and unskilled labor rather than between capital and labor. Initially, the cheapest way to produce Q_0 units of output is at point A, where U_0 units of unskilled labor and S_0 units of skilled labor are employed. Then the rise in the minimum wage increases the slope of the iso-cost line and changes the optimal point on the original isoquant to point B, where U_1 units of unskilled labor and S_1 units of skilled labor are employed. If the level of output was unchanged, the overall impact would be to reduce employment of unskilled workers from U_0 to U_1 and increase employment of skilled workers from S_0 to S_1.

However, it is not plausible to argue that output will remain unchanged. The increase in the minimum wage will increase the cost of producing the good in question. We are certain that the cost rises, because the vertical intercept of C_1 is higher than the vertical intercept of C_0 and the wage of skilled

Figure 7.18 Production, Costs, and the Minimum Wage

An increase in the minimum wage alters the slope of the isocost line. The increased relative price of unskilled labor alters the optimal input combination in favor of skilled labor at the expense of unskilled labor.

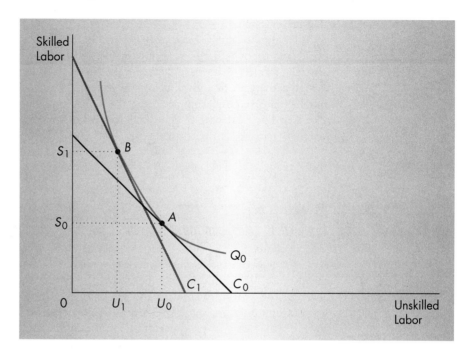

workers is unchanged. The equilibrium level of output will fall, leading to even larger reductions in the employment of unskilled workers. How much output will fall depends on the nature of the production function (how easily skilled workers are substituted for unskilled workers), on the importance of unskilled labor as an input in the production of the good in question, and on the price elasticity of demand for the final good. Therefore, the decrease in the level of employment from U_0 to U_1 understates the employment impact of the rise in the minimum wage.

The loss of employment opportunities by a portion of the unskilled labor market may have serious long-term consequences. If future income depends on the acquisition of on-the-job training, those workers who lose their minimum-wage jobs may suffer a permanent reduction in their lifetime earnings; they never get the training needed to get a better job. This is an argument made by some opponents of the minimum wage.

The foregoing assumes that all firms are equally affected by the minimum-wage laws. This is true when all firms pay the same wages for particular types

The economic effects of minimum-wage legislation are not all positive. Employment and employment opportunities may diminish for some workers.

of labor. Labor markets, however, tend to be segregated geographically, with different wages prevailing in different geographic markets. Firms that must pay greater than minimum wages for unskilled labor will be unaffected by the legislation and benefit from an increase in the minimum wage. They find that their rivals from low-wage regions will experience an increase in their costs of production as the minimum wage rises. This gives the firms in high-wage areas an advantage in the market in which they sell their product.

The effects of input-price changes go beyond their impact on individual firms. The full consequences of such changes depend on the structure of the market in which the individual firms operate. The different market structures are the focus of the next five chapters.

Summary

This chapter provides a crucial link between the theory of production that was developed in Chapter 6 and a theory of firm behavior that will be developed in subsequent chapters. In order to see how firms make optimizing decisions in various market environments, it is necessary to have a clear understanding of production costs. In this chapter we have developed such an understanding by

- presenting an economic view of costs and profits.
- making the distinction between long-run and short-run production.
- developing isoquant and isocost lines and showing how they can be used to develop short-run and long-run cost curves.
- explaining how short-run cost curves relate to long-run cost curves.
- discussing the various factors that can cause the cost curves to shift.

Key Terms

economic cost	explicit cost
implicit cost	historical cost
normal profits	economic profits
isocost line	optimal input combination
long-run expansion path	long-run total cost
long-run average cost	long-run marginal cost
economies of scale	diseconomies of scale
minimum efficient scale	economies of scope
planning curves	variable costs
average variable costs	total variable cost
fixed costs	average fixed costs
total costs	average total costs
marginal cost	plant capacity
short-run expansion path	envelope curve

Sample Questions

Question

Any short-run total-cost curve is drawn so that it lies *on* the long-run total-cost curve at one level of output but *above* the long-run total-cost curve for every other output level. Give a nontechnical, common sense explanation of this fact.

Answer

In the long run, all inputs are variable; therefore, the long-run total-cost curve shows the total cost of producing each level of output, assuming that the cheapest possible bundle of inputs is employed. In contrast, in the short run at least one input is fixed in quantity. Having a fixed quantity of that input is no disadvantage if the firm produces the output for which that quantity is ideal. However, to produce either more or less output means that the firm is constrained to use too little or too much of the fixed input. In either case, the costs will be higher than if the quantity of the "fixed" input could be adjusted to optimal levels.

Question

In both the United States and in England, it is fairly common to have a home garden. However, home gardening in the two countries tends to be done quite differently. In England, crops are "crowded" together, and much time is spent giving each plant tender loving care. In contrast, a garden in the United States which produces the same output typically is much larger but receives much less labor time. Is it possible to explain this difference using the economics of production?

Answer

Yes. In each country, two of the inputs that can be used to produce beans, peas, and other vegetables are labor and land. In either country, the "best" way to produce a given level of output is the cheapest way. However, the relative price of the two inputs differs between the two countries. In England, where population density is high, land tends to be quite expensive. As a consequence, gardeners in Britain tend to buy homes with much smaller yards than their counterparts in the United States. They then spend more time in their small gardens.

In contrast, gardeners in the United States tend to plant large gardens and spend relatively little labor time in gardening activities. What may appear to be a cultural difference between the two countries has an economic explanation. In each country, gardeners tend to use the "best" gardening technique. The technique that is best depends on relative input prices.

Questions for Review and Discussion

1. Explain how explicit and implicit costs are identified.
*2. Why are economic profits an important signal for firms that have an interest in entering a particular market?
3. What does an isocost line represent, and what is the significance of its slope?

4. Explain how output is optimally produced in the context of an isocost and isoquants.

5. What is the relationship between the input price ratio and the marginal rate of technical substitution for an optimizing firm, and what is its significance?

*6. If the ratio of a firm's marginal product of labor to its input price is less than the ratio of the marginal product of capital to its input price, what should the firm do?

*7. What is the long-run expansion path and how is it derived?

8. Graphically derive the long-run average and marginal-cost curves from the long-run total-cost curve.

9. What specific economic problem was addressed by the reorganization of IBM and General Motors, and how did reorganization aim to correct the problem?

*10. The graph of short-run total variable costs has three distinct characteristics. What are these characteristics?

*11. If the level of output is equal to 20 cars, the quantity of labor used is 5 people, and the wage rate is $10 per hour, calculate the average variable cost.

12. How is the U-shape of the short-run cost curves related to the marginal-product curve?

*13. At the minimum point on the long-run average-cost curve, what is the relationship between the long-run marginal cost and long-run average cost?

14. How does a decrease in the price of labor affect the slope of the isocost line? As a result of the lower wage, does equilibrium occur at a higher or lower marginal rate of technical substitution?

Problems for Analysis

1. If you were to compare a company's profits as reported in its income statement with that company's economic profits, would there be a close correspondence? In general, which of the two profit measures would be higher? Can you identify any characteristics of a business that would help explain the divergence between the two measures of profits?

2. If a business firm has to pay workers time-and-a-half for overtime, how does this affect the firm's isocost line?

3. Many years ago, state-supported colleges and universities tended to be much more specialized — there were state teachers' colleges, state agriculture schools, and state engineering schools, all of which offered only a few majors. As time passed, most of the colleges evolved into large universities offering many different fields of study. In implementing these changes, do you think that the education authorities should have considered economies of scale? What about economies of scope?

*4. Suppose that there are two business firms that have access to the same technology, pay the same prices for inputs, and employ the same quantity of inputs. Does this mean that the two firms will necessarily succeed in producing the same amount of output? If not, can you explain this in terms of cost curves?

5. Suppose that you are considering starting a new business. Initially, you expect your sales to be relatively low, but you hope that your product will become popular and that your sales will increase in the next year. Use short-run average-cost curves to show the dilemma you face in committing yourself to a fixed quantity of some input for a two-year period during which you expect to produce markedly different quantities of output.

6. Suppose that a firm's long-run average-cost curve falls initially and then reaches a minimum that extends over a large range of output. What would the firm's long-run marginal-cost curve look like? Draw the long-run marginal-cost curve for a firm whose long-run average-cost curve is positively sloped over its entire range.

Market Structures

8

Competitive Markets

Competition is both an act and an economic model. As an act, competition is a method through which goals are attained. The "results" may be attainment of a prize, maximizing something (such as output, profits, sales, or utility), buying a Ming vase at an auction, or obtaining a government contract. The concept of rivalry as the act of competing underlies virtually all of microeconomic theory and forms the basis for all studies of market functioning. Economists use the word and concept in this ordinary sense but also have a very particular structural model in mind — the market model of perfect competition. Although issues relating to competitive rivalry will be considered, the present chapter is designed to provide an understanding of competition as a market structure. More specifically, the reader should come away from Chapter 8 with

- a basic understanding of the dual concepts of competition as a *static* and structure as a *dynamic* process of rivalry.
- a view of how the competitive process actually works through a thorough analysis of the static structural model.
- an appreciation of the impact of transactions costs on markets and, specifically, on competitive markets.
- insight into the nature and limitations of all economic models, including those that use the adjective *competitive*.

What Is a Competitive Market?

Competition is the heart of microeconomic inquiry. Profit- and utility-maximizing behavior stemming from self-interest creates markets for the goods and services people most desire, thus benefiting society. How are we to understand competition in economic terms? Everyone is familiar with the term *competition* used in ordinary speech. We regularly compete for jobs, in tennis matches, at auctions, and so on. The Big Three automakers compete with the Japanese and the Europeans for the American car buyer's dollars. McDonald's and Burger King compete for the sale of fast food and Coca-Cola and Pepsi for the soft-drink buyer's market. American textile manufacturers struggle to compete with textile imports from Egypt, Hong Kong, and Mexico. In this sense, competition is **rivalry** for a prize of some kind. Such rivalry connotes the attempt to attain maximum advantage (or reward) or minimum disadvantage (or punishment).

Rivalry is the ordinary person's or businessperson's notion of competition and, as will become apparent in Chapter 8, it has an important place in economic theory. Indeed, it is the *process* of competition or ongoing rivalry that economists are actually trying to explain and understand. Unfortunately, change is not so easily captured in simple models. Just as a film editor must examine one frame at a time in a machine (called a moviola) in order to give a motion picture life, so the economist has constructed still pictures of competitive (and not so competitive) markets to create an understanding of the process through which competition takes place.

The Perfectly Competitive Model: Characteristics

The **static theory of competition** is the most famous of all economic models. It is also a no-frills, bare-boned look at the *results* of an *impersonal* competitive process at discrete moments in time. The requirements for the model are stringent in the basic competitive model we discuss in this chapter. The model is "impersonal" in that even though individual buyers and sellers recognize their roles, each individual knows that he or she is too small to affect the outcome. Competition beneficently produces the most desired goods and services, and maximizes social welfare or utility.

Economists identify the standard model of competition as "perfect." The **perfectly competitive model** is "perfect" in the sense that agents (buyers and sellers) are perfectly powerless to influence price, entry and exit are perfectly free, information is perfectly known, and products are perfect substitutes. Such a level of abstraction is necessary as a first step, because making any model more "realistic" and applicable to some specific market case reduces the generality of the theory. Consider the standard characteristics and assumptions in more detail.

Atomism, No Power. Each individual buyer and seller is assumed to have no impact on price. Such atomism also implies that property is widely dispersed and that mutual dependence does not exist. Obviously, firms have the ability to influence price in many real-world markets — Pepsi's advertising and sales obviously have an impact on Coca-Cola's market — but it does not in others such as in markets for many agricultural products (eggs or wheat, for example). In the standard model of perfect competition, however, the price received by any individual seller is completely unaffected by the actions of any other seller.

From the buyer's perspective, moreover, the actions of any single buyer — out of a large number of buyers — is irrelevant to the price that must be paid by any other buyer. No buyer has enough power to affect prices in a perfectly competitive market. A single buyer of milk, for example, is one of millions of buyers. Her purchase of more or less milk over a week or a year will have virtually no impact on the equilibrium price of milk. In other terms, the condition of many buyers and many sellers, or "atomism," implies a lack of market *power* on the part of any participant. One important implication of this assumption is that the seller's demand curve is a horizontal line. The perfectly competitive seller is a **price taker** whose individual actions do not affect the price received for the good or service produced. (This does not mean that production, consumption, or price is unaffected when all buyers or sellers act in concert.)

Free Entry, Free Exit, and Mobility of Resources. One of the most essential characteristics of perfect competition is that *all* resources — material and entrepreneurial — must be able to move freely and costlessly into and out of any market. This explains the fluidity of the competitive system or how profits are "competed away" and losses compel entrepreneurs to leave industries that cannot make a "normal" return on investments.

The requirement that resources be mobile is a very exacting one. In the real world, all entry and exit from businesses entails some costs and restrictions. But the idealized perfectly competitive model requires that labor, capital, and raw materials must be able to move between jobs, geographic areas, and different productions without artificial, legal, or physical restrictions. These conditions do not mean that any real-world competitive market operates with *no* legal framework. Private property (enshrined in law) is certainly critical, as are rules regarding the disposition of property in markets (see, for example, Highlight 8.1).

Highlight 8.1   *Law, Economics, and Incentives: Legal Restrictions on Competitive Markets*

The model of perfect competition is one in which laissez-faire and minimum government regulation are thought to prevail. But no market-maximizing process, including that of perfect competition, takes place (or can take place) in a legal vacuum. All markets function within an institutional framework, and a chief element in that framework is the legal assignment of property rights. Private property is essential to the market functioning of supply and demand. Further, any firm's production and sale of goods and services under *any* market structure carries certain legal responsibilities. A competitive firm's sale of deadly foodstuffs — say, chemically poisoned potatoes — would most certainly carry legal penalties with it.

Importantly, the incentives of firms, their buyers, and all market participants are conditioned by the laws relating to product liability and to judges' interpretation of them. Up until the 1970s and 1980s, old laws dating back to the 1700s held manufacturers liable only for the "intended use" of their products. Punitive damages — those beyond actual costs and damages to consumers — were levied only in circumstances in which negligence and willful neglect could be proved. Liability was traditionally assigned to firms for wrongful actions and/or defective products.

All that changed over the past two decades. Consider an extreme example of competitive firms producing knives. Prior to 1970 or so, a firm that produced a knife that was defective (and knowingly did so) could be sued successfully if that defect resulted in injury, or if injury resulted from any use of the product that was "legitimate" or "intended" by the manufacturer. Product warning labels or instructions concerning intended use and "misuse" of products were common and, in many cases, kept firms from lawsuits.

Liability laws evolved (mainly through judicial decisions) over the past twenty years, so that firms may now be sued for misuse of products. "Fault principles" were replaced by the assignment of "strict liability" of sellers in the courts. Thus a seller firm could be found liable if buyers misused knives and caused injury (in many cases even if a specific warning is included with the product). More importantly, perhaps, punitive-damage awards have risen dramatically and are assessed in a wide variety of cases. Many jury awards reach the tens of millions of dollars in particular cases of "injury" and have no relationship to the actual damage caused by a firm's products or services.

What is the impact on competition of such developments? Naturally, as is well established in common law, buyers deserve some protection from injury because of misrepresentation, willful disregard for safety, and damage from the intended use of products or services. The incentives that are established by such legal principles are (ordinarily) sound. Such liability puts the costs on manufacturing firms to determine the critical attributes of products, such as safety. Because buyers could determine these attributes only at high cost, it makes sound economic sense to assign liability where the costs of assessing the characteristics of products and services are lowest. (The use and disposition of knives is best — that is, at low cost — monitored by buyers, not sellers.)

The problem is that the incentives will be established by extreme laws of strict liability and by high punitive damage awards against competitors. Legal developments often have stark effects on competition and on the number and entry of competitive firms in particular markets. Risk must be compensated for if firms are to enter, and entry is necessary to drive economic profits downward in most fields. Sellers will invest in the safety and "quality" of their products, but only up to a point. As the costs of doing business rise, new entrants will appear on the market only if revenues rise as well. There is some evidence that the current system keeps "good" and important products such as AIDS prevention vaccines off the market.[a] It does not take much imagination to envision the effects of such extreme laws on entry in the machine-tool, pharmaceutical, and aircraft industries. Likewise, the legal profession's interest in maintaining extreme versions of product liability laws may also be easily explained.

Currently, product liability laws fall within the jurisdiction of the individual states, although, since more than 70 percent of U.S.-made products cross state lines, there have been attempts to "federalize" and standardize these laws. Such an attempt (one that failed) was made in the U.S. Senate as recently as 1992. The thirteen European nations comprising the European Community have adopted a uniform Product Liability Directive, and Australia (which contains only six states and two territories) concluded a similar pact. The recurrent themes that underlined the abortive Senate bill were that reform was necessary to reduce unnecessary legal costs, to provide the low-cost incentives of accident prevention described earlier, and to eliminate some of the arbitrary and unfair practices enshrined in the current law. The bill, entitled the Federal Product Liability Fairness Act, failed despite important bipartisan support in Congress. Consumers and all competitive markets would clearly gain by passage of such an Act.

[a] Some of the material for this discussion was derived from Victor E. Schwartz, "Finally, a Chance to Reform Product Liability Law," *The Wall Street Journal* (September 9, 1992), p. A15.

Some legal restrictions restrict the flow of resources into medicine, law, optometry or, in many states, midwifery. These businesses, perhaps for good reasons, are not and, *could* not be, perfectly competitive. Patent restrictions — which may create short-term monopolies in order to encourage inventions and innovations — also fall into this category. Further, we do not ordinarily think of exit being prohibited in markets, but, until deregulation in 1980 (the Staggers Act), railroads were forbidden by law to abandon certain unprofitable routes because they were supposedly in the public interest. Resources could not flow out of the rail transport industry and, for these routes at least, it could not be perfectly competitive.

Note that we have already encountered (in Chapter 7) a technical, or "natural," restriction on perfect competition. When average or unit costs of production decline continuously over larger and larger outputs, economies of scale are said to exist. A moment's reflection tells us that this condition is completely incompatible with perfect competition if that situation is defined atomistically. Many sellers cannot exist under such circumstances, because each seller has an incentive to buy out all other sellers (greater outputs can be produced at lower costs). Under such conditions a "natural monopoly" results and firms will not enter the market.[1] The requirement for perfect competition cannot be met with any such natural or artificial restrictions on entry or exit.

Homogeneous Products or Services. In order to meet the exacting requirements of the abstract perfectly competitive model, all products and services must be **homogeneous**. No product or service sold by one supplier may have any advantage over any other product or service. One piece of tuna, one avocado, or one egg looks and is pretty much like another, at least within some given grade. Such goods would qualify as truly homogeneous products. But real-world competition takes on many dimensions — geographic, in quality, or in financial terms (see Highlight 8.2).

Highlight 8.2   *Time, Products, Ethnic Fast Foods, and Rivalrous Competition*

The very definition of perfect competition raises questions about the nature of products. Some products (fine winter wheat) are clearly homogeneous and perfectly substitutable. But this view of products would arbitrarily restrict the competitive model to few cases. Economic theory also defines a "product" as one whose cross elasticities are high and positive — a percentage change in the price of some good or service A yields a high percentage change in the quantity demanded of some other good B *in the same direction* (see Chapter 4). Higher numbers indicate more substitutability and, using some cut-off number, product groups can be defined. Thus, for purposes of discussing competitive (not *perfectly competitive*) markets, Chevrolets and Hondas or tacos and burgers may be one product.

The assumption of product homogeneity — although useful as an abstraction in the *perfectly* competitive model — hides the interesting and important details of the competitive process based on rivalry. That process *requires* the development of products that vary in quality, location, or point of trade. Consider restaurants. Restaurants — including the purchase of all food consumed outside the home — are one of the most competitive markets in the world. Every decade, hundreds of thousands of formal and informal "sit-down" restaurants enter and exit the food market in the United States alone. In March 1993, the "Subway" chain of sandwich fast-food restaurants was opening 25 stores a week! These restaurants offer a whole spectrum of food, from elegant dining to "street-stand cuisine." In recent times, many of the

---

1. The existence and prevalence of "natural monopoly" conditions have been questioned in recent literature: see Harold Demsetz, "Why Regulate Utilities," *Journal of Law and Economics* 11 (April 1968), pp. 55–65. Also the assumption of "atomism" on the sellers' side has been shown to be unnecessary to obtain "competitive" results if the market is fully contestable: see William J. Baumol, "Contestable Markets: An Uprising in the Theory of Industry Structure," *American Economic Review* (March 1982), pp. 1–15.

Increasing time cost in the household has led families to eat out more often, especially in ethnic restaurants.

new restaurants have been designated fast-food eateries because of the availability of take-out and fast, convenient service. Virtually all of us are familiar with them, and an examination of them provides an important window into the competitive process.

Both supply (cost) and demand factors have shaped and molded the food industry in America over time. An extremely vigorous competition takes place on the basis of both price and quality offerings. An important component of quality is convenience; restaurants of all types offer food without having to prepare it or to purchase the raw materials necessary for meal production. Fast food offered a new dimension in out-of-home meal production with greater time economies and drive-by service.

How do we explain these developments and the evolution of offerings in the highly competitive restaurant market? A recent study focuses on demand factors and on the relative value of time in the household as changing the nature of competition.[a] Clearly the value of household time varies with income or wages, but it also rises with the labor-force participation rate and the proportion of women to men in the work force. Although average real wages have actually declined in the United States since 1970, the sexual composition

[a] Conclusions reached in this discussion are found in Robert B. Ekelund, Jr., and John Keith Watson, "Restaurant Cuisine, Fast Food and Ethnic Edibles: An Empirical Note on Household Meal Production," *Kyklos* 44 (1991), pp. 613-627.

of the labor force was altered drastically. Because historically women have been the primary meal preparers in the household, a rising ratio of females to males takes on clear significance in explaining the opportunity cost of household time.

A statistical study to gauge the impact of this opportunity cost — the value of household time — reveals a number of interesting conclusions.[b] Weighing for other factors such as the price of food inputs for home production of meals, income, and other variables, an increase in the opportunity cost of household time has created a rising proportion of total restaurant meals to all meals consumed by the average household. In addition, the study found that the ratio of fast-food meals demanded to total restaurant meals also rose with increases in the value of time to the household. Supply has responded to changes in the demand for food.

The fierce competition observed in the restaurant–fast-food area has also taken on an ethnic quality. Clearly, immigration to the United States of Hispanics (Mexicans, especially) and Asians, in particular, may be expected to be related to restaurant offerings and to the nature of the competition. In fact, the National Restaurant Association reports that between 1987 and 1990, demand growth at fast-food Mexican restaurants rose by 41.6 percent and in fast-food Asian sources by 31.5 percent. This is in contrast to growth in fast-food pizza and hamburger establishments of only 9.7 percent and –0.8 percent, respectively. Certainly, one reason for the upsurge in ethnic fast foods is the increase in ethnic populations. Another, however, relates to the changing value of time spent on food preparation in the home. It may well be that many ethnic dishes are more time intensive in preparation than more standard fare — sandwiches and simple stews. If that is the case, relative time intensities and the growing opportunity cost of time in preparing such dishes in the home would help explain the growing ethnic restaurant and fast-food competition in the 1990s.

The example of restaurant–fast-food competition reveals that competition is an ever-expanding, ever-changing process. The product here is "out-of-home food consumed" and it does not conform to the stringent homogeneous product assumption of perfect competition. Rather, "food" is a whole spectrum of highly substitutable items — fried chicken, egg rolls, burritos, and pizza. Such an identity has the advantage of bringing home the fact that many important competitive markets include both price and nonprice competition, including quality, location, and service differences.

---

[b] Naturally, other features of household demand, such as time- and labor-saving kitchen inventions (for example, microwave ovens) or the kind of news services demanded by the household, would be driven by the same increased opportunity cost of time.

Variations in product or service qualities from the seller's perspective are too well known to demand comment. Virtually all products and services — computers, medical and dental services, automobiles, tomato soup — are sold in alternative qualities. But products can differ on the consumption side as well. A can of cat or dog food purchased at the supermarket is different from one purchased at a convenience store to feed a hungry pet when the supermarket is closed. Varying time costs to consumers means that the consumption costs of each commodity and service differ between individuals so that, from the buyer's side, products and services are *not* homogeneous. Still, the abstraction of perfect competition sweeps away all of these complications in order to examine a market for goods or services that is alike in every respect to sellers and buyers.

Perfect Knowledge and Certainty. Perfect competition also requires that all market participants have perfect certainty about present and future conditions. Not only that, but knowledge about markets and conditions surrounding markets is costlessly obtained. The so-called **law of one price** is, in large measure, guaranteed by the assumption of perfect information. The sale price in one market for some good or service cannot be higher than in another market if buyers are able to detect a price differential at no cost. If perfect knowledge exists and if transactions take place costlessly to consumers, prices received by sellers cannot be different for the same (homogeneous) product. No one would knowingly pay a higher price when a lower price is available. Moreover, in a highly stylized and abstract world no risk to actions of buyers and sellers could be assumed. This would mean that there would be little or no room for entrepreneurship, because a principal function of the entrepreneur is to take risks. Obviously, this is unrealistic. Firms can take losses or make economic profits in the short run and may even have to cease operations. Entrepreneurs directing firms take risks every day in a number of ways and carry out entry and exit. *Estimated* future demand is often taken into account, along with present demand. Past, present, and future demand *and* supply, for example, must be considered in analyzing actual competitive markets.

A final point to remember is that all markets, competitive and noncompetitive, function within given institutions. The perfectly competitive model described here — particularly the assumption of free entry and exit of all resources — presumes laissez-faire conditions. This means that human and nonhuman resources are free to move into and out of businesses instantly in response to profits or losses. This assumption effectively eliminates all forms of government regulation, including controls over prices, subsidies, taxes, entry, or exit. The assumption of laissez-faire institutions also eliminates the kind of socialistically directed economies such as those that existed in Eastern Europe or the Soviet Union until quite recently.

Market Periods and the Competitive Firm

In Chapter 7, time periods of production were split into a short run and a long run. Over the long run the firm may vary all of its inputs in order to adjust its output. This means that inputs, such as plant size or heavy machinery, may be varied along with labor and raw materials to produce different (smaller or larger) outputs. Recall, further, that the short-run period of production is an amount of time over which fixed inputs (plant and machinery) cannot be varied but over which some inputs (labor or raw materials) can. This distinction will become the basis for an analysis of competitive conditions over long and short runs, but to complete an analysis of markets, one other possibility must be included — the instantaneous short run, or what is sometimes referred to as the **market period**.

Over the market period, each firm's supply curve and, therefore, the market supply curve are vertical. Alfred Marshall (1842–1924), the chief developer of static and equilibrium methods, described the market period for individual (and market) fishing firms in some given locale. These "firms," actually owners of boats, nets, and hirers of labor, were successful or unsuccessful depending on day-to-day fluctuations in weather, water temperature, and the many other factors that affect the supply and demand for fish. As Marshall himself explained:

> The day to day oscillations of the price of fish resulting from uncertainties of the weather, etc., are governed by practically the same causes in modern England [1890] as in the supposed stationary [equilibrium] state. The changes in the general economic conditions around us are quick; but they are not quick enough to affect perceptibly the short-period normal level about which the price fluctuates from day to day: and they may be neglected (impounded in *ceteris paribus*) during a study of such fluctuations.[2]

This means that on any given day or for any time period over which the addition of *any* inputs are impossible, the supply of fish (or any other product) is literally fixed. (Here we must also assume that the commodity is nonstorable — fish totally deteriorate at the end of one day.) Such a situation is depicted in Figure 8.1a, in which the firm's instantaneous market period supply curve is completely vertical.

2. See Alfred Marshall, *Principles of Economics* (London: Macmillan, 8th edition, 1920 [1st edition 1890]), p. 369. Marshall's book is rightly regarded as the first *systematic* treatise on the subject of microeconomic theory. It was written for "businessmen," with strong verbal analysis in the text and many of the formalities in footnotes or in appendixes. It is accessible to today's undergraduates and rewards the reader with many intuitive insights into competitive markets and market processes.

Figure 8.1 Competitive Price at Some Point in Time or Over Time

In panel (a), demand determines prices because the supply curve is vertical as of any given day and catch of fish. In panel (b) the price of fish varies weekly with the particular day's catch.

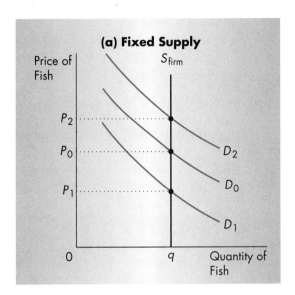
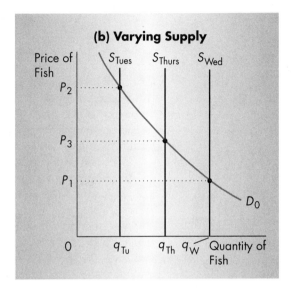

Figure 8.1a depicts the fishing firm's supply curve as of *any* market period, such as any day's catch. (Because all firms in the market for fish face such vertical curves, the industry supply curve is vertical, also, because it is comprised of the horizontal summation of the firms' curves.) In the market-period situation, the demand for fish is the *sole* determinant of the price of fish. If, for example, the price of fish substitutes such as chicken, hamburger meat, or beans falls on a given day, the demand for fish will decline (say to D_1) and the price of fish will fall. Because the supply of fish is nonaugmentable over the market period, it is demand that determines what the fish-selling firm receives as price per pound. The supply of fish determines the quantity sold, whereas demand determines price. (This situation contrasts to virtually all other market situations where both supply and demand determine equilibrium price and quantity.)

An alternative view of "instantaneous" fluctuations in market price over very short periods is to view the supply of fish as fixed on any given day of the week. Each *day* is a market period over which the quantity of fish cannot be altered. Luck, weather, or season may affect these (temporarily) fixed market supplies, as Marshall suggested. These quantities are fixed daily (as in Figure 8.1b) and, on any given day, demand will determine equilibrium price in the market.

We have, of course, only used the foregoing example as an illustration. The actual time period over which supply is fixed may be longer or shorter than a day in any actual market, wherein products may be more or less storable. An automobile manufacturing firm, if it is producing and selling a particular model (the Saturn?) at full efficiency and at the capacity of the plant, would face a market period much longer than a day — perhaps three or four years. Why? Because the supply of autos cannot be adjusted upward without altering some of its equipment or plant size — decisions that would take a good deal of time to actually implement. (Note, however, that automobiles are, to a considerable degree, storable and that supply could be shifted from one period to another.) A pizza-delivery firm, offering the service of auto-delivered pizzas in a college town, could respond to changes in demand by laying off or bringing on delivery personnel in a matter of a few hours. Whatever the market period — years, days, hours, or minutes — supply for the firm is fixed and demand determines price.

An examination of the market period is a reminder of how prices ration existing supplies of a product. Let's reconsider the fish example. If, for example, we assume that the demand for fish is stationary *each day* over a three-day period, price will competitively allocate fixed supplies on any given day. Suppose that a price per pound of fish is established at P_2 because Tuesday's catch constitutes a market period in which quantity is fixed. On Wednesday, however, *fish are caught in greater quantities.* At the high price P_2 (posted on Tuesday), much of the catch will remain unsold. But prices do not remain at P_2 because competing fishing firms would lower price in the attempt to sell their product. Price, therefore, rations the fixed supply (whatever it happens to be) over a market period. In the Wednesday market period, price falls to P_1. On Thursday (given a stationary demand D_0), price rebounds, and so on. Price performs this rationing function, which allocates scarce supplies among those demanders who value products most. (When governments or other institutions prevent prices from performing this function, huge costs may result; see Highlight 8.3.) Over the market period, prices are signals to demanders to buy

---

Highlight 8.3   *Parking Spaces on Campus: The Allocative Function of Competition*

Every university, every college, and many public facilities must somehow allocate parking spaces among competing demanders. At some universities, to the chagrin of both faculty and students, parking spaces are woefully inadequate to meet the demand. A number of devices are used to restrict campus parking to the number of available spaces. The most common device is sticker assignments in which all sorts of "pecking orders" are devised for faculty (eminent scholars, administrators, assistant professors) and students (freshmen, undergraduate students, graduate students). But in many cases, available spaces within the various classes are not "reserved" and stickers amount to no more than a hunting license.

Figure 8.2 Scarce Parking Spaces Allocated According to Full Price

In spite of the *nominal* price of parking stickers, which is below the equilibrium price, scarce spaces Q_S are allocated by both the money price of stickers and the search time for scarce parking spaces.

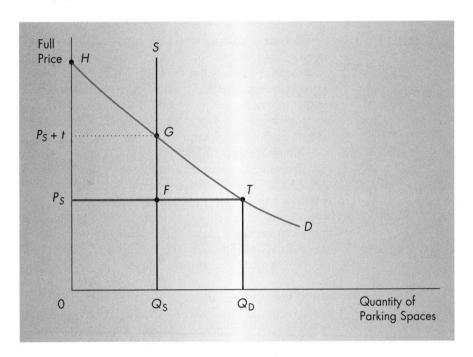

University officials often compound problems with these enforced allocations by invoking other standards of "justice." The chief one, usually devised by a faculty committee, is to keep parking fees "low" in the interests of justice. In the face of low prices, one (extreme) method of reducing demand is to set classes at all hours of the day and night, but this might prove very unpopular for campus bureaucrats. Another method is to maintain the excess demand for spaces by keeping prices low and raising (implicit) prices to faculty and students by imposing stiff fines for parking violations.

The typical problem may be viewed with the help of Figure 8.2, in which some homogeneous demand for campus parking is assumed (that is, faculty, students, and administrators are lumped together in this demand curve). The **full price** of parking is displayed on the vertical axis and the number of spaces is given on the horizontal axis. The supply of parking spaces is assumed to be limited to Q_S. Assume that the (average) price of stickers (hunting licenses) is P_S, a low nominal price set in a spirit of "fairness." The result is an excess demand of $0Q_D > 0Q_S$ or FT at price P_S.

What happens in the market at this low **nominal price** for parking? Vigorous police enforcement, accompanied by heavy fines for violators, could reduce the demand to Q_S, but at the cost of reduced utility and increased fine payments to those who require parking. The **implicit price** of a parking sticker rises. Assuming that the system described in Figure 8.2 remains in place, students and faculty will be forced to "hunt" for a parking space, especially at popular times for classes during the day. The cost to each individual will vary with the time of day and with the *value of time* to an individual. Normally, we would assume that full professors would have higher time costs (proxied by income) than assistant professors or instructors. For all individuals, these costs, along with the nominal price of the sticker, form part of the full price of parking on campus. In effect, the increased full price rations the scarce number of spaces, but at higher costs that are *unappropriated* (not collected by anyone). In other words, the gains to parking are dissipated in waiting and searching time. The full price charged equals $P_S + t$, where t is the opportunity cost of search time for a parking space.

There are a number of possible solutions to the parking problem outlined in Figure 8.2. Spaces could be auctioned to faculty and students alike, with spaces going to the highest nominal price bidders. Wealthy fraternity and sorority members and some freshmen will receive spaces over full professors and administrators, undoubtedly causing outrage. But the university would be richer up to an amount $0HGQ_S$ and could, perhaps, use proceeds to build new spaces. (In the long run, of course, depending on costs, additional parking could be added at the university.) Note that in the "market period" nothing can be changed — parking spaces cannot be added — and costs to the university are approximately zero. Another means would be to randomly allocate $0Q_S$ stickers, charge the nominal sticker price of P_S per sticker, and allow retrading to take place. In this case, those who valued stickers less would be enriched by those who valued them more. Specifically, an amount P_SHGF would be transferred. Whatever the solution, it is important to note that competition could be used to allocate scarce parking spaces over the market period. Imposition of nonequilibrium "just" prices for parking stickers does not mean, moreover, that the competitive market does not work. It does mean that more costly solutions are imposed on the market.

---

greater or lesser quantities of the product or service. But over the same period, firms cannot adjust output in response to different prices received. The firm's ability to adjust inputs, or partially to adjust inputs, in producing its product or service forms the basis for the profit-maximizing (or loss-minimizing) activities of the firm in all other market periods.

Competitive Firm and Industry: Short-Run Statics

The ability of the firm to adjust its output depends entirely on the relative "fixity" of its inputs. As suggested in Chapters 6 and 7, every firm always has a short period in which it can vary some inputs but not others. This conceptual period is of course longer than the market period and shorter than the long run, which is defined as a time when *all* of the firm's inputs can be varied. As detailed in Chapters 6 and 7, marginal and average product of the variable inputs, when applied to fixed inputs, behave according to the law of (eventually) diminishing returns. Two alternative methods of viewing the firm's cost curves in the short run provide information and understanding of profit-maximizing behavior: the total cost–total revenue approach and the marginal cost–marginal revenue approach. Although both approaches yield equivalent information in the final analysis, each provides special insights into the short-run behavior of the competitive firm.

The Total Cost–Total Revenue Approach to Profit Maximization

We will analyze the exact method by which the firm maximizes profits in several ways. The first method is called the **total cost–total revenue approach**, which may be analyzed with respect to Table 8.1, with some of its data plotted

Figure 8.3 Total Cost–Total Revenue Approach to Profit Maximization

The firm produces up to the point at which the difference between total revenue and total cost is greatest (when *TR* > *TC*). This occurs at 8 units of output.

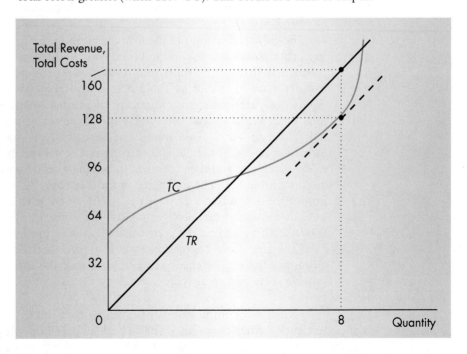

Table 8.1

Market Price	Output	Total Revenue	Total Fixed Cost (TFC)	Total Variable Cost (TVC)	Total Cost (TC)	Total Profit
$20	1	$20	$60	$8	$68	−$48
20	2	40	60	14	74	−34
20	3	60	60	18	78	−18
20	4	80	60	23	83	−3
20	5	100	60	29	89	+11
20	6	120	60	37	97	+23
20	7	140	60	50	110	+30
20	8	160	60	70	130	+30
20	9	180	60	102	162	+18
20	10	200	60	150	210	−10

in Figure 8.3. Table 8.1 provides the data for an individual firm producing some product at a price of $20 per unit. Because the firm is a price taker, it may produce and sell as much or as little as it chooses at $20 per unit. Total revenue, which is calculated in Table 8.1 and graphed in Figure 8.3, is always depicted as an upward-sloping straight line for the firm in perfect competition. This must be so, because market price does not change as output of the firm is increased or decreased.

The cost relationships of the firm are given in the columns designated total fixed cost, total variable cost, and total cost. **Fixed cost** represents the costs of production that, in the short run, do not vary with changes in output. Total fixed cost, as indicated in Table 8.1, is $60 *regardless* of output. Thus, in Figure 8.3, fixed cost is the intercept of the total-cost curve on the vertical axis. **Total variable cost** takes the shape of the total-product curve as variable inputs are added to fixed inputs. Because total product at first rises at an increasing rate, and then at a decreasing rate, total variable costs at first rise at a decreasing rate and then rise at an increasing rate. This is reflected in the data given in Table 8.1. The difference in variable cost is less between the production of the second and third or the third and fourth units than between the seventh and eighth or the eighth and ninth units. Further, because **total cost** is calculated by adding the constant fixed cost of the firm to the total variable cost, the total-cost calculation (see Table 8.1 and Figure 8.3) will exactly reproduce these differences as well. Note that the differences between total variable costs and total costs is precisely the same between all given units of output.

Figure 8.3 combines both the linear total-revenue and the nonlinear-but-rising total-cost functions. These two relationships and their interaction provide the key to the behavior of the firm in the short run. The profit-maximizing firm will always attempt to maximize the *difference* between total revenue and total cost. This occurs at 8 units of output in our example. In graphical terms, profit maximization occurs at the point at which the slope of the linear total-revenue function is just equal to the slope of the total-cost curve. In terms of geometry, maximization obtains where the slope of a line *tangential* to the total-cost curve (which is equivalent to *marginal* cost) is equal to the slope of the (linear) total-revenue curve (equal to *marginal* revenue). As shown in Figure 8.3, profits are maximized when the firm sells 8 units of output, because at that output (see Table 8.1) the firm earns revenues of $160 and spends $130 to produce 8 units. The firm maximizes profits and receives $30. (If sales of the product were in continuous rather than in discrete units, it would be clear that profit maximization occurs at 8 rather than at 7 units of output.)

The Marginal Approach to Profit Maximization

An alternative approach — but one whose results are equivalent — contrasts the marginal revenue that the firm receives and the marginal cost the firm

Figure 8.4 The Competitive Firm Equates Marginal Cost to Marginal Revenue for Profit Maximization
The rational firm manager will always equate marginal cost of production to marginal revenue in order to maximize profits. In the figure, profit maximization occurs at an output of 8 units, yielding a per-unit profit of *GH* and a total profit of *GHKJ*.

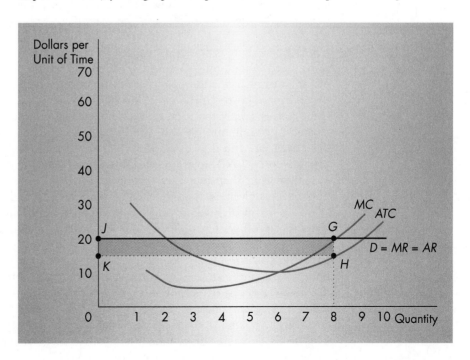

Table 8.2

Market Price (Marginal Revenue)	Output	Marginal Cost (Per Unit)	Average Total Cost	Profit (Per Unit)	Total Profit
$20	1	$8	$68.00	−$48.00	−$48.00
20	2	6	37.00	−17.00	−34.00
20	3	4	26.00	−6.00	−18.00
20	4	5	20.76	−0.76	−2.28
20	5	6	17.80	2.25	+11.25
20	6	8	16.16	3.84	+23.04
20	7	13	15.72	4.28	+29.96
20	8	20	16.24	3.76	+30.08
20	9	32	18.00	2.00	+18.00
20	10	48	21.00	−1.00	−10.00

must pay in order to produce and sell additional output. This approach to the perfectly competitive firm's behavior is summarized in Table 8.2 and Figure 8.4. In Table 8.2, as in Table 8.1, the price-taking firm is supposed to receive $20 for each unit of output sold. This means that the *additional,* or *marginal,* revenue from each additional (unit) sale is $20. Thus, under perfect competition where the firm can sell any amount of output it wants at a constant price, the constant price per unit is also the marginal revenue per unit to the seller (or $P = MR$).

Marginal cost, as noted in Chapter 7, is the addition to total cost as output is increased by one unit. With reference to the specific numbers of our example, the marginal or additional cost of producing the first unit of output is $8, the *marginal* cost of producing the second unit is $6, and so on. **Average total cost** is simply the total cost at any level of output ($TFC + TVC = TC$) divided by the number of units produced or TC/q. Because TC first rises at a decreasing rate and then at an increasing rate because of the influence of total variable cost (TVC), **average variable cost** (AVC) first declines, reaches a minimum, and then increases. Profit obtained on each unit sold (shown in Table 8.2) is given as the difference between price (which is equal to *average,* as well as marginal, revenue under perfect competition) and average total cost. Thus unit profits are a *negative* $.76 *per unit* at an output of 4 ($20 minus $20.76) and a *positive* $3.84 per unit at an output of 6 units ($20 minus $16.16). Total profits are found by multiplying unit profit by the number of units sold. Note from Table 8.2 that both per-unit and total profits are negative at lower levels of output, become positive over some output range, and then turn negative once more.

The key relationship s of the data in Table 8.2 are depicted in Figure 8.4. The firm's demand curve, which is also its marginal- and average-revenue curve, is shown as a flat line at a price of $20. This line indicates that the price-taking firm can sell any or all units of output at the same price, marginal revenue, and average revenue. The typically U-shaped average-total-cost curve (*ATC*) and the associated marginal-cost curve (*MC*) are also drawn in Figure 8.4. The firm (*any* firm, perfectly or imperfectly competitive in nature) follows the following **profit-maximizing rule**: *Produce up to the point at which the marginal cost of an additional unit of output equals the marginal revenue —* equal to price under perfect competition — *in order to maximize profits or minimize losses.*

This central economic relationship is shown in Figure 8.4. In Figure 8.4, profit maximization takes place at an output of 8 units, as it did under the equivalent total revenue–total cost approach to firm behavior. Consider the firm's decision to produce at 7 units of output. At 7 units, the additional revenue from producing one more unit (the eighth) is $20, whereas the marginal or additional cost is just $20. But at a production level of 8 units, the marginal revenue is again $20, but the marginal cost is $32 for producing the ninth unit. No rational entrepreneur would produce beyond 8 units of output, because the addition to cost would be greater than the addition to revenue. Also note from Table 8.2 that although profit per unit is maximized at 7 units, the total profit of the firm is highest when output is 8 units.

Figure 8.4 provides a picture of the same information on the firm's decision. At an output level of 8 units (point *G*), the firm's marginal cost equals the firm's marginal revenue. However, the U-shaped average-total-cost curve is intersected by the marginal-cost function at the low point on the *ATC* curve to the left of the optimum output. At 7 units of output, as noted above with reference to Table 8.2, **unit profits** (the difference between average total cost and average revenue) are highest, but *total* profits are not. **Total profits** (revenues minus costs) are maximized where *marginal cost equals marginal revenue.* (Remember: the equation of marginal cost and marginal revenue exactly corresponds to the equality of the *slopes* of the total-cost and total-revenue curves shown in Figure 8.3.) In Figure 8.4, profit maximization occurs when profits are equal to area *JGHK*. This maximization occurs where marginal revenue and marginal cost are equal at $20 and where the *difference* between total revenue brought in by the firm ($20 times 8 units) and the *total* cost incurred from producing these units ($16.24 times 8 units) are greatest. (Total cost is found by multiplying *ATC* times the number of units sold.) In this and in all cases of firm behavior, output where the difference between total revenue and total cost is maximized (that is, where profits are maximized) coincides with the point at which marginal revenue and marginal cost are equal.

The Marginal Rule and Short-Run Decisions of the Firm

As suggested above, the marginal cost–marginal revenue rule for profit maximization is hard and fast for *all* firms, whether they produce in perfect

Figure 8.5 The Marginal Rule is the Right One for the Firm

At any output other than q_E the firm is not maximizing total profits. All units above q_E that are produced will add more to costs than to revenues. All units lower than q_E will add more to revenue than to costs. Thus the profit maximizer will produce q_E.

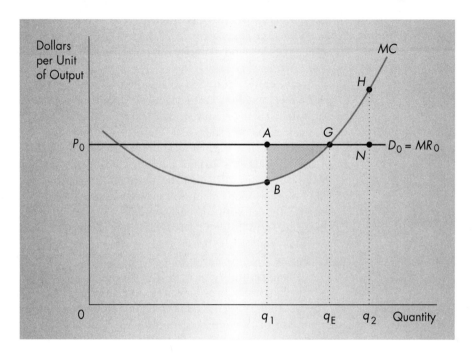

competition or not. That rule provides extremely valuable insight into the short-run workings of the perfectly competitive firm, and we abstract from the details and numbers of Table 8.2 and Figure 8.4 in order to highlight it. Figure 8.5 displays *only* the marginal-cost and marginal-revenue curves from Figure 8.4. We are interested in the constant marginal-revenue curve (which prevails at the price "taken" by the firm) and the rising portion of the marginal-cost curve. At some quantity q_E (which corresponds to points such as G in Figure 8.4), equilibrium is attained because marginal cost equals marginal revenue.

But assuming the firm finds itself producing q_2, what would its behavior be? At q_2 units, the firm is not necessarily "unprofitable." As you may verify from Table 8.2, profits are earned by the firm producing 9 units of output (total profit of $18, to be exact). (The firm incurs losses, not profits, at 10 units, however.) But the firm is not maximizing profits by producing output q_2 because marginal co t exceeds marginal revenue (by amount HN in Figure 8.5). A reduction in ‹ utput will in fact increase profits, because costs are reduced by more than revenues are. Profit-maximizing behavior will therefore create a reduction in output by the firm's managers. Likewise, at all outputs less than q_E, the firm will not be in profit-maximizing equilibrium. At all such outputs, q_1 for example, marginal revenue exceeds marginal cost (by the amount AB in Figure 8.5), and the firm could add to total profits by producing additional output. The *addition* to profits obtainable from increasing output from q_1 to q_E is shown by the shaded area GBA in Figure 8.5. Assumptions concerning the firm's behavior — that the firm will always attempt to maximize profits — ensures that the firm will produce that output at which marginal cost and marginal revenue are equal. Further, it is important to remember that firm optimizing (equating marginal cost and marginal revenue) always occurs within some actual sales environment and that consumer-demanders are part of that environment.[3]

The $MC = MR$ rule of the firm's economic behavior (together with all of the details given earlier) leads immediately to critical principles concerning the firm's short-run optimizing behavior. Specifically, because the firm is a price taker in competitive markets, the rate of output is *always* determined when the firm's marginal cost and marginal revenue are equated. This rule holds whether profits are made or losses incurred, *up to a point*. To illustrate, consider Figure 8.6, which replicates three possible prices that the firm may "take" from the industry.

Price P_0 or (what is the same thing) marginal revenue MR_0 equals marginal cost at an output of q_0. The firm enjoys profits at this level of costs, and revenues and output of $0P_0Mq_0$ (total revenue or price times quantity), less total costs of $0q_0$ times q_0N. Total profits at output level q_0 are then equal to unit profits (MN) times the quantity sold ($0q_0$). For identical reasons, the firm earns profits when its demand curve (as a price taker) falls to D_1 at price P_1. Again the firm maximizes total profits (unit profits AB times output $0q_1$) by following the marginal cost–marginal revenue rule.

But what if demand falls further to D_2, which means that the firm takes a price of P_2 and earns a marginal revenue of MR_2? Clearly, price (or average revenue) will be below average cost by some amount CF (see Figure 8.6) and the firm will incur losses, because total costs at q_2 ($0GCq_2$) are greater than total receipts ($0P_2Fq_2$). But the firm could not do any better than the minimization of losses at output q_2 because the marginal cost–marginal revenue rule still holds. Any addition to output from q_2 (assuming demand curve D_2) would cost the firm more than it brings in terms of revenue. Any reduction of output would, likewise, be unprofitable, because the firm's revenue loss would be greater than the cost reduction. Because the firm cannot do better given the demand curve and cost curves it faces, it will (under certain circumstances) continue producing in the short run, always by equating marginal cost and marginal revenue.

---

3. In real-world competitive markets, information about products and the search for them is not free. The consumer also "optimizes" with regard to search and information. For details on how consumers search for goods and acquire information, see Chapter 13.

Figure 8.6 The Competitive Firm as Price Taker

The firm's profitability will depend on the price it "receives" or "takes" for its product or service. At price P_0 the firm makes profits *per unit* of *MN*. At price P_2 it incurs *per-unit* losses of *CF*. In order to maximize profits or minimize losses, however, the firm always produces at the point at which marginal cost equals marginal revenue.

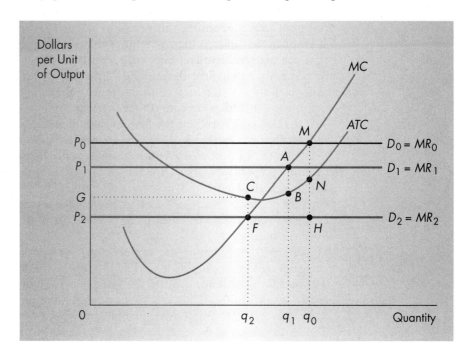

The Firm's Short-Run Supply Curve

Our understanding of the firm's supply curve of output in the short run may be improved by answering the question: "When will the perfectly competitive firm shut down rather than endure losses in the short run?" We have already seen that loss minimization, like profit maximization, requires the equating by the firm of marginal cost and marginal revenue. But when will the firm shut down rather than produce any output?

The analysis represented by Figure 8.7 gives the answer to this question and, along with it, traces out the short-run supply curve for the perfectly competitive firm. Once again assume that industry supply and demand yield alternative demand curves for the firm, but this time the average-*variable*-cost curve (*AVC*) is included. The first of four curves, $D_0 = MR_0 = AR_0 = P_0$, yields a total revenue to the firm of $0P_0Aq_0$ and a total cost of the same amount. The firm is earning a "normal profit" on its sales and is "breaking even." The **break-even point** occurs where average revenue just equals short-run average

Figure 8.7 The Supply Curve of the Competitive Firm is the *MC* Curve *Above* Average Variable Cost

When price is below P_2 in the figure, the firm ceases production. Above *AVC* (at point *C* in the figure) the firm equates marginal revenue and marginal cost to maximize profits or minimize losses. The section of the *MC* curve that lies above *AVC* is therefore the supply curve of the firm.

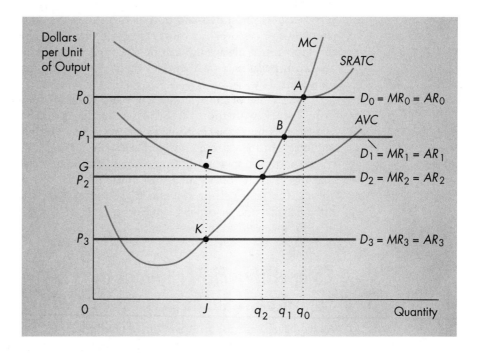

total cost ($AR = SRATC$). At a lower demand and price P_1 the firm is not covering average total cost, although it is more than covering average variable cost. This means that revenues are making some contribution to fixed cost. But when demand falls to D_2 with price P_2 "received" by the firm, the firm is indifferent between shutting down or staying in business.

As shown in Figure 8.7, the firm would equate marginal cost with MR_2 to produce output q_2 in order to minimize losses. But even at this output the firm would only be covering total variable cost, which in this case is equal to $0P_2Cq_2$ — an amount exactly equivalent to the total revenue that the firm takes in. Should demand fall the slightest bit below D_2, the firm will exit the industry, because there is no contribution to fixed cost at D_2 or below. This would occur, for example, at price P_3 in Figure 8.7. As usual, the firm would want to equate marginal revenue and marginal cost in order to minimize losses (at point K in the figure). But at this price the firm's total revenue would be equal to $0P_3KJ$, and the firm's total variable cost would be greater than this revenue at $0GFJ$. Because the firm must pay *all* of its variable expenses in the short run, it must go out of business whenever revenues do not cover them.

Thus the firm ceases production whenever marginal cost and marginal revenue equate at prices below the minimum point (such as *C*) on the firm's average *variable*-cost curve and may exit when price is equal to minimum average variable cost.

The firm's **short-run supply curve** is also traced out in Figure 8.7. It is the upward-sloping line from point *C* on the marginal cost curve. Like all supply curves, it shows the output quantities that the firm will produce at alternative prices over the short run. Note that the supply curve of the firm in the short run is always the marginal cost curve of the firm *above* average variable cost, because, as we saw earlier, the firm will shut down at prices below minimum *AVC*.[4]

The essence of short-term equilibrium is that — temporarily at least — the firm is stuck with the scale of plant that has been built. The firm will, of course, attempt to make the best of matters by maximizing profits or minimizing losses. In the extreme it will, as shown in Figure 8.7, shut down completely. But in the short run the firm will not be able to vary its plant size, a factor that places limits on its ability to efficiently increase or decrease output. As always, the firm will produce at the point at which marginal cost is equal marginal revenue in order to make the best of any situation created by the price it "receives" from the market.

Competitive Firm and Industry: Long-Run Adjustments

As we have seen, the firm is a quantity adjuster in the short run, given some plant size. The firm equates marginal cost to price (remember: price equals marginal revenue under perfect competition), whatever the latter happens to be, so long as it is equal to or above average variable cost. In the long run, the firm also adjusts quantity, but it does so by adjusting the size or scale of the plant it uses. Practically speaking, this means that all of the "fixed" inputs (size of the building, output capabilities of the machinery, and so on) over some time period may be increased or decreased in quantity. The aim of the firm in increasing or decreasing these inputs is not random or perfunctory. The firm seeks to maximize profits by selecting the most efficient-sized plant (lowest cost, given a particular price) in which to produce its output. As in all cases, the firm manager's objective is to maximize profits.

Long-run equilibrium occurs when industry demand and supply are equated and when the firm is only earning a normal profit. Because firms must cover *all* expenses (variable and fixed expenses of the short run) in the long

---

4. We assume that, throughout the decision to continue or suspend production, each firm faces identical and constant input (factor) prices.

run, those that make losses will exit the industry. Further, when profits are above "normal" profit levels (higher than entrepreneurs could make in alternative investments), entrepreneurs are attracted to the industry. New firms come in and industry supply is expanded. The impact on price reduces profits to normal levels for each firm as the number of firms and each firm's output is adjusted. Although this process seems complex, it may be viewed by employing the long-run **envelope curve** relating short-run and long-run cost and plant scales and the marginal cost — marginal-revenue apparatus developed for short-run equilibrium.

Long-run firm adjustments to industry supply and demand may be viewed in Figures 8.8. Panel (a) depicts the industry supply and demand for some good or service. Price settles at P_0 for the industry, and the entire agglomeration of firms produces industry quantity Q_0. Industry price of P_0 is received by the firm that is initially assumed to be producing output q_1 from the scale of plant labeled $SRAC_1$ and $SRMC_1$. If we assume that price P_0 and demand curve $D_0(=MR_0)$ remain constant in the face of our representative firm's actions, the firm depicted in panel (b) is not in equilibrium.

Consider the firm's situation with the cost curves subscripted "1." With that plant size, the firm is earning *losses* of AF per unit. (Total losses are found by multiplying q_1 by AF.) If the firm had to endure these unit and total losses

Figure 8.8 The Process of Long-Run Adjustment for the Competitive Firm

The competitive firm has a whole menu of possible firm sizes in the long run. If price remains at P_0 for a substantial period of time, the firm will adjust output to scale of plant $SRAC_2$ and $SRMC_2$ in order to maximize profits. At that scale, unit profits are GH.

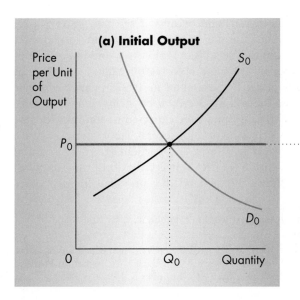
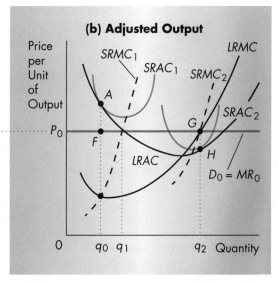

over a long period, it would cease operations because its receipts would not cover total costs. But over a period when adjustments are possible — the long run, as we have called it — the firm faces an array of choices. With reference to the panels of Figure 8.8, the firm may choose to produce any output along its long-run average-cost curve *LRAC*. This is the firm's "envelope," or planning curve, developed in Chapter 7. Each point on the *LRAC* is a point of tangency with a possible short-run average-cost curve. The shape of the *LRAC* (typically U-shaped) is derived chiefly from efficiencies in machinery use and from managerial economies and diseconomies. (The reader may, at this point, wish to review the principles of its construction developed in Chapter 7.) The firm shown in Figure 8.8b, therefore, has a whole menu of choices in front of it. It may go out of business or it may expand output along its planning curve so as to attempt to maximize profits. The theory of perfect competition naturally makes no statements concerning the amount of clock time it takes particular industries to reach long-run equilibrium. Actual time to approach long-run equilibrium will vary with industry conditions. For an example from the recent commercial real-estate market, see Highlight 8.4.

Highlight 8.4   *The Adjustment to Long-Run Equilibrium in the Commercial Real-Estate Market*

Commercial real estate in any large city offers a good example of a competitive market.[a] In such a city, hundreds of owners (corporations, insurance companies, and real-estate development companies) compete to rent office space to business clients. Because their numbers are large, no single owner of office space is able to control the market price.

Because office buildings are durable and because it can take years to plan and construct new office buildings, the time it takes for this particular market to adjust to long-run equilibrium can be considerable. As a consequence, suppliers in this market may experience economic losses for extended periods as the adjustment process takes place. For example, in 1992, owners of office buildings in major cities across the country were experiencing economic difficulties. In many of the cities, the hard times were expected to continue for several years. Table 8.3 summarizes the situation for several major cities.[b]

To understand the high vacancy rate in any particular city, it is useful to consider Figure 8.9. In Figure 8.9, *LRS* reflects the long-run supply of commercial office space, D_0 shows the demand that prevailed for that office

[a] We acknowledge, of course, that zoning restrictions (common in many cities) tend to limit entry in certain sections of the city.

[b] The data reported in Table 8.3 are derived from REIS Reports, Inc., which served as the basis for a story appearing in the *New York Times*. See Neil Barsky, "Commercial Property Market's Troubles May Deepen," *Wall Street Journal* (November 5, 1992), p. B4.

Table 8.3 Commercial Real-Estate Vacancies, 1992
Vacant space and vacancy rates in major cities in the United States were high over the late 1980s and early 1990s.

Market	Vacant Space (millions of sq. ft.)	Vacancy Rate
Midtown Manhattan	154	19.6%
Downtown Manhattan	85	19.1
Chicago	114	19.1
Washington, D.C.	34	8.8
Los Angeles	49	21.8
Boston	36	18.5
Houston	44	17.3
San Francisco	40	11.2
Total/Average	557	18.1

Figure 8.9 Short- and Long-Run Conditions in Urban Commercial Real Estate
Firms supplying commercial real estate expected an increase in the demand for office space in the late 1980s. When the increase failed to appear, the price for such space fell below the long-run equilibrium price.

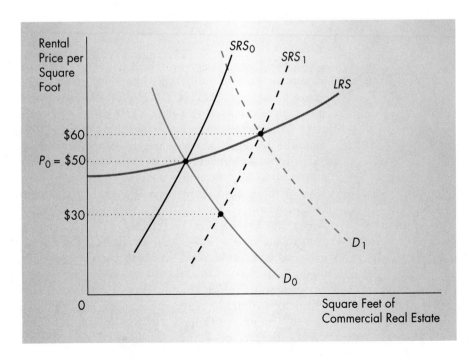

space in the late 1980s, and SRS_0 shows the short-run supply from the stock of office buildings that existed in the late 1980s (see Figures 8.11 and 8.12 and the accompanying discussion for details about the construction of LRS). At that time P_0 represented both the short-run equilibrium price and the long-run equilibrium price.

In anticipation of an increase in the demand for commercial office space to D_1, suppliers built new office buildings, which shifted the short-run supply from SRS_0 to SRS_1. However, because of the economic downturn that occurred, the anticipated increase in demand failed to materialize and the demand remained at a lower-than-expected level like D_0. Instead of rising from $50 to $60 per square foot, the price fell to a new short-run equilibrium price of $30. The consequence is that owners of rental property are currently having difficulty making their mortgage payments.

It is not clear how long the price in those markets will remain below the long-run equilibrium. One possibility is that the economy will improve and cause the demand to increase quickly to D_1. If so, economic losses in commercial real estate will quickly come to an end. However, it is also possible that the demand will remain at its depressed level indefinitely. In that event, supply adjustments will prove necessary to restore long-run equilibrium. Some of the older rental units will be shut down rather than refurbished. Other units may be converted from commercial use to residential use. With this type of adjustment, owners of commercial office space may realize economic losses for ten years or more until a new long-run equilibrium is reached.

In the configuration described in Figure 8.8, the firm's manager would want to *increase* the scale of plant so as to maximize its profits under the constraint of a (fixed) price of P_0. Specifically, the firm will expand output to q_2 along the planning curve $LRAC$. This adjustment will require a larger scale of plant represented in the figure by $SRAC_2$. At this scale of plant (where the short-run average-cost curve associated with an increased amount of capital is just tangential to the $LRAC$ curve at point H), the firm will make economic profits of GH by the unit and total profits of q_2 multiplied by amount GH. Note that the firm decides on this profit-maximizing output by equating *long-run* marginal costs ($LRMC$) to marginal revenue. Once more, the decision of the firm dissolves to the marginal cost–marginal revenue rule, because at the quantity at which $LRMC$ equals marginal revenue (price), the short-run marginal cost also equals long-run marginal cost and price (at point G in Figure 8.8b).

The profits enjoyed by the firm, as depicted in Figure 8.8, are only a temporary phenomenon, given the assumptions of the perfectly competitive model. The industry supply curve does not, as assumed temporarily, remain fixed in the face of output expansions by firms. Specifically, output increases (such as the one to q_2 in Figure 8.8), if undertaken by a significant number of firms, will shift *market* supply rightward, causing a price decrease for *all* firms. New adjustments at the firm level will take place, always in an attempt to maximize profits. The actual length of adjustment time will vary in different markets for goods or services, depending on the nature and costs of the process. But above-normal profits (those higher than the opportunity cost of investment in other areas) will always encourage entry.

Capital may be moved into or out of businesses at different rates, but after the adjustment takes place, all economic (above-normal) profits are squeezed out of the perfectly competitive firms. The long-run equilibrium result is shown in Figure 8.10, where the long-run average-cost curve settles at a point of tangency to the demand curve of the firm. The firm will produce some equilibrium quantity q_E as its share of total industry output at the "received" price of P_E. Note that at point E, the representative firm is in long-run equilibrium because the following equalities hold:

$$SRMC_E = LRMC = SRAC_E = LRAC = P_E$$

Figure 8.10 Long-Run Equilibrium for the Perfectly Competitive Firm

After all adjustments, long-run equilibrium for the firm occurs where $SRMC = LRMC$ and $SRAC = LRAC = $ price. At this point industry output is being produced at the lowest possible cost.

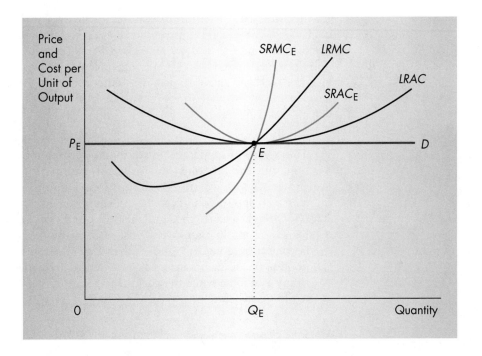

At this grand point of tangency, after all market price and firm adjustments have taken place, the firm is operating at the low point on its long-run average-cost curve. This means that firm output q_E and, by implication, industry output are being produced at the lowest possible cost. Long-run equilibrium also means that all economic profits are eliminated from the market (because $LRAC$ = price or average revenue). How does this result occur? Firms enter the industry in response to the existence of economic profits, and the increased output causes industry supply to shift out. The rightward shift in industry supply causes price to fall. Firms adjust quantity downward and profits per firm fall. This process continues until firm profits fall to zero in static equilibrium.

But, even more important for allocative efficiency, the full opportunity cost of using resources to produce the good or service represented by long-run marginal cost is equated to the price of the good or service in competitive equilibrium. If that price, P_E in Figure 8.10, represents the marginal benefit or utility received by consumers of the good or service, resources are being efficiently and effectively allocated in production. These features of long-run competitive equilibrium help explain the economist's long romance with the idealized model of perfect competition.

Industry and Firm Equilibrium: Factor-Cost Adjustments

In the long run, assuming that technology and other factors remain unchanged, the equilibrium relationship of price and quantity for the competitive firm and industry is determined by what happens to factor costs as *industry* output expands or contracts. Once again we might turn to Alfred Marshall, the inventor of comparative statics, who entertained the question of what might happen in the market for fish when a permanent (long-run) increase in demand takes place:

> The source of supply in the sea might perhaps show signs of exhaustion, and the fishermen might have to resort to more distant coasts and to deeper waters, Nature given a Diminishing Return to the increased application of capital and labor of a given order of efficiency. On the other hand, those might turn out to be right who think that man is responsible for a very small part of the destruction of fish that is constantly going on; and in that case a boat starting with equally good appliances and an equally efficient crew would be likely to get nearly as good a haul after the increase in the total volume of the fishing trade as before.[5]

5. Marshall, *Principles of Economics*, 8th ed., 1920, pp. 370–371.

The impact of market expansion and firm entry into the market, as outlined by Marshall, is clearly determined by what happens to factor input prices as output expands. Certain types of labor (boat builders and trained fishermen, for example) might become scarce as output expands. When this happens, factor prices rise for entering firms and existing firms. These cost increases must be reflected in the cost curves of the firm and, as we will see, in the long-run supply curve of the industry.

What was true of Marshall's fishermen is also the case for modern competitive industries. If, for health reasons, the demand for broccoli or wheat grains permanently increases, more broccoli and wheat will be produced. But under what conditions? The impact on the final price of these products relative to what it was previous to the demand increase will be determined by the impact that the increase in demand for machinery, labor, farm land, and raw-material inputs will have on input prices. That is, of course, also determined by the supply curves of these inputs, which must be included in determining their relative scarcities. If these inputs are relatively substitutable (nonspecialized) among many possible outputs (broccoli and beets, wheat grain and corn), their prices may not rise much, if at all. These features of market expansion, in general, give us two possible cases, both compatible with perfect competition. These two cases are constant-cost industries and increasing-cost industries.

Constant-Cost Industries

As we saw in Chapter 7, changes in technology or changes in input prices will shift the long-run curve upward or downward. An improvement in technology will shift the long-run curve downward, meaning that the same input combinations can produce the same output at lower cost. An increase in input prices will shift the curve upward.

Consider the possibility that the price of inputs to existing and to new (entering) firms does not change over time with entry into the industry. This might be the case in industries that employ nonspecialized inputs that are available in elastic supply with increases in final demand. Such conditions might exist in fields such as agriculture, in which workers with specialized skills or specialized equipment are not necessary to production. As Marshall described it, the "returns" to fishing labor and equipment might yield "nearly as good a haul" after as before the increase in demand. We can see the result for the perfectly competitive firm and industry in Figure 8.11; panel (a) represents the industry supply and demand, and panel (b) depicts a representative competitive firm.

Assume that the industry and its firms all begin in long-run equilibrium, so that industry demand and supply functions (D_0 and S_0) yield industry output Q_0. Industry output is of course composed of the sum of all the representative firms' outputs, or Σq_0. Because all firms in the industry are in long-run equilibrium, equilibrium price P_0 equals minimum *LRAC* and both long-run and

Figure 8.11 The Constant-Cost Industry
In a constant-cost industry, resource prices do not change as the industry changes output levels. The *LRS* of the industry is horizontal.

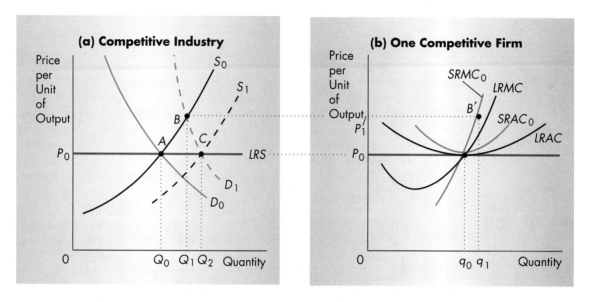

short-run *marginal* cost. What happens now if demand expands to D_1 and remains at D_1 for a long period of time? Clearly, firms will initially respond to the price increase by increasing output along their *short-run* marginal-cost curves $SRMC_0$ to level q_1. Industry output expands along the industry supply curve S_0 to Q_1 and price rises to P_1. (Price is the marginal revenue that each firm equates to marginal cost to determine profit-maximizing output — at B' in Figure 8.11b.)

After the industry demand and price increase, the motivation for change in industry size is in place. Economic profits are being earned by each firm in the industry. (Note that firm profits are the difference between total receipts at price P_1 and total costs read off the *short-run* average-cost curve.) These profits will, with perfect information, bring new firms into the industry. As these new firms enter, industry supply is augmented. As Figure 8.11a suggests, the final resting place of the industry supply curve will be determined by the impact that output expansion and entry have on factor prices (costs to the perfectly competitive firm). If factor costs do not rise for the firms, the end result is a reestablishment of equilibrium for each firm at the low point on the *LRAC* as drawn in Figure 8.11b. Each firm's output returns to q_0, price returns to P_0, and the increase of equilibrium industry output (to Q_2) is accommodated by the entry of *new* firms. Long-run industry supply (the flat line in Figure 8.11a) is shown as the locus of $D_0 = S_0$ and $D_1 = S_1$, or points A and C. It is flat, identifying the industry as one of constant cost.

Increasing-Cost Industries

The other possibility for the perfectly competitive firm and industry is that factor prices may rise as industry output expands. Production characterized by highly technical labor and capital — such as in medical technology or computer research — will often be characterized by increasing costs. Figure 8.12 depicts this possibility. As before, industry demand permanently increases to D_1 from D_0. Once more, representative firms will travel up their *short-run* marginal-cost curves to maximize profits. These higher-than-normal profits will, as in the constant-cost case, encourage entry into the field of firms producing the particular good or service. But this time, entry is accompanied by a rise in the price of factors used to produce the good or service. This factor price rise may originate with scarcities of one or a combination of inputs used to produce the final product. When these cost increases take place for entering firms, however, they also occur as cost increases to existing firms. The entire long-run cost apparatus ($LRAC$ and $LRMC$) rises for each firm after equilibrium is reestablished.

A process of entry similar to the one described in the constant-cost case takes place, but when factor costs rise, the final equilibrium for the firm is at a higher price. In Figure 8.12b the output produced by the representative firm is lower at q_1', but (depending on a host of complex factors) it could conceivably

Figure 8.12 The Increasing-Cost Industry

When resource prices rise as the industry expands output, the *LRS* curve is positively sloped. This means that greater output of the particular good or service can only be had at increasing prices to consumers.

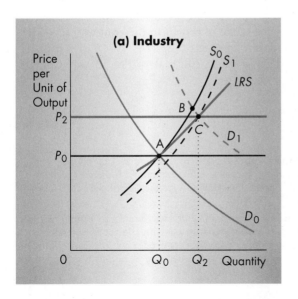

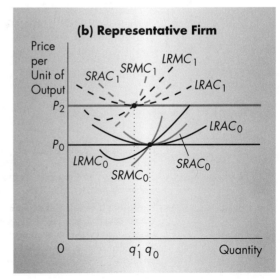

be higher or the same as it was prior to the factor-cost increase.[6] The important point here is that the permanent increase in demand created an increase in industry supply to Q_2 but not without a price increase. (Here Q_2 is the sum of all of the preexisting and new firms' outputs.) Final equilibrium points for the industry are traced out as the line in Figure 8.8a, as the locus of long-run equilibrium prices and quantities. The points trace out a positively sloped long-run industry supply curve (*LRS*). Competitive equilibrium is thus perfectly compatible with the fairly realistic case of rising factor costs with expansions of industry output.[7]

Summary

The mechanics of the perfectly competitive model are straightforward in static terms, but the frequently heard criticism that it is "unrealistic" is unwarranted. It is demonstrable that most firms, whether they meet the exacting definition of *perfect* competition or not, undergo cost and demand changes and influences such as those described in this chapter. All firms hire factor inputs to produce outputs, and all firms experience real cost changes from time to time.

The reader may have perceived a crucial element in the static process described above. It is the actual ease of entry or exit that explains the *speed* with which cost-based equilibrium is restored when disturbed by demand changes. Indeed, in actual examples of competition in real-world markets, it is the speed of the response by entrepreneurs to economic profits that explains how efficient and welfare enhancing markets are or can be. This feature of markets adds a dynamic dimension that is not and cannot be captured in the confines of a static model of competition (or any other market structure). But this does not mean that learning the exacting details of a model of perfect competition is only an exercise or a waste of time. On the contrary, an understanding of the matters discussed in the present chapter is critical in organizing our thoughts about how markets work in the real world. In this chapter, we have

---

6. Principles of substitutability and factor-use response to firm budget changes help explain optimum firm size as factor price changes; see, as an introduction, C. E. Ferguson and S. C. Maurice, "The General Theory of Factor Usage with Variable Factor Supply," *Southern Economic Journal* 38 (October 1971): 133–40.

7. Although Marshall considered the case of factor price *decreases* as industry output expands, the so-called decreasing-cost industry is totally incompatible with competition. A moment's reflection reveals that such a situation would create an incentive for any *one* firm to buy out all other firms in the market, because unit costs would decrease as output is expanded for *any* firm.

- developed an understanding of the meaning of competition both as a static model (that of *perfect* competition) and as a rivalrous process.
- shown, using both total- and marginal-cost and total-revenue approaches to the firm, how rational firms maximize profits and minimize losses.
- discussed the principles of firm management, including a "rule" for shutting down the firm.
- seen how consumers (under competitive and all other market structures) rationally acquire information about products and how they search them out.
- developed the principles of long-run industry supply under competitive conditions.

Key Terms

rivalry	static theory of competition
perfectly competitive model	atomism
price taker	homogeneous goods
law of one price	market period
full price	nominal price
implicit price	total cost–total revenue approach
fixed cost	total variable cost
total cost	average total cost
average variable cost	profit-maximizing rule
unit profits	total profits
break-even point	short-run supply curve
long-run equilibrium	envelope (or "planning") curve

Sample Questions

Question

Why are the prices of goods typically higher at the local convenience store than at the grocery store? Are these goods homogeneous?

Answer

The prices of goods at convenience stores are usually higher than at the grocery store because convenience stores offer services that are not commonly associated with grocery stores. As examples of these services, convenience stores are often open 24 hours each day and are strategically located to minimize the time costs of the customer. When the services offered by convenience stores are taken into account, it is clear that these add to the consumer's valuation of the good, which indicates that grocery stores and convenience stores do not sell homogeneous products.

Question

In an increasing-cost industry, how does the existence of above-normal profits affect potential entrants? Is this the same effect as in a constant-cost industry? Explain.

Answer

The existence of above-normal profits in an increasing-cost industry will attract entrants but at a price to the industry. Entrants in an increasing-cost industry, as opposed to a constant-cost industry, drive up the price of inputs used to produce the good or service. As a result, the long-run-cost curves increase, generating a new, higher equilibrium price.

Questions for Review and Discussion

1. What distinguishes the static notion of competition from the dynamic concept of competition? What is "rivalry?"
*2. Why is the existence of "atomism" among buyers and sellers important in the perfectly competitive model?
*3. Barbers are required by law to be licensed in their field before they can cut hair. Is the market for barbers perfectly competitive? Why or why not? Do you think that barbers in cities engage in "rivalrous" competition?
4. Highlight 8.1 discusses the assignment of liability between consumers and firms. What is the general rule for determining where the liability should be placed? (Hint: Avoidance of liability is costly in terms of resources.)
*5. What do heterogeneous products and services imply about a market and its suppliers?
6. Why is the price of gasoline higher along the interstate than it is in a town? Is this the same product?
7. When analyzing a product in a market period, how is price determined?
8. Highlight 8.3 discussed the common problem of inadequate parking on college campuses. How can spaces be allocated in an economically efficient manner?
*9. How is the total revenue–total cost approach used to maximize a firm's profits? Where is this point located graphically?
10. What is the "profit-maximizing rule" in the marginal revenue–marginal cost approach?
11. What is the break-even point and what is the corresponding level of profit?
*12. When will a firm decide to shut down to minimize losses in the short run?
13. What are the characteristics exhibited in a market that is in long-run equilibrium?
14. What is the role of profit in decisions to enter or exit an industry in the long run?

*15. What is the result of an increase in demand in an increasing-cost industry? What is the slope of the long-run supply curve in this industry?

16. How does the presence of economies of scale affect the perfectly competitive model?

*17. What is the "law of one price?" How is it related to opportunity cost? to full price?

18. What is unique about the supply curve of Marshall's fish market?

19. List three assumptions of the perfectly competitive model that are "unrealistic." Why do economists use a model based on unrealistic assumptions?

20. John makes and sells shoes in a perfectly competitive environment. In order to increase his market share, John plans to increase sales by 10 percent. To cover the increased production costs, John plans to increase the price of his shoes by $1.00 per pair, and thus continue to make a normal rate of return. Will John's plan work? Why or why not?

*21. Why are economic profits only short-run occurrences in the perfectly competitive model? How does your answer relate to industry supply and price?

22. All consumers of fish have downward-sloping demand curves as the result of the law of diminishing marginal utility. True, false, or uncertain: Because the competitive model yields perfectly elastic firm demand curves, the law of diminishing marginal utility does not apply to the competitive model.

23. The St. Nick Christmas Tree Farm makes all of its annual revenue in December. The fixed cost of the operation is $250 per month. Variable costs are equal to $50 a month from February through September, $100 a month in October, November, and January, and $4,500 during the month of December.
    a. If the market price for Christmas trees is $20 a tree, how many trees must the tree farm sell to break even?
    b. Given your answer in part a, what should the firm do if its marginal-cost curve intersects the average-total-cost curve at $Q = 350$?

Problems for Analysis

*1. Assume that the shoe market at both manufacturing and retail levels is perfectly competitive and, further, assume that the demand for shoes at the retail level is elastic. Now assume that a ceiling price below the current market price is placed on shoes at the factory (that is, a maximum price the shoe manufacturer can charge the retail dealer). Will the total revenue received from the sale of shoes at the retail level increase because of the imposition of the ceiling price at the factory level? (Use graphs in your answer.)

2. A parking "problem" exists at Brand X University, as students and faculty well know. The nature of the problem was outlined in a 1988 issue of the school newspaper. Back then, according to the manager of parking services, a "total of 16,562 decals have been issued for 8,661 parking spaces." In each class of parking (one for students, one for faculty), there was roughly 2 decals to 1 space. By fall 1994, in the face of rising enrollment and more faculty, the problem has grown. However, the faculty advisory committee has steadfastly refused to permit yearly parking fees greater than $30.

   a. In general, what are the costs of the current "hunting license" system to students? to faculty?

   b. Provide an estimate of the annual total costs per faculty member of the hunting-license system assuming that one-third of the faculty are assistant professors (earning $32,000 per year), one-third are associate professors (earning $44,000 per year), and one-third are full professors (earning $65,000 per year). Assume that each professor spends an average of 10 minutes per day (5 days a week) searching for a parking place. Each faculty member, moreover, works 40 hours per week.

   c. Suppose that you were free to design other parking-space allocation systems. Outline *two* alternative systems that would improve on the resource allocation currently dictated by Brand X University. Does equity play a role in either system? Explain.

*3. Suppose that the U.S. Health Department announces that eating alligator meat *eliminates* your chances of getting cancer. Assuming the market for alligators is perfectly competitive, what would you expect to occur in the short run and long run to the following:

   a. the industry demand for alligators
   b. profits of alligator farmers
   c. profits of cattle farmers
   d. wages for experienced alligator hunters
   e. the price of alligators
   f. swamp land in Louisiana
   g. the price of alligator-skin shoes.

Monopoly and Price Discrimination

Monopoly theory is the study of market results or outcomes when competition is totally absent. In its barest, static form, monopoly implies that there is only one seller of a unique product or service for which there are no substitutes and that entry into the market for selling that good or service is completely restricted. These conditions imply that the monopoly seller has absolute power, within the limits imposed by willing demanders, to set quantities of the good or service sold and, as a consequence, to set price. Needless to say, these conditions are rarely present in markets and the monopoly seller is, in reality, limited by numerous market and legal factors and features. The present chapter will

* develop a workable concept of monopoly for the reader in which the legal and practical restraints on monopoly power are emphasized.
* present the formal static approach to monopoly theory that is essential to understanding features of real-world markets.
* appeal to the reader-consumer's common experience to present a complete discussion of the most common aspect of "monopoly pricing" — the practice of price discrimination or the charging of different prices for the same or similar goods or services.

What Is a Monopoly Market?

The very word **monopoly** connotes power or control, something sinister, or a devious business plot. Every day media analysts complain of monopoly — by the cable companies over municipal cable TV services, by the Japanese over the foreign-car market, or by some ill-defined "military-industrial-political" complex. All such allegations use the word *monopoly* very loosely, however. A few community cable systems are in fact overlapping and "competitive." The Germans, French, and Swedish would be most surprised to learn that the Japanese have monopolized the import market for automobiles in the United States. Finally, even the least analytical of minds should be able to see that military hardware companies and politicians at all levels of competition and government are constrained by checks of all sorts. Once again, as in the case of the term *competition*, a tyranny of words and meanings afflicts the idea of monopoly.

The term *monopoly* is frequently used in an informal sense, but the word means something very formal and specific to an economist. Far from some loose conception of "power" or "status," the requirements for the static monopoly model of economic theory are as stringent as they were for competition.

The Monopoly Model: Characteristics

Monopoly is the "opposite" of competition in every respect. Instead of the characteristic of the atomistic competitive condition — many sellers — static monopoly theory requires only one seller. (The contrasting condition — one buyer in a market — is called **monopsony**.) The monopolist may sell either a homogeneous product such as aluminum or iron ingots, differentiated products, or different "qualities" of a single product. Obviously a monopoly is not possible if entry can take place in a market. Therefore, there must be some barrier or **barriers to entry** that permit a monopoly to survive. Indeed, the most important key to understanding monopoly in theory or in the "real world" is to be able to analyze the sources of entry control — barriers that keep entrants from the market.

Entry control may take on numerous forms, and it is incumbent on the economist to be able to explain precisely how this factor permits monopoly in a market. Ownership of certain resources may hold the key to certain productions. Prior to World War II, for example, it was said that bauxite, essential in producing aluminum, was controlled by Alcoa. With some exceptions, the DeBeers Company controls virtually all of the gemstone sales of diamonds through outright or contractual control of the world's diamond mines (chiefly in Africa and Australia). **Patents** or copyrights of inventions or intellectual properties are another potential source of monopoly control in markets for goods or services or artistic productions. These controls are normally limited in scope, however, so that monopoly sellers have rights limited to a certain number of years (17 years, in the case of most patents). Close substitutes — for example, prescription-drug markets and markets in which chemicals or processes may be easily simulated — may also emerge to provide viable competition for the patent holder. Patents, further, may be very effective in stimulating inventions and innovations by providing at least some protection to patent holders, so that they will reap the rewards of investments in research and development of new ideas and processes.

Monopoly is also often associated with "bigness." This may be because **economies of scale** exist in certain industries. In modern times there has been very little if any entry into the United States automobile industry (although there has been plenty of foreign competition). Industry activity has been in the opposite direction — toward mergers. If economies of scale exist in automobile production or in any other industry, maximum efficiency — lowest average cost — is not achieved until high volumes of output are attained. The capital requirements for entry into businesses characterized by sophisticated automation are high and discourage entry. Other barriers, in addition to capital requirements, may exist in some markets. High advertising expenditures, for example, may be necessary for entry, although there is little hard evidence in the matter.[1]

One of the most often cited sources of monopoly power is the condition called **natural monopoly**. In this case, economies of scale create conditions in which the average-cost curve (unit costs) continues to decline as output increases. If, initially, there are several or a number of competitors in a market in which natural monopoly exists, common sense tells us that monopoly is the only feasible result. If it is in one seller's interest to merge with another to take advantage of lower unit costs, it is in every seller's interest. One firm will emerge to supply the entire market, because it can do so at the lowest possible average cost of production. The remaining monopoly seller will then raise price by restricting the quantity of the product sold. Thus, in this case, scale economies would "naturally" (that is, because of cost conditions) produce monopoly. Although this theory provides a case for government regulation in the U.S. economy (of such goods as electric and water utilities and cable TV companies), the logic and existence of so-called natural monopoly has been the subject of much recent debate.[2] How is it resolved? Some economic arguments support the existence of unbridled monopoly in markets, whatever the source (see Highlight 9.1).

1. Economists have used and are using a variety of empirical techniques to determine whether such factors as advertising intensity, capital requirements or sunk costs, and economies of scale affect entry into U.S. businesses. The results vary: the majority conclude that advertising may accommodate rather than prohibit entry, whereas significant scale economies and capital requirements restrict entry. See, for example, Ioannis N. Kessides, "Advertising, Sunk Costs, and Barriers to Entry," *Review of Economics and Statistics* (February 1986), pp. 84–95; Robert B. Ekelund, Jr., and David S. Saurman, *Advertising and the Market Process* (San Francisco: Pacific Research Institute for Public Policy, 1988), and Timothy Dunne, Mark J. Roberts, and Larry Samuelson, "Patterns of Firm Entry and Exit in U.S. Manufacturing Industries," *Rand Journal of Economics* (Winter 1988), pp. 495–515. Global competition, from Japan and elsewhere, will naturally expand entry, making the question of barriers in the United States less important.

2. This literature stresses that franchising may be an alternative in that contracts may be let out for bid to low-cost bidders, with franchises "up for grabs" periodically: see Harold Demsetz, "Why Regulate Utilities?," *Journal of Law and Economics* (April 1968), pp. 1–22. Whether regulated monopoly, franchised monopoly, or the totally uncontrolled market produces "better" results depends on the cost and demand conditions in each case and a multitude of other factors.

Highlight 9.1   *The Schumpeterian Vision: Monopoly as an Engine of Progress*

The monopoly model of this chapter deals with a market under static conditions. In one of the most important assessments ever given a functioning capitalist system, Joseph A. Schumpeter featured monopoly as part of the dynamic functioning of the economy. From this perspective, the existence of monopoly was not all bad and, indeed, might have positive features to recommend it.

In a Schumpeterian world, competition is a process of creative destruction. Profits are a signal to entrepreneurs to enter businesses that supply goods and services most desired by consumers. When entry into businesses is risky because of a high probability of losses, entrepreneurs will demand higher prices to supply the goods. Some forms of self-protection will be necessary in a dynamic world. In Schumpeter's words:

> Practically any investment entails . . . certain safeguarding activities such as insuring or hedging. Long-range investing under rapidly changing conditions, especially under conditions that change or may change at any moment under the impact of new commodities and technologies, is like shooting at a target that is not only indistinct but moving — and moving jerkily at that. Hence it becomes necessary to resort to such protecting devices as patents or temporary secrecy of processes or, in some cases, long-period contracts secured in advance.[a]

Included in these "self-protective policies" were railroad rebates and monopoly or cartel price policies that were, like patents, long-run tools of dynamic competition. In Schumpeter's vision, however, only government serves as a significant source of monopoly power. As he clearly noted, "The power to exploit at pleasure a given pattern of demand . . . can under the conditions of intact capitalism hardly persist for a period long enough to matter for the analysis of total output, unless buttressed by public authority."[b] Thus many observed restrictions on the competitive system in a *static* framework (such as those discussed in the present chapter) are efficient over time in that they regulate and encourage the introduction of new and (ultimately) cost-reducing technology. To Schumpeter, the only provider of long-term economic profits associated with output reductions and welfare losses is coercive government regulation in markets.

[a] J. A. Schumpeter, *Capitalism, Socialism, and Democracy* (New York, 1942), p. 88.
[b] Ibid., p. 99.

Whatever the source of monopoly, it is obvious that the formal static conditions must necessarily be modified or qualified in the real world. Monopoly power may, for example, be severely constrained by threatened or potential entry. Markets, in other words, may be contestable even though there is only one supplier of a good or service.[3] The *threat* of entry may have as much impact on the behavior of a monopoly seller as *actual* entry. It is difficult, moreover, to think of a good or service for which there are *no* substitutes. Although each product may have some unique properties, consumers are almost always aware of competitors' products or services (see Chapter 11 on monopolistic competition). Monopolists, furthermore, like other sellers in free and open markets are not guaranteed a market. If there is no demand for a good or service, whether the seller has a unique or patented product or not, the seller will earn no profits and the item will not be produced. No seller, regardless of the degree of monopoly power, can force buyers to buy.

Monopoly and Political Entry Control

Many economists argue that monopoly could not exist without government legislative or legal support of some kind. Franchises, licenses, certificates "of public convenience and necessity," safety regulations, and permits are all devices that government uses to control entry into markets. In addition to public utilities, many businesses and professions, from funeral directors, doctors, lawyers, and pharmacists to hair stylists, carpenters, and electricians, control entry in some manner. Land use, such as zoning restrictions, is also regulated by government at many levels. Appeals to natural monopoly to explain such regulation often fall short of the facts. Regulation is primarily caused by politics and profit seeking by parties that have much to gain from it (see, for example, Highlight 9.2). Politicians have the *power* to grant special

---

Highlight 9.2   *How Local Monopoly Is "Made": The Case of Cable Television*

The term *monopoly* often conjures up visions of large, perhaps global, and distant firms exerting pressures on consumers. Actually, monopoly (especially that created by government) exists in our own backyards or, in the case of cable TV, in our living rooms and bedrooms. Cable television, from its inception, was placed under regulation by the Federal Communications Commission (FCC). Practically, however, local governments were charged with regulating

---

3. Economist William J. Baumol has taken the lead in developing a theory of market contestability that revolves around the question whether a firm's capital is "sunk" — a zero or low opportunity cost of resale — or simply fixed (it can be resold when exiting a market). See William J. Baumol, John C. Panzar, and Robert D. Willig, *Contestable Markets and the Theory of Industrial Organization* (New York: Harcourt Brace Jovanovich, 1982) for details.

Municipal monopolies over cable TV have thwarted competition in the supply of local cable services.

rates and services, because cable was thought to be a "natural monopoly" with significant economies of scale.

Recognizing the inefficiencies of tight municipal regulation of this "supposed" monopoly, the Cable Communications Policy Act of 1984 deregulated portions of cable TV. In particular, municipal cable operators were freed of rate regulation in cases in which "effective competition" — defined as the provision of 30 or more channels with three broadcast signals received in the service area — could be demonstrated. Basic rates rose by 32 percent (average for the nation) between 1986 and 1990, but the increase was accompanied by a 48 percent increase in new channels. These developments were clearly associated with service quality enhancement, but the rapid growth led to some abuses in particular markets. Over-the-air broadcasters (the networks), politicians, and some consumers demanded more stringent controls over the cable industry or a return to "reregulation."

For example, the Federal Communications Commission (FCC) instituted (in July 1991) a more complex test for competition that had the effect of reregulating basic rates in more than half the nation's cable companies. An avalanche of bills was introduced in Congress with sweeping new regulations of rates, cost-raising impositions, and brand-new city powers over proposed **franchises**. U.S. Senate Bill 12 (S. 12) was introduced by Senator John C. Danforth of Missouri in 1991, and a version of it passed the whole Congress (over President Bush's veto) in late 1992. Broadcasters, fearful of cable-company advances in fiber optics systems permitting the implementation of high-density television, were fully supportive of such regulatory initiatives. These networks were able to secure a piece of the profits pie by obtaining regulatory mandates over the cable companies. The major feature is that local cable companies must now carry local (free) network signals and pay network affiliates (local broadcasters affiliated with a major network) for them. Politicians, who (along with networks) convinced citizen-voters that cable rates would be reduced under reregulation, were right out in front of the movement in an election year (1992).

Some economists believe that reregulation of cable TV will only worsen matters. They believe that deregulation of cable markets is the answer and that the partial deregulation of 1984 was not the source of industry problems. Deregulation of cable TV could not be defended if natural monopoly or falling cost conditions existed at the local level. This would mean that more than one cable supplier would be inefficient in providing services to consumers and that a single supplier would provide services at lower cost. Although much evidence on such economies is inconclusive, most studies have failed to find that such conditions exist in municipalities.[a] In fact, evidence suggests that the primary culprit in rising cable rates is the increase in costs and unnecessary expenses imposed on cable companies by local franchisers.

Under the 1984 deregulation agreement, cities stood to gain up to 5 percent of each company's annual gross receipts. However, each city is permitted to extract even more monetary and nonmonetary benefits from cable franchise holders. Examples of unnecessary cost-raising extractions are becoming legion. A cable operator in Sacramento was required to plant 20,000 trees to keep the franchise. In Miami, the cable operator had to agree to provide $200,000 a year for the police department's antidrug abuse campaign in order to get the franchise. Municipalities have intentionally impeded competition by using cable companies as "cash cows" at the expense of consumers. Under the present law, which admits additional rent seekers into the local cable business (for example, network affiliates), the potential for further malfeasance is present. In effect, monopoly is "created" for the benefit of municipal governments, networks, and politicians.

Open competition at the local level may be the ultimate answer to the problems of cable TV. A recent study of price behavior at the city level in California shows that municipalities keep prices high by protecting cable

---

[a] See Kent G. Webb, *The Economics of Cable Television* (Lexington, KY: Lexington Books, 1983) or B. Owen and P. Greenhalgh, "Competitive Considerations in Cable Television Franchising," *Contemporary Policy Issues* (April 1986), pp. 59–77.

franchises from competition and by imposing costs on them.[b] In other recent research, economists conducted a nationwide statistical study contrasting prices in 48 municipalities that allowed openly (overlapping) competitive cable companies with 130 matched cities that did not in 1989.[c] The monthly rate for basic cable services on average was found to be $3.21 lower per month per subscriber for those systems permitting multiple cable suppliers than for comparable systems with a single company. The rate for premium channels was $1.15 lower. Total "deadweight" losses for the entire U.S. economy were estimated at $3.66 billion per year, a sizable sum by any standard.

The changes in the regulatory treatment of cable enacted into law in 1992 may all be in the wrong direction if consumer welfare and protection (along with the encouragement of technological advance) is the object of economic policy. Limitations on open entry by the FCC or Congress may only reinforce the "invented monopoly." Only broadcasters and municipal governments that will increase their tax receipts through regulation will profit. Consumers may pay even higher rates for service to support local governments and politicians. Society could lose irretrievable benefits from the creation of such monopoly.

[b] Thomas W. Hazlett, "The Demand to Regulate Franchise Monopoly: Evidence from CATV Rate Deregulation in California," *Economic Inquiry* (April 1991), pp. 275–296.

[c] See Richard O. Beil, P. Thomas Dazzio, Jr., Robert B. Ekelund, Jr., and John D. Jackson, "Competition and the Price of Municipal Cable Television Services: An Empirical Study," *The Journal of Regulatory Economics* (December, 1993), pp. 401–415.

protections through legislation and they also have the *incentive* to do so — dollars and votes come in handy at reelection time. Businesses, as we will see later in this chapter, will be willing to invest resources up to the value of the potential gain from regulation. Because consumers are widely dispersed and have a small pro rata share in the costs of monopolization through legislation, there is often little organized opposition. (Import tariffs and quotas that help specific groups of U.S. workers at a huge expense to the mass of consumers are often cited as a form of such monopolization.)

Monopoly: Static Analysis

The foregoing considerations must be given weight in any actual case of monopoly control, and there is little doubt that, even in governmentally protected businesses, pure monopoly is extremely rare. But there is little dispute concerning the *theoretical* effects of monopoly organization. Consider some important monopoly characteristics.

Figure 9.1 Demand Curves of the Perfectly Competitive and Monopoly Firms

The demand curve of the perfect competitor in panel (a) is horizontal with an elasticity of infinity. In contrast, the demand curve of the monopolistic firm is (ordinarily) negatively sloped with a range between D_i and D_c in panel (b) of the figure.

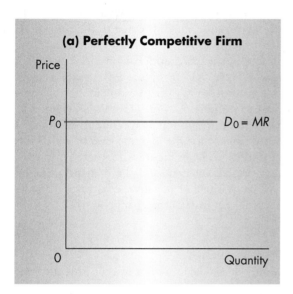

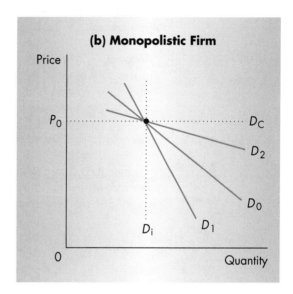

Monopolists as Price Searchers

Just as firms in a competitive industry are price takers (see Chapter 8), the monopoly firm, being the entire industry, is called a price searcher. A **price searcher** is one who "searches" for the right price and output level to maximize profits. Price, in other words, is not imposed on her. Rather, she sets an output level to obtain the price that will maximize monopoly profits. The contrast between the pure competitor and the pure monopolist is shown in Figure 9.1.

In Figure 9.1a the firm is a price taker. The demand curve facing the firm is horizontal, marginal revenue to the firm is equal to the price "taken," and the price elasticity of demand to the firm is infinite — that is, $e_D = \infty$. In Figure 9.1b the monopolist faces a downward-sloping demand curve, with higher quantities associated with lower prices. Note, however, that the elasticity of demand faced by the monopolist can vary. The price-quantity combination shown may be one combination on an infinite number of demand curves between D_C — the competitive curve of infinite elasticity — and D_I, the vertical demand curve of zero elasticity. Here, D_0 and D_1 are two such curves, intermediate between the two extremes. A slight alteration in quantity (price) by the monopolist will have a larger or a smaller impact on price (quantity), depending on the price elasticity of demand that the monopolist faces. Thus, in searching for the right price (by controlling quantity) to maximize profits, the monopolist must take elasticity of demand into consideration. For ordinary negatively sloped demand curves, that elasticity will depend on price.

Monopolists Take Losses on Previous Units Sold. Under competitive conditions, as noted above, the demand, or average-revenue, curve is equal to the *marginal-revenue* curve. This is not so for the monopolist, who must take "losses" or "discounts" on all previous units sold as she lowers price. Consider Figure 9.2 and the related hypothetical data of Table 9.1. In Figure 9.2 a price decline from P_0 to P_1 results in increased sales from Q_0 to Q_1. But monopoly revenues fall (by the cross-hatched area in Figure 9.2) on Q_0 units sold prior to the price decrease and rise by the addition to monopoly revenue from the new units sold at the *new* price P_1. Thus, except for the extreme case in which the demand curve is vertical (like demand curve D_I in Figure 9.1), there is always a *net* change in total revenue when price is lowered and the demand curve is negatively sloped. (Net change will be positive or negative, of course, depending on elasticity of demand.) **Marginal revenue** is the change in total revenue

Figure 9.2 The Monopoly Demand and Marginal-Revenue Curves

A price decrease by the monopoly firm both adds and subtracts revenue from the firm. The monopolist, in effect, takes "losses" on previous units sold at a higher price.

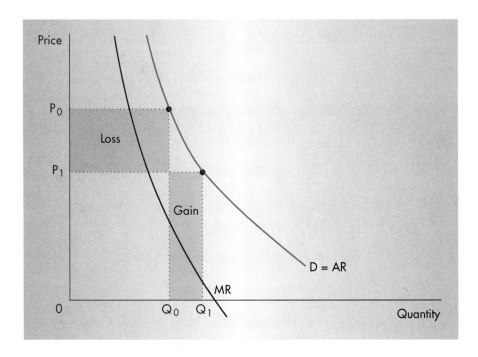

Table 9.1 Revenues, Costs, and Profits for the Pure Monopolist

Column 7 shows the profits that a pure monopolist will earn by charging various prices between $7 and $12. The monopolist will always maximize profits by charging the price at which the marginal cost equals marginal revenue.

1 Rate of Output Q (Units per Day)	2 Price (per Unit)	3 Total Revenue (per Day) (1) x (2)	4 Marginal Revenue ΔTR/ΔQ	5 Total Cost (per Day)	6 Marginal Cost	7 Profit (per Day) (3) − (5)
0				$20.00		−$20.00
			}—$12.00		}—$5.00	
1	$12.00	$12.00		25.00		−13.00
			}— 11.00		}— 4.00	
2	11.50	23.00		29.00		−6.00
			}— 10.00		}— 3.50	
3	11.00	33.00		32.50		0.50
			}— 9.00		}— 5.00	
4	10.50	42.00		37.50		4.50
			}— 8.00		}— 6.00	
5	10.00	50.00		43.50		6.50
			}— 7.00		}— 7.00	
6	9.50	57.00		50.50		6.50
			}— 6.00		}— 7.50	
7	9.00	63.00		58.00		5.00
			}— 5.00		}— 9.50	
8	8.50	68.00		67.50		0.50
			}— 1.75		}—12.50	
9	7.75	69.75		80.00		−10.25
			}— 0.25		}—15.00	
10	7.00	70.00		95.00		−25.00

created by a one-unit change in output. Alternatively, it is the change in revenue divided by the change in output. Under competitive conditions, marginal revenue is always equivalent to price because competitors are price takers. In competitive circumstances, price does not change as more or less units are sold. Under monopoly, in contrast, with a negatively sloped demand curve, additional units can be sold only by lowering price, and price must be reduced on previous units sold. Marginal revenue is less than price for any change in output.

These principles may be given simple numerical expression as in Table 9.1. A monopoly demand curve is expressed in columns 1 and 2 of Table 9.1, in which units produced (per day) are inversely related to price. Total revenue rises as output increases, and marginal revenue — calculated as the change in total revenue with a unit rise in sales — declines as output increases. Clearly, the monopolist must reduce price to sell more output, and therefore she must take a "discount" on units previously sold at higher prices. To sell more than

10 units, price would have to be lowered below $7.00 per unit, causing total revenue to decline and marginal revenue to become *negative*.

Monopoly Revenues and Elasticity. The concept of an addition to revenue from the sale of an additional unit of output suggests the concept of elasticity and its relationship to monopoly revenues. There is, in fact, an exact relationship among price (average revenue), marginal revenue, and elasticity under monopoly conditions (that is, under conditions of less-than-perfect competition). It is given as the following useful expression:

$$MR = P\left(1 + \frac{1}{e}\right)$$

or   (9.1)

$$MR = P + \frac{P}{e}$$

The exact relationship between these magnitudes is given by expression 9.1 and is shown in Figure 9.3, which depicts the *linear* relationships among price, elasticity, and marginal revenue for the monopolist. In Figure 9.3 (which abstracts from costs of production), demand is price elastic in the upper part of the demand curve (between price P_0 and P_M). As price declines from P_0, total revenue rises and marginal revenue falls faster than price does, for reasons given earlier.[4] The important point is that these relationships follow from the definitions of the three concepts. Because elasticity measures the relative response of quantity demanded to a change in price, price reductions from P_0 to P_M cause output to rise by a percentage amount greater than the percentage fall in price. This must mean that total revenue is rising. At the same time, price decreases (given the negative slope of the demand curve) mean that marginal revenue is decreasing. But so long as total revenue is rising, marginal revenue must be positive.

When price reaches P_M, demand elasticity is unitary (a 1 percent change in price yields a 1 percent change in output) and total revenue is at a maximum. When an infinitesimal change in price has no effect on total revenue, marginal revenue is equal to zero, as shown in Figure 9.3. As price falls below P_M, total revenue declines and elasticity is less than 1 (a 1 percent decrease in price leads to a *less* than 1 percent increase in sales). Because total revenue falls as price

4. It can be easily shown that marginal revenue declines twice as fast as price does (for linear curves). If the inverse form of a linear demand curve is of the form $p = a - bq$, where a is the intercept and $-b$ is the slope, total revenue ($p \times q$) is equal to $TR = pq = aq - bq^2$. Because marginal revenue is the rate of change in total revenue as output is increased by some infinitesimal unit, marginal revenue is the derivative of the total-revenue curve, or $MR = a - 2bq$, where the intercept is a and the slope is $-2b$, exactly twice the negative value of the slope of the demand curve.

Figure 9.3 Relationships Among Price (Average Revenue), Elasticity, and Marginal Revenue

When the demand curve is price elastic and price is falling, marginal revenue is positive but falling and total revenue is rising. At unit elasticity, marginal revenue is zero and total revenue is maximized. When demand is price inelastic, price declines are associated with negative marginal revenue and declining total revenue.

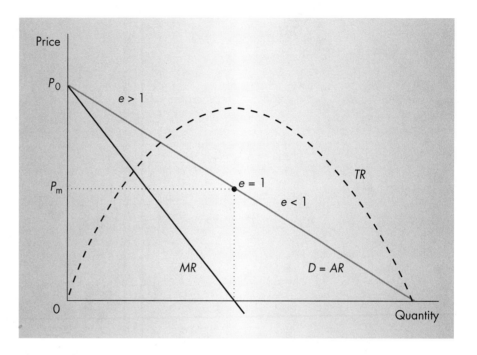

decreases, the marginal revenue associated with price decreases must be negative, as shown in the figure.

This relationship between average and marginal revenue and elasticity for the monopolist is a technical one, but it is fundamental to understanding several important features of monopoly. In particular, it will help us to understand some of the features of the price-discriminating monopolist and, even more fundamentally, why there can be no supply curve for the monopolist in the same sense as that found for the competitive firm and industry.

Short-Run Equilibrium for the Monopolist

Naturally, all firms incur costs in producing goods and services, and we have so far abstracted from them in order to highlight the principles of monopoly revenue. The basic profit-maximizing principle for the monopolist is the same as that of the perfect competitor when costs are added. The monopolist will maximize profits where marginal cost is equal to marginal revenue. But, as noted

Figure 9.4 Equilibrium Occurs Where Marginal Cost Equals Marginal Revenue

Marginal revenue equals marginal cost at point *C* in the figure. Marginal cost exceeds (is less than) marginal revenue at output larger (smaller) than Q_E, and the monopolist is not maximizing profits.

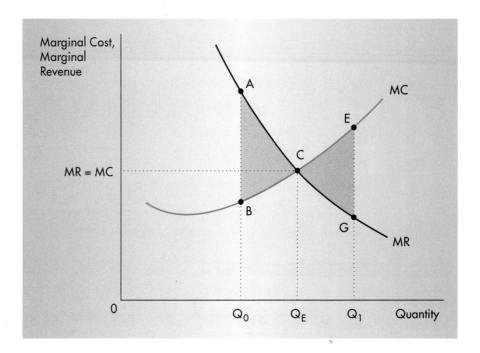

earlier, marginal revenue is not the same as price under monopoly conditions. Equilibrium occurs where the negatively sloped marginal-revenue curve is equal to the marginal-cost curve, as shown in Figure 9.4.

The marginal-cost and marginal-revenue data from Table 9.1 are given abstract expression in Figure 9.4. At some quantity Q_0 the marginal revenue of producing another unit of the good or service is higher than the marginal cost of producing that unit by an amount *AB*. Marginal revenue exceeds marginal cost up to the quantity Q_E. An addition to total revenue equal to the shaded area (approximate triangle) *CBA* could be obtained by raising output to Q_E. Similarly, the monopolist would never choose an output level such as Q_1, because at that level the marginal cost of producing an additional unit of output would exceed the marginal revenue by an amount *EG*. Here reductions in output would be called for in the total amount $Q_1 Q_E$. Total losses would be reduced (net revenues increased) by these actions in the amount *EGC* as shown in Figure 9.4.

Short-Run Price Searching. Profit maximization or loss minimization in the short run takes place as the monopolist searches for price by varying output levels. In

Figure 9.5, as in Figure 9.4, the monopolist maximizes profit by selecting that output at which marginal cost and marginal revenue are equal. Note, however, that in Figure 9.5 the average-revenue (demand) curve and two alternative short-run average-cost curves are included.

The alternative cost curves in Figure 9.5 show that the monopolist may earn either profits (with $SRAC_0$) or losses (with $SRAC_1$) in the short run. In Figure 9.5 the monopolist will earn profits in the amount FHC_0P_0, given the lower average-total-cost curve. Total revenue (FQ_E0P_0) is found by multiplying price or average revenue (P_0) by equilibrium quantity Q_E. The total cost of producing Q_E units of output is calculated by multiplying the average cost of producing Q_E units of output (distance Q_EH in Figure 9.5) by Q_E. Profits are simply the difference between the total revenue brought in by the monopolist and total cost, or FQ_E0P_0 minus HQ_E0C_0, or area FHC_0P_0.

Alternatively, the monopolist might make negative profits (losses) in the short run. If the average-total-cost curve is above the demand curve at the output at which marginal cost equals marginal revenue, the monopolist will incur losses. In Figure 9.5 those losses — calculated in the same manner as the

Figure 9.5 The Profit-Maximizing Monopolist in the Short Run

The monopolist facing cost curve $SRAC_0$ and the demand and marginal-revenue curves shown in the figure will earn economic profits in the amount of FHC_0P_0. Higher short-run average-cost curves will mean lower profits or actual losses (as with $SRAC_1$).

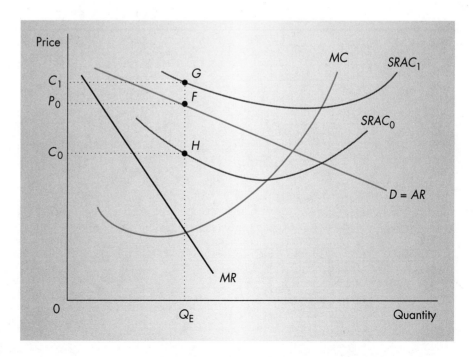

difference between total revenue and total cost above — will amount to GFP_0C_1 because costs per unit are Q_EG rather than Q_EH when the short-run average-cost curve equals $SRAC_1$.

At a more practical level, the possibility of losses reminds us that a monopolist is not guaranteed a market. Not only may a monopolist incur losses in the short run, but she may even be forced to abandon the business altogether. The same principles that apply to the perfect competitor as regards "shutdown" decisions face the monopolist as well. In Figure 9.6, for example, the monopolist will be forced to shut down completely. Total receipts of FQ_E0P_0 do not even cover total variable costs of JQ_E0V_0. Put another way, total losses exceed total fixed costs and the monopolist-entrepreneur is unable to meet her out-of-pocket variable expenses, much less make any contribution to fixed cost of GJV_0C_0. Under these circumstances, the monopolist should abandon production; it is in her interest to do so, because the strategy is said to be loss minimizing. Going out of business will mean responsibility for costs in the amount GJV_0C_0, but continuing operation would obligate the monopoly firm to GFP_0C_0 in outlays.

Figure 9.6   The Monopolist Faces Shutdown of the Firm
The monopolist would face shutdown of her firm if (as in the figure) average variable cost exceeds the demand curve.

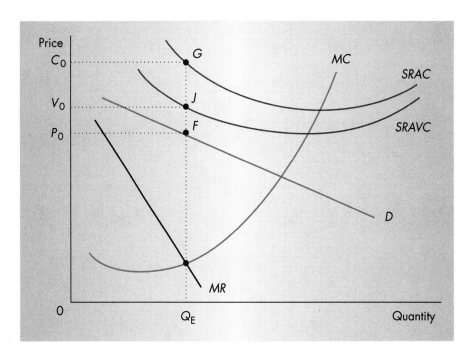

Figure 9.7 Under Monopoly the Marginal-Cost Curve Is Not the Supply Curve of the Firm
Because any given value of marginal revenue may be associated with many different prices, the marginal-cost curve of the monopolist cannot represent quantity supplied at given prices.

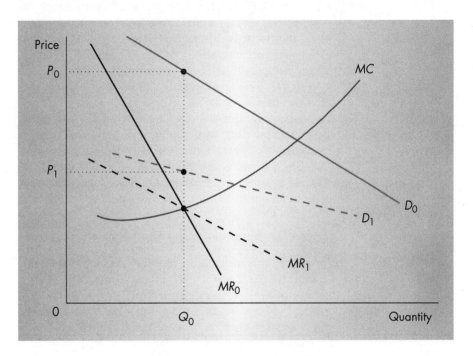

The Marginal-Cost Curve Is Not the Monopolist's Supply Curve. Clearly, going out of business is a self-interested decision. Recall that the decision of the competitive firm to cease operations when price fell below *SRAVC* helped to define the supply curve of the competitive firm — it was the locus of prices and quantities defined by the marginal-cost curve *above* average variable cost. A moment's reflection about the manner in which the monopolist arrives at profit-maximizing equilibrium tells us that this cannot be the case for the monopoly firm.

Under perfectly competitive conditions, the competitive firm's marginal-cost curve traces out the firm's supply curve when price is above average variable cost. When price is *below* average variable cost, the competitive firm (like the monopoly firm discussed here) goes out of business, because receipts are insufficient to pay out even variable costs that must be covered in the short run. (This is the so-called shutdown point.)

While shutdown principles do apply to the monopoly firm, the marginal-cost curve (above or below average variable cost) does not trace out a true supply curve. Consider Figure 9.7, which depicts two possible demand–marginal revenue combinations that could face the monopolist. Because the two marginal-revenue curves MR_0 and MR_1 intersect marginal cost (and each other) at profit-maximizing or loss-minimizing output Q_0, the price associated with Q_0 could be P_0 *or* P_1, depending on which demand curve was facing the monopolist. Reference to the formula relating marginal revenue, price, and elasticity, $MR = P(1 + 1/e)$, tells us immediately that when the marginal revenues are equal (as they are in Figure 9.7 at quantity Q_0) and prices differ, elasticities must be inversely related to the price difference. With reference to Figure 9.7, because $MR_0 = MR_1$ at Q_0, and $P_0 > P_1$, $e_1 > e_0$. Generally, there is a very large (infinite) number of possible prices that could be associated with output Q_0. This fact makes the supply curve of the monopolist indeterminate. By definition, a supply curve links the amounts that a firm would be willing to produce (per unit of time) in a given set of alternative prices. Thus the marginal-cost curve of the monopolist gives us no unique guide to the output decision, because that decision will depend on the particular demand curves faced by the monopoly firm at any point in time. The same problem applies whenever the demand curve or curves faced by the firm are negatively sloped, as in monopolistic competition or oligopoly (Chapter 10).

Long-Run Maximizing by the Monopolist

The foregoing discussion implies, correctly, that the monopolist may well decide to cease operations in the short run. Long-run operation for the monopolist, or for any other firm, will be impossible if total costs are not covered. There are, of course, no fixed costs in the long run — all costs are variable and must be covered if the firm is to remain in business. The monopoly firm is limited by demand for its product even though entry is costly and it has no direct competitors.

The monopoly firm will, however, always attempt to adjust its output to make profits or to break even. Consider the long-run circumstances of a monopoly firm that is breaking even and is earning only a normal profit, as depicted in Figure 9.8. The monopolist is earning only a normal return, but she does this by adjusting the firm's scale of operation to the most efficient level. This means that the monopolist will build a plant scale designated as $SRAC_0$ in order to most efficiently (at lowest cost) produce output Q_E. This is only one size of plant along the envelope or planning curve represented by *LRAC*, but it is the most efficient profit-maximizing one for the monopolist, *given the quantity she produces.* Note, immediately, that though the monopolist is producing efficiently, given demand and marginal revenue, a competitive solution would produce different results if she faced the same cost curves. Competitive conditions and entry would ensure that production would take place for each firm at the low point on the long-run average-cost function. Thus, compared with the pure competitor, the monopolist is operating inefficiently. Unit costs for the monopolist are higher than the minimum long-run costs that would result from competition. Thus, though the monopolist is for

Figure 9.8 Long-Run Equilibrium for the Monopolist

The monopolist maximizes profits by producing at the point at which its short-run marginal cost equals marginal revenue and (simultaneously) at which the long-run average-cost curve is tangential to some short-run average-cost curve. As in the figure, it is the lowest possible cost or most efficient point of the quantity produced (Q_E in the figure).

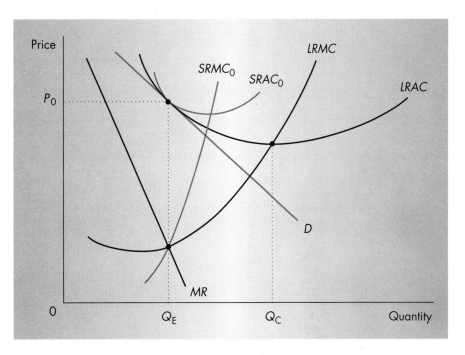

her own profit maximization producing efficiently, the scale level chosen by the monopolist will not (ordinarily) be equal to the one that produces the lowest unit cost under competition. Indeed, the monopolist who selected the output Q_C, corresponding to the lowest unit cost, would be forced out of business as the market is represented in Figure 9.8.

The cost and revenue conditions depicted for the monopolist in Figure 9.8 are only one of a very large number of possibilities. We ordinarily think of the monopolist as a net earner of economic profits, as shown in Figure 9.9, although, as we have seen, there are no guarantees that this is the case. Figure 9.9 shows a demand and cost configuration for a profitable monopolist in the long run.

Again, all possible choices are available along the long-run planning curve, which is a set of tangencies with all possible short-run curves. The monopolist will choose an efficient scale of plant — $SRAC_0$ with $SRMC_0$ — in order to produce profit-maximizing output Q_0. In equilibrium at Q_0, the monopolist equates marginal revenue to long-run marginal cost ($LRMC$). (As noted in

Figure 9.9 A Monopolist Earning Long-Run Profits

The monopolist shown in the figure is earning profits over the long run of FHC_0P_0. In order to maximize profits, the monopolist has bulit the plant represented by the curve $SRAC_0$.

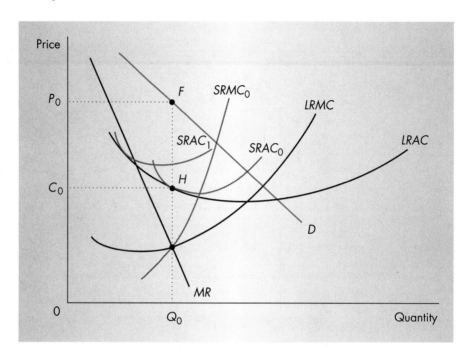

Chapter 8, the short-run marginal cost associated with plant size $SRAC_0$ intersects the $MR = LRMC$ equilibrium at that very point.) Profits, the difference between total revenue and total cost, are equal to FHC_0P_0. These profits depend critically on the lack of entry into the market monopolized by the seller. Should entry occur, profit was competed away as demand was split with new entrants — the demand curve of the monopolist depicted in Figure 9.9 and her associated marginal-revenue curve would shift leftward.

Another aspect of **monopoly profits**, as shown in Figure 9.9, is interesting. Suppose, for example, that the monopolist sells her monopoly rights. Clearly, in some static sense, the bid for the rights would include monopoly profits of FHC_0P_0. But in fact it would include the capitalized value of all the expected future stream of monopoly earnings. Bidders would have to include some assessment of the monopolist's future potential in terms of probability of entry, availability of substitutes, and so on. The net result of a purchase, in terms of the static figure at least, is for the average-cost curve to shift upward to a point of tangency with the demand curve at point F — a position of zero profits for the new owner. Why would anyone want to buy a business for a price that squeezes out all economic profits? Perhaps the buyer believes that he or she can run the monopolized business more efficiently at lower cost. Or perhaps the expectations formed by buyers and sellers with respect to the future prospects for demand differ. Whatever the reason, purchasers or holders of monopoly rights do not necessarily enjoy economic profits. The purchaser is, in effect, charging a price to cover all costs, including the capitalized monopoly right. A miscalculated decline in demand could force the purchaser out of business as the demand (average-revenue) curve falls below long-run average cost.

A Word on Monopoly and Welfare

Economists have assessed the reduction in welfare created by monopoly. The losses to monopoly are, in general, composed of two parts, as shown in the simplified depiction of Figure 9.10. For simplicity, costs are shown as linear in Figure 9.10, with long-run average costs equal to long-run marginal cost. The benchmark in all welfare comparisons is the amount of welfare (or utility) produced under competitive conditions, and in Figure 9.10 the welfare "triangle" is *FJH*. In this simple case, the amount of consumer surplus (*PJG*) is the

Figure 9.10 Monopoly Reduces Welfare of Consumers

Monopoly reduces welfare because it creates a situation in which price is above marginal costs of production. The "deadweight" loss is triangle *FJH*. If the monopolist must compete for the monopoly rights, the (potential) rent-seeking loss may add up to *FHGA*.

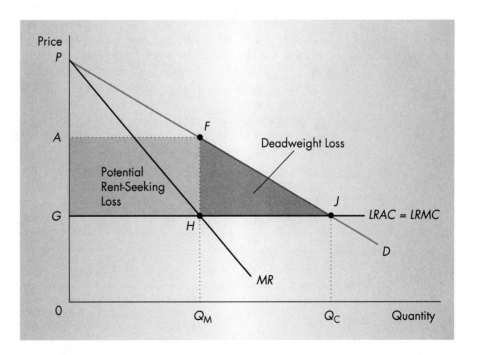

difference between the total amount that consumers would be willing to pay for Q_C units of the goods or service — $0PJQ_C$ — and the amount they have to pay, $0GJQ_C$. However, if the market were organized as a monopoly, with no change in cost or revenue functions, output would be restricted to Q_M and price would rise to $0A$. The amount of consumers' surplus at the monopoly output would fall to *PFA,* and monopoly profits would emerge as the amount *FHGA.* The so-called **deadweight loss** or standard loss arising from monopoly is shown as the darkened area *FJH* in the figure. Deadweight loss develops when quantity traded falls. The marginal value exceeds the marginal opportunity cost for each unit *no longer traded.* These benefits of trade are forgone under monopoly market structures. This loss, variably estimated by economists to be from 3 or 4 percent to over 20 percent of gross domestic product (GDP) in America, is a clear societal loss.[5] It is welfare or utility produced that no one, neither the monopolist nor her consumers, collects.

Two important questions arise in this simple analysis of Figure 9.10. The first, and most obvious, is "Why don't consumers simply purchase the monopoly rights from the monopolist and operate the industry in their own interests?" Apart from questions of scale economies, such a purchase could certainly take place. The monopolist could be bought out for an amount just exceeding *FHGA* by consumers, who would then realize a net gain of the deadweight loss triangle *FJH.* (The economist makes no judgments about distribution, so that the area *FHGA* can go to the monopolist or to consumers.) This would be possible if some way could be found to distribute the net gain *FJH* to consumers, leaving all of them better off. Obviously there will be organizational and **transactions costs** to consider in permitting consumers to buy out the monopolist. These pro rata costs must be lower than the pro rata gains, or consumers will not want to buy out the monopolist. Most economists argue, especially where consumers are numerous and diverse, that these organizational and other costs would swamp any potential gains. Thus, historically, we do not observe very many monopolists being bought out by their consumers.

Another important aspect of Figure 9.10 has already been mentioned in this chapter. That is the question of the origin and stability of the monopoly right, statically represented by area *FHGA.* A proper question might be "How did the monopolist get the monopoly right in the first place, and how is it maintained?" Economist Gordon Tullock and others provide an answer: potential monopolists must demand and compete for the monopoly right through the political process, but in doing so, they must expend resources that

---

5. Economists, through the years, have come up with varying estimates of the loss. Early estimates place the deadweight loss at less than 1 percent of GNP (Arnold Harberger, "Monopoly and Resource Allocation," *American Economic Review* 44 [May 1954], pp. 77–87), but other research puts a much higher value on the loss.

have high opportunity costs to society.[6] Legal fees, expensive lobbying efforts, payoffs to politicians, and financing efforts to maintain the entry control created by regulations or special privileges are all unnecessary expenditures. The good could be had, if such political authority to direct resources was impossible, without any of these expenditures. Groups with sufficient political power who are interested in redistributing wealth through regulation and monopoly creation will do so. These groups may include incumbent barbers, local zoning authorities, electricity producers, funeral directors, Citizens for the Public Interest, or any group with enough money and control over votes to convince politicians that monopoly restrictions should be granted and maintained through time.

Such **rent seeking** creates expenditures that, in effect, wipe out the monopoly gain represented by area *FHGA* in Figure 9.10. Again, combatants for the monopoly right will be willing to expend resources up to their capitalized pro rata share of the gains from the politically granted monopoly right. Naturally, there are circumstances in which those opposed to the granting of the right will also spend resources to fight the granting of monopoly. The net result, if markets for rights function well, is that the area *FHGA*, traditionally considered to be monopoly profits, could *also* be counted, along with traditional deadweight triangle *FJH*, as a loss to society. When these losses from rent seeking and special pleading by groups are counted, the welfare costs of monopoly may be considerably higher than earlier economists thought.

The Theory of Price Discrimination

Monopolists and firms with some monopoly power rarely charge a single price for a product. Rather, firms typically produce a whole range of goods and services that are sold with different "qualities." Strictly speaking, practically all goods are differentiated by the conditions of sale, including location and point-of-sale information, and by the participants to a specific transaction. The practice of selling a product or closely related products to different buyers or groups of buyers at prices *not based on differences in costs of production and sale* is called **price discrimination**. We are all familiar with the phenomenon and do not have to look far for examples.

---

6. See Gordon Tullock, "The Welfare Costs of Tariffs, Monopolies, and Theft," *Western Economic Journal* 5 (June 1967): 224–232. More generally, a whole process involving politicians, gainers, and losers as "rent seekers" in the establishment of regulations, subsidies, and so on, has been described by George J. Stigler, "The Theory of Economic Regulation," *Bell Journal of Economics and Management Science* (Spring 1971), pp. 2–21 and Sam Peltzman, "Towards a More General Theory of Regulation," *Journal of Law and Economics* (August 1976), pp. 211–240. Often, in the context of the Stigler-Peltzman model, consumers are the losers because their pro rata share of the loss from monopoly formation is low and their costs of information and organization are high. This enables certain industries to "capture" the governmental regulatory apparatus for their advantage.

Electric, telephone, and water utilities at local levels charge different prices to home users and to industrial or business users. Airlines (and, formerly, railroads) charge different prices to different groups of demanders on the basis of different services. For example, transcontinental air services from New York to Los Angeles are available for less than $300 (at certain times) but may cost up to $2,500 per trip, depending on the kind of services the buyer obtains — champagne, caviar, and gourmet meals on the $2,500 flight, cattle class on the cheaper flight. Auto manufacturers also play the same game by selling Toyotas, Buicks, and Hondas in many different models with many different options. Budweiser, Busch, and Bud Lite are three different qualities of beer sold at different average prices per six-pack by the same manufacturer — Anheuser-Busch. An American medical center performs organ transplants at no cost for indigents, but charges hundreds of thousands of dollars to an Arab sheik for the same operation. Although some of these examples do not typify pure monopoly, they all involve some element of monopoly and the ability to sell the same or similar products or qualities at different prices. The real question is, Are price differences due to differences in the cost of producing and supplying the goods or services to different consumers or groups of consumers? If the answer is yes, price discrimination is *not* being practiced, but if cost differences do not explain the difference in rates, the firm or firms with monopoly power are practicing discrimination.

Preconditions for Discrimination

As with most concepts, the economist has clear guidelines for explaining and analyzing the issue of price discrimination. Price discrimination, of course, must be profitable to the firm — no one is going to incur costs of selling in two different markets for nothing — but other conditions apply as well.

A Degree of Monopoly Power Is Required. As noted above, some degree of monopoly power must exist before price discrimination can be practiced. The demand curve for the firm must be downward sloping, indicating some ability to control output and therefore price. Because, by definition, purely competitive firms produce homogeneous products and are price takers in markets composed of large numbers of buyers, there is no way that a single firm can discriminate. Price control is, naturally, limited by elasticity of demand. With many substitutes, demand is more elastic (say, for beer) and the firm has some modest control over price. (These markets are said to be "monopolistically competitive" and are analyzed in detail in Chapter 10.) Other "monopolies," such as those over organ transplants or local power services, may have very inelastic demands and may conform more closely to the static requirements of pure monopoly. In these cases, the firm has a large degree of control over price.

The Monopolized Market Must Be Separable. Monopoly may exist without the possibility of increased profitability from price discrimination. In order for price discrimination to be feasible, however, the monopolist's market must be separable in some fashion at low net costs — by artificial creation or naturally through some actual or imputed characteristic or characteristics. This means that (significant) retrading or communications between markets or between consumers in the same market must be limited or prohibited.[7] Without the prohibition, it would do no good for the firm to sell one unit of a product at $5 to individual A and another unit of the same product to individual B for $8. If communication and retrading were possible, individuals A and B would soon catch on. Individual A would buy low and sell to individual B, and the firm would lose the market for the buyers who formerly paid a higher price. Demand for the product from individual A would increase, and demand for the product by B would disappear.

Everyone is familiar with children, adult, or seniors tickets to some sporting or entertainment events and for motel or hotel services. Age is verifiable at relatively low cost to ticket sellers and promoters. But this would be irrelevant for discrimination if age did not proxy some other factor among buyers. Charging higher ticket prices for adults, in contrast to children and senior citizens, is often based on actual and perceived income differences. Other things being equal, the higher one's income, the lower the elasticity or "substitutability" of a good in the buyer's budget.

In other markets, differences are artificially *created* by the monopoly firm. Again, the cost of separating the market cannot be too great, or the additional revenues would be swamped by the costs of making market divisions. This applies to the development of product lines or to the establishment of different qualities of a product or service — high- and low-quality Toyotas or different qualities of beer. Note that it does not matter whether these qualities are "real" or merely created by advertising and sales efforts. This includes the development of travel "classes" on airlines with real service differences (meals, comfortable seats, and so on) or the more ephemeral qualities of cosmetics and makeup ("luscious," more "desirable," "romantic") or restaurants ("superb," "magnificent," "elegant").[8]

In cases in which differences are created by the monopolist, consumers must **self-select** among product alternatives. The consumer must decide

7. Counterfeiting may be an example or a kind of "retrading." Because the government is in charge of investigating counterfeiters of trademarked goods (such as Rolex watches, Gucci shoes and bags, Reebok tennis shoes and equipment) and of transferring fines collected to manufacturers, it may be in some producers' interests to permit some *degree* of counterfeiting. See Richard S. Higgins and Paul H. Rubin, "Counterfeit Goods," *Journal of Law and Economics* 29 (October 1986): 211–230.

8. There is an additional reason why price discrimination is observed more in "services" markets: the practice is allowed under the Robinson Patman Act (enacted in 1936).

whether to buy the high-priced, high-quality item or the low-quality, low-quality model or item (often with many in between). It is the entrepreneur's important task to design different products or qualities so as to maximize profits. Although there may be costs of actual market separation in cases in which markets are naturally divided, the number of consumers is given by the dividing characteristic (age, male or female, and so on), and consumers do not self-select the market they wish to be in. Political barriers, such as between nations, often form the basis for price discrimination (or **dumping**, as it is called when price discrimination takes place by one seller in two or more separate countries). Rules and legal barriers often prevent consumers from self-selecting among products. For an example drawing on *both* of these latter factors, see Highlight 9.3.

Highlight 9.3   *Price Discrimination in Pharmaceutical Markets: Are U.S. Companies "Drug Dumping" in Canada?*

One of the most regulated markets in America is the prescription drug industry. Millions of dollars and years of research are spent on the development of new drugs and potential new drugs by private drug companies. Once the drug is developed, the U.S. Food and Drug Administration (FDA) requires rigorous testing, often for years, before granting approval to the drug company to market the substance. It is obvious that a huge profit payoff is necessary in order to further the process in a market economy. (*How* large profits have to be is another question.)

To encourage such activity, the government grants a patent — exclusive right to produce and market the drug in the United States for 17 years. To compensate companies for delays in getting FDA approval, the patent may be extended in some cases. After 17 years (or more), generic drugs that closely resemble the initial product are, after FDA approval, marketed by *generic* companies. Monopoly profits from exclusive sales of the major pharmaceutical companies are thereby eroded. Competition from (low-priced) generics are estimated to reduce brand-name pharmaceutical prices by one-third to one-half on particular drug products in the first few years.[a] Prices that were once monopolized may approach the cost of production (competitive rates) when 8 or 10 generic substitutes are available. (Generics account for 40 percent of the drug market but take in only 8 percent of total drug revenues, about $4 billion dollars annually.)

[a] Table 9.2 and the accompanying discussion are derived from Milt Freudenheim, "Now the Big Drug Makers Are Imitating Their Imitators," *The New York Times* (September 20, 1992), p. F5.

Table 9.2 Expiring Drug Patents

A sample of expiring drug patents shows the immense profitability of prescription drug sales. Likewise, the size of the vulnerable market provides an indication of the potential value of generic competition.

Date Exclusive Rights Expire		Drug Name	Maker	Use	Size of Vulnerable Market*
1992	Sept.	Procardia XL	Pfizer	Heart	$975
	Oct.	Protropin	Genentech	Human growth hormone	210
	Nov.	Cardizem SR (twice a day)	Marion Merrell Dow	Heart	300
		Cardizem (several times a day)	Marion Merrell Dow	Heart	450
	Dec.	Ceclor	Lilly	Antibiotic	675
1993	Jan.	Lopic	Warner-Lambert	Cholesterol	420
	Feb.	Ansaid	Upjohn	Arthritis	205
	Oct.	Xanax	Upjohn	Anti-anxiety	675
	Nov.	Vepesid	Bristol-Myers Squibb	Cancer	275
	Dec.	Lopressor	Ciba-Geigy	Heart	275
		Naprosyn	Syntex	Arthritis	700
1994	Jan.	Micronase	Upjohn	Diabetes	395
	April	Seldane	Marion Merrell Dow	Antihistamine	850
	May	Tagamet	Smithkline Beecham	Ulcers	775
	Dec.	Cardizem CD (once a day)	Marion Merrell Dow	Heart	600
1995	May	Dilacor XR	Rhone-Poulenc Rorer	Heart	250
	Aug.	Capoten	Bristol-Myers Squibb	Heart	655
	Sept.	Sandimmune	Sandoz	Organ transplant	250
	Dec.	Zantac (original form)	Glaxo	Ulcers	2,450

*Sales (in millions) of the drug that would be vulnerable to competition from generics. Figures are estimates or projections for sales in the United States during the last 12 months before the end of the drug maker's patent protection. *Source:* Milt Freudenheim, "Now the Big Drug Makers Are Imitating Their Imitations," *The New York Times* (September 20, 1992), p. F5. Copyright © 1992 The New York Times Company. Reprinted by permission.

Critics charge that drug companies are virtual monopolists that earn huge economic profits at the expense of the consuming public. Pharmaceutical companies claim that profits are necessary to incur the expense and risk of developing new products, many of which do not pan out. High profits, the companies argue, are also necessary for educating physicians who prescribe the products. Abstracting from the debate over profitability, it is undeniable that the major companies such as Lilly, Pfizer, Upjohn, and Merck have huge revenues at stake when the inevitable day of generic competition dawns. Table 9.2 shows the extent of the revenue at risk for selected drugs on which the patents will expire over the next few years. Clearly, billions of dollars in revenues are in jeopardy for the major companies.

The obvious problem for the big pharmaceutical companies is to keep up revenues in the face of competition. Their solution — in addition of course to developing and marketing new drugs — is to price-discriminate along the lines discussed in this chapter. First consider the possibility of domestic discrimination. Competitors such as Merck and Marion Merrell Dow are planning to market generic copies of their own trademarked products. Thus, for example, Merck will sell diflunisal, the generic name of Dolabid, a $100-million-a-year Merck analgesic, under the banner of West Point Pharma, a new Merck subsidiary. In addition to the trade name, the differences between the trademarked product (Dolabid) and the generic substitute (diflunisal) will only be the *color* of the pill and the color and style of the package! But if the products are identical, how can price discrimination be practiced?

As noted in the text, price discrimination requires that markets be separable and that retrading be limited or prohibited. Although your pharmacist is required to substitute a low-priced generic brand for a high-priced trademarked pharmaceutical, she must sell the higher-priced one if your doctor specifies it. Some physicians may distrust the quality of generics, because slight chemical alterations might in fact produce a weaker drug; so they will continue to prescribe the higher-priced drug. Some consumers, if they are aware of

Table 9.3

Drug price comparison between U.S. and Canada (on May 1, 1991). Prices for the most frequently prescribed pharmaceuticals were significantly lower in Canada than in the United States in 1991.

Drug	Maker	Use	Price Premium in the U.S.
Amoxil	SmithKline Beecham	Antibiotic	+5%
Lanaxin	Burroughs Wellcome	Heart failure	+16%
Zantac	Glaxo	Ulcers	+30%
Premarin	American Home Prod.	Hormone	+162%
Xanax	Upjohn	Anxiety	+183%

possible differences and covered (or partially covered) by a health insurance plan, will demand the high-priced alternative. These market divisions (legal/regulatory) make price discrimination and the extension of profits on trademarked drugs possible.[b]

A second avenue taken by domestic drug companies to exact monopoly revenues through price discrimination is to sell drugs abroad more cheaply than in the United States, a practice called dumping. Drugs, so the argument goes, are dumped at lower prices abroad because markets are separable and demand is often more price elastic because of a larger number of substitutes. There may in fact be some evidence that U.S. drug manufacturers are doing exactly that in neighboring Canada. A recent study for the U.S. House Energy and Commerce Committee, based on comparisons of 121 drugs, found that 23 were priced lower in the United States than in Canada but that 98 were priced lower there by 50 percent or more. (For a sample of the price differences gathered by the U.S. General Accounting Office, see Table 9.3).[c]

U.S. manufacturers were quick to defend themselves against charges of dumping. They charged that the House committee was comparing "sticker prices" in the United States and that price discounts are routinely given to the large health maintenance organizations (HMOs). Also, Canada's health-care system only reimburses patients for the lowest-priced treatment. Clearly, socialized medicine and health care suppresses prices.

Institutions also matter in determining whether price discrimination is actually taking place. The Canadian government encourages competition by permitting generics to compete sooner than allowed in the United States. (Generic copies are allowed to compete after only 7 to 10 years in Canada, whereas the generic companies must wait 17 to 22 years in the United States.) The lower-priced Canadian drugs may only be meeting the competition, given differences in institutions and the health-regulatory structure.

The important questions, with respect to the U.S. drug system, are these: Are profits (however derived) sufficient to cover the costs of new private investment in the development, patenting, and marketing of new drugs? Is there too much regulation in the U.S. drug-certification system? Is more competition in the U.S. system called for, or could a government drug-research apparatus do better?

[b] Note yet another real possibility. Drug companies may be using such price discrimination to weaken or drive generic competition out of the market.

[c] Data and discussion in Table 9.3 are taken from Milt Freudenheim, "Drugs Cost Less in Canada Than in U.S., Study Finds," *The New York Times* (October 22, 1992), p. D1.

Business firms will elect to engage in price discrimination only if they can increase profits by doing so. Figure 9.11 shows how discrimination can increase profits if the demand elasticities of different groups of buyers are different. For simplicity, assume that the buyers of good X fall into two

Figure 9.11 Higher Profits Through Price Discrimination

If a price of $21 is charged in both market A and market B, 190 units will sell in A and 80 units will sell in B. However, the marginal revenue from the last unit sold in market A is $2 compared to $17 from the last unit sold in market B. Profits can be increased by raising the price in market A (where demand is less elastic) and lowering the price in market B so as to equate the marginal revenue in the two markets.

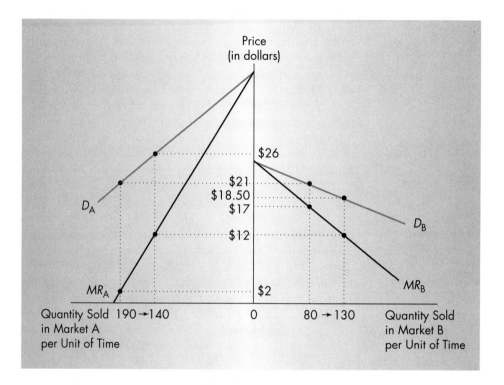

groups, A and B, whose demands are shown as D_A and D_B in Figure 9.11. At every price, D_B is more elastic than D_A. If the seller initially charges a price of $21 to all buyers, a total of 270 units will be sold — 190 to group A buyers and 80 to group B buyers. The last unit sold to buyers of type A yields $2 in marginal revenue, and the last unit sold to type B buyers yields $12 in marginal revenue.

Price discrimination is clearly profitable in this case. Because the marginal revenue in the more elastic market (market B) is higher than the marginal revenue in the less elastic market (market A), the firm can increase its revenues without changing its output by taking units out of market A and selling them in market B. If one less unit is sold in market A, total revenue will fall by about $2. However, if that unit is sold in market B, total revenue will rise by $12, causing total profits to rise by about $10 — the difference between the marginal revenues in the two markets.

The firm in question can increase profits by expanding sales in market B and reducing sales in market A until the marginal revenue in each of the markets is equal. In Figure 9.11 the two marginal revenues become equal when output in market A is reduced by 50 units (from 190 to 140) and output in market B is increased from 80 to 130 units. In order to increase sales to 130 units in market B, the price must be reduced from $21 to $18.50. To reduce sales from 190 to 140 in market A, the seller must increase the price in that market to $26. Instead of selling all 270 units at a price of $21 and generating $5,670 in revenues, the firm obtains $3,640 (140 x $26) from its sales in market A and $2,405 (130 x $18.50) from its sales in market B, for a total of $6,045 in revenues. Because the firm's output (and therefore its total cost) is unchanged, the $375 increase in revenues also increases profits by $375.

If we recall the relationship between marginal revenue and demand elasticity ($MR = P[1 + 1/e]$), we see that whenever the two demands differ with regard to price elasticity, the firm cannot maximize profits by charging a uniform price in each of the submarkets. If the same price is charged in both

Figure 9.12 **Profit Maximization and Price Discrimination**

To determine the most profitable level of output for a firm which engages in third-degree price discrimination, it is necessary to horizontally sum the two marginal-revenue curves. In the graph, ΣMR is the horizontal sum of MR_A and MR_B. The optimal level of output Q_T, is the point at which the marginal cost equals ΣMR.

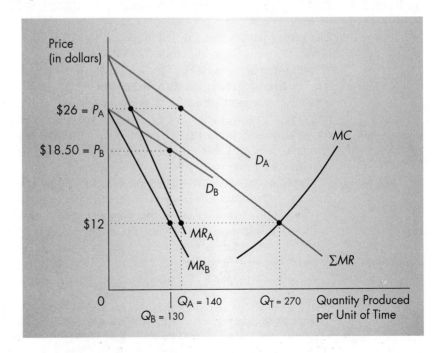

markets, the marginal revenue will always be lower in the less elastic market. Therefore, to maximize profits, the firm must charge a higher price in the less elastic market (market A) and a lower price in the more elastic market (market B).

We see that to maximize profits, a firm must equate its marginal revenue in each submarket. In the situation depicted in Figure 9.11, the most profitable way to sell 270 units is to sell 140 in market A and 130 in market B. However, that graph does not show what the most profitable level of output is. Figure 9.12 shows how to determine this. It reproduces D_A and D_B from Figure 9.11 and the corresponding marginal-revenue curves MR_A and MR_B. The two marginal-revenue curves are summed horizontally to form the summed kinked line labeled ΣMR. This line shows the additional revenue that can be attained from each additional unit of output, assuming that the units are allocated between the two markets in such a way as to equate the marginal revenue in the two submarkets. The profit-maximizing output Q_T is at the point at which the marginal cost equals the sum of the marginal revenues. That last unit has a marginal cost of $12 and it also generates $12 in marginal revenue. The 270 units are allocated between the two submarkets to assure that the marginal revenue in each submarket also equals $12. This occurs when 140 units are sold in market A and 130 units are sold in market B.

Highlight 9.4   *First-Degree Price Discrimination: Kidney Transplants in Europe and India*

The power to discriminate is limited, as noted in the text, by the degree of monopoly power and the ability to effectively separate markets according to differing demand elasticities. In a special case of discrimination, called "perfect" or **first-degree price discrimination**, each consumer pays over his or her maximum demand price for a good or service. Price is in exactly inverse proportion to the elasticity of demand for the item. Some auctions, in a limited way, may exhibit this characteristic, but the conditions for perfect discrimination probably exist, if at all, only for certain services, because services by nature are nontransferable.

Professional services — for example, for highly specialized physicians or lawyers — are sometimes used to illustrate the possibility of first-degree discrimination. Consider some specialized surgical technique — kidney, heart, or lung transplants — as a hypothetical but realistic example. In the United States, the procedure is highly regulated, as is the ordering of the recipients of donated organs.[a] According to rumor, at least, in Europe (especially France), in India, and in parts of Latin America, such operations are available to

[a] Many Americans go abroad for transplants and other medical services (such as for AIDS). Organs such as kidneys may be "harvested" *in vivo* — sold for profit by living donors who only require one kidney. We skirt the issue of the "ethics" or "morality" of using the market

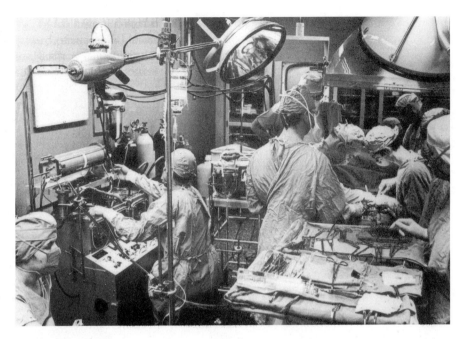

Professional services, such as those of skilled surgeons, offer an opportunity to price-discriminate between buyers.

high-price bidders. Assuming that the operation is available on such terms, and that there is a large and continuous number of "bidders" over some definite time period, the demand curve D_S (or SAR) for surgery, may be drawn as in Figure 9.13.

A highly skilled transplant surgeon in France may face a demand curve as drawn in Figure 9.13. She charges each patient the maximum demand price along the demand curve. Some very anxious and rich patient may pay P_1 for a transplanted kidney or heart-lung combination, P_2 will be paid by some other, slightly less rich or less desperate, patient. Assuming that the marginal and average costs of the operation are constant ($LRAC = LRMC$), the surgeon will price-discriminate all along linear demand curve D_S until price equals P_{MC}. The surgeon takes in a total revenue $0ACQ_{MC}$, of which $0P_{MC}CQ_{MC}$ is cost. The entire amount of the consumers' surplus above costs (area $P_{MC}AC$) goes to the surgeon as profit. One important point to note is that in the case of first-degree discrimination (and in this case *only*), the monopolist is not required to lower the price to higher-price demanders as she moves down the

to supply organs in this example; but see Roger D. Blair and David L. Kaserman, "The Economics and Ethics of Alternative Cadaveric Organ Procurements Policies," *Yale Journal on Regulation* (Summer 1991), pp. 403–452 and Raj Chengappa, "The Organs Bazaar," *India Today* (July 31, 1990), pp. 30–37.

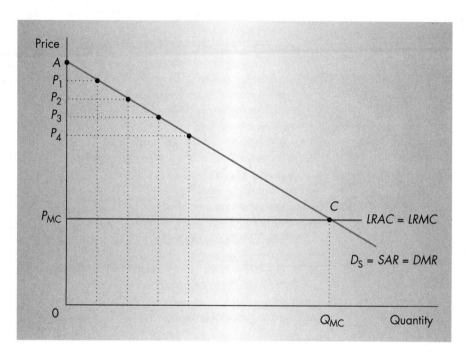

Figure 9.13 Organ-Donor Market Approximates High Degrees of Discrimination
When sellers (surgeons) can bargain individually with buyers of services, the (approximately) maximum demand price may be obtained. Such may be the case with organ transplants.

demand curve and serves other (lower price–lower elasticity) demanders. This means that the demand curve — the simple monopoly's *average* revenue curve *SAR* — and the *marginal* revenue that comes from discrimination (*DMR*) are one and the same![b]

Naturally, it is very costly to discover the exact demand elasticity (from income characteristics or other signals) for each buyer. Techniques to uncover maximum prices, such as auction or bidding schemes, do exist in some markets, however, and the pricing of highly specialized medical services does present a possible example.

[b] The demand curve facing the monopolist — *given* that she is discriminating — will be above the demand curve drawn in Figure 9.12. Also note that the ultimate quantity sold in this case is exactly equal to the quantity that would be sold under competitive conditions, Q_{MC}. Perfect price discrimination, in a static sense, therefore possesses some of the characteristics of competition.

A degree of monopoly power, the ability to separate markets, either naturally or artificially, and different elasticities of demand evaluated at simple monopoly price are clearly *necessary* conditions for the conduct of price discrimination by the monopolist. It must be reemphasized that the actual separation of the markets must be at a cost that is less than the gain to the monopolist from the separation. It is almost always possible to separate markets at some cost to the monopoly seller. The important question is whether the separation is worthwhile in terms of the additional revenue that can be brought in.

Degrees of Discrimination

Another important issue, already encountered in the kidney-transplant example (Highlight 9.4), relates to the so-called degrees of discrimination. This classification system, invented by British neoclassical economist A. C. Pigou (1877–1959), identifies discrimination by three degrees or levels of fineness. In this traditional classification, first-degree discrimination refers to the monopolist's extraction of all consumer surplus from each demander of a *homogeneous* good or service. Pigou argued that the most common form, **third-degree discrimination**, "would obtain if the monopolist were able to distinguish among his customers in different groups, separated from one another more or less by some practicable mark, and could charge a separate monopoly price to the members of each group."[9] The latter type is described (for two markets) in Figures 9.11 and 9.12. The "practicable mark" Pigou refers to includes differences in location (as in our example of drug dumping), in age, or in sex.

An extremely interesting form identified by Pigou, however, is **second-degree discrimination**, which takes place when a firm identifies n markets and charges p_0 to all consumers with a minimum (reservation) price of greater than p_0 but less than p_1; charges price p_1 to consumers with a reservation price of greater than p_1 but less than p_2; and so on. An example of such pricing would be the rental of a Xerox machine and the pricing of special paper for the machine on the basis of the total number of copies made. Another would be the pricing of electricity or phone usage by charging a flat rate plus a "running rate" so that the charge would depend on the amount of use. Everyone who was at least willing to pay the lowest demand price would get to buy the product, and individuals would "self-select" the class they would end up in.[10]

9. A. C. Pigou, *The Economics of Welfare* (London: Macmillan, 1920), p. 279. An excellent contemporary analysis of price discrimination in its many facets is Louis Phlips, *The Economics of Price Discrimination* (Cambridge: Cambridge University Press, 1981).

10. A moment's reflection tells us that this is not true under third-degree discrimination. Consider as an example the dumping of U.S. computer chips in Latin America, where a lower price is charged than to U.S. consumers. There may well be *some* demanders in the United States who would be willing to pay a price above that charged in the Latin America but would not be willing to pay the U.S. price. Those consumers are precluded from the product by location.

In modern economic theory, however, discrimination is thought to occur when different *qualities* of similar products are sold at different ratios of price to the marginal cost of qualities. First-class, business-class, and tourist-class airline tickets are an example, as are differentiated products made by the same manufacturer. Here products are not exactly homogeneous as in the traditional theory, but price discrimination theory is applicable nonetheless. (An introduction to the relation between quality differences and price discrimination is provided in an appendix to this chapter.)

Summary

The static theory of monopoly, although probably inappropriate in describing real-world events, is extremely valuable in identifying real-world characteristics of markets. Pure monopolies fitting the strict static definition are rare or nonexistent, but some aspects of the pure monopoly market fit almost every real-world case. In some realm of influence on buyers, all products have "unique" characteristics and individual firms will have some limited control over price. The phenomenon of price discrimination, moreover, may be the most pervasive characteristic of real-world markets, especially where quality differences are created in conjunction with differential pricing. All of these themes, especially the combination of competitive and monopoly characteristics, are further explored in Chapter 10, which discusses monopolistic competition and oligopolies. Some of the principles we should take from the present chapter, however, are

- an understanding of the meaning of monopoly and an intuitive feeling for where the legal and practical restraints of monopoly power apply.
- a formal understanding of the theory of monopoly behavior in the short and long run.
- the theoretical foundation for price discrimination, a most pervasive practice of real-world monopolies.
- an appreciation for the costs associated with monopolies in our economy and in the global economy.

Appendix: Quality Variability and Price Discrimination

In recent literature, the microeconomic theory of price discrimination has expanded to include the monopolist's selection of quality levels (or

11. R. Mussa and Sherwin Rosen, "Monopoly and Product Quality," *Journal of Economic Theory* 18 (1978): 301–317. The idea that monopolists might manipulate quality (as well as quantity) to maximize profits is a very old one: see the paper by engineer-economist Jules

Figure 9.14 Quality Differences and Price Discrimination

Utility curves for two qualities of a product are given by U_H and U_L in panel (a). When these curves (actually straight lines) are combined with the *MC* curve of supplying quality, first-degree discrimination (if tried) would lead to "defections" from high- to low-quality products. One solution is to lower price to the high-quality demanders and to reduce *quality* to the lower-quality demanders as shown in panel (b).

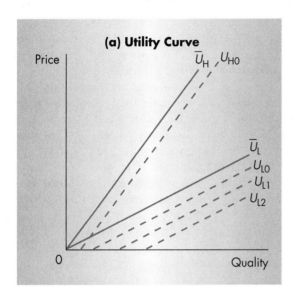
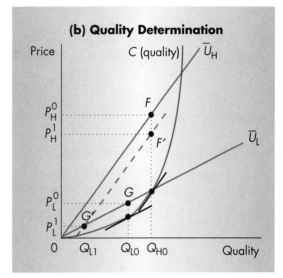

alternative "products") for sale in the market. Perhaps the most important recent contribution in this area is that of economists R. Mussa and S. Rosen, which focuses on the quality decision of the monopolist.[11]

Although the technicalities of the Mussa-Rosen model are fairly complicated, their model may be set out in the simple graphical terms of Figure 9.14. Both panels show the *utility functions* (drawn as straight lines) for two consumers who each buy one unit in a tradeoff between price and quality for some good (or closely related products, Buicks and Cadillacs). The curves, labeled U_H and U_L, are the *reservation* utility functions in the sense that each buyer would be willing to pay some maximum price and no more for each and every level of quality. The slope of the utility curves is the marginal rate of substitution between price and quality for some product or service. If the consumer actually pays this maximum, he or she is left with no consumer surplus and is at the margin of purchase. In Figure 9.14a dashed lines are drawn parallel to each of the reservation utility functions, which represent combinations that would improve the utility of each consumer. On utility

Dupuit, "On Tolls and Transport Charges," *Annales des Ponts et Chaussées* (1849) in *International Economic Papers* (London: Macmillan, 1962), pp. 7–31, or R. B. Ekelund, Jr., "Price Discrimination and Product Differentiation in Economic Theory: An Early Analysis," *Quarterly Journal of Economics* (May 1970), pp. 268–278.

curve U_{H0}, for example, downward and to the right of the reservation utility function, consumer H would achieve a higher level of utility than if she is forced to remain on the function U_H. The same is true for all dashed utility functions to the right of U_L for consumer L. Consumers H and L would each be "better off" to the right of their reservation curves. The valuations of product quality of course differ between the two consumers. Consumer L would only be willing to pay a lower price than consumer H for any level of quality.

In Figure 9.14b, a total-cost curve C (quality) is added to the utility functions of consumers H and L. The cost function is assumed to be convex in quality (marginal costs rise as higher qualities are produced) but constant in quantity (no scale economies then exist). *First*-degree price-discriminating price-quality combinations — in which each consumer pays all of his or her consumer surplus to the monopolist — may be located at F and G, respectively. At F and G, the monopolist would supply qualities Q_{H0} and Q_{L0} to consumers H and L, capturing all of their consumer surplus. These two quality levels are said to be optimal because the marginal cost of providing each quality (shown by the slope of $C(q)$) is equal to the marginal rates of substitution (the slopes of U_H and U_L, respectively) of the two reservation utility curves. Ideally, the monopolist could extract maximum consumer surplus (practice first-degree discrimination) by charging price $P_H{}^0$ to consumer H and $P_L{}^0$ to consumer L. The monopolist would receive the maximum profits possible from selling the two different units of the goods at these prices.

A good look at Figure 9.14b reveals that the initial desires of the monopoly seller cannot be realized. If the monopolist tried to offer qualities Q_{H0} and Q_{L0}, he would only end up selling the low-end product. Clearly, the demander of higher quality would "defect" from point F to point G every time. Why? Because the "self-selecting" consumer H would get more utility at point G than at point F. Point G in Figure 9.14b lies below F — a point below the high-end consumer's reservation utility function (refer to panel (a) to verify this fact). The high-end consumer would *gain* by moving to point G and buying the low-quality product. The monopolist will have to settle for smaller profits if he wishes to divide the market and to discriminate.

Here Mussa and Rosen point to a solution. The monopolist can take a combination of actions to ensure that the markets remain separate, but he must do so at the cost of losing some profits when compared to the first-degree solution. Specifically, according to Mussa and Rosen, the monopolist will *degrade* quality to customer L and lower price but provide quality Q_{H0} to customer H.[12] Such a solution is shown in Figure 9.14b at F' and G'. The

---

12. It should be noted that other solutions are possible — quality may be rendered nonoptimal for high-end consumers (see P. Srinagesh and R. M. Bradburd, "Quality Distortions by a Discriminating Monopolist," *American Economic Review* [March 1989], pp. 96–105) or at *both* ends of a quality spectrum (see T. Randolph Beard and Robert B. Ekelund, Jr., "Quality Choice and Price Discrimination: A Note on Dupuit's Conjecture," *Southern Economic Journal* 57 [April 1991], pp. 1155–1163).

task facing the monopolist is to make unattractive the movement by consumer H to the lower quality. He does that by lowering quality to the initial low-quality buyer, a move which, by itself, would make H's move more unattractive. In addition, to make it more attractive for H to stick with the higher quality, the monopolist lowers price to this consumer from P_H^0 to P_H^1. Both of these moves lower profits to the monopolist somewhat, but some such combination is necessary to preserve market separation and, under the circumstances given by utility and cost curves, profit maximization. The monopolist, in effect, establishes conditions under which self-selection is profitable.

Key Terms

monopoly	monopsony
barriers to entry	patent
economies of scale	natural monopoly
franchise	price searcher
marginal revenue	monopoly profit
deadweight loss	transactions costs
rent seeking	price discrimination
self-select	dumping
first-degree price discrimination	third-degree price discrimination
second-degree price discrimination	

Sample Questions

Question

It has recently been argued in the popular press that the airline industry is moving toward monopolization. Economic theory might suggest otherwise. Do you agree with the press? Explain.

Answer

The airline industry will not become a monopolized industry, because it is a contestable industry. Contestability theory maintains that as long as the threat of entry exists, even if there is only one seller in a market, the seller in the market will not act as a monopolist. The entry and success of Southwest Airlines, which has maintained a policy of nonparticipation in airline price wars, provides evidence of the possibility of entry into the industry. Further, there are substitutes available for travel and shipping, such as trains, buses, and ships. Recently, for example, Amtrak unveiled an express cross-country train that reaches California from Miami in 72 hours.

Question

A. C. Pigou classified price discrimination by a monopolist according to "degrees." Explain the characteristics of the different degrees and provide an example of each type of discrimination.

Answer

Pigou distinguished between first-, second-, and third-degree price discrimination. First-degree discrimination exists when the monopolist is able to charge each consumer his demand price and extract all consumer surplus. Real-world examples of first-degree price discrimination are rare but might hypothetically arise for an individual who discovers and sells a cure for AIDS, or for an organ transplant as discussed in the chapter. Second-degree price discrimination exists when the consumers self-select their class. One example is the decision to buy a product in bulk and receive a "quantity discount" or to buy the product on an as-needed basis and at a higher price. An individual who pays a flat fee for a given quantity of electricity and who can elect to buy more at different rates is another example. Finally, third-degree price discrimination exists when consumers are separable by the monopolist by such factors as age, sex, eye color, location, and so on. Examples include charging different prices for movie tickets to people with blue and brown eyes or drink specials for women but not for men.

Questions for Review and Discussion

1. What distinguishes a monopolist from a competitive firm regarding the goods and services that they sell?

*2. Patents and copyrights are important to a monopolist. What do these represent in the market and why do they help a monopolist?

3. Some economists believe certain industries exhibit economies of scale throughout their range of output. What are industries called that exhibit this characteristic and what are some examples of such industries?

4. Why are utilities such as electricity, water, and gas typically provided by only one firm in a city or region? Is this efficient?

5. Explain the impact of potential entry on a monopolist's behavior.

*6. Because a monopolist is the only seller in a market, how is price determined?

7. Show graphically a monopolist who is earning a loss in the short run.

*8. Why is monopoly regarded as inefficient in production when compared to a competitive firm?

9. Show graphically the areas of profit and deadweight loss that occur when a formerly competitive market is monopolized.

*10. What is price discrimination? Explain the preconditions for discrimination to occur.

11. Explain "perfect" price discrimination in the context of organ transplants.

*12. Given the inefficiencies and welfare loss associated with monopolies, why might economists support giving monopoly status to pharmaceutical companies in the form of patents on certain drugs?

*13. What role, if any, do you think advertising might play in creating and maintaining monopoly power?

*14. Monopolies have absolutely no incentive to operate in a cost-minimizing manner. Is this statement true or false? Explain.

15. Can perfectly competitive firms (discussed in Chapter 8) practice price discrimination? Why or why not?

16. List and explain the requirements for effective price discrimination.

17. Other things being equal, monopoly power tends to be stronger in service industries than in manufacturing. Is the statement true or false? Explain.

*18. If a competitive industry became monopolized, would its total revenues inevitably increase? Explain.

19. How does the slope of the demand curve affect monopoly profits?

20. Explain the inefficiencies created in the political process by firms trying to obtain legal monopoly status.

Problems for Analysis

1. The U.S. Postal Service is a monopolist (in first-class mail delivery but not in all markets). Laws prohibit any substitute firms from delivering first-class mail and from use of your mailbox by any firm but the Postal Service. With such a degree of monopoly power, why doesn't the service price-discriminate on the basis of income or age? What type of price discrimination *is* practiced by the Postal Service?

2. There is a thriving medical-pharmaceutical industry just across the U.S. border in Mexico. Tijuana, Mexico — just south of the California border — is a very popular spot for medical treatment of all kinds, including AIDS treatment, dental work, and cancer therapies. With the principles of monopoly and price discrimination in mind, analyze the following hypothetical questions or statements (it might be helpful to reread Highlights 9.3 and 9.4):

   a. The American Medical Association is considering new laws and regulations restricting the U.S. licensing of physicians who received training in Mexico or in Caribbean medical schools. The AMA charges that these schools produce "substandard" doctors.

   b. The American Pharmaceutical Association issues press releases suggesting that drugs purchased across the border — though they are produced and labeled by American companies — are tainted or are of lower quality than those purchased in the United States.

   c. The Food and Drug Administration (FDA) takes steps to require the Postal Service to more closely inspect packages from Mexico suspected of containing prescription drugs.

3. The prices charged by supermarkets in poor, dangerous, and ill-kept urban areas are very often higher than those charged by the same stores in high-income and well-policed areas of the same city. Such cases are often cited as examples of price discrimination against the poor. With the tools of this chapter, analyze this allegation.

*4. Owners of major-league baseball teams are effectively monopolists in the sale of tickets in their franchise area. However, many of them price tickets so that there is excess capacity (unsold seats) for most games. Is it wise for them to pursue such a pricing policy?

*5. Is it possible for price discrimination to occur both in markets for goods and in markets for services? In which case would you expect price discrimination to be more frequent? Why?

6. Suppose that you are the manager of an airport and that you have decided to allow only one car rental company to locate on premises. Can you show graphically how you might go about determining how much to charge for the exclusive right to operate at that location?

7. To the best of our knowledge, all state-supported universities charge higher tuition to out-of-state than to in-state students. Do you think this pattern of prices (higher prices for out-of-state students) would exist if the university were attempting to maximize profits? Explain.

8. Highlight 9.1 describes the Schumpeterian notion of the competitive process. What is the role of monopoly in this view?

9. Highlight 9.2 explained that regulation of the cable industry actually increases monthly cable rates. Explain why rates rise as a result of the regulation of local cable franchises by municipal governments.

10. Pharmaceutical companies in the United States have been accused of "dumping." Explain what dumping is and how it occurs.

10

Imperfect Competition and Strategic Behavior

When the economist abandons the market extremes of perfect competition and pure monopoly, one central fact of real market functioning must be recognized: the actions of any single competitor will be felt by other competitors. In the extreme case of duopoly, the actions of one competitor will clearly be felt by the other, but all competitive actions must be taken into account whenever competition is "imperfect." Strategic behavior — alternative plans of action and responses to actions — is the central part of this process called imperfect competition. After reading this chapter, you should have a basic understanding of such aspects of strategic behavior as

- the role of product differentiation in the model of monopolistic competition in which many sellers compete on nonprice bases,
- some basic principles underlying small-numbers strategy called the Cournot-Nash model of duopoly,
- the foundations of game theory as they relate to nonprice competition, especially to the provision of different qualities of goods, alternative locations, and product differentiation,
- some general principles relating to the short and (often) unhappy life of cartels.

What Is Monopolistic Competition?

The "abstract" static nature of market models of competition and monopoly has been closely examined in Chapters 8 and 9. The assumptions of these models, as has undoubtedly occurred to readers, are quite limiting. Where, for example, do the strict definitions of monopoly or competition apply in the real world of business and industry? In truth, economists have always been at pains to find good examples of competitive markets in which the behavior of one firm has *no* effect on the industry, or of monopoly in which the firm and the industry are one. Most especially, the assumption of homogeneous products or services violates most common experience. Of course, simplifying assumptions are useful in analyzing certain problems. Difficulties occur when assumptions and models get too far away from market realities.

Even Augustin-Antoine Cournot, the inventor of the formal market models of competition and monopoly, was aware that behavioral assumptions in these cases were simplistic. Cournot clearly understood the possibilities of **strategic behavior**, in which the sales of one firm have an impact on the profits and the output-maximizing quantity produced by other firms.[1] We examine his duopoly model of *two* firms later in this chapter, but it is important to note that Cournot hit on a central problem in analyzing most market behavior — that firms adopt strategies in order to position themselves in the market. Although the object of Cournot's specific strategy was output alteration, it has become recognized that the firm's profit-maximizing strategy may include many other dimensions as well. As noted by twentieth-century economists such as Edward H. Chamberlin, Joan Robinson, and Harold Hotelling, the firm's strategies to increase profits can include numerous dimensions other than quantity adjustments. Specifically, firms can differentiate products or services, alter the qualities of products or services offered, or locate so as to maximize demand or lower demand elasticity for their specific wares. Direct price competition — always a strategy when we depart from models of perfect competition or monopoly — is but one of a large number of possible methods that a firm can use in attracting demanders to its product or service.

The Static Model of Monopolistic Competition

Some degree of interdependence between perfect competition and monopoly exists in *all* market models. More interdependence means that one firm's actions have a greater effect on the sales of other firms in the industry. Where there are large numbers of firms competing in widely dispersed markets, the actions of one firm may have an inappreciable effect on the sales and profits of all of the others. The effects of a new entrant on existing firms may vary in an industry in which products vary in quality. The introduction of a new and expensive luxury automobile will have a "primary" effect on competitors in the luxury car market, with a smaller "secondary" effect on other firms producing

---

1. Economists have given the name *conjectural variation* to the conjecture that one competitor makes about another's behavior. Augustin Cournot (1801–1877) was the first but certainly not the last writer to deal with this central question. Later mathematicians and economists toyed with his idea (Joseph Bertrand in 1883, F. Y. Edgeworth in 1897), but it was not until the mid-twentieth century that the matter of strategy and conjecture received a central place in economic literature. Cournot's idea was the basis for game theory, a formal model of strategic behavior that was set forth in 1944 by John von Neumann, a mathematician, and Oskar Morgenstern, an economist, in a book entitled *The Theory of Games and Economic Behavior*.

autos of lower quality. In markets in which quality competition or **product differentiation** is not particularly relevant, such differences may not exist. Each market takes on the character of a special case. A host of models have been suggested by economists from Cournot to the present. The theory of monopolistic competition is one such model.

Chamberlin's Model

E. H. Chamberlin suggested a model in 1933 that has remained popular in representing some market cases between competition and monopoly. A model of **monopolistic competition** applies where a large number of firms sell somewhat differentiated products (or product qualities) and where entry and exit are unrestricted. The "monopolistic" element of this model exists in the uniqueness of the product or product quality that each firm produces, and the "competitive" aspect relates to the ease of entry and exit and to the large number of competitors. A static theoretical apparatus has built up around Chamberlin's idea.

Assumptions of the Model. The model described by Chamberlin shares the competitive characteristic of large numbers of competing firms. Sellers are assumed to be numerous and of small size so that **collusion** is costly, as it is under perfectly competitive conditions. This does not mean that collusion or collusive activity to engage in strategic behavior is impossible, just that it is costly to arrange. This large-number situation is the competitive element in the model.

Monopolistic competitors, although numerous, are not price takers as firms under perfect competition are. Each seller differentiates his or her product so that firms all sell slightly different goods or services. These close-substitute products (or product qualities) may be manipulated by sellers, thereby creating **nonprice competition**. Sellers of toothpaste or makeup, for example, are in control of their product design, sales location, quality, and contents. They may, even in the presence of close substitutes, alter these product attributes in order to garner customers. This product differentiation will give each firm some control over price, so the firm's demand curve is downward sloping. Under monopolistic competition, the firm therefore not only has some control over price but is free to engage in nonprice competition as well. The "uniqueness" of the product or service is the monopolistic element in the model of monopolistic competition.

Nonprice Competition. The forms of nonprice competition are numerous. Almost any attribute of a transaction between buyers and sellers — from the smile of the salesperson to the availability of the good at a given time and/or location — are aspects of nonprice competition. Often consumers are offered different combinations of price and nonprice aspects by sellers. Full-service retail sellers of computers, equipment, and software often sell their wares at higher nominal prices, although the same items are available at "cut-rate" prices from discount stores or catalogues. In the latter case, demonstrations and after-purchase assistance are either not available or only available at high cost. The provision of presale and postsale information and service is only one form of nonprice competition.

The most popular forms of nonprice competition are the creation of actual or perceived differences in the products themselves. Detergent, makeup, automobiles, or brands of toothpaste are either actually different or perceived to be different by consumers. A flood of new kinds of makeup or toiletries appear on the market every year. Are these products actually different, or are the differences established in the minds of consumers? Some actual differentiation is part of the process, but many products are "branded" by sellers to signal actual or created differences from competitors. Tide detergent, Coca-Cola, Velveeta cheese, and Frito-Lay are all examples of branded products. Advertising (discussed below) is a part of the process of differentiating products and services in the consumer's mind. Brand allegiance is what creates the "monopoly" element in monopolistic competition and gives each seller some limited control over price and output.

Another important part of nonprice competition is location. Sellers have every incentive to locate where they expect sales. Burger, pizza, and chicken fast-food restaurants; typing, copying, and fax services; and bookstores typically agglomerate around colleges and universities. High rents and other factors may force sellers of competing products to locate farther away from the demand center. In order to induce buyers to come for their products, the stores more distant from the campus may lower prices. The typical "convenience" store, for example, charges higher prices than the supermarket for items such as coffee, soft drinks, or beer because of location (and speed of service). Location is a primary form of nonprice competition.

The reader can undoubtedly think of a great number of other ways in which sellers can create mini-monopolies. Packaging, service, location, after-sale repairs, the provision of information, and myriad other factors are the subject of nonprice competition between sellers. Each of these factors permits an individual seller to differentiate the product or service for consumers, but there is a high degree of substitutability. This means that the firm's demand curve is not infinitely elastic, as it is under perfectly competitive conditions. Because there are close substitutes, the demand curve will be more elastic than in the monopoly case.

Absence of Entry Barriers. Under monopolistic competition, there is an absence of entry barriers. As in the perfectly competitive model, we assume that there are no artificial entry barriers, such as government regulations or restrictions. Further, there are no barriers to entrants or potential entrants in the acquisition of inputs. This does not mean that entry is free. Firms entering a monopolistically competitive market, like those who attempt entry in any market, must bear costs. Machinery, equipment, and resources, including labor resources, must be purchased. Under monopolistic competition, moreover, costs will include those associated with product differentiation. Research and development costs for new products and, most particularly, advertising and other selling costs must be incurred in order to enter markets. These advertising costs do not exist under the assumptions of the perfectly competitive model. But despite these "additional" costs, entry is assumed to be free under monopolistically competitive conditions, as it was in perfect competition.

Advertising and Monopolistic Competition

When products must be differentiated by service, physical appearance, quality, or location, advertising necessarily comes into play. Chamberlin himself recognized the key role that advertising played in the model of monopolistic competition. Modern research confirms the central role of advertising in market functioning and in the provision of information about products and services.[2] Simply put, it usually "pays to advertise," because the activity exerts an impact on the demand curve of the firm and therefore on the firm's revenues.

Figure 10.1 depicts typical (downward-sloping) demand curves of a monopolistically competitive firm. Assuming that the initial demand curve is D_0, the firm has the option of using advertising to increase sales of its product. Assuming that the expected marginal returns from engaging in some form of advertising are greater than the marginal costs, the firm will advertise. In a market with differentiated products, advertising (if successful) will have the effect of shifting the firm's demand curve rightward. The particular nonprice attributes emphasized in the new advertising (location, service, product or quality characteristics) will mean that at price P_0 in Figure 10.1, customers will demand a greater quantity. This means that the demand curve shifts from D_0, perhaps to D_1.

Note, however, that the consumers' decision to buy more of the product is often accompanied by greater allegiance to the product as well. In economic terms, advertising also aims at making the consumers' demand for the differentiated product less elastic. In Figure 10.1, the seller aims to make demand less elastic at price P_0, thus giving himself or herself more control over price and revenues. This phenomenon is tantamount to a rotation of the demand curve around point A in Figure 1, from D_1 to D_1'.

---

2. Huge vats of ink have been used in analyzing the pros and cons of advertising as an economic activity. Earlier economists, especially those married to static models of competition, have generally condemned advertising as unnecessary (in many cases) and as wasteful in most situations. Modern research has placed advertising at the nexus of supplying information to consumers and as an invaluable part of the market process; see Robert B. Ekelund, Jr., and David S. Saurman, *Advertising and the Market Process* (San Francisco: Pacific Research Institute for Public Policy, 1988).

Figure 10.1 Demand Curves for the Monopolistically Competitive Firm

Advertising in the monopolistically competitive firm is an attempt to shift the demand curve outward from D_0 to D_1. It also tends to differentiate the product (reducing price elasticity) and rotate the demand curve from D_1 to D_1'.

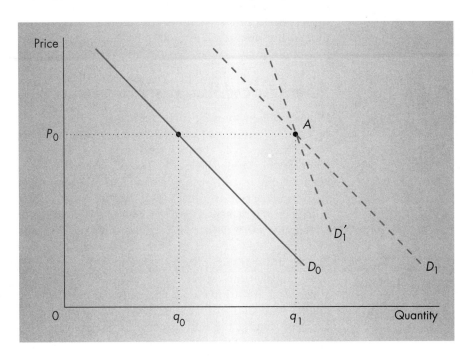

The impact of advertising as a provider of information will differ (sometimes subtly) by type of product and by the profile of the consumer, but the basic reason why a monopolistically competitive firm uses advertising is described simply in Figure 10.1.

Price Competition and the Firm's "Strategy"

Although nonprice competition is a principal component of the monopolistically competitive firm's arsenal of competitive devices, price competition also comes into play. There is naturally a strategy in finding a market niche among many competing sellers. Location or subtle variations in the product will often be used. But price changes on the part of the firm may provoke reactions by the "competition." Further, it is important to note that the firm may also be affected by nonprice and price competition from other firms in the market. The firm's demand curves in Figure 10.1 could shift leftward and become more elastic as other firms increase advertising and change products, location, and so on. The entry of new firms with slightly different products, locations, (or the like) will also have these effects. Moreover, competing firms may also lower the price they charge for given products. If they do so, the demand for the products of rival firms will shift to the left.

These factors indicate that, even in markets with a large number of firms, the actions of each firm may provoke reactions from other firms. Although the pro-rata share of the total output of any one firm may be small, that firm's price and nonprice policies will not be entirely independent of the other sellers with whom that firm shares the market (see Highlight 10.1).

Highlight 10.1 *Hurricane Andrew and Goodwill Strategies for the Imperfectly Competitive Firm*

There is a tendency to make a distinction between price strategy and nonprice strategy (such as advertising, location, and product differentiation) in discussing strategic behavior by imperfectly competitive firms. However, in some cases firms can adapt their current pricing policy to achieve the ends usually attained through nonprice actions. Specifically, firms at times find that by keeping current prices low, they can create goodwill, which leads to future increases in the demand for their product. When it is cheaper for a firm to achieve a given increase in future demand by lowering current prices than by advertising, we should expect a firm to exploit this opportunity.

One example of such an opportunity occurred in south Florida following Hurricane Andrew in the fall of 1992. Any time a hurricane strikes, much of the damage to homes and other buildings is to roofs and windows. Unless roofs and windows can be patched quickly, water damage from future rain is likely to be more devastating than the initial wind damage. For that reason, a huge increase in demand for plywood occurs after any hurricane. In fact, the increase in demand may take place before the hurricane arrives as residents rush to board up their windows in anticipation of damaging winds. This was the situation in south Florida in late August 1992.

How did the area suppliers of plywood react to the situation? Given the huge increase in demand, one possibility would have been to increase the price of plywood. Because, in the very short term, it would have been possible for suppliers to sell all the plywood they could possibly deliver at prices as much as five times the normal price, a drastic price increase would have been consistent with short-term profit maximization. However, several of the major building supply companies in the area adopted a quite different policy.[a] Home Depot, a large Atlanta-based retailer of building supplies, adopted a policy of charging a price for plywood equal to the price Home Depot paid to its suppliers plus the

---

[a] Information concerning plywood prices was obtained from Steve Lohr, "Lessons From a Hurricane: It Pays Not to Gouge," *The New York Times* (September 22, 1992), pp. D1, D5.

Home Depot, a building-materials firm based in Atlanta, Georgia, built goodwill by keeping prices low after Hurricane Andrew devastated South Florida in 1992.

costs it actually incurred in shipping the plywood. In doing so, Home Depot opted to forgo all profits from the sale of plywood as a goodwill gesture. Home Depot also negotiated with its major suppliers and got both Georgia-Pacific and Louisiana-Pacific to agree to freeze wholesale plywood prices in south Florida at the prehurricane level.

Although spokespersons for Home Depot suggested that they were "only doing what was right," there is no doubt that the company was acutely aware of the future benefits of holding prices down ("doing well by doing good"). Jeff Barrington, manager of Home Depot in Kendall, Florida, was quoted as saying, "This will pay us back — people will remember," and one of their plywood customers said, "If they [Home Depot] had spent $50 million on advertising, they couldn't have bought the goodwill they got by doing this." This estimate may be exaggerated, but there is no doubt that Home Depot attained many loyal customers through their actions.

The actions of Home Depot, Georgia-Pacific, and Louisiana-Pacific were in sharp contrast to those of the many independent "firms" who showed up selling plywood (as well as ice and water) from the backs of pickup trucks. Because these firms had no plans to remain in business in the area for long, they had no financial incentive to keep prices down. Accordingly, they acted as short-term profit maximizers. Although they were widely referred to as "price gougers," these small firms did provide a valuable service to the victims of the area. The plywood they delivered worked just as well as that sold by Home Depot in patching roofs and windows. The option to buy plywood from the "price gougers" made residents of south Florida better off than they would have been in the absence of such sellers. The authorities in south Florida generally recognized this, so they did nothing to stop the independents. Their actions were in sharp contrast to those of the local authorities in Charleston, South Carolina, following Hurricane Hugo. The Charleston government passed emergency legislation that froze prices at prehurricane levels. The legislation not only discouraged independents from shipping badly needed supplies into the area, but also reduced the opportunities for established firms to gain favorable publicity by acting in the public's interest.

Consider the firm's pricing policies. In terms of strategy for any one firm, consider Figure 10.2, which shows two demand curves for the individual firm. The two demand curves are marked $D_{perceived}$ and D_{actual} in Figure 10.2. They represent, respectively, the demand curve as perceived by the firm and the actual demand curve — one that includes all industry reactions to the price actions of the firm in question.

What would be the impact of an attempt to increase market share by a decrease in price from P_0 to P_1? If the firm thinks it is acting alone, it will perceive that quantity demanded will expand from q_0 to q_1 — that is, along the more elastic demand curve segment *EG* in Figure 10.2. But that action by the firm might elicit a response from competitors in the industry. When the price reductions of the initial firm are detected, other firms may join in the game by reducing their prices as well. These competing firms want to forestall a decline in their sales. Thus the actual demand curve that the initial firm will follow is labeled D_{actual}. It is clearly less elastic than the firm's perceived curve. The firm could increase sales from q_0 to q_2 along the actual curve, following segment *EB*, which is clearly less elastic. Note that these effects are from price changes alone and that, in assessing them, all product differentiation and other forms of nonprice competition are held constant. These strategic factors play important roles in the understanding of the many possible kinds of equilibria in imperfect competition. One important equilibrium model is that suggested by Chamberlin himself for monopolistic competition.

Monopolistic Competition in the Short Run

Short-run equilibrium under monopolistic competition is easily described. Over the short run, the monopolistically competitive firm — one with many competitors selling a product differentiated in one or more ways — will either make profits or losses, depending on costs and demand. These two possibilities

Figure 10.2 Strategic Pricing Behavior

A firm that initially sells q_0 units at a price P_0 may believe that it can reduce price and move along its perceived demand curve. However, if rival firms also lower their prices, the firm may find that it operates along the actual demand curve instead of the perceived demand curve. If the other firms match the price cut, sales will rise to q_2, not q_1.

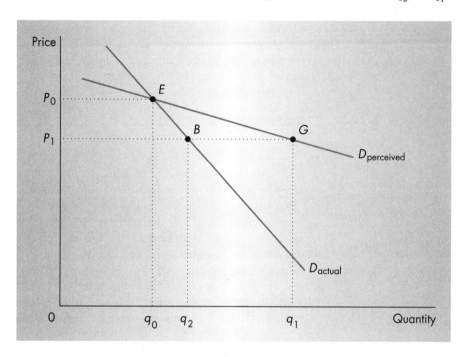

are depicted in Figure 10.3. Conceptually, there is little difference between the possible short-run equilibria described here and for the monopoly firm as described in Chapter 9. The monopolist, of course, faces no competition and the monopolistic competitor faces much. Therefore, demand curves of the latter kind of firm are likely to be much more elastic. But the underlying principles of short-run profit maximization and loss minimization are exactly the same. The monopolistically competitive firm, like all firms, equates marginal revenue and marginal cost in deciding the profit-maximizing output to produce.

In Figure 10.3a the firm earns profits of $P_0 FGC_0$ at output q_0. Changes in the elasticity of demand for the firm would change the picture, however. Figure 10.3b, for example, shows that losses are a possibility. As always, the firm equates marginal cost and marginal revenue, but in the case depicted, the firm would not earn profits. The monopolistically competitive firm with the demand, revenue, and cost curves shown in Figure 10.3b would endure total losses in the short run of $C_1 GFP_1$. The same principles that apply to "shutdown" under competition and monopoly apply to this firm as well. The

Figure 10.3 Economic Profits and Losses by the Monopolistically Competitive Firm

Depending on the cost and demand configurations, the firm may enjoy economic profits (panel a) or economic losses (panel b).

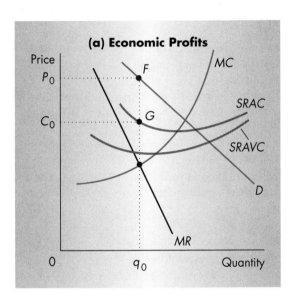

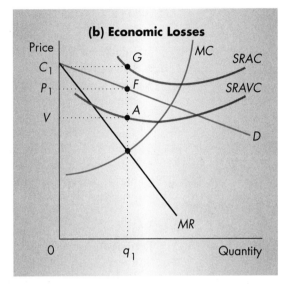

firm is covering total variable costs $(Aq_1 0V)$ with its revenues of $Fq_1 0P_1$, so it stays in business in the short run.[3] Going out of business would cost it more than "gutting it out" over the short run with prospects of demand and revenue increases.

Chamberlin's Long-Run "Tangency" Solution

An understanding of basic principles of monopolistic competition makes it obvious that there are not one but many possible models and equilibrium solutions under this market structure. The assumption of a large number of small firms of roughly equal size does not always hold. In reality, some smaller number of firms typically dominate markets (with perhaps a large number of fringe competitors). The soft-drink or beer markets may constitute examples. Location often gives one or a small number of firms big advantages. There is also the matter of costs. There is no reason to believe that all firms face the same cost or enjoy equal managerial efficiency.

3. Note that in *all* cases of imperfect competition, including monopolistically competitive models, the true supply curve of the firm is *not* the marginal-cost curve above average variable cost (as in perfect competition). The reasons are the same as those analyzed in Chapter 9 on monopoly. Put differently but equivalently, marginal revenue and price are not the same whenever competition is not perfect.

In spite of these problems, economists persist in depicting the tendencies that might continue under monopolistic competition, strictly and (admittedly) unrealistically defined. A "minimalist" model of monopolistic competition, one that approximates Chamberlin's 1933 conception, would include the following assumptions:

- An industry exists in which many competing sellers provide highly substitutable but slightly differentiated products or services,
- Each seller faces identical demand and cost conditions,
- The selling firms all react the same way — each firm believes that its demand curve is more elastic than it turns out to be (as shown in the analysis of Figure 10.2),
- The number of firms is fixed, both before and after the final equilibrium position is attained; entry with new products simply does not take place,
- The amount of product/quality differentiation does not change over the period analyzed, which means that the competitive process is limited to price manipulations.

Figure 10.4 Zero-Profit Equilibrium for the Monopolistically Competitive Firm

Assuming no entry barriers, economic profits will entice new firms to enter a monopolistically competitive market. Their entry will depress the demand curve for each of the firms from *D* to *D'*. The tangency occurs at point *F* in the figure.

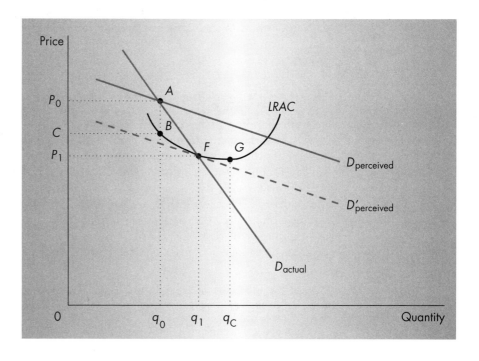

A model conforming to these conditions is presented in Figure 10.4.[4] It depicts both perceived and actual demands for the typical firm in monopolistic competition, along with a "typical" long-run average-cost (*LRAC*) curve. (For clarity, marginal-revenue and marginal-cost curves are left out of Figure 10.4.) If one representative seller of (say) 75 sellers finds herself at point *A*, she may attempt to increase sales along $D_{perceived}$. At point *A*, which corresponds to profits of $ABCP_0$, the seller will want to expand sales along the more elastic demand curve to increase profits. The perceived demand curve is, for reasons given above, more elastic than the actual curve. Attempts to increase sales by this one firm will be met by actual price competition (remember: the degree of differentiation is held constant, as is the number of firms). But the perceived demand curve of any one firm — such as the one shown in Figure 10.4 — is drawn up under the assumption that all other close competitors hold prices constant.

When competitors lower prices, the representative firm experiences a leftward shift in its demand curve. This means that quantity demanded actually expands along demand curve D_{actual} down the segment *AF* in Figure 10.4. Progressive price reductions are met with strategic price declines by the competition, creating leftward shifts in the firm's demand curve. The process ends when the firm's new perceived demand curve is exactly tangent to the long-run cost curve (at point *F* in the figure). The firm's perceived curve, in effect, slides along the actual industry demand curve until the position given by $D'_{perceived}$ is reached. The behavioral dynamics of this model guarantee that profits will be squeezed out of the system in the long run. This solution, in which no firm earns economic profits, is known (for obvious reasons) as the Chamberlinian tangency solution.

The "tangency solution" is but one possibility among a large range of outcomes in monopolistically competitive markets. We have merely *assumed* that initial profits exist in the system and that all firms are alike. If these conditions ever existed, profits would surely cause (with unimpeded entry) *new* firms to enter with differentiated products announced by advertising. These actions would, just as surely, elicit advertising and nonprice competitive responses from the initial price-cutting firm. From a strategic sense, moreover, only imbecilic sellers would continue to assume that their attempted price reductions would have no impact on the behavior of competitors in the face of consistent and continuous evidence to the contrary.

Most particularly, the assumption that there exist large numbers of competitors of roughly equal size selling slightly different products is particularly unrealistic. In reality, we tend to observe a small number of larger firms

---

4. Figure 10.4 and the accompanying argument are similar to that used by Chamberlin himself. See Edward H. Chamberlin, *The Theory of Monopolistic Competition: A Re-orientation of the Theory of Value* (Cambridge, Mass.: Harvard University Press, 8th ed., 1962 [1933]), p. 91.

competing with a larger number of smaller firms. The size distribution of firms within a market will have stark implications for strategic behavior (as we will see later in the chapter) and for consumer welfare. The model does serve, however, as a way of organizing thinking about markets that conform roughly to the assumptions of monopolistic competition. It is a study of market "tendencies." One advantage is the ready comparison that the tangency model allows between perfect competition and monopolistic competition.

Efficiency and Monopolistic Competition

Economists have been enamored of the perfectly competitive model for generations. If price is a measure of the value placed on the last unit consumed by buyers, and long-run marginal cost is the true opportunity cost of resources used to produce that last unit (so $P = LRMC$), efficiency is achieved under perfect competition. Also, when the low-cost and most efficient scale of plant is used at its optimum rate of output (since $P = minimum\ LRAC$), consumers get the product or service at the lowest possible cost. Finally, free entry assures that profits will always be squeezed out of the system ($P = AR = LRAC$).

The tangency model of monopolistic competition shares some, but not all, of these characteristics. Clearly, if the dynamics of the tangency solution obtain, profits will be driven out of the system. In Figure 10.4, for example, zero profits are assured at point F, because price "slides" down the actual demand curve of the monopolistically competitive firm. In the process, the perceived demand shifts leftward until a tangency is reached with the long-run average-cost curve. At price P_1 and output rate q_1, the firm earns no economic profits.

Note, however, that price exceeds long-run *marginal* cost at point F, which means that too few resources are dedicated to production under monopolistic competition. Moreover, critics of monopolistic competition observe that although the firm is producing efficiently at point F (from the *firm's* perspective, that is), *social* welfare is not maximized. Although the firm has adopted its low-cost scale of plant to produce q_1 (where some short-run curve is tangent to the $LRAC$ curve at F), there is excess capacity. Production in that scale of plant is not being pushed to the point of minimum average cost. Only at point G would there be no excess capacity, because the minimum $SRAC$ of that plant would equal minimum long-run average cost.

It is important to note that these criticisms stem from the comparison of an idealized competitive model (Chapter 8) and an equally idealized tangency solution under monopolistic competition. That is, the criticisms are really directed toward some (never realized) equilibrium states. Further, the criticism has cogency only because the demand curve of the perfectly competitive firm, *selling homogeneous products*, is perfectly elastic. When product differentiation is brought in, as it is in monopolistic competition, that small element of "monopoly" *must* create inefficiency and excess capacity. Modern economists put little faith in the comparison with perfect competition and note that under dynamic conditions, ever-new and varied products and services offered to consumers have a value of their own. Consumers seem to prove over and over by their choices that variety (differentiated products) is of clear value. Thousands (maybe hundreds of thousands) of new products are purchased by consumers in monopolistically competitive markets every year — a testament to the consuming public's interest in variety and choice.

Quality and Imperfect Competition

Variations in quality are the very factor that is the foundation of a negatively sloped demand and therefore of static inefficiency when any form of imperfect competition, including monopolistic competition, is compared to *perfect* competition. Quality variations are also the essence of the competitive process in real-world markets. Existing or new companies develop and market hundreds of thousands of new "brands," or new qualities of existing brands, or new products or services each year. Canned soups, for example, are offered in hundreds of varieties, with the Campbell company offering more than 100 kinds of soup to consumers (see Highlight 10.2). Virtually all kinds of products and

---

Highlight 10.2   *Brand Proliferation and Imperfect Competition: Has Product Variation Run Amok?*

Seemingly bewildering displays of products greet the consumer at the modern American supermarket. Thousands of products are sold and thousands more are introduced every year. A recent study found that, in 1991 alone, massive quantities of new brands, new flavors, new sizes, or other variations on established brands were introduced by business entrepreneurs. For example, 64 spaghetti sauces, 69 disposable diapers, 103 snack chips, 54 laundry detergents, and 91 cold remedies were all new to the market in 1991.[a]

Brand "variations" in type or quality are most common. You may now purchase spaghetti sauce plain, with green peppers, with three different kinds of cheeses, with beef, with pepperoni, and in a host of other variations. Critics of the market system attack such product proliferation as unnecessary, costly, and of little value to the consumer or to the economy. However, such criticism belies a misunderstanding of the system.

Big consumer-product-oriented companies such as Procter & Gamble, Johnson & Johnson, or Kraft Foods have every incentive to maintain "market

[a] Data according to Marketing Intelligence Service Ltd., Maples, N.Y.; reported in Gabriella Stern, "Multiple Varieties of Established Brands Muddle Consumers, Make Retailers Mad," *Wall Street Journal* (January 24, 1992), pp. B1, B2.

share" and profitability for company stockholders by differentiating their products. The question is, Does such differentiation increase consumer welfare? The answer (at least in many cases) is a resounding yes! This is especially so in markets characterized by repeat purchases and monopolistic competition.

Most product differentiation or quality variations do not come free to consumers and are offered only at added cost. Most often, the "plain" or "classic" variety (Coke?) remains available. The subjective evaluation of the consumer concerning the new product or variety will turn on whether the change (improvement?) is, in utility terms, sufficient to overcome the additional charge for the product or service. If it is, the consumer buys and his or her dollar votes encourage such variety. If not, the producer/seller discontinues the new brand.[b] Moreover, successful innovations in product or packaging — such as the new detergent concentrates — are immediately imitated by other producers.

What critics of innovation and differentiation seem to misunderstand is that the market system, in responding to the particular demands of consumers and groups of consumers, is creating greater welfare for consumers. If there is no increase in utility, consumers will not buy a new product at a higher price. The ideal (perhaps) would be the ultimate in product differentiation — that each and every consumer gets exactly the product or service he or she wants. Because of resource scarcity and opportunity cost, this is not possible. The truth is, however, that the market system that allows trial, error, and fishing by producers and sellers for new variations or products to entice consumers comes closest to the ideal. Restrictions on this system are more likely to harm consumers than to help them.

[b] This view of the role of product differentiation and the growth of variety in markets is not shared by all. See Michael Spence, "Monopoly, Quality, and Regulation," *Bell Journal of Economics* 6 (Autumn 1975): 417–429 or William Comanor, "Vertical Price Fixing, Vertical Market Restrictions, and the New Antitrust Policy" *Harvard Law Review* 98 (1985): 983–1002. Some critics argue, Spence and Comanor included, that inframarginal consumers might not value the innovation but will be forced to pay for it anyway. This result is not likely in the case of monopolistic competition, however, because competitors will always be ready to profit from reintroducing the earlier variety.

services are sold in alternative qualities. If they went unconsumed (not demanded), such proliferation would not take place. Obviously, consumers want variety, and firms in monopolistically competitive markets are eager to give it to them.

Along with variety and quality differences, however, come some potential problems. Do monopolistically competitive sellers (or *any* sellers of nonhomogeneous products) have an incentive to act fraudulently in promising alternative qualities of a good? Unfortunately, there is no unequivocal answer to this question. Generally speaking, the larger the number of competing firms in a market, the lower the probability of seller fraud. But this statement does not mean that consumers cannot be bamboozled by sellers in pursuit of profits.

It is easy to construct examples by which, in a number of successive periods, sellers may profitably degrade the quality of a given product.[5] After a period of selling high-quality goods, for example, a seller may be tempted in future periods to cut costs by clandestinely lowering quality while continuing to market the product under the same name and at the same price, under the assumption that buyers will be slow to catch on. Sellers, moreover, may use advertising in conscious attempts to misrepresent the characteristics of products or services. But a number of factors limit this possibility. Obviously, under conditions of monopolistic competition with large numbers of substitutes, it would be extremely difficult to fool consumers for long when purchases are repeated often. A firm would not last long by selling bad or impure gasoline or food products. But the ability to hoodwink consumers is also related to the informational characteristics that surround goods. There is a classification system that illustrates some important issues related to quality and information.[6] It divides goods into three classes of quality characteristics — search, experience, and credence. (For some evidence concerning the information-providing role of advertising and goods/buyer "types," see Highlight 10.3.)

Highlight 10.3   *Information, Goods Types, and the Demand and Supply of Yellow-Pages Ads in Tourist Cities and College Towns*

Information provision, of which advertising is a big part, is a prime characteristic of the market process, as was suggested in the chapter text. Information is both demanded by consumers and supplied by seller-producers in a wide variety of settings and circumstances. Information tends to be supplied efficiently — that is, the marginal value it produces will be equal to the marginal cost of producing it. The evidence of efficient production of information is everywhere. For example, we do not expect to find expensive perfume advertised in *Sports Illustrated*, but we do find ads for tennis shoes and golf bags there. *Gourmet* magazine, likewise, is unlikely to carry ads for tennis shoes, but devotes plenty of ad space to food blenders. There are sound economic

---

5. We have already analyzed this possibility in Chapter 9 by showing that (in static terms) a monopolist may intentionally degrade quality to "low-demand" type consumers in order to eliminate the defection of high-quality demanders to the goods of lesser quality.

6. Economist Phillip Nelson first dichotomized goods into search and experience components. Two of his papers form the basis for the modern view of advertising as a vehicle for information provision: see Nelson, "Information and Consumer Behavior," *Journal of Political Economy* 78 (1970): 311–329 and "Advertising as Information," *Journal of Political Economy* 82 (1974): 729–754. These papers, moreover, are accessible to the general reader and are highly recommended.

reasons why beach-resort restaurants and bars use airplane banners to inform sunbathers of their "specials" and services.

Advertising and the informational content of ads will vary on the basis of buyer characteristics, product characteristics, and advertising outlet. Economist David Laband analyzed the Yellow Pages as an outlet for information using a set of search and experience goods (as defined in this chapter).[a] Consumers rely on quality information in ads when buying infrequently purchased and high-priced items (**search goods**), but for cheaper, more frequently purchased items, a large stock of information has been gathered through purchase and consumption (**experience goods**). Clearly, consumers will receive more "quality signaling" for search goods than for experience goods, in the form of information about licensure, certification, membership in a professional association, or experience of the seller.

Buyer characteristics also play a role in the quantity of quality information provided in equilibrium. Information about goods and services can be self-provided, of course, but the cost of self-provision can be higher or lower, depending on the buyer's situation and circumstances. With these considerations in mind, Laband compared the Washington, D.C., and Baltimore Yellow Pages for ads of both low-price repeat-purchase (experience) goods and high-price, infrequently purchased goods and services (search goods). In both locations Laband found quality signaling (measured by the information provided in ads) of experience goods to be significantly greater than for search goods. Moreover, the more mobile population of Washington, D.C. apparently demanded and was supplied with significantly more information in both search and experience good categories. Why? Because self-provision of information about the existence and availability of *all* goods and services is more expensive for more mobile, transient populations, like that of Washington, D.C., than for the more stable population of Baltimore.

A more recent study of information provision in the Yellow Pages adds the **credence good** category.[b] Credence goods are goods whose quality is not determined either before or after purchase. In this study, a sample of ten goods for each category was employed. This time, however, matched pairs of tourist/nontourist and college/noncollege towns proxied buyer mobility and the opportunity cost of self-provision of information regarding all goods and services. In general, the statistical results of these tests conform to the earlier results of Laband. In virtually all cases and in all cities, the intensity of information provision (certification, license, experience, and so on) was higher for experience and credence than for search goods. Buyer characteristics (those

---

[a] See David Laband, "Advertising as Information: An Empirical Note," *Review of Economics and Statistics* 68 (1986): 517–521.

[b] Robert B. Ekelund, Jr., Franklin G. Mixon, Jr., and Rand W. Ressler, "Advertising, Information, and Goods-Buyer Characteristics: An Empirical Study" (Manuscript, Auburn University, 1992).

living in tourist towns compared to nontourist and college towns compared to noncollege towns) also had predictable effects on the relative informational content of advertisements. Buyers in nontourist Minneapolis, Minnesota, were supplied with relatively less information in all categories than those in San Francisco, California, a well-known tourist mecca. Similarly, buyers in college towns Princeton, New Jersey, and Chapel Hill, North Carolina, were given more Yellow Page information than those in their matched city pairs Paterson, New Jersey, and Burlington, North Carolina.

Naturally, other factors may affect the quantity of information. Income levels also proxy the opportunity cost of the buyer's time, for example. In this regard, two *tourist* cities of significantly differing incomes — San Francisco and New Orleans — were analyzed. Because the relative opportunity cost of time to a San Franciscan (with an average annual income of $21,086 in 1987) and to a New Orleanian ($13,130 in 1987) are significantly different, one would expect Yellow Pages information intensity to be significantly greater in San Francisco. The study found exactly these results, indicating that income differences in cities of similar buyer characteristics have an impact on the amount of hard information (experience, licensing, certification) produced in Yellow Pages advertisements separated by classification of product. In short, Yellow Pages advertisements appear to be supplied efficiently: more information is supplied concerning products and services where the opportunity cost of search is higher, and where the value of information is greater.

Search goods are goods with observable characteristics that may be determined *prior* to purchase. Many or most of the characteristics of such goods as books, clothing, or an apartment will be known to consumers before purchase. Advertising of quality characteristics of search goods may be cheaply verified by consumers, so there is little incentive on the part of sellers to mislead in the case of search goods. Even so, advertised hyperbole — "the most exquisite food in town" — may be used to mislead consumers. Such false claims, however, will readily backfire on sellers if the good is produced under monopolistic competitive conditions and if the item (restaurant meals) is a repeat-purchase item. Moreover, the quality of the goods and services we purchase is not obtained solely from seller advertising. A firm's reputation is critical to its success, and information about the firm is often readily available from friends, relatives, and independent rating agencies (the local newspaper reviews restaurants, *Consumer Reports* independently rates thousands of products, and so on).

Some qualities (even for search goods) cannot be determined by consumers until *after* purchase. Those goods with large numbers of important qualities discoverable only during or after actual consumption are called experience goods. Even though the authenticity of quality information is hard to discern with experience goods and though the possibility for fraud is even greater, advertising nevertheless provides a valuable role in informing consumers of the *existence* of goods and services.

A third type of good has been identified by economists.[7] Credence goods — whose quality is unknown both before and after purchase — are an extreme type of experience good. Do we really know the quality of a medical "physical," even after we have had one? Or has our automobile really been fixed after repairs have allegedly been made? Did the love potion work or were our prayers answered? Economists agree that the probability of fraud is highest with these types of goods.

Information and Imperfect Competition

The kind and availability of information demanded by consumers will depend both on the goods "type" as discussed above and on the price of the product. Other things being equal, the higher the price of the product or service, the more resources the consumer will invest in information about product or service quality. Advertising reduces the full cost of exchange. In an ideal equilibrium, suppliers of goods and services will supply a utility- and profit-maximizing quantity of information to consumers. Seller-provided information is part of a process by which the full price of the product is minimized by consumers and profits are maximized by producer-sellers. For their part, consumers will demand information about the existence and quality of goods and services as a function of their own profiles and characteristics. High-income or very mobile individuals, for example, will demand more information of greater intensity, whereas low-income or locationally sedentary consumers will demand less information.

Through time, sellers have invented numerous and clever methods of signaling consumers concerning the existence and quality of products. The very names Toyota, Steinway, Wendy's or Heinz conjure up certain visions of quality. Branding is one extremely important method of certifying and signaling quality to consumers. Brand names earn reputations, and reputation has enormous value in the marketplace. This is true for all kinds of goods, including search and experience goods. Other devices are used to provide product assurances to consumers. Guarantees, warranties, buy-back arrangements, and trade-in assurances are very common. These are devices to effectively support quality assurance when information about quality is difficult or expensive to convey to buyers. Although product quality may be unknowable or carry a high price of discovery to consumers, the monopolistically competitive market adjusts with an incredible number of devices and inventions to give consumers what they want at low full prices.

7. Credence goods and their characteristics are discussed in Michael R. Darby and Edi Karni, "Free Competition and the Optimal Amount of Fraud," *Journal of Law and Economics* 16 (1973): 67–88.

Small Numbers and Strategy: Duopoly and Oligopoly

So far in this chapter we have analyzed seller strategies when any one seller's pro rata share of the market is small. But sellers undertake the same kind of price and nonprice strategies when the firm's pro rata share of the market is relatively large. We could debate what "relatively large" is, but in the case of many industries, such as automobiles, local hamburger restaurants, or aluminum fabricators, the actions of one seller will clearly have important effects on the demand and profits of the other sellers. Other things being equal, the smaller the number of competitors, the greater the impact that actions of any one seller will have on the other. With a smaller number of competitors, the opportunity for strategic behavior is much larger than under monopolistic competition. These strategies, like those with larger numbers, will involve choices regarding quality, product, price, location, and promotion. As we will see, results will vary in models of duopoly, oligopoly, or cartels, depending on the assumptions we make about the competitors involved. Several classic game-theory examples will illustrate the problems encountered in analyzing strategy when there are a small number of rivals. The first deals not with firms but with prisoners.

The Prisoner's Dilemma

An important illustration of strategies when numbers are small — in this case, two — is the so-called **prisoner's dilemma**. The dilemma is illustrated by the hypothetical capture of two criminals, Thelma and Louise, caught in the act of burglary. Assume that the burglary itself carries a penalty of 3 years in prison, but police suspect the two of a more serious crime, which could carry a 15-year prison term. Immediately after capture for burglary, Thelma is separated from Louise and each is given the following "deal": If *both* confess to the more serious crime, each gets 9 years in prison, but if one confesses and the other doesn't, the one who confesses goes free and the other gets 15 years. If *neither* confesses, both get 3 years in prison (the penalty for burglary). These options are summarized in a payoff matrix in Table 10.1, which displays Thelma's options across the top and Louise's vertically at the left. The table is easy to read. It shows the consequences of each of the four possible outcomes of this game. For each outcome, the first entry gives Louise's penalty and the second one gives Thelma's penalty. For example, if Louise refuses to confess and Thelma confesses, the entry (15 years, 0 years) tells us that Louise is sentenced to 15 years in prison and Thelma goes free.

How would the two act in this dilemma? It all depends on how each of the prisoners assesses the situation. Suppose that you are Thelma. If you think Louise is going to confess, you are clearly better off confessing. Your confession would give you 9 rather than 15 years. If, on the other hand, you think

Table 10.1 The Prisoner's Dilemma

If Louise confesses to the crime and Thelma does not, Louise goes free and Thelma gets 15 years; the opposite is also true. In the most likely scenario, both confess and get a 9-year term.

Louise's Strategies	Thelma's Strategies	
	Confesses to Serious Crime	Refuses to Confess
Confesses to Serious Crime	9 years, 9 years	0 years, 15 years
Refuses to Confess	15 years, 0 years	3 years, 3 years

Louise would *refuse* to confess, you should still confess. If you are right, you (Thelma) will go scot-free instead of getting a 3-year sentence by refusing. You will therefore have an incentive to confess regardless of what you expect Louise to do. Louise has the same incentive. Given the prisoner's dilemma, therefore, Thelma and Louise both confess and each gets a prison sentence of 9 years.

A number of points are relevant relating to the solution depicted in Table 10.1:

- Collusive behavior by Thelma and Louise is not possible because the two women are sequestered immediately after capture and — once they have confessed — they do not get the chance to "play the game again." It is a one-shot, nonrepetitive game.
- Suppose instead that Thelma and Louise were given an opportunity to discuss and formulate strategy. Clearly, the best strategy is to refuse to confess. Even then, the decision not to confess would require confidence that the other would not cheat on the agreement by confessing.
- Cheating in these kinds of games is a real possibility, because if either one "cheats" and confesses with the other remaining silent (in a second round), she could get off with no prison time rather than the 3 years.
- Once the decision is made and the outcome known (both confess), neither regrets her decision. Given that Thelma (Louise) confesses, does Louise (Thelma) want to change her decision? Naturally not, since refusing to confess would add six years to her prison term.

The example of the prisoner's dilemma appears stylized and artificial, but it contains the kernel of all problems in **duopoly-oligopoly** (small-numbers bargaining) behavior. A better result (lower prison term, higher profits) may be had by collusion, but the probability of successful collusion is lowered by the reward of successful cheating. Under a certain set of assumptions about behavior, such as those contained in the prisoner's dilemma, some intermediate solution is to be expected. How does this translate into business behavior?

Duopoly Behavior and Game Theory: The Cournot-Nash Model

As the prisoner's dilemma suggests, predicting the outcome of strategic behavior is very complex. The larger the number of players or the more alternatives each player faces, the more complex game-playing, in general, becomes. But a slightly more complicated model (one with two "players" and three alternatives) will add to our understanding of this kind of strategic behavior. The kinds of strategies involved are called **Cournot-Nash strategies**, after inventors Augustin-Antoine Cournot, a nineteenth-century French economist mentioned earlier in the chapter, and contemporary mathematician John Nash.

Consider two business competitors, Toyota and Nissan, who are trying to determine the most effective (maximum profit) advertising strategies for selling high-powered sports cars. Strategy X is to spend very little on advertising, Y implies a moderate advertising budget, and Z implies very heavy advertising. Table 10.2 outlines the three possible strategies in horizontal (Toyota's choices) and vertical (Nissan's choices) fashion. Thus there are nine possible combinations of marketing choices. The payoff for each is expressed in millions of dollars of profit, with Nissan's profits listed first. (Naturally, the choices could just as easily relate to auto design, equipment offerings, or any other competitive margin.) For example, if Nissan chooses strategy Y (moderate

Table 10.2 The Cournot-Nash Solution
If the two firms are able to cooperate (both pursue strategy X), joint profit will be maximized. However, a more likely solution is for both to pursue strategy Z — the Cournot-Nash solution — in which joint profits are lower.

Nissan's Strategies	Toyota's Strategies		
	X	Y	Z
X	$800, $800	$620, $962	$440, $1088
Y	$962, $620	$728, $728	$494, $800
Z	$1088, $440	$800, $494	$512, $512

X: very little advertising
Y: moderate advertising
Z: very heavy advertising

advertising) and Toyota chooses Z (heavy advertising), Nissan's profits are $494 million and Toyota's are $800 million.

The analogy to the solution of the prisoner's dilemma, *given that there is no collusion between Toyota and Nissan*, is perfect. The two competitors, in a one-shot or one-time game, will each end up with strategy Z. Regardless of which strategy Toyota employs, Nissan's profits are greatest by selecting strategy Z. The same is true for Toyota. We should not then be surprised to find that the combination (Z, Z) is chosen.

The result of the game is the same as the prisoner's dilemma, but the intermediate solutions permit us some additional insights into small-numbers strategy. Assume now that the game is played by Nissan and Toyota period after period. Even the dullest of firm managers will recognize that collusion or cooperation will increase each competitor's payoff. Indeed, collusion is to be expected in the situation described by Table 10.2, in which both Toyota and Nissan would share the joint profit-maximizing amounts of $800 million each (solution X, in which both companies spend little on advertising). But even this solution leaves room for some opportunistic behavior on the part of one or both of the competitors. A look at the table tells us that *either* competitor could improve his or her position by defecting from the (X, X) solution. If Nissan cheated by employing strategy Y (earning $962 million in profits, as contrasted to the joint maximizing return of $800 million), Toyota could punish Nissan by immediately moving to strategy Z. At (Y, Z), Toyota would regain lost profits but would force Nissan to lowered returns (to $494 million). Once cheating begins, we can verify that Toyota and Nissan would return to the Cournot-Nash solution (Z, Z) and the process (in repeated "trials") would begin over again.

A competitor may "signal" the other from the Cournot-Nash solution. This may be done by taking short-term losses for one or more periods and raising the other's returns. This would be a signal that both could improve their joint profits by returning to the strategy (X, X). Such signaling is most likely where open collusion is illegal and carefully watched by antitrust authorities. Although it is clearly in the profit interests of the competitors to collude, the likelihood of success is dependent on two basic factors:

1. Collusion is more difficult when the number of rivals is large and when the products sold by the rivals are differentiated.
2. When firms compete on a number of margins such as product quality, service, and variety, the possibilities of some kind of joint profit maximization through collusion is significantly reduced.

An examination of the prisoner's dilemma or the Cournot-Nash solution to the duopoly problems, although a highly stylized view of a particular situation, contains many lessons for the study of small-numbers strategic behavior. Duopoly and oligopoly theory, to a large extent, are general ideas that must be adapted to a large number of special cases. Each case is, in effect, a hybrid.

Figure 10.5 The Hotelling Model of Firm Location

Assuming that transportation costs are proportional to distance, the firm located at point *M* will be at a cost advantage in serving buyers between *Q* and point *F*. The seller located at *G* will have a cost advantage for the remaining buyers.

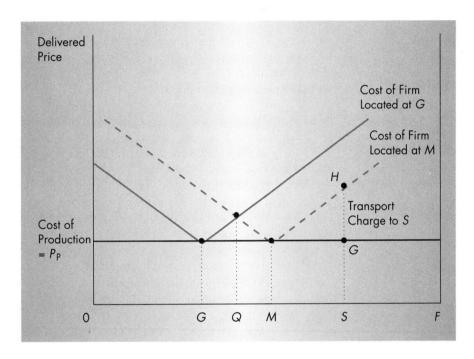

This does not mean that the study of oligopoly theory is useless but simply that no generally applicable principles pertain to each and every case. An understanding of the Cournot-Nash approach to game theory is invaluable in analyzing real-world cases.

Variety and Agglomeration: The Hotelling Solution

A number of other classic models of strategic duopoly behavior contain important insights. A particularly interesting (and unique) model is that offered by American economist Harold Hotelling.[8] That model tells us something about why businesses locate as they do and, by generalization, why products often appear so alike. Hotelling began by assuming that buyers of some commodity (say, video camcorders) were evenly and equally distributed along a linear "strip" market such as 0*F* of Figure 10.5. Further, he assumed that each of these demanders has a completely inelastic demand for *one* unit of the

8. The classic Hotelling paper discussing duopoly and location is "Stability in Competition," *Economic Journal* 39 (March 1929): 41–57.

commodity, which must be transported to demanders at some cost per mile. Thus the total cost of videocams is equal to the cost of producing them (assumed to be P_p in Figure 10.5) plus the constant transport rate per mile times the number of miles.

Assume that, initially, one firm is serving the market and is located at the midpoint along the distance $0F$. At the midpoint, M, the firm is producing videocams at an average cost of P_p. On either side of M, videocams cost P_p plus the total transport charge to that point.[9] To deliver to a customer at location S, the total cost is distance SH. The amount GH is the transport charge added to the production price.

The question for a second firm considering entry into the market is where to locate in order to maximize market share. Suppose, hypothetically, that the second firm locates at point G and faces the same transport charge to distant demanders as the initial firm. Which buyers can this firm serve at a cost below that of the first firm? Because the second duopolist enters at a point west of the initial firm, the initial firm has a "protected market" to the right of the midpoint M. Clearly, the price that the firm at G would have to charge for videocams to the east of point M would exceed the charge of the initial firm at M. In this sense, that part of the firm's market is protected. If the second firm actually located at point G, the total market covered by the second firm would be $0Q$. That total market would consist of the "protected" part $(0G)$ plus a portion (GQ) over which the second firm would have a transport advantage. Still, the firm at the midpoint would serve a larger market than the one at G $(QF > 0G)$.

What is the moral of all this? As Hotelling argued, the duopolists are not in a locational equilibrium. The entrant would want to move *closer* to the initial firm, that is, closer to point M. By doing so, the firm could increase its market share. This kind of locational movement would take place no matter where the initial firm located. The second duopolist would always want to locate at an adjacent point so as to maximize market share. A moment's reflection reveals that *both* firms would locate next to each other at point M in equilibrium (where market share is one-half for each firm).

A number of important aspects of this solution may be observed. The first is simply a reminder that the solution is *duopolistic*, with the very existence of equilibrium determined by the presence of only two competitors. Think of it. A third competitor enters next to the existing competitors at point M. One of the competitors would then have *no* market. He or she would be sandwiched in between the other two, soon moving outside of one of them, capturing another competitor who would then want to move outside the other two, and

---

9. In exact terms, total price (production + transport fees) to any consumer at any distance D from the production point would be $p + tD$, where t = a constant unit transport charge for the good.

so on without end or equilibrium.[10] This is not so, of course, if the proper analogy to the competitive situation is a *circle* rather than a straight line, as in Hotelling's particular example.

Despite the limited nature of Hotelling's solution, the basic principle Hotelling discovered is thought to be applicable in a wide range of important situations. Hotelling himself believed that it explained why agglomeration takes place in the marketplace and in the world of ideas. It may explain, for example, why there is little variety in the production of certain products (autos, cornflakes), why all the auto dealers in many towns are located on adjacent lots, and why Protestants and Catholics as well as Republicans and Democrats (in Hotelling's famous view) are becoming more alike. Hotelling's model, although not a particular solution in any specific case, is extremely provocative in orienting thought to the problems faced with small numbers in a variety of market and nonmarket situations.

The Secret and Rocky Life of Cartels

A **cartel** is any formal or informal organization or combination to restrict output. The goal of the cartel is to adjust total industry output so as to maximize joint profits. Collusive solutions, such as those at (X, X) in Table 10.2, are the object of cartelization. Obviously, the achievement of advertising restriction or output restriction to maximize joint profits requires (a) successful price fixing and (b) some method of distributing output shares among the cartelized firms. These two goals of the cartel and its management are exceedingly difficult to achieve.

When we think of cartels, international cartels immediately come to mind. Such cartels — for oil (OPEC) or coffee — are well-known, *legal*, open, and formal organizations. For years, world pharmaceutical and chemical markets have been divided by large multinational corporations. But much cartel activity is secret, *illegal*, and difficult to detect. The Justice Department and the Federal Trade Commission enforce antitrust laws against price fixing (and market sharing), as when General Electric and other electrical equipment manufacturers were prosecuted for illegal price agreements on the sale of generators to municipalities in the 1960s.

Cartel activity in the United States is generally legal and subtly conducted. Groups such as the national and state medical associations, the national and state bar associations, local barbers, morticians, and a host of other

---

10. In the *linear* Hotelling model, transport costs are not minimized when both competitors end up at the midpoint. (They would be minimized if each located at one-quarter the distance from either end of the line.) In a circular model of location and competition, firms would have the incentive to locate in optimal fashion. Envision a circular area with evenly dispersed competitors. Wherever an initial competitor locates, a second competitor would locate 180 degrees opposite the first. A third would locate on either the east or west side of the circle, and so on. In such a model, transport cost is minimized.

professional and trade organizations are cartels. Many (such as the AMA) set entry requirements and effectively fix prices by controlling the supply of physicians. Much of this activity is "sold" to the public as promoting quality, setting standards, and so on. The economic effects, however, have been cartelization of the medical industry, along with monopoly prices for these services to American consumers.

Cheating and Cartel Enforcement

Just as our analysis of duopolistic behavior within a model of game theory led to cheating (even if collusion is attained), cartels must face the same problem. The problem may again be viewed as one of individual versus group incentives (similar to the Chamberlin model developed in Figure 10.4). Figure 10.6 depicts two demand curves faced by a firm in a cartel situation. Assume that a "cartel manager" has been able to calculate the joint profit-maximizing cartel price for all of the members and to allocate to each firm its share of the output. Further assume that demand curve DD is the pro rata industry demand curve of the firm (allocated according to some share or quota technique) and dd is

Figure 10.6 Cartel Demand

Cartel demand DD shows each firm's sales if the other firms match their price reductions (cheating is detected). Demand curve dd shows sales at each price if cheating is undetected by rivals.

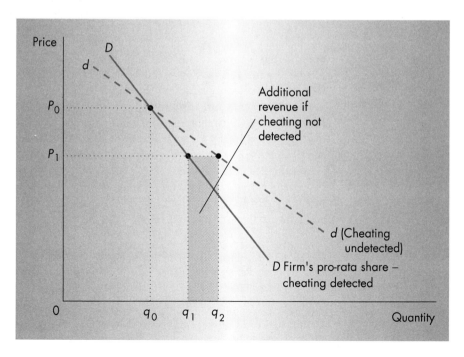

the firm's demand curve if it cheats undetected. Demand curve *DD* shows how much the firm will be able to sell at each price if the other firms charge a price of P_0. If cheating is detected, the other firms in the cartel will *lower* prices in retribution, although the demand curve for the firm would clearly be more elastic if cheating is not detected. The firm thus faces a dilemma: it might increase sales and profits if it cheats, but if undercover dealings are detected, it will be punished as other members of the cartel cut prices. Clearly, if the benefits of cheating are high or if the cost of detection is high, the firm will attempt to gain at the other firms' expense. The practice may well lead to the dissolution of the cartel.

This simple example points up the fragility of cartels. The incentive to cheat is always there, even in a well-run cartel. Although a cheating firm may be successful in the short run (going undetected), the possibility for profitable long-run cheating is lower. Other firms in the market will obviously begin to notice declines in sales or profits. Rivalrous responses to price cutting may in fact result in a return to the competitive solution ($P = LRAC$) for the entire industry. However, the increased profits available to cartelization will often lead the cartel to find mechanisms through which quasi-stable agreements among the firms can be reached and to spend resources to control incentives to cheat.

What are some of these agreements? Cartels must find a way to divide industry output among the members and to fix prices in a manner that carries the lowest probability of cheating and price defections. Often the firm (or country, in the case of the OPEC oil cartel) will be allocated sales on the basis of its precartel share of the market. Another method — one which in some circumstances may reduce the cost of secret price cutting and cheating — is the geographic allocation of markets by which firms take a segment of the market and operate as a monopolist in that area. The allocation of market shares, especially where firms overlap, is made easier if the cartel product is homogeneous.

Nonprice Competition

When products are themselves not homogeneous or when nonprice competition is significant, cartel enforcement is rendered considerably more difficult and expensive. Eventually, such nonprice competition may lead to the impossibility of maintaining a cartel (see Highlight 10.4). In some cases the cartel

Highlight 10.4   *Colbert and the Calico Cartel*

History provides us with many examples of the success and failure of cartelized forms of market organization. French mercantilism under Louis XIV's minister Jean-Baptiste Colbert (1619–1683) is an especially ripe source of examples.

Colbert designed a system of controls in international trade and in the domestic economy that would rival any in history. These controls provided revenues and spoils to the monarch and aristocratic retainers that would be the envy of any modern dictator.

One primary source of monopoly revenues to the Crown was in the production and sale of textiles in the French economy. Colbert, with the support of the king, set up an elaborate system of "inspectors of manufacturers" (*intendents*) to monopolize and oversee production and to secure meticulous observance of the industrial regulations laid down. These regulations were incredibly detailed, and the details were tailored to restrict the various means, such as product differentiation, that cartel members could find to increase their market share. On the matter of textiles, consider only one small example of the details: "The fabrics of Dijon and Selongey were to be put in reeds $1\frac{3}{4}$ ells wide, a warp was to contain 44 x 32 or 1408 threads including the selvedges, and when it came to the fulling-mill, the cloth was to be exactly one ell wide."[a]

All went well until a technological innovation came along. When printed calicoes became popular, the state went to great lengths to prevent their production, import, and consumption. Why? As mentioned in the text, the existence of nonprice competition will tend to dissipate cartel profits. Even if prices are controlled, consumers will buy on the basis of quality and variety (nonprice competition). As such, nonprice competition had to be suppressed by Colbert or the created monopoly would, eventually, provide no revenues. And Colbert *did* suppress competition. Before an absolute ban was placed on French calico production in 1681, Colbert tried to regulate it. Colbert failed in spite of extreme retributions against "cheaters" on the cartel. On one occasion in Valence (France), according to one authority, "77 [cheaters] were sentenced to be hanged, 58 were to be broken upon the wheel, 631 were sent to the galleys, one was set free and none were pardoned" for violating the rules.[b] None of it prevented the internal dissipation of returns from the cartel, and an absolute ban on printed calicoes went into effect. The end result, according to some observers, was to retard the development of the French textile industry until the nineteenth century. But the experience also affirms the principle that the management of economic regulation, which creates a cartel, is less costly when the industry produces a homogeneous product.

[a] Eli Heckscher, *Mercantilism,* trans. Mendel Shapiro, vol. 1 (London: George Allen & Unwin, 1934), pp. 160–161.

[b] Ibid., p. 173.

agreement may be to set price and to permit nonprice competition to allocate market shares, although the practice may lead to the ultimate dissolution of the organization. Airline rates were controlled by the Civil Aeronautics Board, for example, prior to deregulation in the late 1970s. But *everything* cannot be controlled. Individual airlines began offering enhanced service, including gourmet meals, more frequent flights, services providing greater flyer convenience, and so on. These factors had the effect of increasing the costs of air service, eroding the (legal and regulated) cartel's profits. Market shares shifted because of nonprice competition, but the financial stability of many lines was threatened. Deregulation ensued and provided us with the lesson that price-setting cartels that permit nonprice competition will tend to dissolve through profit dissipation over time.

Cartel Instability: Some General Observations

Is collusion feasible, and under what conditions will collusive (joint profit-maximizing) conditions survive in markets? There are no hard-and-fast answers, but economists have identified certain factors that influence the stability of a cartel.[11] These include product (or service) differentiation, the numbers of buyers and sellers in the market, whether the industry is in growth or decline, and the turnover of buyers and sellers. Consider each of these briefly.

As we have already seen, collusive agreements are easier (less costly) to come to and to maintain when the products sold are homogeneous. Nonprice factors play a much less important role when products are homogeneous and firms will not be able to compete away market shares through advertising, location, quality differentiation, or other means. Many services are, by nature, differentiated and are therefore less likely, other things being equal, to be cartelized. In general, the smaller the number of sellers, the more likely that a collusive agreement may be reached and maintained. The costs of organizing a cartel and of making group decisions will rise (at an increasing rate) with the number of firms in the cartel.

When there are a large number of small buyers, collusion is more likely to be successful. Large buyers will find it in their interests to induce sellers to give secret price cuts and other difficult-to-detect concessions. Further, it is in seller's interests to "make deals" where high returns are at stake. Cartels, other things being equal, are easier to form and maintain in growing industries or economies than in declining industries. When a particular line of business (or all business in an economy) is in decline, excess capacity develops, creating seller incentives to cheat on the cartel.

The lower the turnover of buyers, the more likely the success of collusion. Buyers become known to competing sellers, thereby reducing the information

---

11. The classic paper in this area is by the late American Nobel laureate (1982) George Stigler. Stigler's "A Theory of Oligopoly," *Journal of Political Economy* 72 (Feb. 1964): 44–61 is accessible to the reader at the intermediate theory level.

costs associated with policing the arrangement. With frequent turnover of buyers, sellers can more easily cheat on a collusive agreement. There are high costs of detection of cheating when buyers change frequently. Likewise, successful collusion is less likely when sellers are replaced frequently; the cost of holding the arrangement together becomes higher and higher as seller turnover increases.

These general rules are only illustrative of factors that would encourage or discourage cartels; there are undoubtedly many other factors. Purely private agreements tend to be the most unstable, especially if government uses vigorous antitrust enforcement through the Federal Trade Commission and the Justice Department. When firms "run for cover" or must operate secretly, the possibilities for successful collusion decline precipitously.

Businesses and industries seeking cartel organization often have recourse to government (see Chapter 9). In return for relinquishing some control over profits, output quality, or prices, some private cartels may obtain legal status. This legal status is often accompanied by entry control and the outlawing of price competition. The government in effect provides low-cost enforcement for the cartel organization.

Summary

Market models of imperfect competition run the gamut from large numbers and slightly differentiated product markets to smaller numbers and a homogeneous product. In each of the many cases, competition involves strategic behavior. But strategic behavior introduces numerous complexities to the problem of analyzing business and industrial organizations. Whether or not successful collusion and profit maximizing through time is possible or feasible (without government legal support) is problematic. These cases do tell us that in the real world — where products and product qualities are differentiated, where location and service are variables, and where real flesh-and-blood sellers compete on many nonprice margins — models of perfect competition or pure monopoly are not as descriptive as those that utilize assumptions concerning strategy. In the present chapter we

- developed a number of alternative models that featured product differentiation and strategic behavior,
- discussed the classic Chamberlinian model of monopolistic competition, where large numbers and product differentiation are assumed,
- detailed the foundations of small-numbers strategy that has become "game theory" and showed how it applies in economic situations,
- developed some general considerations that relate to all cartel behavior when the number of competitors is relatively small.

Key Terms

strategic behavior	product differentiation
monopolistic competition	collusion
nonprice competition	search good
experience good	credence good
prisoner's dilemma	duopoly
oligopoly	game theory
Cournot-Nash strategies	cartel

Sample Questions

Question

How does the number of buyers and sellers in a market assist or prevent the success of a cartel?

Answer

The number of buyers and sellers influences the success of a cartel by making collusion easier or more difficult for cartel members. The larger the number of small buyers in a market, the less likely it becomes that a collusive arrangement will be detected. The cartel is also more likely to be successful when there is a small number of sellers, which makes organization and monitoring less costly. The smaller the number of buyers, the easier it is to detect cheating.

Question

What is a Cournot-Nash solution, and why do participants in a "prisoner's dilemma" model arrive at such a solution?

Answer

A Cournot-Nash solution is the joint profit-maximizing solution in which the participants in a one-time prisoner's dilemma model are prevented from colluding. The solution is attained because it strategically minimizes potential losses (or jail time) when uncertainty exists about the other participant's behavior in the absence of collusion.

Questions for Review and Discussion

*1. What are the monopolistic and competitive elements of Chamberlin's model of monopolistic competition?

2. Suppose that a pet store decides to offer obedience training free of charge with the purchase of a pedigree dog. What type of competitive strategy does this represent?

3. Explain why advertising intensity differs by location when consumers in the different cities have similar demographic characteristics.

4. Why will a firm follow the *actual* demand curve as opposed to the *perceived* demand curve?

*5. Show graphically a monopolistically competitive firm that earns losses in the short run. Will this firm shut down in the short run?

*6. Why do some economists view the tangency solution as inefficient?

7. What economic motive explains the proliferation of new products each year in the grocery store? Do consumers benefit from product diversification?

*8. Explain how the quality of a good is discerned for search goods, experience goods, and credence goods.

9. The medieval Roman Catholic Church specialized in the assurance of salvation. Given the classification scheme in question 8, what type of good is salvation?

10. The quality of a good can be assured to consumers by a variety of methods. Identify the different ways that firms ensure quality for consumers.

*11. In a two-person, one-time, prisoner's-dilemma situation, what is the optimal strategy for each prisoner? Explain.

12. What theory explains why you are likely to find a McDonald's, Burger King, and Wendy's located next to each other?

13. Cartels exist in many industries. How are cartels promoted as beneficial to consumers, and do they actually help or hurt consumers?

14. Why did Colbert regulate and eventually ban the production of printed calicoes?

*15. Identify and explain the factors that influence the stability of collusive arrangements.

Questions for Analysis

*1. If a single firm in a monopolistically competitive market undertakes advertising, the effect may be to reduce the price elasticity of that firm's demand. Could you make an argument that, when all firms advertise, the price elasticity of the demand curve faced by each firm is increased, not decreased?

2. Evidence from monopolistically competitive markets shows that rival firms sell a number of differentiated products at prices that are similar — but not identical. Suppose that the government enacted a law requiring all firms to charge the same price. (For example, all brewers could be required to charge a price of $8.00 per six-pack.) If such a law were enacted, what effect would you expect it to have on the degree of product differentiation? Explain. Would the law benefit consumers or harm them?

*3. "One reason that it is harder for an oligopolist to decide what price to charge than it is for a monopolist is that it is harder for an oligopolist to identify his demand and marginal-revenue curves." Do you agree or disagree? Explain.

4. Table 10.2 shows that when both firms elect strategy X (spend little on advertising), their profits will be higher than if they both adopt either strategy Y or Z, in which advertising costs are higher. Does higher advertising necessarily lead to lower overall profits by firms in the industry?

5. Physicians generally favor policies that ban or greatly limit advertising by physicians. Tobacco companies oppose policies that limit advertising of tobacco products. Do you think that the physicians are acting sensibly from an economic perspective? What about the tobacco companies?

6. It has been said that there are two major causes of cartel failure — greed and the *fear* of greed on the part of other cartel members. Do you agree with this statement?

7. Suppose that two individuals, Jim and Sue, are accused of stealing computers and vandalizing cars at a local university. If convicted, Jim and Sue will face a jail sentence. If each confesses, the jail time will be seven years. If Jim confesses and Sue does not, Jim receives a two-year sentence and Sue receives a ten-year sentence. If neither confesses, then each goes to jail for five years. Construct the prisoner's dilemma matrix and determine the outcome, assuming this is a one-time deal with no collusion.

8. The price of a good sometimes provides information about the quality of the product. What are some other means of determining quality for search, experience, and credence goods?

11

Market Structures: Issues and Applications

Various market structures, from competition to pure monopoly, including market situations in between, were discussed in Chapters 8, 9, and 10. Now we may proceed to analyze some of the numerous issues and innovations that may illuminate how markets of diverse kinds may function in the real world. A few of the aspects that we will treat — information and product search — apply to practically all structures. Others — antitrust enforcement and regulation of monopoly — are fairly specific to oligopoly and monopoly markets. Mastery of this chapter should lead to an understanding of

- the role of information and consumer search in markets of all types,
- the consequences of transactions in which one party (such as a used-car salesperson) has a good deal more information than other parties (car buyers),
- some general policy principles in antitrust enforcement that are raised by modern theories of markets,
- the effects of regulation of so-called natural monopolies such as telephone, electrical, and local water supply services.

Market Structure: An Introduction

An economic theory of market structures provides the backdrop for the economist's analysis of production and exchange in the real world. How efficient are markets that we trade in day after day? Do some structures produce some goods at lower costs than others? Will government control or regulation bring about a better result than unregulated, unfettered market forces? For example, should there be more government regulation and control in order to establish environmental standards, "fairer" prices for cable TV, or more "equitable" phone, utility, or airline rates?

There are more questions here than can be answered in a single chapter, a single book, or a whole collection of books. However, there are some elements in contemporary economic theory that point toward answers to questions such as these. It is probably fair to say that modern research into the economics of information, consumer search, full price, and the importance of service and quality to consumers has (on balance) revolutionized economic assessments of market structures. Along with this "revolution" has come a reassessment of public policies toward antitrust and regulation. Before we turn to a brief examination of policies directly relating to market structure, consider the role of information once more and its relationship to consumer well-being and to how markets function.

Information and Markets

As we have repeatedly emphasized in this book, all exchange involves costs. The money price for any good or service is only one element in the sacrifice required of consumers in making purchases. In order to buy a can of soup and a box of crackers, we must be willing not only to pay the money price, but also to expend real resources in getting to the supermarket (gas, tires, car wear, and so on) and to spend time on the trip. Often the value of time is proxied by the consumer's wage rate, but leisure (or nonwork) time also has value. The total or full price to consumers of goods and services thus includes all of these factors — the actual dollars spent plus the opportunity cost of resources (time, gas, and so on) used in the act of purchase.

A Search Model

The idea of full price is given life in a well-known model of **consumer search**.[1] For all consumers, *the acquisition of information or knowledge about the prices (or qualities) of goods and services is costly.* Furthermore, price dispersions will exist in all markets in a world in which information is not perfect. How many times have you bought an item, only to find out that it was available elsewhere at a lower price? Consumers are not stupid when they pay a higher-than-necessary price. Rather, price dispersion — with the possibility of lower prices than the one actually paid — results from the fact that buyers do not have full and complete information about the price distribution offered by sellers. Naturally, the consumer would buy from the low-price seller if he or she was aware of the

---

1. The classic treatment of information and search was developed by Nobel laureate in economics George Stigler, "The Economics of Information," *Journal of Political Economy* 69 (June 1961): 213–225. In the traditional treatment presented here, consumers embark on a price search (that is, a search for a low price), but the model could as easily be framed in terms of quality or some other good or service characteristic.

Figure 11.1 Optimal Search Time

The cost of search is depicted by *MCS*. A rational consumer searches for lower prices so long as the benefits of search on the margin exceed the costs. For a relatively uninformed buyer, the marginal benefits of search are depicted by MBS_0, and the optimal amount of search is S_0. For a better-informed consumer, the benefits of search (MBS_1) *are lower* and the optimal search time (S_1) is shorter.

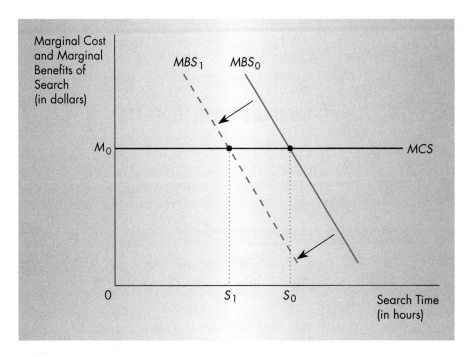

seller's existence and all other things were equal. Often, consumers do not buy from the low- (nominal-) price seller because of the real resource sacrifices that must be made to obtain price information.

These principles may be reduced to a simple model of consumer choice. Figure 11.1 depicts optimal consumer search, in which search time (in hours) is set against the marginal costs and the marginal benefits to search in some market. As mentioned earlier, search costs include the value of commodities (gas, auto wear and tear, and so on) sacrificed in order to search, plus the (usually more important) value of time that is sacrificed. The value of time could be represented by the value of forgone income or of leisure time to the consumer.

Naturally, no one is going to spend time and resources looking for products without some reward, and the benefits to search are real enough. Where we assume quality as given, the benefits to search are in discovering a lower price for the product than the best price currently known to a potential buyer. The more knowledge or information the consumer possesses concerning the price distribution, the less likely he or she is to discover a lower price. Alternatively, given some initial stock of information, the marginal benefits to additional search time declines as the consumer spends more time looking for lower prices. It becomes steadily less probable that a consumer will find a lower price as he or she acquires more information by search.

Assume that the cost of search is constant in terms of hours spent. In Figure 11.1, in which search time is measured on the horizontal axis and marginal cost (and benefit) is measured on the vertical axis, a constant-cost assumption corresponds to the flat marginal cost of search curve *MCS*. Marginal benefits to search, *MBS*, described earlier, fall as more time is spent in looking for a lower price for some good. Note, in Figure 11.1, that benefits remain positive as the consumer spends more hours searching but that the marginal benefit falls along MBS_0. At the intersection of MCS_0 and MBS_0 the net benefits of search to the consumer are maximized. Additional hours of search after time S_0 would cost the consumer more in resources and time value than any potential benefit from the possibility that a lower price would be found.

The impact of advertising and other types of information provision may be analyzed using Figure 11.1. Recall that the consumer starts out with some initial state of knowledge about the price distribution surrounding the provision of some good or service. That initial state of information may, of course, correspond to total ignorance concerning the price of some particular item. Given that initial state of information (possibly none), the consumer gains new information with search. Suppose that MBS_0 is drawn with regard to some information state of the consumer for some particular item. Further, assume that the optimal search, given that initial state, is S_0 hours (say, six hours) for some good. If the lowest price found for the good is $350 and if the entire opportunity cost from search (time plus other resources) is $7.50 per hour, the full price of the good or service purchased will be $395.

What, then, is the impact of additional information on the consumer? Information concerning the price of goods (or quality or whatnot) may be obtained from many sources. Advertising (such as the Yellow Pages, newspapers, TV, magazines, billboards) is often the main provider of information about particular goods and services. Price information is also often obtained from friends and relatives. A new and improved initial stock of information will lower the benefits of search for lower and lower prices to consumers, reducing the optimal amount of search time used in acquiring a product. But although the benefits to product search fall in terms of finding a lower price for the item, the total amount of resources used up by the consumer in looking for the "right" good or service also falls. Suppose, with reference to Figure 11.1, that price advertising in the newspaper increases the initial stock of information possessed by the consumer, so that the *MBS* curve shifts from MBS_0 to MBS_1. *Every* hour of search now necessarily yields less *new* information about price. Optimal search time falls by two-thirds, from S_0 (6 hours) to S_1

(2 hours). If the nominal price of the good described above remains at $350, full price falls from $395 (with 6 hours of search time) to $365 (with only 2 hours of time spent on search). Advertising and other devices for providing information therefore reduce the amount of time consumers spend in "looking for the best deal," thereby reducing the full price paid for the item.

Naturally the form and nature of search and the demand for information for particular goods and services will be conditioned by the nature of each particular item. As we saw in Chapter 10, search, experience, and credence goods have particular characteristics that will cause consumers to invest in more or less information prior to purchase. In general, given some initial stock of information, the higher the price of a good or service, the greater the search time. Moreover, the consumer's wealth or income must also be considered, with higher-income individuals bearing higher marginal search costs. Advertising and other means of information provision will ordinarily lower either money prices or time costs or both.[2] Further, costly information and search directly imply that price dispersions will exist in *any* market, *including* markets that are fully competitive.

Asymmetric Information: The Lemons Problem

A type of market failure related to information may exist in some markets. The nature of some products — automobiles, VCRs, refrigerators, and the like — may mean that in the secondary or resale market sellers may possess more information than do buyers. In other words, buyers and sellers possess asymmetric information. For such items, a "lemons problem" is said to exist wherein mutually beneficial trades fail to take place because price becomes an inaccurate signal of quality. The typical "lemon" problem relates to used automobiles, where the seller knows quality but the buyer does not.[3]

Consider the resale of almost-new automobiles that are initially of high, medium, and low quality. (It is often alleged, for example, that autos produced on Mondays or on Fridays are of inferior quality; in England such cars are called "Mondays"!) A seller of a used car knows the quality because he has been able to test the car thoroughly. Consumers, however, can only judge the quality of the car *after* the purchase, although they may know the *average* quality of all cars traded. An examination of such a market may mean that *no* cars will be traded.

Figure 11.2 shows demand and supply curves for, say, cars that have been used for only six months. The curves in this case, however, take on a special

2. Note that much brand advertising — Fritos, Camels, and the like — never mentions price. We should not jump to the conclusion that such advertising carries no information. Knowledge of the existence of products also has some value to consumers.

3. The "lemons" problem was made famous by economist George A. Akerlof, "The Market for 'Lemons': Quality Uncertainty and the Market Mechanism," *Quarterly Journal of Economics* (August 1970): 488–500.

Figure 11.2 The Market for Lemons

When buyers use the price as a measure of quality, decreases in the price of a good will lead to decreases in the demand. Starting at a price of P_0, a reduction in price to P_1 may decrease demand from d_0 to d_1. If so, the surplus at P_1 may be larger than the initial surplus at P_0.

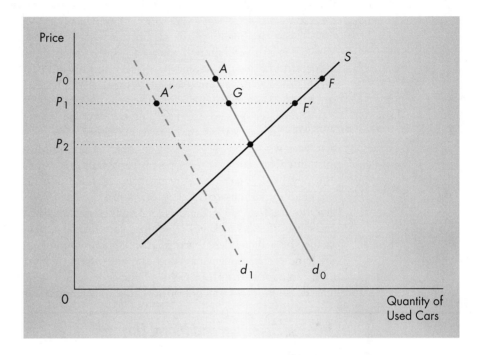

interpretation. Clearly, because sellers know the quality of their used cars with a good deal of certainty, the quality as well as the quantity of the cars offered will increase with price. This means that as price falls, *high-quality sellers will drop out of the market* and only low-quality sellers will remain.

Consumers generally will be suspicious of any seller wishing to sell an automobile after owning it less than a year. More importantly, buyers will take price as a *signal* of quality, with high prices signaling higher-quality autos and low prices signaling "lemons." Thus the demand curve for the consumers of used cars takes on a peculiar interpretation, because there is a clear connection between price and the probability of being sold a lemon. When the prices offered by sellers become lower, buyers become more suspicious that the autos offered are lemons. Lower prices lead to increasingly suspicious buyers and to reduction in the average quality of the cars offered for sale. The lemons situation could lead to no trade or to reduced trade, as illustrated in Figure 11.2. If price is p_0 in Figure 11.2 at some initial time period, excess supply would exist in some amount AF, assuming demand curve d_0 and supply curve ss. In a typical market, price would fall to equilibrium (P_2), eliminating excess supply. This may not happen in the case of used cars, however. As price begins to fall, the demand curve for used cars itself begins to shift leftward. Why? Because the demand for such cars is, in part, a function of the probability of getting a lemon, which is in turn a function of price. As the price falls below P_1, potential sellers of higher-quality cars will drop out of the market. The buyers know this, so as the price falls (say, to P_1) they will revise downward their expectations about the quality of the cars being sold. With the assumed quality being lower, demand will fall, perhaps to d_1. Rather than eliminating the surplus, the reduction in price might lead to a larger surplus of $A'F'$ compared to an initial surplus of AF. Buyers and sellers, particularly high-quality auto sellers, appear stuck and, eventually demand for used cars might disappear completely!

The reader may appropriately object that she has herself purchased a used car and that she knows that many hundreds of such goods are traded every day. She would be right. Most markets containing asymmetric information introduce certain practices to prevent failure. Some such devices include "money-back guarantees," warranties, service contracts, and leases. Easily obtainable market-provided information services such as *Consumer Reports* give the used-car buyer hard facts on (average) repair records. Buyers in many cities may (for a small fee) have used cars formally or informally evaluated for quality by independent parties. Also, seller reputation counts a great deal in the lemons situation. Most used cars are offered through *new* car dealers who have reputations to protect. All of these devices have evolved to mitigate the market failure that comes about because of asymmetric information.

Adverse Selection and Moral Hazard

A few related problems arise very often in the sale of insurance. The first is the problem of **adverse selection**. In setting insurance rates, the insurance industry assembles masses of data that enable them to determine how often the *average* 35-year-old female visits the doctor, how much damage the *average* 17-year-old driver causes each year by wrecking his car, and so on. On the basis of this information, insurance companies are able to determine insurance rates that are actuarily sound — rates that generate enough revenue to pay the claims of the average individual. However, only a sampling of the individuals within any group buys insurance.

Neither an individual insurance company nor the insurance industry as a whole can be assured that their customers will be average. In fact, the average buyer of insurance is likely to be a bad risk. The reason for this is that an insurance rate that is actuarily sound for an average customer will appear expensive to buyers who are good (low) risks and cheap to buyers who are poor (high) ones. As a consequence, high-risk buyers are likely to purchase insurance in greater proportions than low-risk buyers. From the seller's perspective, the group that selects insurance is an adverse sample of the entire group.

Adverse selection is just one example of asymmetric information, or the lemons problem. An individual buyer of insurance has better information about the risks of insuring him or her than does the seller of insurance. Accordingly, those who are eager to buy insurance tend to be "lemon buyers." Insurance companies have to raise rates to account for adverse selection. But higher rates only exacerbate the adverse selection problem. In the extreme, it may be impossible for insurance companies to sell certain types of insurance at rates that are actuarially sound.

A related problem that plagues the insurance industry is the problem of **moral hazard**. Once someone buys insurance, his behavior is likely to change, because his losses are now covered by insurance. A person who takes great care to lock his home or car before he has theft insurance may stop doing so after obtaining insurance. Because insurance reduces the cost of risky behavior, an insured person is likely to engage in more risky behavior. The ironic result is that the actual losses of those who are insured tend to grow as a direct consequence of their being insured!

The insurance industry is not helpless in dealing with either of these problems. By insisting on coinsurance provisions and deductibles, they are able to reduce but not totally eliminate moral hazard and adverse selection. In addition, they can eliminate much adverse selection by marketing group policies rather than individual ones.

Antitrust and Microeconomic Theory

Market-structure analysis, such as that contained in Chapters 9, 10, and 11, has also been used extensively in the application of economic theory to policy. However, the application of static theory has raised important and ongoing issues. For pedagogical purposes there is an "old" view of the microanalytics of antitrust and regulation based on a kind of static analysis of markets, and a "new view" that reaches out for broader concerns in economic theory. The differences between these views may be made by succinctly addressing several important issues in the contemporary economics of antitrust concepts and enforcement.

The Concentration Issue

Economists have always been concerned with business concentration. An "old" view of markets with empirical reference to the real world was developed within a **structure-conduct-performance** sequence of industrial organization. This view arose in the 1940s and prevailed through the 1970s. The idea, which formed the basis for much antitrust legislation and opinion both before and after this period, was closely tied to the static models of market structure discussed in this text.

In the old view, industry "structure" is determined by the number of firms in an industry, the type of products produced by those firms, the number of consumers for the industry's products, and the existence of entry barriers to the market. It is easy to see how the concept of structure fits into our definitions or categories of markets: many sellers of a homogeneous product means a "competitive structure," few large sellers of a homogeneous or heterogeneous product means "oligopoly structure," one seller must mean "monopoly," and so on. Within the nexus of these definitions, economists of the "old" view then *pre-decide* conduct and performance on the basis of industry structure. Armed with easily observable structural characteristics such as the number of firms, kind of product(s), and so on, the analyst could argue that certain types of conduct and performance necessarily follow certain characteristics. Small numbers of large firms selling a certain type of product would necessarily bar entry, reduce quantity, and increase price to noncompetitive levels. The entry bars would include high advertising expenditures, brand proliferation, and capital requirements. After the entry barrier was erected, the firms would resort to monopoly pricing, which would have deleterious effects on consumer welfare and on the allocation of resources.

These views were encapsulated in the formal concepts of business concentration. Aggregate concentration — the percentage of business assets held by the top 100 firms in America — is one familiar measure. But of far more relevance for antitrust enforcement is the so-called **concentration ratio**. A concentration ratio is calculated by assessing the percentage of sales accounted for by the top 4 or 8 firms in an industry. An industry is defined in a Standard Industrial Classification scheme developed by the Department of Commerce. Typical concentration ratios in such industries are given in Table 11.1. In this table the 4-firm or 8-firm ratio measures the share of total sales that the top 4 or 8 firms held in the market in 1963, 1977, 1982, and 1987. A concentration ratio of 100 ($CR = 100$) means that the top 4 or 8 firms sell the output of the entire market. A CR of 60 for 4 firms means that the top 4 firms account for 60 percent of market sales.

The concentration ratio — the centerpiece of the structure-conduct-performance view of industrial organization — forms the basis for antitrust guidelines for horizontal mergers. **Horizontal mergers** are mergers between firms in the same line of business or selling similar products — Pepsi-Cola and 7-Up, R. J. Reynolds and Phillip Morris, and so on. Merger guidelines were set up by the Department of Justice's Antitrust Division in 1982, based on a single-number index that summarized market structure. That number is the **Herfindahl-Hirschman Index** or

$$H = S_1{}^2 + S_2{}^2 + \cdots S_n{}^2$$

where S is firm 1's percentage share of the market sales and where there are n firms in the market. The value of H will always be between 10,000 and 0. Under (defined) competitive conditions, in which each of a very large number

Table 11.1 Selected Concentration Ratios in Manufacturing

Concentration ratios measure the share of sales held by the largest four or eight firms in an industry. The data shown here represent a selected group of manufacturing industries for the years 1963, 1977, 1982, and 1987. In some industries — such as men's and boys' suits — the concentration ratio increased through the years, suggesting that the largest firms obtained a larger share of total industry output. In some cases — such as jewelry and precious metals — the ratio fell, suggesting a more competitive situation.

| | Concentration Ratios | | | | | | | |
| | 1963 | | 1977 | | 1982 | | 1987 | |
	Four-Firm	Eight-Firm	Four-Firm	Eight-Firm	Four-Firm	Eight-Firm	Four-Firm	Eight-Firm
Meat packing	31	42	19	37	29	43	32	50
Fluid milk	23	30	18	28	16	27	21	32
Cereal breakfast foods	86	96	89	98	86	97	87	99
Distilled liquor	58	74	52	71	46	68	53	75
Roasted coffee	52	68	61	73	65	76	66	78
Cigarettes	80	100	—	—	—	—	92	—
Men's and boys' suits and coats	14	23	21	32	25	37	34	47
Women's and misses' dresses	6	9	8	12	6	10	6	10
Logging camps and contractors	11	19	29	36	30	37	18	24
Mobile homes	—	—	24	37	24	39	30	44
Pulp mills	48	72	48	76	45	70	44	69
Book publishing	20	33	17	30	17	30	24	38
Pharmaceutical preparations	22	38	24	43	26	42	22	36
Petroleum refining	34	56	30	53	28	48	32	52
Flat glass	94	99+	90	99	85	97	82	—
Ready-mix concrete	4	7	5	8	6	9	8	11
Blast furnaces and steel mills	48	67	45	65	42	64	44	63
Metal cans	74	85	59	74	50	68	54	70
Electric lamps	92	96	90	95	91	96	91	94
Radio and TV receiving sets	41	62	51	65	49	70	39	59
Motor vehicles, car bodies	—	—	93	99	92	97	90	95
Jewelry, precious metals	26	33	18	26	16	22	12	18
Pens and mechanical pencils	48	60	50	64	41	62	49	65

Sources: U.S. Department of Commerce, Bureau of the Census, *Census of Manufacturers* (Washington, D.C.: U.S. Government Printing Office, 1977): U.S. Department of Commerce, Bureau of the Census, *Concentration Ratios in Manufacturing* (Washington, D.C.: U.S. Government Printing Office, 1982, 1987).

of firms sells a very small percentage share of the market, the *H* value will be close to zero. Naturally, if there is only one firm in the market, that firm sells 100 percent and the *H* value is 10,000.

The so-called guideline is that the Justice Department will look into mergers when the industry *H* value is 1,800 or more (a number that would occur if four firms accounted for approximately 50 percent of the market). Note that the calculation is made postmerger (after the proposed merger takes place). Further, if the *H* value is 1,800 or more and a merger will raise the value by 100 or more, the merger will be challenged. In less-concentrated markets with *H* values of 1,000 or less, mergers that increase the value by 200 or more will ordinarily elicit antitrust action. *H* values above 1,000 and 1,800 ("moderately concentrated" markets) will only be challenged when the post-merger index rises by more than 100 points.

International Competition and Market Structure

All broader notions of competition and the competitive process must include international competition against domestic firms. The four-firm *domestic* concentration ratio for automobiles, to use an obvious example, would provide little information on the actual competitive conditions in the United States. Japanese and European manufacturer-exporters would be most surprised to learn that the top four U.S. firms supplied 100 percent of the market! To make matters even more complex, many foreign firms establish production and assembly plants in the United States. Indeed, one of the leading producers of automobiles in the United States is Honda.

Although there is much dispute concerning free versus fair trade in politics and business, one fact is clear. Imports — like broader notions of competition discussed in this chapter — act as a kind of antitrust enforcement on firms. The impact of foreign competition must be included in any of the new theories of the competitive process. (For an analysis of the competitive impact of foreign production, see Highlight 11.1.)

Highlight 11.1 *The Impact of Imports on Domestic-Market Competition*

The government counts only domestic production in computing the concentration ratio for any particular industry. For that reason, four-firm and eight-firm concentration ratios may inform us about the level of concentration in *production* in that industry, but this often gives a quite misleading picture about concentration in *sales*. The reason for this apparent discrepancy is that imports play an important and increasing role in the U.S. economy. Many of our industries are highly concentrated in production but much less concentrated in terms of sales.

To see why this is the case, it is useful to consider a few particular industries in which production is extremely concentrated. The steel, auto, and petroleum industries serve well for this purpose.[a] Production in each of the

Imports, such as these Hondas at a storage yard in New Jersey, have stimulated competitive reactions in U.S. production and sale of goods and services.

three industries has been concentrated for many years. In the auto industry, the three largest domestic producers produced over 90 percent of domestic production in every year from 1960 to 1987. Over the same period, the four largest firms accounted for about one-half of domestic steel production and about one-third of domestic oil production. But what is the role of imports in the three industries? In 1960 the role was small, because imports accounted for about 2 percent of the steel sales in this country, about 5 percent of auto sales, and about 18 percent of the petroleum sales. Since then, the percentages have grown rapidly. Today we import about 22 percent of our cars, about 20 percent of our steel, and about 40 percent of our oil. As a consequence, for each industry the four largest *sellers* in our market control a smaller share than they did thirty years ago. The presence of foreign firms in our market has greatly reduced the market power of the largest firms in these three industries and in many other industries as well.

[a] For an interesting economic analysis of these three industries (and others), see Walter Adams, *The Structure of American Industry*, 8th ed. (New York: Macmillan Publishing Company, 1990).

It is interesting to note that foreign firms have grown to importance in each of the three markets *despite* U.S. policy to limit imports. Imports in all three of the industries have been curtailed both by tariffs and quotas that have been imposed by the United States, and this has kept the level of competition lower than it would otherwise have been.

It is somewhat ironic that the same trade restrictions that have reduced actual levels of competition have created the impression of increasing competition. Because of the trade restrictions, several Japanese auto companies have built auto plants in the United States. Whatever the number of cars that are produced in the plants, it is almost certain to be less than the number that would have been produced in Japan and exported to the United States *in the absence of trade restrictions*. However, because the output from those foreign-owned plants is included in the calculation of domestic concentration ratios, our trade restrictions have reduced the actual level of competition in the U.S. markets at the same time that they reduced domestic concentration ratios.

In many small countries in the world, domestic markets are too small to support industries that consist of very many firms of reasonable size. If those countries wish to enjoy the benefits of a competitive market system, it is imperative that they "import" competition by welcoming imports to their markets.

New Views of Market Processes. Modern microeconomists, especially those concerned with industrial organization, present a very cogent critique of the old view of industrial organization and of the tools that it has spawned (such as the Herfindahl index). One aspect of their criticism is to attack the narrow definition of industry on which concentration ratios and Herfindahl indices are based. Consider the concentration ratio for some product, say roasted coffee, in Table 11.1. The four-firm ratio rose from 52 to 61 to 65 between 1963 and 1982, and to 66 between 1982 and 1987. Does this mean that the industry is becoming more concentrated and less competitive? Critics argue that such a conclusion is potentially spurious on a number of grounds. A major problem with concentration ratios as a measure of competition is that they ignore the fact that competition takes place on many margins. Tea, soft drinks, beer, wine, and a host of other products compete for the coffee drinker's dollar. Substitute products abound for most items. "Cereal breakfast foods" — listed as an industry by the Commerce Department — meet competition from a myriad of other sources. Although the four firm concentration ratio for cereal breakfast foods was 87 in 1987 (it was 99 for the eight firms!), the ratio itself gives a totally inaccurate picture of actual competition in the breakfast-food market. Bread, eggs, bacon, fruit, fast foods of many kinds and varieties substitute for cereal at breakfast. Sales concentration has no predictable link with actual competition, and any simple assessment of the "number of powerful firms in the market" also fails to provide such a link.

Even if the Commerce Department's industry classification scheme has merit in identifying a closed market with few important "outside" substitutes, such as tobacco products, the implied analogy to competitive conditions is questionable. The concentration ratio may mask extremely vigorous competition between firms in any given market. The eighth-largest firm (in terms of sales) may readily move up to fourth place, the number-one firm may, as a result of effective competition, fall to the number-three slot, and so on. Competition, or rather the competitive process, may thus be viable and alive in particular markets, in spite of a high concentration ratio.

Advertising and the Market Process. Focusing on the number of firms in an industry, together with some indication of the relative importance of these firms (through sales, employment, or some other indicator), means viewing competition in static, partial-equilibrium terms. (Such a view seems to apply to a large portion of the antitrust laws; see Highlight 11.2.) As valuable as these

---

Highlight 11.2   *The Robinson-Patman Act and Microeconomic Theory: Restricting Competition by Law*

One of the most obvious confrontations between the antitrust laws and modern economic notions of market structure is called the Robinson-Patman Act. Passed in 1936 as a "Depression-inspired" piece of legislation, the act was a populist measure against the growing chain-store movement, which was proving harmful to the less-efficient small retailers. The law states that discrimination in price is unlawful between different purchasers of goods of like grade and quality where the effect *may* be to lessen competition in some substantial manner or to create a monopoly. If the price difference is due to differences in cost or if the seller offered a lower price in "good faith" to meet a competitor's price, the discrimination is not illegal.

Although the law seems straightforward enough, many microeconomists condemn it as anticompetitive. As we have already seen in Chapter 9, some forms of price discrimination may actually *increase* output. To the extent that this happens, consumer welfare could be increased. Therefore, there is a persistent objection that the Act actually has anticompetitive effects and reduces consumer welfare. To see this, consider a firm that cuts price in one geographic market in order to compete with a local rival. Is such behavior predatory and anticompetitive in nature, or are we merely observing the competitive process in action?

In order to answer this important question, it is only necessary to analyze the classic case brought under the Act: the Utah Pie Case of 1967.[a] Utah Pie sued Continental Baking Company, the Carnation Company, and the Pet Milk Company for price discrimination in the Salt Lake City area. Utah Pie built plants in Salt Lake City in 1957 and quickly established a huge market share in the frozen pie market: Pet, Carnation, and Continental (national producers), producing pies in California for the Salt Lake City market, responded by cutting prices below the prices they charged elsewhere. However, Utah Pie continued to charge the lowest price. Market shares over the relevant period were as follows:

	1958	1959	1960	1961
Utah Pie	67%	34%	46%	45%
Pet	16	36	28	29
Carnation	10	9	12	9
Continental	1	3	2	8
Others	6	19	13	8

The effect of this competition was a downward trend in prices. The structure of average pie prices were as follows:

	Early 1958	1961
Utah Pie	$4.15	$2.75
Pet	4.92	3.46
Carnation	4.82	3.30
Continental	5.00	2.85

In spite of such evidence, the Supreme Court (incredibly) ruled for Utah Pie. Even though Utah Pie maintained a large market share, continued to make a profit, and continued to charge the lowest price, the Court ruled that there was damage to competition. Note that proof of *actual* injury to competition is not necessary under the **Robinson-Patman Act.** The courts can award treble damages for a violation if a plaintiff merely shows that there is a "reasonable possibility" that price differences "may" have such an effect.

Modern microeconomists dealing with market structure see this law (and other laws) as a welfare program for small and inefficient businesses. The actions of Pet, Carnation, and Continental are rivalrous and competitive in nature. Indeed, Utah Pie had led some of the price decreases in the Salt Lake City market. The law, in the opinion of most, is blatantly anticompetitive and inimical to consumer welfare and economic efficiency.

[a] *Utah Pie Co. v. Continental Baking Co.,* 386 U.S. 685, 699 (1967).

models are, accuracy suffers when competition is not viewed as a "rivalrous" activity. In this view, as we have already seen to some extent, practices such as advertising lose much of their character as a barrier to entry. Advertising — like other big and sunk investments — can be a barrier to entering certain markets, especially consumer product markets with well-known brands. But advertising may also serve as a means for efficient entry into a market by providing information that would encourage consumers to switch from traditional products to newer ones. Viewing consumers as hapless tools of advertisers supports the idea that advertising primarily (like high capital requirements) protects markets from competition. Alternatively, advertising may be depicted as a tool for providing information to the consumers — information on which consumers may base rational decisions that have the power to erode monopoly power and the sales of incumbent firms. Careful empirical analysis is required to assess the effects of advertising in particular cases.

Monopoly and Efficiency

An important question that is ignored in the literature on the structure, conduct, and performance relates to the sheer size of firms. Is "bigness" necessarily a signal of damage to society? The old view holds that concentration necessarily inhibits consumer welfare through output and price controls.

Figure 11.3 The Potential Advantages of Monopoly

A monopolist, through superior efficiency, may be able to reduce production costs from P_C to MC_m. If so, economic welfare under monopoly may be greater than under the competitive alternative.

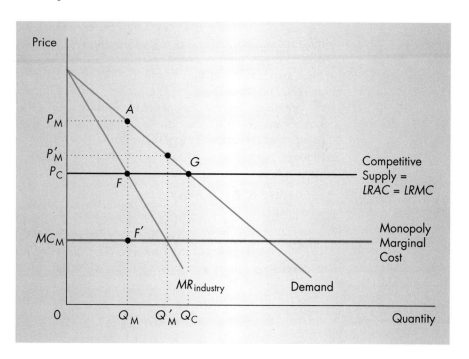

A newer view, held by many economists, proposes that size per se is no index of inefficiency.[4] In short, there is a meaningful and real tradeoff between any output restrictions and welfare reductions that come from market power and the efficiency-creating lower costs created by size.

This view is illustrated in simple terms in Figure 11.3. The figure contrasts competitive and monopoly organization with a given demand for some product. Under competitive conditions, supply produces a price of P_C and an output of Q_C. Competitive supply corresponds to the $LRMC$ ($= LRAC$) function under simplifying assumptions. The substitution of monopoly for competition in the market (in the old view) would have deleterious welfare effects on consumers. Given that costs remained at competitive levels after monopolization, the deadweight loss triangle would amount to AFG when price is raised to P_M and output curtailed to Q_M. In this case consumer welfare is transferred to the monopolist in the amount of monopoly profits ($P_C P_M AF$), and society is the net loser.

4. See, in particular, Robert H. Bork, *The Antitrust Paradox: A Policy at War with Itself* (New York: Basic Books, 1978).

Newer microanalytic thinking focuses on competition as a rivalrous process. The new view revises the traditional scenario in several important respects. Firms in oligopolistic industries could not raise prices above costs over any appreciable period without some kind of superior efficiencies. Without these efficiencies, competing firms would enter, eroding supernormal profits and, in the process, decentralizing the industry. A market process always pits efficiency from increased size against the market restrictions and welfare reductions that size creates. Cost reductions are associated with higher industry concentrations — that is, with larger firm size.

The potential relevance of size efficiencies may be illustrated with Figure 11.3. If more large-scale firms are also more efficient, cost curves will fall below what they would be under competition. These efficiencies mean a reduction in costs to MC_M. (Demand is assumed to remain steady as firms grow in size and concentration.) Assuming output restrictions to Q_M, the lower costs of the bigger firms create cost efficiencies in the amount $P_C FF'MC_M$. (In fact, a price-maximizing monopolist would increase output to Q'_M and lower price to P'_M.) These cost efficiencies must be compared with the loss in consumer surplus due to monopoly (area AFG) in order to compare a few concentrated firms (or just one) with a large number of decentralized firms in any given industry.[5]

Microeconomics and Vertical Integration

Skepticism about static models of market structure by adherents to the "new" microanalytics of industry structure carries over to issues of vertical integration. **Vertical integration** is the formal or informal relationship between firms at successive levels of production or distribution. Full integration connotes full ownership of the upstream input or manufacturing stage of production and of the downstream, final good or retail marketing of the product. The fully integrated firm is *one* firm in a legal and contractual sense. If, for example, Exxon manufactures gasoline from raw oil inputs, transports it through Exxon-owned facilities, and sells gas through Exxon filling stations at the corner of your block, the firm would be said to be fully integrated.

Many other arrangements are possible, however. Manufacturers or sellers of fine china, gasoline, breakfast cereals, toothpaste, motel services, or almost any product must choose how to assemble, manufacture, and market their goods. Rather than buy certain raw-material inputs through contractual affiliation, firms may choose to own raw-material suppliers outright. In lieu of full downstream ownership of service-station retailers, Exxon may determine the optimal locations of filling stations in a city or state and franchise the Exxon emblem (and gasoline) to separate owners of the stations. The examples

5. There is, of course, an issue related to the possible redistribution of income from consumers to producers. The redistribution may matter to society, but economists are primarily concerned with increasing the total net gain.

from such items as fast foods, low-price motels, and carpet cleaning are even more obvious. The firms are related by rigid or loose contractual arrangements of some kind. In these cases, either upstream or downstream independent firms purchase inputs (burger patties, napkins) or outputs (Wedgewood china, Exxon gasoline) from other firms in return for specified obligations. These obligations may include selling a product only in a prespecified territory or at some minimum or maximum price. (Some of these arrangements might be deemed illegal, as we will see later in this section.) The obligations may be to purchase a certain minimum or maximum quantity of the product for resale or to advertise and provide sales promotion or after-purchase service to customers.

A Simple Model of Vertical Integration

Although the number of actual forms of vertical integration is infinite, a simple model can show market interrelationships between integrated firms. Figure 11.4 is based on an upstream firm and a downstream firm existing in some given market. For our purposes it does not really matter whether the upstream firm is a raw-material input and the downstream firm is the final-product manufacturer or whether the upstream firm simply wholesales a final product to a downstream retail seller. Assume, further, that both firms exhibit no economies or diseconomies of scale, and that their average costs equal their marginal costs ($AC_U = MC_U$, $AC_D = MC_D$), as shown in Figure 11.4.

First assume, with reference to the figure, that both stages are competitive and that they are independent of one another. The competitive result is achieved when the two (independent) average- and marginal-cost curves are added together to give $AC_{total} = MC_{total}$. Price for competitive upstream and downstream arrangements is equal to $0T(0D + 0U)$ in Figure 11.4 and quantity is at Q_C.

An interesting question arises from both a theoretical and a policy viewpoint when one of the stages is not competitive. If *either* the upstream or the downstream stage is monopolized and there is **full ownership integration** of the two stages, output falls to Q_M and price rises to the monopoly level, $0M$. One firm equates marginal cost and marginal revenue to maximize profits — shown at monopoly level $TMGF$ in Figure 11.4. But what happens if one of the two stages is monopolized and the firms are fully independent of one another?

Suppose that the upstream firm is a monopoly and the downstream firm is competitive and that the market is characterized by perfect information. The upstream firm simply charges the downstream firm a unit price equal to $(0M - 0D)$ or DM. When aggregate average costs are added together by the downstream firm, they are equivalent to AC_M or $0D + DM$. The price charged for the product is $0M$, and the upstream monopolist extracts a total of $TMGF$ in monopoly profits from the market, the same as if the firms were totally

Figure 11.4 A Graphical Model of Vertical Integration

If the upstream and downstream stages of production are both organized competitively, the equilibrium price will be $0T$ and the equilibrium quantity will be Q_C. If either of the stages is monopolized, the price will rise to $0M$ and output will fall to Q_M regardless of whether vertical integration is permitted.

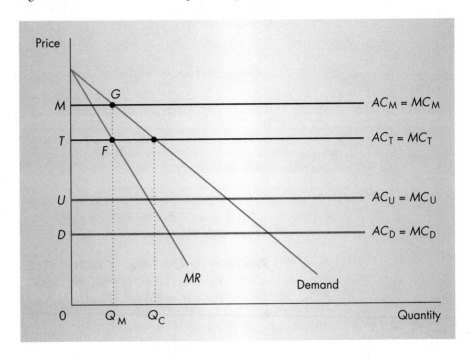

integrated. Using simple logic, the same result holds true if the downstream firm is the independent monopolist.[6] The lesson: monopoly at one stage of production usually means a monopoly result in the market, notwithstanding actual ownership arrangements. Further, **divestiture** — where stages of production are split by antitrust authorities — will not do any good. The monopoly outcome will prevail.[7]

6. If the downstream firm is the monopoly, a monopoly price $0M$ will be calculated and total profits will be $TMGF$, the same as if the upstream firm were a monopoly or if there were full integration. If both firms were independent and monopolies, a bilateral monopoly bargaining situation would result.

7. See Joseph J. Spengler, "Vertical Integration and Antitrust Policy," *Journal of Political Economy* 58 (1950) for the original statement of the model in the text. These results must be modified when there are economies or diseconomies of scale. See Roger D. Blair and David L. Kaserman, "Optimal Franchising," *Southern Economic Journal* 48 (1982) and "Vertical Control with Variable Proportions: Ownership Integration and Contractual Equivalents," *Southern Economic Journal* 46 (1980).

The Legal Treatment of Vertical Integration

There are many forms of integration, as we noted earlier. The selection of any particular form, however, will usually be related to the minimization of cost. Why, for example, would Holiday Inns of America choose to franchise its name, architectural design, and other features to retail franchise buyers rather than establish and fully own its inns throughout the nation? Why would you, as a lawyer or a medical professional, hire "temporary" typing services rather than contract for a regular typist position within your firm? The simple answer is the correct one: it is cheaper to do so. You will choose to hire out, rent, or fully integrate on the basis of cost minimization.

Many other arrangements that at first appear monopolistic or restrictive of competition are often the result of cost minimization. These are the so-called price and nonprice vertical restraints that are forbidden or severely limited by antitrust laws and the courts. **Vertical restraints** are composed of a number of possible arrangements and agreements between firms (manufacturers and wholesalers, manufacturers and retailers, franchisors and franchisees, and so on) that limit marketing options in return for specific services. Consider the two most common forms of restraints: price restraints or resale price maintenance (RPM) and exclusive territories as a downstream nonprice restraint.

Resale Price Maintenance (RPM) and Nonprice Restraints. The courts have, for many decades, roundly condemned the practice called **resale price maintenance**, or RPM. RPM is simply a manufacturer's requirement for downstream sellers (often retailers) *not* to sell products at prices lower than some stipulated level. The use of such practices has been declared per se illegal by the federal courts as a form of restrictive (and noncompetitive) price fixing.

Likewise, restraints on downstream firms may be regarded as "nonprice" in nature. One of the most common forms of such restraints is the provision of **exclusive territories** to wholesalers or retailers in some given area. Some very common examples exist in the beer and automobile industries, in which downstream wholesalers (in beer) and retailers (in automobiles) are restricted to sell within given areas of cities or other geographic regions. This practice has met mixed reactions in the courts.

What microeconomic rationale(s) could justify such arrangements? Why would upstream manufacturers want to keep retail prices high if profit maximization was their goal? Wouldn't their sales rise if retailers engaged in discounting? Why would you give some retailer an exclusive territory from which to sell your product? Wouldn't sales be maximized if firms (selling Budweiser or Miller beer) were able to price-compete for customers in overlapping sales territories? Wouldn't consumers be harmed by each of these "restrictive" practices?

The answer being given by a number of economists is that, when the *full value* of the product to consumers is considered, neither price restraints nor nonprice restraints can be easily condemned. To understand why requires a careful consideration of the role of advertising.

The Role of Advertising. Economic efficiency may be achieved with nonprice restraints if local firms can more cheaply create and place local advertising for national brands. Without a guaranteed exclusive local territory local firms would have little or no incentive to promote or advertise. Why? Other firms would "free ride" on the firm or firms that advertise. This means that they would cash in on the benefits of the advertising (by increased sales of the product) but would not have to incur costs to do so. The result would be less-than-optimal advertising of the product from the perspective of the manufacturer, that is, less-than-maximum profits. In addition, consumers would suffer from too little advertising, which is a principal means of acquiring price and nonprice information about goods and the conditions of sale.

Free Riding, "Discounts," and Promotion. The question of **free riding** is interrelated with the production of other services as well. Wholesalers and retailers perform many other tasks for manufacturers. These "promotional investments" might include training of salespersons, the provision of attractively decorated showrooms of adequate size, delivery and repair services, stock maintenance of the final product and replacement parts, after-purchase service, and a host of other tasks and duties. We are all familiar with these promotional investments, and, at least implicitly, we all recognize the inherent problem to sellers of such products. What is to prevent some discount sellers — Kmart, Wal-Mart, and a host of others — from letting customers and potential customers go first to a full-service dealer to get expert advice about competing products and then selling the product at a lower nominal price? The discount price does not reflect the cost of providing all of the presale information and services that are often associated with products.

Free-riding behavior permits a discounter to sell a product at a nominal price that is lower than the full price that the consumer would be willing to pay. The difference between nominal and full price is made up for by those merchants who increase the valuation of the good to consumers through advertising, demonstrations, and so on. When these services are not bundled with the product, discount retailers (or wholesalers) have every incentive to price-compete, often driving the full-service sellers out of business in the long run. The establishment of RPM and exclusive territories is an attempt to prevent such "free riding" and to support increased full value of products or services to consumers. Note that such price and nonprice restraints apply only to **in-brand competition** (Chevrolet versus Chevrolet), not to **interbrand competition** (Chevrolet against Ford or Nissan). Such restrictions provide incentives for dealers of products to provide high-quality service. Although RPM limits price competition, it provides a mechanism by which active full-price competition may take place. Critics of such practices suggest that they are simply attempts to monopolize. Modern microeconomic theory suggests that such restraints may be in the welfare interests of all parties to exchange — manufacturers, retailers, and consumers as well.[8] (For one case study of geographical restraints among wholesalers, see Highlight 11.3.)

Highlight 11.3   *Exclusive Distribution of Beer: The Strange Case of Indiana*

Most economists believe that, in general, markets tend to evolve in the direction of economic efficiency. Unregulated and otherwise unfettered markets, in other words, are expected to provide competitive prices and optimal levels of service and quality. This evolution takes on many forms, in a seemingly infinite number of variations on market structure. One of the most interesting and misunderstood variations deals with so-called vertical restraints. As noted earlier, vertical restraints are simply any terms, agreements, or contracts between a manufacturer and a distributor-wholesaler of a product that specify the conditions under which the product can be sold at wholesale and retail. These terms may include minimum price or quality standards, the requirement that distributors provide certain services to customers, the assignment of exclusive territories for purposes of sale, or a combination of such conditions.

The argument that vertical restraints are procompetitive is straightforward and is based on free-rider effects. Economic logic suggests that no given manufacturer would choose a distribution system in which quality and point-of-sale services would seriously deteriorate. The reason is that sales would decline. Exclusive distributors are, because of the free-rider problem, necessary to control the quality of some *final* products. For example, full-service dealers who provide technical data about product performance, warranty terms, and so on, would be injured if customers were able to make their purchase decision at one location and then buy from a nearby dealer who, because it did not supply such ancillary services, could sell the same product at a discount. The argument applies, *mutatis mutandis* (Latin for "the differences having been considered"), to the sale of intermediary products. A distributor dealing with retail stores that buy from multiple suppliers of the same item will lose incentive to rotate stocks, to carry sufficient inventory in order to meet normal (or special) customer demands, to participate in promoting and developing brands, and to provide informational services to retailers. Exclusive distributorships also encourage sales and service to small retailers and permit wider brand selection and the introduction of new brands to consumers.

---

8. The fundamental study of the competitive advantages of nonprice vertical restraints is Lester Telser, "Why Should Manufacturers Want Fair Trade?," *Journal of Law and Economics* 3 (1960). Also see Howard Marvel, "Exclusive Dealing," *Journal of Law and Economics* 25 (1982).

The marketing and sale of individual brands of beer through the vertical device of exclusive territories has been the choice of beer manufacturers for many decades. Forty-nine states either mandate or permit such systems, whereas one state and one state only, Indiana, prohibits them. Economists, therefore, are given a unique case study to assess the effects of the absence of exclusive territories on efficiency and consumer welfare.

Prior to 1967, Indiana wholesalers rarely sold out of their own territories. Then the *Schwinn* decision was handed down by the Supreme Court.[a] This decision found exclusive territories to be illegal per se and held that the use of nonprice restraints, such as exclusive territories, in any market was unlawful. After this decision, several Indiana wholesalers began to "transship" — to sell beer outside their territories. After *Schwinn* but before the *Sylvania* decision (which overruled *Schwinn*), the Indiana Alcoholic Beverage Commission adopted an administrative rule (Rule 28) prohibiting brewers from granting an exclusive territory to a beer wholesaler.[b] Therefore, transshipping of beer has proceeded apace in Indiana.

The effects of transshipping have been dramatic. In 1970 there were approximately 200 beer wholesalers in Indiana. By 1986 that number had shrunk to 122, and in 1990 there were about 75. The reduction in the number of competitive wholesalers in specific locales is even more telling. In 1977, prior to the rapid growth of transshipping, Indianapolis had seven beer wholesalers. In 1990, it had only two. Lake County, near Chicago, the second-most-populous area of the state has only one wholesaler, and other high-population areas (Lafayette and Muncie, for example) have none.

The increase in transshipping has clearly destroyed a large number of traditional wholesalers. From an economic perspective, transshipping is eliminating the market's ability to provide services to manufacturers as well as to retailers and final consumers. These events are occurring in predictable fashion: Single-brand, traditional wholesalers are caught in a cost-price squeeze. Costs of providing retailers *of all sizes* with services such as regular (and irregular) delivery, stock rotation, retail-shelf placement, special products such as draft beer, new-product introductions, and promotions must be borne by traditional wholesalers in the face of transshippers who charge lower prices but who do not provide these services in optimal amounts if they provide them at all.

[a] *U.S.* v. *Arnold, Schwinn and Co.*, 388 U.S. 365 (1967). Although the legal rule has been relaxed, criticisms of nonprice vertical restraints continue.

[b] *Continental T.V.* v. *GTE Sylvania* 433 U.S. 36 (1977). In this decision, the legality or illegality of exclusive territories was judged by the "rule of reason." The Court argued that exclusive distributorships could be procompetitive in some industries, citing the free-rider problem and some of the quality benefits that can be induced by the assignment of exclusive territorial agreements. This opinion was furthered in 1982 by the Federal Trade Commission's decision in the *Beltone* case, which held that exclusive territories "may increase local merchandising, promotion and service activities of wholesalers, and might increase output" (*Beltone Electronics Corp.*, FTC 68 [1982]).

Because Indiana statutes require beer wholesalers to provide the same price to all customers, traditional wholesalers have an incentive to reduce service to all accounts and, most particularly, to reduce or eliminate service and sales to small, unprofitable (less than ten-case) accounts. Retail outlets of some brands are reduced or eliminated, thereby diminishing consumer choice and welfare. Wholesalers who earlier had incentives to seek out and service new accounts, especially small accounts with growth potential, no longer have a strong reason to engage in these activities. The prohibition of exclusive territories in Indiana has had and will continue to have predictable effects in the beer market:

1. a reduction in consumer choice and welfare from the restricted retail availability of brands, indicating a higher full price for beer to consumers,
2. a reduction in some brand sales and a decline in interbrand competition at retail because of disincentives of wholesalers to promote brands,
3. reduced quality of service to retailers.

In short, it is difficult to understand how transshipping is in anyone's interest — consumers, retailers, traditional wholesalers, or manufacturers — save those of the large multi- or all-brand transshippers themselves.

Markets and Regulation

New views of microeconomic theory have upset traditional views of antitrust policy. In addition, they have transformed economic assessments of regulated markets. An "old" view of regulation — one that places the existence of natural monopoly at the center of the case for regulation — is being replaced by a "new" view centered in broader notions of competition.

Natural Monopoly and the Traditional Approach to Regulation

The fundamental idea of antitrust revolves around the notion that competition could exist in a market. In this view, competition is "thwarted" by combinations in restraint of trade, by untoward mergers, by collusive price fixing (including price discrimination), and by other noncompetitive business practices. The thrust and intent of antitrust policy, whether or not it has had such results, is to *restore* competition to these markets by interventions on behalf of competition. The rationale for regulation is quite different. It is an explicit admission that, because of conditions of natural monopoly or some other kind of market failure, competition cannot exist. Thus some of the outcomes of perfect competition must be imposed on an industry by an administrative body of regulators.

Regulation and the Natural-Monopoly Argument. The familiar natural-monopoly argument rests on the following logic: Because unit (average) costs for each and every firm fall over output spans great enough to serve the entire market, mergers will take place until a monopolist "naturally" emerges. Although a single firm could in this case be an efficient supplier to the entire market, the unregulated firm will eschew competitive price and output levels and will "naturally" raise price and reduce quantities to monopoly levels. Thus some form of administrative control is necessary in order to achieve competitive efficiency.

The familiar argument is set out simply in Figure 11.5. Here the long-run average-cost and long-run marginal-cost curves of one firm fall over a large span of output, intersecting the market demand curve at points E and F, respectively. The underlying logic of the natural-monopoly argument is clear: The firm (indeed, each firm) has an incentive to expand output because the unit cost of all units produced declines with such increases. Once market dominance is achieved, however, the firm will decrease output to Q_M and raise price to P_M in order to maximize profits. Whether scale economies leading to natural monopoly exist in any given industry is debatable. Evidence on this issue is mixed, so economists differ as to the actual presence of such economies

Figure 11.5 Natural Monopoly Regulation

An unregulated monopolist would charge a price of P_M and sell Q_M units of output. It might be possible to improve efficiency by regulating the firm and requiring it to charge a lower price of P_{AC} or P_{MC}.

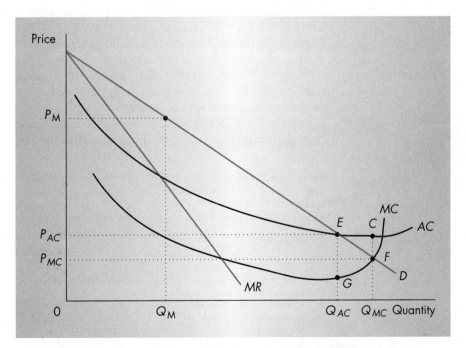

in any particular case. What is *not* debatable is that the argument, until very recently, has been at the base of much utility regulation at the federal, state, and local levels.[9]

Marginal-Cost Pricing and Regulation. If regulation were to become a substitute for competition and if competitive efficiency were the criterion on which to base rates for utilities or other services, regulators should impose a marginal-cost solution. With respect to Figure 11.5, the regulatory agency would force the firm to price at P_{MC} to produce Q_{MC}. But this solution is clearly not feasible under private property ownership. The firm would be *forced* to take losses of *CF* per unit (see Figure 11.5) and would be able to sue the government for confiscation of property without due process of law under the Fifth and Fourteenth Amendments to the Constitution. Either the firm would have to be nationalized, or subsidies equal to the firm's losses would have to be paid.[10]

Regulation and Average-Cost Pricing. In many countries, natural monopolies have been either nationalized or provided with government subsidies in order to allow the use of **marginal-cost pricing.** However, U.S. regulatory policy has been to set price equal to **average cost** across *all* markets within a single regulated firm so that total costs equal total revenue. In Figure 11.5 such a solution is depicted at P_{AC} and Q_{AC}. By setting the price equal to P_{AC}, the regulatory agency allows the regulated firm sufficient revenue to cover all its costs, which include a normal "profit" on its investment.[11] In this fashion, the requirement of a subsidy is eliminated.

On the surface, this type of regulation appears quite sensible. There is some inefficiency because the price exceeds the marginal cost (this inefficiency is represented by triangle *EFG* in Figure 11.5), but this loss may be quite small.

Despite its apparent potential, this type of regulation has not worked particularly well. One major problem with allowing the regulated firm to charge a price equal to its average cost is that the firm has little or no incentive to keep its costs as low as possible. If the regulated firm intentionally allows its costs to be higher than those represented by the average-cost curve in Figure 11.5, the

9. We do not wish to imply that this is the *only* justification for regulation. Other kinds of market failure — externalities and common pool problems — explain the source of much regulation, including environmental regulation that inspired the Occupational Safety and Health Administration (OSHA) and the Environmental Protection Agency (EPA).

10. Interested readers might wish to work through the classic paper by Harold Hotelling, "The Relation of Prices to Problems of Taxation and Railway and Utility Rates," *Econometrica* 7 (1939).

11. When the allowable rate of return exceeds the actual cost of capital, a number of inefficiencies may be built into regulation: see Harvey Averch and Leland L. Johnson, "Behavior of the Firm Under Regulatory Constraint," *American Economic Review* 52 (December 1962).

regulatory response will be to allow the price to increase to cover the unnecessarily high costs. In the extreme, costs might be allowed to rise so much that the regulated price exceeds the unregulated monopoly price P_M. Accordingly, this type of regulation has succeeded in preventing natural monopolies from earning economic profits, but it has not been nearly as successful in keeping down prices to consumers.

A second major problem inherent in natural-monopoly regulation is that it has protected incumbent firms and industries from competition by new firms using new technologies. The railroads may have been a natural monopoly early in their history. However, by the 1930s trucking and barge companies had developed the potential to provide stiff competition for the railroads. Not long afterward, air transportation also emerged as a viable competitor. The emergence of these competing modes of transportation should have brought an end to railroad regulation. Instead, the regulatory authorities reacted by protecting the railroads from this competition by imposing minimum-price regulations on the new competitors. Such protections create massive inefficiencies and maldistribution of resources. Most particularly, modern theories of regulation have emphasized the *political* nature of the regulatory process.[12] Vote-collecting incumbent politicians are willing to supply, and business and industry have a positive demand for, regulation *completely apart from any issues of natural monopoly*. Trade regulation at the local level, most professional regulation (nurses, physicians, lawyers, and so on), and regulation of morticians and funeral directors would be difficult to explain without recourse to political and private-interest interaction.

Other economists minimize the impact of "politics" on the regulatory process, at least in particular markets. They argue that some forms of regulated pricing — using incentive schemes and multipart tariffs — have potential in promoting consumer welfare. As usual, empirical analysis must establish the benefits and costs of particular institutional arrangements concerning the supply of particular goods and services.

Franchising

Market **franchising** has become a popular method of "loose" vertical integration in private markets. In public markets, especially at the local level, franchising has been implemented in place of regulation or government operation for a number of "public" services. Fire-protection service, cable-television services, water supply, garbage collection, and a number of other common items are "let out" for public bidding in some cities across the United States. Scottsdale,

---

12. For the basic discussion of the public interest theory of regulation, see George J. Stigler, "The Theory of Economic Regulation," *Bell Journal of Economics and Management Science* (Spring 1971) and Sam Peltzman, "Toward a More General Theory of Regulation," *Journal of Law and Economics* (August 1976).

Figure 11.6 Franchise Bidding for a Natural Monopoly

Some cities issue franchises for the right to operate natural monopolies. If the bidding is based on the willingness to provide service at the lowest price, a bid of P_{AC} will be the winner. Bidders would be willing to pay up to $P_M FGA$ dollars for the franchise rights if they were then free to charge any price — that is, the monopoly price P_M.

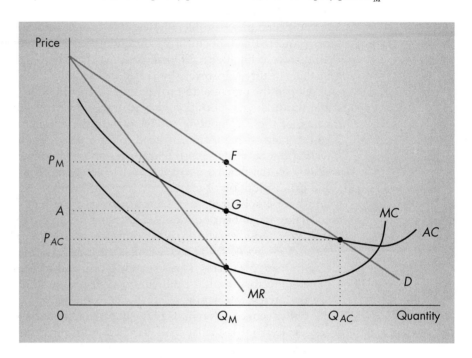

Arizona is famous as a contemporary example, but examples of such methods of supplying "public" goods go back many centuries.[13]

The microanalytics of such bidding for the entire "field of service" are straightforward. First, government must possess the property rights to supply some good or service. Once the rights to supply are secured by government, the government may attempt to supply the good itself or it may auction off the rights to supply the good or service for a limited period of time. In such an auction, the right to provide the service goes to the firm offering to do so at the lowest price. Suppose that the demand and the production costs are those represented by Figure 11.6. Further assume that there is an elastic supply of competitive bidders who are willing to supply the municipality with these services. For the competitive bidding process to work, resources used in the

---

13. The idea is a very old one: see Edwin Chadwick, "Results of Different Principles of Legislation and Administration in Europe; of Competition for the Field, as Compared with Competition within the Field of Service," *Royal Statistical Society Journal* (1859).

production process must be available to all bidders at competitive market prices, and the cost of collusion among the actual and potential bidders must be prohibitively high.[14]

Given these assumptions and depending on the bidding method chosen, several solutions may result. If bidders were required to serve all willing demanders, the winning bid would be P_{AC} in Figure 11.6, because economic profits would exist at any higher price. Such a process would approximate competitive price and output levels. (Recall that these would not be the same as *marginal*-cost pricing.) A more cynical solution would occur if the municipality set up a process with no absolute requirement to serve and asked for lump-sum amounts from bidders, with the franchise as a "prize." In this case, bidders would be willing to offer an amount $AP_{M}FG$ for the franchise. This is the largest amount that the government could bring into the public coffers. Naturally, there would be a welfare loss to consumers of the good or service from such a bidding-contracting structure, which generates a monopoly outcome.

Critics of franchise bidding point to the related problems of resource duplication and to the inability to devise a long-term optimal contract between government and the winning bidder. In terms of contracting, for example, it may be impossible to devise a contract in which all important potential sources of dispute are covered. If some sort of "board" must be set up to administer complex contracts, critics say, the whole franchise-bidding apparatus begins to look like traditional cost-plus regulation. In this view it is not obvious that franchising avoids the major problems of regulation.

Defenders of public franchising argue that resource duplication, capital transfers, and other problems that are supposed to be associated with franchise bidding may be handled with appropriate market arrangements. Critics claim that the problem of duplication lies primarily in the means of transporting the product to the final consumer. The extensive network of power lines running from the production source to the consumer in the case of the utility industry is an obvious case in point (the same may be true of cable TV lines). The problem may be solved, perhaps, by auctioning off rights to use such public facilities in the same manner as many states auction off the rights to supply services at state parks and state office buildings.

Whether or not franchising would work as an alternative to traditional regulation (that is, administration of firms or an industry on a cost-plus basis) in all cases is problematical. Surely, it works in *some* cases of federal, state, and local "public" service provisions. Governments routinely let out infrastructure constructions, defense, and space-related hardware and facilities contracts to low-cost bidders. Virtually all local governments supply some goods (cable TV, for example) using a franchising apparatus. As budgets tighten and as

14. The modern version of the idea originated with Harold Demsetz, "Why Regulate Utilities?," *Journal of Law and Economics* (April 1976).

government feels the pinch, lower costs and enhanced consumer welfare might be had by supplying more "public" goods through franchising. Sometimes such policies are identified with **privatization**, but in the case of franchising, government retains the property rights over supply. Many questions remain unanswered regarding the relative effectiveness of markets versus government ownership or regulation in providing goods and services to consumers. The debate is, of course, ongoing.

Contestable Markets and Laissez-Faire

As we have seen throughout this book, there is some tension between static, situational notions of competition and the dynamic, multidimensional view of the competitive process. In the latter view, product differentiation, quality variation, and all of the many elements of nonprice competition are considered important aspects of the competitive process. As noted in the first section of this chapter, a dispersion of prices for some good does not necessarily connote a noncompetitive situation. The idea that unregulated markets may function more efficiently than commonly thought is supported even more directly by microeconomic theory. Two related theoretical developments in this area are limit-entry pricing and contestable-market theory.

Limit-Entry Pricing. Consider a firm supplying some good under natural-monopoly conditions in a laissez-faire economy. As in Figure 11.7 and according to the logic we have described in this chapter, the firm might be tempted to restrict output and raise price to the monopoly level (corresponding to P_M and Q_M in Figure 11.7). But what if there are possible contenders for the market? If there are no barriers to entry, potential entrants are likely to enter the market if the price charged by the initial firm is greater than the average cost to the potential entrants. For that reason, the initial firm may adopt a different pricing policy. Rather than charging a price of P_M and attracting entry, the initial firm may opt for a price sufficiently low to deter entry. Assuming that potential entrants can produce at a cost of P_{LE}, that is the limit-entry price. By lowering the price from P_M to P_{LE}, the initial firm is able to deter entry by new firms.

The theory of **limit-entry pricing** suggests that a policy of allowing entry into natural-monopoly markets may achieve results similar to the idealized results of regulation. Relatively free entry may motivate the initial firm to charge a price similar to the regulated price. This policy may therefore yield most of the advantages of traditional regulation without entailing any of the serious disadvantages.

Contestable Markets. A related idea that gives support to the limit-entry pricing argument is **contestable-market theory**. Three contemporary economists — William J. Baumol, John C. Panzar, and Robert D. Willig — have shown that

Figure 11.7 Limit-Entry Pricing

If outside firms are permitted to enter the market and compete with a "natural monopolist," the monopolist might be motivated to lower the price (say to P_{LE}) to discourage new firms from entering the market. If so, the mere threat of entry may be sufficient to keep the price near the regulated price of P_{AC}.

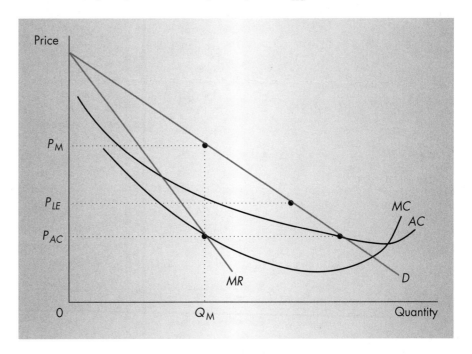

even if only one firm exists in a market, the competitive price may be charged and competitive output sold.[15] The market is said to be contestable if entry and exit are totally free (but not costless) to all potential firms. Rather than focusing on the old problem of natural monopoly, the idea of contestability centers on cost conditions within an industry.

Consider Figure 11.8, which is conceptually similar to Figure 11.7. If price is above the competitive level (P_C), say at P_S, entry will be assured, provided that potential entrants may come into the market on a par with the existing incumbent firm. Supernormal profits will generate entry into this market, forcing the former monopolist to reduce price. Either the former firm or the new entrant will then exit, because both firms would otherwise experience losses and exit is costless.

15. See William J. Baumol, John C. Panzar, and Robert D. Willig, *Contestable Markets and the Theory of Industry Structure* (New York: Harcourt Brace Jovanovich, 1982).

Figure 11.8 Contestable Markets

If a market is contestable, entry and exit are costless. In that event, new firms enter whenever the price exceeds the competitive level to take advantage of temporary profits.

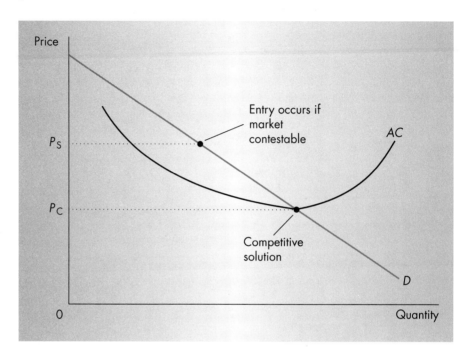

The entire argument for contestable markets rests on the nature of cost. In any line of business, costs may be "fixed" or they may be truly "sunk." Totally **sunk costs** are those with a zero opportunity cost — meaning that entry into some business would entail high nonrecoverable costs to investors. Once incurred, these costs are lost forever in the sense that they are irrecoverable. Some capital costs (for a dam or airport) and some "variable costs" (such as advertising) are said to have these properties. Such properties would obviously limit contestability and raise the price that incumbent firms could charge without encouraging entry. Many industries, however, are thought to be characterized more by fixed rather than sunk costs. In such cases (airlines are a good example), capital and equipment that might require millions of dollars in investment are not sunk in any realistic sense. Used airplanes and transport equipment are sold every day on secondary markets. As such, sunk costs are not thought to be an important problem in many industries, meaning that contestability may be a real possibility.

When combined with other elements in the competitive market process, limit pricing and contestability theory are replacing old notions of market "structure." In these microeconomic conceptions, the firm maximizes long-run profits while providing benefits very close to competitive levels. It is fair to note that long-run monopoly is not to be expected under laissez-faire conditions in any event. Monopoly power is the product of specific demand and cost conditions that are applicable at one point in time. Through time, demand may increase or technologically driven costs may decrease, permitting new entrants to the market. Alternative products or qualities of products may also alter the incumbent's elasticity of demand. In virtually all such cases, monopoly power (if any existed to begin with) deteriorates.

Although considerations such as those outlined here turn traditional competitive theory on its head, the study of static theories of market structure is nonetheless of great value. These theories have anchored analysts' thinking about markets for more than one hundred years. The more modern approach is a supplement of growing importance. The design of public policy, especially relating to antitrust and regulation, requires careful assessments of all elements in markets.

Summary

In this chapter we have discussed the policy implications of two contrasting views of markets. In the old view, a static theory of markets was developed. As a consequence, major emphasis was placed on the structure of an industry. Industries that were highly concentrated were viewed as incapable of performing well. Accordingly, adherents of the old view endorsed strict interpretation and enforcement of antitrust laws in an attempt to improve the structure of industries. Where it was impossible to change the structure of an industry or where it was unfeasible to do so (as in the case of natural monopoly), strict economic regulation was advocated.

The new view of markets emphasizes the dynamic nature of competition. Accordingly, less concern is placed on industrial structure so long as new firms are relatively free to enter markets. This view sheds new light on specific types of industry conduct such as advertising, price discrimination, and vertical mergers and restrictions by emphasizing their potential to increase market competition. As a consequence, adherents of the newer view are skeptical about using either antitrust enforcement or economic regulation to improve economic efficiency. Both policies are viewed as being essentially unnecessary, and are viewed as causing great potential harm.

This chapter treated a number of modern elements that affect full price and the competitive process and, ultimately, public policies that deal with antitrust and regulation. Specifically, we analyzed

- the role of information in the full-price calculations of individuals in any market structure,
- possibilities for nonoptimal trades in markets characterized by asymmetric information advantages held by sellers over buyers,
- some of the contrasts between old views and new views of antitrust policies,
- issues concerning forms of regulation, franchising, and deregulation that are raised by contemporary microeconomic theory.

Key Terms

consumer search	asymmetric information
adverse selection	moral hazard
market structure	structure-conduct-performance
concentration ratio	horizontal merger
Herfindahl-Hirschman index	Robinson-Patman Act
vertical integration	full ownership integration
divestiture	vertical restraint
resale price maintenance	exclusive territories
free riding	in-brand competition
interbrand competition	marginal-cost pricing
average-cost pricing	cost-plus regulation
franchising	privatization
limit-entry pricing	contestable market
sunk cost	

Sample Questions

Question

On the basis of concentration ratios presented in Table 11.1 for 1982, the cereal-breakfast-food industry (four-firm $CR = 86$, eight-firm $CR = 97$) and the flat glass industry (four-firm $CR = 85$, eight-firm $CR = 97$) appear to be nearly identical with regard to concentration. Does this mean that the two industries would necessarily have a similar Herfindahl index?

Answer

No. The following table shows *hypothetical* sales percentages for the firms in the two industries, which are consistent with the reported concentration ratios.

	FIRM									
Industry	#1	#2	#3	#4	#5	#6	#7	#8	#9	#10
Cereal	65	10	6	5	4	3	2	2	2	1
Glass	23	22	21	19	3	3	3	3	2	1

However, the Herfindahl index for the cereal industry is 4424, but for the flat-glass industry only 1856. The more equal the sales of the four largest firms, the next four largest firms, and so on, the smaller will be the Herfindahl index, given the four-firm and eight-firm concentration ratios.

Question

In the past twenty or so years, various election reforms have been implemented in the United States. One of these reforms is to limit campaign spending, which, in effect, is a limitation on political advertising. In arguing for this reform, proponents have contended that such limits reduce the advantage to incumbents. Do you agree?

Answer

Whether you agree or disagree should depend on whether you view advertising more as a barrier to entry or as a means of entry. The former view would suggest that, if allowed, incumbents will advertise heavily, making it nearly impossible for nonincumbents to capture a majority of the vote. The alternative view that advertising is a means of entry suggests that allowing challengers to advertise heavily makes it easier for them to succeed in overcoming the normal advantages of incumbency.

Questions for Review and Discussion

*1. When asymmetric information exists in a market, what are the consequences of a decrease in the price of the product? Explain.

2. What is the concentration ratio and what is its primary purpose?

*3. What is the basis for many economists' belief that the Robinson-Patman Act benefits small businesses and is anticompetitive?

4. The existence of monopoly and the resulting price increase from the competitive level are viewed in the static view as decreasing social welfare. How does the newer microanalytic view differ?

5. When full ownership integration exists and monopoly exists in production, which stage of production must be monopolized? What happens to output in this situation?

*6. Why do many full-service retailers argue in favor of exclusive territories?

7. Explain why modern microeconomic theorists maintain that price and nonprice vertical restraints may actually enhance the welfare of all parties to an exchange.

8. What is the focus of antitrust policy and how does this differ from the aim of regulation?

*9. What is the drawback of marginal-cost pricing in a natural-monopoly situation? How is the problem solved?

10. How is the regulatory process politicized? Is a license to practice medicine part of this process? What about the bar exam that lawyers must pass to practice law? Explain.

11. When the provision of a good or service is let out to bid, who holds the property rights to provide the good or service, and what assumptions must be made for a bidding process to occur?

*12. What pricing strategy might be adopted by a monopolist who faces the threat of entry? Explain this strategy and its goals.

13. What are sunk costs and how are they important in the context of contestable markets?

14. How does transshipping in the Indiana beer industry negatively affect other beer wholesalers? Why do some economists argue that exclusive territories are preferred in this case?

Problems for Analysis

1. "If other buyers of a product are well informed about the distribution of prices, you should spend little or no search time in buying that product." Agree or disagree.

2. Suppose that a new firm enters an industry and quickly becomes the industry's largest producer with 40 percent of the output. Assuming that the other firms in the industry continue to sell the same quantity as they did previously, what will happen to the four-firm concentration ratio? to the eight-firm concentration ratio? to the Herfindahl index?

3. Suppose that an industry is initially characterized by an upstream monopoly and by perfect competition in the downstream market. Suppose also that there are some cost savings associated with a vertical merger. (Refer to Figure 11.4, and assume that the upstream monopolist is able to perform the downstream activity at a cost that is one-half of the competitive cost $0D$.) How should consumers feel about the upstream monopolist acquiring the downstream competitors?

4. Suppose that you own a camera shop and find yourself spending a lot of time demonstrating various cameras to potential buyers, who then go out and purchase a camera for a lower price from a local discount store. Can you think of any ways of preventing the discounter from free-riding on the services you provide to customers?

*5. Traditional public-utility regulation consists of having the regulators constantly adjust prices so as to assure that the regulated firm can break even. With reference to Figure 11.5, this would consist of setting the price at P_{AC} and keeping it there until the firm experienced losses or economic profits, then the price would be adjusted upward or downward, respectively. An alternative type of regulation would be to set the price at P_{AC} and then keep it there for several years. Can you think of any advantages to the use of this alternative regulatory scheme? any disadvantages?

6. One way of making markets perform more efficiently is to make them more contestable. In the minds of many critics, certain "markets," such as public schools, the post office, and local cable television, are not functioning very efficiently. Is it possible to make these markets more contestable?

7. The insurance industry is under attack for using age, sex, and other factors in setting premiums. How would the adverse-selection problem be changed if insurance companies were compelled to charge uniform premiums for all buyers?

Resource Markets

12

Competitive Resource Markets

A market that commands a great deal of attention (especially among college seniors) is the job market. How much difficulty will graduates have finding a job? Will they be able to find employment in a desirable location? What will those jobs pay? These questions and many others are answered in the labor market, one of many resource markets.

Although resource markets vary in their particulars, certain basic principles underlie the operations of these markets. These basic principles can be organized using the market structures presented in Part IV of this text. At one extreme are competitive resource markets, in which homogeneous resources are traded between numerous buyers and sellers, each of which is free to enter or leave the market, and none of which is able to influence the market price. Moving away from this extreme takes us to imperfectly competitive resource markets, in which one or more of the characteristics of the perfectly competitive market are absent.[1] We will defer investigation of imperfectly competitive resource markets while we focus our attention on the operation of competitive resource markets. The objectives of this chapter are to develop an understanding of

- the nature of resource demand.
- firm and market demands for inputs.
- individual and market labor-supply curves.
- the unique characteristics of the labor market.
- the markets for nonhuman resources.

The Demand for Inputs

The demand for productive resources is fundamentally different from the demand concept that has thus far dominated our study of microeconomic analysis. Preceding chapters have dealt exclusively with consumer demands —

1. For example, a market in which there is one seller of a resource would be a monopoly. A market with just one buyer of a resource is a monopsony.

the demands for finished goods and services. Consumer demand is based on the utility that comes from the consumption of products and is derived from constrained utility maximization, or optimizing behavior. Resources, on the other hand, do not make direct contributions to individual utility. The demand for resources is based on their indirect contributions to the process of satisfying human wants. Although much of this section on the demand for resources refers to the employment of labor, the principles developed apply to the demand for all resources.

The Derived Demand for Inputs

The demand for an input is a **derived demand**. It is derived from the demand for the good or service that is produced using the resource. There are demands for accountants, robot welding machinery, oil, and other productive resources, because consumers have demands for the goods and services produced with the aid of these resources. If the demand for a product disappears, the demand for resources used to produce the product also disappears. For example, the demand for machinery used to press vinyl record albums has all but disappeared as the compact disc has become the music-industry standard.

The derived demand for inputs is grounded in the profit-seeking behavior of producers. Two factors figure prominently in this behavior and serve as the basis for the demand for inputs:

1. *The productivity of the input.* Because the input is demanded for the output that it produces, the greater the productivity of the input, the greater the desire for the input. Because economic decisions are made at the margin, the marginal product of the input will be involved in explaining the demand for inputs.
2. *The revenues from selling the product.* These revenues affect the profitability of purchasing/employing resources and determine the quantity of a resource demanded.

The manner in which these two factors interact to define the demand for a resource is revealed by considering the demand for a resource by a profit-seeking firm.

Firm Demand

The competitive marketplace puts a number of constraints on firms operating in the market. Firms operating in competitive *product* markets (discussed in Part IV) must contend with large numbers of buyers and sellers of homogeneous outputs. This turns the firms into price takers, accepting the market price for each unit of output that it produces. The only factors subject to firm control are (1) the level of output to produce and (2) the quantities of resources necessary to produce the output.

This chapter is concerned with competitive *resource* markets. Firms facing competition in a resource market must contend with large numbers of buyers and sellers of a homogeneous resource. The homogeneity of inputs and the large number of market participants leaves everyone a price taker. Resources are traded at market-determined prices, and the only decision is what quantity to buy or sell. Your expanding knowledge of economics should tell you that the analysis of these decisions will be more accessible if it is presented within the short-run/long-run framework.

Short-Run Firm Demand. The relationship between the price of a resource and the quantity of that resource demanded is derived from the optimizing behavior of the firm. The basic input-demand relationship can be illustrated with the profit-maximizing actions of a firm operating with a single variable input. Chapter 9 showed that, in the short run, the competitive firm operates where output price (P) equals marginal cost (MC), provided that price is greater than average variable cost. The firm's output decision is settled along the short-run firm supply curve, which is the portion of the marginal-cost curve that is above the average-variable-cost curve. In the short run, each level of output will be associated with a unique amount of the variable input. The marginal-cost curve indirectly defines this relationship. Chapter 8 showed that the marginal-cost curve was the inverse of the marginal-product (MP) curve multiplied by the price of the variable input. Where the variable input is labor (L) whose price is w, the marginal-cost curve is defined as $MC = w(1/MP_L)$.

The basic short-run relationships,

$$P = MC \quad \text{and} \quad MC = w \, \frac{1}{MP_L}$$

can be used to derive the short-run firm demand for labor. Each equation has marginal cost on one side of the equation. Because output price and the inverse of the marginal product multiplied by the input price are both equal to marginal cost, they are equal to each other. Thus we are able to write

$$w \, \frac{1}{MP_L} = P$$

Rearranging terms by multiplying both sides of this equation by the marginal product of labor, we can define the short-run firm demand for labor (or any variable input). Although this equation may seem rather antiseptic, there is an economic rationale underlying the relationship.

Rational behavior is optimizing behavior, and in generic terms, the optimal level of an activity is the point at which the marginal benefits and marginal costs of the activity are equal. The activity that concerns us here is the employment of a variable input. Consider the problem faced by the owner of a car-wash, who must decide how many workers to hire, as illustrated in Table 12.1. The cost of hiring an additional worker is the market-determined wage — say, $8/hour — which translates to $64/day. Because additional workers can be

Table 12.1 The Employment Decision

Workers are hired up to the point at which the marginal cost of employing an additional worker equals the marginal benefit. For every number of employees less than nine that the employer gains by hiring additional workers, the marginal benefits are greater than the marginal costs.

Number of Employees (L)	Marginal Cost of Additional Employees ($64 per Day = $8 per Hr x 8 Hrs per Day)	Marginal Product MP_L (Additional Cars Washed per Day)	Marginal Benefit of Additional Employees ($ per Day = $P_W MP_L$)
4	$64	9	$144
5	64	8	128
6	64	7	112
7	64	6	96
8	64	5	80
9	64	4	64
10	64	3	48
11	64	2	32

hired without an increase in the wage rate (the firm is a price taker) the marginal cost of additional employees is constant at $64/day, as reflected in the second column of Table 12.1. The marginal benefit of hiring additional workers is the product of two effects. The direct effect of hiring an additional worker is an increase in output, or in economic terminology, the marginal product of labor (MP_L). The marginal product of carwash labor is illustrated in the third column of Table 12.1. The carwash owner, however, does not want the additional output for its own sake; she wants the money that can be earned by washing cars. When the competitive price of a car wash (P_W) is $16, the marginal benefits of hiring additional workers are as illustrated in the fourth column of Table 12.1. The carwash owner finds that profits will rise by $80/day when the fourth worker is hired, because the marginal cost of the worker is $64/day and the marginal benefits are $144/day. Profits rise for each additional worker until the ninth worker is hired, at which point the marginal benefits just equal the marginal costs.

The marginal benefit of employing a variable input is the revenue earned by selling the additional output produced by the input and is called the **value of the marginal product** (*VMP*) of the input. The value of the marginal product is equal to the marginal product (*MP*) multiplied by the price of the output (*P*), or $VMP = (P)(MP)$. A value-of-the-marginal-product curve is formed by multiplying a marginal-product curve by the price of the output. A *VMP* curve for labor can be found in Figure 12.1. The only difference between Figure 12.1 and a graph of an *MP* curve is what is measured on the vertical axis. Multiplying the *MP* curve by price simply changes the vertical

Figure 12.1 A Firm's Demand for Labor in the Short Run

The VMP_L curve is the demand for labor by a competitive firm. The firm employs the quantity of labor for which the market wage equals the value of the marginal product of labor. The firm takes the wage as given and goes out to the VMP_L curve to find the optimal quantity of labor to employ.

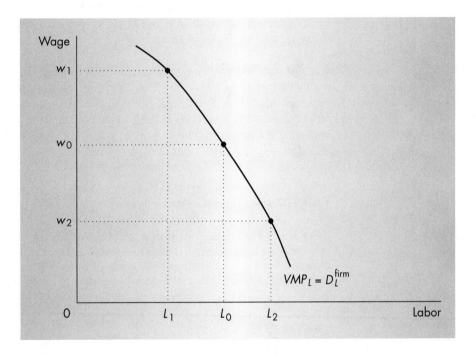

scale from output to dollars; otherwise the graph is unaffected. Obviously, the curve illustrated in Figure 12.1 does not look like an *MP* curve. The VMP_L curve in Figure 12.1 includes only the downward-sloping and positive portions of the *MP* curve.[2]

The VMP_L curve is the short-run firm demand curve under competitive conditions when labor is the only variable input. Optimal input use occurs where the input price equals the value of the marginal product. At a price of w_0, the profit-maximizing firm hires L_0 units of labor. If the price of labor rises to w_1, the firm reduces employment to L_1. If the price of labor falls to w_2, employment expands to L_2. Given a wage, the value of the marginal-product curve defines the quantity of labor that the firm will hire. Any curve that

---

2. For our purposes, Figure 12.1 encompasses the range of *MP* in which production is in stage II. Stage II production occurs where marginal product is less than average product and marginal product is positive. This segment of the *MP* curve is the only one illustrated, because it is irrational to operate outside of stage II.

defines the relationship between the price and the quantity demanded, *ceteris paribus*, is a demand curve.

The *VMP* curve is the input demand curve when the firm operates in competitive markets for both inputs and output. Note that the firm's demand for a resource slopes downward and the value of the marginal product also slopes downward, because of the principle of diminishing marginal productivity. A declining marginal product is the cause of the downward slope of the input demand curve in the short run.

Long-Run Firm Demand. The long-run decisions facing the firm are complicated by the variability of all inputs. The short-run response to a change in resource prices occurs along a marginal-revenue-product curve. The long-run adjustment to the same price change will involve changes in all inputs. Tracing the impact of the long-run adjustments on the employment of one resource traces out the long-run firm demand for a resource. Figure 12.2 summarizes this process.

Figure 12.2 A Firm's Demand for Labor in the Long Run

The long-run demand for labor by a firm is the locus of such points as A and B, at which the firm optimizes the use of all inputs. The long-run adjustment to a fall in the price of labor from w_0 to w_1, will usually entail an increase in the use of capital. The increased use of capital increases the marginal product of labor and the *VMP* curve shifts upward with L_2 units of labor employed when the wage rate is w_1.

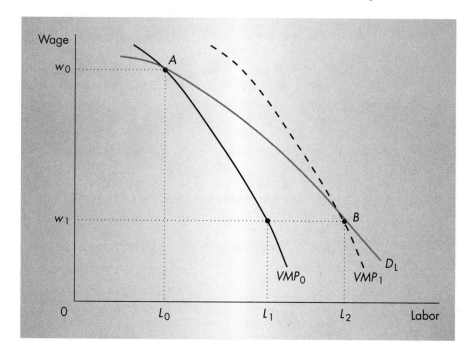

Begin with an initial long-run equilibrium at point A in Figure 12.2, where the firm hires L_0 units of labor at price w_0. A fall in the price of labor to w_1 induces a short-run adjustment along the original *VMP* curve, denoted VMP_0. The decline in the price of labor also shifts the firm's marginal-cost curve down. Because long-run equilibrium occurs where price equals marginal cost, the change in the price of labor leads to an increase in output. This increase in output generally (assuming an upward-sloping long-run expansion path, limited substitutability between inputs, and fixed technology) requires an increase in the use of labor *and* capital. The increase in the use of capital will usually increase the marginal product of labor, shifting the value of the marginal-product curve for labor to the right, from VMP_0 to VMP_1. A new equilibrium will occur where the new value of the marginal product equals the new wage. The lower price of labor, coupled with the higher value of the marginal product of labor, generates a new long-run equilibrium at point B, where w_1 equals VMP_1.

Points A and B in Figure 12.2 are two points on the firm's long-run-demand-for-labor curve. These two points show the price- and quantity-demanded combinations for two long-run equilibria. Other prices of labor will lead to different long-run-equilibrium combinations of labor and capital and different *VMP* curves. Where each price of labor equals the corresponding value of the marginal-product curve, a long-run-equilibrium quantity of labor is found. Linking these price- and quantity-demanded combinations traces out the competitive firm's long-run demand-for-labor curve, labeled D_L in Figure 12.2.

Market Demand

The market demand for a resource shows the quantities of the resource demanded at alternative input prices, *ceteris paribus*. It is found by summing the quantities demanded at each price for each of the firms participating in the market. The derivation of the market demand curve for an input differs markedly from the process by which product demand curves were derived. In Chapter 2 the market demand for consumer goods and services was shown to be the horizontal sum of the individual demand curves. The market demand for inputs, however, is not the horizontal sum of individual demand curves. Individual firm demands are derived demands and will be affected by events in the market for the output. The process by which the market demand curve is derived is illustrated in Figure 12.3.

The derivation of the market demand curve begins with some initial equilibrium. Point A in panel (b) serves as an initial equilibrium in the labor market. At a price of w_0 for labor, each firm, as illustrated in panel (a), will employ L_0 units of labor where the price of labor equals the initial value of the marginal product of labor, VMP_0. The industry as a whole employs ΣL_0 units of labor, the sum of each firm's employment at a wage of w_0. A fall in the price

Figure 12.3 The Market Demand for Labor

The market demand for labor is the locus of points such as A and B in panel (b), where the sums of the quantities employed by the industry are plotted against their respective wage rates. Each firm (panel a) experiences a decline in the value of the marginal product as industry employment and output expand and the price of the product declines.

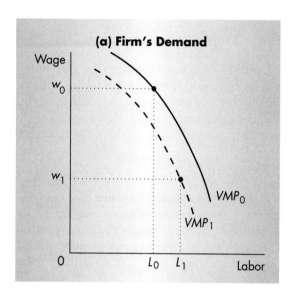 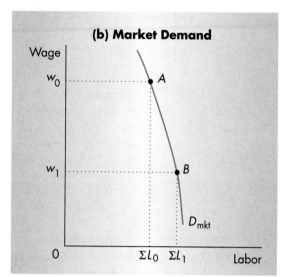

of labor to w_1 induces an increase in the quantity of labor demanded by each firm. Individually, each firm expands employment by moving along its individual demand curve, VMP_0, and the output of each firm increases. Although the output of a single firm has no impact on the product market, increased production by all firms will reduce the price of the product. The falling product price reduces the value of the marginal product of labor, and the VMP curve shifts leftward to VMP_1. Each firm will be in equilibrium where w_1 equals VMP_1 and individual firm employment has expanded to L_1. The industry as a whole will be in equilibrium at point B in panel (b), where industry employment has expanded to ΣL_1 units of labor. The market-demand-for-labor curve (D_{mkt}) will be the locus of points at which alternative combinations of wage and industry employment trace out the curve, such as the curve connecting points A and B in Figure 12.3.

Determinants of the Market Demand for Resources

The only variables that were allowed to change in the derivation of the demand curve illustrated in Figure 12.3 were the price of the resource and the price of the output. All other variables affecting demand were held constant. The list of the factors that must be held constant to derive an input demand curve bears a striking resemblance to the list of the determinants of product demand compiled in Chapter 2. The determinants of resource demand include the demand for the product, technology, the prices of related inputs, the number of buyers, and any other factor that affects the profitability of employing resources. The effects that these determinants of resource demand have on the market demand for labor operate through the value of the marginal product of resources.

A change in the demand for a product will shift the demand for inputs that can be used to produce the product. For example, an increase in the demand for autos will increase the demand for autoworkers. Similarly, a decrease in the demand for sugar reduces the demand for sugarcane and sugar beets. An increase (decrease) in the demand for a product will increase (decrease) the price of the product and increase (decrease) the value of the marginal product. The change in the value of the marginal product is equivalent to the change in the demand for the resource.

Technological change will have a direct effect on the demand for resources. Technological change that increases the marginal product of an input increases the demand for the input by shifting the *VMP* curve upward. Improved tools and machinery increase the productivity of the workers who use the tools, and the demand for the workers will increase. The latest medical technology, for example, increases the productivity of physicians, which increases the demand for doctors' services.

A change in the price of a substitute or a complement will alter the demand for a resource. An increase (decrease) in the price of a substitute increases (decreases) the demand for a resource. The demand for skilled workers will rise with an increase in the equilibrium wage of unskilled workers, and the demand for natural gas will fall with a decline in the price of coal. An increase (decrease) in the price of a complement will decrease (increase) the demand for a resource. The demand for bricklayers will fall with an increase in the price of brick, and a decrease in the price of laser printers will lead to an increase in the demand for laser printer paper.

The demand for a resource also varies with the number of firms that employ the resource. Job creation goes hand in hand with the formation of new businesses. The U.S. defense buildup of the 1980s spawned many new defense-related companies, and the demand for resources rose accordingly. An increase in the number of buyers will increase the demand for the resource. The increase in the demand for defense-related inputs was occurring as the demand for inputs used to produce oil was falling. The demand for oilfield workers and equipment fell during the 1980s as a falling price of crude oil drove many independent oil producers into bankruptcy.

Resource-Demand Elasticity

One conclusion that we can draw from the foregoing discussion is that resource demand obeys the law of demand: there is an inverse relationship between price and quantity demanded. Although this information will be sufficient to answer many questions, some questions will require knowledge of the quantitative relationship between the price of an input and the quantity of the input demanded. In some situations, the ability to predict the magnitude of the quantity response to a price change is vital. The Boeing Corporation will be very interested in how American Airlines will respond to an increase in aircraft prices. The elasticity of resource demand provides such information.

The Elasticity of Resource Demand.   **Resource-demand elasticity** measures the impact of a change in price on the quantity of a resource demanded. An elasticity coefficient is calculated by dividing the percentage change in the quantity demanded by the percentage change in the price, or

$$E_{RD} = \frac{\%\Delta Q_{RD}}{\%\Delta P_R}$$

where Q_{RD} is the quantity of the resource demanded and P_R is the price of the resource. The terminology developed in Chapter 3 applies to resource-demand elasticity as well as product-demand elasticity. Resource demand is

- *inelastic* when the elasticity coefficient is less than the absolute value of 1,
- *unit elastic* when the elasticity coefficient is equal to the absolute value of 1, and
- *elastic* when the elasticity coefficient is greater than the absolute value of 1.

Determining the numerical value of the elasticity of resource demand will require precise information on the position and slope of the resource-demand curve, information that is often lacking in real-world situations.

Determinants of Resource-Demand Elasticity.   Certain rules of thumb can be used to estimate the elasticity of resource demand when the quantitative dimensions of the demand curve are unknown. The elasticity of resource demand can be gauged by (1) the elasticity of demand for the final product, (2) the amount of time buyers have to adjust to the price change, (3) the ease with which inputs can be substituted for one another, and (4) the resource's share of the total costs of production. Each of these determinants of resource-demand elasticity have a predictable effect on the problem at hand.

The demand for a resource will increase in elasticity along with the demand for the final product. If the demand for air travel is elastic, the demand for aircraft will also be elastic. An increase in aircraft prices will decrease the supply of air transportation by increasing the marginal cost of producing air travel. An elastic demand for air travel will result in relatively large reductions in the number of passengers and a relatively large reduction in the number of aircraft needed to carry the passengers. An aircraft price increase when the demand for air travel is elastic results, *ceteris paribus*, in a relatively large decrease in the quantity of aircraft demanded, which implies an elastic demand for aircraft.

The producer's ability to substitute one input for another will have a direct bearing on the elasticity of resource demand. Consider the demand for Boeing aircraft. If airlines can easily substitute McDonnell-Douglas or Airbus aircraft for Boeing products, any change in the price of Boeing aircraft will have a relatively large impact on the quantity demanded. The demand for pilots, on the other hand, tends to be inelastic. Although it may become possible to build a fully automated aircraft, it seems likely that the traveling public would be unwilling to accept a pilotless airplane. The airlines have a fixed-proportions production function: one pilot to one airplane. The inability to substitute for pilots creates an inelastic resource demand. The demand for a resource will be more elastic if it is easier to substitute for the resource in production, and less elastic as substitutability declines.

The more time producers have to adjust to a price change, the more elastic resource demand will be. This rule of thumb is an extension of the ability to substitute for resources. The firm will be able to develop or find more substitutes if it has more time to adjust to a price change. The demand for flight crews has been elastic over the long run as aircraft makers have used technological advances to automate cockpits and reduce the size of flight crews.

Finally, the greater the resource's contribution to the total costs of production, the more elastic resource demand will be. A change in the price of a resource that makes up a large share of the total costs of production will cause a relatively large change in the supply of the product. The relatively large change in the supply of the product will, other things being constant, cause a relatively large change in the quantity of the resource demanded. Reversing this logic, the demand for a resource that represents a small fraction of the total costs will be relatively inelastic. This interpretation of this rule of thumb has come to be known as the Importance of Being Unimportant. For an application of resource demand elasticity, see Highlight 12.1.

Highlight 12.1　*Resource-Demand Elasticity: Energy*

The energy market provides ample opportunity for examining resource-demand elasticity. Energy is an input into virtually every production process and is purchased by virtually every business and household. Businesses use energy directly as an input when it powers machinery (lathes, assembly lines, and so on) or promotes chemical reactions/changes (smelting iron ore to make steel). Businesses also use energy as an indirect input to improve the working environment (lighting, cooling, and heating). Households use energy to produce services consumed by the household. The two major components of household energy use are for residential consumption (lighting, heating, and cooling) and transportation. The many uses of energy and the significant changes in the price of oil that occurred during the 1970s and 1980s provide useful examples of each of the rules of thumb relating to resource-demand elasticity.

The public response to the oil price shocks of the mid-1970s indicated a relatively inelastic demand for energy, most notably in the demand for gasoline. The inelastic demand for gasoline was derived from an inelastic demand for personal transportation. The relatively low gas prices of the 1960s had promoted transportation independence. The family car was the primary mode of transportation, and there were few alternatives. The lack of alternative modes of transportation translated into an inelastic demand for personal transportation and an inelastic demand for the inputs (particularly gasoline) required in the production of transportation services. The demand for energy in the form of gasoline was inelastic.

The demand for energy from specific sources tends to be elastic. This is particularly evident in the residential demand for energy associated with home heating. There are a variety of options for heating one's house: electricity, natural gas, fuel oil, solar, geothermal, and other sources of heat. The demand for any one of these sources of heat will be elastic because there are relatively readily available substitutes. A rise in the price of natural gas will, in time, induce the installation of electric heat pumps or other means of heating. The easier it is to substitute other inputs, the more elastic resource demand will be.

An industrial example of the impact that substitutability has on the demand for energy can be found in the production of aluminum. Primary production of aluminum (from the natural resource bauxite) is extremely energy intensive. Higher energy prices induced a substitution of previously processed aluminum for production of aluminum from bauxite, because melting and recasting existing aluminum stocks requires much less energy than the production of aluminum from bauxite. Higher energy prices made it profitable to recycle aluminum. In 1960 none of the processed aluminum was recovered, but by 1980 16.7 percent of the processed aluminum was being reprocessed, with secondary sources of aluminum accounting for 21 percent of all aluminum production. By 1988, 31.7 percent of aluminum was being reprocessed, accounting for 35 percent of all production.[3]

The examples just cited involve adjustments to energy price changes, and it takes time for economic units to implement these adjustments. In the long run, the demand for a resource will be elastic. Given enough time, operators of power plants can switch to alternative fuels when the price of one fuel rises. Additionally, over time drivers will purchase more fuel-efficient cars when the price of gasoline rises. Rising residential energy prices induce investment in insulation and more energy-efficient appliances. In the long run, research will

---

3. The data on the aluminum market are taken from U.S. Bureau of the Census, *Statistical Abstract of the United States: 1991,* 111th ed. (Washington, D.C., 1991).

lead to the development of energy-saving technology, allowing for greater reductions in energy use.

Buyer responsiveness to changes in energy prices will depend on energy's share of total production costs. The demand for energy will be more elastic where energy expenditures are a large share of total cost. This principle is reflected in the changes in the aluminum market discussed in the preceding paragraph. The importance of energy in the primary production of aluminum led to expansion of the secondary market for aluminum. Where energy is a small share of total costs, the demand for energy will be relatively inelastic. The demand for energy used for lighting will be relatively inelastic, because light is produced at relatively low cost. This fact is offered for those who tend to leave lights on and who live with people who habitually turn lights off.

Even though most of the discussion of resource demand has been cast in terms of the demand for labor, the principles developed apply to the demand for any productive resource. Labor was cited repeatedly because of labor's importance in the determination of income. In the aggregate, employee compensation accounted for 73 percent of the income generated in 1989. The relative scale of labor income underlies the emphasis that this chapter places on the labor market.

The Markets for Human Resources

Labor markets are characterized by a demand for labor (as discussed) and a supply of labor. Chapter 9 showed that the basis for the market supply of a final good or service is the sum of individual supply curves, which are based on the marginal cost of producing the product. The same holds true for the supply of any input. The market supply of an input will be the sum of individual supply curves. Individual supply functions reflect the optimizing behavior of individual resource owners. Rational resource suppliers base their supply decision on the marginal costs of their decisions, and as discussed in Chapter 8, these costs are evaluated in terms of forgone alternatives. This section focuses on the optimizing behavior of suppliers of labor, leaving the supply of other resources for consideration in a later section.

The derivation of labor supply relies on a number of simplifying assumptions:

1. This section treats labor as if it were a homogeneous commodity; that is, we assume that all workers and all employment opportunities are identical.
2. In keeping with the focus of this chapter, we will also assume that the market is perfectly competitive. Large numbers of buyers and sellers result in all market participants taking the market price of labor, the wage rate, as given.

3. Finally, labor suppliers are confronted with only two uses for their time; they can

   - work at the prevailing wage rate
   - not work and devote their time to leisure activities.

This final assumption serves as the basis of the individual's labor-supply decision.

The Supply of Labor

Income from the sale of labor services is the major source of income in any economy. Wage earners are motivated not by money in itself but by those things that money can buy. Because consumer behavior is explained by the utility-maximizing model, individual labor supply can also be explained using this framework. Individual labor supply traces the quantity of labor supplied at alternative wage rates.

Labor Supply and Utility. The simplified version of the problem facing the individual supplier of labor is to allocate time between work and leisure activities. Leisure contributes to utility directly, because leisure time is used for recreational or other utility-producing pursuits. Work time contributes to the individual's utility indirectly via the goods and services that can be purchased with the income earned from the sale of labor services. The individual's problem is to find the combination of work time and leisure time that maximizes utility. This problem can be analyzed using the indifference curves introduced in Chapter 3.

The indifference curve approach to labor supply is based on a utility function that uses income (M) and leisure (ℓ) as the variables that determine the level of utility. This version of the utility function takes the mathematical form $U = U(M,\ell)$. An indifference curve taken from this utility function shows the alternative combinations of income and leisure that provide equal levels of satisfaction. An example of an income-leisure indifference curve is the curve labeled U_0 in Figure 12.4. The indifference map that includes U_0 will exhibit the usual properties of indifference maps discussed in Chapter 4. The most important of these are that indifference curves (1) are downward sloping, (2) have a decreasing slope,[4] (3) do not intersect, and (4) represent higher and higher levels of satisfaction the farther they are from the origin. The utility-maximizing individual will be in equilibrium at the point that corresponds to the highest indifference curve attainable, given the constraints faced by the individual.

---

4. The decrease in the slope of the indifference curve indicates a diminishing marginal rate of substitution. The individual's willingness to substitute leisure for income declines as the quantity of leisure consumed rises and the level of income falls.

Figure 12.4 Labor-Supplier Equilibrium

The indifference curve U_0 indicates the alternative combinations of income and leisure that provide the same level of utility. The time constraint T_0 shows the alternative combinations of income and leisure that the individual can obtain each day by working at a wage of $10. Utility is maximized at E_0, where the indifference curve is tangent to the time constraint.

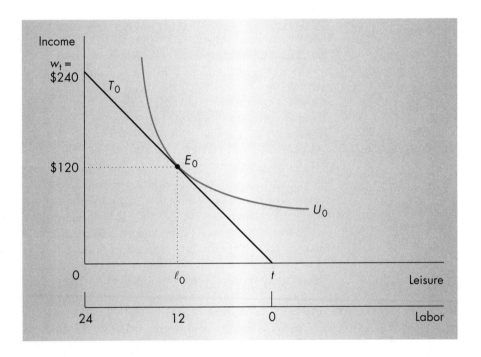

The Time Constraint. Utility-maximizing suppliers of labor are constrained by the amount of time they have to allocate between labor and leisure. Given that there are (by assumption) only two uses for time, there is a one-for-one trade-off between work time and leisure time. If t represents the total amount of time available to an individual and ℓ represents leisure time, time spent at work (L) will be equal to the difference between t and ℓ, or $L = t - \ell$. Although this equation demonstrates the one-for-one tradeoff between work and leisure (increasing ℓ by one hour reduces L by one hour), it cannot be used to solve the utility-maximization problem, because time devoted to work does not explicitly enter the individual's utility function.

Work time enters the utility maximizer's decision making through its impact on income. Income (M) is defined as

$$M = wL$$

where w is the wage rate and L is the number of hours worked. Substituting the expression $(t - \ell)$ for L produces the equation

$$M = w(t - \ell)$$

This equation defines the **time constraint**: the alternative combinations of income and leisure that are available to the individual. Graphically, the time constraint becomes the line labeled T_0 in Figure 12.4. Suppose that T_0 shows the daily time constraint of 24 hours. If the individual chooses to devote all time to leisure ($\ell = t = 24$), income will be zero and the individual will be at the horizontal intercept of T_0. If no leisure is taken, the individual is at the vertical intercept of T_0 and earns income equal to wt, or \$240, when the wage rate is \$10 per hour. The time constraint serves the same function as the consumer's budget constraint introduced in Chapter 4. The points along T_0 show the alternative combinations of income and leisure that can be "purchased" with the available time.

Individual Equilibrium. The time constraint shows the available combinations of income and leisure, whereas the indifference map indicates the individual's preferences regarding alternative combinations of income and leisure. The utility-maximizing supplier of labor will be in equilibrium where an indifference curve is tangential to the time constraint, or at point E_0 in Figure 12.4. Point E_0 represents the highest level of satisfaction that can be obtained with the individual's resources, because all other combinations of income and leisure along T_0 are on lower indifference curves. At this point the individual consumes ℓ_0 (12) units of leisure and the remaining time $(t - \ell_0 = 12)$ is devoted to work, producing $M_0 = w(t - \ell_0) = \$120$ of income. The quantity of labor supplied (L_0) can be found graphically as the horizontal distance between t (the horizontal intercept) and ℓ_0 (the equilibrium quantity of leisure).

Individual Labor Supply. The equilibrium point in Figure 12.4 defines one point on the individual's supply-of-labor curve. At a wage equal to w, the individual supplies (other things being constant) $L_0 = t - \ell_0$ units of labor. The individual labor supply curve can be found by altering the wage rate and observing what happens to the equilibrium quantity of labor supplied. The mechanics of this process are illustrated in Figure 12.5.

Panel (a) uses the information contained in Figure 12.4 to define an initial equilibrium. Initially, the wage is w_0, the time constraint is T_0, and the individual is in equilibrium at E_0, where the quantity of labor supplied is $L_0 = t - \ell_0$. The price-quantity combination (w_0, L_0) is one point (S_0) on the individual labor supply curve (S_{Labor}) in panel (b). An increase in the wage rate to w_1 rotates the time constraint outward to T_1 and produces a new equilibrium at E_1. The equilibrium quantity of leisure falls to ℓ_1 and the equilibrium quantity of labor supplied rises to $L_1 = t - \ell_1$. The new equilibrium wage-quantity combination (w_1, L_1) forms a second point (S_1) on the labor supply curve. The other points on the labor supply curve are found by using all of the alternative

Figure 12.5 Individual Labor Supply

Panel (a) shows the effects of an increase in the wage rate. The higher wage rotates the time constraint outward and generates a new equilibrium. The two equilibria in panel (a) represent two points on the individual labor supply curve in panel (b). The movement along the supply curve from S_0 to S_1 is composed of a substitution effect — the movement from E_0 to E_A in panel (a) — and an income effect — the movement from E_A to E_1.

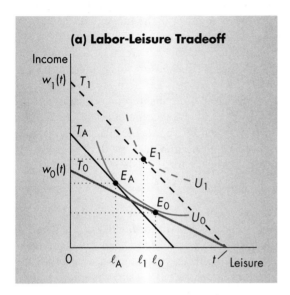
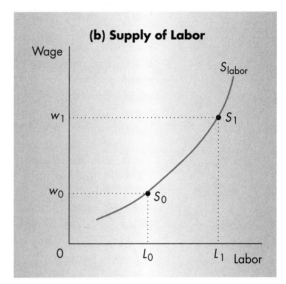

wage rates, finding the alternative equilibrium quantities of income and leisure, and solving (by subtracting ℓ from t) for the equilibrium quantity of labor supplied. The indifference map of panel (a) has higher wages, leading to greater quantities of labor supplied, and the individual depicted in Figure 12.5 has an upward-sloping labor supply curve.

The slope of an individual's supply-of-labor curve depends on the relative magnitudes of the substitution and income effects introduced in Chapter 4. A change in the price of labor changes the slope and position of the time constraint. This alters (1) the equilibrium combination of income and leisure and (2) the individual's level of satisfaction. The total effect of the price change (from w to w_1) shown in panel (a) is the change from point E_0 on indifference curve U_0 to point E_1 on indifference curve U_1. The substitution and income effects are identified by finding the time constraint that (1) reflects the new wage rate and (2) is tangent to the original indifference curve. These two conditions are met by the time constraint labeled T_A.[5] The substitution effect is

5. Note that T_A and T_1 are parallel. The slope of the time constraint is equal to the wage rate. This is why an increase in w makes the time constraint steeper. Because T_A and T_1 are parallel, they have the same slope and both reflect the new wage faced by the supplier of labor.

the movement along indifference curve U_0 from E_0 to E_A, where constraint T_A is tangent to the original indifference curve. The increased payment to labor induces a substitution of labor for leisure, decreases the quantity of leisure consumed from ℓ_0 to ℓ_A, and increases the quantity of labor supplied from $L_0 (=t-\ell_0)$ to $L_A (=t-\ell_A).$[6]

The increase in the quantity of labor supplied is the direct result of the higher relative price of leisure. The income effect is the movement from E_A to E_1 as the individual uses the higher wage rate to reach a higher level of satisfaction on indifference curve U_1. The income effect increases the quantity of leisure consumed from ℓ_A to ℓ_1, indicating that leisure is an income-normal good, and the demand for leisure increases as income increases. The total effect of a change in the price of labor on the consumption of leisure is the sum of the substitution effect (ℓ_0 to ℓ_A) and the income effect (ℓ_A to ℓ_1). For the individual depicted in Figure 12.5, the positive income effect does not fully offset the negative substitution effect, resulting in a decrease in the quantity of leisure consumed and an increase in the quantity of labor supplied. Consequently, the individual's labor supply curve is upward sloping.

Backward-Bending Labor Supply. The properties of indifference maps say nothing about the relative magnitudes of income and substitution effects. It is theoretically possible for individual preferences to entail income effects that are, in absolute terms, greater than substitution effects. Preferences for an individual who fits this scenario are illustrated in Figure 12.6a. This hypothetical supplier of labor is confronted with the same wage rates as the individual depicted in Figure 12.5. The substitution effects are the same in each graph, with the amount of leisure consumed declining from ℓ_0 to ℓ_A as the wage rate rises from w to w_1. The worker in Figure 12.6, however, experiences a large, positive income effect and the consumption of leisure rises from ℓ_A to ℓ_2. The income effect, in this case, swamps the substitution effect, and the total effect of the price change is an increase in the quantity of leisure consumed (ℓ_2 in Figure 12.6 is greater than ℓ_1 in Figure 12.5). The increased consumption of leisure comes about through a reduction in the quantity of labor supplied. Although the labor supply curve may slope upward for wage rates below w, it will slope downward for wage rates greater than w. The individual's labor-supply curve bends backward, as illustrated in Figure 12.6b.

The slope of an individual's labor supply curve is an empirical matter, because the theory behind the relationship is ambiguous with regard to the slope. In practice, the slope of an individual's labor-supply curve will depend on individual preferences and the relative level of wages. Those who enjoy only simple pleasures may have a backward-bending labor supply. A modest level of

---

6. Alternatively, the wage rate can be viewed as the price of leisure, because it is what is forgone when leisure is consumed. A rise in the price of leisure leads, by the law of demand, to a decrease in the quantity of leisure demanded, and a simultaneous increase in the quantity of labor supplied.

Figure 12.6 Backward-Bending Labor Supply

Panel (a) illustrates an indifference map for someone for whom leisure is a strong income-normal good. The increase in the wage rate causes the usual substitution of labor for leisure. The higher income obtained from the higher wage rate increases the consumption of leisure via the income effect. The income effect is larger (in absolute terms) than the substitution effect and the quantity of labor supplied falls with the higher wage. The labor supply curve bends backward, as in panel (b).

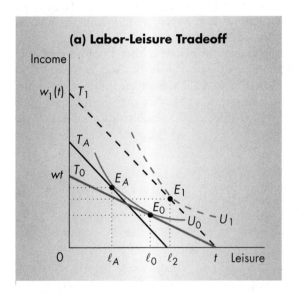

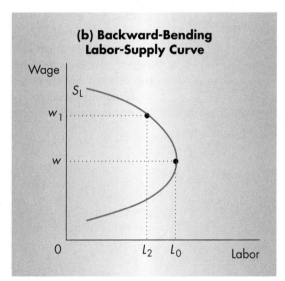

income will be sufficient to meet their needs, and any increase in the price of labor will reduce the quantity of labor supplied. This will also be true for more materialistic workers if the wage rate gets high enough. How many hours (per week for every week) will you work if you can earn $5 per hour? How about $50,000 per hour? Intuitively, it seems likely that there will be a wage rate at which everyone's labor supply curve bends backward. The crucial empirical question is, Are market wage rates near the point at which an increase in wages will reduce the time devoted to the labor market?

This analysis of the labor supply problem has ignored many relevant features of real-world labor markets (in addition to those assumed away at the beginning of this section). For one thing, workers may not be able to schedule the exact number of hours that they would most like to work. Although the practice of job sharing is available, few employers offer this new approach. Another factor that has been overlooked is the impact of taxes on the labor-supply decision.

Taxes and the Labor-Leisure Tradeoff. The relative magnitudes of the substitution and income effects play an important role in determining the effect of a tax on labor income. An income tax reduces the net return to labor and rotates the time constraint inward. Figure 12.7 illustrates the impact of a 25 percent flat-rate tax, holding the marginal tax rate (the fraction of additional dollars in earnings taken in taxes) constant. The tax leaves the horizontal intercept of the time constraint unchanged (the individual can always consume t hours of leisure), whereas the vertical intercept falls by a proportion equal to the tax rate (the vertical intercept decreases by 25 percent, from wt to $0.75wt$). The change in the time constraint incorporates a change in its slope (creating a substitution effect) and inward rotation that moves the individual to a lower indifference curve (creating an income effect).

The substitution effect is the change in behavior that would occur if an individual were presented with the new relative price but was constrained to the original indifference curve. In Figure 12.7 the substitution effect is the movement from E_0 to E_A, as the consumption of leisure rises from ℓ_0 to ℓ_A. The lower net wage (and lower price of leisure) causes a substitution of leisure for

Figure 12.7 Income Taxes and Labor Supply

An income tax rotates the time constraint inward, resulting in a new equilibrium at E_1. The movement from the original equilibrium at E_0 to E_1 is composed of a substitution effect (from E_0 to E_A) and an income effect (from E_A to E_1). The total effect of the income tax is to increase the consumption of leisure and reduce the quantity of labor supplied.

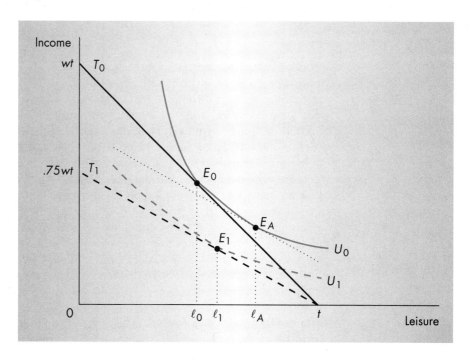

income, and the quantity of labor supplied falls. The post-tax equilibrium then depends on the income effect. Given that leisure is income normal, an income tax will reduce income and reduce the amount of leisure consumed. The new equilibrium quantity of leisure will be somewhere to the left of ℓ_A. If the income effect is smaller than the substitution effect, the equilibrium will be at some ℓ_1 that is greater than ℓ_0, as illustrated in Figure 12.7. The income tax reduces the quantity of labor supplied, gross income falls, and tax collections are reduced. If the income effect is greater than the substitution effect, the equilibrium quantity of leisure consumed falls and the quantity of labor supplied increases. Gross income actually increases and tax collections rise (see Highlight 12.2).

Highlight 12.2 *Welfare, "Workfare," and the Labor-Leisure Tradeoff*

The welfare system is one of the more controversial economic issues. How can a system dedicated to improving the lives of the least fortunate generate such controversy? An analysis of the economic effects of welfare can shed some light on the source of controversy. A deeper understanding of the debate can be gained by contrasting the current system with workfare and a negative income tax. Naturally, application of particular programs to groups of welfare recipients requires careful study of numerous elements, only some of which are economic. But microeconomic theory is capable of providing important insights into the problem.

Traditionally, welfare programs provide a subsidy to those with no income. The subsidy augments the options faced by the supplier of labor. In addition to the time constraint showing alternative combinations of income and leisure that may be consumed, welfare allows the individual to select a combination that includes the subsidy, no work, and all leisure. These options are illustrated in Figure 12.8, in which the usual time constraint is T_0 and the welfare program adds point A to the individual's choice set. Point A is an option because the individual can choose to go on welfare, collect the subsidy (which provides $\$S$ in income), and have t units of time for leisure. One of the controversial aspects of the welfare system is illustrated in the figure. The individual whose preferences are illustrated in Figure 12.8 would, in the absence of welfare, be in equilibrium at point E_0, work $L_0 = t - \ell_0$ hours, and earn income equal to S. The indifference map and time constraint were contrived to set the initial equilibrium earnings equal to the subsidy. The welfare option adds point A to the individual's choice set, which lets the individual reach indifference curve U_1, corresponding to a higher level of satisfaction. Point A is preferred to point E_0 because it provides the same amount of income but allows for more leisure. Welfare involves a disincentive to work. Welfare recipients aren't necessarily

Figure 12.8 Welfare, Workfare, and Labor Supply

Public-assistance programs add options to the individual's income-leisure tradeoff. Welfare adds point *A* as an option by offering $S in public assistance, with no need to supply labor. The individual depicted reaches a higher indifference curve by accepting welfare. The option added by workfare depends on the number of hours of public service required of the recipient. Points *B*, E_0, and *C* are the workfare options when the workfare service requirement is L_B, L_0, and L_C hours, respectively.

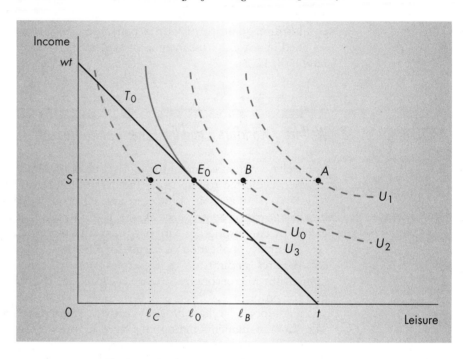

lazy, they are simply responding rationally (that is, maximizing their utility) to the economic constraints that they face.

The workfare concept was developed to diminish the disincentive to work that is inherent in traditional welfare programs. Workfare adds a work requirement as a condition of public support. Welfare recipients must perform some set amount of public service to qualify for public assistance. The effects of this program are also illustrated in Figure 12.8. Workfare leaves the time constraint unchanged but changes the option regarding public support. If workfare requires L_B hours of labor, the recipient will have ℓ_B hours of leisure remaining. The workfare option adds point *B* in Figure 12.8 to the individual's labor-leisure tradeoff. A workfare program that keeps the subsidy at $S and requires L_B hours of public service shifts the welfare option horizontally from point *A* to point *B*. The individual whose preferences are illustrated by the indifference curves in Figure 12.8 is better off (that is, moves to a higher indifference curve) by accepting workfare. The impact of workfare depends on the public-service requirement. A workfare program that requires L_0 hours of public service will leave the individual indifferent between workfare and working for $S in income. A workfare requirement of L_C hours of public service and a subsidy of $S would present the individual with point C in Figure 12.8 as the public-assistance alternative. Those faced with constraint T_0 would be *worse* off (because they would be on indifference curve U_3) by going on workfare.

Both welfare and workfare suffer from a common defect. The programs add options to the individual's choice set that are defined by single points (points A, B, and C in Figure 12.8) that are not on the time constraint. An attempt to increase income through labor-market activity results in the loss of all public support. The all-or-nothing aspect of public income-support programs subjects the recipients to a tax, equal to their welfare benefits, for entering the labor market. Not surprisingly, some people have an incentive to remain on welfare when faced with a 100 percent marginal tax rate.

The negative income tax is a program that eliminates the prohibitive tax on the labor income of public-assistance recipients. A negative income tax program would provide a basic subsidy, which is reduced by a fraction (called the negative income-tax rate) of earned income. For example, suppose that the base subsidy is $5,000 and the negative tax rate is 50 percent. Someone with no earned income would receive $5,000 in welfare benefits. Someone who earns $1,000 would have his or her subsidy reduced by $500 (50 percent of earned income) for total income of $5,500 ($1,000 earned income plus $4,500 in welfare benefits). The negative income tax gives individuals an incentive to work, because working increases their income. Under traditional welfare and workfare programs, earning $1,000 would cost the individual $5,000 in lost welfare benefits.

The effect of the negative income tax on the individual's choice set is illustrated in Figure 12.9. The negative income tax confronts the individual with a time constraint composed of line segments AC and CD. Individuals who do not work start at point A. Those who choose to work see their income increase as they move along the line between points A and C. Their incomes increase because their subsidy is reduced by a fraction of earned income. Individuals at point C are at the break-even point. Their earnings are such that the negative income tax exactly offsets their subsidy. Optimizing behavior leads the individual to the indifference curve that is tangential to this constraint. Indifference curve U_3 is positioned to illustrate the advantages of the negative income tax. The individual reaches a higher indifference curve (that is, is better off) by working L_3 ($= t - \ell_3$) hours, earning income equal to $w(t - \ell_3)$, and receiving a subsidy equal to $M_3 - w(t - \ell_3)$. Society is better off by the reduction in the subsidy paid to the individual. The negative income tax provides incentives to work, improves the standard of living for the poor, and reduces the cost of the welfare program.

Figure 12.9 The Negative Income Tax

The negative income tax provides a basic subsidy of S to provide the option at point A. The individual can increase income by working, because the program reduces assistance by a fraction of earned income, allowing an individual to choose any point on the line between A and C. Point C represents the break-even income, where the subsidy has fallen to zero and the individual's income consists entirely of earned income.

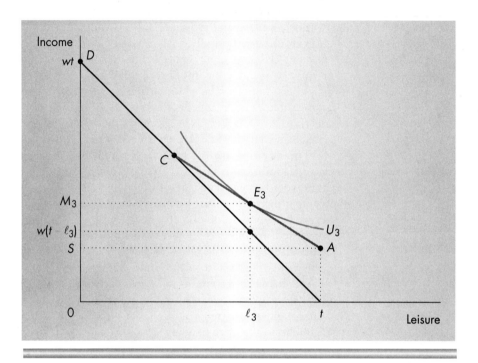

The Market Supply of Labor

The version of the labor market that we have been developing in this chapter is no different from the idealized markets of Chapter 4. Independent, self-interested buyers and sellers acting within a price system generate an economic order in the form of a market equilibrium. Labor-market equilibrium is determined by the interaction of the market demand for labor (as defined previously) and the market supply of labor.

Market behavior is always the aggregate of individual behavior. The market supply of labor is the horizontal sum of individual labor-supply curves. The horizontal summation of the individual supply curves adds the quantity supplied by each individual at each wage rate. Because the individual supply curves hold everything except the wage rate constant, the market supply will indicate the quantity of labor that will be supplied at alternative wage rates, other things being constant. A change in one of the "other things" held constant will lead to a change in the supply of labor.

The *ceteris paribus* component of the labor-supply curve includes everything that affects the aggregate willingness to work. Chief among these will be the number of labor-market participants, taxes on labor income, and leisure opportunities. The influx of women into the labor force that began in the 1960s has increased the supply of labor. The personal income tax, social security, and medicare tax all reduce the supply of labor by reducing the net benefits of employment. Finally, changes in the alternative uses for one's time will affect the labor-supply decision. Parents drop out of the labor market to devote their time to the not-so-leisurely activity of child rearing.

Labor-Market Equilibrium: A Simplification

The labor market will be in equilibrium when the quantity of labor demanded equals the quantity supplied. This occurs at the wage rate defined by the intersection of the supply and demand for labor, or w_E in Figure 12.10. Wage rates above the equilibrium wage create a surplus of labor, and unemployed workers will bid wages down in their efforts to find employment. Wage rates below the equilibrium wage result in a labor shortage in which employers will bid wages

Figure 12.10 Labor-Market Equilibrium

The idealized labor market is in equilibrium at the intersection of the supply and demand for labor; L_E units of labor will be supplied and demanded at the equilibrium wage w_E.

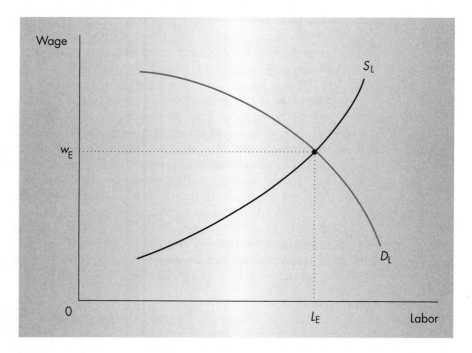

up to fill open positions. The optimizing behavior of individuals (employers and employees) guides the labor market to an equilibrium. The market-determined equilibrium wage becomes the price taken by labor demanders and labor suppliers in their decision making.

At the margin, labor-market participants have attained their respective goals when the competitive equilibrium is reached. The firm operates at the point at which the costs of hiring additional workers (the wage rate) equal the benefits of hiring additional workers (the value of the marginal product of labor) and profits are maximized. Workers operate at the point at which the benefits of an additional hour of labor (the wage rate) equal the costs (measured in terms of forgone leisure) of selling the labor time, and utility is being maximized.

The labor-market model just developed is grossly simplified. The implication that all workers earn the same rate of pay is clearly unrealistic. Although continuing to focus exclusively on competitive markets, we drop the assumption regarding the homogeneity of labor to find an explanation of the wage differentials observed in real-world labor markets. It doesn't take much experience to realize that workers and employment opportunities are incredibly diverse. This diversity leads to market segmentation and wage differentials.

Labor-Market Segmentation

Trade in labor services occurs through an interconnected system of segmented labor markets. Economic activity in these markets reflects the decision making of subsets of the working population concerning subsets of the alternative employment opportunities. The interconnectedness of these markets arises from the mobility of resources across market boundaries. These boundaries are usually drawn along occupational or geographic lines.

Occupational Segmentation. On one level, labor markets are segmented by occupational requirements. Employment opportunities and workers can be classified by the attributes (skills, mental capacity, personal characteristics, and so on) necessary to fulfill the responsibilities of a position.[7] Occupational segmentation in labor markets occurs when all employment opportunities with a given set of job requirements (the demand side) and all workers who possess the necessary attributes (the supply side) are considered separately. The numerous combinations of necessary job attributes and the diversity of the work force translate into severely fragmented markets. Defining markets by occupations can range from the very broad — teachers — to the very narrow — people who teach college economics. The breadth of the market definition often depends on the nature of the problem at hand.

---

7. Contemporary employment practice has evolved to include job descriptions to explicitly define these attributes and the responsibilities of the position.

Geographic Segmentation. On another level, labor markets are separated geographically. Labor is unique in that the owner (supplier) is inseparable from the productive powers of the resource. Although the owners of capital, land, and natural resources may go where they will, the owners of labor must be physically present at the job site.[8] Transportation costs, the wage rate, and time constraints put limits on the spatial dimensions of labor markets. Geographic segmentation of labor markets appears where the costs (measured in terms of forgone opportunities) of traveling to a job site exceed the benefits. In practice, these boundaries depend on the particular job, geographic area, and individual. Although some might view a thirty-minute commute as long, others would view it as trivial. There is even the case of the radio personality who commuted between a morning show in Dallas and an afternoon show in Chicago.

Labor-Market Equilibria and Wage Differentials

Each labor market moves toward an equilibrium, and that equilibrium depends on the equilibria in other markets. Self-interested behavior promotes equality across employment opportunities as competition eliminates profitable reallocations of resources. If wage rates are the only difference between jobs, wage differentials elicit entry into high-wage markets and exit from low-wage markets. The increase in supply in the former and the decrease in supply in the latter continue until wage rates are equalized. However, because workers and jobs differ, equal wages will be inequitable. The equality created by competition takes all aspects of jobs and workers into account. Labor markets are in equilibrium when the net economic benefits of alternative employments are equal. Net economic benefits equal the difference between benefits and costs, where benefits and costs include all aspects of employment, pecuniary and nonpecuniary. **Wage differentials** exist to compensate for nonwage differences between employment opportunities.

Wage Differentials: Pecuniary Considerations. Wages vary to compensate for differences in net money earnings. The net money income of an employment opportunity equals the difference between all receipts and all job-related expenses. Wage rates vary to the extent that employment opportunities differ in job-related expenses and potential income. These two aspects of employment can go a long way in explaining wage differentials.

---

8. Some readers might question this assertion. Futurists and a few innovative employers consider telecommuting the work environment of the future. Telecommuting is the electronic transfer of a product from one location (usually a remote office or the worker's home) to another (usually the home office). This frees the employee from having to travel to the employer's location by moving the job site to a location of the employee's choice.

Every employee bears some cost in the performance of his or her job. Some jobs require outlays just to meet the day-to-day responsibilities of the position. Workers who provide their own tools, uniforms, or any item necessary to fulfill the duties of their job must be compensated, in terms of their alternatives, for their expenses. Moreover, most jobs have some minimum set of qualifications. Employees often acquire these qualifications prior to employment through education and training. Employees who have so invested must be compensated for this investment with higher wages. Finally, the geographic segmentation of markets brings cost-of-living differentials into the equation. Because workers must reside close to the job site, regional competition for labor will increase wages in high-cost-of-living areas. *Ceteris paribus,* wage rates rise or fall to compensate for differences in job-related expenses.

Gross income is a function of a number of variables in addition to the wage rate. Consequently, competition will vary the wage rate to compensate for differences in these other variables. One of these other considerations is the regularity of employment. A portion of the relatively high hourly rates paid to construction workers is to compensate for the irregularity of construction work. Another consideration is future income. Workers will accept lower current pay when the job presents opportunities for promotion, career advancement, and higher future income. This is particularly true of entry-level jobs in which on-the-job-training prepares workers for more challenging (and better-paying) positions.

Wage Differentials: Nonpecuniary Considerations. The inseparability of the resource (labor services) from the owner (worker) makes nonpecuniary considerations a major factor in the equilibria of labor markets. Wages adjust to compensate workers for the job characteristics that directly affect the utility of the worker. Many of these characteristics are inherent in the position. Jobs that are boring, hazardous, strenuous, stressful, or that have any attribute that reduces the worker's utility will have to pay a premium to attract workers. The workplace environment will also affect the utility of workers. Firms that offer friendly, air-conditioned, and/or peaceful workplaces will, *ceteris paribus,* be able to attract workers at lower wages. Because workers must also reside near the job, locational factors will influence wage rates. Climate, proximity to friends and family, and recreational opportunities are but a few of the many locational factors affecting the allocation of resources among labor markets. Competition in labor markets will force workers to pay (via lower wages) for those aspects of employment that yield utility. The segmented labor markets will be in equilibrium when wages have adjusted, both occupationally and geographically, to equalize the net benefits, both pecuniary and nonpecuniary, of employment.[9]

---

9. The discussion of wage differentials is predicated on competitive labor markets. If the labor market is not competitive, discrimination may be the cause of wage differentials.

The Markets for Nonhuman Resources

Although labor is the major source of income, it is not the only productive resource. All other productive resources are conveniently grouped together as nonhuman resources. We can treat nonhuman resources as a separate class because they all have a common characteristic: the productive powers of the resource are separate from the owner. Because the supplier need not accompany the resource to the job site, nonpecuniary factors will be much less important in the operation of markets for nonhuman resources. These markets will tend to focus on the financial bottom line. Thus the allocation of nonhuman resources is best described using the profit-maximization model.

Although nonhuman resources share an important characteristic, they do possess characteristics that permit finer classification. Inputs that are the output of one firm but require further processing before they are ready for final consumers fall under the general heading of **intermediate products**. Capital includes products that are (1) used to produce other products and (2) durable. Finally, natural resources, including land, are inputs whose origins predate production activities but require some processing before they can be utilized in production. Each of these categories of resources will be discussed separately in the remainder of this chapter.

The Markets for Intermediate Products

Markets for intermediate products operate on the same principles as the market for any resource. When the market is competitive, the price of an intermediate product is determined by the interaction of supply and demand. The market for flour can be used to illustrate the operation of such a market. The demand for flour is a derived demand, for example, one that is derived from the demand for baked goods. Flour is purchased by both households and bakeries to be processed into pies, cakes, cookies, and so on. The price that bakers are willing to pay for flour reflects the value of baked goods. Flour is supplied by profit-seeking flour mills. Because mill owners do not have to accompany their product into the kitchens of bakers, the decision to supply is based solely on the marginal costs of producing flour. Supply and demand produce an equilibrium at which the price of flour equals its marginal production costs.

Transfer Pricing. A special case arises when the buyer and seller of an intermediate product are subsidiaries of the same firm. **Transfer pricing** examines the process by which intrafirm prices are set. Consider the case of a firm with one division that produces flour and another that produces baked goods using flour supplied by its corporate sibling. The price of flour will be contentious if the divisions are operated independently and divisional compensation is tied to divisional profits. High flour prices are beneficial to the milling division, whereas low prices benefit the bakery division, and vice versa. Optimal pricing requires setting the price of flour equal to its marginal cost.

Figure 12.11 Transfer Pricing

The profit-maximizing level of pie production occurs at the point at which marginal revenue equals marginal cost. The marginal cost of producing pies is the sum of the marginal baking costs (MC_B) and marginal flour milling costs (MC_F). Profits are maximized when the transfer price of flour is equal to the marginal costs of producing flour. A higher price for flour increases the profits of the milling division at the expense of the baking division.

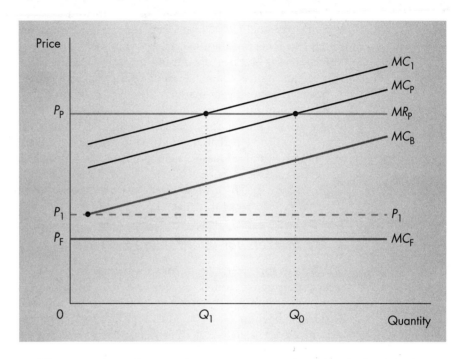

The optimality of marginal cost pricing is explained with the aid of Figure 12.11, which shows a vertically integrated firm's participation in the pie market. The pie market is competitive, with the equilibrium price of pies at P_P. The marginal cost of producing pies (MC_P) is the sum of the marginal cost of producing flour (MC_F) and marginal baking costs (MC_B). The firm maximizes profits by producing Q_0 pies, where the price of pies equals total marginal costs. If milling and baking operations take place in different subsidiaries, the optimal price of flour is equal to the marginal costs of producing flour, or P_F. If the flour division sells flour to the baking division at price P_1, the marginal cost of producing pies rises to MC_1 and the bakery subsidiary produces Q_1 pies, less than the profit-maximizing quantity of pies. The flour division benefits at the expense of overall firm profits.

Transfer Pricing: International Considerations. Transfer pricing becomes a creative art when the subsidiaries are located in different countries and are subject to different regulations. Multinational corporations can increase their net profits by shifting "reported" profits from countries with high tax rates to countries with low tax rates. Reported profits are shifted by having subsidiaries in high-tax locations (1) pay higher transfer prices for the intermediate products they purchase or (2) receive lower transfer prices for the intermediate products they sell.

Transfer prices can also be used to circumvent international trade restrictions. Some nations impose import duties on products that fail to meet domestic content requirements. Automobile shipments from Canada to the United States are exempt from import duties if a specific percentage of the car's value was created in Canada. If Honda assembles cars in Canada from parts manufactured in both Canada and Japan, it can increase the domestic content by reducing the price that its Canadian subsidiary pays for parts manufactured by its Japanese subsidiary.

Capital

In economics, capital consists of anything produced that augments, for multiple periods, the production of goods and services. The economic interpretation of this concept is malleable, taking in both tangible and intangible aids to production. Buildings, tools, equipment, and inventories are examples of capital that have a material existence. Education and training are examples of capital (called human capital) that are intangible. Education and training can be viewed as capital, because they are produced (learning is a production process in and of itself) and they contribute to the production of other goods (over the life of the worker) by increasing the productivity of those who invest in them.[10]

The analysis of the capital market is shaped by the three characteristics noted before. Capital is (1) productive, (2) durable, and (3) produced. The productivity of capital is the basis of the demand for capital. The durability of capital means that demanders of capital look at its future productivity as well as its current contribution to output. Durability also means that it is important to distinguish between the stock of capital (the quantity of capital that exists at some point in time) and capital flows (the change in the stock of capital that occurs over time). Finally, because capital is produced, its supply will be based on its costs of production.

The Supply of Capital. When capital is produced under competitive conditions, the market supply of capital will be the sum of each producer's marginal-cost curves. Profit-maximizing producers of capital, who operate under the constraints of a competitive market, take the market price as given and equate that price to the marginal costs of producing capital. The only difference between

10. The economic definition of capital excludes money and financial assets by requiring a direct influence on output. At best, money plays an indirect role in production by virtue of its ability to purchase productive resources.

"Something's got to go, Fenton.
You, me or this inventory—and it's
not going to be me."

the supply of capital and the supply of any other produced good is the result of
the durability of capital. The short-run supply of capital is the existing stock
of capital and will be vertical. The long-run supply indicates how the stock of
capital changes when the price of capital changes. Figure 12.12 illustrates the
relationship between the short-run and long-run supplies of capital.

The long-run supply of capital defines the quantity of capital that will be
produced at alternative prices. If the price of capital is P_0, the stock of capital
will, in the long run, adjust to quantity K_0. In production theory, the essence
of capital is its fixity in the short run. The short-run supply of capital is perfectly inelastic at the existing capital stock, as indicated by the curve labeled SRS_0
in Figure 12.12. A change in the price of capital, say to P_1, has no short-run
impact on the stock of capital because the quantity of capital is fixed in the
short run. In the long run, a rise in the price of capital causes a movement
along the long-run supply (the quantity of capital increases to K_1) and a rightward shift of the short-run supply (from SRS_0 to SRS_1).

Figure 12.12 The Supply of Capital

The long-run supply of capital (*LRS*) reflects the marginal costs of producing capital goods. The short-run supply of capital SRS_0 reflects the fixity of capital in the short run and is vertical. An increase in the price of capital causes a movement along the long-run supply and a rightward shift of the short-run-supply curve.

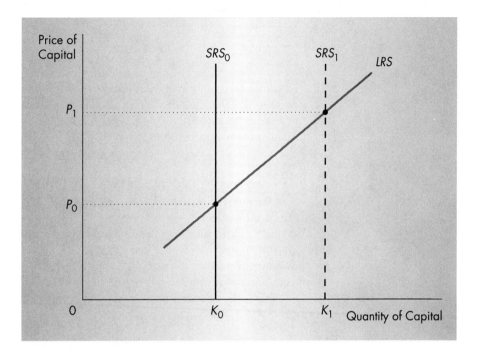

The Demand for Capital. The demand for capital, like the demand for any resource, is a derived demand. It is derived from the demand for the output produced with capital and is based on capital's contribution to the revenues of the firm. The profit-maximizing firm uses capital up to the point at which the price of capital equals the value of the marginal product of capital. For other inputs, the *VMP* equals the marginal product of the input multiplied by the price of the output. The *VMP* of capital is different because capital is durable and produces additional output over its useful life span. Because capital provides a flow of additional revenue that occurs over time, the value of the marginal product of capital must take a concept called the "time value of money" into account.

The Time Value of Money and the Demand for Capital. A dollar today is not equal in value to a dollar at some point in the future. The current dollar can be converted into an interest-earning asset that will be worth more than a dollar in the future. This is the essence of the **time value of money**. When dollar amounts are separated in time, they must be adjusted for the time value of money before they can be compared. One method of adjustment converts all dollar amounts to their future equivalents. The **future value** (*FV*) of a dollar sum is its present value (*PV*) plus the interest that can be earned over time. If interest is compounded annually[11] at a rate of *r* percent per year for a period of *t* years, the relationship between the future value and the present value is given by the equation

$$FV = PV(1 + r)^t$$

A second method for adjusting for the time value of money converts all future amounts to their current equivalent through a process called discounting. Discounting calculates the current dollar sum, the **present value**, which, when invested in an interest-earning asset, will generate a given future amount. The present value of a future sum is given by the formula

$$PV = \frac{FV}{(1 + r)^t}$$

where *r* is the interest rate and *t* is the number of time periods separating the present from the future.

The value of the marginal product of capital is the present value of the additional revenues that accrue over the life of the capital. The additional revenues for a period that is *t* years in the future will be the price of the output during that period (P_t) multiplied by the marginal product of capital in period *t* (MP_t). When the interest rate is *r* percent, the present value of the future additional revenue will be equal to

$$PV_t = \frac{P_t MP_t}{(1 + r)^t}$$

If capital has a useful life of *n* years, the value of the marginal product of capital is the sum of each of the present values for each of the *n* years, or

$$VMP_K = \sum_{t=1}^{t=n} \frac{P_t MP_t}{(1 + r)^t}$$

The Market for Capital. A competitive market for capital operates on the same principles as any other competitive market. The supply of capital (which depends on the costs of producing capital) and the demand for capital (which depends on the value of the marginal product of capital) determine an

---

11. Interest is compounded when interest is paid on previous interest earnings. If $100 was invested at 10 percent interest, the $100 will be worth $110 in one year (the original $100 plus 10 percent of $100). If interest is compounded for 2 years, the $100 will be worth $121 at the end of the second year. Interest earnings in the second year equal 10 percent of the original $100 plus 10 percent of the first year's interest of $10, for an additional $11 in interest.

equilibrium price of capital. Price-taking buyers and sellers follow their individual interests in responding to the market-determined price, with capital being allocated to its highest-valued uses. The capital market does differ from other markets in its adjustment to changes in supply and demand. This adjustment is complicated by the perfectly inelastic short-run supply of capital (see Highlight 12.3).

Highlight 12.3   *Booms, Busts, and Capital Markets*

The oil industry offers a classic example of what happens to a resource market when an industry goes through a boom/bust cycle. A key input in the production of oil is the drilling rig used to drill the oilwell. Figure 12.13 illustrates the market for drilling equipment. Supply curve LRS_R reflects the costs of constructing drilling rigs. Demand curve D_{R0} is the value of the marginal product

Figure 12.13 The Market for Drilling Rigs
The long-run supply of rigs is slopes upward, reflecting rising costs of building rigs. In the short run, the price of rigs is determined by demand because the quantity is fixed. The boom in drilling activity caused by rising oil prices drove the price of existing rigs above the costs of producing a new rig. The oil bust and declining demand for rigs drove rig prices below their preboom level.

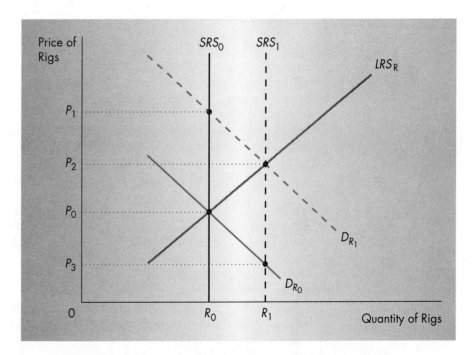

Oilfield roughnecks in Texas know well the sting of booms and busts in the oil market.

of drilling rigs that prevailed prior to the rise in price of oil that began in the mid-1970s. The supply and demand for rigs established an equilibrium at price P_0 and quantity R_0.

The rise in the price of oil increased the demand for drilling rigs to D_{R1} by increasing the value of the marginal product of rigs. The price of existing drilling equipment rose to P_1, the VMP of the existing stock of drilling equipment. New drilling equipment was selling at a price of P_2, the point at which the increased demand (D_{R1}) intersected the long-run supply (LRS_R). Competition among rig builders kept the price down to marginal costs. The market for drilling rigs was characterized by an unusual price regime: used equipment cost more than new equipment. Why would anyone pay more for a used machine? Used equipment was available for immediate use, whereas new equipment was back-ordered. Purchasers of new equipment had to wait up to two years for delivery. Used equipment brought in money immediately, whereas buyers of new equipment had to wait two years before their equipment could begin to bring in additional revenues. It was rational to pay a premium for the ability to enter the market immediately.

Over time, the increased demand for rigs and the long-run response of rig builders increased the stock of drilling equipment to R_1. Time also brought the oil bust of the mid-1980s. The falling price of oil decreased the demand for drilling rigs and put downward pressure on the equilibrium price of rigs. Because the short-run supply of rigs was fixed at SRS_1, the decrease in demand pushed the market price of rigs to P_3, a price that was well below the preboom price. Operators of drilling equipment saw a rapid depreciation in the value of their capital. Although this was devastating to rig owners, it was disastrous for those who had loaned the money used to buy the rigs in the first place. Drilling operators declared bankruptcy by the score and banks repossessed drilling rigs. Because the market price of rigs had fallen, the rigs were worth far less than the loan balances. One of the side effects of the decline in the price of oil was the failure of a record number of banks in energy-producing states.

Although the supply-and-demand approach is useful in explaining the pricing of capital equipment, it offers little insight into the way investment decisions are made. Insight into this process is gained by looking at the internal rate of return for an investment opportunity.

Internal Rates of Return. Traditionally, investment decisions are made by comparing the rate of return on an investment opportunity with the cost, measured in percentage terms, of the project. The opportunity cost of investing in a project is the return that the firm can earn from its next best investment opportunity. The firm always has the option of lending its funds, at prevailing market interest rates, to other investors. Therefore, the market interest rate is the opportunity cost of investing in a particular project. The benefits of an investment opportunity is measured by the **internal rate of return** for the project. The internal rate of return is the rate of interest that sets the net present value of the project equal to zero.

Every investment opportunity entails a stream of future revenues and an obligation to meet future expenses. Rational project analysis requires the conversion of all revenues and costs to their respective present values to correct for the time value of money. The **net present value** (*NPV*) of a project is the difference between the present value of revenues and the present value of costs, or

$$NPV = \sum_{t=1}^{t=n} \frac{R_t}{(1+r)^t} - \sum_{t=1}^{t=n} \frac{C_t}{(1+r)^t}$$

where R_t and C_t are the revenues and costs, respectively, in year t; r is the interest/discount rate; and n is the life of the project in years. The internal rate of return is the discount rate (r) that sets the net present value of the project equal to zero.

The internal rate of return on a project shows the break-even rate of return for the project. If the current interest rate is *less* than the internal rate of return of the project, the investor profits by undertaking the project. If the current interest rate is *greater* than the internal rate of return, the investor profits by avoiding the project. Rational investors calculate the internal rates of return for all of their projects, rank these investment opportunities by their internal rates of return, and undertake those for which the internal rate of return exceeds the opportunity cost of the investment.[12]

Natural Resources

For analytical purposes, land and natural resources are included in one broad category. Both are "gifts" of nature in that, at some level, their existence is independent of human actions. Although the "original" productive powers of land and natural resources are a gift, few are useful in their natural or raw state. Land and natural resources usually need improvement, extraction, harvesting, refinement, processing, transportation, or some other form of modification before they can contribute to the production of goods and services. All of these activities are included in the operation of resource markets.

Natural-resource markets are driven by the supply and demand for particular resources. Natural-resource demand is based on the value of the marginal product of the resource, where the nature of the *VMP* depends on the durability of the resource. Because land provides productive services for an extended period of time, its *VMP* is the present value of future additions to the user's revenues.[13] Other natural resources are consumed in the short run and their *VMP* need not be discounted.

Natural-resource supply can be viewed as the sum of two costs: the opportunity cost of the resource in its natural state and the costs of converting the resource from its natural state into a form suitable for productive use. Conversion costs are identical in form to the production costs discussed in Chapter 8. Resources are expended in the process (mining, harvesting, extracting, shipping, and so on) that transforms natural resources into usable forms. Conversion costs are also independent of other characteristics of natural resources.

Natural resources do differ in the opportunity cost associated with the resource in its natural state. These differences center on whether the resource is renewable, nonrenewable, or recyclable. The opportunity costs of raw, renewable resources are the costs of reproducing the resource. The opportunity cost inherent in harvesting a pine forest is the cost of replanting and growing replacement trees. The opportunity costs of raw, nonrenewable resources is the present value of the highest-valued future use of the resource. Because the resource cannot be replaced, the alternative to using it in current production is to save it for future production. The current supply of oil reflects production

---

12. The foregoing has ignored the fact that investment opportunities vary in the amount of risk associated with each project. Risk-averse investors will require a premium to compensate for bearing risk.

13. The remainder of this section excludes further comments on the market for land. Because land is immobile, there are monopoly elements in the price of land. Locational considerations force us to defer the discussion of the price of land to the next chapter.

expectations concerning the future price of oil. Taking the opportunity cost of the resource into account reduces the supply of renewable and nonrenewable resources by adding the opportunity cost of the raw product to the marginal costs of converting the resource from its raw to a usable state.

Recycling resources is fundamentally different from using renewable and nonrenewable resources. The conversion costs associated with recycled resources involves reprocessing a finished product, a task that may be more costly than the original processing. Moreover, the opportunity costs of the resource work to offset the conversion costs. The alternative to recycling a resource is to pay for its disposal. Recycling avoids the disposal costs, and these savings are deducted from conversion costs to determine the supply of the resource.

The operation of a natural-resource market is depicted in Figure 12.14. The position of the demand curve is determined by the value of the marginal product of the resource, and the position of the supply is determined by the sum of the conversion and opportunity costs of the resource. Together, supply

Figure 12.14 Natural-Resource Markets

The price of natural resources is established by the demand (value of the marginal product) for the resource and supply (the marginal opportunity costs) of the resource. Where the latter is depicted by S_0, the resource is priced at P_0, and Q_0 of the resource is used. Where the marginal opportunity costs are S_1, the resource is not used in production.

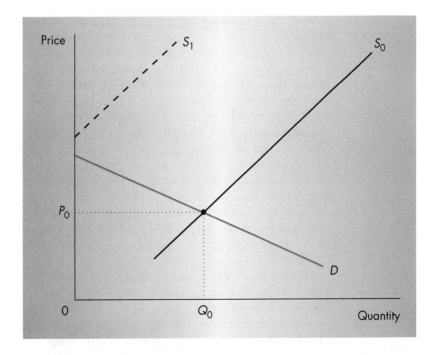

and demand determine the equilibrium price and quantity traded in the market. One such equilibrium is illustrated by the intersection of demand curve D and supply curve S_0. Supply curve S_1 is included to represent a situation that could develop in a natural-resource market. Supply curve S_1 represents a case in which the price that buyers are willing to pay is everywhere less than the marginal costs of using the resource. In one example, the costs of reprocessing might be so high that, even when the savings in disposal costs are included, recycling is not economically feasible. This situation could also arise where the future uses of the resource are so valuable that the resource is conserved (that is, current use is forgone) for the future use.

Resource Prices and Economic Rents

The competitive resource market achieves an equilibrium at the point at which supply intersects demand. The price determined by this intersection is the result of optimizing behavior on the part of resource buyers and resource sellers. For the employer, the cost of the last unit of the resource employed just equals the additional revenues generated by the employment of that resource. The owner of the marginal resource receives a price that just equals the marginal opportunity cost of providing the resource. Although these equalities are true at the margin, the diversity of resources implies that some resource owners are paid a price that exceeds their opportunity costs. This premium is what economists call an economic rent.

The theoretical limit of the economic rent concept is the **pure economic rent**. A resource owner earns a pure economic rent when the resource has no alternative uses. Because opportunity costs are defined as the value of the next-best alternative, the sale of a resource that has no alternative uses incurs no opportunity costs. The supply curve for such a resource is vertical, and the price is determined solely by demand. Because costs are zero, the entire payment received by the resource owner is an economic rent.

A concept that is similar to the pure economic rent is the quasi-rent. **Quasi-rents** are short-run windfalls that accrue to the owners of capital. This concept is similar to the pure economic rent in that the supply of capital is fixed (vertical) in the short run. Any increase in the demand for capital drives the price above the marginal cost of producing capital, conferring a short-run bonus to the owners of capital. This short-run divergence between the price and marginal cost of capital is a quasi-rent. Quasi-rents are transitory because any short-run profit will, under conditions of competition, be eliminated by the entry of competitors. The case of the fluctuating price of drilling rigs discussed before is an example of quasi-rents.

A third rent concept is the **inframarginal rent**. Resource prices equal their marginal costs only at the margin. The diversity of resources implies that other resources will have other opportunity costs. Those with opportunity costs that exceed the market price will take their higher-valued alternatives and opt out of the market. Those with lower opportunity costs will take part in the market and earn returns that exceed their opportunity costs. The difference between the price and the opportunity cost is a rent. Because these resources are within the margin, the rents earned by their owners are called inframarginal rents.

Inframarginal rents are illustrated in Figure 12.15. The market price (P_0) is determined by the intersection of supply and demand. The suppliers to the left of quantity Q_0 are the inframarginal sellers. The supply curve indicates the minimum payment (that is, the opportunity cost) necessary to induce the suppliers into the market. A particular supplier receives an inframarginal rent equal to the vertical distance between the price and his position on the supply curve. Adding the inframarginal rents of each of the suppliers generates the shaded area in Figure 12.15. The area above the supply and below the market price is the total inframarginal rents earned in the market.

A fourth rent is the **monopoly rent**. This type of rent was discussed in Chapter 11, where monopolistic markets were introduced. Monopoly rents are applicable to resource markets when the market is not competitive, the subject of the next chapter.

Figure 12.15 Inframarginal Rents

When the price of a resource is P_0, resource owners receive total payments equal to the rectangle under the price. The total opportunity costs of using the resource are the area under the supply curve. The shaded area is the inframarginal rents, the difference between total earnings and the total opportunity cost of using the resource.

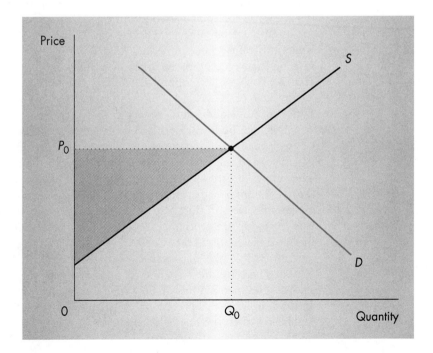

Summary

- The demand for resources is a derived demand. Resources are purchased for their ability to produce output that consumers want to purchase. Producer willingness to pay for a resource is a function of the additional revenues from selling the output obtained from a resource.
- The short-run firm demand is the value of the marginal product of a resource, the *VMP*. The *VMP* equals the price of the output multiplied by the marginal product of the input. The long-run firm demand accounts for changes in the marginal product of a resource arising from changes in the usage of all inputs. The market demand for a resource is the sum of the quantities demanded at alternative prices of the resource.
- The market demand for a resource depends on (1) the demand for the output, (2) technology, (3) the prices of related inputs, and (4) the number of employers.
- Resource demand elasticity measures the responsiveness of resource buyers to a change in the price of a resource. Resource demand becomes more elastic with increases in (1) the elasticity of demand for the product, (2) the ease of substituting among inputs, (3) the time producers have to adjust to a price change, and (4) the resource's share of total cost.
- Resource supply depends on the marginal costs of using the resource. The marginal cost of devoting human resources to production is the value of alternative uses of the individual's time. The marginal costs of using non-human resources are the opportunity costs of producing the resource or diverting the resource from other uses.
- The supply of labor reflects individual utility maximization, subject to a time constraint. The individual labor supply is the result of finding the income-leisure combination that maximizes utility subject to a time constraint. The market supply of labor is the horizontal sum of individual supply curves.
- Labor-market equilibrium occurs at the wage that equalizes the quantities of labor supplied and demanded. The labor market is segmented, both occupationally and geographically, with wage differentials compensating for pecuniary and nonpecuniary differences between the markets.
- The supply of intermediate products is based on the marginal costs of producing the intermediates. A special case, called transfer pricing, arises when an intermediate product is traded between two subsidiaries or divisions of one firm. Optimal pricing requires the intermediate to be priced at its marginal production costs.
- The analysis of the market for capital is complicated by the durability of capital. The long life of capital requires calculating the present value of the value of the marginal product of capital to evaluate the demand for capital. In the long run, this present value will equal the marginal costs of producing capital when the market is competitive.

- Natural resources are classified as renewable, nonrenewable, and recyclable. The supply of natural resources reflects the marginal opportunity costs of the current use of the resources. Competitive markets will account for these opportunity costs in the pricing of natural resources.
- Economic rents are payments in excess of opportunity costs. A pure economic rent is earned when a resource has no alternative uses. The short-run fixity of some resources creates quasi-rents, temporary excess payments that will be eliminated by the adjustment to a long-run equilibrium. Inframarginal rents arise when participants in a resource market have different opportunity costs. A monopoly rent is earned when barriers to entry prevent competition from reducing the price to opportunity costs.

Key Terms

derived demand	value of the marginal product
resource-demand elasticity	time constraint
wage differentials	intermediate products
transfer pricing	time value of money
future value	present value
internal rate of return	net present value
pure economic rent	quasi-rent
inframarginal rent	monopoly rent

Sample Questions

Question

Starting salaries are on the order of 5 to 40 percent lower for many kinds of professional workers in San Francisco, and in the Bay Area generally, than they are in a number of U.S. cities of comparable size (such as Minneapolis/St. Paul). How can this be so if markets for these professionals (accountants, lawyers, and so on) are assumed to be competitive?

Answer

As noted in the chapter, competitive markets do not require uniformity in pecuniary wages. San Francisco is, for many people, one of the most desirable places to live in the United States. The principle of equalizing differences in wages suggests that total compensation in all occupations must be equal under purely competitive conditions. Because housing is known to be relatively high-priced in the Bay Area (and in California generally), lower wages probably underestimate real compensation differentials. These seeming disparities in total compensation suggest that real (nonpecuniary) factors are at work to explain different compensations of professionals. Locational preference, lifestyle differences, scenic beauty, and many other factors help explain wage differences, especially if the differences persist over long periods of time (time enough for supply and demand to adjust). If markets are truly competitive, we would expect total compensation to be the same in the same occupation in San Francisco and in Minneapolis/St. Paul.

Question

Jane earns $250 per hour as a medical consultant to large hospital complexes. Joe earns $22.50 per hour as a skilled cabinet maker. A 10 percent increase in both Jane's and Joe's hourly wage has the following effects on their individual labor supplies: Jane works more hours, Joe works fewer hours. Does this result violate common sense or economic principles?

Answer

An individual's labor-supply curve cannot be determined solely from economic theory. We cannot know for certain which wage would induce a particular person to enter the labor market. Similarly, the economist cannot say for certain whether a rise in any individual's hourly wage would induce her to supply more or less labor time. The reason, as outlined in this chapter, is that wage-rate changes (which change the relative tradeoff between income and leisure) have both income and substitution effects that work in opposite directions. Utility maximization by the individual suggests that it is perfectly rational to respond to a wage increase by working more or by working less. When the substitution effect dominates the income effect, the individual (such as Jane) works more. When the opposite holds (Joe's case), the individual works less. Both are rational responses. Individual tastes and preferences determine the result in each case. Economic theory only explains the possible responses.

Questions for Review and Discussion

*1. Explain the concept of derived demand and cite three examples of derived demand.

*2. Explain the concept of the value of the marginal product and the rationality of employing a resource up to the point at which the resource price equals its *VMP*.

3. Derive the long-run firm demand for a resource. Compare this derivation with the short-run demand curve.

4. What are the primary determinants of resource demand? Show how each affects the market demand for a resource.

*5. What is meant by the elasticity of resource demand? How is it calculated? What factors affect the elasticity of resource demand?

6. Illustrate and explain the optimizing behavior of an individual supplier of labor. What is the laborer's objective? What is the constraint?

*7. Illustrate and explain the substitution and income effects of a change in the wage rate. How do these effects relate to the slope of the labor-supply curve?

8. Illustrate and explain the impact of taxes and subsidies on the individual decision to supply labor.

*9. What causes labor-market segmentation? How does this segmentation relate to wage differentials?

10. Illustrate and explain the pricing of intermediate products.

11. Illustrate and explain transfer pricing.

*12. How does the demand for capital differ from the demand for other resources? How does the time value of money relate to the demand for capital?

13. Illustrate and explain the effects of a change in the demand for capital. Distinguish between the short run and the long run.

14. How do the supplies of renewable, nonrenewable, and recyclable resources differ? Explain in terms of the components of the marginal cost of supplying each category of natural resources.

15. Explain the differences between economic rents, pure economic rents, quasi-rents, inframarginal rents, and monopoly rents.

Problems for Analysis

1. Analyze the market for computer programs in light of the revolutionary changes that have occurred in the computer market over the last twenty years.

*2. Illustrate and explain the impact of overtime pay on the individual labor supplier's time constraint. What will happen to the number of hours worked as income increases?

*3. The entertainment industry faces major changes in the 1990s. Direct-broadcast satellite transmissions and fiber-optic cable-television networks will greatly increase the number of available television channels. What impact will this have on the labor-leisure tradeoff? Illustrate.

4. At one time, the U.S. government held the price of gold at $35 per ounce. The price of gold has since risen as high as $800 per ounce before settling in the $300-per-ounce price range. Trace the impact of these price changes on the price of gold-mining equipment. Distinguish between short-run and long-run adjustments.

5. Some agricultural interests are promoting grain alcohol as a vital renewable energy source. Analyze the supply of grain alcohol as a source of energy.

6. Consider the current problem regarding the recycling of plastics. The market is woefully underdeveloped with respect to the potential supply. The problem is complicated by the fact that plastics represent an excellent source of energy when burned in a cogeneration facility. Analyze the market for recycled plastics.

13

Imperfectly Competitive Resource Markets

Although the theory of competitive resource markets may be very useful, it cannot be used to explain the operation of all input markets. Multi-million-dollar contracts for athletes and land that sells for the equivalent of $1 billion an acre are but two examples in which the perfectly competitive model might be inappropriate. Part IV of this text presented an array of market structures with perfect competition at one extreme and monopoly at the other. One characteristic of the competitive market is the absence of market power, the inability of a market participant to influence the price of the commodity. The amount of market power increases as we move away from the competitive ideal toward the pinnacle of market power, the monopolist. This chapter investigates the consequences of market power wielded by resource-market participants. The learning objective of this chapter are to examine

- the effect on resource prices and employment of market power exercised by buyers.
- the effect on resource prices and employment of market power exercised by sellers.
- the effect on resource prices and employment of the simultaneous exercise of market power by buyers and sellers.
- price discrimination in resource markets.
- the economic effects of unions.

Market Power and Resource Demand

An economic actor's ability to influence prices is always a matter of degree. The degree to which market participants can affect prices tends to rise as the number of economic actors falls and the relative size of each actor rises. The larger the buyer's or seller's share of the market, the greater their impact on the market price. The limiting case of this phenomena is where a buyer or a seller is the sole participant in a market. This extreme case of market power will be used to motivate the analysis of market power on the operations of resource markets. The market power of resource buyers manifests itself in two ways: the ability of the firm to influence (1) output prices and (2) input prices.

The Resource Demand of a Product Monopolist

The ability to influence output prices impacts the resource market through the demand for resources. The profit-maximizing firm equates the price it pays for a resource with the **marginal-revenue product** of the resource in determining the optimal amount of the resource to employ. The marginal-revenue product is the additional revenues attributable to the employment of an additional unit of a resource. Mathematically, the marginal-revenue product equals the marginal product of the input multiplied by the marginal revenue of the output. Other things being constant, a monopolist will employ fewer resources than a competitive industry because its marginal-revenue product is less than the competitive industry's marginal-revenue product. This difference is illustrated in Figure 13.1.

The difference between the marginal-revenue product of a monopolist and the marginal-revenue product of a competitive industry lies in the marginal revenue of the respective market structures. Because competitive firms are

Figure 13.1 Monopoly and the Demand for Resources

In panel (a), we see that the monopolist's marginal revenue lies below the demand. Panel (b) shows the marginal-revenue curve for some resource (R) both for a competitive industry (MRP_C) and for a single monopolistic firm MRP_M. Because MR lies below D in panel (a), MRP_M lies below MRP_C in panel (b).

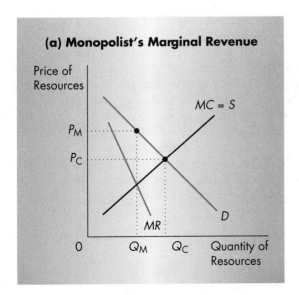

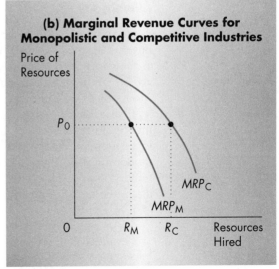

price takers, the firm's marginal revenue equals the price of the product. The marginal-revenue-product curve for the competitive industry (MRP_C) will be equal to the price, which is taken from the output demand curve, multiplied by the marginal product of the resource. Graphically, the MRP_C curve in Figure 13.1b is found by multiplying the demand curve D in Figure 13.1a by a marginal-product curve. The monopolist, on the other hand, faces a marginal-revenue curve that lies below the demand curve.[1] The marginal-revenue product for the monopolist (MRP_M in Figure 13.1b) equals the marginal-revenue curve (MR) in Figure 13.1a multiplied by the marginal product of the resource. Because the MR curve is everywhere below the D curve, the MRP_M curve will be everywhere below the MRP_C curve. The marginal-revenue product of the monopolist will be less than the marginal-revenue product of the competitive industry.

The impact of this difference is also illustrated in Figure 13.1. For any given resource price, the monopolist employs fewer units of the resource. When the price of the resource is given, the firm equates the resource price with the marginal-revenue product of the resource. At a price equal to P_0, a competitive industry would hire R_C units of the resource, whereas the monopolist would hire R_M (which is less than R_C) units of the resource. The reduced employment is a result of the monopolist exerting its market power. The monopolist restricts output from competitive level Q_C to Q_M, as shown in Figure 13.1a. This increases the price and profits of the monopolist. Because output is lower, the industry requires fewer resources to produce the output and employment falls accordingly. The use of market power by either sellers or buyers reduces the level of economic activity and alters prices to advance the interests of those who possess market power.

Monopsony

A **monopsony** exists when there are many sellers of an input but only one buyer. The effects of monopsony can be predicted if we consider monopsony as the mirror image of monopoly. Market power reduces the level of economic activity in the market and alters the price to benefit those with market power. Monopolists and monopsonists both use their market power to reduce the level of economic activity. The reduction in economic activity benefits the monopolist by increasing the price of what the monopolist sells. The reduction in economic activity benefits the monopsonist by reducing the price the monopsonist pays for inputs. Although it may be easy to predict this outcome, understanding the effects of monopsony requires a closer look at the self-interested behavior of a monopsonist.

---

1. The monopolist's marginal revenue is less than the price, because it must reduce price to sell additional units of the output. This reduction in price drives the marginal revenue below the market price of the good.

The resource-market effects of monopsony originate in the input decisions of the resource buyer. Optimal input usage of a profit-maximizing firm occurs at the point at which the additional costs of employing an input equal the additional revenues. Previous models of resource-market behavior portrayed the actions of price-taking employers. The individual competitive firm faces a resource-supply curve that is horizontal at the prevailing market price of the resource. The cost of employing additional units of the resource equals the price of the input when there are numerous small buyers. When there is only one buyer, the additional costs of expanding employment diverge from the price of the resource. This feature of monopsony requires the introduction of an additional economic relationship: marginal-factor cost.

Marginal-Factor Cost. **Marginal-factor cost** is the change in the total expenditures on an input caused by increasing input usage by one unit. Marginal-factor cost diverges from the price of the resource whenever the firm's actions influence resource prices. As the sole buyer, the firm's input supply curve is also the *market* supply curve. The resource-market monopsonist determines both the level of employment and the market price of the input. A change in the firm's input usage changes the level of employment and the market price of the input. It is this change in the market price of the input that causes the divergence between marginal-factor cost and input price.

Figure 13.2, in which the supply of the resource is labeled S_R, graphically illustrates marginal-factor cost. Suppose that the firm is employing R_0 units of the resource and is considering expanding input usage to R_1. Expanding input usage will drive the price of the resource from P_0 to P_1 as the firm moves along its (and the market's) input supply curve. When employment is R_0, the costs of employing the resource equal the price P_0 times the quantity R_0. Graphically, these costs can be represented by the area of the rectangle bounded by points 0, P_0, A, and R_0.[2] Expanding employment to R_1 increases the costs of employing the resource to the area of rectangle $0P_1BR_1$. The additional costs of this expansion equal the sum of areas P_1CAP_0 and R_0CBR_1. The area of rectangle R_0CBR_1 equals the cost of employing the additional (R_1-R_0) units of the resource and is equal to the new, higher market price times (R_1-R_0). The area of rectangle P_1CAP_0 equals the costs of paying the higher market price to those resources that were already employed by the firm.[3] The additional costs of expanding employment from R_0 to R_1 are greater than the market price of employing R_1 units of the resource. The

---

2. The area of the rectangle is equal to the side of the rectangle that lies along the vertical axis multiplied by the side that lies along the horizontal axis. The distance from the origin to P_0 is the price of the resource, and the distance from the origin to R_0 is the quantity employed. Price times quantity employed equals the costs of employing the resource.

3. This analysis presupposes that the firm does not discriminate in employment. All resources are paid the same market price for the resource.

Figure 13.2 Resource Supply and Marginal Factor Cost

Assuming an upward-sloping resource supply curve (S_R), higher prices are required to obtain larger quantities of the resource. Therefore, the decision to employ an additional unit of the resource causes costs to rise by more than the price of the resource.

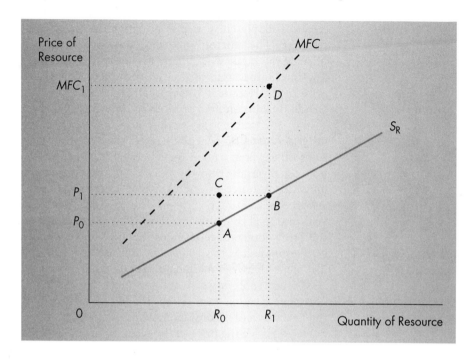

marginal factor costs of R_1 units of the resource will be at some MFC_1 greater than P_1. Calculating the additional cost of moving along the supply curve and plotting the result generate the MFC curve in Figure 13.2.[4]

The relationship between the supply curve and the marginal-factor cost curve can also be demonstrated with a numerical example. The first two columns in Table 13.1 show a linear supply curve for some particular factor. The third column shows the total cost of employing each of the six possible quantities of the input, and the fourth column shows the marginal-factor cost of each additional unit of the input.

---

4. Marginal-factor cost takes the algebraic form

$$MFC = P + R \frac{\Delta P}{\Delta R}$$

where P is the price paid for an additional unit of the resource, R is the original quantity employed, and $\Delta P/\Delta R$ is the change in the price of the resource from expanding employment. When R_1 in Figure 13.2 equals $R_0 + 1$ (a unit change in employment), P in the foregoing equation equals the area of rectangle $R_0 CBR_1$, and $R(\Delta P/\Delta R)$ equals the area of rectangle $P_0 P_1 CA$. Because R and $\Delta P/\Delta R$ are both positive, MFC must be greater than P.

Table 13.1 Factor Costs to the Monopsonist
The marginal-factor cost of employing inputs rises to the monopsonist.

Price	Quantity Supplied	Total Factor Cost	Marginal-Factor Cost
$5	0	$0	—
$6	1	$6	$6
$7	2	$14	$8
$8	3	$24	$10
$9	4	$36	$12
$10	5	$50	$14

For example, in order to hire three units, the firm must pay a price of $8, for a total cost of $24. The decision to employ one additional unit will drive the price up to $9 and cause the total cost to rise from $24 to $36. The marginal-factor cost of the fourth unit is $12, even though the price is $9. This is so because the price of each of the initial three units of the factor also rises by $1. Table 13.1 shows clearly that, after the first unit is hired, the marginal-factor cost exceeds the price.

Equilibrium Employment Under Monopsony. The input decision of the monopsonist will reflect rational, optimizing behavior: undertake any activity to the point at which the marginal benefits equal the marginal costs. The marginal benefits of employing additional units of a resource are the marginal-revenue product. When the resource market is monopsonistic, the marginal costs of employing the resource are the marginal-factor costs. The monopsonist optimizes the use of a resource by employing that quantity for which marginal-factor cost equals marginal-revenue product. This criterion is satisfied at point A in Figure 13.3, where the profit-maximizing quantity of the resource is R_0. This quantity will be supplied if the monopsonist offers price P_0, as indicated by point C on the resource supply curve.[5]

A number of points must be made about the equilibrium of a monopsonist:

1. *The monopsonist does not have a resource demand curve.* A demand curve implies alternative quantities purchased at alternative prices. The monopsonist has only one profit-maximizing (and therefore equilibrium) price-quantity combination. That equilibrium point corresponds to a point on the resource supply curve.

---

5. Note the methodological similarity to the monopolist's decision making. Both the monopsonist and the monopolist take the curve that is marginal to the curve illustrating their trading partner's willingness to trade, and find the point at which the curve that reflects their willingness to trade intersects that marginal curve.

Figure 13.3 A Monopsonistic Market for Resource

Faced with the resource supply curve S_R and the marginal-revenue-product curve *MRP*, a monopsonistic firm will hire R_0 units of the resource and pay a price of P_0.

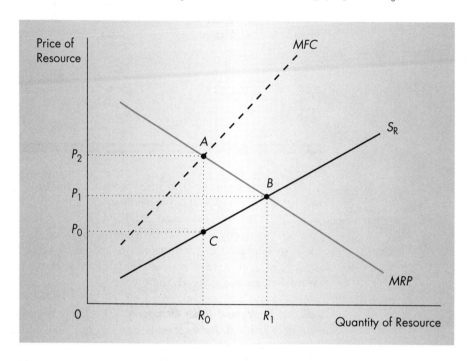

2. *The monopsonist restricts employment and reduces the price of the resource.* If the monopsonist depicted in Figure 13.3 had acted like a competitive firm and treated the price of the resource as its marginal cost of employing additional units of the resource, the firm would have employed R_1 units of the resource at a price of P_1. The market power of the monopsonist results in reduced employment and lower factor prices.

3. *Monopsonistic equilibrium involves monopsonistic exploitation.* The monopsonist pays a price that is less than the input's contribution to the revenues of the firm, the marginal-revenue product. The difference between the price (P_0) and marginal-revenue product (P_2) is captured by the firm and is part of the economic profits earned by the firm.

The monopsony model is a benchmark representing one extreme in the array of possible resource-market structures. The monopsony price and level of employment represent a worst-case resource-market scenario. This equilibrium is the lower limit for the level of employment and resource prices when the resource buyer exercises market power. Real-world examples of monopsony generally require a very narrow definition of a resource market. Given the diversity of resource markets, finding a monopsony would involve restricting the market to a specific time, place, and resource. An example of a monopsony might be the market for college professors in the typical college town (one big employer) during a given semester or quarter.

Even the most restrictive market definition will usually involve more than one employer. A somewhat more realistic example of buyer-side market power is that which occurs in most college towns where there is one large employer (the university) and many small employers (the small-business owners in the surrounding community). Many college students and other residents of college towns have noticed the relatively low wages that prevail in the typical college town. The level of wages in these markets can be explained by what is known as dominant-firm price leadership.

Dominant-Firm Price Leadership

Price leadership occurs when some market participant sets a price and others follow this pricing strategy. **Dominant-firm price leadership** develops when one side of a market has one large participant who has many small rivals. In resource markets, one variant of this model looks at the pricing behavior of a large employer — called the dominant firm — and the impact of this behavior on its rivals and the market. The dominant firm is large enough to influence the market price of the resource. The other firms are so numerous that no single one of them has any impact on the market price and takes the price set by the dominant firm as given. Because the small firms are price takers, they are referred to as the **competitive fringe**. The outcome of this market structure is determined by the optimizing behavior of the dominant firm.

The graphical representation of the dominant-firm price leadership model begins with three basic economic relationships: the market supply of the resource, the resource demand of the fringe firms, and the marginal-revenue product of the dominant firm. The market supply appears in both Figures 13.4a and 13.4b as the curve labeled S_{mkt}. The demand of the fringe firms is obtained by horizontally summing their marginal-revenue-product curves to obtain the curve labeled D_{fringe} in Figure 13.4a. The dominant firm's marginal-revenue product is the curve labeled MRP_{dom}, in Figure 13.4b.[6] If the dominant firm were to act as a price taker, the market demand for the resource would be the horizontal sum of D_{fringe} and MRP_{dom}, or the curve in Figure 13.4a labeled D_{mkt}. The market outcome of competition between the dominant firm and the competitive fringe would be the competitive price and quantity, or P_C and Q_C, respectively, in Figure 13.4a. Note that this outcome is dependent on the dominant firm ignoring its market power, so the curve labeled D_{mkt} is of use only to compare the dominant-firm equilibrium with the competitive equilibrium.

---

6. Two graphs are used to present this model to avoid cramming all of the necessary information into one diagram.

Figure 13.4 Dominant-Firm Price Leadership

When the dominant firm acts as a price taker, the market equilibrium occurs at the competitive price P_c and quantity Q_c, as illustrated in panel (a). To exercise its market power, the dominant firm subtracts the fringe demand from the market supply to determine its supply curve S_{dom}, as illustrated in panel (b). The dominant firm then equates the marginal factor cost curve that is associated with the dominant firm's resource supply curve to find the optimal employment level, Q_{dom}. The dominant firm then sets a price P_d using the supply faced by the firm.

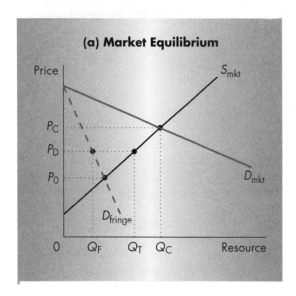

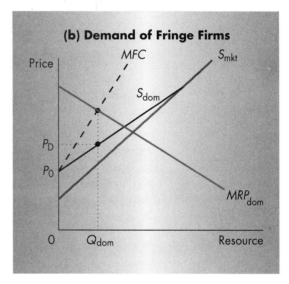

Although the rational dominant firm will exercise its market power, it does not have the power to set monopsonistic prices. The dominant firm's ability to set resource prices is limited by the presence of the competitive fringe. The fringe firms will take whatever price the dominant firm sets and purchase the quantity that corresponds to that price on the fringe demand curve. The dominant firm will be left with that portion of the quantity supplied (at the price set by the dominant firm) that is not purchased by the competitive fringe. The dominant firm faces a supply curve that is determined by the horizontal difference between the market supply and the fringe demand.

The supply curve faced by the dominant firm is illustrated in Figure 13.4b by the S_{dom} curve. When the price is P_0, the fringe quantity demanded equals the market quantity supplied and the dominant firm is unable to purchase any of the resource at that price. When the price is at the vertical intercept of the D_{fringe} curve, the dominant firm has the entire market supply to itself. Between these two prices, the quantity supplied to the dominant firm is the horizontal distance between S_{mkt} and D_{fringe}. This horizontal distance (measured at each price) is drawn and labeled S_{dom} in Figure 13.4b.

The supply curve faced by the dominant firm will be sloped upward, because the quantity supplied to the dominant firm is the difference between the upward-sloping market supply and the downward-sloping fringe demand. As we learned with monopsony, the firm that faces an upward-sloping supply curve also faces an upward-sloping marginal-factor cost curve that is above the supply curve. The dominant firm optimizes its usage of a resource by employing that quantity at which the marginal-revenue product equals the marginal factor cost, or quantity Q_{dom} in Figure 13.4b. The dominant firm pays price P_D, corresponding to the price from its supply curve S_{dom} for the quantity Q_{dom}. The competitive fringe takes this price as given and purchases quantity Q_F as determined by the fringe demand and illustrated in Figure 13.4a.

The total quantity of the resource employed is the sum of fringe and dominant-firm employment, or Q_T in Figure 13.4a. This amount is equal to Q_F plus the difference between fringe demand and market supply at price P_D. Note the difference between the competitive equilibrium (price P_C and quantity Q_C) and the price leadership equilibrium (price P_D and quantity Q_T). The quantity employed and the equilibrium price are both reduced when the dominant firm exercises its market power.

An example of dominant-firm price leadership might be found in the market for elementary and secondary school teachers. Elementary and secondary education is produced by a mixture of public and private schools. Price leadership will tend to develop in communities in which there is a single public school district and a number of small, independent private schools. In 1989, public schools nationwide employed 2.36 million teachers, and their private counterparts employed 377,000 teachers.[7] If the local market for teachers follows this public/private mix, the public school district would employ 86 percent of all teachers, and the private schools would share the remaining 14 percent. The dominant firm (the school district) would set a teacher pay scale and each of the fringe employers (the private schools) would pay according to that schedule.

Discrimination

Another pricing scheme that reduces resource costs is price discrimination. Factor-market price discrimination entails the payment of different prices for identical productive services. The firm that practices this form of price discrimination is able to increase its profits by extracting some (or all) of the producer surplus that resource suppliers are receiving. The firm wishing to capture these rents must do the following:

- *Possess market power.* The ability to influence factor prices (that is, market power) is a prerequisite for price discrimination, because the competitive firm simply pays the market-determined price. Once the decision to price-discriminate is made, the profit-maximizing price structure will reflect supplier responsiveness to factor-price changes — that is, the elasticity of factor supply.

7. Source: *Statistical Abstract of the United States,* 1991.

- *Face resource suppliers with differing supply elasticities.* Although the firm may be able to control factor prices, factor suppliers control the quantity supplied. The responsiveness of the quantity supplied to a change in the factor price will affect the prices paid by discriminating employers.
- *Be able to classify resource suppliers according to their supply elasticities.* The optimal pricing scheme can be implemented if and only if the firm is able to identify the supply elasticities of specific resource suppliers or groups of suppliers.
- *Be able to segregate the resource suppliers.* A discriminatory price regime creates the potential for profitable exchanges. The price differentials that discrimination creates allow arbitragers to profit from buying at low prices and reselling at high prices, unless they can be prevented from doing so.

Arbitragers make discrimination all but impossible in markets for non-human resources. An important characteristic of nonhuman resources is the separability of the resource owner and the productive powers of the resource. This separability will lead to the elimination of discriminatory price differentials. Suppose red-headed sellers of machine tools are paid more for their product than blonds, when the productivity of machine tools is independent of hair color. Red-headed arbitragers can profit by purchasing the output of blond machine tool manufacturers and reselling the output to discriminating machine-tool buyers. Arbitragers bid up the prices paid to blond machine-tool manufacturers. The sales by red-headed arbitrageurs will bid down the price received by red-headed suppliers, and the discriminatory price scheme breaks down.

In contrast, the markets for human resources, by virtue of the inseparability of the owner from the productive power of the resource, are candidates for effective price discrimination. Wage discrimination can prevail because those workers who are discriminated against cannot arbitrage their labor services. Consequently, the theory behind the practice of factor-market price discrimination will be portrayed using labor-market examples. These examples include third-degree and first-degree wage discrimination.

Third-Degree Wage Discrimination. **Third-degree wage discrimination** occurs when the labor market is segregated into two or more groups and the wages paid to each group are determined separately. Figure 13.5 illustrates the discriminatory actions of a monopsonist practicing third-degree discrimination. The firm employs labor that can be segregated into two groups, the supplies for which are S_A and S_B. Summing S_A and S_B horizontally generates the total supply of labor S_T. Because each of the three supply curves slopes upward, the additional expenditures resulting from movements along the supply curves are shown by the respective marginal-factor-cost curves MFC_A, MFC_B, and MFC_T.

Figure 13.5 Third-Degree Wage Discrimination

The nondiscriminatory monopsonist pays the same wage w_0 to both types of labor. This wage is determined by the intersection of the marginal-revenue product and the total marginal-factor cost MFC_T. The discriminating monopsonist employs the same total number of workers, but the number and wages of each labor type is adjusted to equate the marginal-factor cost in each labor market.

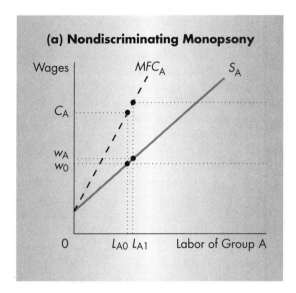

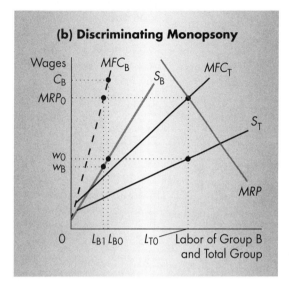

Finally, the marginal-revenue product of labor is assumed to be the same for both types of labor and is represented by the MRP curve.[8]

The nondiscriminatory monopsonist ignores the separate supply curves and makes its employment decision based on the aggregate curves S_T and MFC_T. The profit-maximizing firm will equate marginal-revenue product and marginal-factor cost and employ L_{T0} units of labor. The combined supply curve S_T indicates that L_{T0} units of labor can be employed if a wage equal to w_0 is offered. This wage will attract L_{A0} units of type A labor and L_{B0} units of type B labor, as determined by the separate supply curves.

The nondiscriminatory equilibrium leaves available a profitable reallocation of resources. If the labor types are treated separately, the marginal-factor cost of employing L_{A0} units of type A labor is C_A, and the marginal factor cost of

8. Discrimination occurs when different prices are paid for the same service. Different marginal-revenue products imply that the services are different and that any wage differential is not necessarily discriminatory.

employing L_{B0} units of type B labor is C_B, C_B being greater than C_A. Reducing employment of type B labor by one unit reduces costs by C_B and revenues by MRP_0. Increasing employment of type A labor by one unit increases costs by C_A and revenues by MRP_0. These two actions leave revenues constant, reduce costs (by the difference between C_B and C_A), and profits rise accordingly. The profitability of this reallocation is predicated on differential treatment of the workers. Profits rise if and only if wages are set by referring to the separate supply curves. The firm must raise the wage paid to type A workers in order to attract more of them, but it can lower the wage paid to type B workers because it wants to reduce their number. Profits rise because the marginal cost of hiring additional type A workers is less than the marginal cost of type B workers. The firm saves more by terminating type B workers than it has to spend by employing more type A workers. The reallocation continues until the marginal factor cost of employing the two labor types are equalized.

The discriminating monopsonist is in equilibrium when the marginal-factor costs of each labor type equal each other and the marginal-revenue product. The firm begins by equating the combined marginal-factor cost (MFC_T) and marginal-revenue product to determine the equilibrium marginal-revenue product, or MRP_0, in Figure 13.5. The employment of each labor type is expanded until the marginal-factor cost of each group of workers equals MRP_0. This occurs when the employment of type A and type B labor equals L_{A1} and L_{B1}, respectively. Each labor type is then paid a wage determined by the separate supply curves. A wage equal to w_A is necessary to attract L_{A1} units of type A labor, whereas w_B is required to employ L_{B1} units of type B labor.

Supply Elasticity and Discrimination: A Digression. Labor-supply elasticity can be used to explain the wage differentials that exist under wage discrimination. The elasticity of labor supply is the relative responsiveness of labor suppliers to a change in the wage rate. It is defined as the percentage change in the quantity of labor supplied divided by the percentage change in the wage rate, or

$$e_{LS} = \frac{\%\Delta LS}{\%\Delta W}$$

The elasticity of labor supply will have a direct bearing on the marginal-factor cost of an input. The marginal factor cost of labor has two components: the payments to additional employees and the expense of passing a higher wage along to existing employees. The former is simply the (higher) wage required to increase the quantity supplied, and the latter is determined by the change in the wage rate. The new wage and the change in wages are both related to the elasticity of labor supply. *Ceteris paribus,* the less elastic the supply, the higher the new wage, and the greater the change in wages, will be. Consequently, the marginal-factor cost will be relatively high when the supply of labor is relatively inelastic. Because the discriminating monopsonist reduces the employment and wages of those whose marginal-factor cost is relatively high, the group whose labor supply is relatively inelastic will experience lower wages under wage discrimination.[9]

The theory of wage discrimination implies that those who are least responsive to wage changes will experience lower wages. What factors contribute to a relatively inelastic supply of labor? Two considerations are the availability of alternative employment opportunities and the costs of changing jobs. The supply of labor tends to be inelastic when prospects of finding alternative employment are limited. Those with very specialized skills or relatively few skills are, other things being constant, more likely candidates for discrimination. The supply of labor also tends to be inelastic when the costs of changing jobs is high. Those who would have to relocate to take another job will tend to be less responsive to wage changes because of the moving expenses. Whatever the source of the unresponsiveness, those whose supply is relatively inelastic will be paid lower wages when the employer is able to segregate the labor market. For an example, see Highlight 13.1.

Highlight 13.1 *Salary Compression and the Issue of Age Discrimination*

A persistent source of controversy in American universities is the issue of salary compression. Salary compression occurs when the differential between the pay of experienced professors and that of new professors is very low (or even negative). As an example, a survey of salaries for economics professors in 1992 revealed that, at institutions with Ph.D. programs in economics, newly hired assistant professors received an average starting salary of $45,813. The average salary among assistant professors who had on average worked for about five years was $44,441, and that of associate professors (average experience of over ten years) was $53,071.

---

9. This proposition can be demonstrated algebraically. Rewriting the expression for *MFC* in footnote 4 to conform with the labor market, we obtain $MFC = w + L(\Delta w/w\Delta L)$. Multiplying the right-hand side of this equation by w/w permits us to write

$$MFC = w \left[\frac{w}{w} + \frac{L}{w}\left(\frac{\Delta w}{\Delta L}\right) \right]$$

which can be rewritten as

$$MFC = w \left(1 + \frac{L\Delta w}{w\Delta L} \right)$$

The $L\Delta w/w\Delta L$ term is equal to the inverse of the supply elasticity, so we can write

$$MFC = w \left(1 + \frac{1}{\varepsilon_s} \right)$$

Given the *MFC*, a lower (more inelastic) ε_s translates into a lower *w*.

At colleges and universities at which no graduate programs in economics were offered, the average entry salary for a new assistant professor was $39,446. Current assistant professors earned an average of only $30,791, and associate professors had an average salary of $43,557.

The reaction to this salary structure is mixed. Some current assistant and associate professors adopt the view that high salaries by newly hired assistant professors strengthens their bargaining position when it comes to future salary negotiations, so they favor salary compression. Others argue that money is wasted on new, inexperienced faculty when it should go to reward those with more experience. In fact, many universities have been sued for age discrimination because of their compressed salary structure.

A number of factors contribute to an economic understanding of salary compression. However, monopsonistic wage discrimination almost certainly plays a role. When a college or university seeks to hire a new assistant professor, they are generally looking for someone who is just finishing a Ph.D. program. Those persons are generally young and mobile — willing to move to almost any part of the country for employment. Generally they do not own homes, many are unmarried, and most do not have children. Accordingly, the labor supply of this group of prospective employees tends to be quite elastic.

In contrast, current assistant professors and associate professors tend to be far less mobile. Often they have ties to the community in the form of spouses who work, children in school, and homes on which they are paying mortgages. All of these factors tend to increase the costs to them of moving to a new job. Therefore, their labor supply tends to be much less elastic.

Salary compression is therefore entirely consistent with the type of behavior we would expect from a monopsonistic college or university with an interest in minimizing its costs of staffing faculty positions. Such an institution would want to cut back on the employment of the group with the less elastic labor supply, because their marginal factor cost is high. This explains low salaries to experienced faculty and high salaries to new faculty.

First-Degree Wage Discrimination. **First-degree wage discrimination** is discrimination carried to its theoretical limit. This form of discrimination segregates the labor market to the point where each worker is a separate market. One-on-one negotiations take place, and each worker is paid the lowest possible wage. This minimum payment will equal what the individual can earn in his next best alternative — that is, the opportunity cost of accepting the job. A heterogeneous labor market will include individuals with heterogeneous alternatives. In this case, first-degree discrimination will lead to each worker earning a different wage.

The market effects of first-degree wage discrimination are demonstrated with the aid of Figure 13.6. Each point on the supply curve in Figure 13.6 represents a different individual, with the individuals ranked by their opportunity costs. This ranking yields an upward-sloping supply curve where the

Figure 13.6 First-Degree Wage Discrimination

The firm that practices first-degree discrimination pays each worker a wage that is just equal to its opportunity cost. Paying employees their opportunity cost transforms the supply curve into a marginal-factor cost curve. Total wages paid are equal to the shaded area. The monopsonist captures the inframarginal rents Aw_1B that would have been earned by the workers.

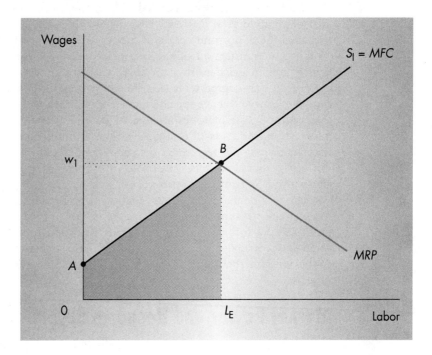

firm must increase its wage offer to attract additional employees. Because each individual is treated separately, the wage paid to the last worker hired is higher than that paid to the other workers. Previously hired workers are paid the wage that was just sufficient to hire them. This pricing scheme converts the labor supply curve into the marginal-factor-cost curve.[10] The firm then hires the quantity of labor for which the marginal-factor cost equals the marginal-revenue product, or L_E in Figure 13.6.

10. In mathematical terms, the marginal-factor-cost curve is determined by the equation

$$MFC = w + L \frac{\Delta w}{\Delta L}$$

When first-degree discrimination is practiced, the $\Delta w/\Delta L$ term is zero (the higher wages are not passed on to other workers) and the marginal-factor cost is equal to the wage of the last worker hired. Because the wage of the last worker hired is determined by the labor supply curve, the marginal-factor cost and the labor-supply curves coincide.

The firm depicted in Figure 13.6 pays wages ranging from A (the wage paid to the first worker hired) to W_1 (the wage paid to the last worker hired). Between these extremes, the wage rate rises along the supply curve with total wage payments equaling the shaded area under the supply curve. In the absence of discrimination, each of the L_E workers would have been paid a wage equal to W_1, with total earnings equal to the area of rectangle $0W_1BL_E$. If these earnings had been received, the portion of the total represented by the area of triangle AW_1B would have been inframarginal rents, earnings that exceeded the opportunity costs of the resource owners. First-degree wage discrimination transfers all of the inframarginal rents from the workers to the firm, so it increases the firm's profits by that amount.

Perfect first-degree wage discrimination is never possible. To practice it, a firm would have to have specific knowledge of each worker's next best alternatives. Although it may be possible to collect such an enormous amount of information, the costs of doing so would undoubtedly outweigh any benefits that the firm would receive by discriminating. The firm would end up spending any potential savings on private investigators' efforts to track down the alternative employments of prospective employees.

The first-degree-wage-discrimination model is illustrative of the discriminatory extreme and does provide some insight into wage negotiations. The profit-seeking firm seeks to minimize its costs and tries to pay the minimum wage that workers will accept. An effective labor negotiator must be cognizant of this fact, whether he represents himself, another individual, or a large group of workers.

Market Power and Resource Supply

The ability to influence resource prices is not limited to the demand side of resource markets. Sellers of resources may exercise market power as well. The ability of sellers to influence the price of a resource varies from the price-taking behavior of competitive sellers (as detailed in the previous chapter) to the price-setting power of a monopolist. This section investigates the actions of resource-market monopolists.

Resource Monopoly

The theory of resource-market monopoly differs from the theory of product-market monopoly (covered in Part IV) in only one detail: the demand faced by the monopolist. The demand for the resource is derived from the demand for the good or service produced with the resource. The price that buyers will pay for the resource will be limited to the additional revenues generated from employment of the resource. The demand faced by a single seller of a resource is, like the demand faced by any resource owner, the marginal-revenue product of the resource.

The price of a resource controlled by a single seller is set to maximize the net returns to the owner of the resource. The marginal benefits to a seller, as discussed in previous chapters, are the marginal revenues. These additional revenues are indicated by the curve that is marginal to the marginal-revenue-product curve. The *MR* curve in Figure 13.7 indicates the marginal revenues of selling the resource *R*. The seller's marginal costs are the marginal opportunity costs of using the resource. These costs are represented by the *MC* curve in Figure 13.7, which, under competitive conditions, would be the market supply of the resource. The monopolistic resource supplier sells the quantity at which the *MR* and *MC* curves intersect, or R_M in Figure 13.7. The price of the resource is then set at the price that the buyer is willing to pay for quantity R_M, as determined by the demand curve. This will be price P_M in Figure 13.7. A competitive resource market would have employed R_C units of the resource at a price equal to P_C. The resource monopolist, in contrast, reduces employment and raises the resource price.

The rational resource supplier yearns for a monopoly over the sale of his resource. The market power inherent in a monopoly increases the net income of the resource owner. The monopoly returns, however, will inspire entry into

Figure 13.7 Resource Monopoly
The monopolistic resource supplier equates marginal cost and marginal revenue, restricts the quantity of the resource employed, and raises the price of the resource.

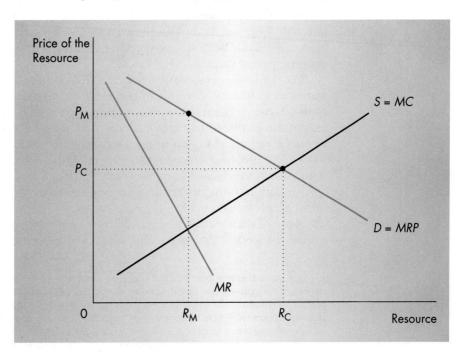

the resource market, increasing the quantity of the resource supplied and driving resource prices toward the competitive level. Resource-market monopolies will be transitory unless something prevents entry into the resource market. Barriers to entering resource markets can be natural (as in the case of land) or artificial (as in the case of organized labor). We will discuss the monopoly aspects of land before going on to the market power of labor unions.

Land

The tradition in economics is to use land as a generic term that includes natural resources. The previous chapter went against this tradition by dealing with natural resources separately. This chapter follows this unconventional approach by looking at the market for land, in which land is synonymous with space. Land contributes to the production of goods and services, both directly and indirectly. Land makes a direct contribution, via the productive powers of the soil. This aspect of land is consistent with land as a natural resource and can be analyzed using the theory of natural resources presented in Chapter 12. Land makes an indirect contribution to output in the form of the space necessary to undertake production.

Land and Space. All economic activity has a spatial dimension, because all economic actors must be somewhere. The parties to a potential exchange, however, are often in different places. When this occurs, the costs of overcoming the distance between traders makes location an important market characteristic.[11] Locational considerations inject an element of monopoly into the market for land, because any specific parcel of land occupies a unique and exclusive part of space.

The market for land can be analyzed from a number of perspectives. One way is to view land in terms of the total quantity of space available. This approach can be illustrated with a graph, Figure 13.8a, which puts the surface area of the earth on the horizontal axis. In this approach, the supply of land would be vertical and equal to the amount of the earth's surface that is above water. The supply of land can shift left as land becomes submerged or shift right as land is reclaimed from the ocean. Although this approach may provide some insight into the market for land, it presents such a big picture that many useful details are obscured.

Some of these details are revealed by taking a use-specific approach to the market for land. This approach examines the quantity of land devoted to a

11. In some circumstances, location is the *only* important characteristic. When the market trades a homogeneous commodity among many small buyers and sellers (that is, under competitive conditions), the only difference among rivals will be their location. A fairly close approximation of this sort of market is the retail sector of the economy, which encompasses many small and a few large organizations. This is the economic logic behind the old saying "There are three important factors in retailing: location, location, and location."

Figure 13.8 Two Views of Land

Panel (a) views land in terms of the total area available. The supply of land is perfectly inelastic at the earth's current surface area. Panel (b) examines the supply of land for a particular use — in this case, residential lots. An increase in demand for residential space increases the price of land and attracts land from alternative uses.

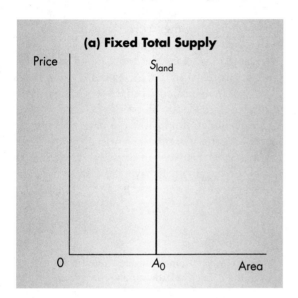

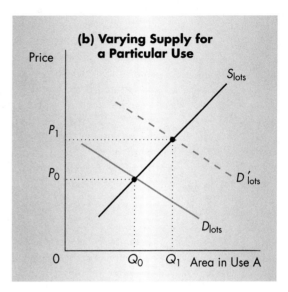

particular use. The demand for land in a particular use will be the marginal-revenue product of land in that use. The curve depicting the supply of land for the particular use will slope upward, because higher prices will encourage landowners to shift their resources from alternative uses of their land. This approach provides flexibility, because the particular use can be defined very broadly or very narrowly. A broad view of land use would analyze the market for agricultural land. A narrow definition of land use would examine the market for land used to grow potatoes or the market for commercial office space in Toronto.

The particular use approach can be used to explain the conversion of farmland to residential land that is sometimes called urban sprawl. A rising demand for housing, which accompanies urban population growth, increases the demand for land devoted to residential use. The demand for residential space might increase from D_{lots} to D'_{lots} as illustrated in Figure 13.8b. This puts upward pressure on the price of residential lots, which is increased through the development of surrounding land, usually farmland. The quantity of residential space is increased as land is transferred from agricultural to residential uses. Although the particular-use approach is flexible, it may obscure the monopolistic elements in the market for land.

Locational Monopolies. A third approach to the market for land is a variation on the first two approaches. This approach investigates the alternative uses of a particular tract of land. The quantity of land available in a particular plot is fixed, with the supply curve being vertical, as illustrated in Figure 13.9. The property will have alternative uses, with the demand for the land in each use represented by a different marginal-revenue-product curve. The curves MRP_A and MRP_B in Figure 13.9 represent two uses for the land. The land will ultimately be allocated to its highest-valued use, with the price being set by the marginal-revenue product of the land in that use. Of the two alternative uses illustrated in Figure 13.9, the land will be allocated to those whose marginal-revenue product is MRP_B and the price of the land will be P_B.

The location of the parcel of land will determine, in large part, the number of alternative uses for the property and the marginal-revenue product of the land in the alternative uses. Land that is relatively inaccessible (in terms of distance from economic actors and/or terrain) will have the fewest uses and will be, *ceteris paribus,* relatively inexpensive. Land that is close to centers of

Figure 13.9 The Price of Land

The price of a particular piece of property is determined by the value of the property in its highest valued use. Given the perfectly elastic supply, the price is determined by the marginal-revenue product of the land in its best use.

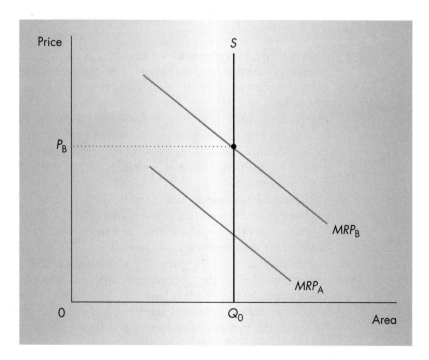

economic activity will have many uses, some of which will involve relatively high marginal-revenue products. The price of such land will be relatively high. Land in downtown Tokyo is a prime example of the effects of **locational monopolies**. This land is extremely expensive, because Tokyo is the center of both government and business in Japan (see Highlight 13.2).

Highlight 13.2   *Inventories and the Price of Space in Japan*

In the ongoing debate concerning trade between Japan and the United States, some observers point to Japanese management as a partial explanation of the trade imbalance that exists between the two countries. Managers in Japan appear to be particularly adept at organizing production. Two often-cited examples of the superiority of Japanese business practice are "just-in-time" scheduling and the low defect rate of Japanese products as they come off the assembly line. These two aspects of Japanese business practice are interrelated and can be traced to the price of land in Japan.

Land prices in Japan are among the highest in the world. One survey of Japanese property-tax rolls found the cheapest property to be valued at $1 million per acre. The high price of land is derived from market conditions that are peculiar to Japan. Japan has one of the world's highest standards of living and a population that is approximately half that of the United States. The relatively wealthy citizens of Japan reside on an island nation whose land area is approximately equal to that of Montana. The relative scarcity of land is compounded by the mountainous terrain of the Japanese islands. Mountains account for approximately 80 percent of Japan's land area.

Just-in-time scheduling, in which inputs are delivered just before they are needed, is a rational response to high land prices. Traditionally, firms keep inventories of inputs for which resources are purchased beforehand and stored until needed. The firm's inventory can be viewed as an input, because production cannot proceed without the necessary inputs. The demand for this input, like the demand for any input, will be downward sloping. The level of inventories will fall as the price of inventories rise. The price of inventory is the cost of maintaining the inventory, an element of which is the cost of constructing storage space. The high price of land in Japan leads firms to economize on storage space by adopting just-in-time scheduling and minimizing inventory levels.

Japanese industry's record of exceptionally low defect rates is no accident. Just-in-time scheduling is an alternative to inventories if and only if the inputs can be reliably fed into the production process. If a shipment contains defective parts, some mechanism must be developed to remove the defects from the production process. The process of sorting out defects takes both

The Japanese have adapted to scarce land resources by adopting "just in time" schedules of input deliveries. The price system thereby economizes on the use of scarce space.

time and space and disrupts the just-in-time schedule. Japanese suppliers have to develop efficient quality-control practices to survive in an economy in which space is at a premium.

Unions

A **labor union** is an agreement among workers to cooperate on issues of mutual concern. Workers form a cartel that acts like a monopolist in the market for labor services and promotes the interests of the members of the union. These interests include, but are not limited to, wages, fringe benefits, job security, and working conditions. Because union members and their employment opportunities are heterogeneous, labor unions are complex economic institutions that exhibit great diversity in structure and conduct. Although a thorough study of unions is beyond the scope of a course in intermediate microeconomics, it is possible to use familiar economic concepts to develop a basic understanding of union behavior. The analysis of unions views a union as a single economic organism (separate from its members) and begins by identifying the objectives of the organization.

Union Objectives. The objectives of a union are easy to identify but difficult to specify. Because unions represent labor suppliers, union activity will reflect the underlying motivations of their members. As the previous chapter showed, the actions of labor suppliers can be analyzed within the utility-maximization framework. Thus union activity can be expected to increase the utility of union members. In the simplest terms, the objective of a union is to maximize the net economic benefits accruing to its members from employment.

This statement of union objectives is necessarily vague. Determining the optimal economic conditions for a large group of workers is exceedingly complex. One complexity arises from the number of factors, both pecuniary and nonpecuniary, that affect the utility of workers. Workers benefit from higher wages and benefits, greater job security, and better working conditions, to name just a few of the factors that affect the utility of labor suppliers. In a world in which scarcity requires choice among alternatives, one problem for a union is to find the optimal combination of the factors that affect the utility of workers. This problem is complicated further by the diversity of union members. Different workers will have different preferences. Members who would have little difficulty obtaining another job care a lot about wages and much less about job security, whereas those who would have difficulty finding another job care a lot about job security and less about wages. The union will have to reconcile conflicts among members as well as conflicts between members and their employers.

Although it is easy to say that unions promote the interests of workers, it should be remembered that unions are no different from other economic organizations. Someone within the union must make decisions on behalf of the union. Unions are directed by self-interested individuals, and the interests of union leaders may conflict with the interests of the union members. This is identical to the separation-of-ownership-and-control problem that may arise in corporations. It is incumbent upon the individuals in an organization to devise mechanisms to ensure that those who make decisions on behalf of the organization exercise their power in the interests of the organization. Unions use the ballot box to curtail the self-interested behavior of their leaders. Union leaders are elected by the membership and must satisfy the members to continue in their leadership positions. Union leaders can expect reelection by promoting the interests of at least a majority of the union rank and file.

The means to union ends can be either direct or indirect. Unions advance the interests of workers directly through contract negotiations with employers and other activities that take place within the labor market. Unions can also affect the labor-market outcome indirectly by going beyond the usual confines of the market to alter fundamental market conditions. These two paths to union goals are illustrated by assuming that higher wages are the sole concern of unions. Although this is a gross simplification, it does provide insight into union activity.

Unions and Wages. The union that elects to make wages its sole concern must first set a wage goal. The union, like any other monopolist, does not have absolute power over prices, because it is constrained by a demand curve. The

Figure 13.10 Unions and Income

A union might pursue a monopoly price strategy and set employment where marginal revenue equals marginal cost. This strategy results in wages being set at w_0, and maximizes the net returns to the workers. Alternatively, the union might pursue a strategy that maximizes the total earnings of union members. Earnings are maximized at the point at which the marginal revenue is zero and wages are w_1.

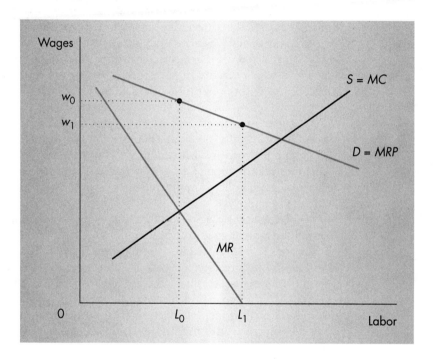

wage goal of a union will be the price/quantity combination on the marginal-revenue product of labor curve that best serves the interests of its members. The optimal union wage, however, is subject to interpretation. Two possible interpretations of the optimal union wage are illustrated in Figure 13.10.

One solution to the optimal-wage question is the monopoly solution. The union acts as a monopolist and sets the wage (W_0) from the demand curve for the quantity at which marginal cost equals marginal revenue. This wage maximizes the net economic returns to suppliers of labor by restricting employment to L_0. An alternative wage goal would be to maximize the total amount paid to workers. In Figure 3.10 this occurs at wage W_1, where marginal revenue equals zero.[12] Each worker earns a lower wage as employment expands to L_1.

---

12. If marginal revenue is positive, an increase in quantity increases total revenues and total earnings. Earnings and revenues are at a maximum when marginal revenue is zero.

A decrease in wages from the monopoly wage results in a more-than-proportionate increase in employment, and total earnings rise. Either of the these wages, or some other wage, can serve as the union's wage goals. The union must determine an optimal wage that takes the wage/employment tradeoff into account.

Once the optimal union wage is determined, the union must undertake actions to achieve its goal. The four parts of Figure 13.11 illustrate a hypothetical labor market and the actions that bring about a higher market wage. Panel (a) illustrates the initial market conditions. The supply of labor is S_0 and the demand for labor is D_0. Supply and demand set an initial equilibrium wage at W_0, and L_0 workers are employed. For analytical purposes the union's wage goal is set at W^*. The union can bring about an increase in the wage to W^* by (1) increasing the demand for labor, (2) reducing the supply of labor, or (3) setting a minimum wage at which union members will work. These strategies are illustrated in panels (b) through (d), respectively.

Panel (b) shows the increase in demand necessary to achieve an equilibrium wage of W^*. This strategy is particularly desirable, because it also increases employment from L_0 to L_B. There are a number of ways to increase the demand for labor:

- Because the demand for labor is a derived demand, *an increase in the demand for the output* will increase the demand for the input. The International Ladies' Garment Workers Union's ad campaign asking consumers to "look for the union label" will, if successful, increase the demand for union labor by increasing demand for the clothing produced by union workers.
- *Union support for import quotas and tariffs* is another way they can increase the demand for their services. Import restrictions decrease the supply of foreign products and increase the demand faced by domestic producers. This increases the demand for domestic (union) labor.
- *Unions also support legislation that limits competition from other labor suppliers.* For example, minimum wage laws increase the demand for union labor by increasing the price of nonunion labor, a substitute.
- Finally, because the demand for labor is equivalent to the marginal-revenue product of labor, *an increase in the marginal product of labor will increase the demand for labor*. For example, training programs that increase the productivity of union workers increase the demand for those workers.

A union that is unable to increase wages by increasing the demand for labor may increase wages by reducing the supply of labor. With demand at D_0, an equilibrium wage of W^* will prevail if supply is reduced to S_1 as in Figure 13.11c. The union can achieve a reduction in the supply of labor by restricting entry into the market. One way to restrict entry is simply to limit the number of members. The number of new union cards is fixed, so that there is a surplus of prospective union workers. Another way of restricting entry is to raise the

Figure 13.11 Achieving Union Wage Goals

Panel (a) shows the relationship between the market wage w_0 and the union's wage goal W^*. The wage goal can be achieved by increasing the demand for labor, as shown in panel (b). The goal may also be reached by decreasing the supply of labor as shown in panel (c). Finally, a wage of W^* can be achieved by eliminating price competition among the workers. This entails an agreement among workers not to work for less than the wage goal.

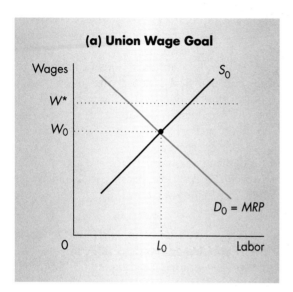

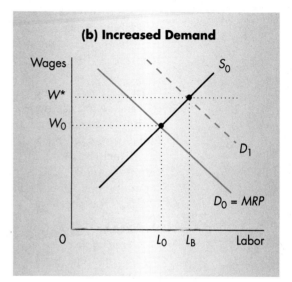

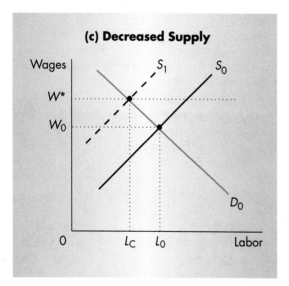

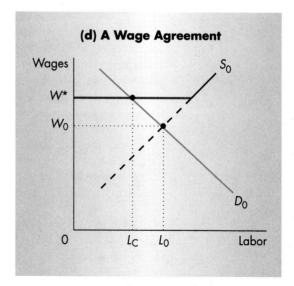

costs of entering. Unions that have training or apprenticeship programs as prerequisites to union membership are effectively raising the costs of getting into the union. Regardless of the means by which entry is restricted, the union raises wages at the expense of employment. Restricting the supply of labor from S_0 to S_1 reduces employment from L_0 to L_C.

If the union can neither increase demand nor reduce supply, it can still achieve its wage goals by eliminating price competition. This strategy requires the cooperation of the union rank and file. Members must agree not to work for less than the optimal union wage. The agreement to withhold labor unless union wage demands are met makes the supply of labor horizontal at the desired wage, as indicated in Figure 13.12d. This strategy puts employment at L_C (the same result as restricting the supply of labor), but the lack of entry restrictions means that the quantity of labor supplied (L_0) will be greater than the quantity demanded. The surplus of union labor requires some means of allocating the available jobs among the union members. Seniority rules, by which the most senior members have first priority, are one means of allocating the relatively scarce job openings. Regardless of its form, the union must come up with some means of allocating the available work to prevent unemployed union members from resorting to price competition (that is, working for less than the union wage) and undermining union wage goals. Many of the professions in America — some of them directly affecting important aspects of our lives — are effectively unionized. Examples include legal and medical services (see Highlight 13.3).

Highlight 13.3   *The American Medical Association: A "Union" at Work*

Medical associations have the lofty goal of protecting the health-care consumer by assuring the quality of health care provided to patients. Although the policies and practices of medical associations may indeed enhance the quality of health care, they often have the side effect of protecting the health-care provider from the forces of competition. Although the American Medical Association and its state and county affiliates may not fit the usual public image of a union, they do employ the tactics used by unions to limit competition and raise wages.

The AMA and its affiliates have been unusually successful in restricting entry into the health-care profession. The path to a health-care career is long and arduous. Those wanting to be physicians must get into and through medical school and a residency program, both of which are accredited and, to some extent, controlled by the AMA. A monopolist seeking to reduce the supply of labor would set high admission standards for those entering the market. This might explain why it is so difficult to get into medical school. Prospective doctors must also obtain a license before they can practice medicine, because unlicensed doctors face criminal sanctions. Licensing requirements include exams conducted under the auspices of state medical associations. These policies clearly restrict the supply of physicians.

Medical associations also attempt to eliminate price competition among doctors. Local medical associations have codes of conduct that often define advertising as unethical. Bans on advertising make it more difficult for health-care consumers to compare prices, which reduces price competition in the market. Doctors who engage in this "unethical" conduct (advertising) are subject to sanctions, including the denial of access to local hospitals.

The AMA also relies on government to increase the demand for physicians through indirect channels. The laws regulating the market for prescription drugs effectively increase the demand for physicians. Consumers are required to obtain a prescription from a licensed physician to gain access to these important health-care inputs. States also have laws that restrict the activities of other health-care professionals, such as midwives. Reserving the provision of certain services to doctors when other health-care professionals could provide those services increases the demand for licensed physicians.

Although most of the regulations sponsored by the AMA can be justified on the basis of protecting health-care consumers, the impact on the market is undeniable — it results in less competition and higher prices. All of this is particularly pertinent to debates concerning health-care in the United States. Fostering competition among doctors has yet to be offered as part of the solution to the high cost of health care.

In practice, unions employ all three strategies (increasing demand, reducing supply, and eliminating price competition) to achieve union wage goals. Each of these strategies raise wages above the competitive level. The impact of these strategies need not be exactly as illustrated in Figure 13.11. The analysis of union wage strategies depicted in Figure 13.11 assumed that the buyer or employer was a passive market participant with no influence on wages. As the first part of this chapter discussed, the buyer of resources may possess market power as well. The remainder of this chapter is devoted to examining what happens when a monopolist confronts a monopsonist — a market situation called **bilateral monopoly**.

Bilateral Monopoly

The resource-market monopolist uses its market power to generate higher prices by reducing employment of the resource. The monopsonist uses its market power to reduce employment as well, but the goal is to reduce resource prices. The one-on-one confrontation between a monopsonist and a monopolist that occurs under bilateral monopoly will generate a level of employment that is below the competitive level. Restricting employment advances the interests of both the buyer and the seller who are seeking to increase profits.

A decline in the level of employment, however, is the only definite conclusion that can be reached in the analysis of bilateral monopoly. (The precise level of employment may be determined when the monopolist and the monopsonist maximize joint profits and are able to bargain.) Under all circumstances, the model is inconclusive regarding the price of the resource.

A bilateral monopoly is depicted in Figure 13.12, which is a combination of Figures 13.3 and 13.7. The supply curve S reflects the marginal costs to the resource owner of selling the resource. The demand curve D indicates the marginal-revenue product accruing to the buyer from employing the resource. The monopolist equates the marginal revenues from selling the resource (as determined by the demand curve) with its marginal costs to find the price/quantity combination that is to its advantage. The optimal solution for the monopolist is to sell R_1 units of the resource at price P_1. The monopsonist, on the other hand, wants to buy R_2 units of the resource at price P_2. This optimum is where the marginal factor cost of employing the resource (as determined by the supply of the resource) equals the marginal-revenue product, with the price being taken from the supply curve.

Figure 13.12 Bilateral Monopoly

A bilateral monopoly is composed of a monopolist and a monopsonist. The monopolist wants to sell R_1 units of the resource at price P_1. The monopsonist wishes to employ R_2 units of the resource at price P_2. The optimum for each is inconsistent with the optimum of the other, and both diverge from the competitive equilibrium at R_C and P_C.

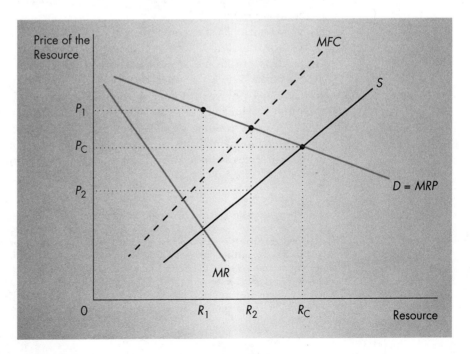

Figure 13.12 illustrates the basic indeterminacy that arises under bilateral monopoly. The price/quantity combinations that optimize the respective fortunes of the two market participants are different. Both desire a level of employment that is below the competitive level (R_C in Figure 13.12), but the specific optimal quantities are different unless assumptions are made concerning joining profit maximization between the two parties to the exchange.[13] More importantly, the optimal prices are vastly different. The monopolist would like a price that is above the competitive level, whereas the monopsonist wants a price that is below the competitive level. The solution to the bilateral monopoly problem will depend on the relative bargaining abilities and strengths of the two parties. The side that employs the more effective negotiator will get an agreement that comes closer to its ideal solution.

Ordinarily, bilateral monopoly results in an inefficient allocation of resources. The market power that pervades the market is used to reduce employment below the efficient, competitive level. There are circumstances, however, in which the creation of bilateral monopoly can bring about a competitive equilibrium. Introducing monopoly into a monopsonistic market or monopsony into a monopolistic market will bring about a competitive equilibrium in which the new market power is used to counteract existing market power.

Suppose that a resource market is dominated by a monopsonist, as in Figure 13.13a. The monopsonistic buyer reduces employment to R_0 and the price of the resource falls to P_0. Organizing the resource owners into an effective monopoly creates market power that can be used to counteract the power of the monopsonist. If the newly organized resource sellers refuse to sell for a price lower than P_C (the competitive price), the buyer will face a market supply that is horizontal at P_C and continues out to point A on the market supply curve. This horizontal stretch is the key to eliminating the power of the monopsonist. When the price of a resource is constant, the marginal-factor cost of employing the resource is equal to the price. Under these conditions, the profit-maximizing monopsonist (who operates where marginal-factor cost equals marginal-revenue product) will use R_C units of the resource (the competitive employment level) and pay the competitive price. In this case, the monopoly serves as a **countervailing market power** to the monopsonist.

---

13. Where negotiations to obtain joint profit maximization between an upstream monopolist and a downstream monopsonist are possible, quantity is in fact determinant. Quantity is determined where the net marginal-revenue product of the input is equal to the marginal cost of producing the input. Any other value for the corresponding quantity would permit both buyer and seller of the input to increase profits. The price of this "intermediate" good serves to divide the maximized rents between the two parties. See the excellent exposition of this problem in Roger D. Blair, David L. Kaserman, and Richard E. Romano, "A Pedagogical Treatment of Bilateral Monopoly," *Southern Economic Journal* 55 (April 1989): 831–41.

Figure 13.13 Countervailing Market Powers

Panel (a) shows how monopoly power can be used to offset monopsony power. The sellers of the resource organize and set a price that is above monopsony price P_0. Similarly, panel (b) illustrates how monopsony power can be used to offset the power of a monopolist. The cooperation of buyers can push the price below monopoly price P_0.

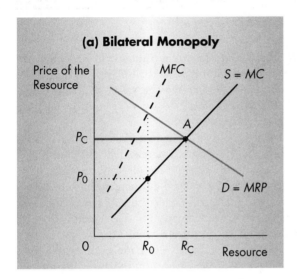
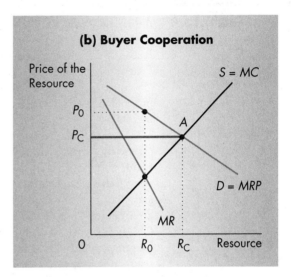

Figure 13.13b illustrates how a monopsony can counteract the power of a monopoly. The market is initially monopolistic, with employment at R_0 and the resource price at P_0. Creating a monopsony gives the buyers the ability to confront the power of the monopolist. The buyers can jointly refuse to pay more than P_C, the competitive price of the resource. The demand faced by the sellers becomes horizontal at P_C and remains so out to point A. As shown previously, a horizontal demand curve generates marginal revenues that are equal to the price. The profit-maximizing monopoly equates marginal revenues and marginal costs and sells R_C units of the resource at the price set by the monopsony. The power of monopsony is used as a countervailing force in the market.

The foregoing discussions illustrate situations in which market power can be used to diffuse market power. The key to attaining the competitive solution is the motivations of the newly formed block of market power. In each case, competitive equilibrium arises because that is the solution dictated by the new player in the game. Achieving the same results in the real world requires the creation of a monopolist or a monopsonist who will resist the natural temptation to use their market power for their own benefit. If the economists' assumption of rationality is correct, the attempt to create a countervailing power will ultimately result in a bilateral monopoly in which the outcome depends on the relative bargaining strengths of the market participants. Such is the case in a number of important businesses affecting consumers, including organized baseball (see Highlight 13.4).

Highlight 13.4   *Monopsony and Unions: The Case of Professional Sports*

Recent years have been very good to professional athletes. On average, the salaries of major-league baseball, football, and basketball players have risen by almost 20 percent per year. For example, the average salary of major-league baseball players went from $241,000 in 1982 to over $1 million per year in 1993.

Numerous factors have played a contributing role. Fan interest and fan attendance has been rising, and this has led to increases in the number of teams and a corresponding increase in the demand for player services. In addition, lucrative television contracts have also caused an increase in demand for star players. However, much of the increase is the result of new bargaining arrangements that were negotiated after the formation of player unions.

In the early days of professional sports, there were no players' unions. League executives drew up rules, which effectively made each professional team a monopsonist in hiring players. Players were drafted by a single team and remained the "property" of that team throughout their career unless they were traded. Because players were unable to negotiate with other teams, they were forced to accept their team's pay offer unless they elected to pursue an alternative career. This system led to economically predictable results — players were paid much less than their marginal-revenue product. In fact, estimates by Gerald W. Scully suggest that salaries amounted to less than 20 percent of the marginal-revenue product.[a] Famous players like Mickey Mantle received annual salaries of about $100,000 despite bringing in nearly $1 million of extra revenue to the league.

Dissatisfaction on the part of certain players led to the formation of a players' union that challenged the reserve clause. This was the league rule that tied players to a single team throughout their career. New contracts were negotiated that greatly increased a player's freedom to negotiate with more than one team. Accordingly, the monopsonistic power of the teams was ended, and player salaries soared to between 50 and 100 percent of their estimated marginal-revenue products.[b]

[a] Gerald W. Scully, "Pay and Performance in Major League Baseball," *American Economic Review* 64, 2 (1974).

[b] See Paul M. Sommers and Noel Quinton, "Pay and Performance in Major League Baseball: The Case of the First Family of Free Agents," *The Journal of Human Resources* 17 (1982).

Players' salaries in professional sports are the result of the interplay between monopsony buyers and players' unions.

This does not mean that player salaries will necessarily remain at current levels. Team owners have a continuing interest in breaking the players' union, or at least in curtailing its power. In the current environment in which many teams face financial troubles, team owners will prove tough to bargain with in upcoming negotiations because they have relatively little to lose if a strike or lockout occurs. On the other hand, the high player salaries (combined with short careers) mean that the players will want to avoid a strike. For these reasons, future contracts are likely to reduce the monopoly power of the player unions and increase the monopsonistic power of the league.

Summary

In many resource markets, individual buyers or individual sellers (or both) have some market power — their actions affect the market price of the resource. In such cases, the competitive model of factor markets that was developed in Chapter 12 does a poor job of explaining the pattern of factor prices that develops. In this chapter, we have developed alternative market models to explain how large employers use their market power. Specifically, the chapter showed how

- the monopsony model is used to examine the behavior of a firm that is the sole employer of labor or other productive resources.
- the dominant-firm, competitive-fringe model explains the behavior of one large firm that competes with numerous small employers for labor and other productive resources.
- monopsony firms are able to increase their profits by engaging in various types of wage discrimination.
- labor unions and professional organizations are able to affect factor prices by acting as monopolists in the supply of specific types of labor and, by so doing, to reduce employment and output and to increase the price of goods and services.
- how monopoly on *both* sides of the market affects price and quantity through bilateral bargaining.

Key Terms

marginal-revenue product
marginal-factor cost
competitive fringe
first-degree wage discrimination
labor union
countervailing market power

monopsony
dominant-firm price leadership
third-degree wage discrimination
locational monopoly
bilateral monopoly

Sample Questions

Question

How do the elasticity of demand for a product, the availability of substitutes, and union labor as a proportion of total costs affect the elasticity of demand for union labor?

Answer

The elasticity of demand for union labor is positively related to both the elasticity of demand for a product and the availability of substitutes. Union labor as a proportion of total costs and the elasticity of demand for union labor are inversely related, however, so that the larger the percentage of a firm's total costs attributed to unions, the more elastic is the demand for union labor.

Question

Why were labor unions in the forefront of opposition to the North American Free Trade Agreement (NAFTA), passed in 1993 and put into effect in 1994?

Answer

In general, the objective of all unions is to maximize the net economic benefits flowing to its members from employment. Because unions have long been a political force in U.S. politics and policies and the NAFTA treaty was perceived as having free-trade effects between low-wage Mexico and high union wages in the United States, it is not surprising that many union leaders opposed the agreement. Free trade inhibits the ability of unions to pass on wage demands in the form of higher prices to domestic consumers. (Free trade tends to lower prices to consumers for goods in the U.S. economy.) Because unions have political power, they may be expected to oppose any policies (such as free trade) that would reduce their net economic position and to support those policies (such as minimum wages) that would improve that position.

Questions for Review and Discussion

*1. What is monopsony? How is the phenomenon related to monopoly in output markets?

*2. Why does marginal-factor cost slope upward to the monopsonist?

3. Why is the employment of inputs restricted by the monopsonist?

4. Do the conditions for the strict definition of monopsony ever exist in the real world? Explain.

5. What is the dominant-firm model and how does it relate to problems of monopsony and employment? How, for example, does the dominant-firm model relate to the hiring of teachers in private and public schools?

6. Present a model of third-degree monopsony discrimination in employment. Does the monopsonist hire more or less labor than the competitive firm? Explain fully.

*7. How is monopsony discrimination related to labor or resource-supply elasticity? Explain with an example.

*8. What is the very practical reason why first-degree discrimination in employment is rarely if ever actually practiced in the real world?

9. Discuss the market for land (broadly interpreted to include natural resources) in view of the total quantity of space available (see Figure 13.8).

10. How does land in downtown Tokyo represent a locational monopoly?

*11. Do unions create unemployment? If so, what is the impact of unions on the wage and incomes of nonunionized workers?

*12. How are professional organizations such as the American Medical Association, the American Bar Association, or state nursing associations similar to labor unions?

13. What are the primary goals of labor unions? How do they achieve these goals?

14. What is bilateral monopoly? How is price determined in this model?

Problems for Analysis

*1. At most universities faculty salaries are based partly on rank and seniority but primarily on the basis of productivity. Because productivity is hard to measure, many professors feel that they are underpaid relative to other faculty members. One specific allegation is that faculty members who have roots in the community — particularly those whose spouse is also a faculty member — are systematically paid less than comparable faculty members with weaker ties to the university. If you were the administrator of a large university with monopsony power in hiring faculty and were interested in conserving university funds spent on faculty salaries, how would you treat faculty members who had strong ties to the university? Use a graph to explain your answer.

2. When you go to your doctor for your annual flu shot, the shot is almost always given by a nurse — rather than by the doctor. There are many other medical tasks — checking blood pressure, taking blood samples, and so on — that are performed by both physicians and nurses. However, nurses consistently earn much less than doctors, even when they perform the same tasks. Can you explain this wage differential in terms of an economic model? What changes would be necessary in order for the wage differential between doctors and nurses to diminish or disappear? Why haven't these changes been made?

*3. Some observers have noted the historical trend toward urbanization in certain countries with alarm. It is their view that continued population growth in countries like Mexico will lead to more and more agricultural land being converted to housing, with the inevitable result being a decline in food production and an increase in hunger and starvation. For this reason, they argue that to prevent starvation, the Mexican government must enact regulations to prohibit further conversion of land from agricultural to residential uses. What is your assessment of this argument? Can you use a graphical model to support your assessment?

4. There is a tendency to depict labor unions and the companies that hire union labor as antagonists. However, in some cases the economic interests of the two groups coincide. Can you use Figure 13.12 to identify certain types of policies that serve to achieve both union goals and company goals? Are there other types of policies on which the two groups are likely to be in sharp disagreement?

The Role of Government
in Markets and International Trade

14

Government, Markets, and Welfare Analysis

Few people can get through a day without being affected by some aspect of government decision making. Whether it is through the tax code, government spending policies, or government regulations, the choices we make as consumers and producers are invariably influenced by government. In spite of this pervasiveness, the influence of government has, with the exception of the discussion of regulation in Chapter 12, taken a back seat in the presentation of microeconomic theory through the first five Parts of this text. This chapter brings government under the microscope of economic analysis to gain a better understanding of government's impact on the market. Although some of what follows will be a review of material that was introduced previously, this chapter seeks to provide a deeper understanding of these topics and introduce some concepts that will be developed further in the next chapter. The objectives of this chapter are to

- provide insight into the motivations of government decision makers,
- present cost-benefit analysis and welfare analysis as a means of evaluating government intervention,
- use welfare analysis to evaluate the impact of taxes and subsidies,
- use welfare analysis to evaluate the impact of price controls.

This chapter looks at the *how* and *what* of government's impact on the market. The *why*, or justification, of such intervention is reserved for the next chapter.

Public Choice

Government activity is the result of public decision making, or what economists call **public choice**. Government, like all other economic organizations, is not some separate entity with a will and life of its own. Any economic organization, however complex, is a collection of individuals. The actions of government therefore will be influenced by, and reflect the motives of, those who make decisions on behalf of the organization. At the core of the economist's view of public decision making is the notion of rational self-interest. Rational self-interest can be used to explain the behavior of voters, politicians, and bureaucrats.

The profit-maximization hypothesis will be noticeably absent from the analysis of public decision making. Government agencies and public bodies are part of the not-for-profit sector. This sector is organized so that maximizing the difference between revenues and costs does not normally enter the decision-making process. Employees of not-for-profit organizations have no claim on any revenues that may remain after operating expenses have been paid. The public sector goes so far as to impose criminal sanctions on those who attempt to convert public residuals to private use. Although passing laws does not totally eliminate a banned activity, the general prohibition against profit seeking in the public sector does take the profit-maximization hypothesis out of the public-choice model.

The analysis of public decision making looks at the behavior of three fundamentally different public-sector actors: voters, politicians, and public employees who are not elected. Voters determine who will exercise the power to make (or change) law. Politicians are elected to fill the highest public offices and write the laws that define the broad framework for government activity. This framework is then interpreted, implemented, and administered by public employees. The motivations and activities of each of these three groups have a direct bearing on government activities in the marketplace.

Voters

In a representative democracy, the individual citizen's role in government decision making is an indirect one. Although voters are occasionally called upon to make decisions on specific issues through referenda, the voting public is usually restricted to selecting who will make the final decision on the many questions that come before the government. The problem for the voter is to determine which politicians to support. The self-interest axiom implies that voters will select the candidates who support legislation that promotes their interests (both pecuniary and nonpecuniary). An important assumption of the public choice model is that individuals vote for the candidates who are closest to their own position on the "issues." An issue that is near and dear to the hearts of everyone is their source of income. Those who earn their income in an industry (defense, agriculture, housing, automobile) will tend to vote for politicians who support that industry.

Rational self-interest has other implications for voter behavior. One is that voting, if evaluated in purely pecuniary terms, is irrational. The rational economic actor undertakes an activity as long as the marginal benefits of the activity exceed the marginal costs. In the voting booth, the marginal benefits of participating are effectively zero when measured in dollar terms. Because elections are very rarely settled by one vote, the expected impact of an individual's vote is nil. The marginal costs of voting (the value of the voter's time and resources spent going to and from the polls) are clearly positive. If the public were to base its decision to vote on purely monetary factors, no one would vote, because the lack of pecuniary benefits leaves no incentive to vote. This is at least a partial explanation for low voter turnout. Those who do vote must be motivated by nonpecuniary considerations such as the satisfaction gained from fulfilling one's civic duty.

Another implication of rational self-interest, as it applies to voting, is rational ignorance. The infinitesimally small chance that one vote will change an election limits the resources that rational economic actors will expend in voting. Elections often entail many complex issues. The costs of being fully informed on even a few of the issues will usually be large. Rational voters will economize on the acquisition of information and may make a political choice from a position of relative ignorance.

Politicians

The actions of those who hold or aspire to elective office can also be cast in the utility-maximization framework. People who pursue a career in politics must, if they are rational, expect a higher level of utility from a political career than from their alternatives. The rewards of a political career include (but are not limited to) salary and benefits, the perks of political office, the utility of being in a position of power, and the satisfaction of helping others. Those who seek the rewards of a life in politics must first be elected and then reelected to maintain this career path. Election and then reelection will be first and foremost in the minds of politicians.

The process by which politicians seek and attain elective office bears a striking resemblance to the supply-and-demand model. Politicians demand votes and need a majority of the votes to ensure election or reelection. Voters supply votes to the politicians who meet their "price," where the voter's price is a position on the issues. This marketlike process is described in the median-voter model, which offers an economic explanation of the election process and election results.

The Median-Voter Model

The **median-voter model** is a simplified model of political campaigns. Its simplest form assumes (1) a single-issue campaign, (2) voters evenly distributed between the extremes of the issue, and (3) only two candidates for the political office. Suppose that a political campaign focuses solely on defense spending and that defense spending can vary from nothing to $500 billion. An evenly distributed electorate would have one voter favoring each level of defense spending between these two extremes. This situation is illustrated with the aid of Figure 14.1. The line in panel (a) represents the alternative levels of defense spending, and each point on the line represents the position of a different voter. For convenience, the issue is displayed in $50 billion increments, with

Figure 14.1 The Median-Voter Model

Panel (a) illustrates voter preferences regarding defense spending when those preferences are evenly distributed between $0 and $500 billion, with the median voter being at *M*. If candidates adopt positions *A* and *B* in panel (b), and if voters cast their ballots for the candidate closest to their own position, the candidate at *B* wins the election. The candidate at *A* can win the election, as in panel (c), by adopting a position at *A'* and moving closer to the median voter.

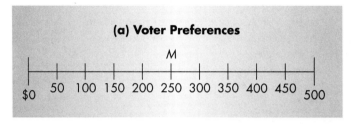

(a) Voter Preferences

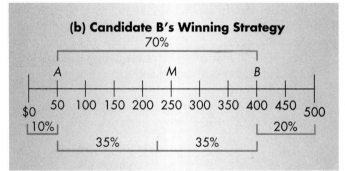

(b) Candidate B's Winning Strategy

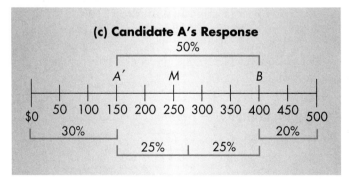

(c) Candidate A's Response

each increment representing the preferred position of 10 percent of the electorate. Our attention will focus on the median voter. The median is a statistical concept referring to the point at which 50 percent of the population lies on either side. The median voter is at point *M*, halfway between the extremes of no defense spending and $500 billion in defense spending. The median voter becomes all-important when people vote for the candidate whose position on the issue is closest to their own.

Suppose that the race is between a candidate who favors spending $50 billion on defense and a candidate who proposes a $400 billion defense budget. These two candidates would be at points *A* and *B*, respectively, on the defense-spending continuum of panel (b). When ballots are cast for the candidate that is closest to one's own position, the election goes to the candidate who proposes a $400 billion defense budget. The candidate at point *A* gets the support of the 10 percent of the people who favor $50 billion or less in defense spending. The candidate at point *B* gets the vote from the 20 percent who favor $400 billion or more in the defense budget. The two candidates then split the 70 percent of the voters who are between points *A* and *B*, for an additional 35 percent of the vote each. All voters who prefer less than $225 billion in defense spending vote for candidate A; those who prefer more than $225 billion vote for candidate B. The candidate who favors $400 billion in defense spending wins with 55 percent of the vote.

The election will always go to the candidate that is closest to the median voter. Suppose that the candidate at point *A* adopts a $150 billion defense budget to get to point *A'* in panel (c). If the other politician remains at point *B*, this move garners the support of the 30 percent who favor $150 billion or less in defense spending plus half of the 50 percent that lie between the positions of the two candidates on the defense issue. The politician's new stand on defense produces a winning majority (55 percent) of the votes. Moving toward the median voter's position is a winning political strategy.

This feature of the election process will not be ignored by the candidates. Politicians that are able to discover and adopt the median position will achieve their election/reelection goals. This tendency does create difficulty for voters. As candidates stake out the median position, voters will find it increasingly more difficult to distinguish between the candidates on the basis of the issues. Politicians will then try to "help" the electorate by pointing out how their rivals differ from the median. One obvious result of this strategy is the negative campaign, in which candidates depict their rivals in the worst possible political light.

As the **median-voter model** demonstrates, politicians respond to voters. Those who do not participate in the election process minimize their political influence. Those who align themselves with others who share political concerns and then vote as a block increase their political influence. This is the foundation for the power of special-interest groups. A group of like-minded voters can present a unified political front that promises to get out the vote and increase their political influence. The special-interest group may convince the politician that theirs is the median position. Special-interest groups will be particularly effective when the opposition is disorganized and politically inactive. The politician is bombarded by special interests to vote in favor of policies conveying economic advantages to one group or another. Lobbyists representing these interests fill county courthouses, state capitals, and Washington, D.C. We leave to the reader to decide whether this activity is "democracy in action" or a subversion of democratic principles. The economist does observe such behavior, however, and notes that it tends to skew economic benefits from the many to the few (see, for example, Highlight 14.1).

Highlight 14.1   *Markets and Special Interests: In-Kind Payoffs and the Lobbying of State Politicians*

Economists have long pondered the relationships between economic efficiency and democratic political processes.[a] Problems of what social goods to provide and in what quantities would be lessened if all who are affected by some political decision had an equal voice or vote in its determination. But American democracy is based on a system of representation in which (at periodic intervals) individuals elect their representatives to serve for given periods of time. Monitoring costs (keeping track of the activities of your politicians) are fairly high for most individuals over this time period. Your own personal stake in the majority of decisions made by your politicians is typically small, so that you remain "rationally ignorant" of the way that he or she votes. Not so for some organized groups of interests whose fortunes are directly affected by decisions of your politician.

Concentrated interests on the part of particular groups of individuals — as against the wider public interest — are represented by lobbyists in all political venues. Lobbyists and political action committees (PACs) for particular groups cover every conceivable interest at one level of government or another. Examples include real estate, physicians (the American Medical Association), defense industries, teachers, postal workers, banking and financial institutions, textiles, petroleum, labor unions, and virtually any other interest for which legislation or regulation can affect economic benefits or costs in a positive or negative fashion.

Clearly, effective lobbying takes place. It would be difficult otherwise to explain many local, state, or federal allocations and subsidies, such as water subsidies in the West or supercolliders in Texas or inland waterways in the South. *How* such activity takes place is another question. If politicians are self-interested, as modern public-choice economists believe, they will always make policy with an eye to reelection and enrichment. Because the direct transfer of money for votes is fairly easy to detect, politicians must rely on other kinds of transfers and perquisites. Interest groups are often able to deliver blocs of votes, as mentioned in this chapter, or to finance campaigns by a variety of means. Most proposed reform focuses on changing methods of campaign finance.

But there are numerous other ways to pay off politicians for economic interventions that benefit special interests. For example, it would be a rare representative or senator specializing in banking or transportation legislation

[a] Most recently a new field in economics called public choice has emerged to study the interface between economic theory and politics. Its chief modern exponents are Nobel laureate James Buchanan of George Mason University and Gordon Tullock of the University of Arizona.

Political payoffs from lobbyists may take many forms, including "free" meals for local, state, and federal politicians.

who did not have opportunities to work for the industry he or she regulated after retiring from politics. Family members or business partners and associates of the politician, moreover, may be in position to accept payoffs.

Economic-resource distortions — allocations that would not occur with other forms of representation — may take many other forms. Although most of the attention has been fixed on cash and other bribes, many forms of in-kind transfers are in fact used. Overt cash bribes attract attention and invite regulation, but lobbying efforts may be indirect, as when trips, fancy (or not-so-fancy) meals, transportation or limo services, employment of relatives or business associates, or golf rounds are provided for legislators.

Recent research into in-kind perquisites of state politicians has produced convincing results. When allowance is made for per-capita income and other key variables, state capital cities have been shown to contain a larger per-capita percentage of sitdown (nonfast-food) restaurants than paired randomly chosen same-state cities with similar income characteristics.[b] The bigger the budget of

[b] See Franklin G. Mixon, Jr., David N. Laband, and Robert B. Ekelund, Jr., "Rent Seeking and Hidden In-Kind Resource Distortion: Some Empirical Evidence," *Public Choice* 78 (1994): 171–185.

the state (the more opportunities for profit seeking by special interests) and the more full-time lobbyists in the state, other things equal, the more restaurants the city has. The same goes for golf courses!

What are the costs of such lobbying by special interests? First there is the cost to society of skewing regulations and goods towards concentrated interests and not to the public interest. But there is a direct cost as well. In the sample of 47 state capitals, there are a total of 9,635 *additional* restaurants for the capital cities solely because of their political status as capital cities. A lower-bound estimate of resource distortion from restaurant payoffs is suggested by multiplying 9,635 times the average start-up cost per restaurant. Then there are also 286 additional golf courses to consider!

There are many forms of political payoffs from special interests. More hidden in-kind rent seeking may be expected where functions and funding are shifted away from the federal level and to cities and states. Cruder, lower-cost forms of payoffs may be expected where the gains from special treatment are lower. In smaller communities, lunch at McDonald's or Wendy's or a weekend fishing vacation may do the trick. Whatever the case, such special-interest legislation and regulation will likely have negative benefits for voter-consumer-taxpayers at large.

Elected officials decide the questions that come before the legislature. Politicians serving in the legislature provide answers to these questions in the form of legislation that enables specific government actions. It is then the responsibility of public employees to follow through on the designs of the legislature. The economic motives of public employees also have a strong impact on the implementation of government decisions.

Public Employees

Public employees are the ones who are directly responsible for implementing public policy. These suppliers of labor are in a curious position. They are expected to function efficiently but they get little reward for doing so. Public employees are not residual claimants and have no claim on any excess of public revenues over government expenditures. The civil servant who reduces the costs of running government and makes government more efficient may get little in return and may even be penalized. The agency that has funds remaining at the end of its budget period may find its allocations cut in the future. The structure of government employment does not lend itself to great economy, because the rewards for efficiency are few, whereas the costs of promoting efficiency may be great.

The public sector has one overriding constraint: agencies cannot spend more than is allocated to them by the legislature. This constraint, however, says nothing about the objectives of government agencies. The objectives of an organization depend on the motivations of the people within the organization, and public-sector employees are no different from their private-sector counterparts. The hypothesis of rational self-interest is just as applicable to public employees as to private employees. Utility maximization is the model of choice for analyzing the actions of public employees. Bureaucratic decision making will reflect the preferences of civil servants. What contributes to the utility of public employees? It may be the satisfaction derived from a job well done. There is nothing that prevents the bureaucrat from striving to meet the objectives of a political decision at the least possible cost, but the public sector is structured in such a way that cost-minimization is simply not necessary. It has also been suggested that bureaucrats maximize their budgets. Budget-maximization can become the objective when the size of the agency's budget is directly related to the utility of those working within the agency. If salaries, perks, and power grow with the agency's budget, we can expect pressure for budget increases from civil servants. Public employees might also pursue personal objectives at public expense. A bureaucrat who has a fondness for pre-Columbian art may allocate government money to promote this style of art.

Regardless of the motivations that underlie government decision making, actions will be taken on the public's behalf. These actions often have an impact on the operation of markets. The analysis of government intervention requires some means of evaluating the impact of government. The following section discusses two methods for evaluating the impact of government.

Evaluating the Impact of Government

Some mechanism that gauges the effects of government decision making is needed to evaluate the impact of government. There are two widely used techniques for evaluating government activity. Cost-benefit analysis is used widely within government to determine the effectiveness of government action. Economists use a technique called welfare analysis to evaluate the impact of both private and public decision making. We will look at cost-benefit analysis before turning to the technique that will be employed in the remainder of this chapter.

Cost-Benefit Analysis. **Cost-benefit analysis** is simple at the conceptual level. The net economic benefits of an activity are calculated by finding the difference between the total costs and total benefits of the activity. If there are no spending limits, the decision maker should undertake all projects that have a positive net benefit. If the decision maker is under a budget constraint, the projects with the highest ratio of marginal benefits to marginal costs should be undertaken. Although this method of evaluating government intervention may seem straightforward, there are some significant difficulties in implementing this procedure.

The problem with cost-benefit analysis lies in measuring the costs and benefits of a project. An accurate appraisal of net benefits requires an accounting of all economic costs and all economic benefits. Consider a construction project to control flooding along a river basin. Flooding can be controlled by building a dam to regulate the amount of water flowing through the river. The runoff from heavy rains is trapped behind a dam and released when there is no threat of flooding. The costs and benefits of this project might seem straightforward. A first approximation of the costs would include the expenses of building the dam and the costs of acquiring the land behind the dam that will be flooded by the project. (The project controls temporary flooding in one area by permanently flooding another.) The benefits of the project will be the flood damages that are prevented by the dam and flood-control lake. Although this is an accurate accounting of the direct effects of a flood-control project, indirect effects must also be considered.

There are significant indirect benefits and indirect costs of a flood-control project. The project creates a lake that is, in itself, a valuable resource. Lakes have many recreational uses (fishing, boating, and so on) that consumers value. Creation of the lake also means that some land may become more valuable lakefront property, an unintended consequence of controlling downstream flooding. The water collected behind the dam also embodies potential energy that can be harnessed by including a hydroelectric plant within the dam.

It so happens that the indirect benefits of the project also add to the indirect costs of the project. The operation of the dam for flood-control purposes requires raising and dropping the level of the water in the lake to counteract intermittent rainfall. The unpredictable water line compromises the recreational uses of the lake. It's difficult to build a lakefront resort when the lakefront is constantly changing. Moreover, reducing the amount of flooding in the river basin is not universally beneficial. Although flooding causes damage to some downstream property, some property benefits from occasional flooding. Flooding leaves behind matter that is rich in nutrients and increases the productivity of agricultural land. Eliminating all flooding imposes a cost on downstream farmers.

The attempt to define the costs and benefits of a flood-control project highlights two important distinctions: private versus social costs and private versus social benefits. The private costs and private benefits are the consequences of an activity that accrues to the participants in the activity. Social costs and social benefits are consequences of an activity, whether or not they accrue to the participants. Social costs diverge from private costs when someone other than those who are directly involved bears part of the costs. These third-party costs are called external costs. Social benefits diverge from private benefits when a third party receives a portion of the benefits from an activity. These benefits are called external benefits.

Although we will defer a full discussion of external costs and benefits to the next chapter, recognize that cost-benefit analysis requires the compilation of all social costs and benefits. The remainder of this chapter will assume that there are no external costs and no external benefits, so that market supply and demand curves reflect the social costs and social benefits of market activity.

Welfare Analysis. **Welfare analysis** is a technique employed by economists to evaluate economic activity. Like cost-benefit analysis, welfare analysis takes social costs and social benefits into account to gauge the net benefits of an activity. Welfare analysis is cost-benefit analysis that has been adapted to fit the supply-and-demand model. This adaptation interprets supply and demand curves graphically to measure the net benefits of market interaction. The net benefits of economic activity are identified as those accruing to consumers and those accruing to producers.

The consumers' share of the net benefits of economic activity is the difference between the total benefits of consumption and what consumers pay to acquire those benefits. Figure 14.2 illustrates these amounts graphically. Panel (a) illustrates a market equilibrium at which quantity Q_E is traded at price P_E. Consumers pay an amount equal to price times quantity to purchase Q_E units of the good. Total consumer expenditures are equal to the area of the shaded rectangle ($0P_EBQ_E$) in panel (b). The total benefits of consumption are derived from the demand curve. The height of the demand curve at each quantity indicates what people are willing to pay for each additional unit of the good. This is a measure of the marginal benefits from consumption. Summing each of the marginal benefits produces the total benefits from consumption. This summation is represented by the area under the demand curve from the vertical axis out to the equilibrium quantity. The shaded area in panel (c), or the area of the trapezoid $0ABQ_E$, is a measure of the total benefits of consuming Q_E units of the good. The benefits of consumption exceed the costs of consumption by the area of triangle P_EAB in panel (d). The area of the triangle under the demand curve and above the equilibrium price is called the **consumers' surplus**: the net benefits accruing to buyers.

The remainder of the net benefits from market activity is captured by producers in what is called **producers' surplus**. Figure 14.3 illustrates the derivation of this surplus. The first panel of this figure illustrates the same equilibrium as illustrated in Figure 14.2. The total revenues received by producers equal price times quantity traded, or the area of rectangle $0P_EBQ_E$ in panel (b). Note that the amount paid by consumers equals the amount received by producers. When the supply curve reflects the marginal costs of producing the good, the area under the supply curve equals the total costs of production. Summing the marginal costs of producing each unit generates an amount equal to the area of the shaded portion of panel (c). The net benefits accruing to the producers — that is, the producers' surplus — is the difference between the shaded areas of panels (b) and (c). The producers' surplus is the area of triangle CP_EB in panel (d).

The notion of producers' surplus may seem inconsistent with a competitive market. If long-run competitive equilibrium is characterized by zero economic

Figure 14.2 Consumer Surplus

Panel (a) illustrates the market equilibrium at which consumers purchase quantity Q_E at price P_E. Total expenditures by consumers are the shaded area in panel (b). Total benefits received by consuming the good are the shaded area in panel (c). Consumer surplus is the difference between total benefits and total expenditures, or the shaded triangle in panel (d).

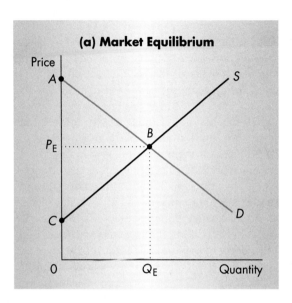

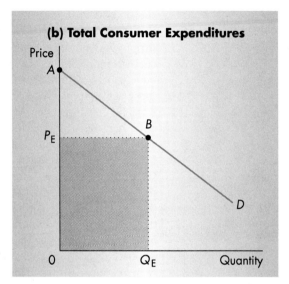

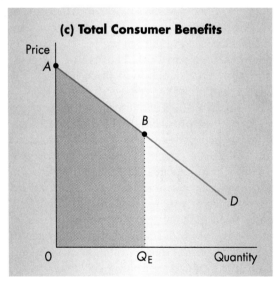

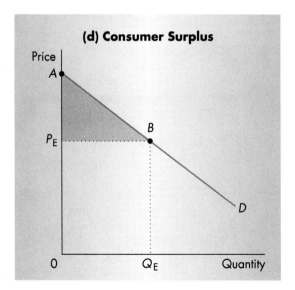

Figure 14.3 Producer Surplus

Panel (a) illustrates the market equilibrium at which producers sell quantity Q_E at price P_E. Total revenues received by sellers are the shaded area in panel (b). The total costs of producing the good are the shaded area in panel (c). Producer surplus is the difference between total revenues and total costs, or the shaded triangle in panel (d).

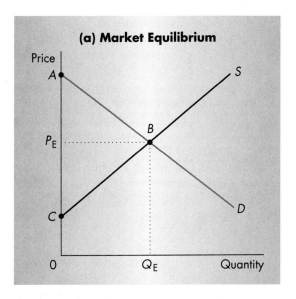

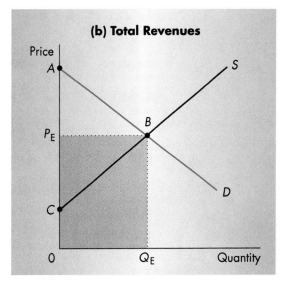

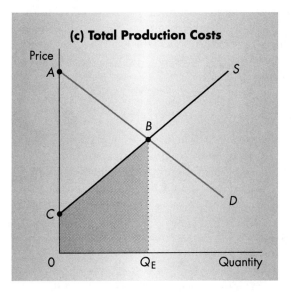

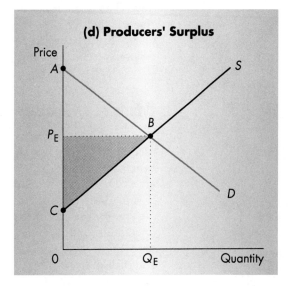

profits, where is the surplus? The producers' surplus in a competitive industry is captured by suppliers of resources in the form of inframarginal rents. The producers' surplus arises because the supply curve slopes upward. Higher prices are required to attract more resources into the industry. The higher resource prices are passed along to all resource suppliers, granting an inframarginal rent to the suppliers.

The net economic benefits of market interaction, also called **economic welfare**, is the sum of the producers' and consumers' surpluses. Graphically, economic welfare is measured by the triangle to the left of the intersection of the supply and demand curves in Figure 14.3a, or triangle *ABC*. If the market supply and demand curves reflect the social costs and social benefits, respectively, a competitive market will maximize economic welfare. This proposition is illustrated by considering the welfare effects of taxes, subsidies, and price controls. These forms of government intervention may alter the prices paid by consumers, the prices received by producers, or the quantities traded in the market. Changes in any or all of these aspects of market equilibrium alter the net economic benefits of market activity. The remainder of this chapter uses the concepts of consumer surplus, producer surplus, and economic welfare to analyze the impact of government intervention.

Taxes and Subsidies

The fiscal operations of government have a pervasive impact on an economy. The taxing and spending functions of government affect markets in a variety of ways. This section concentrates on the impact of taxes and direct subsidies. These activities alter the prices paid by buyers and the prices received by sellers. Because buyers and sellers respond to prices, this will alter the level of economic activity taking place in a market and alter the net benefits of that activity. We begin with an analysis of taxes.

Principles of Taxation

The basis of a tax can be traced to one of four basic principles: the benefits received, the ability to pay, paternalism, or political expediency. The benefits-received principle collects taxes from those who receive the benefits of government activity. This principle underlies taxes on gasoline and air travel that fund the construction of highways and airports. The ability-to-pay principle argues that those who are most able to pay taxes should fund government operations. This argument underlies the progressive income tax. Individuals with higher incomes pay a higher percentage of their income in taxes. Paternalism, in which the government seeks to protect individuals from themselves, may be the idea behind the "sin" taxes on tobacco and alcohol. The government protects people by making certain products more expensive. Finally, some taxes are assessed out of political expediency. Funds are necessary for the operation of government, and the public-choice model predicts that these funds will be collected from those with the least political influence.

Types of Taxes. Governments resort to many devices to generate the funds necessary to finance their operations. Personal income taxes, business income taxes, sales taxes, property taxes, social security, and Medicare taxes are but a few of the sources of government revenue. Although each of these taxes may differ in their particulars, there are similarities that permit analytical simplicity. Taxes can be classified by the relationship between the amount of the tax and the object of the tax. This organizational scheme permits the classification of taxes as lump-sum, excise, or *ad valorem*.

A **lump-sum tax** is a fixed dollar assessment against economic units (individuals, households, or firms). Many states impose a business franchise fee that takes a fixed sum from each firm wishing to operate in the state. An **excise tax** collects a fixed dollar amount per unit of the good. The gasoline tax is an excise tax in that the tax is expressed in cents per gallon. Finally, an ***ad valorem* tax** takes a percentage of the market price per unit of the good. Sales, property, and income taxes are all expressed as a percentage of the market value of a transaction and fall within the *ad valorem* category of taxes.

Ad valorem taxes dominate the practice of tax collection. *Ad valorem* taxes are popular because their proceeds are adjusted for inflation automatically. A doubling of market prices will double the amount of the tax collected, because the tax is a percentage of the market price. Excise taxes, on the other hand, produce a declining real revenue when inflation is a persistent problem, because the tax is expressed in dollar terms. Lump-sum taxes are relatively scarce in the overall tax scheme. The public-choice model can be used to explain this feature of the tax landscape. Lump-sum taxes affect every member of the class subject to the tax and, if the amount of the tax is significant, will motivate each member of the class to work against its passage or for its repeal.[1] It will be difficult to build a political consensus in favor of lump-sum taxes.

The Market Impact of Taxes. Supply-and-demand analysis is easily adapted to illustrate the market effects of excise and *ad valorem* taxes. The impact of a tax is illustrated by shifting one of the market curves vertically by the amount of the tax. Figure 14.4 illustrates this process. Panel (a) analyzes the impact of an excise tax collected from sellers. The firm must pay a fixed amount per unit of the good that it sells. The imposition of a tax equal to $t per unit means that the firm must collect an additional $t for each unit sold to obtain the same revenue per unit it received before the tax. This shifts the market supply upward by the amount of the tax. The after-tax supply curve $(S + t)$ will be

---

1. A lump-sum tax that is both high (in money terms) and broad (in terms of the number of persons affected) can generate an extreme reaction from the public. This occurred when the British government imposed a head tax and riots broke out in opposition to the tax.

Figure 14.4 The Market Effects of Taxes

Panel (a) shows the impact of an excise (per unit) tax imposed on sellers, and panel (b) shows the effects of a similar tax imposed on buyers. The prices paid and received are the same regardless of the collection method. Panels (c) and (d) show the effects of sales taxes collected from sellers and buyers, respectively. Again, the impact of the tax is independent of the collection mechanism.

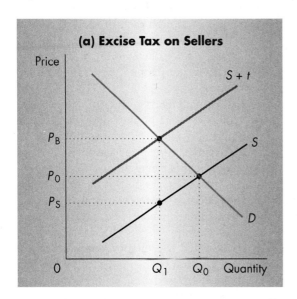

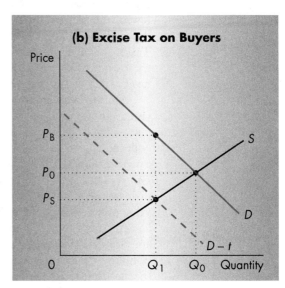

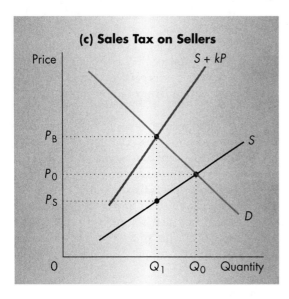

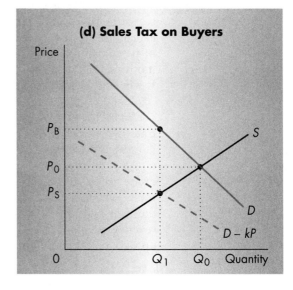

parallel to the pre-tax supply (S) because the amount of the tax is constant. The after-tax supply results in a lower equilibrium quantity (Q_1 versus Q_0), a higher price paid by buyers (P_B versus P_0), and a lower price to sellers ($P_S = P_B - t$ versus P_0).

Panel (b) illustrates the impact of an excise tax collected from buyers. A tax of $\$t$ that is assessed against each unit purchased by a consumer shifts the demand curve downward, from D to $D - t$, by the amount of the tax. The amount that buyers are willing to pay to sellers is reduced by the amount of the tax. Because the dollar amount of the tax is constant, the after-tax and original demand curves will be parallel. The after-tax demand produces an equilibrium quantity of Q_1, at which the seller receives P_S, and the buyer pays P_B, which is equal to P_S plus the tax.

Panels (c) and (d) illustrate the impact of an *ad valorem* tax assessed against sellers and buyers, respectively. The tax on sellers shifts the supply curve upward, whereas the tax on buyers shifts the demand curve downward. Each curve moves vertically by the amount of the tax where the amount of the tax varies with the quantity. The after-tax supply curve in panel (c) diverges from the pre-tax supply curve as the quantity supplied increases. The higher prices necessary to increase the quantity supplied increase the amount of the tax, because the tax is a percentage of the price. The after-tax demand curve in panel (d) converges with the pre-tax demand, because the lower prices necessary to increase the quantity demanded decrease the amount of the tax. In both cases, the after-tax equilibrium is characterized by lower equilibrium quantities, higher prices for buyers, and lower prices for sellers.

The market effects of a lump-sum tax are somewhat more difficult to illustrate. Figure 14.5 illustrates the optimizing behavior of an individual economic unit when the pursuit of some objective (illustrated by the O curves) is curtailed by some constraint (illustrated by the C curves). If the economic unit in question represents a consumer, the O curves can be considered indifference curves and the C curves budget lines. If the economic unit in question is a producer, the O curves represent isoquants and the C curves isocost lines. The equilibrium for the economic unit will occur at a point of tangency between an objective curve and the constraint. A lump-sum tax causes a parallel, inward movement of the constraint (from C_0 to C_0^*) because the tax is independent of all other variables. The tax reduces, *ceteris paribus,* the level of economic activity by pushing the economic actors to an equilibrium that is closer to the origin. If the economic actor portrayed in Figure 14.5 is a consumer, the demand for both products decreases.[2] If the economic unit portrayed in Figure 14.5 is a producer, the producer's supply decreases as the total cost of producing each level of output increases. Reducing the disposable income of consumers or increasing the fixed costs of producers reduces market activity.

2. The results of using Figure 14.5 to analyze the effect of a lump-sum tax on a consumer reflect the implicit assumption that both goods are income normal. The decrease in demand arises because the quantity consumed falls as income falls. A lump-sum tax would increase the demand for income-inferior goods.

Figure 14.5 Lump-Sum Taxes

A lump-sum tax shifts the economic actors' constraint inward and parallel to the original constraint. The new constraint pushes economic actors to lower levels of their objective.

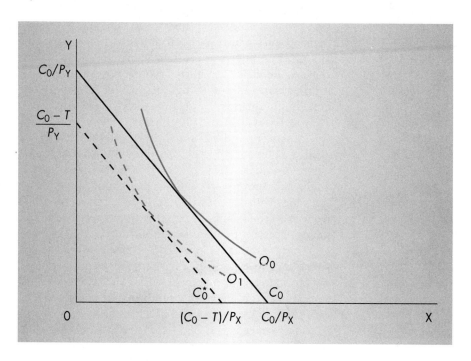

The Welfare Effects of a Tax

Although the impact of taxes may be quantitatively different, the qualitative impacts of different types of taxes are the same. The equilibrium quantity falls and the tax drives a wedge between the price paid by buyers and the price received by sellers. These market effects also lead to a change in consumers' and producers' surpluses. These welfare effects of a tax are illustrated in Figure 14.6.

The pre-tax equilibrium involves a consumers' surplus equal to the area of triangle P_0AB and a producers' surplus equal to the area of triangle P_0BC. The imposition of a tax drives a wedge between the buyer and seller. The after-tax equilibrium will be the point at which the vertical distance between the supply and the demand is equal to the amount of the tax, or at quantity Q_1 in Figure 14.6. Consumers pay P_B to purchase the new equilibrium quantity with a new consumers' surplus equal to the area of triangle P_BAD. Producers receive a price equal to P_S with a new producers' surplus equal to the area of triangle

Figure 14.6 The Welfare Effects of a Tax

A tax of $P_B - P_S$ reduces consumers' surplus by $P_0 P_B DB$, and reduces producers' surplus by $P_S P_0 BF$. The tax generates revenues of $P_S P_B DF$ leaving a net welfare loss of *FDB*.

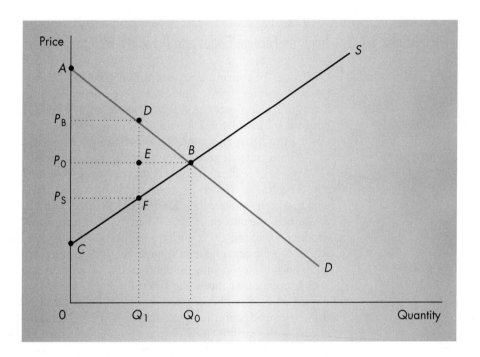

$P_S FC$. Consumers' surplus declines by an amount equal to the area of $P_0 P_B DB$. Producers' surplus declines by an amount equal to the area of $P_S P_0 BF$. Both consumers and producers experience a welfare loss because of the tax.

The welfare effects of a tax are overstated by simply summing the losses in consumers' and producers' surplus. Part of these losses are captured by government in the form of tax revenues. The tax generates government revenue equal to the tax times the after-tax equilibrium quantity. In Figure 14.6, this amounts to the area of rectangle $P_S P_B DF$. The receipts generated by the tax can be viewed as a transfer of wealth from producers and consumers to government. The rectangle $P_0 P_B DE$ is a decrease in consumers' surplus that is captured by government, whereas the rectangle $P_S P_0 EF$ is a decrease in producers' surplus that is also captured by government. The government, however, does not obtain the entire change in consumers' and producers' surpluses. The triangle *BDF* is wealth that is lost by consumers and producers but not recaptured by government. This triangle represents what is called the deadweight welfare loss of the tax. There is a net loss in welfare because the level of economic activity changes.[3] The level of economic activity changes with the imposition of tariffs as well, which are nothing but another kind of excise tax (see Highlight 14.2).

Highlight 14.2   *Taxes on Foreign Goods and Economic Welfare*

With one exception, taxes are universally unpopular. The one exception is taxes on foreign firms. The many proponents of tariffs and import duties, as taxes on foreign-made goods are called, argue that these restrictions on international trade are good for the economy. An analysis of the welfare effects of tariffs shows that this is not the case and goes a long way to explain how the proponents of trade restrictions come to that position.

Figure 14.7 illustrates the domestic market for a good that is traded globally. The home country is assumed to be a price taker in the global market, which sets the price at P_0. Domestic consumers purchase quantity Q_0, with a consumers' surplus of P_0HC. When the domestic supply curve is S_D, domestic producers will sell Q_{D0}, with a producers' surplus of P_0FG. Foreign producers will satisfy the remainder of the market with imports amounting to $Q_0 - Q_{D0}$.

The imposition of a tariff raises the domestic price by the amount of the tax. A tariff of $\$t$ raises the price to P_1, where $P_1 = P_0 + t$, as illustrated in Figure 14.7. The higher price reduces domestic consumption to Q_1, increases domestic production to Q_{D1}, and reduces imports to $Q_1 - Q_{D1}$. The welfare effects of the tariff include changes in consumers' and producers' surpluses and the proceeds of the tariff. The tariff generates revenues equal to the amount of the tax times the quantity imported, or the area of rectangle $ABDE$. Consumers' surplus at the higher price is P_1HB, which is a decrease of P_1BCP_0. Producers' surplus, on the other hand, increases by P_0P_1AF for a total equal to GP_1A. The loss in consumers' surplus more than offsets the gain in producers' surplus and the revenues from the tariff. The tariff results in a deadweight loss equal to the sum of triangles BCD and AEF. This deadweight loss means that the economy is worse off. Why, then, is there support for tariffs?

Ordinarily, a tax transfers wealth from consumers and producers to government. The welfare effects of a tariff are different, because domestic producers are exempt from the tax. Consequently, the redistribution of wealth is from domestic consumers and foreign producers to domestic producers and government. This pits domestic consumers against the domestic producers in the debate over tariffs. Producers, including their suppliers, benefit from the tariff,

---

3. A tax on a market in which one of the market curves is perfectly inelastic will not entail a deadweight welfare loss. Because one side of the market will be totally unresponsive to a price change, the level of economic activity (that is, the equilibrium quantity) will be constant. A tax in this instance transfers all of the lost consumers' and producers' surplus to government.

Figure 14.7 The Welfare Effects of a Tariff

A tariff of \$t per unit raises the domestic price to P_1. Domestic producers experience an increase in producers' surplus of $P_0 P_1 AF$, whereas consumers' surplus declines by $P_0 P_1 BC$. The tariff generates tax revenues of $EABD$ for a net welfare loss of $FAE + DBC$.

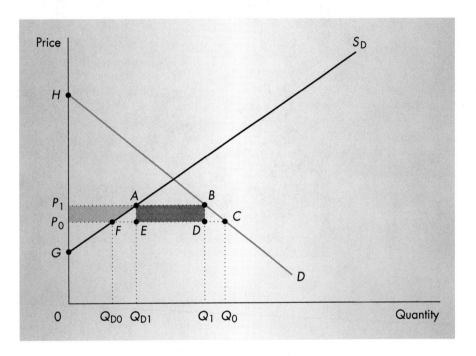

and the self-interest axiom predicts that they will support such restrictions on international trade. One doesn't have to look very hard to find the self-interest behind a Michigan politician's support for tariffs on Japanese automobiles or an Oklahoma politician's support for a tax on imported oil.

Although any restriction on international trade will result in a deadweight welfare loss, different trade policies will have differential effects on the distribution of wealth. This aspect of trade policy can be illustrated by analyzing the impact of an import quota, a restriction of the quantity of goods that may be imported. Suppose that the market depicted in Figure 14.7 is subject to laws that restrict imports that have an effect equivalent to the tariff discussed above. Trade in the good would be free of taxes, but imports would be limited to an amount equal to $Q_1 - Q_{D1}$. The restricted market would achieve an equilibrium at which the quantity supplied (the sum of imports and domestic production) equals the quantity demanded, or at a price equal to P_1, the same price produced by the tariff.

Taxes on imported goods, such as Toyotas, benefit some domestic interests but have negative welfare effects on society in general.

The welfare effects of the quota are almost the same as the tariff. Consumers experience a decrease in consumer surplus equal to $P_0 P_1 BC$, whereas producers' surplus increases by $P_0 P_1 AF$. The market also suffers from a deadweight loss equal to the sum of triangles BCD and AEF. The only difference between the tariff and the quota is in the distribution of rectangle $BCDE$. Under a tariff, this portion of the loss in consumers' surplus is transferred to government. Under a quota, the foreign producers capture this rectangle, because the price of their goods rise to P_1 as a result of the restriction on the forces of competition. It wasn't skill on the part of U.S. negotiators that produced an agreement that led Japanese automobile manufacturers to voluntarily restrict exports to the United States. When given a choice between tariffs and export restrictions, exporters will always choose a quota, because they are the beneficiaries of the redistribution of wealth from consumers.

Taxes alter the behavior of economic actors, disrupt the efficient operation of competitive markets, and reduce economic well-being. If taxes are bad for the economy, it might seem that the opposite of taxes — subsidies — must surely be good for the economy. An analysis of the welfare effects of subsidies will show that the world is not symmetrical. The fact that one activity is harmful does not mean that its opposite will be beneficial.

Subsidies. Government subsidies are benefits provided to economic actors and take the form of cash subsidies or in-kind subsidies. In-kind subsidies are goods or services that are provided to the recipient at no cost or below cost. Cash subsidies are money payments to beneficiaries. Although cash and in-kind subsidies may have different impacts on the well-being of individuals, as was demonstrated in Chapter 5, their market effects are qualitatively identical. Consequently, the remainder of this section will focus on the market effects of cash subsidies.

Cash subsidies take the same basic forms as taxes. Lump-sum subsidies pay a fixed amount to the beneficiary. Aid to Families with Dependent Children (AFDC), which provides income to families that qualify for the program, is an example of a lump-sum subsidy. Subsidies are also paid on a per-unit basis, so that recipients receive cash payments that are related to their respective levels of market activity. Per-unit subsidies are being used to solve the problem of used tires.[4] Some states now pay tire recyclers, who shred used tires for reuse, a fixed amount per tire that is shredded. Finally, subsidies are also paid as a percentage of the amount spent on an activity. The most common forms of the percentage subsidy are federal income tax deductions. Taxpayers get a reduction in their tax liability (the equivalent of a cash payment) that is equal to a percentage of their deductible expenses.

The market effects of a subsidy are exactly the opposite of the market effects of a tax. Whereas a tax on consumers will reduce market demand, a subsidy paid to consumers will increase demand. Subsidizing producers, on the other hand, increases market supply by shifting the supply curve downward. Although taxes and subsidies have opposing influences on the market, they are identical in one respect. Each drives a wedge between the price paid by the buyer and the price received by the seller. The relationship between these two prices under a subsidy is the reverse of the situation under a tax. The price received by sellers equals the price paid by buyers plus the amount of the subsidy.

Welfare Effects of a Subsidy. A change in the prices faced by market participants will change the level of market activity and the well-being of market participants. Figure 14.8 analyzes the welfare effects of a subsidy. The subsidy increases the price received by sellers to P_S and reduces the price paid by buyers to P_B, where the difference between P_S and P_B equals s, the amount of the subsidy. The increase in price to P_S increases the quantity supplied, whereas the decrease in price to P_B increases the quantity demanded. The subsidized market is in equilibrium when the level of output is Q_1.

---

4. Used tires present a particularly difficult disposal problem. They are not biodegradable and tend to rise to the surface when buried. Traditionally, used tires have been simply piled into "mountains" that pose a serious fire hazard.

Figure 14.8 The Welfare Effects of a Subsidy

A subsidy equal to $P_S - P_B$ increases consumers' surplus by $P_B P_0 BE$ and increases producers' surplus by $P_0 P_S DB$. The subsidy costs taxpayers $P_B P_S DE$ and exceeds the gains in consumers' and producers' surplus by BDE, the net welfare loss.

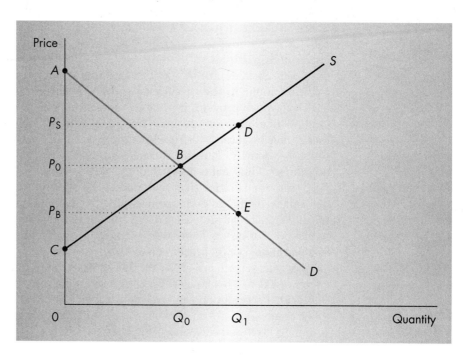

The expansion of market activity that is created by the subsidy increases both consumers' and producers' surplus. The lower price paid by the buyers and the higher quantity demanded increase consumers' surplus by $P_0 BEP_B$. The higher price received by sellers and the increase in the quantity supplied increase producers' surplus by $P_S DBP_0$. This increase in welfare is not achieved without cost. The subsidy program requires a government expenditure equal to the subsidy multiplied by the equilibrium quantity. The subsidy illustrated in Figure 14.8 costs the taxpayers an amount equal to rectangle $P_S DEP_B$. Examination of Figure 14.8 reveals that the cost of the subsidy exceeds the combined increases in consumers' and producers' surplus by an amount equal to triangle BDE. This triangle represents the deadweight loss because of the subsidy.

Subsidies, like taxes, result in a reduction in economic welfare. This welfare loss comes about because of an imperfect transfer of wealth. The subsidy transfers wealth from taxpayers to the consumers and producers who participate in the market. Wealth is destroyed because the costs of producing the additional output (measured by the area $Q_0 BDQ_1$) exceed the benefits of the additional output (measured by the area Q_0BEQ_1). The deadweight loss is the difference between the costs and the benefits of the additional output. Subsidies in the American economy, of course, take many forms. Home ownership, for example, is one of the chief subsidies to the average U.S. citizen, as discussed in Highlight 14.3.

Highlight 14.3   *Subsidizing Home Ownership*

Home ownership remains a major part of the American dream. The federal government has a longstanding policy of facilitating homeownership. Government has encouraged home buying with indirect subsidies in the form of tax deductions. Homeowners are able to deduct the interest paid on home mortgages and state and local property taxes from gross income in figuring their taxable income, thereby reducing their tax liability and the net costs of owning a home. These two deductions reduce government tax revenues by about $50 billion per year — a sizable bonus for homeowners. What are the market and welfare effects of these tax breaks?

The deductibility of property taxes increases the demand for owner-occupied housing by reducing the net cost of homeownership. The deductibility of mortgage interest increases the demand for homes by decreasing the price of a complement of homeownership, the mortgage. This deduction also increases the demand for mortgages by reducing the net cost of having a mortgage. Thus a thorough investigation of this issue requires an examination of both the housing and the credit markets. The market effects of the tax breaks for homeowners are illustrated in Figure 14.9.

Panel (a) illustrates the changes occurring in the credit market in which homebuyers obtain their mortgages. The mortgage-interest deduction increases the demand for loans to D'_L, which results in a higher volume of loans (L_1 versus L_0) and a higher interest rate (r_1 versus r_0). The net interest rate paid by mortgagees falls because borrowing reduces the mortgagees' tax liabilities. The lower effective interest rate and higher mortgage loan volume translate into an increase in consumers' surplus for those who borrow to purchase a home.

Homebuyers, however, are not the only participants in the credit market. People borrow for reasons other than buying a home, and borrowers who cannot deduct their interest payments face the higher interest rate. This reduces the consumers' surplus of those who do not receive the credit subsidy. The credit market is also made up of lenders who are the suppliers of credit. The higher equilibrium interest rate increases the producers' surplus accruing to the suppliers of credit. Higher interest rates increase the profits of firms that provide loans and the return to those whose savings provide the money that is loaned out.

Figure 14.9 Housing Subsidies

The deduction for home mortgage interest increases the demand for loans and increases mortgage interest rates, as shown in panel (a). The deduction decreases the net costs of a complement to home ownership and increases the demand for housing, as shown in panel (b). The price of housing rises as a result of the subsidy to mortgagees.

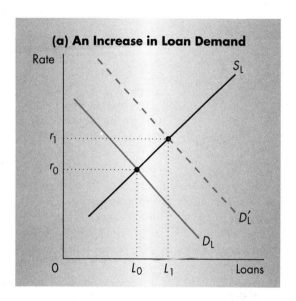

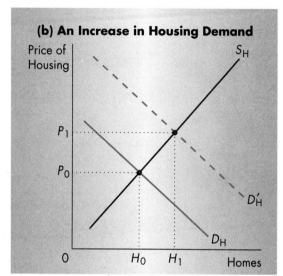

The tax breaks for homeowners also increase the demand for housing. The increased demand for housing increases the equilibrium quantity of housing (the ultimate goal of the tax breaks) and the equilibrium price of housing. It is ironic that a policy designed to extend homeownership results in higher home prices. The higher market price of housing notwithstanding, the policy increases the consumers' surplus of homeowners as well as the producers' surplus accruing to homebuilders. Like any subsidy, the tax policy increases the economic well-being of buyers and sellers. The losers are the taxpayers, who have to make up the $50 billion hole that the tax deductions create in the government budget.

Direct subsidies (in which the government sends someone a check) are not the only means of granting the benefits associated with a subsidy. Historically, the government has often tried to accomplish the same ends by direct control of market prices. The indirect subsidization of buyers and sellers via price controls creates, as the next section demonstrates, its own set of wealth transfers and welfare effects.

Price Controls: Welfare Effects

The market effects of price controls were established in Chapter 2, with real-world examples of these effects detailed in Chapter 5. Laws that establish a minimum price, a **price floor**, consistently create surpluses. The above-equilibrium price increases the quantity supplied and reduces the quantity demanded. The surplus persists as long as the price is held above equilibrium. Laws setting maximum prices, or **price ceilings**, create shortages by increasing the quantity demanded and decreasing the quantity supplied. A shortage continues until the price is allowed to rise to its equilibrium level. Legal limits on market prices disrupt the efficient operation of the price mechanism. These disruptions have not been a deterrent to the imposition of price controls. An examination of the welfare effects of price controls provides some insight into the public's apparent willingness to evade the laws of supply and demand.

The Welfare Effects of a Price Floor

A price floor drives a wedge between market participants. The above-equilibrium price reduces the quantity demanded to Q_D, and increases the quantity supplied to Q_S, as illustrated in Figure 14.10.[5] The welfare effects of this action include direct and indirect components.

The direct effect is the result of the higher price and lower quantity traded within the market. The price floor reduces consumers' surplus by P_0P_FDB, because a smaller quantity is purchased at a higher price. The producers are subject to two opposing influences. Producers' surplus increases by P_0P_FDE (from the higher price received for the quantity sold) and also falls by BEF (from the decrease in sales from Q_0 to Q_D). The net effect of these changes is a loss equal to BDF. This net loss is the sum of P_0P_FDB and BEF (the loss to consumers and producers) minus P_0P_FDE (the gain to producers). Note that the producers' gain is at the expense of consumers.[6] The price floor transfers wealth from consumers to the producers who are able to find buyers in the price-controlled market. These producers represent one group that will definitely favor price floors.

A price floor also involves indirect effects. The indirect effects of a price floor depend on the means by which the minimum legal price is maintained. One means of supporting a price floor is to prosecute those who trade at prices below the legal minimum. Perfect enforcement of the legal minimum price may help eliminate "illegal" trades and prevent the development of a surplus.

5. Note that the wedge between market participants is horizontal when price controls are imposed, in comparison to the vertical wedge caused by taxes and subsidies.

6. Also note that the welfare effects of a price floor are identical to the deadweight loss because of a tax. The only difference between the two is the distribution of wealth. The two would be identical if the tax proceeds were rebated to producers.

Figure 14.10 The Welfare Effects of a Price Floor

The effects of a price floor depend on the means by which prices are supported. If enforcement of the floor precludes production of a surplus, the welfare loss is *FDB*. If government buys total production at the price floor and resells at the price consumers are willing to pay for the output, the welfare loss is *BGH*.

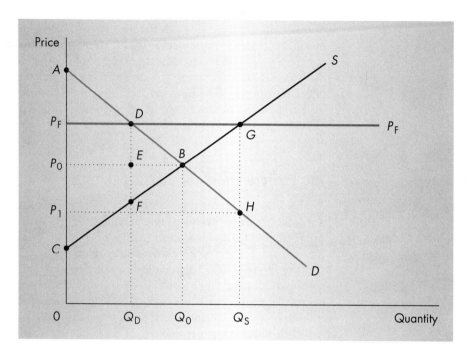

Although firms might want to produce Q_S at the price floor, they will produce Q_D because that is all the market will absorb when the price floor is enforced. A surplus fails to materialize, because it is always unprofitable to produce goods or services that cannot be sold. This method of maintaining price floors adds the costs of enforcing the price floor to the direct welfare loss discussed earlier. Enforcement costs are added to the welfare loss from the price floor, because they represent resources consumed in the operation of the market.[7]

Another means of maintaining a price floor is to have the government purchase any surplus that develops in the market. This action removes the surplus

7. It is far-fetched to believe that any law can be perfectly enforced, thereby eliminating all criminal activity. This is especially true of price controls. Price controls set the stage for "victimless" crimes in which all parties to the criminal activity take part voluntarily. When price controls are in place, those taking part in illegal trades do so because the trade makes each party better off — in spite of the violation of the price controls. Such crimes are seldom reported to the authorities. The authorities are also hampered in their effort to enforce price controls by the sheer number of transactions that must be monitored to prevent illegal trades.

from the market and dissipates the pressure for reductions in the price of the commodity and "illegal" trading. This approach requires the use of government funds to buy up the surplus, which in Figure 14.10 will amount to $Q_D DGQ_S$ (P_F times the surplus) and grants government control over the surplus. The indirect welfare effects of this policy will depend on what the government does with the excess production. The main options are to destroy, store, or sell the inventory of surplus goods created by the price floor.

The least harm is done when the government sells the surplus. This tactic, if applied to the market depicted in Figure 14.10, drives the price down to P_1 and turns the government into an exclusive broker for the good. The combination of a price floor and government surplus sales presents buyers with two options: buy from the private sector at P_F or buy from the public sector at P_1. Because the government's price is less than the private sector's, consumers will prefer the government as a source of the product. Private suppliers will soon find that the government is the only buyer willing to pay the price floor. Industry output will be purchased by government and resold to the public at a discounted price.

The welfare effects of this scheme can be illustrated with the aid of Figure 14.10. The price floor results in Q_S being purchased by government and resold to the public at P_1. Private suppliers are paid $0P_F GQ_S$ for a producers' surplus of $CP_F G$, an increase of $P_0 P_F GB$ over the competitive equilibrium. Buyers pay $0P_1 HQ_S$ for Q_S units of the good for consumers' surplus of $P_1 AH$, an increase of $P_0 BHP_1$. These increases in producers' and consumers' surplus are achieved through an indirect subsidy. The government spends $0P_F GQ_S$ to buy the output and resells it for $0P_1 HQ_S$, for a net expenditure of $P_1 P_F GH$. This indirect government subsidy exceeds the gains in consumers' and producers' surplus by BGH. The net welfare loss generated by this price-support scheme will equal the BGH triangle plus the costs of financing the government's brokerage operations.

Supporting price floors with government purchases and then reselling the surplus mitigates the welfare loss of the price-support program. The government sales let consumers benefit from the increased production. Other uses of the surplus preclude this mitigating effect. A government that stores or destroys the excess production compounds the direct welfare loss associated with the price floor with an indirect loss. The purchase and store program adds an indirect welfare loss equal to the costs of the purchase program plus the costs of storing the surplus. The purchase-and-destroy program adds an indirect welfare loss equal to the costs of the purchase program plus disposal costs. The net welfare losses of these two approaches equal the direct loss plus government expenditures to acquire the surplus (the sum of BDF and $Q_D DGQ_S$ in Figure 14.10, respectively) plus the costs of implementing the disposition of the surplus.

The three schemes for maintaining a price floor via government purchases of the surplus yield different welfare effects. The buy-and-store approach entails a welfare loss of BDF plus $Q_D DGQ_S$ plus the storage costs. The purchase-and-destroy method incurs a welfare loss of BDF plus $Q_D DGQ_S$ plus the costs of disposing of the surplus. The buy-and-resell scheme results in a welfare loss of BGH plus the costs of administering the brokerage operations. Of these three options, the buy-and-resell plan minimizes the welfare loss of the price support program. A comparison of Figures 14.8 and 14.10 reveals that the welfare effects of the buy-and-resell option are similar to the effects of a direct subsidy. A per-unit subsidy equal to P_F minus P_1 will generate the same market results as a price floor of P_F with the government buying and reselling the surplus. The only difference between the two programs will be in administrative costs. The direct subsidy will result in a lower welfare loss if the costs of administering the subsidy program are lower than the costs of buying and reselling the surplus to maintain the price floor.

The Welfare Effects of a Price Ceiling

A price ceiling, if it is effective, sets a maximum legal price that is below the market equilibrium price. The below-equilibrium price creates a shortage by increasing the quantity demanded and reducing the quantity supplied, as illustrated in Figure 14.11. A price ceiling set at P_C results in a quantity supplied equal to Q_S, a quantity demanded equal to Q_D, and a shortage equal to the difference, $Q_D - Q_S$. Because the government's attempt to control prices changes the level of economic activity, it also has an effect on the level of economic welfare. The determination of these welfare effects is simplified by separating them into direct and indirect components.

The direct welfare effects of a price ceiling are found by ignoring any secondary or side effects of the price controls. This part of the analysis assumes that the legal price is perfectly enforced and that all trades occur at the legal, below-equilibrium price. The reduced price and quantity created by the price ceiling result in a transfer of wealth from producers to consumers. The price ceiling reduces producer surplus by $P_C P_0 BF$. The change in consumer surplus is the net effect of two demand-side effects. Consumers gain an amount equal to $P_0 EFP_C$ from purchasing quantity Q_S at the controlled price. However, consumers lose an amount equal to BDE, because the quantity purchased is also reduced by the lower price. The net market impact of the price ceiling is a deadweight loss equal to BDF, the losses in consumers' and producers' surplus of BDE and $P_C P_0 BF$, respectively, minus the gain in consumers' surplus of $P_0 EFP_C$. Note that the gain to consumers is at the expense of producers. It should come as no surprise that calls for price ceilings often originate from the buyer side of the market. Those who maintain their ability to buy the product are better off under the price ceiling.

Indirect welfare effects of a price ceiling arise from the rationally self-interested behavior of those who want to participate in the market. The price ceiling creates a shortage that the price system is prohibited from eliminating. Because price cannot be used to allocate the available output among consumers, some other rationing mechanism must develop to take its place. The

Figure 14.11 The Welfare Effects of a Price Ceiling

The effects of a price ceiling depend on the effectiveness of the price controls. If enforcement of the ceiling precludes illegal trades, the welfare loss is *FDB*. If all trades occur illegally, the welfare loss is less than *FDB* with a redistribution of wealth from consumers to producers.

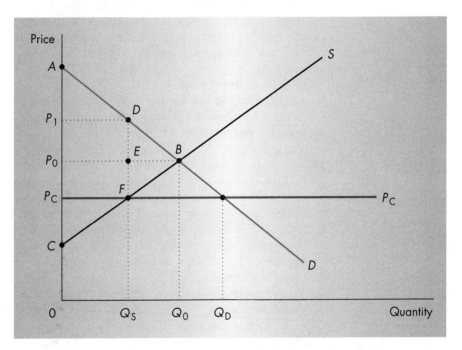

nature and magnitude of the indirect welfare effects depend on which rationing scheme is adopted. Among the alternatives are queuing, illegal or black-market trading, and discrimination. Each of these rationing schemes involve costs that are not incurred when prices alone allocate goods. These rationing costs represent an indirect welfare loss.

The nonprice rationing scheme that people are most familiar with is queuing, or waiting in line. Queuing is the natural outgrowth of the convergence of a shortage with the standard practice of first come, first served. When facing a shortage, prospective buyers arrive early to secure a spot near the front of the line and then wait to be served. The scarce product is then allocated to those who are willing to wait the longest. The time spent in queues is a resource that has alternative uses, and its expenditure is an additional cost in the operation of the market. Rationing by waiting reduces the net benefits of market activity by the value of the time that consumers spend standing in line.

An alternative to line-standing is to break the law and pay more than the ceiling price. The slopes of the market curves indicate that there are buyers and sellers who are, price controls notwithstanding, willing to trade at prices above the legal maximum. It is just a matter of getting the "criminals" together in underground, or "black" markets. The black market will increase the quantity traded in the market as the (higher) black-market prices stimulate production. The new equilibrium output, however, will be less than the competitive equilibrium. The very nature of black-markets make it impossible for them to achieve the competitive solution. The criminal sanctions that illegal traders face, among other problems, prevent the level of activity from expanding to the competitive level. Although illegal trading does reduce the deadweight loss associated with price ceilings, it also alters the distribution of wealth. The higher black-market prices transfer some of the consumers' surplus to the producers.

A price ceiling precludes price rationing, but nothing requires first-come-first-served or black-market distribution of the product. The price controls grant the sellers the power to determine the rationing criteria. This frees the sellers to discriminate in the distribution of the good. The available output is sold to whoever (1) is willing and able to pay the controlled price and (2) meets criteria established by the seller. When confronted with excess demand for their product, sellers can exclude buyers on the basis of their race, sex, age, religion, personal appearance, personality, or any other characteristic.

Distributing the output based on seller preferences affects the efficiency of the market. The discriminatory seller determines who receives the gain in consumer surplus that comes from buying at the lower controlled price. Sellers have neither the ability nor an incentive to maximize the consumers' gain. The gain in consumers' surplus, P_0EFP_C in Figure 14.11, is maximized if and only if the buyers who value the product most (as indicated by the price that they would pay) are allowed to purchase the available output. When output is distributed to please the seller (or on any basis other than price), consumers' surplus is reduced. Discrimination in a market operating under the constraint of a price ceiling aggravates the welfare loss associated with price controls.

Summary

This analysis of price controls and the preceding analysis of taxes and subsidies assumed that markets are efficient. It should come as no surprise, then, that any deviation from the market equilibrium will result in a welfare loss. What would happen to the analysis if the market were not efficient? As noted previously, externalities will detract from the efficiency of the competitive market. The next chapter will consider the impact of government in cases of market failure, the inability to generate an efficient outcome. In this chapter, we have developed

- a brief analysis of the incentives of politicians within the economic theory of public choice.
- several methods — cost benefit and welfare analysis — of evaluating government programs and policies.
- a theory of taxation and subsidies.
- the theory of price controls within a welfare context.

Key Terms

public choice

cost-benefit analysis

consumers' surplus

economic welfare

excise tax

price floor

median-voter model

welfare analysis

producers' surplus

lump-sum tax

ad valorem tax

price ceiling

Sample Questions

Question

How are special-interest groups, such as the National Rifle Association or the American Medical Association, advantaged in the voting process?

Answer

In the median-voter model, individuals who do not participate in the political process by voting obviously minimize their direct influence. But indirect influence through the formation of coalitions of "like interest" is possible. Because politicians respond to voters or to perceived voter influence, individuals may bond together with some strongly felt interest or interests and lobby politicians — with promises of votes or influence — to pass legislation. When opposition to these interests is weak or ineffective, such voter blocs will be most influential in skewing votes to particular interests. Whether or not the activities of these blocs improve overall benefits to society is questionable.

Question

Assume that the enactment of the North American Free Trade Agreement in late 1993 has the effect of reducing Mexico's import tariffs on U.S. goods as well as U.S. tariffs on Mexican goods. Using the analysis surrounding Figures 14.6 and 14.7 in this chapter, analyze the welfare effects of the tariff reduction to either Mexican or American consumers.

Answer

The effects of a tariff reduction are directly analogous to the welfare effects of a reduction in excise tariffs. For American consumers, lowering and ultimately eliminating tariffs on particular goods will lower the price of such goods. Expanding demand (when price falls) will increase both consumer and producer surplus. There will be a redistribution from domestic producers (and their resource suppliers, including labor) and the U.S. government (which heretofore collected revenues from the tariff) to Mexican producers and domestic consumers of the product(s). The great debate over the passage of NAFTA is easy to understand when the "winners" and "losers" of tariff reductions in the United States are identified.

Questions for Review and Discussion

1. In the public-choice model, explain the role voters play in the utility-maximization process of politicians.
2. Why is the median voter significant in the political process, and how does he figure into politicians' hopes for election?
3. It often seems that cost-benefit analysis is a direct method of evaluating government policy. What are some of the disadvantages of this approach?
4. Suppose that the government decides to build a highway (financed with tax revenue) in front of your house. The highway would decrease your property's value. Explain what type of costs will result from this decision.
*5. How does welfare analysis differ from cost-benefit analysis?
6. Explain how consumer surplus and economic welfare are determined.
7. Show graphically: consumer surplus, producer surplus, and economic welfare.
*8. Why are *ad valorem* taxes the most favored type of tax by the government?
9. Explain the impact of a decrease in an excise tax.
10. What welfare effects result from taxation?
11. Explain how tariffs and quotas differ regarding welfare effects.
*12. What are the similarities and differences between taxes and subsidies?
13. The mortgage-interest deduction that exists for homeowners generates changes in the housing market. What are these changes?
*14. In the past, the government has supported farmers by setting a minimum price on milk. What type of price control is this and what are the effects?
15. Rent control is one price control that is frequently used in leasing apartments. What type of price control is this, and what are some of the consequences that might develop in the market for apartments?

Problems for Analysis

*1. It is common to group some taxes under the simple title of "sin taxes." These are taxes on goods and services that can be harmful to the consumer. Tobacco, alcohol, and gambling are the usual objects of sin taxation. (Note that such goods are "legal" but that societal representatives have determined that the consumption of the goods should be restricted.) What are the market effects of such taxes? the welfare effects? How might consumers be helped (or harmed) by the imposition of sin taxes?
2. The 1986 Tax Reform Act passed by the U.S. Congress included a special 10 percent tax on luxury items: expensive cars, jewelry, fur coats, and yachts. What were the effects of these taxes on the markets for luxury items? The sellers of luxury items complained about having to bear the burden of these taxes. Show that, under normal market circumstances, the tax would be borne by both the buyers and the sellers. In 1993 many of these taxes were repealed. Can you explain why?

3. The deductibility of home-mortgage interest is, in effect, a subsidy to homeowners. Their taxes are reduced by a fraction of the mortgage interest that they pay. What impact does this have on the market for owner-occupied housing? What would happen in the rental housing market if tenants could deduct their rent from their taxes?

4. Usury laws are a fairly common feature of economic life. What happens to the operation of credit markets when the equilibrium interest rate is above the legal limit? Include the direct and side effects of the price ceiling in your analysis.

5. Teen age unemployment rates — especially those of minority teens — are relatively high, even during periods of low unemployment in America. Do minimum-wage laws (assume them to be above the equilibrium wage) have anything to do with this unemployment problem? Explain. What are the welfare effects of such minimum-wage laws?

C H A P T E R

15

Market Failure, Externalities, and Public Goods

Adam Smith's dictum that if we all act in our own self-interest, we will promote the aggregate social good holds in a variety of cases. Most markets work in this manner. A long tradition in economics, reaching back to philosopher-economist Jeremy Bentham (1748–1832), holds that markets fail in some circumstances. This chapter is an introduction to the major channels through which markets might fail to provide goods efficiently and to promote the general welfare. Here, using important real-world examples, we will analyze

- the source of alleged market failures in so-called spillover and third-party effects to free exchange.
- the theoretical manner in which economists have dealt with economic problems related to externalities.
- the nature and theory of so-called public goods — goods that private markets do not supply in efficient quantities but that are nonetheless wanted by the public.
- the critical interplay between the provision of public goods and the redress of externalities, on the one hand, and the political system or structure that public choice works through on the other.

How Do Markets Fail?

Practically speaking, the vast body of theory in microeconomics concerns markets, how they are described, and how they function. We have seen throughout this text that, judged from the perspective of static efficiency and welfare criteria, markets may be either efficient or (as with monopoly) inimical to efficiency and welfare maximization. In general, we have seen that the elimination of artificial barriers to entry is conducive to efficient results in markets. In this respect, the existence of monopoly is a kind of **market failure** — one in which artificial (manmade) or natural barriers prevent efficient market functioning.

Numerous economists of the past have argued that the market can fail in other ways. Most frequently, market failure is the result of the complete or partial failure to define property rights. Most environmental problems and problems related to resource depletion are the result of such market failures. For example, certain endangered species of fish (including some species of the redfish) and turtles are completely off limits to fishermen in the Gulf of Mexico. Because there are no defined property rights to the fish, the take is on a first-come-first-served basis. Each fisherman has the incentive to catch as many fish as possible and the result is the so-called problem of overfishing. Most endangered species — for example, the African elephant, the Indian tiger, or the California condor — fall into this category. In this **common-pool problem**, what belongs to everyone belongs to no one. There is no incentive to conserve these resources, because they are not "owned" by anyone.

The same is true of the air. Because no individual or nation owns the air, the incentives to pollute go unchecked. No one would think of littering her house or yard, but since the pro rata share of littering costs to you are low in public places such as Yellowstone Park, we tend to observe a pile-up of litter. These effects may be positive as well. If you build a beautiful and viewable garden or Christmas or Hanukkah display, you are creating benefits to non-paying observers for which you cannot charge.

The Problem of Externalities

The foregoing problems are called externalities, and a whole branch of microeconomic theory has emerged to address them. An **externality** is simply the benefits or costs that apply to an economic entity's behavior that are not expropriatable or borne by that entity. An entity may be an individual, a firm, or a government agency. Clearly, planting a beautiful garden is a **positive externality** — where the individual or economic entity creates benefits to others without receiving any compensation for them. A **negative externality** is, as in the case of pollution, an activity that imposes costs on others without compensation to them. Those who live downstream from a polluter or close to a smoke-belching factory may well understand such costs.

Not all externalities — in fact, very few of the many that occur — require or deserve attention. Many everyday activities and behavior create both positive and negative externalities. Happy and concerned friends or coworkers may unfailingly create some pleasure or joy for all they meet without being compensated (or adequately compensated). Alternatively, you might endure a friend's smoking habit or use of obnoxious perfume. Such externalities exist for everyone everyday. Whether or not these are relevant — requiring some action to obtain efficiency — depends on how trivial they are. You may be willing to pay a friend or coworker $5 per week to stop using perfume or cologne, whereas that person would require $20 not to lose utility. In this event, the externality will not be corrected and it *should* not be corrected. The payment would cost more than it would be worth to correct the externality.

Likewise, you might get a monetary benefit of $25 per month to get your neighbor to plant more flowers closer to your property. If the neighbor required $40, the flowers would not be planted.

Relevant externalities exist when there is enough of a problem or benefit to create an effective demand for change. If your neighbor only required $20 to plant the flowers, bargaining would take place, a deal would be struck, and the flowers would be planted. When benefits exceed all costs, the externalities are "corrected."

One essential problem concerning relevant externalities is the determination of how they are to be addressed. Clearly, using the foregoing trivial examples, government may step in to regulate the individual's planting of flowers — with a statute or law requiring your neighbor to plant more flowers. But we have seen that if you benefit more from the additional flowers (in a monetary sense) than the planting would cost your neighbor, the externality would, through purely private interests and actions, be internalized. In terms of relevant externalities, the answer is not often so simple. Who owns the property rights to air? The owner is able to place costs on other parties. If a factory owner has the rights, individuals around the factory must bear the cost of polluted air and water. If the citizens surrounding the plant own the rights, they would be able to force the plant to reduce pollution through costly control devices or cease production altogether. Who gets the rights and what are the consequences? More generally, what are the various means through which externalities may be controlled and "internalized" so that positive net harm is mitigated or positive net benefits rewarded?

A number of means have been proposed for addressing relevant externalities. They include

- purely private internalization through the legal assignment and definition of property rights.
- the so-called Pigouvian taxation of negative externalities and the subsidization of positive ones.
- sales of the rights to create negative externalities.
- administrative regulation of industry.

The possibilities for the internalization of externalities were raised in a profound statement of the dual nature of the externality problem by Ronald H. Coase.[1]

---

1. Ronald H. Coase, "The Problem of Social Cost," *Journal of Law and Economics* 3 (October 1960): 1–44. Coase, the Nobel laureate in economics in 1991, established an entire new branch of microeconomics, called "law and economics," with this single paper. The branch is concerned with such questions as the efficiency of legal rules, the evolution of common law, and the impact of liability placement. Most major law schools in the United States now teach courses in the subject, which integrates microeconomic and legal principles in order to assess the question of efficiency.

The Coase Theorem: Privatizing Externalities

Common ownership, as noted initially, is at the heart of most problems of externalities. Common ownership, moreover, means that rights are not assigned to any particular party, so that limits are not put on behavior. Consider the problem of a firm that is an upstream polluter of water. Further, assume that downstream farmers use the water for household purposes and irrigation. Clearly we would be tempted to say that a negative externality is placed on the downstream farmers by the polluting firm. But think of the problem from the firm's perspective. The negative externality *would not exist* if the farmers had not settled along the river. Should the downstream farmers invest resources in cleaning up the polluted water? Should the firm compensate the farmers for the pollution clean-up? Coase came up with a famous answer and analysis of the question.

A Generalized Model. In order to understand the **Coase theorem**, consider a generalized problem with economic entities A and B involved. These entities could be individuals, firms, or a combination of an individual and a firm. Figure 15.1 shows the total impact of A's actions — as yet undefined — on A's total payoff, as well as the impact of A's actions on B's total payoff. Further, consider that A's actions have a negative impact on B's payoff, so that we are considering a *negative* externality. (Remember, however, that the very existence of B contributes to the existence of an externality.) The vertical axis measures the total payoff for A and B and the payoff for the combination of A + B.

As A's actions progress to some ultimate value, Q_N, A's total payoff rises at a decreasing rate. A's *marginal* benefit is shown by the tangent to the total payoff curve (TP_A in Figure 15.1). As A's actions progress, B's total payoff (TP_B) declines at an increasing rate. If A has full property rights in his or her actions, A's activity will be pushed to line Q_N where A's total payoff is maximized and B's payoff minimized. Conversely, if B owns property rights, A is completely unable to act and (insofar as A's possibly adverse actions are concerned) B's payoff is maximized with A's payoff minimized.

The "social maximum" is the simple sum of the positive and negative payoffs to A and B. Note that the point Max on the social payoff curve occurs at the point at which the action level of A is at A_0. The critical question is, How do we get there? Begin at Q_N, where A is assigned the property rights but where negotiations between the two parties are possible. A slight decrease in A's actions that are harmful to B has a large marginal improvement in B's payoff but only a *slight* reduction in A's payoff. B would therefore be willing to pay A to reduce his actions incrementally because, in monetary terms, it would be in his interest to do so. Likewise, if B holds the property rights, (at A's action equal to zero in Figure 15.1), A would receive a large marginal increase in his payoff if B permitted A to act incrementally, whereas B would lose little

Figure 15.1 The Coase Theorem — A Generalized Model

A's actions have a detrimental effect on B. Hence B's total payoff falls as A's rises. When A's actions reach a level of A_0, the sum of A's and B's payoffs are maximized.

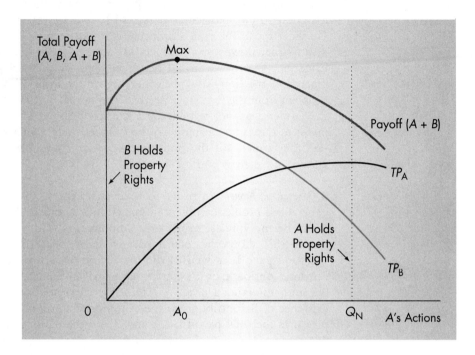

in a marginal sense. A would therefore bribe B to permit the incremental action. Bargaining would end, in either case, where the social benefit is maximized — where A's actions are given as A_0. The model conforms to Coase's assumptions that the costs of negotiation and bargaining are zero. In this case, note that private arrangements guarantee that the social optimum is reached. It does not matter who owns the property rights so long as the parties can negotiate costlessly.

The Coase Theorem: An Example. The generalized model of the workings of the Coase theorem may be made more understandable with a concrete example. Our example may be drawn from a large variety of circumstances: a chemical plant exuding malodorous fumes and gases, a noisy neighbor, a water or air polluter, or secondary smoke. Consider a now-common example — the attempt to make an office building smoke-free. This time, however, let benefits and costs be expressed in marginal terms. In Figure 15.2 the problem of smokers and nonsmokers is outlined in terms of marginal costs and marginal benefits to work hours of permissible smoking versus hours of smoke-free environment in some office building. If there is an eight-hour workday in the building, there are 480 minutes of smoking (or nonsmoking) possible.

Figure 15.2 The Marginal Costs and Benefits of Smoking

Smokers create an "externality" on nonsmokers, but the presence of nonsmokers equally creates an externality on smokers. If negotiation between parties is allowed, a solution at smoking level T_E would be feasible.

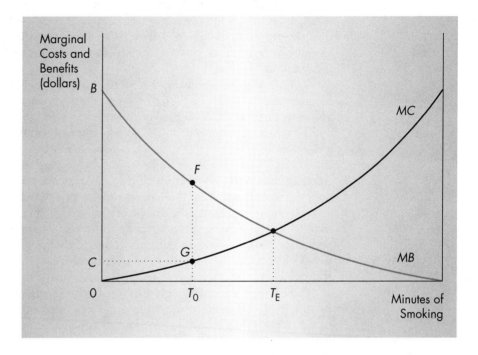

The marginal benefits to smokers, the *MB* curve in Figure 15.2, are positive but declining as a function of the number of minutes that smoking is permitted over the workday. The marginal costs to nonsmokers, the *MC* curve, are positive and rising at an increasing rate as the number of minutes of smoking rises over the eight-hour day. All benefits and costs are expressed in dollar terms. Fundamentally, the logic is identical to that of the generalized model of Figure 15.1. Economic efficiency would not be served if *either* smokers' or nonsmokers' rights are forced to the extreme. If smokers have rights and negotiations are not possible, the marginal costs to nonsmokers will exceed the marginal benefits to smokers past time period T_E. If smoking is prohibited, with no bargaining possible between the two groups, economic efficiency and welfare are likewise reduced.

If smokers and nonsmokers are free to negotiate, exactly T_E minutes of smoking will be permitted. If less time were permitted, say T_0, the marginal benefits will exceed the marginal cost to nonsmokers. Because the total benefits and total costs are the integrals under the marginal curves at time T_0, the total benefits exceed total costs by an amount $0BFG$ — more than enough money to bargain with nonsmokers for additional smoking time. A freely negotiated equilibrium takes place at T_E minutes of smoking.

There are a number of characteristics of this equilibrium and the more general one described in Figure 15.1:

1. In Coasian logic, *neither* smokers *nor* the presence of nonsmokers is, by itself, responsible for the creation of the externality. Externalities are two-way affairs because they would not exist except for the presence of both parties simultaneously. (A little reflection will reveal that this is true of *all* externalities.) Pejorative or judgmental statements about one group or the other take us out of the realm of positive science and into the mire of normative statements about "justice."

2. Following observation 1 and the simple logic of choice, *it does not matter in terms of overall efficiency where the liability or property rights are placed* in order for the externality to be internalized. So long as negotiations and a "marginal" approach to the situation are permitted, an optimal solution will occur no matter who gets the rights. If smokers have the rights in the foregoing illustration, nonsmokers will respond by bribing them to reduce smoking time to T_E. Conversely, if nonsmokers have property rights in the situation, smokers will have the wherewithal to provide monetary expression for their desire for smoking time. Monetary transfers will bring the bargainers to a time of T_E, *or* technologies may arise to prevent or mitigate problems in the first place.[2] No real-world solution, because of the nature of benefits and costs, is "all or nothing" — intermediate solutions (with some smoke-free time and some smoking time) are to be expected.

3. Although a very large number of relevant externalities may be addressed by simply placing liability and letting market forces settle the optimal amount of the activity, high transactions and negotiating costs between parties will make that impossible in a number of extremely important cases. We have already noted that, in general, it is impossible to apportion and assign rights to the air. The problems of air pollution or acid rain are therefore unlikely to be solved by liability assignment and internalized market mechanisms (see Highlight 15.1). The same is true of the preceding water-pollution example.

Highlight 15.1   *Smog Futures and "Cash for Clunkers": Air Pollution and Innovative Solutions*

One of the most difficult and important of all modern problems generated by externalities is air pollution. Air quality problems abound in a number of forms. Acid rain, for example, causes the chronic rusting of infrastructure (such as bridges and public monuments). Smog produces a variety of physical ailments, especially those related to bronchial diseases. Holes in the ozone layer

---

2. Note that technology could feasibly eliminate the externality. Smoke-free areas of restaurants and buildings, sophisticated smoke-removal equipment, and air-conditioning systems are all designed to eliminate the problem.

Air pollution is one of the best-known externalities in our
society. A number of innovative solutions have been proposed
for dealing with the problem.

may be producing global warming and cataclysmic climatic changes. A rising
incidence of skin cancer among people living in the lower parts of South
America has, for example, been blamed on increased ultraviolet exposure from
the sun.

These unwanted and horrifying glimpses of things to come are the result
of an externality that has only become relevant in recent centuries. The
Industrial Revolution and the growth in population have made air pollution a
relevant externality in modern life. Unfortunately, there is no practical way to
relate a unit of air to any individual, and this means that there are few, if any,
means of defining property rights to the air. When property rights cannot be
defined, as noted in the chapter, no one has an automatic incentive to conserve. Everyone, rather, has the incentive to produce the negative externality,
because his or her pro rata share of the social cost is small.

All of this translates into an explanation for purely governmental solutions to the various problems created by the externality of air pollution. *All of these solutions are imperfect and all of them create costs.* The best solutions, from an economic perspective, are those that produce the largest net benefit — the most bang for the buck. (Recall from the chapter and from basic economics that it would be inefficient to eliminate air pollution or any externality entirely.) Consider some wise and perhaps not-so-wise approaches to forms of air pollution.

Smog is the number-one air-pollution problem in major cities around the globe. Both the federal government — through the Environmental Protection Agency (EPA) and a number of other agencies — and state governments regulate air quality in the United States.[a] Regulations in the form of emission standards on automobiles and on industry are the cornerstone of these policies. In general, the toughest air-quality laws in place are in California. These laws often exceed EPA guidelines and are more stringent than in all of the other states. Even with the most stringent regulations in America, standards were only being met one out of every two days in the Los Angeles area in 1992. Regulations are costly to enforce and maintain for government administrative bureaucracies, so that a combination of innovations — some involving incentives in the private sector — are being tried at all governmental levels. Here are a few of them:

Pollution limits may be set with permits sold to the highest bidder, as noted in the chapter. Adjustments to the Clean Air Act in 1990 — administered by the EPA — allow the EPA to issue permits to utilities to emit specific quantities of sulfur dioxide. Sulfur dioxide is a major ingredient in acid rain and in smog. The effect of these permits, auctioned off annually, will be to provide businesses with incentives to clean up pollution. Importantly, however, business will *be able to choose and/or develop* their own technology to limit emissions. In a distinctly market-oriented approach to the problem, companies with low-grade emissions will forgo the use of their permits and instead sell them to polluters with higher-grade emissions. Polluters will, in effect, pay market penalties for their activities. A ready market in permits means that "smog futures" may be traded just like gold, petroleum, or hog-belly options contracts. Both the Chicago Boards of Trade and the New York Mercantile Exchange are interested in running such a market in government-issued permits.

---

[a] Some groups believe that the EPA is not stringent enough in implementing and enforcing environmental policy. In 1991, for example, coalitions of environmentalists, individual states, and the American Lung Association threatened to sue the EPA for failing to clean up lung-killing urban smog. Unfortunately, scientific evidence on this matter — evidence that would shed light on costs and benefits of more stringent policies — is, as in the case of global warming, in debate among experts. See Linda Kanamine, "Coalition: EPA Not Cleaning Up Smog," *USA Today* (July 26, 1991), p. A3.

Although the state of California and the city of Los Angeles support such devices, their efforts and those of the federal government extend far beyond attempts at market implementation. The EPA has issued a cleanup timetable of three to twenty years for 100 U.S. cities, with possible "fixes" including more and tougher vehicle-inspection standards, development of cleaner and alternative fuels, and carpooling and greater reliance on urban transit. A subway system has been begun in Los Angeles, where auto emissions are a chief factor in smog production. In addition, the state has placed restrictions on such consumer items as barbecue grills, charcoal fire starters, and lawn mowers. In 1992 the Bush administration even proposed a "cash for clunkers" program under which older cars, those produced before 1980 and especially pre-1971, would be purchased by cities or private companies and destroyed.

All of these innovations are interesting and potentially of value in dealing with the externality. Economists, however, are by nature skeptical. Bureaucracies of all kinds tend to ignore the full costs of their actions. In 1992, for example, the EPA attempted to require the posting by businesses, large and small, of intentions to change marginal emissions. This would allow environmental bureaucrats to hold hearings on each and every change. The law would apply to dry-cleaning establishments and bakeries, in addition to larger manufacturers and refiners. Economists question whether the costs of such a law, particularly to small businesses and consumers, would be reasonable.[b]

Other features of environmental regulations cause economists some pause. Why, for example, should car buyers and owners in Nevada or Idaho have to pay for pollution control when they do not create a relevant externality? Should the standards mandated in California — admittedly a state with a problem — be required of an entire nation? It does no good, moreover, to argue that environmental activists are rationally concerned about the costs that are shifted to business and consumers from increased regulation. They, as well as such not-for-profit agencies as the American Lung Association, are pursuing their own self interests, often in the form of expanded bureaucracies. For the economist, it is inconsistent to argue that the tobacco companies or electrical utilities are self-interested but that the EPA, OSHA, and the American Cancer Society are not. At bottom, all public policy aimed at control of externalities is enacted in the theater of politics. All government solutions should be judged with that fact in mind.

---

[b] Mexico City, arguably the most polluted urban area in the world, has taken extreme measures to eliminate its air pollution, trying to enact in a few years what the United States has not been able to accomplish in twenty or thirty. The impact on industry and employment has been dramatic, with many firms, including a large General Motors truck-assembly plant, moving to other locales. It is important to note that every policy to eliminate an externality has tradeoffs in terms of costs.

No matter where the liability is placed — on upstream polluting firms or on downstream farms or users of water — a solution by which the market internalizes the externality is not ordinarily practical. The transactions and bargaining costs of collecting enough money from widely dispersed farmers to bribe polluters, or an acceptable scheme by which firms can bribe the downstream injured, may be "too high" in order to get to the Coase solution.[3]

Non-Coasian Solutions

Through time a number of other means of internalizing externalities have emerged. Virtually all of the attempts to address these problems of market failure involve larger or smaller measures of government involvement. The most famous of these "solutions" is one proposed by neoclassical economist A. C. Pigou.[4]

The Pigouvian Tax-Bounty Argument. At the base of most government "solutions" to the problem of market failure is the approach of taxing negative externalities and subsidizing positive externalities. This process is described for competitive markets in Figure 15.3. The underlying analysis of taxes and subsidies (bounties, in old English) is quite simple. When only the private costs of an action are considered, either "too much" or "too little" of products or services that engender externalities are being produced.

The Negative Externality. Consider a negative externality such as pollution. In Figure 15.3a, the polluting industry's marginal-cost curve (actually the summed marginal-cost curves of all of the competitive firms) is drawn under two assumptions — that full costs (private and social) are considered (MSC) and that only private costs (MPC) are included in the cost calculation. When only the purely private costs of the industry's actions are taken into account, the marginal-cost curve is designated MPC, or **marginal private costs**. Output of the industry, under these assumptions, is Q_0.

But when the external costs imposed by the industry's pollution — cleanup costs and the like — are fully accounted for, the "full" marginal cost curve to society of producing additional units of the good or service (for example, chemicals, paper, polyethylene) is designated by the curve MSC, or marginal

3. Such schemes will always be compromised by so-called free riders — those individuals who will seek to benefit from a provision without paying for the benefit. In the example of the text, it would be difficult to get downstream individuals to reveal exactly the amount they would be willing to pay to bribe the upstream polluter. In fact, the incentive to under-reveal the value of clean water would be low or nonexistent, an example of the free rider. Why contribute when you expect others to do so?

4. In *Wealth and Welfare* (London: Macmillan, 1912) and again in the *Economics of Welfare* (London: Macmillan, 1920), Pigou discussed the possibility of market failure, the MSB/MSC apparatus discussed hereafter, and the probable necessity for government intervention.

Figure 15.3 The Pigouvian Tax-Subsidy Solution

Divergences between private and social costs and benefits may be addressed with taxes or subsidies. In panel (a) a pollution tax of *FG* would raise price and reduce quantity to reflect the full social cost of the activity. In panel (b) a subsidy would have the effect of adjusting price and output to account for the social benefits that production of the good creates.

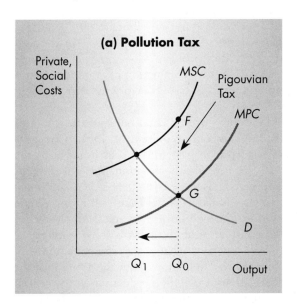

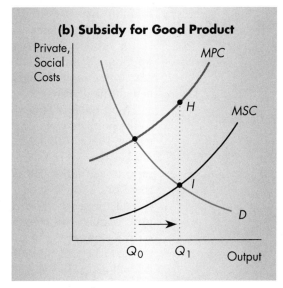

social costs. The government, recognizing this externality, imposes a per-unit tax on firms in the industry. A tax in the amount of *FG* per unit of output produced will raise the *MPC* to *MSC*, thereby reducing the amount produced from Q_0 to Q_1. (Ostensibly the proceeds of the tax are used to pay for cleaning up the environment, water, soot, medical expenses, and so on.)

The Positive Externality. In the opposite case of a positive externality, the marginal private and social cost curves for the industry (and for firms) are reversed. One often-cited positive externality relates to health-promoting vaccinations. It is clearly in the individual's interest to vaccinate herself against polio, typhoid fever, and other contagious diseases. Doing so also increases the probability that others will be safe (though they are not vaccinated). Thus an alleged positive externality results. The marginal private costs do not include this positive benefit and are therefore gauged as "too high." A per-unit subsidy does the trick and increases the industry supply curve of vaccinations to *MSC*, where the quantity of vaccinations rises from Q_0 to Q_1. (The nature of the subsidy does not concern us here. A per-unit subsidy in the amount *HI* in

Figure 15.3b may be paid to individuals who obtain vaccinations as a rebate. Or the amount may be paid on a per-unit basis to clinics or physicians who vaccinate demanders.)

There are a number of interesting and important features of this **"Pigouvian" solution**. Depending on elasticities of demand and supply, both suppliers and demanders will share in the payment of the tax. Further, the Pigouvian solution, like the one proposed by Coase, is not an all-or-nothing solution. The simple assignment of property rights with bargaining, as well as the unit tax or subsidy solution to the externalities problem, does not yield extreme solutions. And this is to be expected. The *total* elimination of pollution or acid rain, for example, would cost more in terms of resources forgone than it would benefit the demanders of clean water or air.

A central problem in this and in other governmental-bureaucratic solutions to the problem of externalities is the knowledge requirement. In the Coase situation, simple liability must be levied (or property rights established) and the market takes care of the rest. In the tax-subsidy situation, the government seeks to get individuals or firms to behave as if the cost curve is *MSC* and must therefore know the exact extent of the externality. Take pollution. Where should the tax be placed? How does the *output* of a chemical or petroleum plant correlate with the pollution emitted? Should the tax be on the *output* or on the emissions? Further and more critically, what is the optimal amount of the tax? The technical relationships may be well known, but the amount of the tax will depend on the correct estimation of pollution reduction on the part of beneficiaries — a most difficult task. In addition, different-sized plants will have different per-unit Pigouvian taxes.

In terms of a positive externality such as vaccinations, the spillover benefits to society from an additional vaccination must be given some monetary expression, a calculation that is extremely difficult in practice. Practically any government activity can be defended with the allegation that high transactions costs justify taxes, subsidies, or other interventions for economic efficiency. In such arguments, high transactions costs are eliminated by low-cost government intervention. But many of these hypothesized cases have no basis in fact (see Highlight 15.2).

Highlight 15.2   *President Clinton and the Beekeepers: Imaginary Externalities*

The U.S. presidential campaign of 1992, like all political contests, produced a great deal of rhetoric and promises. The campaign literature of both major political parties promised to trim the federal budget and to reduce bureaucracies. (Too often, as noted by American humorist Will Rodgers, the pre-election "season of promises" becomes the post-election "season of alibis".) A relatively minor budget item — targeted for ridicule and elimination by candidate Bill Clinton — was the federal honeybee subsidy.

The honeybee subsidy, which cost a total of $18.6 million to the federal government in 1991, was established in 1952, not to stimulate bee or honey production, but to foster the joint product of bees — the pollination of fruit and nut crops. The subsidy, in the form of high-rate loans to beekeepers that are repaid at low rates, affects 3,000 to 5,000 beekeepers in North and South Dakota, California, Florida, and Washington.[a] In 1990, the General Accounting Office, an arm of investigations for Congress, recommended abolishing the bee-subsidy program. The GAO argued that fruit and nut growers that needed bees could buy or rent them.

GAO arguments did not faze the beekeepers in their response to Clinton's proposal. According to Don Schmidt of Winner, SD, president of the American Beekeeping Federation, beekeepers would not survive without the (approximately) $0.08 per pound subsidy. There were even intimations that the United States would lose fruit and nut production to China, where bee-keepers are paid the equivalent of a dollar a day. (An estimated $9.7 billion worth of crops per year are pollinated by bees in the United States.) American apiaries and, by implication, fruit and nut producers in the United States, would be put out of business by unfair foreign competition, it was argued.

Clearly, for defenders of the program, an externality is the prime justification for the beekeepers' subsidy. And there *is* an obvious externality in the Coasian sense — bees pollinate fruits and nuts, gathering nectar to produce honey in the act of doing so. But the leap to subsidies is incorrect in this case. For years, economists *themselves* offered the bee-pollination case as a prime example of externalities justifying government interventions.[b] It was "obvious" to many that the benefits of pollination could and would not be recompensed by farmers or (equally "obvious") that beekeepers could not or would not pay for the nectar that bees gathered from the trees and plants. Under such circumstances, not enough fruits, nuts, or honey would be produced. After all, nature could not be controlled by markets. Only government could adjust for the vagaries of nature!

Economist Stephen Cheung, in a now-classic paper published in 1973, showed that the case for government intervention with subsidies in the bee, fruit, and nut business was a "fable."[c] Cheung showed that elaborate contractual arrangements between farmers and beekeepers were long routine. The conclusion that the pollination-honey market was efficient (*without* the government subsidy) was the product of a detailed empirical study of the Washington state plant and bee industries conducted in the spring of 1972. Some plants do not require bees for pollination but yield high amounts of nectar for honey (mint is an example). Some plants, such as apple trees, do

[a] See "Trying to Sweeten Up Clinton To Keep a Honey Bee Subsidy," *The Washington Post* (November 24, 1992), p. A19.

[b] Two examples are J. E. Meade, "External Economies and Diseconomies in a Competitive Situation," *Economic Journal* 52 (1952): 54 and Francis M. Bator, "The Anatomy of a Market Failure 72 *Quarterly Journal of Economics* (1958): 364.

[c] Steven N. S. Cheung, "The Fable of the Bees: An Economic Investigation," *Journal of Law and Economics* 16 (1973): 11–33.

require bees for pollination but produce little or no surplus nectar. Still other plants yield high amounts of nectar *and* require pollination by bees. An example of this reciprocal externality is alfalfa. In all cases studied by Cheung, the pricing and rental rates of beekeeper services and the contractual arrangements governing nectar and pollination services were consistent with the efficient allocation of resources.

Hives of bees are movable resources. Beekeepers begin pollinating almonds in California in early spring and move northward to Washington in late spring to pollinate apples and soft fruits (including late-blooming cherries). Evidence that the market functions — that pollinating services are bought and sold — is no farther away than the Yellow Pages in some Washington and California cities. Rental prices received by beekeepers may be in terms of honey, a money fee, or a combination of money and honey. (The money fee or the honey payment may be positive or negative.)

Cheung was able to show that in the same season and with bee colonies of about the same strength, rental prices per hive "obtained from different farms or by different beekeepers will be roughly the same whether the hive is employed for pollination, for honey production, or for a combination of both."[d] This means that there is a strong *negative* correlation between the pollination fee — the money value of the rent — and the expected honey yield — the in-kind value of the rent.

Other fascinating implications follow from Cheung's study. Apiary rents (paid by the beekeepers) are always observed where the use of hives provides no valuable pollination services. Where little surplus honey is produced (over and above that required to maintain the hive) and pollination services are valuable, higher rents are paid to the beekeepers by farmers. Apiary lease and pollination contracts between beekeepers and farmers routinely deal with provisions regarding the number and strength of hives, time of delivery of the bees, removal of hives, rental fees per hive, the protection of bees from pesticides, and the strategic placement of hives. Cheung found that customs (such as the "custom of the orchards") emerged that deal with the foraging behavior of bees (which means that neighboring orchards might be benefited from bee rentals) and with the problem of pesticides. Such customs are merely "informal contracts." In all, the evidence is consistent with the efficient production of both honey and pollination services.

Government intervention, in the form of subsidies, is inappropriate and unnecessary in this market. President Clinton's first impression, that the subsidy could be eliminated, is the correct one. An agricultural spending bill passed in October of 1993 did in fact eliminate $16 million in honey support payments. If the quantity of pollination services or honey falls below that demanded, the market will ensure that more bees or nectar are supplied.

[d] Cheung, "Fable," p. 24.

Each case in which externalities supposedly justify government intervention must be carefully documented and evaluated. Otherwise economic policy is created out of sheer fabrication.

Other Solutions

Some attempt to integrate market forces into the externalities problem is given in the proposal that "pollution rights" be sold. The bidding process would thereby permit the sale of rights to pollute the environment, with the proceeds (ostensibly) going to clean up the pollution. Under this system, the government would set an allowable amount of pollution — the optimal quantities signified in the foregoing technical analysis. The advantage would be that the polluting firms would be able to decide whether to pay for the right to pollute by some given amount or to install pollution-control equipment. The nature and kind of equipment installed would be entirely up to the firm's management, and the incentive for the firm would be, in all cases, to minimize costs.

Choice is built into the system when pollution rights are auctioned off to firms. The firm may choose to buy the rights or it may select from an array of possible pollution-control technologies or devices carrying different cost

"It's a letter from the Food and Drug
Administration."

estimates. The problems with this solution, however, are similar to those of the tax-subsidy scheme. What is the optimal level of pollution? Again, it depends on how individuals *value* pollution — a knowledge requirement of government. The behavior and performance of polluting firms must also be monitored by the government and the rules must be enforced. These kinds of costs must be added to the costs of the pollution in order to obtain the total costs of the clean-up.

The most draconian approach of all to the pollution problem is direct regulation. In this solution, firms cannot choose to pollute or not to pollute or decide on the pollution-control technology. Under such forms of regulation, such as those administered by the Environmental Protection Agency (EPA) and the Occupational Safety and Health Administration (OSHA), *rules,* rather than discretion, are prescribed by government bureaucratic agencies. Each firm must use EPA- or OSHA-prescribed technology to clear up pollution or to establish a safe, hazard-free work environment.

At first blush, the regulatory solution might seem to be an efficient one to the externalities problem. Equipment is installed and pollution is abated or workplace safety achieved. Without the element of choice, however, economic efficiency is unlikely to be achieved. If the technology to control the externality is optimal at the start of regulation, it is unlikely to be optimal through time. The reason is that the incentive for firms to develop new technology to control pollution or to establish new levels of workplace safety is reduced or eliminated with direct regulatory mandates. A potentially worse economic problem is that some firms in an industry — usually large and efficient firms — will seek and demand direct regulation to increase smaller rivals' costs, sometimes putting them out of business.[5]

All solutions involve specific costs and benefits. When the inefficiencies and costs of some government taxing or regulatory schemes are considered, market forces (left alone) often do as well or almost as well in providing redress of the externality. No solution will be perfect. Many environmental and ecological problems — saving the northwestern spotted owl, for example — are blatantly politicized.

Government solutions may be necessary in some instances, but private internalization of some externalities is perfectly possible, especially in the presence of strong profit motives. New technology in ocean agriculture is an example. The vagaries of nature, plus pollution and overfishing of common property resources, have explained the uncertainties in the amount and quality of certain seafood crops over the years. Included in these crops are lobster, clam, shrimp, and other ocean products. High-tech pond culture has made the "private" production of many of these products viable in recent years.

---

5. There is good evidence that such behavior is related to OSHA restrictions. See Ann P. Bartel and Lacy Glenn Thomas, "Predation through Regulation: The Wage and Profit Effects of the Occupational Safety and Health Administration and the Environmental Protection Agency," *Journal of Law and Economics* 30 (October 1987): 239–264.

A principal example is the Atlantic LittleNeck Clam Farms operation at James Island, South Carolina. Private clam production is emerging in the face of increasing demand by major restaurant and seafood restaurant chains for dependable supplies of quality clams. The Atlantic LittleNeck company, with the help of marine biologists, engineers, and management experts, plans to supply up to 20 percent of the total U.S. market for clams after reaching full production levels in 1995.[6] Aquaculture, which is the farming of fish and shell-fish such as clams, is the fastest-growing segment of American agriculture. Private farms yielded $761.5 million worth of products in 1990 — four times the value produced in 1980.

It is likely that a variety of approaches, governmental and Coasian private solutions, such as in clam farming, will continue to be used in attacking such market failures. (Sadly, even well-meaning policies may fail to save some species; see Highlight 15.3.) Clearly, the microeconomic theory devoted to such questions will remain as a foundation in identifying problems in many of these areas.

Highlight 15.3   *Will an Ivory Ban Save the African Elephant?*

The fascinating and (inexplicably) lovable African elephant is a favorite of children and zoo-goers everywhere. Unfortunately, an externality in the form of a common pool problem has created a growing fear of extinction of the species. Consider some recent statistics. Data suggest a continentwide decrease in the number of elephants by 30 percent in only 8 years (from 1.2 million in 1981 to 760,000 in 1988). The decline of specific populations in parts of Africa is shocking. Consider estimates of the decimation in the following countries.[a]

Country	1979	1989
Central African Republic	63,000	19,000
Kenya	65,000	19,000
Mozambique	54,800	18,600
Sudan	134,000	40,000
Tanzania	316,300	80,000
Zaire	377,700	85,000
Zambia	150,000	41,000

6. Some of the problems and pitfalls of such productions are discussed in Joe Earle, "Banking on Millions of Clams," *The Atlanta Journal and Constitution* (November 29, 1992), pp. R1, R9 from which these data are taken.

[a] Phillip Shabecoff, "Seeing Disaster, Groups Ask Ban on Ivory Import," *The New York Times* (June 2, 1989), p. 19.

It is not clear, given economic incentives, that a total ban on
ivory sales will best preserve the African elephant.

Part of the problem is undoubtedly that the biological characteristics of
elephants (such as a long gestation period) lead to slow population replacement. The essential problem, however, is an externality created by the common pool — that which belongs to no one will soon be gone. The elephant
produces hide, meat, and, most importantly, valuable ivory from its tusks.
Ivory poaching has become a way of life and a means to prosperity for many
Africans. Good intentions and help from outside agencies have not been
enough in most countries to protect the elephant on its way to extinction. An
ivory ban, honored by most nations, has been implemented by world conservation organizations, again with every good intention. But an ivory ban may not
do the trick when economic incentives are considered.

An ivory ban, if it is not totally enforced and honored around the world,
may in fact hasten the demise of the elephant, at least according to some

economists.[b] Although the ban may temporarily alleviate pressures on elephant populations, it will also (if not very effective) drive the price of ivory up, encouraging more intense poaching and improved poaching technology. The total ban on ivory sales, although laudable in intent, does nothing to eliminate the poacher. Goodwill and enforcement monies, especially in poor Central and East African countries, may be at a premium insofar as the security of the elephant is concerned.

Innovative solutions followed in some Southern African nations, such as Zimbabwe and Botswana, include economic factors and take incentives into account. These countries have calculated the biologically optimal number of elephants in specific habitats, used property-rights assignments, and permitted the limited and scientific harvesting of elephant ivory to finance wildlife conservation programs. Hunting rights are given to farmers who harvest elephants themselves or sell the rights to others. (Elephants themselves create negative externalities by competing with farmers for land and crops in some regions.) Incentives to create picture safaris are also being implemented. It is too soon to tell what long-run effects these incentive-driven policies might have, but the data are promising. Populations *grew* from 1981 to 1989 by 38,000 elephants in Botswana and by 2,000 in Zimbabwe.[c] In practically every other African country, populations declined. Saving the elephant from a common-pool disaster may require a variety of solutions. Economic incentives, along with biological considerations, are surely part of any rational approach.

The Problem of Public Goods

A specialized branch of microeconomic theory has also built up around the related problem of the demand and supply of **public goods**. Adam Smith believed that government should supply only those goods that were widely regarded as necessary but that would not be supplied by the private sector (or would be supplied in nonoptimal quantities). But (a) *why* would such goods not be supplied in private markets and (b) how do we determine which goods are widely regarded as "necessary"?

Public-Good Characteristics

The modern theory of public goods attempts to more accurately identify answers to both these questions. A number of goods, as we have seen, are associated with some kind of externality. Although all citizens in a particular

---

[b] See Michelle McKeever, "The Economics of Conservation: African Elephants and the Ivory Trade" (Auburn University thesis, 1991).

[c] Data from "Saving the Elephant," *Economist* (July 1, 1989), p. 16.

urban locale might agree that street lighting is desirable for safety or security reasons, a purely private market might not guarantee that such lighting will be provided or provided in some optimal amount. Clearly, some citizens would refuse to contribute toward a private "lighting fund." They would attempt to free-ride on neighbors, expecting them to provide the lighting services. This free-rider effect — a kind of externality — would mean that the private market is unable to provide the good in quantities that *in the absence of the free rider* would be desired by demanders.

Public goods are often characterized by this free-rider effect, but an even more fundamental characteristic is associated with consumption conditions of public goods. In this regard, a public good might be distinguished from a private good in that, for the latter, consumers compete for additional units of the good or service. If I go to the supermarket and purchase more oranges on some given day at some given time, there are *fewer* oranges for all other buyers. If you buy more Toyotas or more office visits at the doctor, less is available for me and other consumers. These are examples of **competing consumption**. A moment's reflection tells us that, for public goods, the opposite is true. An additional nuclear submarine or missile adds to my consumption of defense, but it *adds to your consumption as well.* Across a number of consumers, the addition of a streetlight would provide **complementary** (or noncompeting) **consumption** of lighting services.

The simultaneity of consumption associated with public goods does not apply to private-goods provision. Here, the definition of appropriate "units" of the good is important. A "unit" is that minimum quantity of the good necessary to provide more than one consumer with a simultaneous bundle of services. Further, that unit distinguishes the good in question from all other goods. Clearly, two dozen computers could satisfy 24 users with a bundle of "services." These services — calculation, expression, word processing, and so on — could be consumed simultaneously by 24 individuals in the case cited. But the appropriate unit is the individual. At one time one computer is capable of providing these services to only one user. A unit of computers is therefore a purely private good. Alternatively, a "Star Wars" defense unit is a public good, because it provides "safety from surprise attack" to more than one individual at one time.

These differences may be expressed symbolically. If the total consumption of a good such as umbrellas is Q_T (and umbrellas are a private good), the total consumption may be expressed as

$$Q_T = q_1 + q_2 + \cdots q_N$$

where the lower-case q's represent each individual's consumption. Clearly, in this instance, the more umbrellas one individual consumes, the fewer will be available for others. In the public-good case — say, expenditures on national defense — total consumption of the good Q_T is expressed as

$$Q_T = q_1 = q_2 = \cdots q_N$$

where any production level of the good is consumed equally and simultaneously by all consumers.

The characteristic of simultaneous consumption is essential to the definition of a public good. Other characteristics are often related to but are not unique to public goods. It is often said that another characteristic is the practical inability to exclude nonpaying demanders from using the good in question. The ability to exclude, however, is an illusive matter. Even in national defense, exclusion for nonpayers may be possible. You, as a nonpayer, may be shipped off to some desert island far away from the United States. Further, and more practically, it may always be possible to exclude nonpayers from such "public" items as police and fire protection. Before the advent of public fire-protection services at the local level, insurance companies placed medallions on the houses of payers and actually provided such services. The presence of the medallion was necessary for actual protection, because nonpayers of fire insurance were excluded.[7] The point is that some exclusion may be possible even in the case of goods that are widely regarded as public. Exclusion will take place until the marginal benefits of practicing it are outweighed by the marginal costs.

Yet another characteristic related to simultaneous or "communal" consumption is the zero-marginal-cost criterion. If a good is public in the sense that consumers do not compete among themselves for additional units of the good, the marginal cost of supplying the good to one extra demander is zero. Thus the marginal cost necessary to extend defense protection in the form of a nuclear sub to another consumer is effectively zero. But this characteristic is not unique to public goods, because some goods in the private sector approximate these cost conditions. A bus or subway ride may be such a good. Once the decision to run the bus or subway for some particular journey has been made, the marginal cost of including an additional passenger (up to some point, of course) is effectively zero. Thus, although exclusion and zero or low marginal cost of additional users are related to communal consumption, they are not unique to public goods.

A Model of Public Goods

The principal model used to analyze public goods — one developed by economists Howard Bowen in 1943 and Paul Samuelson in 1954 — has clear analogies to a particular case in the microeconomics of *private* goods.[8] Ever since classical writer John Stuart Mill's *Principles of Political Economy* in 1848,

7. See Fred S. McChesney, "Government Prohibitions on Volunteer Fire Fighting in Nineteenth-Century America: A Property Rights Perspective," *Journal of Legal Studies* (January 1986), pp. 69–92.

8. The Bowen-Samuelson solution was developed by Howard R. Bowen in "The Interpretation of Voting in the Allocation of Resources," *Quarterly Journal of Economics* (November 1943), pp. 27–48 and by Nobel laureate Paul A. Samuelson, "The Pure Theory of Public Expenditures," *Review of Economics and Statistics* (November 1954), pp. 387–389.

economists have analyzed goods that are jointly supplied, as noted in Chapter 2. The careful reader of the **joint-supply** discussion in that chapter will immediately recognize the similarities between the market for steers (or cattle) and the market for public goods. If cattle or steers are produced, not only is edible beef made available but hides come to the market as well. When cotton is produced, both cotton fiber and cotton seed (for making cottonseed oil) result. The reader may think of many private goods that are supplied in this manner.

The key to the analogy between these purely private goods and public goods is in the manner in which demand curves are added. First consider the private-good case in Figure 15.4. The figure shows a private good with characteristics of joint supply — steers that produce hides and beef. A bit of reflection tells us that the production of beef and hides is of a *noncompeting* character. If person A demands additional hides (beef) in some given market, there are *fewer* hides (beef) left for all other demanders. Such consumption is competitive by nature. However, if demand in the whole market for hides rises, the total demand for steers increases, as shown in panels (b) and (c) of Figure 15.4. Does this *decrease* the quantity of edible beef produced? The answer is that the quantity of edible beef produced *increases* with an increase in the demand and supply of hides.

All of this is shown in Figure 15.4, where the demand curves for hides and beef are presented in panels (c) and (f). Note that these demand curves are derived in the ordinary fashion — they are the product of a horizontal summation of the individual demanders of hides and beef. The aggregate demand curve for hides is found by adding the quantities demanded by all demanders. Here the total market is represented by only two individual demands, in panels (a) and (b) for hides and in (d) and (e) for beef. If hides and beef are produced in fixed proportions (that is, Quantity Produced of Hides/Steers = Quantity Produced of Beef/Steers = 1), a *vertical* addition of the "aggregate" demands for hides D_H and beef D_B produces a demand for steers D_S in panel (g) of Figure 15.4. This joint demand for steers is the combined product of the demand for both components of the good.[9]

In order to fully understand the aspect of this market that is important in the public-goods case, consider an increase in demand for one of the goods, such as hides. If, as shown in panel (b), the demand for hides increases (from d_{H1} to d'_{H1}), the total demand for hides increases. When this happens, a new and higher demand for steers results. The vertical summation of D'_H and the unchanged beef-demand curve D_B now produces a higher demand for steers, D_S' in panel (g). Given the simplifying assumption of constant average cost shown in that panel ($AC = S$), more steers are put into production over the long run because supernormal profits, in the amount FG in panel (g), open up in the steer market. The central point is that *more, not less, beef is produced* with

9. The production of multiple goods (or bads) from a single process is not confined to two products. Many by-products may be obtained, including air or water pollution.

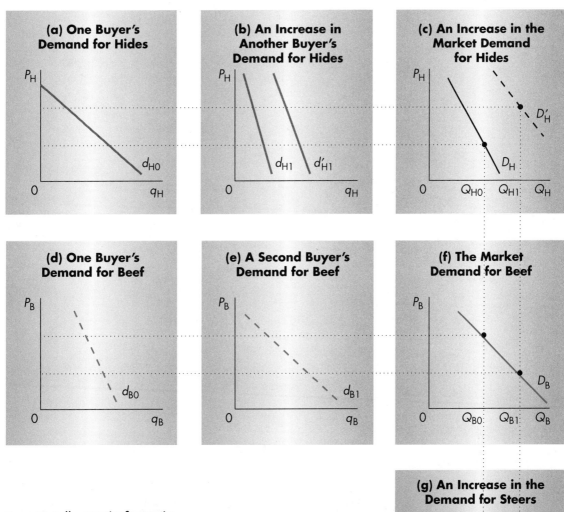

Figure 15.4 Noncompeting Consumption

The market demand for beef and the market demand for hides are obtained by horizontally summing individual demands. The horizontal summation across panels (a) and (b) produce the demand for hides in panel (c). Similarly, the demand for beef in panel (f) is found by summing across panels (d) and (e). The demand for steers, however, is obtained by adding the market demands for beef and hides vertically (panels (c) and (f) are added to obtain the demand for steers in panel (g)). Beef and hides do not compete with each other in consumption, so as more steers are produced, an increase in the demand for one lowers the price of the other.

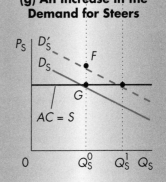

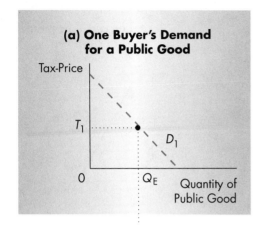

(a) One Buyer's Demand for a Public Good

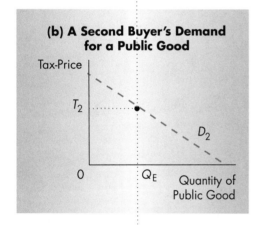

(b) A Second Buyer's Demand for a Public Good

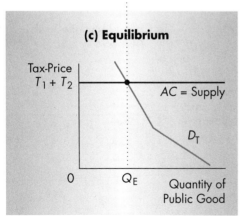

(c) Equilibrium

Figure 15.5 Public-Good Supply and Demand

As in all cases of noncompeting consumption, the demand for the public good D_T (panel c) is obtained by the vertical addition of D_1 (panel a) and D_2 (panel b). For efficiency, Q_E is produced, and demanders are charged tax prices of t_1 and t_2.

the increase in the demand for hides. The lucky consumers of beef experience a price decrease shown along the demand curve for beef, and the demanders of hides must pay a higher price.[10]

In most respects, the public-good case is directly analogous to the characteristics of the steer market. In Figure 15.5 a purely public-good equilibrium is shown for, say, national defense. Instead of two distinct products, however, the demand or marginal preference curve of each individual for national defense is for the *same* good. (Note that national defense could be represented by some specific good — "Star Wars," Patriot Missiles, and so on — with no loss of generality.) It is not necessary, and it is probably not the case, that the marginal valuation of an additional unit of national defense is the same for every individual. Indeed, in the post–USSR/Cold War world, there are probably stark differences in the valuations of national defense in the United States.

The technicalities of the public goods model are simple. As shown in Figure 15.5, national defense (street lighting, fire or police services) demands are added vertically to produce a total demand D_T in panel (c). In this case of noncompeting consumption, the addition of one more missile or one more tank would provide additional national defense to *all* demanders (who would, in general, value that additional amount at different rates). This important feature of public-goods markets is shared with the private-goods case: additional steers means both more hides and more beef. Further, just as optimality in the private-goods case requires the production of a single quantity of steers and multiple prices for the jointly supplied goods hides and beef, the same applies in the public-goods case. Only *one* quantity of national defense is provided to all citizen-demanders, and strict optimality demands that differential tax rates be charged for the services (t_1 and t_2, respectively). Any attempt to recoup costs with some single average tax rate will create nonoptimality in the form of two separate quantities demanded for national defense (see the later discussion of such a possibility).

Politics and Public Goods

The theoretical assumptions of the **Bowen-Samuelson public-goods model**, while readily understandable, do not easily translate into actual practice. Rational provision of public goods requires (a) that they be identified as such (with characteristics such as we discussed above) and, (b) that they be provided on the basis of sound cost-benefit principles. Some degree of "publicness" (given the various characteristics) is necessary or the good, if desired by consumers in sufficient quantities, would be provided in and by the private sector. Even if the good is "public," however, some measure of costs and benefits is necessary before any optimal quantity of the good is produced.

---

10. These price changes are the result of our constant-cost assumptions. Under conditions of increasing cost, other outcomes are possible.

Cost calculation — although often difficult in practice — is relatively as easy as such computations in the private sector. The problem, of course, is the revelation of public-good demands. In private markets, buyers directly reveal their demands with the proverbial dollar votes. If "votes" are insufficient to cover costs, the good or service disappears. In the market for public goods, however, discovery of demands is rendered extremely difficult if not impossible. One problem, of course, is the so-called free-rider effect. If individuals believe that they will pay taxes approximating their demand price, they have every incentive to *under*-reveal demands for any public good (defense, street lighting, and so on). Citizen surveys are of little help. Voting processes at federal, state, and local levels are thought to be of most promise in establishing demand revelation for public goods, but voting, too, carries much critical baggage.[11] If *each* issue could be voted on separately, the process might accurately reveal preferences. The simple fact, however, is that people elect representatives who are called on to express preferences on many different issues in a representative democracy and in an environment of incomplete information. A referendum process (or through elected representatives when they are focused on a particular issue) may more closely represent demander choice on marginal increases of a public good. Economists interested in public goods and public choice have developed a "median-voter model" in order to deal with the question.

The Median-Voter Model. The standard **median-voter model**, discussed at length in Chapter 14, is easily applied and is related to public-goods provision. Voter preferences for the provision of some public good will not be exactly equal (see Figure 15.5, for example). If, however, voter preferences follow a normal distribution, the median voter, clustered in the middle of the distribution, will always carry any referendum. Consider Figure 15.6, which presents a simplified median-voter model with demands for some public good set against price.

Some quantity Q_0 of the public good will be evaluated differently according to the normal distribution. Median-voter demand, designated TD/n or the pro rata share of the total demand accounted for by the median voter, will evaluate that quantity as Q_0 at point A. Demanders who exhibit a lower evaluation of the good — say, those represented by D_1 — have a lower evaluation of quantity Q_0. Some will have higher evaluations than the median voter. The important point is that at A, the evaluation of the median voter is higher than at C, which is the pro rata tax share to all taxpayers receiving the good. That pro rata cost is AC/n, which equals, for simplicity, MC/n in Figure 15.6.

The median-voter model indicates that in any majoritarian voting process (such as a town-hall meeting), proposals to provide some quantity above Q_0

11. Importantly, voting does not and cannot accurately represent utility or welfare. Consider a simple referendum on "liquor by the drink" in a local community and suppose it passes 51–49 percent. Those composing the majority may hold only mild preferences *for* the referendum, whereas those in opposition may harbor intense feelings about the matter. In utility terms the measure would be defeated.

Figure 15.6 Public Goods and the Median Voter

Preferences for a public good will not be the same for all voters. However, if preferences are normally distributed, the median voters will always carry a referendum to determine the quantity provided of the good (Q_E in the figure).

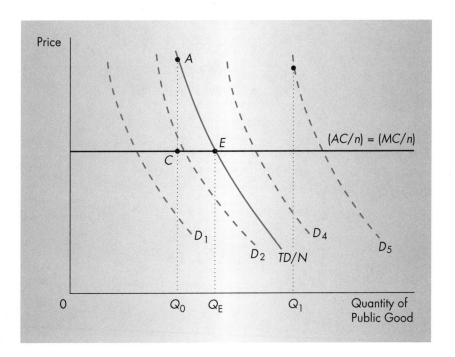

will always pass, whereas those that propose to supply a quantity of the good above Q_E, such as Q_1, will fail to carry. The quantity of the good preferred by the median voter (Q_E) will always carry over any other proposal. This means that — to the extent that voters directly express preferences on *particular* public goods or on *discrete additions* to the stock of public goods — voting may well proxy marginal valuations. But voting, as we noted at the outset of our discussion, rarely involves only one issue. In a U.S.-style democracy, such techniques are as yet impractical, and "representative voting" or the "sequence" of issues taken up will create a very imperfect filter of consumer-voter preferences for goods and services. Nevertheless, voting has widespread positive appeal as an approximation of preferences.

Tax Shares and Public-Goods Provision. The microeconomics of public-goods provision reaches certain limits in the political process. A contrast always exists between strict microeconomic "efficiency" criteria and the allocation of tax shares and the means of paying for public goods. A simple example may clarify some of the problems that all such provisions entail.

Consider a relatively small, closed community that is considering providing fire protection publicly. Note that although there are aspects of "publicness"

Figure 15.7 The Demand and Supply of Fire Protection

The total demand for fire protection, D_T, is the sum of both poor and wealthy voters. Efficient provision takes place when each separate group of voters is charged a tax equal to their marginal valuation of fire protection.

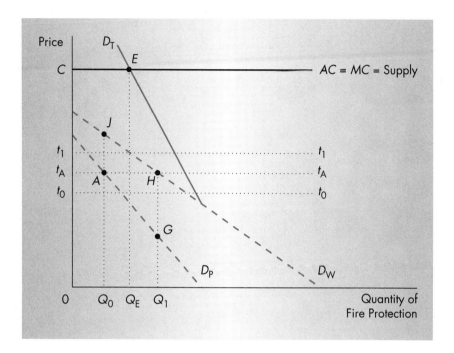

concerning the provision of fire protection services, these services are not pure public goods (approximated by, say, national defense).[12] Nevertheless, we portray them as such.

In Figure 15.7, demanders of fire-protection services are dichotomized into two groups: wealthy and poorer, designated D_W and D_p, respectively. Although demands for fire protection may differ for reasons other than differences in wealth, the distinction is useful. Note that the effective demand price for fire protection along D_W is everywhere above the demand curve D_p in Figure 15.7. The public nature of fire protection — the addition of one new fire engine is assumed to add to *everyone's* fire protection — should also be noted. In this case, as in the pure case described in Figure 15.5, the demand curves must be added vertically. Thus, D_T is the vertical sum of D_W and D_p.

Bowen-Samuelson public-goods equilibrium requires that the same quantity of fire-protection services be provided to *both* groups simultaneously. That

---

12. Further, assume that fire-protection services are homogeneous, although we all know that this is not ordinarily the case. Those next door to the fire station get "higher-quality" service.

criterion is reached where everyone receives the same (pro rata) protection at level Q_E.[13] At this point the *total* demand for fire-protection services equals the supply price of such services (again, assuming constant $AC = MC$). In full Bowen-Samuelson equilibrium, moreover, differential tax prices (t_1 and t_0) for wealthy and poor must be charged. This is so because these tax prices exactly represent the marginal valuation of each group of demanders.

Consider the problems with economic and practical efficiency when the Bowen-Samuelson scheme is *not* followed. Although the total cost of producing fire services ($0CEQ_E$) may be covered by charging some common *average* tax price to all fire-service demanders ($0t_aAQ_0 + 0t_aHQ_1$, for example), the result, in terms of economic efficiency, would be chaos. Which quantity of protection would be produced if average tax price t_A (in Figure 15.7) was charged to all demanders? The less wealthy demanders would want quantity Q_0, but the wealthy would try to hold out for quantity Q_1. The issue then becomes, Who is victorious at the ballot box? Clearly, the wealthy would like to impose a quantity of Q_1 fire services on all citizens, but at that larger quantity the marginal valuation of poorer demanders would only be Q_1G in Figure 15.7. If the poor win the election or referendum and Q_0 is provided, a nonoptimal provision would be made to the wealthy, because their marginal valuation Q_0J would exceed the tax price t_A. In *either* case, tax receipts are not guaranteed to cover the costs of service. Although other solutions are possible when communities are not, as we have assumed, "closed," virtually all public-goods provision that does not select a single quantity that is sold on a differential basis of marginal valuations is doomed to some inefficiency.[14]

The idea that voting — even under ideal circumstances — produces optimal or efficient public-goods supplies implies that the political process is unaffected by special interests. (See, for example, the discussion of public choice in Chapter 14.) In reality, politicians are, in some part, self-interested. At local, state, and federal levels, goods and services are often provided in response to special interests rather than to the majoritarian interests of voters. In any real-world analysis, the purely theoretical world of public-goods economics must be tempered with an understanding of the realities of politics and political influences.

13. Once again we leave aside some thorny questions concerning the content of Q_E. Obviously, Q represents a whole basket of inputs to fire protection — engines, fire houses, location, water-main distribution, and so on.

14. An extremely interesting variant of the model described in Figure 15.7 is obtained when movement from community to community is allowed. The imposition of an average tax rate (such as t_A in Figure 15.7) may result in specific forms of urban mobility. Those in wealthier groups will move to communities supplying Q_1 of fire protection, whereas poorer citizens will seek out cities offering Q_0. There are many reasons for particular movements, but "voting with one's feet" for public goods is one of them. See the seminal paper by Charles M. Tiebout, "A Pure Theory of Local Expenditures," *Journal of Political Economy* (October 1956), pp. 416–424.

Market Failure and Public Policy: Postscript

Microeconomic theory, as this book has strongly maintained, is a powerful tool in analyzing and understanding markets. As suggested in the present chapter, however, economic theory best explains the functioning of *private* markets. Without question, Adam Smith's belief that individual self-interest leads to maximized social welfare and efficiency is a characteristic of freely competitive arrangements. Numerous chapters of this book have emphasized that much of the economy is typified by competitive markets in the broadened sense of "rivalry."

The present chapter is an exception. Any scientific defense of market interferences by government must be premised on market failures of some kind. Monopoly, to the extent that it exists and *persists*, *may* constitute an example. But the presence of externalities — particularly negative externalities such as pollution, environmental hazards, species endangerment, and so on — highlights a potential role for government in market functioning. The theoretical possibilities outlined for public goods — those where free-rider problems are overwhelming — constitute yet another area for government.

For their part, however, many economists tend to be suspicious of interventions based on nonmarket hypotheses. Although poor judgment in private markets is met with (often rapid) failure, there is virtually no reliable way to gauge the extent of the demand for public goods or the benefits or costs attached to externalities. Demands are not revealed in these markets, although political demands for redistributions are. Even if there were a satisfactory process for collecting demand information, the "under-revelation" problem would come into play. Even more perplexing, perhaps, is the simple identification of an externality or a *public* good. Scientists have debated, and will continue to debate, the existence and extent of global warming or damage from second-hand smoke. (Even if we know that some externality exists, the actual *extent* of the problem must be known before rational and efficient action may be taken.)

For these good reasons, economists most often take an eclectic and skeptical attitude toward public policies that claim to redress externalities or to provide public goods. Market failure, in the first place, means that unfettered markets lead to nonoptimal provision of some desirable goods and services. In this sense, markets are not perfect. Experience with direct government interventions, likewise, does not always lead one to believe that discretionary controls or rules will provide any more efficiency in these "failed" markets than a laissez-faire approach would have. This is especially so when politics enters the picture.

The role of the economist is to assess markets on an individual basis and to try to develop rational criteria on which to base policy decisions. One major purpose of this chapter has been to outline some of the theoretical criteria that the economist typically uses in developing judgments about the economic efficiency and welfare produced in markets. The menu of possible policy advice is diverse: from total noninterference, to regulation, to a reorientation of property-rights assignments as practiced by Coase, to franchising and "privatization." Each and every logical (and empirical) tool at the economist's disposal must be used in order to understand and analyze any specific market, and, even more, to suggest policy changes to promote economic efficiency.

Summary

Adam Smith's belief that the behavior of self-interested market participants also promotes the public welfare is challenged when markets fail. This chapter examined the various ways in which markets might fail to establish a maximum of welfare to consumers and to society at large. Our discussion included

- an evaluation of positive and negative externalities or "third-party effects" that might occur in markets.
- the identification of public goods and an evaluation of how they might be financed.
- an analysis of the impact of taxes and subsidies in markets in which positive and negative externalities may exist.
- the extent to which externalities might be "internalized" by property-rights assignments.

Key Terms

market failure   common-pool problems
externality   positive externality
negative externality   relevant externality
Coase theorem   marginal private costs
Pigouvian solution   public good
competing consumption   complementary consumption
joint supply   Bowen-Samuelson public-goods
median-voter model   model

Sample Questions

Question

Suppose that you are an urban planner in charge of controlling congestion on *existing* major expressways through your city. Further suppose that you have determined that one particular stretch of roadway is most heavily congested between 7 A.M. and 6 P.M. but far less so during other hours. How might you use economic tools to analyze the problem and to propose solutions (at least theoretically)?

Answer

The economist has a variety of tools with which to analyze the situation described. The Pigouvian tax-subsidy argument outlined in this chapter helps explain the source of the problem. In particular, the marginal social cost of driving on this stretch of highway exceeds the marginal private cost, because each driver tends to ignore the "externality" or disutility created by being on the road. The Pigouvian solution is a congestion tax sufficient to bring the number of cars using the road to a point at which crowding is eliminated. The optimal congestion toll would be higher between 7 A.M. and 6 P.M. than for the other period. A graph similar to Figure 15.3a may be used to analyze the situation. Another possible solution would be to privatize the road, allowing the highway to be priced under competitive conditions. In this case, the model of "competing" versus "complementary" consumption would be relevant. Each solution would have to account for enforcement and metering costs.

Question

Is there an economically effective manner of taxation for financing particular public goods — such as the now-defunct supercollider or a new type of military airplane? How would the economist analyze the provision of such goods? What are some of the problems involved in the "economic solution"?

Answer

Theoretically at least, there is an economic approach for analyzing the provision of a particular public good (once it is decided that the good really is "public" — that is, characterized by noncompeting consumption). That approach would involve the vertical summation of all of the demands for the public good (the supercollider, for example) and allocating "tax prices" to each individual demander or to each group of demanders (see Figure 15.5). These individuals or groups would then pay their demand price for the optimal quantity of the good in the form of a tax. The optimal price and quantity of the public good would then be assured. Unfortunately, the very act of determining the individual or group's demand curve for the public good is fraught with difficulties. Individuals (or groups) will have every incentive to under-reveal demands if they know that their taxes will be determined by their revelation. In other words, no foolproof method exists for allocating the tax prices.

Questions for Review and Discussion

1. Why are private parks typically better maintained than public parks?
*2. What type of externality exists for residents of a dark street when a neighbor installs a streetlight? Explain.
3. How is it determined whether a negative externality will be corrected?
*4. When trying to solve an externality problem to achieve the socially optimal solution, why is the issue of who owns the property rights unimportant to society as long as they are assigned to one of the parties?
5. What is meant by internalizing an externality?
*6. How does a Pigouvian solution differ from a Coasian solution to solving externality problems?

7. Why do some economists maintain that an ivory ban will exacerbate the extinction of the African elephant?

8. Suppose that Mark and Bob are both Atlanta Braves fans. If they both desire to purchase season tickets, what is the nature of their consumption?

*9. What are the two essential characteristics of a public good?

10. When two goods are the products of a joint supply model, what happens to the price of one good when the demand for the other increases?

11. In a Bowen-Samuelson equilibrium, how are tax prices assessed and why?

12. Why would it be inefficient to charge an average tax price in a Bowen-Samuelson case? Use a graph to illustrate your answer.

*13. In deciding to provide a public good, the government often attempts to determine the demand for the good. Why do some demanders have an incentive to understate their demand for the good?

14. Why are economists often skeptical of government policies enacted to control externalities?

*15. Hotels often have a weekday and weekend clientele. Are these demands for hotel rooms competing or complementary?

Problems for Analysis

1. The Kemps Ridley sea turtle, found in the Gulf of Mexico, is an endangered animal. It has been decimated by extensive fishing in the Gulf. Why is the turtle on the endangered list? What might be done to save the turtle? How many turtles do you think should be saved? Explain.

*2. It is sometimes argued that private (for-profit) parks and recreational areas are characterized by less pollution and congestion than are public parks and recreational facilities. Does the assignment of property rights have anything to do with this assessment? If you agree with the assessment, why aren't state and national parks privatized? Do good reasons exist for public provision? What are they?

*3. "Instead of regulating airline safety, the government should make airlines completely liable for preventable accidents!" Comment.

4. The Japanese have developed innovative provisions of recreational facilities. In response to outdoor crowding on beaches, the probability of bad weather, sickness from polluted seas, dangers of skin cancer from ultraviolet radiation, and other "outdoor" maladies, the ingenious Japanese entrepreneurs have developed and constructed three enormous indoor resort complexes with manmade beaches and snow-capped peaks. "Oceans" have been constructed with retractable roofs for surfing in good weather. Wave machines create waves to satisfy the professional surfer. For lovers of winter sports, a skidome has been constructed with a drop of 80 meters. New and varied kinds of indoor recreation facilities are being planned. Are these examples of internalized externalities? Why or why not?

Exchange and Gains from International Trade

The principles of demand and supply were established in the first four chapters of this book. Mutually beneficial trade between individuals was highlighted in Chapter 4. But anyone who has followed the news in recent years is aware of the growing importance of trade on a larger scale — for example, between the United States and other countries. In contrast to countries like Italy, the Netherlands, the United Kingdom, and Switzerland that have long histories of extensive trading arrangements, the United States has only recently become heavily dependent on international trade. Because of the sheer size of its economy, the United States has been an important player in world markets, at least since World War II. However, until fairly recently, the international sector (imports and exports) made up a small proportion of our economic activity — just thirty years ago, less than 4 percent of the goods we purchased were imported. Since then, things have changed. Now, about 10 percent of all the goods we purchase are imported, and nearly all of our goods contain some imported components. As a consequence, we have quickly been made aware of the importance of the international sector.

Most of us are unclear about the effects of international trade — in part because it is all relatively new to us. A consequence is that we are unsure how to assess statements concerning international events. Headlines that say, "North American Free Trade Agreement to Cost 400,000 Jobs," "Strong Dollar Harming U.S. Economy," or "U.S. Must Shape Up to Compete in World Market" both alarm and confuse us. The purpose of this chapter is to help end this confusion about international trade. Specifically, we will

- develop two basic models of international trade.
- provide an explanation of the pattern of trade that is observed in the world and show the effect of trade on jobs, wages, and living standards in both the importing and exporting country.
- examine the economic impact of policies like tariffs and quotas that limit international trade.

- develop a model of the foreign-exchange market in order to gain an understanding of trade imbalances (trade deficits or surpluses) and to see how
  changes in the exchange rate affect various economic interests, including
  those of all ordinary citizens.

The Effect of Imports and Exports on Domestic Market Equilibrium

The mere fact that international trade is a subject of controversy suggests
either that it affects different groups differently or that different groups perceive its effects differently. In considering changes in a nation's trade policies
with other nations, people in that country ask certain questions: How will the
new policy affect my job security? Will it increase or decrease my chances of
getting pay raises in the future? Will the new policy lead to an increase or a
decrease in the number of jobs in this country? What effect will it have on the
number of "good" jobs? What affect will it have on the prices I pay for goods
and services? Will it improve the quality of the products I buy? What will
happen to overall living standards in this country if the policy is enacted?

To answer these questions, it is useful to consider the impact of the proposed change in policy on the market equilibrium. For example, consider a
country that previously has been totally isolated from world markets — it is
neither an importer nor an exporter. Then, suppose that this "home" country
opens its economy and allows foreign goods to be imported and domestic
goods to be exported. To see the economic consequences of this policy
change, consider the home market for some good (say, cars) in Figure 16.1. In
that figure, D_{home} is the home demand for cars. It shows the number of cars
that domestic buyers are willing to purchase at each price. Similarly, S_{home}
shows the supply of cars by all home producers as a group. In the absence of
car imports or exports, the market will clear at P_0 ($20,000) with 8 million
cars produced and sold each year.

Now, suppose that the home economy is opened to foreign trade and that,
as a consequence, foreign sellers ship their cars to the home country. This will
cause the supply of cars that is available to home buyers to increase from S_{home}
to S_{total}, where S_{total} is the horizontal sum of S_{home} and S_{for} (the foreign supply).
As a consequence of the imports, the equilibrium price of cars will fall to P_1
($18,000) and the equilibrium quantity will rise to 9 million cars. Of the 9
million cars bought and sold at that price, 6 million will be produced by home
producers (at a price of $18,000, 6 million is the quantity they are willing to
supply) and the remaining 3 million cars will be imported. The imports benefit
domestic consumers by enabling them to buy cars at a lower price. However,
allowing imports harms domestic producers, because they sell fewer cars at
lower prices. Workers in the auto and related industries will experience a loss
of jobs and lower wages.

Figure 16.1 The Effect of Imports on the Domestic Market for Cars

Without imported cars, the equilibrium price would be $20,000 and 8 million cars would be bought and sold. With imports, the price falls to $18,000, home buyers buy 9 million cars, 3 million of which are imported.

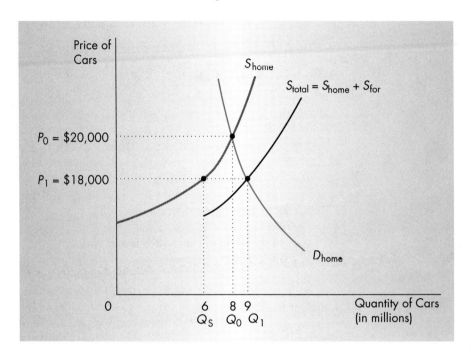

The effect of opening the home economy to foreign trade will be quite different in other industries that become export industries. Figure 16.2 depicts the effect of exports on the wheat industry. Before trade, the home market clears where D_{home} and S_{home} intersect, at a price of $6.00 per bushel and an equilibrium quantity of 640 million bushels. However, the export of wheat reduces the supply that is available to the home market to S' and causes the equilibrium price to rise to $8.00. At that price, home producers produce 680 million bushels and export 160 million bushels. The remaining 520 million bushels are sold to home buyers. Wheat exports harm home consumers (who pay a higher price for wheat) and benefit domestic producers, who sell more wheat at a higher price.

On the basis of straightforward demand and supply analysis, we can see why trade policy is controversial. Changes in policy that lead to changes in the volume of world trade harm some groups while benefiting others. However, our analysis fails to explain the **pattern of trade** that will develop under free-trade conditions — it doesn't explain which goods or which types of goods will be imported or which types will be exported. Therefore,

Figure 16.2 The Effect of Wheat Exports on the Domestic Wheat Market

If domestic producers are prohibited from exporting wheat, the equilibrium price will be $6 per bushel. Once they are allowed to export, the price will rise to $8. Domestic buyers will reduce their consumption to 520 million bushels, and domestic producers will sell their remaining 160 million bushels abroad.

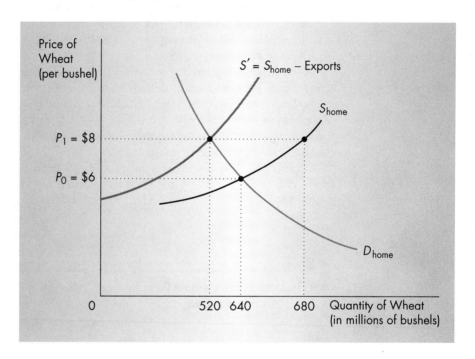

supply-and-demand analysis is inadequate to enable us to predict the impact of a change in trade policy on any particular group of buyers or sellers. For some evidence about the impact of foreign trade on employment in various industries, see Highlight 16.1. To understand the pattern of trade, we need to develop more sophisticated models of world trade.

Highlight 16.1 *Trade and Employment*

Arguments about trade policy inevitably become arguments about jobs. Opponents of trade argue simply that every time we buy something from abroad, we destroy the jobs that would have been created domestically had the product been built in the United States. By this standard, trade must destroy jobs. However, the issue is certainly more complex than this. When a country decides to participate in world markets, it must recognize that the resulting pattern of jobs will be quite different than in the absence of trade. Some industries will flourish, and others will not be able to survive against foreign competition. It is extremely difficult to predict what type of jobs and how many of them will be created in the process of international trade.

Table 16.1 presents estimates of the percentages of jobs created and destroyed in various industries by international trade during the 1970s.

Based on these estimates, we see that trade has had dramatic impacts on the number of jobs in different industries. It is no wonder that our trade policy is subject to such controversy.

Defenders of free trade often find themselves arguing that free trade will create more jobs than it will destroy. Although that may well be the case, one should not lose sight of the fact that the major advantage of free trade is that it destroys jobs — it enables us to obtain goods from abroad by working fewer hours than it would take us to do the same task at home. In this sense, trade is like a technological improvement.

Before we develop theoretical models to explain the pattern of world trade, it is useful to have some knowledge about the current pattern of trade. Table 16.2 lists the volume of U.S. imports and exports of certain important

Table 16.1 Percentage Change in Employment in U.S. Manufacturing Resulting from Foreign Trade

Industry	Percentage Change in Employment Because of Imports and Exports
Footwear	−15.9
Motor vehicles	−11.1
Electrical components	−7.8
Leather products	−6.3
Apparel	−6.3
Radio and television equipment	−5.7
Miscellaneous manufacturing	−5.0
Furniture and fixtures	−4.5
Service industry machines	5.7
Miscellaneous electrical machinery	6.6
Electrical and industrial equipment	7.1
Miscellaneous machinery	8.0
Aircraft and parts	12.8
Office, computing and accounting machines	16.1
Engines and turbines	17.8
Construction and mining machinery	19.9

Source: R. Z. Lawrence, "Can America Compete?" (Washington, D.C.: The Brookings Institution, 1984), pp. 58–59.

Table 16.2 U.S. Exports and Imports

	Exports			
	1985		1991	
Product	Value (in Billions)	Percentage of Total Exports	Value (in Billions)	Percentage of Total Exports
Agricultural products	19.2	9.0	21.1	5.3
Coal	4.5	2.1	4.6	1.2
Food	10.1	4.7	17.5	4.4
Tobacco	1.3	0.6	4.6	1.1
Textiles	1.5	0.7	4.1	1.0
Apparel	1.0	0.5	3.7	0.9
Lumber	2.7	1.3	6.5	1.6
Paper products	3.9	1.8	9.2	2.3
Chemicals	21.8	10.2	41.5	10.3
Petroleum & coal products	5.4	2.6	7.0	1.8
Rubber & plastic products	2.8	1.3	7.0	1.8
Stone, clay, & glass products	1.8	0.8	3.5	0.9
Primary metal products	4.7	2.2	15.2	3.8
Nonelectrical machinery	37.5	17.6	65.3	16.3
Electrical machinery	18.9	8.9	42.3	10.6
Transportation equipment	38.0	17.9	76.2	19.0

	Imports			
	1985		1991	
Product	Value (in Billions)	Percentage of Total Imports	Value (in Billions)	Percentage of Total Imports
Agricultural products	7.5	2.2	6.1	1.3
Fish & marine products	3.6	1.0	4.6	0.9
Petroleum & natural gas	35.9	10.4	42.4	8.8
Food	12.5	3.6	16.3	3.4
Textiles	3.6	1.1	7.1	1.5
Apparel	15.7	4.6	25.5	5.3
Lumber	5.1	1.5	5.2	1.1
Furniture	3.2	0.9	5.1	1.1
Paper products	7.5	2.2	10.4	2.2
Chemicals	12.8	3.7	23.0	4.8
Petroleum & coal products	18.3	5.3	11.1	2.3
Leather & leather products	7.7	2.2	10.7	2.3
Stone, clay, & glass products	4.3	1.3	5.6	1.2
Nonelectrical equipment	31.3	9.1	55.6	11.5
Electrical machinery	38.0	11.0	58.6	12.1
Transportation equipment	65.9	19.2	88.0	18.2

Source: U.S. Bureau of the Census, *Statistical Abstract of the United States,* 1992 (Washington, D.C.: U.S. Government Printing Office, 1992), p. 487.

categories of goods. In examining the entries in Table 16.2, it is important to realize that there are currently many restrictions on international trade that affect the volume of imports and exports. The pattern of trade that would emerge under a policy of perfectly free international trade may differ greatly from the existing one.

The Ricardian Trade Model and the Principle of Comparative Advantage

By far, the simplest model for explaining the pattern of trade is the **Ricardian Trade Model.**[1] It has been used extensively by economists since 1817. The Ricardian Model addresses the simplest possible case of world trade. It considers a world consisting of two countries, which produce either of two goods using a single input, labor. Further, it assumes a very simple, proportional relationship between the amount of labor used to produce either of the two goods and the amount of output that is produced.

For example, suppose that the two countries are home (H) and foreign (F), and that the two goods are wine (W) and linen (L). Further, assume that the home country has a labor force of 1,200 workers and the foreign country has a labor force of 2,400 workers. Also, assume that the **unit labor requirements** — the amount of labor necessary to produce one unit of output — are as reported in Table 16.3. In the home country, it takes 3 workers a day to produce 1 unit of wine and 2 workers a day to produce 1 unit of linen; in the foreign country 12 workers are required to produce 1 unit of wine and 3 workers are required to produce 1 unit of linen.

Table 16.3 Comparative Labor Requirements in Two Countries for Wine and Linen
Countries differ not only with regard to the size of their labor force but also in the number of workers that are required to produce a unit of different goods like wine and linen.

	Labor Force	Unit Labor Requirement for Wine	Unit Labor Requirement for Linen
Home	1,200	3	2
Foreign	2,400	12	3

1. This model was developed by the famed British economist David Ricardo. It was included in his *Principles of Political Economy and Taxation,* which was published in 1817.

With this information, we can graph the production-possibilities frontier — the line showing the maximum possible combinations of the two goods that can be produced — for each of the two countries. Panel (a) of Figure 16.3 shows the home country's production-possibilities frontier. With a labor force of 1,200, the largest quantity of linen that the home country can produce is 600 units, because that country's unit labor requirement for linen is 2 workers. If the country produces 600 units of linen, it is unable to produce any wine, because its entire labor force is employed in linen production. Point *A* in panel (a) of Figure 16.3 represents this combination of goods.

If, instead, the entire labor force were employed producing wine, wine output would equal 400 units. In order to produce 400 units of wine, linen production must be reduced to zero, as at point *B* in panel (a). In addition to points *A* and *B*, any other point on the straight line connecting *A* and *B* also represents another combination of the two goods that the home country can produce. For example, point *C* represents the production of 450 units of linen and 100 units of wine, which is possible because the 450 units of linen would employ 900 workers, and the 100 units of wine would require the employment of the remaining 300 workers.

The slope of the straight-line production-possibilities frontier connecting points *A* and *B* is −1.5. This has a very important economic interpretation: it shows the opportunity cost of an additional unit of the good on the

Figure 16.3 **Production-Possibilities Frontiers for the Home and Foreign Country**
The line connecting points *A* and *B* shows different combinations of wine and linen that the home country can produce. The line connecting *A'* and *B'* does the same for the foreign country. If the countries specialize and trade, they can attain points like *D* and *D'*, which are beyond their production-possibilities frontiers.

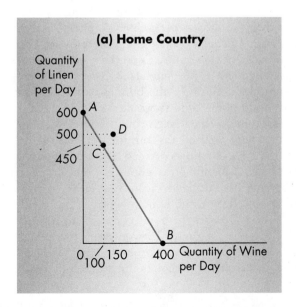

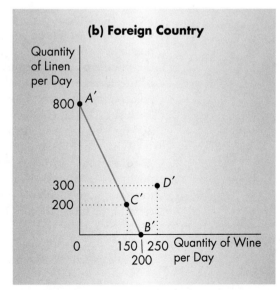

horizontal axis (wine, in this case) in terms of the good on the vertical axis. For the home country, each additional unit of wine costs 1.5 units of linen.

It is important to note that this example reflects constant costs — no matter how many units of wine are produced, the opportunity cost of an additional unit of wine is 1.5 units of linen. This also implies that the cost of producing additional units of linen is also constant. In order to expand linen production by 1 unit, 2 workers must be moved from the wine industry to the linen industry, and this will cause wine output to fall by $\frac{2}{3}$ of a unit. It is helpful to remember that the cost of linen in terms of wine is always the inverse of the cost of wine in terms of linen. The opportunity cost of the good on the vertical axis in terms of the good on the horizontal axis is the *inverse* of the slope of the production-possibilities frontier.

For the foreign country, the production-possibilities frontier is depicted in panel (b) of Figure 16.3. If the entire labor force of 2,400 workers is used to produce linen, 800 units of linen can be produced, because each unit requires 3 workers. Similarly, the maximum amount of wine that the foreign country can produce is 200 units, because each unit requires 12 workers. Any point on the straight line connecting points A' and B' in Figure 16.3 also represents other combinations of linen and wine that the foreign country can produce. The slope of this production-possibilities frontier is −4, which means that the opportunity cost of each additional unit of wine that is produced in the foreign country is 4 units of linen. Correspondingly, the opportunity cost of each unit of linen that is produced in the foreign country is $\frac{1}{4}$ of a unit of wine. Just as was the case for the home country, the cost of either wine or linen, in terms of the other good, is constant. That is, it does not vary with the level of wine or linen output.

In the absence of trade, each of the two countries would be able to consume only what it was able to produce for itself. Their consumption choices would be limited to points on their production-possibilities frontiers. Exactly which point would be selected would depend on tastes and preferences. One possibility would be for citizens of the home country to produce and consume the bundle of goods represented by point C in Figure 16.3a, and for citizens of the foreign country to produce and consume the bundle represented by point C' in panel (b). Citizens in the home country would have 450 units of linen and 100 units of wine to consume; in the foreign country there would be 200 units of linen and 150 units of wine available for consumption.

What would be the impact if the two countries decided to specialize in one good and trade with the other country for the other good? On the surface, it might appear that the home country has nothing to gain from trade with the foreign country. After all, in absolute terms, the home country is more efficient in the production of both goods. It takes the home country only 3 workers to produce 1 unit of wine, whereas it requires 12 workers in the foreign country. In the home country it takes 2 workers to produce 1 unit of linen, but it takes 3 in the foreign country. However, although the home country has an **absolute advantage** in the production of both goods (its unit labor requirement is lower than the foreign country's unit labor requirement for both wine and linen), mutually advantageous trade between the two countries is possible. To see this, it is necessary to understand the **principle of comparative advantage.** According to this principle, each of the two countries can benefit if it specializes in the good in which it has a comparative advantage and obtains the other good (in which it is said to have comparative disadvantage) from its trading partner. If a country has a comparative advantage in the production of a particular good, then its opportunity cost of producing that good is lower than the opportunity cost for the trading partner of producing the same good would be.

In this particular example, the opportunity cost of producing a unit of wine in the home country is 1.5 units of linen, and the opportunity cost in the foreign country is 4 units of linen. The home country has a lower opportunity cost in wine production, so we say that the home country has a comparative advantage in wine production.

If we focus attention on the production of linen, the opportunity cost at home is $\frac{2}{3}$ of a unit of wine; but in the foreign country the cost of 1 unit of linen is only $\frac{1}{4}$ of a unit of wine. Therefore, the foreign country has a comparative advantage in the production of linen, because its opportunity cost of producing linen is lower than that of the home country. According to the principle of comparative advantage, each country can benefit if the home country specializes in wine (the good in which it has a comparative advantage) and the foreign country specializes in the production of linen (the good in which it has the comparative advantage).

In terms of Figure 16.3, this suggests that, as an alternative to producing and consuming bundle *C*, the home country should specialize in wine by producing bundle *B*. Similarly, instead of producing bundle *C'*, the foreign country should specialize in linen by producing bundle *A'*. Then the foreign country should trade some of its linen for the home country's wine. In considering trade between the two countries, any number of exchanges are possible. However, certain exchanges run counter to the interest of the home country; others will run counter to the interests of the foreign country. In distinguishing trades that are beneficial from those that are not, it is useful to think of the **terms of trade.** Terms of trade means the number of units of the imported good that the home country receives for each unit of the exported good. In this case, we are asking how many units of linen the home country receives for each unit of wine it exports. It should be clear that the "better the terms of trade" (the larger the number of units of linen the home country receives for each unit of its exported wine), the more advantageous trade will be for the home country. The reverse is true for the foreign country. However, the terms of trade must fall within certain limits in order for trade to be mutually advantageous — the price of wine cannot be too low for the home country or too high for the foreign country.

The limits within which the terms of trade must fall in order for trade to be mutually advantageous are determined by the opportunity cost of producing wine in the two countries. Here, the limits are 1.5 units of wine (the cost of wine in the home country) and 4 units of linen (the cost of wine in the foreign country). To see why, consider terms of trade outside this range. For example, consider a trade of only 1 unit of linen for 1 unit of wine. Such an exchange would be counter to the home country's interest. It costs the home country 1.5 units of linen to produce each unit of wine. The home country would be crazy to sell the wine for less than its opportunity cost of 1.5 units of linen. Similarly, the foreign country can produce its own wine at a cost of 4 units of linen. It would be counter to its interest to pay more than 4 units of linen for 1 unit of wine.

The home country would like to strike a deal so that it receives the highest possible price for its wine (4 units of linen), and the foreign country would like to pay the lowest possible price for wine (1.5 units of linen). How much each country gains from trade depends on what the terms of trade turn out to be. For the sake of argument, let's suppose that the countries negotiate with each other and strike a deal in which the foreign country pays 2 units of linen for each unit of wine. Further, suppose that the foreign country agrees to buy 250 units of wine at that price. The home country then produces 400 units of wine, and trades 250 units of wine for 500 units of linen. The country can consume the remaining 150 units of domestically produced wine and the 500 units of imported linen. In Figure 16.3a, the home country is able to consume the bundle labeled *D*. Note that bundle *D* is beyond the home country's production-possibilities frontier. Getting to point *D* enables the home country to consume 50 more units of linen and 50 more units of wine than it was able to produce for itself at point *C*.

The same exchange that enables the home country to consume a bundle of goods beyond its production possibilities frontier enables the foreign country to do the same. In Figure 16.3b, instead of producing and consuming bundle *C'*, the foreign country now produces bundle *A'* and consumes *D'*. Bundle *D'* consists of the 300 units of linen that remain after trading 500 units to the home country, plus the 250 units of wine that the foreign country buys from the home country. Compared to bundle *C'*, the foreign country is richer by 100 units of linen and 100 units of wine. This particular exchange provides gains to the foreign country that are twice those of the home country. If more favorable terms of trade had been negotiated, the gains would have been larger to the home country and smaller to the foreign country. However, the important point is that at terms of trade that lie between the opportunity costs of the respective countries (between 1.5 units of linen per unit of wine and 4 units of linen per unit of wine), both countries can gain.

It may seem impossible that trade enables both countries to consume at some point beyond their respective production-possibilities frontiers. To see how it is possible, we must understand the gain in efficiency that trade provides. Prior to trade, wine was produced in each country. However, each of the 150 units of wine produced in the foreign country came at a cost of 4 units of linen. If wine production is reduced by 1 unit in the foreign country, enough additional labor is made available to produce 4 additional units of linen. If, at the same time, wine production is increased in the home country by 1 unit, the reduction in linen output is only 1.5 units. The switch of 1 unit of wine production from the foreign country to the home country enables total linen production to rise by 2.5 units — the difference between the cost of producing wine in the high-cost country (4 units of linen) and the low-cost country (1.5 units of linen). It is simply inefficient to produce wine abroad at a cost of 4 units of linen when it can be produced at home at a cost of only 1.5 units of linen. Similarly, it is inefficient to produce linen at home at a cost of $\frac{2}{3}$ of a unit of wine when that linen can be produced abroad at a cost of only $\frac{1}{4}$ of a unit of wine. Whenever comparative advantages exist, the failure of the two countries to specialize will result in an inefficient pattern of production, with their total combined output being lower than is possible.

This raises the question, When will a comparative advantage exist? We saw that in the numerical example of production summarized in Table 16.1, there were comparative advantages. In that example, the home country was 1.5 times as efficient in linen production (its unit labor requirement for linen was two-thirds that of the foreign country), whereas it was 4 times as efficient in the production of wine. In other words, its productive advantage differed in the two industries. So long as this is the case, a pattern of comparative advantage will exist. If the home country is 10 times as efficient in producing one good and 100 times as efficient in a second good, the home country will have a comparative advantage in the second good, whereas the foreign country has a comparative advantage in the first. A pattern of comparative advantage will always exist unless one country is a clone of the second country (the unit labor requirements are the same for both countries) or if one country is uniformly more or less efficient at the production of both goods than is the other.

The Terms of Trade in the Ricardian Model

In our previous example of comparative advantage, we discussed a case in which the terms of trade were determined through negotiation between the two countries, with a specific quantity of linen being traded for a specific quantity of wine. In fact, goods and services are seldom traded on world markets — they are bought and sold. Also, the prices at which the goods and services are bought and sold are determined through the interaction of demand and supply — not through negotiation between representatives of the two countries. What this means is that the terms of trade are market-determined.

To see how this process works, we need to consider the demand and supply of wine and linen in each of the two countries. In the home country the cost of each unit of wine is 1.5 units of linen. Therefore, so long as the price of

Figure 16.4 The Home and Foreign Wine Markets

The supply curve S_H shows the supply of wine in the home market. Assuming domestic demand D_H, the equilibrium relative price at home will be $P_W/P_l = 1.5$, and 240 units of wine will be produced and sold. The foreign equilibrium will be at $P_W/P_l = 4.0$, with 100 units of wine produced and sold.

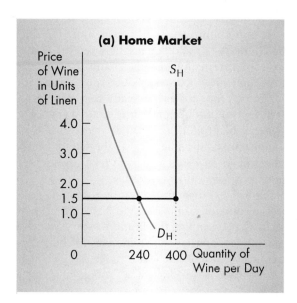

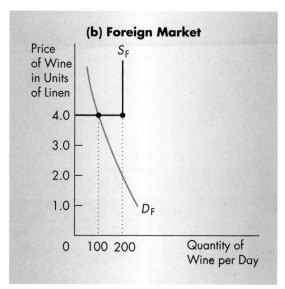

wine is less than 1.5 times the price of linen, it would be more profitable to produce and sell linen than it would be to produce and sell wine. If P_W/P_C is less than 1.5, the quantity of wine that would be produced and offered for sale would be zero. On the other hand, at any relative price of wine to linen above 1.5, only wine would be produced. This supply curve S_H is depicted in panel (a) of Figure 16.4. At a relative price of less than 1.5, no wine is supplied; at any price above 1.5, 400 units of wine (the maximum amount the home country can produce) are supplied. At a relative price of 1.5, any quantity of wine between 0 and 400 units will be offered for sale, because it is equally profitable to supply wine and linen.

The supply curve for the foreign country S_F is shown in panel (b) of Figure 16.4. In the foreign country, wine is four times as expensive to produce as linen, so no wine is produced at relative prices of less than 4.0. At relative prices above 4.0, *only* wine is produced.

Assuming that the demand for wine in the home country is represented by D_H, the equilibrium relative price at home would be 1.5. The equilibrium quantity of wine would be 240 units. Similarly, in the foreign country, with a demand of D_F, the equilibrium price would be 4.0, and the equilibrium quantity of wine would be 100 units.

If the two countries then became open to trade, instead of having two separate national markets there would be a single world market. The world supply curve S_W would be the horizontal sum of the home and foreign supply curves (S_H and S_F); the world demand D_W would be the horizontal sum of D_H and D_F.

The world demand and supply curves are shown in Figure 16.5. There, the equilibrium relative price is 3.0, and the equilibrium quantity of wine is 400 units, all of which is produced in the home country. The foreign country in turn is totally specialized in the production of linen. Given S_W, the terms of trade are determined by the demand for wine. The greater the demand for wine, the higher the equilibrium price and the more favorable the terms of trade to the home country. The weaker the demand for wine, the worse the terms of trade to the home country. In Figure 16.5, if demand for wine fell to D_W', the terms of trade would fall from 3 to 2 units of linen per unit of wine.

To see more clearly how a change in the terms of trade affects the two countries, we can return to the production possibilities frontiers for the countries. They are reproduced in Figure 16.6; line AB in panel (a) is for the home country and line $A'B'$ in panel (b) is for the foreign country. Suppose that

Figure 16.5 The World Market for Wine

The world supply curve S_W is obtained by summing the home supply and the foreign supply horizontally. The world demand is obtained by horizontally summing the home and foreign demand. Initially, when world demand is D_W, the equilibrium P_W/P_ℓ will be 3. Should world demand drop to D_W', P_W/P_ℓ will fall to 2.

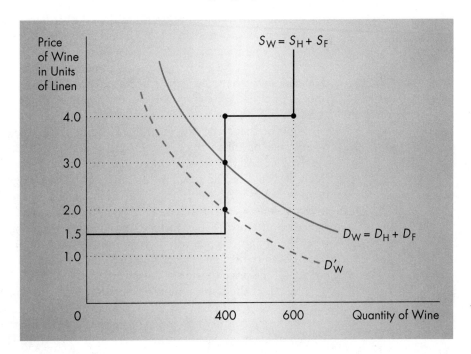

Figure 16.6 Consumption-Possibilities Frontiers

With free trade, the home country can specialize in wine where it has a comparative advantage and trade along a consumption-possibilities frontier. The better the terms of trade, the greater will be the home country's gains from trade.

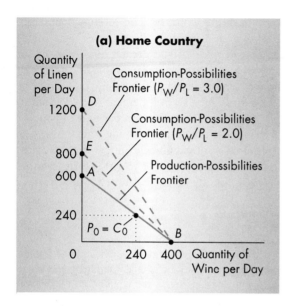

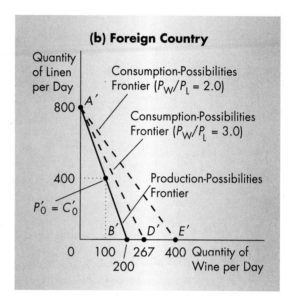

initially the two countries refuse to trade and that demand for wine in the two countries is as depicted in Figure 16.4. The home country will produce at point P_0, where wine output is 240. Without trade, the country consumes what it produces, so point P_0 is also the bundle consumed in that country. For that reason, we have also labeled that point as C_0 to represent the initial level of consumption. For the foreign country, point P_0' is the initial production and consumption point.

Suppose that trade is opened up. In equilibrium, the price of wine relative to the price of linen will be 3 given the world demand and supply depicted in Figure 16.5. At this relative price, the home country will produce only wine. Point B would be the new production point. The foreign country's new production point is A', where it produces only linen. With trade, the two countries are no longer constrained to consume the combination of the two goods that they produce. For each unit of wine that the home country exports, it receives enough revenue to purchase 3 units of linen. Starting at point B, the country can trade along the line labeled BD in panel (a). The slope of that line equals -3, the price of wine relative to the price of linen. It is useful to think of the line BD as the home country's **consumption-possibilities frontier** at that relative price. Each point on BD represents a combination of wine and linen that the home country is able to consume if it produces at point B and obtains 3 units of linen for each unit of wine it sells abroad. At this relative price, the foreign country's consumption-possibilities frontier is $A'D'$, which shows the different bundles that country can consume by producing bundle A' and obtaining 1 unit of wine from the home country for each 3 units of linen. The slope of the foreign consumption-possibilities frontier is also equal to -3.

At an equilibrium relative price of 3, each country is able to move along a consumption-possibilities frontier that lies beyond its production-possibilities frontier. Therefore, each country can specialize according to the principle of comparative advantage and trade to obtain a larger bundle of goods than it could possibly produce for itself.

How would a shift in demand affect the two countries? Consider the decrease in wine demand from D_W to D_W' in Figure 16.5. As a consequence, the price of wine relative to the price of linen falls from 3 to 2. The home country continues to specialize in wine and the foreign country in linen. However, the home country now receives only enough revenue from each unit of wine to buy 2 units of linen. Starting at point B in Figure 16.6, the home country can now move up along the new consumption-possibilities frontier labeled BE, the slope of which equals -2. The terms of trade have worsened for the home country, and its gains from trade are smaller along BE than they were along BD. The reduction in the price of wine enables the foreign country to obtain 1 unit of wine for 2 instead of 3 units of linen. As a consequence, it can produce at point A' and trade down along its new consumption-possibilities frontier labeled $A'E'$. The terms of trade have improved from this country's perspective, and it is richer along $A'E'$ than it was along $A'D'$.

Changes in the world demand for wine affect the gains from trade for the two trading countries. Increases in the demand for wine make the home country (the wine exporter) richer and the foreign country (the wine importer) poorer; decreases in wine demand have the opposite effect. So long as the equilibrium relative price of wine lies between 1.5 and 4, both countries will gain from trade. If demand for wine were to fall sufficiently to drive the world price down to 1.5, all the gains from trade would go to the foreign country, and the home country would be limited to consuming along her own production-possibilities frontier. If demand for wine rose sufficiently to drive the world price to 4 or above, all the gains would go to the home country.

Limitations of the Ricardian Model

There is much to be said for the simple Ricardian model of world trade. Most importantly, it presents the notion of comparative advantage in as clear a fashion as possible. Prior to Ricardo, arguments in favor of free trade were limited to examples in which one country had an absolute advantage in one good and the other country had an absolute advantage in a second good. The Ricardian model makes it possible to extend the argument for free trade to cases in which one country has an absolute advantage in both goods.

However, the model has at least two important disadvantages: (1) It is unable to explain a typical pattern of production in which both countries produce some of both goods. For example, the United States continues to produce cars in the face of imports from Japan; Japan imports U.S. beef but still produces beef. (2) It implies that trade based on comparative advantage makes everyone in the two countries better off. It therefore fails to provide insight into the adamant opposition to free trade that is often observed. To understand this opposition, we need a more sophisticated model of trade.

The Specific-Factors Model of International Trade

Since Ricardo, many advances have been made in the study of international economics. Today economists are able to construct elaborate models that can predict (though not with great confidence) the economic impact of free trade on narrow groups in an economy. For our purposes, such elaborate models are neither necessary nor useful. We can use a much simpler model to answer the questions at hand. One such model is called the **Specific-Factors Model of Trade.**[2].

The Specific-Factors Model assumes that there are two goods, two countries, and three factors (inputs) used to produce the two goods. However, one of the factors is useful only to produce one of the goods; a second factor is useful only to produce the other good. The two factors are called the specific factors. The third factor is used to produce both goods, and it is called the shared factor.

For example, we might consider the production of cars and wheat, when labor is used to produce both goods, but land (or terrain) is used only in the production of wheat, and capital (equipment) is used only to produce cars. The home country is assumed to have a labor force of some specific size L, a certain amount of terrain T, and a fixed amount of capital K. We can make similar assumptions for the foreign country, in which the labor force, quantity of terrain, and stock of capital are represented by L^*, T^*, and K^*.

In comparison to the Ricardian Model, it is more difficult for this model to derive each country's production-possibilities frontier, because it is not reasonable to assume a linear relationship between the number of workers employed in the production of each good and the output of that good. The production of cars entails the employment of capital in addition to labor, so we would not expect car production to be in proportion to the number of workers employed. Instead, we would expect that the use of additional labor to produce cars will lead to increases in car production that get smaller as the number of workers increases. Because there is a fixed amount of capital, as we add more and more workers each worker has less capital to work with. A large workforce implies more sharing of equipment and therefore less productivity

---

2. This model was developed by Paul Samuelson, "Ohlin Was Right," *Swedish Journal of Economics*, (1971), pp. 365–384, and by Ronald Jones, "A Three Factor Model in Theory, Trade, and History" in Jagdish Bhagwati et al., eds. *Trade, Balance of Payments, and Growth* (Amsterdam: North-Holland, 1971), pp. 3–21.

Figure 16.7 Total-Product Curves

The solid total-product curve shows the number of units of cars that can be produced by using different numbers of workers in conjunction with 100 units of capital. The other total-product curve shows the same thing, assuming that the workers have 150 units of capital to work with. In both cases, total output of cars rises as the number of workers increases, but at a decreasing rate. With a labor force of 1,000 workers, 3,000 cars is the maximum number that can be produced if there are only 100 units of capital available.

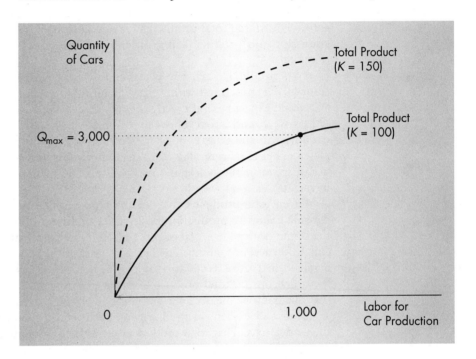

per worker. This type of relationship between the amount of labor employed and the amount of output produced is depicted in Figure 16.7.[3]

In the figure, increases in the number of workers employed in car production (L_C) lead to increases in the output of cars. However, as L_C rises, Q_C rises at a decreasing rate. This means that the marginal product of labor (the

3. In Figure 16.7 the marginal product of labor begins to diminish with the second worker. In fact, initially the marginal product of labor may well increase. If we have such a large stock of capital and a very small number of workers, adding a worker may provide an opportunity for increased specialization in production with little offsetting disadvantages from having less capital per worker. If so, the marginal product of the second worker may be larger than that of the first worker. However, as the work force is increased, the fixed stock of capital will eventually lead to a decrease in the marginal product of labor. Here, we ignore that possibility and assume that the marginal product declines with the second worker. In Chapter 6 when the total-product curves were introduced, the marginal product increased and then decreased.

increase in car output resulting from each unit increase in L_C) declines as L_C rises. Extra workers contribute less and less to output because, with a fixed stock of capital, there is less equipment available per worker. In Figure 16.7 the home country is assumed to have a labor force of 1,000 workers and a capital stock of 100 machines. The largest number of cars that can be produced by that country per year is 3,000.

If that country had a larger stock of capital, its ability to produce cars would be greater. The higher the stock of capital, the higher the total-product curve. The dotted total-product curve in Figure 16.7 shows how many cars the country could produce using different quantities of labor with 150 units of capital.

We can also look at the wheat industry, in which different amounts of labor (L_W) can be used with a fixed quantity of terrain (T) to produce wheat. We would expect to find exactly the same type of relationship between L_W and Q_W as we found above between L_C and Q_C — as the number of workers employed in the wheat industry is increased, the output of wheat will also increase, but at a decreasing rate. Just as in the car industry, the marginal product of labor in the wheat industry will decline as the number of workers is increased.

Given total-product curves of the type depicted in Figure 16.7, we can derive a country's production possibilities frontier. Suppose, for example, that the home country has a labor force of 1,000, a capital stock of 100 machines, and 1,000 acres of terrain. Further, assume that the total-product curves are as depicted in Figure 16.8. In that figure, ignore the northeast quadrant, and focus first on the total-product-of-wheat curve in the northwest quadrant. In that quadrant we measure the amount of labor employed in the wheat industry L_W from right to left on the horizontal axis, and the output of wheat Q_W on the vertical axis. That total-product curve reflects a diminishing marginal product of labor: 200 workers can produce 4,000 units of wheat and 500 workers can produce 8,000 units; 800 workers can produce 11,000 units, and if the entire labor force of 1,000 workers is employed, wheat output will be 12,000.

The total-product curve for the car industry is depicted in the southeast quadrant of the same graph. There, L_C is measured on the vertical axis (from top to bottom), and Q_C is measured from left to right on the horizontal axis. This total-product curve is also drawn to reflect a diminishing marginal product of labor. On that graph we see that car output rises from 0 when L_C is 0 to 1,000, 2,000, 2,700, and 3,000 as L_C is increased to 200, 500, 800, and finally 1,000 workers.

We are now ready to derive the production-possibilities frontier in the northeast quadrant. Note first that in the southwest quadrant we have drawn a straight 45-degree line connecting point A, where L_W equals 1,000, with point E, where L_C equals 1,000. Each point along that line represents a different allocation of labor between the two industries. Point A represents using 1,000 workers to produce wheat and no workers to produce cars. At point B, 800 workers are allocated to wheat, 200 to cars. Similarly, at points C, D, and E, the labor allocation to wheat falls to 500 workers, 200 workers, and 0 workers, whereas the allocation to cars rises to 500, 800, and finally 1,000 workers.

We are now in a position to see how much output of each of the two goods we can get from each possible allocation of labor. Allocation A would yield 12,000 units of wheat and 0 units of cars. This point is labeled A' in the northeast quadrant of Figure 16.8. Allocation B (800 workers in the wheat industry and the remaining 200 in cars) would yield 11,000 units of wheat and 1,000 units of cars. This combination of the two goods is labeled B' in Figure 16.8. Similarly, the labor allocations labeled C, D, and E can be used to produce the combinations of output labeled C', D', and E'. The curve connecting points A' through E' is the home country's production-possibilities frontier.

In sharp contrast to the production-possibilities frontier implied by the Ricardian Model, the Specific Factors Model yields a nonlinear production-possibilities frontier. As we move down along it from point A' to point E', the slope changes. The first 1,000 cars require only a 1,000-unit reduction in

Figure 16.8 The Derivation of the Production-Possibilities Frontier

The production-possibilities frontier in the northeast quadrant is derived from the total-product curves in the northwest and southeast quandrants. Each point labeled A through E in the southwest quandant shows a different allocation of the 1,000-person labor force between car and wheat production. Allocations A through E lead to output combinations A' through E', respectively, on the production-possibilities frontier.

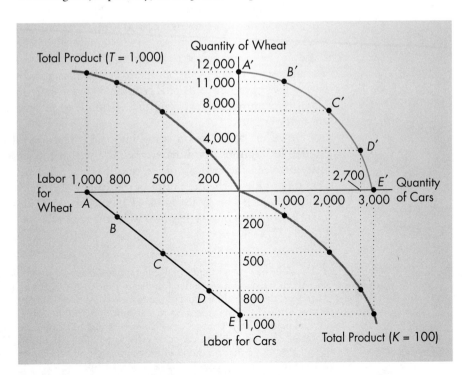

wheat production. However, the second 1,000 cars require a 3,000-unit reduction in wheat production. The cost of producing cars in terms of wheat continues to rise as we expand car production, with the last 300 cars coming at a cost of 4,000 units of wheat. The opportunity cost of producing cars rises from a very low level of (perhaps) 0.5 units of wheat to (perhaps) 25 units of wheat as car production rises from 1 car to 3,000 cars.[4]

Just as was the case in the Ricardian model, the production-possibilities frontier implies a specific supply curve. If we consider various relative prices of cars (P_C/P_W), car producers would be unwilling to offer cars for sale unless the relative price was equal to the opportunity cost. Because the first car costs 0.5 unit of wheat, it would be supplied only at a relative price of 0.5 or above. At a relative price of $P_C/P_W = 1.5$, it would pay to produce only 1,000 cars. As the relative price of cars rises from 0.5 to 25.0, the quantity supplied would rise from 0 cars to 3,000 cars. Figure 16.9 depicts the supply ccurve of cars that corresponds to the production-possibilities frontier in Figure 16.8. Assuming a demand for cars of D_C in Figure 16.9, the equilibrium relative price will be 4, and the equilibrium quantity will be 2,000 cars per year. That equilibrium point, corresponding to point C on the production-possibilities frontier in Figure 16.8, implies that 500 workers are employed in each of the two industries.

We can also consider the production-possibilities frontier of a second foreign country. There are several possible reasons why the foreign country's production-possibilities frontier might differ from that of the home country. The population in the foreign country might be either larger or smaller, or the workers in that country might be systematically more or less efficient than those in the home country. In saying that they are more or less efficient, we are suggesting that a given number of workers in the foreign country, working with a given amount of capital, could produce either more or fewer cars than could that number of workers in the home country working with the same amount of capital.

However, to focus on some important features of the Specific Factors Model, let's ignore any differences in the size of the labor force or in productivity between the two countries. Specifically, let's assume that the two countries differ only in the quantities of the specific factors. Compared to the home country (which has 1,000 units of terrain and 100 units of capital), assume that the foreign country has 500 units of terrain ($T^* = 500$) and 200 units of capital ($K^* = 200$).

---

4. The slope of a straight line connecting points A' and B' would be –1.0. Compared to that line, the production-possibilities frontier is a bit flatter at point A' and a bit steeper at B'. Therefore, the opportunity cost of the first car is *less* than 1 unit of wheat and the opportunity cost of the 1,000th car is *more* than 1 unit of wheat. Similarly, the slope of the line connecting points B' and C' is –3.0, which implies that the 1,000th car costs *less* than 3 units of wheat whereas the 2,000th car costs *more* than 3 units of wheat. For the sake of concreteness, let's assume that the slope of the production possibilities frontier at points A', B', C', D', and E' is –0.5, –1.5, –4.0, –8.0, and –25.0, respectively.

Figure 16.9 The Market for Cars in the Home Country

The supply curve of cars S_C, was obtained from the production-possibilities frontier in Figure 16.8. Because the first car produced has an opportunity cost of 0.5 unit of wheat, the quantity of cars supplied at a relative price below 0.5 is 0. The graph shows that 2,000 cars are supplied at a relative price of 4, because that is the number of cars that can be produced at an opportunity cost of 4 units of wheat or less. Assuming demand D_C, 4 is the equilibrium relative price.

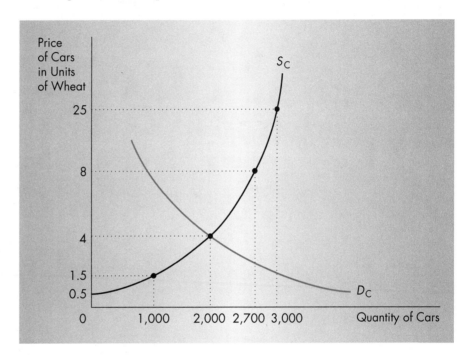

The foreign country's production-possibilities frontier is derived in Figure 16.10 using the same technique that we used earlier for the home country. To emphasize the difference between the two production-possibilities frontiers, Figure 16.10 also includes the home country's total-product curves and production-possibilities frontier.

The foreign production-possibilities frontier is also nonlinear — it becomes steeper as we produce greater quantities of cars. The reason that the opportunity cost of producing a car increases as the number of cars is increased is the same as for the home country. As the number of cars rises, we use workers who are increasingly productive at wheat production and decreasingly productive at car production.

The foreign production-possibilities frontier differs from that of the home country in one important way; it is flatter. This means that cars tend to be cheaper to produce in the foreign country than at home. However, this does not mean that it is always cheaper to produce an additional car in the foreign

Figure 16.10 The Derivation of the Foreign Production-Possibilities Frontier

Here, the same method that was used in Figure 16.8 is again used to derive a production-possibilities frontier, but for the foreign country. The only difference between the two countries is that the foreign country has more capital but less terrain. The home production-possibilities frontier is presented for the sake of comparison.

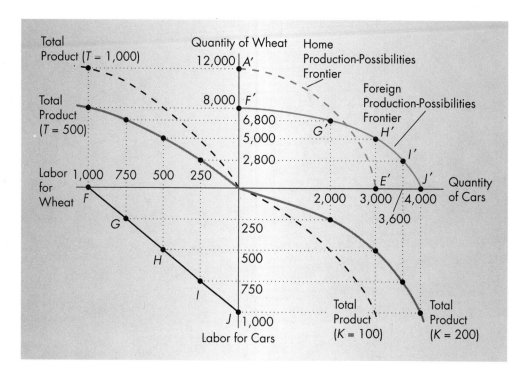

country. If we compare the bottom portion of the foreign production-possibilities frontier with the top portion of the home production-possibilities frontier, we see that the foreign one is steeper. If the foreign country produces a lot of cars, their cost will be higher than the cost to us if we produce a small number of cars.

From the two production-possibilities frontiers, we see that the home country can produce at most 12,000 units of wheat or 3,000 cars. On average, the home country must give up 4 units of wheat for each additional car. However, the cost is not 4 units of wheat for each car. As we saw earlier, the first car costs only 0.5 unit of wheat; the last one costs 25 units of wheat. The foreign production-possibilities frontier shows that they can produce at most 8,000 units of wheat and at most 4,000 cars. On average, cars cost 2 units of wheat in the foreign country. Again, the cost varies from a number much lower than 2 at point *F'* to a number much greater than 2 at point *J'*. For the sake of concreteness, let's assume that the slope of the foreign production-possibilities frontier is 0.10 unit of wheat at *F'*, 1 unit at *G'*, 2 units at *H'*,

Figure 16.11 The Market for Cars in the Foreign Country
The foreign supply of cars is drawn to reflect the production-possibilities frontier from Figure 16.10. Assuming a foreign demand of D^*_C, the equilibrium P_C/P_W in the foreign country is 2.0, and the equilibrium quantity is 3,000 cars.

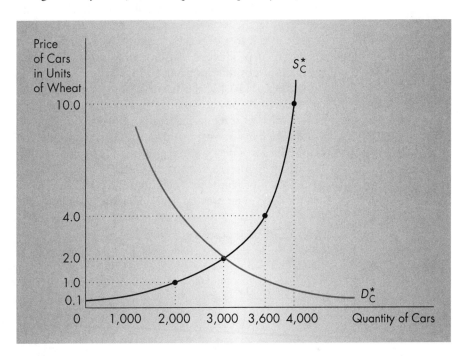

4 units at I', and 10 units at J'. If so, the foreign supply curve is S_C^* in Figure 16.11. Assuming demand curve D_C^* in the foreign country, the domestic equilibrium in the foreign country would be at a relative price of 2, with 3,000 cars produced. This is represented by point H' on the production-possibilities frontier in Figure 16.10. In the absence of trade, this country would produce 5,000 units of wheat and 3,000 units of cars during each time period, and the citizens of the country would buy and use that bundle of goods.

Comparative Advantage in the Specific-Factors Model

In the Specific Factors Model, there is some ambiguity to the notion of comparative advantage. To determine which country has a comparative advantage in cars (which country has the lower opportunity cost), we need to know how many cars are produced in each country. However, given the home and foreign demand assumed in Figures 16.9 and 16.11 respectively, the foreign country has a comparative advantage in car production. At its initial production level of 3,000 cars, the last car produced in the foreign country has an opportunity cost of 2 units of wheat; in the home country, where 2,000 cars are being produced, the last car has an opportunity cost of 4 units of wheat. Because the opportunity costs differ, there are gains from trade. The foreign country can expand its production of cars, moving down its production-possibilities frontier. At the same time, the home country can reduce its production of cars and increase its production of wheat. Production of cars would be expanded in the foreign country and contracted at home until there is no difference in the cost of producing cars. In other words, the two countries would change their production patterns until they reached points on their respective production-possibilities frontiers that have the same slope.

In Figure 16.12, the home country would reduce its production of cars and increase its production of wheat, moving up along its production-possibilities frontier to some point to the northwest of point *C′*. The foreign country would increase its car production and move down along its production-possibilities frontier to some point to the southeast of point *H′*.

Using Figure 16.12, we can determine that the home country will reduce car production and the foreign country will increase car production, but we cannot determine how large the increases and decreases in production will be.

Figure 16.12 Output Adjustments Under Free Trade

Without trade, the home country will produce output combination *C′*, and the foreign country will produce combination *H′*. The slope of *H′* is less than the slope of *C′*. With free trade, the foreign country will expand car output and move down its frontier to a point like *I′* or *J′*. The home country will reduce car production and move to some point higher on its production-possibilities frontier, such as *D′* or *E′*.

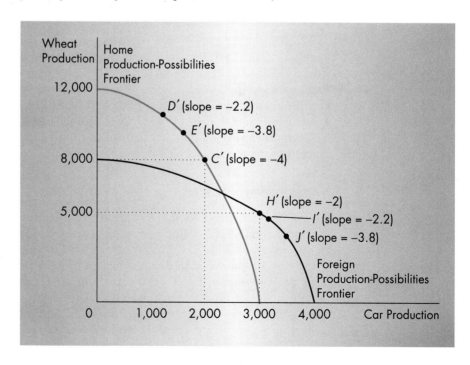

One possibility would be for the home country to reduce car production by a lot and move all the way up to point D', where the opportunity cost of the last car produced is 2.2 units of wheat. The foreign country could then expand car production by a very small amount — moving down its production-possibilities frontier to point I', where the cost of the last car is also 2.2 units of wheat. At points D' and I', there would no longer be any difference in opportunity costs.

Alternatively, the home country could reduce its car production by much less, moving to a point like point E' while the foreign country increases its product a lot and moves to point J'. At points E' and J' the two countries again have the same opportunity cost of producing cars, but in this case the cost is 3.8 units of wheat.

To determine precisely how many cars each of the two countries will produce with a policy of free trade, we once again turn to demand and supply. Figure 16.13 reproduces the demand and supply for wheat in each of the two countries, and adds the two demand curves and the two supply curves horizontally to obtain the world demand D_W and the world supply S_W.

In Figure 16.13, the equilibrium price is 3.0. At that price, consumers in the home country wish to buy 2,100 cars, and home producers are willing to produce 1,500 cars. The home country has a shortage of 600 cars.

In the foreign country, buyers are willing to purchase 2,900 cars, and car producers are willing to sell 3,500 at a relative price of 3. The home shortage is equal to the foreign surplus, and the total number of cars that are demanded at the equilibrium price is 5,000 — the same number that are offered for sale.

To raise the revenue necessary to pay for the 600 imported, the home country exports 1,800 units of wheat. In Figure 16.14, the home country is depicted in panel (a). Point P_0 on its production-possibilities frontier represents the combination of cars and food that the home country would produce and consume without trade. With trade, the home country is able to obtain foreign cars at a price of 3 units of wheat. Accordingly, it moves up along its production-possibilities frontier to point P_1, its new production point. At point P_1 the slope of the production-possibilities frontier is negative 3, and the home country produces 9,850 units of wheat and 1,500 cars.[5] Instead of consuming that bundle of goods, the home country exports wheat and imports cars, moving down along the line labeled AB, the **consumption-possibilities**

---

5. If you are wondering how we know that wheat output at point P_1 is exactly 9,850 units, the answer is that we don't. However, within limits we can pinpoint the amount of wheat the home country is able to produce if car output is 1,500. Starting at P_0, where wheat production is 8,000 units, we reduce car production from 2,000 to 1,500. Each car that we no longer produce provides labor that is used to produce wheat. Because the slope at P_0 is -4.0, the first unit reduction in car production enables us to produce 4 more units of wheat. However, successive reductions in car output lead to smaller increases in wheat production. The last unit reduction leads only to a 3-unit increase in wheat production. Because each of the 500 cars that we give up enables us to produce between 3 and 4 more units of wheat, total wheat production will increase by some amount between 1,500 and 2,000 units. The 1,850-unit increase that we show in Figure 16.14 falls within this range.

Figure 16.13 Equilibrium in the World Market

At a relative price of 3.0, world demand for cars equals world supply. At that price, there is a shortage in the home market represented by the distance from point A to point B. In the foreign market there is an equal surplus represented by the distance from point C to point D.

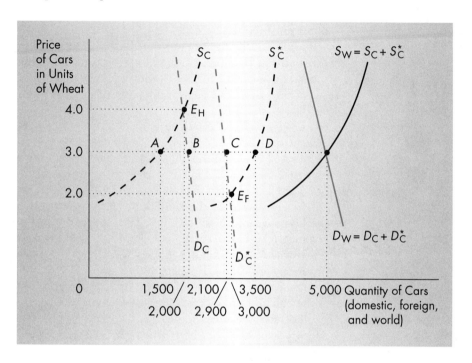

frontier. If the country produces bundle P_1 and is able to buy or sell cars on the world market at a price of 3 units of wheat, the line AB shows the different combinations of wheat and cars that the country can obtain through trade. At that price, consumers in that country would prefer 2,100 cars. That quantity is obtained by moving down the consumption-possibilities frontier from point P_1 to point C_1, the new consumption point. Point C_1 differs from point P_1 in that it contains 600 more cars but 1,800 fewer units of wheat.

To see the effect of world trade on living standards in the home country, we need to compare point P_0 with point C_1. Point P_0 is the best the home country can do if it is self-sufficient. However, if it can specialize on the basis of comparative advantage and trade, it can attain point C_1, which contains 50 more units of wheat and 100 more cars.

Panel (b) shows the effects of specialization and trade on the foreign country. Before trade, it produces the bundle of goods represented by P_0^*. When trade develops and the foreign country is able to sell cars at a price of 3 units of wheat, it expands its car production and reduces its wheat production, moving down its production-possibilities frontier to point P_1^*, where the last car produced costs 3 units of wheat. The foreign country then exports 600 cars to

Figure 16.14 The Adjustment to a Free Trade Equilibrium

Without trade, the two countries would produce the combinations of goods represented by P_0 in the home country and P_0^* in the foreign country. With free trade, the countries would adjust their production to points P_1 and P_1^*. They would then export the good for which they have a comparative advantage and import the other good so they consume combinations C_1 and C_1^*.

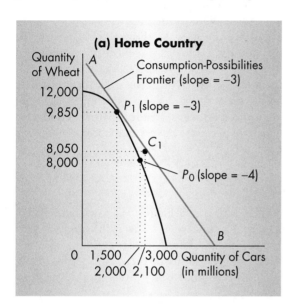
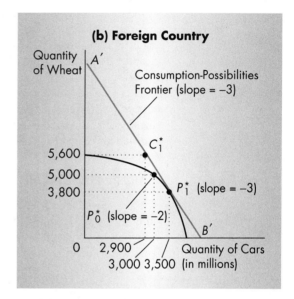

the home country and imports 1,800 units of wheat from the home country, moving up along the consumption-possibilities frontier to point C_1^*. This new consumption point lies outside its production-possibilities frontier and enables it to consume 600 more units of wheat but 100 fewer cars than it could when it was self-sufficient.

By enabling each of the two countries to consume a bundle of goods beyond its production-possibilities frontier, international trade raises average living standards. However, this does not imply that everyone in both countries is made better off. In the home country, free trade leads to an increase in the production of wheat and a decrease in car production. Therefore, it leads to an increase in demand for terrain, the input that is specialized in the wheat industry. Landowners gain by being able to obtain higher rents for their land. At the same time, owners of capital suffer. That input is used only to produce cars, and car production falls because of foreign competition. This leads to a decrease in demand for capital and to lower returns to owners of capital.

Unfortunately, the Specific Factors Model is not able to show what effect trade has on the real wage of labor — the shared factor in our example. Because wheat output rises, the marginal product of labor falls in the wheat industry and laborers experience a reduction in purchasing power over the exported good. At the same time, their marginal product rises in the car industry, where output is reduced, and their purchasing power for cars is increased.

Because all workers can buy more of the imported good but less of the export-ed good than before trade, we cannot determine unambiguously whether their living standard has improved.

In the foreign country, free trade would have different effects. Car produc-tion would rise, and wheat production would fall. This would cause a decrease in the demand for terrain and an increase in the demand for capital. Capital owners would benefit, and terrain owners would suffer.

The Specific Factors Model can also be used to show the impact of free trade on consumers. In the home country, trade has the effect of lowering the price of cars, the imported good, but raising the relative price of wheat, the exported good. Domestic consumers of cars will enjoy a larger consumer surplus as a consequence of the price reduction. Wheat buyers in the home country will face a higher relative price after free trade, so their consumer surplus will fall. Similarly, free trade will harm car buyers in the foreign country and benefit wheat buyers in that country.

Extensions of the Basic Trade Models

The Specific Factors Model provides a nice explanation of how trade affects different broad groups of people within a country. However, the model is very simplified; in the real world there are many different classes of inputs that are used to produce goods and services, and few if any of them are specific to any particular industry. Nonetheless, it is possible to apply the specific findings from our model to real-world examples.

When we consider trade from the perspective of different types of income earners, we find that free trade benefits those who supply a *disproportionately* large percentage of their inputs in industries that become net exporters. If we are interested in how accountants, welders, or machine operators will fare under free trade, we need to determine whether the firms they work for pro-duce the types of goods in which the home country has a comparative advan-tage. For almost every occupation, some workers are currently employed in industries in which we are at a comparative disadvantage; and those jobs are likely to be lost as we move toward freer trade. Other workers in the same occupation will be employed by firms that produce goods (or services) in which we have a comparative advantage. The movement toward free trade will enhance their job security and their chances for rapid advancement, and it will create new job opportunities for others of the same occupation. For some occupations, the net effect will be an increase in jobs, in job security, and in pay. For other occupations, the net effect of trade will be a loss of job security and perhaps an increase in unemployment (see Highlight 16.2). Because many people have much to gain, and others have much to lose, it is no wonder that trade policy is so controversial. However, in assessing trade policy it is impera-tive to keep in mind that there are net gains from free trade. Countries can enhance overall living standards through a free-trade policy, despite the fact that some are harmed by those policies.

Highlight 16.2 *The Pattern of Trade and the Endowment of Resources: Japan and the United States*

Models of trade like the Specific Factors Model suggest that comparative advantage is determined largely by differences in the pattern of resource endowments in different countries. There are a number of reasons one should not expect resource endowments to fully explain the current pattern of world trade, one major one being that trade restrictions, like tariffs, interfere with trade and have an impact on patterns of production. Even if the models are correct, factor endowments will not fully explain trade patterns if trade patterns are determined politically and not through the forces of comparative advantage. However, it is interesting to compare the trade pattern of different countries with their respective resource endowments. Table 16.4 shows the endowments of certain resources for Japan and the United States.

In our discussion of the determinants of comparative advantage, we argued that a country's relative proportions of different resources were of primary importance. To interpret Table 16.4, it is important to stress two facts: of the six inputs listed, the United States held about 29 percent of the world's total and Japan held about 11 percent. We therefore have to consider the numbers listed in the table relative to the overall resource holdings of the country. A country is said to hold a given factor intensively only if its proportion of that factor exceeds its proportion of all factors as a whole.

From the table we can see that the United States holds about 33 percent of the physical capital — which is a slightly high amount given that the United States holds 29 percent of all resources. U.S. holdings of skilled labor and of arable land are about in line with its overall holdings of resources. Its relative proportion of semiskilled labor is low, its proportion of unskilled labor is extremely low, and its proportion of research and development scientists is very high.

Table 16.4 Shares of World Resources

The entries show each nation's total as a percentage of the world total.

Country	Physical Capital	Skilled Labor	Semiskilled Labor	Unskilled Labor	Arable Land	R & D Scientists
U.S.	33.6	27.7	19.1	0.19	29.3	50.7
Japan	15.5	8.7	11.5	0.25	0.8	23.0

Source: Data derived from Robert J. Carbaugh, *International Economics,* 4th ed., (Belmont, California: 1992). Wadsworth Publishing Company, Table 4.2, p. 66. Reprinted by permission.

American agriculture, given U.S. technology and resource endowments, is the most efficient and productive in the world.

This pattern of endowments would imply a strong comparative advantage to the United States in goods that use a high proportion of scientists, and a somewhat weaker comparative advantage in goods that are capital intensive. It would also suggest that the United States is at a comparative disadvantage in goods requiring much semiskilled labor and at a strong comparative disadvantage in goods that require the use of a lot of unskilled labor.

With about 11 percent of the total resources, Japan is highly endowed in scientists and physical capital (more so than the United States). Japan's endowment of semiskilled labor is in line with its proportion of all resources, and it has a disproportionately small amount of arable land and unskilled labor.

What do we know about the trade pattern of the two countries? Table 16.5 shows the ratio of each country's exports to imports for each of five broad classes of goods and services.

Economic theory implies that we should find ratios greater than 1.0 (which means that the country's exports exceed its imports) in industries that require the intensive use of the inputs held in disproportionately high amounts by that country. The high numbers for technology-intensive goods both for the United States and Japan are certainly consistent with economic theory. The small fractions (0.39 for standardized goods and 0.38 for labor-intensive goods) for the United States are not surprising given that our endowments of both semiskilled and unskilled workers are so low. Japan's ratios for these two products are, perhaps, a bit higher than one would expect.

Table 16.5 Ratios of Exports to Imports

Country	Technology-Intensive Goods	Standardized Goods	Labor-Intensive Goods	Services	Primary Goods
U.S.	1.52	0.39	0.38	1.50	0.55
Japan	5.67	1.09	1.04	0.72	0.04

Source: Robert J. Carbaugh, *International Economics*, 4th ed., (Belmont, California: 1992). Wadsworth Publishing Company, Table 4.3, p. 67. Reprinted by permission.

The fact that the United States is a net exporter of services and Japan is a net importer probably reflects differences in the types of skilled labor in the two countries. Japan's education system tends to be more technologically oriented, whereas the American system places a greater emphasis on liberal arts and business training. Both countries are net importers of primary goods. Japan's ratio is minute because it is a net importer of both agricultural products and fuels; we are a net importer because our fuel imports exceed our agricultural exports.

The Economics of Protectionism

Up to this point, our discussion has focused on the two extremes of trade policy — no trade on the one hand, and completely free trade on the other. To this end, in previous sections we used both the Ricardian Model and the Specific Factors Model to contrast free trade with no trade. However, debates over trade policy are seldom over these two policy extremes. Instead, they are focused on **protectionist** policies to restrict but not eliminate foreign trade. The two major ways that nations restrict trade is through the imposition of tariffs or quotas. A **tariff** is simply a tax on imported goods. A **quota** is a limitation on the quantity of imports to some specific number.

In addition to tariffs and quotas, there are many other ways in which countries can restrict imports. In recent years, many countries have turned increasingly to the use of these alternatives. For example, a government that has been advocating free trade may find itself under pressure to reduce imports of some particular good like cars, textiles, or shoes. Given its stated opposition to trade restrictions, it is understandably reluctant to impose either a tariff or a quota. Instead, that government might negotiate a **"Voluntary" Export Restriction** (VER) with a trade partner under which that country "voluntarily" limits its exports to some particular quantity. For example, the Reagan administration, which adamantly advocated free trade, negotiated a VER with Japan that continues to limit the number of cars that Japan ships to the United States. If you think that a VER is simply a disguised quota, you are essentially correct.

In addition to VERs, another means of limiting foreign trade is through the enactment of **domestic-content legislation.** Domestic-content legislation requires that goods sold in a country have a certain percentage of "domestic content." By domestic content, we mean domestic parts or domestic labor content.

The effect of such legislation may be to increase the cost of producing goods that are exported to the United States, thereby reducing their quantity. If, for example, the United States is at a comparative disadvantage in producing auto parts or assembling cars, legislation that requires the use of such parts or labor as a condition of sale in the U.S. market will clearly reduce the flow of "foreign" cars into our market.

The government of a country can discourage imports in many other ways. Customs searches can be carried out so as to damage imported goods or to delay the shipment of perishables. In addition, safety regulations can be designed to make it difficult for foreign firms to comply.

A Graphical Model of Trade Restrictions

One way to examine the consequences of trade restrictions is to use a graph like the one in Figure 16.13. It depicts the demand and supply curves for the home and foreign countries as well as the world demand and supply. It would be possible to use that graph to illustrate the consequences of, say, the imposition of a tariff on imported cars by the home country. However, there is no easy way to do this, and the graph is already so cluttered that the addition of new demand or supply curves to reflect the impact of the tariff would undoubtedly lead to greater confusion.

There is one additional problem with using Figure 16.13. We cannot use that graph to illustrate the impact of a specific tariff of, say, $4,000 per car, because the vertical axis measures the *relative* price of cars, not the dollar price. We could use that graph to illustrate the effect of a tariff of one unit of wheat per car, but it is rather bizarre to think of such a tariff.

Fortunately, it is fairly easy to devise a graphical model that overcomes these two problems. Until now we have considered models of the world in which there were only two goods. In such a model the two goods are so closely interrelated that it made no sense to think of a change in the price of one good without considering the impact on the other good. That was why we always thought in terms of relative prices rather than money prices. However, if we broaden our analysis to a world in which there are many goods, a change in the market for any one good need not have substantial repercussions on other markets. If the money price of all other goods remains constant, any change in the money price of the good in question will imply a similar change in its relative price. Therefore, in an example with many goods, we can appropriately consider demand and supply models in which prices are measured in dollar terms rather than in relative terms.

Panel (a) of Figure 16.15 shows the home country's demand and supply for cars with the price expressed in dollar terms. The equilibrium price is $20,000. That graph emphasizes the country's domestic surplus and shortage of cars at prices above and below $20,000. For example, at a price of $28,000, the distance between the points labeled *A* and *B* is the car surplus at that price. Similarly, at a price of $24,000, the surplus of cars is the distance between points *C* and *D*.

In panel (b), the curve labeled *XS* graphs these surpluses. At a price of $28,000, the excess supply is shown as the distance between points *A'* and *B'*, which is identical to the distance between points *A* and *B* in panel (a). The excess-supply curve shows the magnitude of the home country's surplus at each price above $20,000. At a price of $20,000, the excess supply is zero.

At prices below $20,000, there will be shortages in the home market. At a price of $16,000 the shortage is the distance from point *F* to point *G*, and at $12,000 the shortage is the distance from *H* to *I*. The excess-demand curve (*XD*) in panel (b) shows the domestic shortage at each price below $20,000. The distance from *F'* to *G'* in panel (b) is equal to the distance from *F* to *G* in panel (a).

Figure 16.15 Excess-Supply and -Demand Curves

At any price above the equilibrium price, there is a surplus. In panel (a) the suplus at $24,000 is equal to the distance *CD*. The Excess Supply (*XS*) in panel (b) shows the size of that surplus at each price. For example, distance *C'D'* equals distance *CD*, and so forth. Below the equilibrium price there is a shortage, an excess of demand. The shortage at each price in panel (a) is shown in panel (b) as the Excess Demand (*XD*). For example, *FG* = *F'G'* and *HI* = *H'I'*.

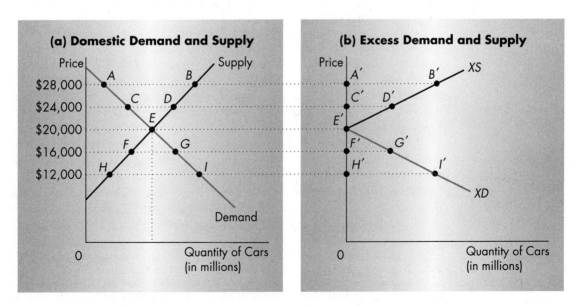

The purpose of developing excess supply and excess demand curves is that under conditions of free trade, a country's **excess supply** curve is identical to that country's supply-of-exports curve, and its **excess demand** curve is identical to its demand for imports.[6] In Figure 16.15, at a price of $28,000, home buyers would be willing to buy the number of cars represented by the distance out to point *A*, but home suppliers would be willing to sell a number of cars equal to the distance out to point *B*. The distance from *A* to *B* would represent the number of cars that home producers would not be able to sell at home, and this would therefore be the number of cars it would be willing to export. Each point on the home country's excess-supply curve shows how far domestic demand falls short of domestic supply. That excess equals the number of cars home producers would desire to sell abroad.

Similarly, the excess-demand curve shows the amount by which domestic demand exceeds domestic supply at each price below the domestic equilibrium. If, at a price of $12,000, domestic buyers want to buy the quantity of cars represented by point *I*, but the number supplied by domestic producers is only the number represented by point *H*, the difference between those two numbers is the number of cars home consumers would be willing to import.

Figure 16.16 shows how excess demand and supply curves can be used to illustrate the equilibrium level of imports and exports under conditions of free trade. Panel (a) shows the demand and supply of cars in the home country; the equilibrium price is $20,000.

In that graph, panel (c), demand and supply in a foreign country are shown. The foreign equilibrium price is $12,000. If you are a bit troubled by thinking of the equilibrium price in some foreign country (perhaps Japan) as being some number of American dollars, you should be. It would make more sense to express the price in terms of the Japanese currency, the yen. However, once we know the current exchange rate at which yen can be converted to dollars, we can easily convert any yen price into the dollar equivalent. Assuming that the exchange rate is 120 yen per dollar, a price of $12,000 is equivalent to a price of 1.44 million yen (120 × 12,000 = 1,440,000). Therefore, the demand curves in panel (c) show how many cars Japanese buyers are willing to buy and how many cars Japanese producers are willing to sell at yen prices 120 times as high as the dollar prices that are shown on the vertical axis in panel (c). Given that the foreign equilibrium price is $12,000 (or 1.44 million yen), at higher prices there would be a surplus of cars in Japan, and at lower prices there would be a shortage of cars.

Now, turn your attention to panel (b) of Figure 16.16. The excess-demand curve shown there is the excess-demand curve for the home country, in which the domestic equilibrium price is higher than that in the foreign

---

6. This graphical model ignores the costs of shipping between countries. To include such costs, all that is necessary is to displace the excess-supply curve upward by an amount equal to the unit shipping costs. This graphical model treats importers and exporters as price takers. Again, the model can be fairly easily adapted to reflect situations in which buyers or sellers have market power.

Figure 16.16 The Use of Excess Demand and Supply to Determine the World Equilibrium
Panel (a) shows home demand and supply. The home country's excess demand is drawn in panel (b). Panel (c) shows foreign demand and supply. The foreign excess supply is also shown in panel (b). In panel (b) we can see that at a price of $15,000, the foreign country's surplus (2 million cars) is equal to the home country's shortage. Therefore, $15,000 is the world equilibrium price.

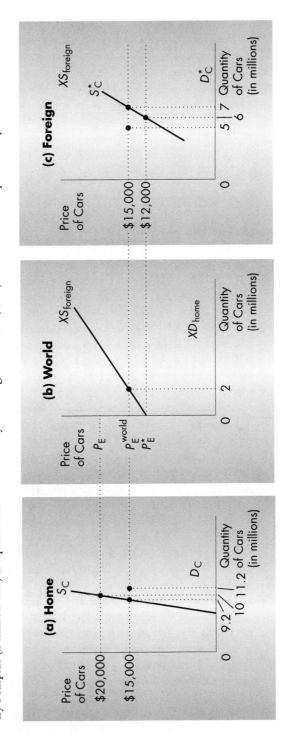

country. That excess-demand curve shows how many cars buyers in the home country would be willing to import at each price.

The excess-supply curve shown in panel (b) is Japan's excess supply; it shows how many cars Japan is willing to export at each price above its domestic equilibrium of $12,000. We see that Japan's excess supply is equal to our excess demand at a price of $15,000. At that price, Japanese producers are willing to supply 2 million cars to American buyers, and American buyers are willing to import 2 million cars. Therefore, the world equilibrium price is determined by the intersection of the home excess demand and the foreign excess supply.

With free trade, the United States will import 2 million cars, and the equilibrium price in the United States will be $15,000. We see in panel (a) that at a price of $15,000, American buyers are willing to buy 11.2 million cars, whereas American producers are willing to supply 9.2 million cars. The shortage of 2 million cars is eliminated by imports.

In the Japanese market, the equilibrium price under free trade is also $15,000. At that price, Japanese producers are willing to produce 7 million cars and Japanese consumers are willing to buy 5 million. The 2 million car surplus is eliminated by exporting cars to the United States.

Figure 16.16 shows clearly how free trade compares with no trade in each country. Without trade, the equilibrium price in the United States would be $20,000, with American buyers buying all 10 million cars that are produced domestically. Under free trade, the price falls to $15,000 and American buyers increase their purchases to 11.2 million cars. In response to the price reduction, American producers cut their quantity supplied from 10 million cars to 9.2 million. American producers are worse off (they sell fewer cars at a lower price), but consumers of cars in the United States are better off. We should note that *all* car buyers in the United States benefit — not just the 2 million buyers who purchase imported cars but also the 9.2 million buyers who buy American cars for a price of $15,000. Had it not been for free trade, the same cars would have brought a price that was $5,000 higher.

In Japan, the effect of free trade is to drive car prices up from $12,000 to $15,000 (from 1.44 million yen to 1.8 million yen). This price increase induces consumers in Japan to reduce their purchases by 1 million cars (from 6 million to 5 million), and it induces Japanese producers to increase their car production from 6 million to 7 million. Car producers in Japan are better off as a consequence of free trade, but Japanese consumers are worse off.

In this particular example, we have depicted the home country as the high-price country, which leads it to become an importer. If we were to focus on another good (perhaps wheat), the home country may well be the low-price country. In that event, we could construct the home excess supply and the foreign excess demand and find a new equilibrium price above the home equilibrium. The effect of free trade on the U.S. wheat industry would be analogous to the effect of free trade on the Japanese car industry. It would lead to higher wheat prices and increased wheat production, which would benefit U.S. producers but harm U.S. consumers.

Now, let's see how our excess-supply–excess-demand model can be used to analyze various trade restrictions. Figure 16.17 shows home and foreign car markets that are identical to those depicted in Figure 16.16. Therefore, *XD* and *XS* in panel (b) are identical to *XD* and *XS* in Figure 16.16. With free trade, the equilibrium price would again be $15,000. What would the consequences be if the home country engaged in protectionist practices? For example, what if the home country imposed a tariff of $4,000 per car on imports? Chapter 2 presented the economics of taxation. A tariff is simply a tax applied to imported goods. Here, we are considering a per-unit tax on imports. This tax raises the cost to the suppliers of imported cars by $4,000 per car, and it therefore displaces the supply of imports (Japan's excess-supply curve) upward by the amount of the tax. In Figure 16.17 this causes the excess supply to shift from *XS* to *XS'*.

As we learned when we studied the economics of taxation, a tax imposed on sellers falls partly on sellers and partly on buyers, depending on the slopes of the demand and supply curves. Therefore, the $4,000 tariff causes the equilibrium price to rise, but not by the full $4,000. In Figure 16.17 the new equilibrium *E'* is at a price of $17,500, where home buyers are willing to purchase only 1 million imported cars. By reducing the number of imported cars from 2 million to 1 million, the tariff causes the price to rise in the home country. With imports of 1 million, $17,500 is the only price that brings equilibrium to the home market.

But what about the foreign market? Although it may seem that the imposition of the tariff should raise prices there as well, we have to focus on the quantity of exports to see what happens to the foreign price. In the absence of exports, the foreign market clears at a price of $12,000, and the higher the quantity of exports, the higher the market-clearing price. Under conditions of free trade, when exports amounted to 2 million cars, the equilibrium price was $15,000. However, the tariff reduces the quantity of exports to 1 million cars, so it also reduces the equilibrium price in the foreign market. At a price of $13,500, the surplus in the foreign country is 1 million cars, so $13,500 is the equilibrium price.

It may seem strange that the foreign producers sell their cars for $17,500 in the foreign market but for $13,500 in the home market. However, keep in mind that the $17,500 they receive is a gross price, not a net price. For each car they export for $17,500, they have to surrender $4,000 to the home government. This means that, after the tariff, the net price of a car sold in either market is $13,500.

Our analysis suggests that the imposition of a tariff causes the volume of trade to fall from 2 million cars to 1 million. With fewer imports, the price in the home country rises. Home producers increase their production of cars from 9.2 million under free trade to 9.6 million after the tariff is imposed. Therefore, the tariff benefits producers by enabling them to sell more cars at a higher price. It harms consumers by increasing the price of cars.

The home country's decision to impose the tariff also has important consequences in the foreign market. It causes their price to fall, with producers

Figure 16.17 The Effects of a Tariff

Here we compare free trade with restrained trade. A tariff of $4,000 per car is imposed on imports. This displaces the excess-supply curve upward by $4,000. In panel (b) we see that the new equilibrium point is *E'* (instead of *E*), and we see that imports fall from 2 million cars to 1 million. Equilibrium in the home market is where excess demand is 1 million cars (distance *AB*) and that is at a price of $17,500. The foreign market clears at a price of $13,500 where their surplus (*A'B'*) is also 1 million cars.

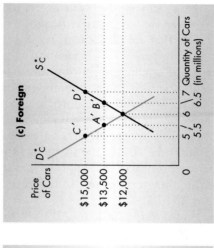

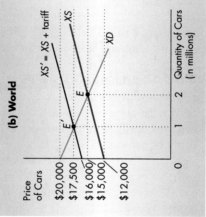

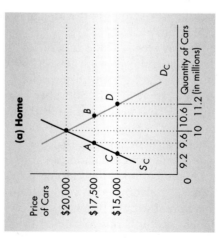

reducing their production from 7 million cars to 6.5 million. Consumers benefit because they are able to buy 5.5 million cars for $13,500 instead of 5 million at $15,000.

The Effects of Nontariff Trade Restrictions

Other protectionist policies have an impact that is similar to a tariff. For instance, we could consider the imposition of a 1-million-car quota or the negotiation of a voluntary export restriction under which Japanese producers agree to limit car exports to the home country to 1 million. (For an analysis of Japan's VER program on cars, see Highlight 16.3.) Given the home demand and supply, the 1-million-car quota and the 1-million-car VER will each have essentially the same impact as the $4,000-per-car tariff. Why? Because all three of these measures reduce home imports from 2 million cars to 1 million cars. In doing so, they all cause the price to rise from $15,000 to $17,500. The major difference in the three programs is that the tariff generates revenues to the home country's government.[7]

Highlight 16.3 *Voluntary Export Restrictions on Japanese Autos*

In the late 1970s and early 1980s, U.S. car production dropped sharply and U.S. car imports rose. Very quickly, Japanese producers increased their share in the U.S. market from less than 20 percent to about 30 percent of U.S. car sales. The consequence was a large drop in auto employment and large financial losses by U.S. auto producers that pushed the Chrysler Corporation to the brink of bankruptcy. As a consequence, a huge amount of pressure mounted on the new Reagan administration to get tough with Japan. However, that administration had come into office with a strong commitment to free trade, and the president was hesitant to suggest the enactment of either tariffs or quotas. Instead, the Japanese government and auto producers were induced (presumably under the threat of more drastic action) to agree to a "voluntary" reduction in their car sales in the United States. Japanese producers were limited to sales of 1.68 million cars in 1981–1983 and 1.85 million cars in 1984 and 1985.

The impact of this program was immediate. Car prices rose quickly, and U.S. auto producers moved into the black and were making record profits by

---

7. Under each of the restrictions, car prices will be $4,000 higher in the United States than in Japan. This $4,000 markup on cars shipped to the United States is captured by the U.S. government under the tariff program. Under a quota or a VER, this profit will be captured by Japanese exporters or American importers, depending on how the permits to import or export cars are allocated.

1985. The cost fell on auto consumers in the United States. Various estimates placed the price impact of the import restriction at between $600 and $1,700 per car, and the resulting reduction in consumer surplus clearly exceeded gains to U.S. auto producers.

The most surprising of the program's effects was on Japanese auto producers. Initially, they were quite adamant in their opposition; but when they saw car prices rising sharply in the U.S. market as they curtailed their exports, their reaction changed. It became apparent that U.S. demand for Japanese cars was sufficiently inelastic that, by restricting exports, the Japanese producers were able to increase their profits in the U.S. market. What the VER had done was to halt the Japanese auto companies from acting as competitors in selling cars in the United States. Those competitive actions had succeeded in increasing Japan's share of the U.S. market, but it had come at the cost of a greatly reduced profit margin. When they were forced to cut back the number of cars sold to the United States, the increase in unit profits more than offset the drop in the number of cars sold. In essence, what the VER succeeded in doing was to induce Japanese producers to behave as a cartel.

It is not surprising that since 1985, when the United States stopped requesting extensions in the agreement, the Japanese have voluntarily continued to restrict exports. In making these "concessions," the Japanese have stressed their eagerness to avoid trade friction with the United States. Many observers suspect that their real reason for making the concessions is that doing so increased their profits.

There are at least two other repercussions of the voluntary export restriction that are unfortunate. One is that since its enactment, Japanese producers have changed the mix of cars they ship to the U.S. market from small, fuel-efficient models to luxury models. There is good reason to believe that Japan's relative advantage was greater in the smaller models, so this move represents a movement away from efficiency.

A second repercussion is that it has led Japanese auto companies to produce cars in the United States. Currently, Japanese companies produce nearly as many cars in the United States as they ship from Japan to the United States. This production pattern is not necessarily consistent with the principle of comparative advantage.

From the perspective of the foreign country, each of the three policies has a similar effect. They all reduce the volume of exports from 2 million cars to 1 million cars, so each policy causes the equilibrium price in the foreign country to fall from the free-trade equilibrium of $15,000 to $13,500. Producers and consumers in the foreign country fare equally under all three programs.

We have seen that protectionist policies harm certain groups (consumers in the importing country and producers in the exporting country) and benefit other groups (producers in the importing country and consumers in the exporting country). Rather than stopping there, we can attempt to compare the gains and losses to the various groups. To do so, we can use the concepts of consumer surplus and producer surplus. The notion of consumer surplus was covered in Chapter 4. **Consumer surplus** is a measure of the surplus that consumers attain by purchasing goods. In that chapter we saw that one way of measuring consumer surplus was as the area under the demand curve but above the price line. For example, at the equilibrium price of $20,000 in Figure 16.18, consumers would receive a surplus equal to the area of triangle *ABC*. At a price of $15,000, consumers would buy 11.2 million cars and receive a consumer surplus equal to the area of triangle *AIG*. Therefore, a policy that causes the price to drop from $20,000 to $15,000 and enables consumers to increase the purchases of cars from 10 million to 11.2 million will enable them to increase their surplus from triangle *ABC* to triangle *AIG*. The change in consumer surplus, *CBIG*, shows how much consumers benefit from this change in policy.

Figure 16.18 The Effect of a Tariff or Quota on Consumer Surplus and Producer Surplus
Either a tariff or a quota can reduce imports to 1 million cars and drive the equilibrium price up from $15,000 to $17,500. This harms domestic consumers and benefits domestic producers. However, the loss in consumer surplus (the area bounded by *DFIG*) exceeds the gain in producer surplus (the area bounded by *DEHG*).

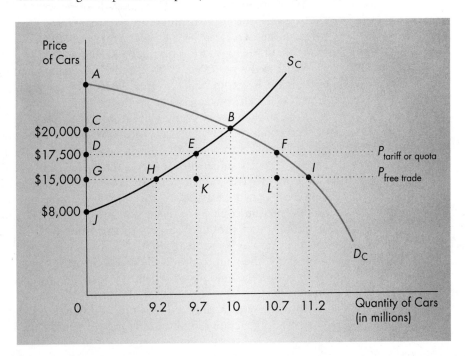

A similar concept, **producer surplus,** provides a means of measuring the gains producers attain by being able to sell different quantities at different prices. The supply curve S_C shows the marginal cost of producing cars. Any time a car can be sold for more than its cost, the producer profits. A measure of this surplus is the area below the price line but above the supply curve. For example, when the price is $20,000, producers sell 10 million cars. According to the supply curve, the cost of producing the cars ranges from $8,000, the number of dollars (represented by point *J*) for the first car, up to $20,000 for the final car produced and sold. The difference between $20,000 and the cost of each car is the producer surplus.

At a price of $20,000, the producer surplus is the area *CBJ*. If the price drops to $15,000 and output falls to 9.2 million cars, the producer surplus will fall to the area *GHJ*. The difference between the two surpluses represents how much producers are harmed (how much surplus they lose) because of free trade.

We can use these concepts to review the gains and losses from free trade and to evaluate protectionist policies. Initially, suppose that there is no trade and that the equilibrium price is $20,000. The consumer surplus is area *ABC* and the producer surplus is area *CBJ*. Then, suppose that free trade is permitted. The price will fall to $15,000, consumers will increase their consumption to 11.2 million cars, and their consumer surplus will rise to the area *AIG*. The movement from no trade to free trade enables consumers to gain the area *CBIG*. That area represents the increase in consumer surplus.

What about producers? With no trade, producer surplus is area *CBJ*. With free trade, producer surplus falls to area *GHJ*. Therefore, the difference between the two areas, area *CBHG*, represents the loss to producers as a consequence of the move from no trade to free trade.

What is the net effect of free trade? The gain to consumers (area *CBIG*) exceeds the loss to producers (area *CBHG*) by the area *BIH*. That area represents how much consumers and producers as a group gain under free trade.

We can then use consumer and producer surplus to analyze the net effects of protectionism. Suppose that initially we have a policy of free trade and that the government then enacts either a tariff or a quota, which reduces the volume of imports sufficiently to drive the price from $15,000 up to $17,500. Consumer surplus will fall from the area *AIG* to the area *AFD*. The difference between the two areas, *DFIG*, measures the loss to consumers. How does the producer's gain compare with the consumer's loss? The imposition of the tariff or quota causes producer surplus to rise from *GHJ* to *DEJ*. The increase in producer surplus is the area *DEHG*.

Clearly, the gain to producers is less than the loss to consumers. The area *EFIH* shows the amount by which the loss to consumers exceeds the gain to producers.

In the case of a tariff, there is one additional element we should consider — tariffs do generate revenue to the government of the home country. In this particular example, the revenues collected are $4,000 for each of the 1 million cars imported, for a total of $4 billion. In evaluating a tariff, we have to decide whether this revenue is worth the net cost to consumers and producers. In contrast to the tariff, neither quotas nor VERs generate any revenue to the government of the home country, although they do generate revenues to importers or exporters who obtain a permit to import or export a car.

We will not take the time to work step by step through an analysis of the impact of different trade policies on consumer surplus and producer surplus in the exporting country. We will summarize the results and suggest that you work through the details yourself. If the low-cost country goes from isolationism to free trade, the increase in producer surplus will exceed the decrease in consumer surplus. If the home country then engages in protectionism, consumers in the export country gain, but their gain is less than the loss to producers in that country.

The economic arguments in favor of free trade are quite powerful. However, because some parties gain from protectionism, there will always be some political pressure to enact protectionist measures. The net effect of trade restrictions, however, is to lower overall living standards.

Trade Imbalances and the Exchange Rate

Most Americans are acutely aware that the United States has had a large trade deficit with Japan and other countries in recent years. Many Americans, even those who really don't know what a trade deficit is, are convinced that it is a major economic problem. Critics have identified a large number of factors that, they argue, have caused the problem. Among other causes, they have placed the blame for the trade deficit on unfair trade practices by Japan, on laziness and incompetence by U.S. workers and management, on the failure of our education system to produce an adequate number of technically competent graduates, on the failure of the U.S. government to assist U.S. businesses in their efforts to export, on the failure of Americans to save, on the refusal of the Japanese to consume, on the failure of the U.S. government to balance its budget, and on the exchange markets that produce an overvalued dollar.

This is not the place to address all these arguments. Nor is it the place to engage in a comprehensive analysis of either exchange rates or trade imbalances. What we intend to do here is to use rather basic microeconomic analysis, first to gain an understanding of trade imbalances and then to see how exchange rates are determined. Finally we will examine the connection between trade imbalances and exchange rates.

Most people "know" that a trade deficit occurs when we import more than we export. However, it is impossible to import more than we export. Every transaction has two sides, even those between parties in different countries. At least in an accounting sense, every transaction involves the exchange of things of equal value. Therefore, in any time period when citizens of one country obtain $50 billion worth of various things from another country (when their imports from that country are worth $50 billion), their exports must total $50 billion in order to pay for their imports.

To take a simple example, suppose that the only transaction that occurs between the United States and Japan in some time period is that a car importer buys one car and sends the Japanese producer an IOU for $20,000. During that period of time, the U.S. imports $20,000 worth of cars and exports $20,000 worth of assets (IOUs). It is simply impossible for total imports to exceed total exports.

What, then, does it mean to say that the United States has a trade deficit? It means that the dollar value of certain types of imports exceeds the dollar value of the same type of exports. Specifically, it means that the dollar value of the goods and services that are imported exceeds the dollar value of the goods and services that are exported. We should note immediately that for this to be the case, exports of things other than goods and services must exceed imports of things other than goods and services. When someone refers to the trade balance, that person is almost always talking about the balance on the current account. Traditional accounting practices for international transactions distinguish between current-account transactions and capital-account transactions. In essence, the **current account** is where goods and services transactions are recorded; the **capital account** records the other transactions, which are financial in nature.

In any international transaction, something is brought into the country and something is sent out. Goods and services are recorded on the current account, other things on the capital account. Total exports must equal total imports, but total exports of goods and services need not necessarily equal total imports *of goods and services.*

Suppose that an American businessman ships a $5 million check to Toyota to pay for new cars. This transaction would be recorded as a $5 million import on the current account and a $5 million export on the capital account. Suppose that Toyota then takes the check and uses it to buy a piece of real estate in California, where it plans to build an office complex. The sale of real estate (an asset) would be recorded as an export on our capital account. The receipt of the check would be recorded as an import on the capital account. Total imports on the current account would be $5 million and total exports would be zero. On the capital account we would have $10 million in exports and $5 million in imports. This would represent a $5 million deficit on the current account — our exports of goods and services exceed our imports by $5 million. At the same time we would have a capital-account surplus of $5 million. Total exports of assets ($10 million worth) exceed total imports ($5 million) by $5 million. Any imbalance that exists on one account is offset by an opposite imbalance on the other account. If we have a large **trade deficit** with Japan, then we also have a large current-account deficit and an equally large capital-account *surplus.* In very simple terms, we have been exporting assets (stocks, bonds, real estate, and the like) to pay for the goods and services (cars, electronic equipment, and so on) that we import. Our total imports equal our total exports, but our imports of goods and services far exceed our exports *of goods and services.*

What is the connection between trade imbalances and exchange rates? To answer, we need to understand the market forces through which exchange rates are determined. Currently, most countries allow their currency to fluctuate in world markets, with the price (the exchange rate) being determined by demand and supply. For a particular example, consider the exchange rate between the yen and the dollar. Some individuals who initially hold yen would like to obtain dollars, presumably to spend in the United States. At the same time, others who hold dollars would like to obtain yen to spend in Japan. **Foreign-exchange markets** are where the two groups interact and establish market-clearing exchange rates.

Because most of us are more accustomed to thinking of the exchange rate as yen per dollar, it is easier for us to view the exchange market as the market for dollars. Demanders of dollars are those who wish to obtain dollars to buy American goods and services as well as American assets. In other words, the demanders of dollars plan to use the dollars they purchase either to import American goods and services (which appear on the current account) or to import American assets (which appear on the capital account). Suppliers of dollars are those who wish to obtain yen to buy goods and services (current account transactions) or to buy Japanese assets.

Initially, ignore any demanders of dollars who wish to buy American assets and any suppliers of dollars who wish to obtain Japanese assets. The only demand we consider is demand for dollars to buy American goods and services; the only supply we consider is the supply of dollars to obtain yen to buy Japanese goods and services.

Turn now to Figure 16.19 and note that we are measuring dollars on the horizontal axis and the price of the dollar in terms of yen on the vertical axis. The supply curve depicted there is labeled *goods and services.* It shows the number of dollars that are supplied for yen at each exchange rate in order to buy Japanese goods and services. We see that at an exchange rate of 50 yen per dollar, holders of dollars are willing to sell $250 billion per year to obtain yen to buy Japanese goods and services. At that exchange rate we are willing to import $250 billion of goods and services, so our current-account imports at that exchange rate would amount to $250 billion. Each point on the supply curve shows how large our current-account imports from Japan will be at the corresponding exchange rate.

Let's turn our attention now to the demand curve, labeled *goods and services.* That demand curve shows how many dollars holders of yen are willing to buy at each exchange rate in order to buy American goods and services. At 120 yen per dollar, they are willing to buy $350 billion to spend on American goods and services; at an exchange rate of 100 yen per dollar, they will buy

Figure 16.19 The Exchange Rate and the Current Account Balance

At an exchange rate of 100 yen to the dollar, holders of dollars would sell $400 billion to obtain yen to buy $400 billion worth of Japanese goods and services. At that exchange rate, holders of yen would spend $400 billion on U.S. goods and services, so the current account would balance. At higher exchange rates, our spending on their goods and services would exceed Japanese purchases of U.S. goods and services, and a deficit would exist on the current account.

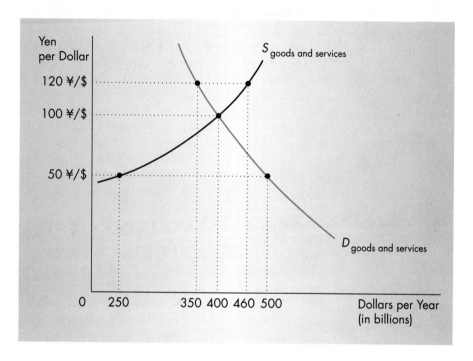

$400 billion of our goods and services, and at an exchange rate of 50 yen per dollar, they will be willing to buy $500 billion of American goods and services.

From Figure 16.19, we can determine what the current account balance will be at each exchange rate. At an exchange rate of 120 yen per dollar, holders of yen would elect to buy $350 billion to spend on American goods and services; holders of dollars would be willing to sell $460 billion to buy Japanese goods and services. At that exchange rate our current account imports would total $460 billion and our current account exports would total $350 billion. We would therefore have a current-account deficit of $110 billion.

As the exchange rate falls, the quantity supplied of dollars decreases, and our purchases of Japanese goods and services decline; the same decline in the price of the dollar leads the Japanese to increase their spending on U.S. goods and services. A weakening of the dollar leads to increases in our exports of goods and services and decreases in our imports of Japanese goods and services, so it leads to a reduction in our current-account deficit. Given the demand and supply in Figure 16.19, at an exchange rate of 100 yen per dollar, we are willing to spend $400 billion on Japanese goods and services; the Japanese are willing to spend $400 on our goods and services. At that exchange rate, our current account would be in balance. At exchange rates *below* 100 yen per dollar, Japanese spending on U.S. goods and services would exceed our spending on their goods and services, so we would have a surplus on the current account equal to the difference between the demand and supply curves. At an exchange rate of 50 yen per dollar, our current account surplus would be $250. In this framework, a current account deficit is caused by the exchange rate being above 100 yen per dollar, or, using the jargon of international trade, by the dollar being "too strong."

To see why the exchange rate need not be 100 yen per dollar, focus on Figure 16.20. The figure reproduces the demand and supply of goods and services from Figure 16.19.

However, in Figure 16.20, we see that what determines the equilibrium exchange rate is the *total* demand and supply, not just some *component* of demand and supply. In exchange markets, buyers of dollars seek to obtain dollars, not just to buy American goods and services but also to make capital-account purchases. Similarly, holders of dollars do not sell dollars solely to buy Japanese goods and services. They also sell dollars to obtain Japanese assets. Therefore, the equilibrium exchange rate can be above or below 100 yen per dollar, depending on the size of the asset component of the demand and supply.

In Figure 16.20, S_{total} is obtained by horizontally summing the goods-and-services component of the supply curve that we discussed earlier plus S_{assets}, which shows how many dollars' worth of Japanese assets holders of dollars would be willing to buy at each exchange rate. In Figure 16.20, adding S_{assets} does not markedly shift the supply curve outward, which indicates a relatively weak demand by Americans for Japanese assets. The total demand, D_{total}, is obtained by adding the Japanese asset demand to their goods and services demand. Here D_{total} lies far to the right of $D_{goods\ and\ services}$, indicating that Japanese demand for American assets is strong relative to our demand for their assets.

In Figure 16.20 the equilibrium exchange rate is 120 yen per dollar. At that exchange rate, the current account deficit is $110 billion — holders of dollars spend $460 billion on Japanese goods and services, whereas the Japanese spend only $350 billion on U.S. goods and services. At that exchange rate our capital-account surplus is also $110. Because our total spending in Japan is $570 billion, $460 billion of which is on Japanese goods and services, the remaining $110 billion must be used to purchase Japanese assets. Our exports of assets total $220 billion — the difference between the total Japanese spending of $570 billion and the $350 billion they spend on U.S. goods and services.

Figure 16.20 The Equilibrium Exchange Rate
Equilibrium in the exchange market occurs where total Japanese demand for U.S. dollars to buy U.S. goods, services, and assets is equal to our total supply. If their demand for our assets is quite strong and our demand for their assets is relatively weak, the equilibrium exchange rate (120¥/$) will lead to a U.S. current-account deficit of $110 billion per year and a U.S. capital-account surplus of equal size.

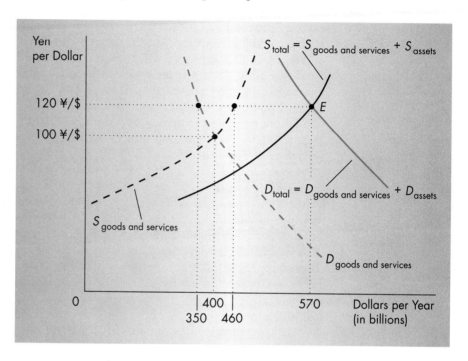

Now, let's return to the question of what causes a country to experience a current-account deficit. In Figure 16.20 we can see that anything that decreases Japan's demand for our assets will reduce our trade deficit; anything that increases our demand for Japanese assets, or that increases Japanese demand for our goods and services, or that reduces our demand for their goods and services will have the same effect.

It is important to note two final points: (1) Our attempt to explain a current-account deficit does not imply our endorsement for the notion that such a deficit is necessarily a problem. Under many circumstances, it is advantageous for a country to run a deficit. (2) It probably makes no sense to worry inordinately about a large trade imbalance with any one country. If specialization according to comparative advantage takes place, there is no reason why a given country should not have large current-account deficits with certain trading partners and offsetting current-account surpluses with other trading partners.

Summary

In this chapter we have seen that the economic consequence of exchange between individuals or companies in different countries is essentially identical to that of trade between two individuals or companies within the same country. In either case, voluntary exchanges tend to improve the well-being of both the buyer and the seller. We have seen that attempts by the government to regulate international trade tend to lower living standards. This conclusion is perfectly in line with our previous analysis of government interventions in domestic markets.

In reaching this conclusion, this chapter has focused on important differences between international trade and domestic trade. In particular, we have

- developed two complementary models of international trade that illustrate the principle of comparative advantage and explain the benefits of specialization and trade in accordance with comparative advantage.
- developed a graphical model that shows the economic impact of trade restrictions like tariffs, quotas, and voluntary export restraints.
- introduced the notion of a foreign-exchange market and shown how the flow of imports and exports relates to the foreign-exchange market.

Key Terms

pattern of trade	Ricardian Trade Model
unit labor requirements	absolute advantage
principle of comparative advantage	terms of trade
consumption-possibilities frontier	Specific-Factors Model of Trade
protectionism	tariff
quota	Voluntary Export Restriction
domestic-content legislation	excess supply
excess demand	consumer surplus
producer surplus	current account
capital account	Trade Deficit
foreign-exchange market	

Sample Questions

Question

According to the Ricardian Trade Model, is it possible for two countries with identical production-possibilities frontiers to specialize and engage in mutually-advantageous trade? Answer the same question using the Specific Factors Trade Model.

Answer

The Ricardian Model of Trade implies constant opportunity costs and a linear production-possibilities frontier. Therefore, each country has the same opportunity cost of producing each good. With no difference in opportunity costs, there are no comparative advantages and no possible mutual gains from trade.

In contrast, the Specific Factors Model implies that each of the two goods is produced under conditions of increasing costs. Therefore, even though each country has the same production-possibilities frontier, the two countries will not produce at the same point on that frontier unless the pattern of demand is the same in each country. Assuming that demand for good X is stronger in the home country, production of X will initially be larger at home than in the foreign country. The home country will thus find its opportunity cost of X to be greater, causing the foreign country to have a comparative advantage in X and the home country to have a comparative advantage in Y. The two countries can trade advantageously if the foreign country increases its X production and the home country reduces X production, with the foreign country then exporting good X and importing good Y.

Question

Suppose that the United States decides to impose an import tariff on Japanese-made cars that is sufficiently large to completely end imports from Japan. What impact would this have on the yen/dollar exchange rate?

Answer

Initially, a major component of the dollar supply in the foreign-exchange market is from U.S. importers who supply dollars to obtain yen to purchase Japanese cars. The imposition of the tariff will eliminate this component of the dollar supply and cause the dollar to rise against the yen.

Questions for Review and Discussion

1. It is sometimes argued that the decision to open an economy to international trade benefits consumers in that country but harms producers. Do you agree?

*2. In Figure 16.1, with free trade the home country imports 3 million cars. Suppose that in the home country the production of 3 million cars would employ 30,000 workers in "good" jobs. Do you agree that free trade costs the home country 30,000 "good" jobs?

3. A diplomat from a small country once expressed opposition to free trade because "his country was at a comparative disadvantage in the production of all goods." Is it possible to change the unit labor requirements in

Table 16.3 in such a way that the foreign country has a comparative disadvantage in both wine and linen? Explain.

*4. A country wants the best possible terms of trade. Does this mean that an ideal trading partner is a country in which workers are exceedingly productive? A country in which workers are exceedingly *un*productive? Can you think of an ideal characteristic of a trading partner?

5. In Figure 16.5, regardless of whether the world demand is D_W or D_W', the home country specializes entirely in wine and the foreign country specializes entirely in linen. Can you draw a demand curve that would lead the foreign country to produce some wine? Can you draw a demand that would lead the foreign country to produce *only* wine?

6. The home country whose production-possibilities frontier is depicted in Figure 16.8 is assumed to have 1,000 units of terrain, 100 units of capital, and 1,000 workers. What would happen to its production-possibilities frontier if the capital stock increased to 150 units? What if the labor force increased to 2,000 workers?

*7. Suppose that a country's stock of capital rises. What effect, if any, will this have on the country's opportunity cost of producing wheat? Explain.

8. The supply curve for cars depicted in Figure 16.9 is based on the home country having 100 units of capital. What would happen to that supply curve if the country's capital stock increased?

*9. Suppose in Figure 16.12 that the two countries produce the combination of wheat and cars indicated by the point at which the two production-possibilities frontiers intersect. Is that an efficient pattern of production? Explain.

10. Suppose that the home country initially produces the bundle of goods represented by P_0 in panel (a) of Figure 16.14 and that the foreign country initially produces the bundle represented by P_0^*. Suppose that the two countries refuse to change their production pattern. Would it be possible for the two countries to trade profitably without first altering their production? Does the position of a country's consumption-possibilities frontier depend on whether it alters its production pattern when it enters into international trade?

*11. Suppose that in Figure 16.16 the foreign demand for cars rises. What will happen to the number of cars imported by the United States?

12. Figure 16.17 shows that the imposition of a tariff of $4,000 per car reduces the number of cars that the home country imports. Is it possible to impose a tariff that would eliminate all car imports? How large would such a tariff have to be?

*13. Suppose that the United States has a capital-account surplus of $120 billion and that we import $480 billion worth of goods and services. Can you tell how many dollars' worth of goods and services we export?

14. Currently the United States has a fairly large current-account deficit with Japan. What would happen to that deficit if the United States became less willing to acquire Japanese assets? Use a graph to explain.

Problems for Analysis

1. The United States is currently in the process of establishing free trade with Mexico and with Canada. Of the two countries, which do you think will turn out to be the better trading partner? Why?

*2. The Ricardian Model of international trade considers only two goods. Suppose that, in addition to wine and linen, the two countries also produce corn. Does the notion of comparative advantage make any sense in a world of more than two goods? Explain.

3. One issue that is proving to be a major obstacle to world trade agreements is agricultural subsidies. In addition to the United States, Japan, and Canada, many of the members of the European Community, such as France and Italy, subsidize agricultural production. One consequence of these policies is that each of the countries attempts to export large surpluses of its subsidized farm output. The other countries view this as unfair. Use a graphical model to analyze the economic consequences of export subsidies. Specifically, how would it affect the United States if Mexico subsidized the export of tomatoes to the United States?

4. Countries throughout the world differ widely with regard to the combinations of productive inputs they possess. Some countries are atypical in that their resource endowment consists of large quantities of one or two productive inputs and minute quantities of other inputs. For example, France and Japan have large amounts of technically skilled labor and lots of capital but little unskilled labor; India has a lot of unskilled labor and fertile land, but little skilled labor or capital. Other countries (perhaps Mexico, Spain, and Poland) are more typical in that their endowments of productive inputs are more in line with the world as a whole. Do you think typical countries like Poland or atypical countries like India have the most to gain from trade? Explain. Is the United States a typical country or is it an atypical one?

*5. Prior to the reunification with East Germany, West Germany was richly endowed with capital and skilled labor and had relatively little unskilled labor. Not surprisingly, West Germany exported much of what it produced and imported much of what it consumed. In contrast, East Germany was a country with much good land and a lot of unskilled or semiskilled labor but with little skilled labor or capital. Do you think that unified Germany will be as dependent on trade as West Germany was? Explain.

6. Imagine a situation in which the United States trades freely with Japan and U.S. car imports total 2 million per year. Suppose that Japanese auto producers adopt new techniques for producing cars that are substantially more efficient than current ones. How will Japan's technological advance in car production affect the United States? Use a graph to explain your answer.

7. Suppose again that under conditions of free trade, the United States imports 2 million cars per year from Japan. If, for some reason, we wanted to reduce imports to 1 million cars per year, there are at least two ways of reaching this goal. One is to impose a tariff on Japanese cars that is just sufficient to reduce our imports to 1 million cars. A second way is to impose a 1-million-car quota on imports from Japan. From the U.S. perspective, does it make any difference which of the two policies is adopted? Explain.

8. Suppose that the United States passed a law that limited foreign investments in the United States. What effect would this law have on the price of the dollar in exchange markets? How would this affect our imports and exports of goods and services?

Answers to Selected Questions and Problems

Chapter 1

Questions for Review and Discussion:

1. The primary reason for the failure of the Soviet system to satisfy consumer demands was that the costs and benefits faced by decision makers in centrally planned economies did not reflect economic reality. Experience has shown that the efficient production, distribution, and exchange of goods and services in an economy occur most readily in a market economy in which the price mechanism is allowed to function freely.

3. If you are considering spending an hour watching soap operas, there are many alternative uses of that time. You could watch a news show, study for an hour, clean your room, play basketball. Just because some of the alternative uses may have no value to you does not imply that watching the soap operas has no cost. The cost of watching the soap operas is the highest-valued alternative use because that is what you would have done had you not watched the soap operas.

4. One must also consider the opportunity costs faced by the individual consumer. If we are observing a corporate executive who must do her household shopping the one hour after work but before picking up her children from daycare, then the discount store may not be the cheaper place to shop, given the high opportunity cost placed on her time.

7. The shared living area in such arrangements involves many of the problems associated with public goods — goods for which consumption cannot be blocked. The upkeep and cleanliness of the area, although for the benefit of all involved, may be ignored because property rights are not clearly established.

10. Whether or not the act is consciously undertaken, most students make decisions as to how much time to spend studying for an exam at the margin. For example, facing constraints on the time that can be devoted to preparing for one of many exams, a student will allocate time among subjects so as to maximize the total gain on all exams. After you graduate, you may consider entering a professional program or going on to graduate school. In making this decision, you are likely to consider the type of job you will be able to obtain *without* further education. In this way, you will be considering the marginal costs of additional education, which means that your decision will be based on marginal analysis.

11. Yes. The benefits of theft are the goods taken from their rightful owner. Costs are related to the probability of being caught, prosecuted, and sentenced or maybe even shot as an intruder. To alter the behavior of a thief, you can install a burglar alarm or other anti-theft device to increase the probability of capture. Video cameras in convenience stores also serve the

purpose of increasing the probability of being caught by the police. Signs telling shoplifters that the store will prosecute may also deter crime.

13. A seniority system does not encourage quality performance. Performance will be only good enough to avoid getting fired. Because police officers are employed to capture criminals and gather sufficient evidence for prosecution, it may be better to base police officers' pay on the number of criminals captured, prosecuted, and sentenced.

Problems for Analysis:

1. (a) An alternative expression might be "Drive 95! Save Time!" Such alternatives reflect the multidimensionality of choice. For each individual, the benefits from saving lives, time, or any other valuable resource must be evaluated at the margin.

   (b) First, it is necessary to clarify the meaning of "well" in the expression. If "well" refers to equating marginal benefits and marginal costs, then the statement holds true from an economic point of view. For example, in studying for an exam that is not a vital part of your final grade, you must consider the opportunity cost of the time that could be devoted to another subject in order to allocate time between the two in such a manner as to achieve the maximum total benefit.

3. Probably not. Suppose that without detectives, theft would cost the manager $250,000 per year. Even if she could completely eliminate theft by hiring four detectives at an annual cost of $160,000, the decision to do so might not be rational. She would also have to consider how much theft would occur with fewer than four detectives in order to determine at what point hiring detectives no longer pays on the margin.

Chapter 2

Questions for Review and Discussion:

1. An individual demand curve shows how much of a particular good a consumer will desire at each given price level; a market demand curve reflects the purchase decisions at alternative prices for all buyers in the market. In order to obtain the market demand curve for a single commodity, we sum the individual demand curves horizontally across prices. For example, if at a price of $2 consumers A, B, and C choose to buy 1, 2, and 3 hamburgers, respectively, then the total market demand for hamburgers at that price is 6.

4. Because flour is an input into the final product of pizza, an increase in its price will translate into an increased cost of pizza. Each individual supplier of pizza will face a higher marginal cost, which will result in a decrease in individual supply curves and a corresponding shift in the market supply curve. Such a shift causes the price of pizza to rise and results in a decrease in quantity demanded.

5. As shown on the accompanying graph, if the market price temporarily falls below the equilibrium level, then the quantity offered for sale will fall short of the quantity demanded at that price ($Q_S < Q_D$). The excess demand will induce suppliers to increase price and produce more. As producers are induced by the higher price to offer more for sale and consumers are prompted by the higher price to buy less, equilibrium in the market will be restored (P^*, Q^*).

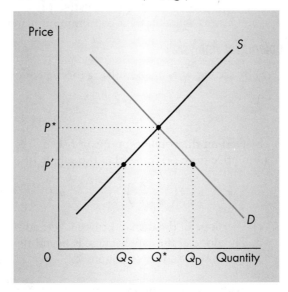

8. In effect, tougher regulations on entrance into a profession tighten the supply and thereby allow those who are already established to procure higher prices for their services. Barbers and carpenters therefore have incentives to push for higher licensing requirements in their respective fields. When entry into a profession is unrestricted, the effect is to reduce the average wage rate to all participants in that market.

9. The demand curve illustrates the maximum prices one is willing to pay in order to acquire various quantities of some good or service. If we assume that an individual is rational, then the marginal-benefit curve is identical to the individual's demand curve where marginal benefits are expressed in dollars. The supply curve shows how many units a seller will be willing to sell at each possible price. To a price-taking seller, price is equal to the marginal revenue of selling additional units. Profit maximization occurs at the point at which marginal revenue equals marginal cost. Therefore, the marginal cost curve gives us the profit-maximizing quantity at each and every price. If we assume that sellers desire to maximize profit, the supply curve is the same as the marginal-cost curve.

11. Tennis balls and rackets are complementary goods. An increase in the

price of rackets can therefore be expected to result in a decrease in the demand for tennis balls.

13. An increase in across-the-board drug enforcement would have the effect of making high-potency drugs less expensive relative to their low-potency counterparts. This results from the fixed cost imposed on both goods by the increased risk encountered by lawbreaking. Increased enforcement translates into higher transport costs across the board, and the full price of illegal drugs rises. As the relative price of high-potency drugs falls, many buyers will alter their consumption patterns accordingly.

Problems for Analysis:

1. (a) By setting $q_D = q_S$ and solving for the equilibrium price we obtain

$$p = \frac{(a + n)}{(m + b)}$$

(b) Finding the equilibrium quantity requires us to substitute the equilibrium price from (a) into either the supply or demand equation:

$$q_D = a - b\left(\frac{a + n}{m + b}\right) \quad \text{or} \quad q_S = m\left(\frac{a + n}{m + b}\right) - n.$$

(c) The slope of the demand curve is $-b$ and the intercept is a.

(d) The slope of the supply curve is m and the intercept is $-n$.

5. Using a graph similar to Figure 2.15, we can answer both parts of this question.

a. In the initial equilibrium, the equilibrium quantity of turkeys is Q_E. The price for whole turkeys is P_W. Breasts and legs are priced at P_B and P_1, respectively.

b. An increase in the demand for turkey breast shifts the demand curve for turkeys from the initial demand of EFG to $E'F'G'$. The new equilibrium quantity is Q_E' and the price for whole turkeys remains at P_W. The price for turkey breast increases to P_B', while the price for wings falls to P_1', as expected.

Chapter 3

Questions for Review and Discussion:

5. The marginal rate of substitution (MRS), which is the slope of the indifference curve, represents the maximum amount of good Y a consumer is willing to give up to obtain an additional unit of good X. A diminishing MRS corresponds to a decreased willingness to give up units of good Y for additional units of good X as consumption of X increases. As illustrated in the text, convexity implies that an indifference curve gets flatter as we move down along it and, therefore, that the MRS decreases.

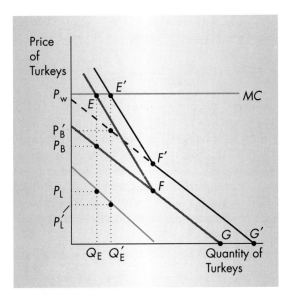

7. When a consumer is faced with a choice between economic goods and bads, the resulting indifference curves will be positively sloped. For example, a nonsmoker considers secondary smoke to be a bad but views income as desirable. As illustrated in the diagram, if a person is subjected to increased smoke inhalation and utility is to be held constant, more income is necessary to compensate for having to consume the bad — we move northeast along the indifference curve.

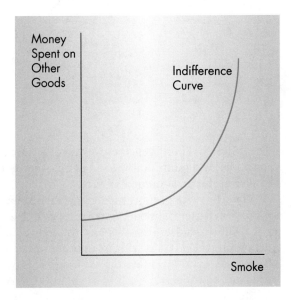

9. Income can be defined as $M = P_X Q_X + P_Y Q_Y$. Dividing both sides by P_Y and solving for Q_Y we get

$$Q_Y = \frac{M}{P_Y} - \left(\frac{P_X}{P_Y}\right) Q_X$$

which is the budget line. The intercept is M/P_Y and the slope is the ratio of prices or $-(P_X/P_Y)$.

11. When the budget line is steeper than the indifference curve, as at point A in the accompanying graph, the marginal cost of X (which equals the slope of the budget line) exceeds the marginal benefit of X (which equals the slope of the indifference curve). To maximize utility, purchase less X. The optimal consumption bundle is at point E, where the indifference curve and the budget line have the same slope.

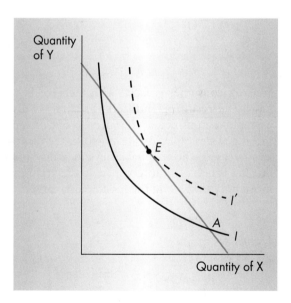

14. The MRS for indifference curves incorporating a composite good illustrates the maximum dollar value of all other goods a consumer is willing to give up for an additional unit of good X.

15. A fall in the price of food will decrease the slope of the budget constraint, making it flatter. The amounts of food and wine consumed at the new price will depend on the shape of the individual's indifference curves. By definition, the MRS of all three consumers will be equal in equilibrium, because all consumers face the same prices; however, quantities consumed need not be equal.

Problems for Analysis:

4. Much like the *Playboy* and *Playgirl* examples cited in the text, the marginal utility obtained from buying *Sex* is diminished if prepurchase viewing of its revealing photos is allowed. If customers are prevented from "browsing" through the contents of the book, the marginal utility at the time of purchase is higher than it otherwise would be.

8. No. As shown in the accompanying graph, the price change alters the slope of the budget constraint, making it steeper. An increase in income will cause a parallel shift of the budget constraint outward. Budget line *MM'* reflects the change in both income and price. The slopes of the budget constraint and indifference curve will no longer be equal at point *D*. The consumer can still purchase bundle *D* but instead will choose a bundle such as *Z* and reach a higher indifference curve.

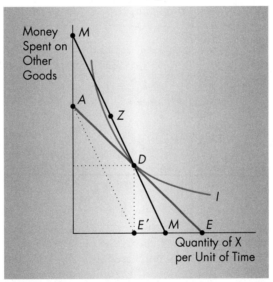

Chapter 4

Questions for Review and Discussion:

2. A price-consumption curve shows the relationship between the price of a good and the consumer's purchases of it. The slope of this curve tells us whether demand is elastic, inelastic, or unit elastic. The curve is constructed by drawing a line connecting the optimal points on alternative budget constraints. A negative slope indicates that demand is elastic, and a curve with a zero or positive slope reflects a unit-elastic or inelastic demand, respectively.

3. When constructing a demand curve from the information provided in an indifference map and an initial budget line, we are holding constant income, tastes and preferences, and the prices of other goods. In this manner we are able to determine the consumer's response to variations only in the price of the good in question — say, clothing. Allowing the price of clothing to vary and taking the utility-maximizing commodity bundles from the indifference map, we can then plot the demand curve showing the different quantities of clothing demanded at the various prices.

5. Assuming that steak is a normal good, the income and substitution effects will reinforce one another and result in an increase in the consumption of steak. Even if one were to claim that steak is an inferior good, the substitution effect would override the income effect and consumption would increase.

8. In order to calculate the price elasticity of demand, we must first find

$$\% \text{ change in quantity} = \frac{180}{(320 + 500)/2} = \frac{180}{410} = 0.44$$

$$\% \text{ change in price} = \frac{-\$10}{(\$65 + \$55)/2} = \frac{-\$10}{60} = -0.166$$

and then we compute

$$e_D = \frac{-0.44}{-0.166} = 2.65$$

10. The interpretation of a downward-sloping portion of the price-consumption curve is that with a reduction in the price of X, spending on other goods decreases, whereas spending on X rises. In order for this to occur, the quantity of X purchased must increase by more than enough to offset the price reduction. If the percentage change in quantity is greater than the percentage change in price, the implication is that demand is elastic.

12. If we know the price elasticity for the good in question, we can determine the effect of a price change on total expenditure. If demand is elastic, price increases will result in a decrease in total expenditure on the good or service. Total expenditure on the good will rise following a price increase if demand is inelastic. In the case of unit elasticity, no change in total expenditures results from either an upward or a downward change in price.

14. As illustrated in the graph, the tangency points between the budget line and the indifference curve will initially fall to the left of the original point as income rises but will eventually shift to the right.

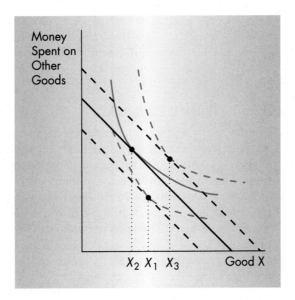

16. The two measures of consumer surplus may differ because the demand-curve approach includes the income effects of price changes, whereas the indifference-curve approach excludes such effects. Although the difference between the two may be small, the measurements will only coincide when the income effect of a price change is zero.

17. Because the slopes of indifference curves indicate a consumer's willingness to give up one good in order to obtain an additional unit of another good, the relative slopes of two individuals' indifference curves tell us the opportunities for trade available between the two. As long as the slopes of the two curves differ, there is an incentive for trade to continue. When the slopes are equal, there is no gain to be had from trade.

Problems for Analysis:

2. The cross-elasticity of demands for parakeets and canaries is calculated as

$$\ell_{CP} = \frac{\text{\% change } Q_d \text{ of X}}{\text{\% change in price of Y}} = \frac{12/[(23+35)/2]}{5/[(15+20)/2]} = 1.448$$

A positive cross-elasticity implies that the two birds are substitutes and, therefore, that a rise in the price of one of them will result in an increase in the demand for the other. We are assuming that the demand for parakeets did not change and that the rise in the price of parakeets caused the demand for canaries to increase such that (at the original price of canaries) purchases rose from 23 to 35.

12. Yes. The law of demand states that price and quantity demanded are

inversely related, other things being constant. Increasing household income violates the *ceteris paribus* assumption and causes an increase in demand rather than a movement along the demand curve.

Chapter 5

Questions for Review and Discussion:

3. At the below equilibrium price shortages will occur; that is, quantity demanded will exceed quantity supplied. In an unregulated market, forces would act to bring quantity supplied and quantity demanded into equilibrium. This shortage will persist until either the ceiling is removed or supply and demand change to eliminate the surplus. Producers of the fruit are clearly hurt as prices are held artificially low. Consumers, except for the few who are still able to purchase the limited number of oranges or grapefruit, are also injured as they are forced to do without a product for which they are willing to pay. Consumers may be forced to compete for the limited number of goods in some type of nonprice rationing scheme. Producers of substitutes for oranges and grapefruit may realize a gain as shortages in those markets translate into increased demand for their substitute product.

4. If a government desires to decrease the consumption of some particular good or service, the tax-rebate scheme is appropriate. Altering relative prices will cause consumption of the taxed good to fall. Rebating the tax revenue increases the income of those paying the tax, but the after-tax consumption will still be below that of pre-tax levels. If the rebates were directly tied to consumption, no change in behavior would result. Equal rebates, however, are not based on a particular individual's consumption, so the incentive to alter consumption of the taxed good is effective.

8. The families who benefit most from the current system of subsidiary public education are the families whose tastes and incomes are such that the quantity of education they would purchase for their children is similar to the quantity provided by public schools. In contrast, families who would choose much larger or much smaller quantities of education than that provided by the public schools benefit little.

Problems for Analysis:

1. School districts differ with respect to the amount of education they provide and the taxes that are assessed. Each jurisdiction therefore provides the family with a consumption point that represents the number of units of education provided by the local schools and a number of dollars to spend on other goods equal to the family income minus local school taxes. Therefore, if a family can attain a higher indifference curve by moving to another jurisdiction, it may make sense for the family to incur the costs associated with the move.

4. The students would have an incentive to avoid parking tickets. Each student will receive a rebate equal to the average fine for all students. Because the parking behavior of any one student will have a minor impact on the student average, each time a student receives an additional ticket the student will incur a cost almost equal to that of the fine because the rebate will barely increase.

Chapter 6

Questions for Review and Discussion:

1. The major advantage of team production is that it enables individual workers to become highly specialized, thus increasing their productivity. The major disadvantage is that shirking is likely to increase, because it becomes more difficult to detect.

3. The formation of a partnership is a good way to deal with shirking, because it forms a direct link between the firm's financial success and the financial rewards to each partner.

7. The total-product-of-labor curve shows the maximum amount of output possible with different quantities of labor, holding the quantity of all other inputs constant. Typically, a total-product curve goes through three ranges. Initially, it rises at an increasing rate. In an intermediate range, it rises at a decreasing rate until it reaches a maximum. Beyond that point, the use of additional workers causes output to fall.

11. The decision to employ labor in stage III is incompatible with profit maximization. In stage III the marginal product of labor is negative. It makes no sense to spend money employing additional workers if the effect is to reduce output.

13. Assuming that units of capital are measured on the vertical axis, the marginal rate of technical substitution is equal to $\Delta K/\Delta L = -3/5 = -0.6$. This number tells us that, in this range of input usage, one can keep the level of output constant by adding three-fifths of a unit of capital each time that labor is reduced by one unit.

14. Returns to scale measure the proportionate change in output relative to a proportionate change in all inputs. If some percentage change in all inputs leads to a larger percentage change in output, returns to scale are increasing. If the resulting percentage change in output is smaller than the percentage change in inputs, there are decreasing returns to scale. Constant returns to scale exist when the percentage change in output is equal to the percentage change in inputs.

Problems for Analysis:

2. Large firms do have a problem with shirking by inspectors. To solve this problem, they devise ways of tracing poor inspection to a particular inspector. For example, clothing manufacturers have inspectors place an

identifying number ("inspected by #22") in the pocket of clothing. Car manufacturers place identification numbers on cars, which enable them to determine which workers and inspectors were responsible for defective cars. Restaurant chains employ anonymous inspectors who pose as customers in order to detect establishments that fail to maintain quality standards.

3. Hostile takeovers are most likely to occur when existing management fails to operate the firm so as to maximize profits. Stock prices reflect current corporate profits and expectations about future profits. If management fails to maximize current or future profits, the price of its stock will be lower as a consequence. This lower price provides an opportunity for a corporate raider to buy the company's stock, improve the profitability of the firm, and make a large profit from the resulting run-up in the price of the stock.

Chapter 7

Questions for Review and Discussion:

2. The presence of economic profits in an industry shows that resources invested there earn higher returns than elsewhere. Although there is no guarantee that economic profits will continue in the future, profit-seeking investors are always looking for an opportunity to realize an above-normal return on their investments.

6. The firm should employ less labor and more capital. An additional dollar spent on capital will cause output to rise by more than output will fall as a consequence of spending one dollar less on labor. Therefore, the decision to spend more on capital and less on labor will cause output to increase at no additional cost.

7. The long-run expansion path shows optimal combinations of input usage for each level of output, assuming a fixed level of technology and a fixed set of input prices. To derive an expansion path, we construct a series set of parallel isocosts, each reflecting a different level of resource expenditure. Along each isocost, we find the point of tangency with an isoquant. These points reflect the cost-minimizing method of producing each level of output, and a line connecting these points is called an expansion path.

10. The first important characteristic of a total-variable-cost curve is that it passes through the origin. This shows that the total variable cost of producing zero units of output is zero dollars, because units of the variable input would not be employed if the firm elected to produce no output.

   The second important characteristic is that, initially, total variable costs rise at a decreasing rate. When we discussed short-term average-product-of-labor curves (Chapter 6), we saw that, initially, the average product of labor increased. In this range, Q/L is rising. If Q/L is rising, L/Q is falling. The total variable cost is equal to $L \times w$. If L/Q falls as Q rises, the number of dollars spent on labor increases as output rises, but at a decreasing rate.

The third important characteristic is that, beyond some point, the total-variable-cost curve rises at an increasing rate. This occurs because the average-product-of-labor curve eventually declines.

11. The total variable cost is equal to wL. The average variable cost is wL/Q. Therefore, $\$10(5)/20 = \$50/20 = \$2.50$.

13. They are equal. If the marginal cost is below the average cost, the average cost must be falling. If the marginal-cost curve is above the average-cost curve, the average-cost curve is rising. At the minimum point on the average-cost curve, the average cost is neither rising nor falling, so the marginal cost must equal the average cost.

Problems for Analysis:

1. An income (profit) statement is compiled by subtracting *explicit* costs from revenue. Because the statement ignores *implicit* costs, the reported profit figures exceed the true *economic* profits by an amount equal to the implicit costs. Therefore, income statements of firms systematically overstate economic profits.

The extent to which profits are overstated depends on the extent to which the firm uses resources that are owned by the firm.

4. The output of the two firms will not necessarily be equal. Production theory tells us that there is some maximum level of output that can be produced by either of the firms, given the assumed quantities of resources. However, because of shirking and other inefficiencies, each of the firms is likely to produce less than the maximum possible amount. How much less depends on the degree of inefficiency.

The proper interpretation of a cost curve is that it shows the lowest possible cost (either average or total) of producing each level of output. In this sense, cost curves are frontiers that represent complete efficiency. The two firms in question are likely to operate at some point above the cost curve because of inefficiency.

Chapter 8

Questions for Review and Discussion:

2. If a buyer has the power to influence the price, then the buyer cannot determine how many units of a good he would be willing to buy at any particular price unless he knows how many units he could buy at other prices. The same is true for producers in their decision to offer goods for sale. The market demand and supply curves on which the competitive model is based make sense only when "atomistic" buyers and sellers have no control over the price.

3. The market for barbers is not perfectly competitive. One reason is that

licensing requirements prevent free entry into the market. In addition, individual barbers have some control over their price, because they offer somewhat differentiated products at geographically separated locations.

There is much rivalry between barbers. Every barber is aware that other barbers provide quite similar services, so they are motivated to minimize waiting time, engage in witty conversation, and so forth, to keep current customers and attract new ones.

5. Heterogeneous products or services indicate that a market is not *perfectly* competitive. However, the broad range of choice is evidence of rivalry by competing firms trying to survive or get ahead in a highly competitive market.

9. Profits are the difference between total revenue and total cost. To determine where profits are maximized, you have to determine the level of output at which total revenue exceeds total cost by the widest margin. This occurs at the point at which the slope of the total-revenue curve is equal to the slope of the total-cost curve.

12. A firm always has the option of shutting down and limiting its losses to its fixed costs. Therefore, it should shut down whenever all the alternatives to shutting down result in losses that exceed the firm's total fixed costs. This occurs whenever the firm is unable to generate a total revenue that is sufficient to pay the total variable costs at any positive level of output.

15. In an increasing-cost industry, the expansion of output by the industry has the effect of increasing the price of inputs used in that industry. The consequence is that the long-run industry supply curve slopes upward because the average cost increases as industry output increases.

17. The law of one price says that if information is perfect and if there are no transactions costs, a single price will prevail across the market for all buyers and sellers.

This law is closely related to the notion of opportunity cost. The opportunity cost of selling an item to a particular buyer is, at minimum, the price (marginal revenue) that can be obtained by selling to another buyer. No one will sell at a low price if he knows that he can sell at a higher price.

In a world in which there are transactions costs, the law of one price pertains to the full price. If a good is available across town for $10, the highest price I can obtain for it is $10 plus the transactions costs associated with going across town to buy the item.

21. Free entry assures that economic profits are only a short-run phenomenon. If economic profits exist in the short run, new firms will enter. This will increase the industry supply and drive the price down until economic profits are eliminated.

Problems for Analysis:

1. The imposition of a price ceiling at the wholesale level reduces the quantity of shoes shipped to shoe retailers. Therefore, it reduces the number of shoes that can be sold at the retail level. Because the demand for shoes at the retail level is elastic with respect to price, the price at the retail level will rise but by a percentage that is less than the percentage reduction in the number of shoes sold. Total revenue to shoe retailers will therefore fall.

3. The results would be as follows:
   a. The industry demand would increase in both the short and long runs.
   b. In the short run, the profits of alligator farmers would rise. In the long run, entry of new firms would decrease the equilibrium price and (probably) increase the costs of harvesting alligators, which would eliminate economic profits.
   c. In the short run, cattle farmers would incur economic losses (negative profits) as demand switched to alligator meat and away from beef. In the long run, firms would exit the beef industry, and profits would return to normal levels.
   d. Because initially there is a fixed supply of experienced alligator hunters, the price would rise in the short run. In the long run, more alligator hunters would gain experience, causing the wage to fall, though probably not to the initial level.
   e. The price of alligators will rise in the short run. In the long run, new firms will enter the industry, causing the price to fall. Whether the price will stabilize above the initial level, at the initial level, or below the initial level depends on whether the industry is an increasing-, constant-, or decreasing-cost industry.
   f. The price of swamp land in Louisiana will rise in the short run. It will remain higher in the long run unless there is sufficient swamp land elsewhere to accommodate the increase in alligator farming.
   g. Alligator skin is jointly supplied with alligator meat. The increase in the production of alligator meat will lead to an increase in the supply of alligator skins, causing the price to fall in the short and long run. The supply of alligator shoes will rise because of the decrease in the price of an input, causing the price of alligator shoes to fall.

Chapter 9

Questions for Review and Discussion:

2. Patents and copyrights represent barriers to entry. They are important because they enhance a firm's ability to preserve its monopoly position.

6. As the only seller in a market, a monopolist is able to search along its demand curve and select the price-quantity combination that is most

profitable. To do this, the monopolist produces the quantity of output at which its marginal revenue equals its marginal cost. The firm then charges the price that will induce buyers to buy that quantity of output.

8. Efficiency requires production of each good or service at the level at which the marginal benefit to consumers (the market demand) is equal to the marginal cost. To maximize profits, a monopolist produces at the point at which marginal revenue equals marginal cost. Because the monopolist's marginal-revenue curve lies below the market demand curve, this leads to a less-than-optimal level of production.

10. Price discrimination occurs when different buyers are charged different prices for the same product. In order to profitably engage in price discrimination, the seller must have some monopoly power, sell to buyers who differ in their willingness to pay for the product, and be able to prevent resale.

12. Although it is inefficient to permit an existing product to become monopolized, this does not mean that it is inefficient to grant monopoly power to the developer of a new product. If pharmaceutical companies are enabled to enjoy monopoly profits from the sale of new drugs, these companies are provided with an incentive to carry out research and development.

13. Advertising can be used to gain and maintain the loyalty of buyers to a particular product brand. In this way it might increase the monopoly power of the firm that undertakes the advertising. However, advertising is also used by firms that attempt to enter a market in competition with a monopolist. All things considered, advertising probably does more to reduce monopoly power than it does to create that power.

14. False. A monopolist that fails to minimize costs may be able to earn economic profits, but such behavior is inconsistent with maximizing economic profits. Monopolists can always increase their profits by reducing their costs, so they have every incentive to do so.

18. No. The monopolist will charge a price above the competitive equilibrium and sell less than the competitive equilibrium quantity. What happens to total revenues depends on the demand elasticity. The monopolist will end up producing at some point at which demand is elastic, whereas the competitive equilibrium may have been at an elastic, unitary elastic, or inelastic point on the demand curve. Therefore, it is possible for the total revenues to increase, decrease, or remain unchanged.

Problems for Analysis:

4. It is wise for the owners to price tickets so that they equate marginal revenue and marginal cost. If this occurs at a price of $25 per ticket with 40,000 tickets being sold per game, the pricing policy is wise even though the stadium might have a capacity of 60,000 seats. The owner could lower the price and sell more tickets, but it would reduce profits.

5. It is possible to discriminate in both types of markets. However, it is impossible to increase profits by price-discriminating unless resale can be prevented. Because it is generally impossible to resell services (I can't transfer my haircut or my oral surgery to you) but much easier to resell goods, price discrimination should be more frequent in the service sector.

Chapter 10

Questions for Review and Discussion:

1. Chamberlin's model is similar to the competitive model in that it assumes free entry. It is similar to the monopoly model in modeling the firm demand as downward sloping.

5. The firm depicted in the accompanying graph produces Q_0 units of output, sells at a price of P_0, and realizes an economic loss. This firm's total revenue exceeds its total variable costs, so it should remain in business in the short run. If the firm's demand is below its AVC, then the firm should shut down in the short run.

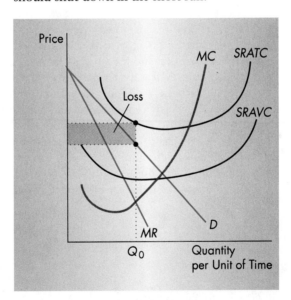

6. The tangency solution depicts an industry with a large number of firms, each producing on the downward-sloping portion of the average-cost curve. Neglecting the value of choice to consumers, this model suggests that consumers would be better off if product differentiation was eliminated, causing the price to fall to the minimum point on the average-cost curve.

8. The quality of a search good is discerned from advertising and from

research done by the prospective buyer. The quality of an experience good is discerned from past experience in using the good. The quality of a credence good is never really discerned, even after purchase and use.

11. Each prisoner has an incentive to behave in a noncooperative way. In the Thelma-and-Louise example (Table 10.1), each is better off confessing, regardless of what the other does.

15. Cartels are more stable when it is hard for member firms to cheat on the cartel agreement without being detected. Cartels that sell a homogeneous product tend to be more stable than those that sell differentiated products, because undetected nonprice cheating is an ongoing problem if the product is not homogeneous. Cartels are more stable if there is a small number of members, because it is easier to detect both price and nonprice cheating with fewer participants.

Questions for Analysis:

1. Yes. As rival firms increase their advertising in an attempt to acquaint more and more buyers with their product, the effect is to increase the extent to which typical buyers are aware of the presence of competing products. Therefore, an unintended consequence of advertising is that buyers become better informed about alternatives, which increases the elasticity of their demand for a particular product.

3. Agree. Although it is easy to draw a market demand curve on a blackboard, it is extremely difficult to estimate real market demand curves. This makes the job of a monopolist difficult. But the job of an oligopolist is even *more* difficult. The oligopolist not only needs to know the market demand but also has to try to anticipate the price policy of his rivals. Even if he succeeds in determining the position of the market demand curve, he will fail in his attempt to estimate his own demand curve unless he correctly anticipates the behavior of other firms and the reaction of buyers to that behavior.

Chapter 11

Questions for Review and Discussion:

1. In markets in which only the seller has reliable information about the quality of the good being offered for sale, a reduction in price causes buyers to fear that the product is a "lemon." Decreases in the price lead to decreases in demand. In the extreme, sales of the item fall to zero.

3. If a firm is interested in expanding beyond its own market area to compete with an established firm elsewhere, a very attractive strategy is for the firm to offer its products at low prices in the new market. However, such pricing practices are often declared illegal under the Robinson-Patman

Act. To the extent that the act frustrates firms in their attempt to enter new markets, it succeeds in protecting established firms and is anticompetitive.

6. Full-service outlets have higher costs than discount stores, which sell products while providing little service to the buyer. Unless the full-service outlet is given the exclusive right to sell in a certain area, it will be unable to compete with the discounters. Customers who are interested in buying a particular product (perhaps a computer or a camera) will go to the full-service outlet to obtain detailed information about the product, and then buy from a discounter. Afterward, they may call on the full-service outlet for warranty work and other services. The discount stores are able to free-ride in providing information and customer services, and full-service outlets may disappear from the market.

   Full-service outlets argue that customers prefer higher prices and full service to low prices and no service. Unless exclusive territories are established, customers will be deprived of the price/quality combination they prefer.

9. In the case of natural monopoly, the market demand is likely to equal the marginal cost at a point at which marginal cost is below average cost. If a price equal to marginal cost is established, the regulated monopolist will be unable to break even, so some type of subsidy will prove necessary.

   A solution to this problem is to set the price equal to average cost at the point at which the demand crosses the average-cost curve. This results in a level of output that is less than the efficient level, but it avoids the need to subsidize the enterprise.

12. Such a firm may practice limit-entry pricing. This is a strategy by which the monopolist elects to establish a lower price than the one that would maximize short-run profits. By keeping the price low, outside firms may be deterred from entering the market. The firm sacrifices current profits to increase future profits.

Problems for Analysis:

5. There are some advantages. If the regulatory process quickly adjusts the regulated price to assure that the regulated firm never enjoys profits or suffers losses, the firm has no incentive to minimize costs. Whether output is produced at a cost of $5 per unit or $10 per unit, profits will be the same — zero in both cases. However, if the price is fixed at some level for an extended period, the firm is given a strong incentive to minimize costs. This regulatory scheme may bring about lower prices to consumers. If so, it will be preferred by all affected parties.

   This proposed change has some disadvantages. If the firm faces unavoidable cost increases (if the prices of inputs rise), the firm will suffer economic losses and could be driven into bankruptcy.

7. Young males have more auto accidents than their female counterparts. As a consequence, they pay higher insurance premiums. If auto companies were forced to offer collision insurance at uniform rates to young men and women, the rates would initially fall for men and rise for women. The proportion of men who would elect to buy the insurance would rise, whereas the proportion of women with insurance would fall. The problem of adverse selection would be made worse.

Chapter 12

Questions for Review and Discussion:

1. Inputs are of value to a firm only to the extent that their employment generates output of final goods that are demanded by consumers. Demand by the firm for these inputs is derived from the demand for the final goods.

    Examples are endless. The demand for carpenters is derived from the demand for new homes. The demand for open land on which to build a new golf course is derived from the demand to play golf. The demand for cattle is derived from the demand for beef.

2. If a firm employs an additional unit of any input, it will be able to produce more output and generate more revenue. The value of the marginal product of that unit of input is the extra revenue that results from the sale of the additional output. If the employment of an additional farm worker causes wheat output to rise by 50 bushels per day and the farm's revenue to increase by $400 per day, the value of the marginal product is $400. It would be irrational not to hire that worker if the daily wage is less than $400. If the wage of farm workers is $80 per day, the farm could increase its profits by $320 per day by employing an additional worker. It should continue to add workers until the value of the marginal product falls to $80.

5. The elasticity of resource demand is a measure of the responsiveness of the quantity of the resource demanded to changes in the resource price. Specifically, it equals the percentage change in the quantity of the resource demanded divided by the percentage change in the resource price.

    The elasticity of demand for a particular resource depends on the price elasticity of demand for the final product, the amount of time buyers have to respond to the change in the resource price, the availability of easily substitutable inputs, and the importance of the input in determining the cost of the final good.

7. To understand an individual's response to a change in the wage rate, it is useful to think of the substitution effect and the income effect. If an individual's wage rate falls, the effect is to reduce the cost of leisure, which

induces the worker to substitute leisure time for work time. It also reduces real income, which can affect the decision to consume leisure.

In the accompanying graph, at an initial wage rate of w_0, the individual maximizes utility at point E_0 where he consumes l_0 units of leisure. When the wage rate falls to w_1, the constraint becomes flatter, and utility is maximized at point E_1 where l_1 units of leisure are consumed. The substitution effect is the movement from E_0 to E_A, and the income effect is shown by the movement from E_A to E_1. In that graph, leisure is a normal good, and the income effect works in the opposite direction of the substitution effect. However, because the substitution effect swamps the income effect, the reduction in the wage rate reduces work time and increases leisure time.

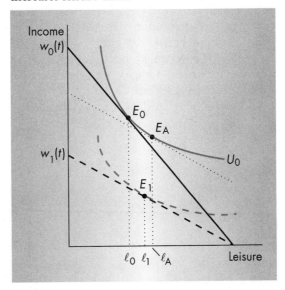

9. Labor markets are segmented because workers differ with regard to their skills, occupations differ with regard to the skills that are required, and both workers and jobs have a geographic dimension. There is not just one big labor market in which a single, uniform wage rate is determined. Instead, there are hundreds of thousands of labor markets that determine the wage of certain types of workers in certain areas. These markets are interconnected by the willingness and ability of workers to move from location to location and from occupation to occupation and by the willingness of businesses to relocate and to modify the skills required to fill a particular job.

12. Capital provides productive services over a long period of time; other inputs generally yield services only in the current time period. Therefore, the current demand for capital is affected by the future value of the capital

equipment. A major determinant of the future value of capital is the time value of money. The higher the market interest rate, the higher the discount that must be placed on future yields from capital equipment.

Problems for Analysis:

2. The accompanying graph shows the situation of a worker who is paid $10 per hour for the first 8 hours worked per day and then $15 per hour for overtime. The effect of premium pay for overtime is to change the constraint from the straight line *DC* to the kinked line *ABC*.

  What will happen to the number of hours worked when premium pay for overtime is introduced depends on the indifference map. For a worker who initially elects to work 8 or fewer hours, a premium for overtime will either increase or have no impact on the number of hours worked. (To confirm this, draw an indifference curve on the graph that is tangential to *DC* at points between *B* and *C*.) For an individual who initially selects some point between *D* and *B*, the offer of premium pay for overtime can increase, decrease, or have no impact on the number of hours worked. The substitution effect will be toward more work time, but the income can work either way, depending on whether leisure is normal or inferior.

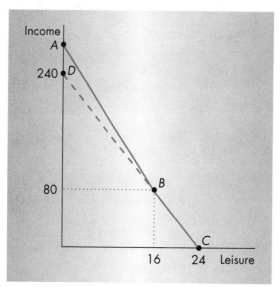

3. To the extent that a greater number of television channels makes leisure time more desired, indifference maps will be affected. Specifically, indifference curves will become steeper, reflecting the increased willingness to give up income for leisure. With steeper indifference curves, workers will tend to select points farther down their constraints, where the quantity of leisure is greater.

Chapter 13

Questions for Review and Discussion:

1. Monopsony is a market situation in which there are many sellers but only one buyer. A monopsonist is similar to a monopolist in one important way — each can affect the market price. By increasing output, a monopolist depresses the selling price; by employing less of an input, a monopsonist is able to reduce the price of that input.

2. A monopsonist is a price maker — the more of an input the monopsonist buys, the higher the price that must be paid. Because the monopsonist faces the upward-sloping market supply curve for each input, the marginal-factor-cost curve also slopes upward.

7. Discriminating monopsonists behave in a way that is closely analogous to a discriminating monopolist. In the case of a discriminating monopoly, prices are raised in a less-elastic market and lowered in a more-elastic market. Similarly, a monopsonist lowers wages in a less-elastic market and raises them in a more-elastic market, compared with the nondiscriminatory outcome. By reducing the employment of workers whose supply is inelastic, the monopsonist can drive the wage down markedly. He can then hire more workers whose supply is elastic without having to raise the wage by much.

8. To engage in perfect wage discrimination, you must determine the lowest wage at which each worker is willing to continue to work. If you negotiate separately with each employee, every one will have an incentive to overstate her reservation wage. The time that you would have to spend determining the true reservation wage (assuming that this would ever by possible) would be so great as to make the search impractical (noneconomical). A monopsonist has an incentive to obtain some information about employees and to engage in some wage discrimination, but it would never pay to devote enough resources to practice perfect wage discrimination.

11. To attract members, unions have to succeed in raising wages. To do this, they must increase demand for the labor services of union members, reduce the supply of those services, or prevent price competition among their membership. If they are able to increase demand for union membership, they can also increase the employment of their members. Otherwise, they can drive up wages only by reducing the level of member employment.

   If the union raises wages by restricting supply or by preventing wage competition, the demand for nonunion labor (a substitute for union labor) rises. If, however, the union is able to drive wages up by increasing demand, it is likely to switch demand from the nonunion sector to the union sector. In that case, employment and income in the nonunion sector will fall.

12. Included in the various goals of each of these organizations is the promotion of the economic well-being of their membership. The means by which they can achieve this goal are identical to those available to labor unions. Although their rhetoric might be very different, they too work to reduce supply and increase demand.

Problems for Analysis:

1. Suppose that we can conveniently divide faculty into two categories — those with strong community ties and those without such ties. For the first group, the decision to move elsewhere for alternative employment is a costly one. Not only would another university have to come up with a much better offer to get such faculty to move; the current employer could reduce their salary substantially before inducing them to move elsewhere. As a group, their labor supply is relatively inelastic.

   A university administrator seeking to conserve resources tries to avoid giving pay increases to those who will remain in their position without such raises. The administrator will lose fewer faculty if he denies pay raises to those with community ties than by denying pay raises to the more mobile group.

3. Figure 13.9 shows that the use of any particular parcel of land is determined by the marginal-revenue product of that parcel in alternative uses. As population rises, the marginal-revenue product of land used for housing will increase. However, the rise in food prices that accompanies population growth will also increase the marginal-revenue product of the land in agriculture. This means that population growth will lead to rising land prices — it does not mean that government regulation is necessary to prevent conversion of farmland to housing.

Chapter 14

Questions for Review and Discussion:

5. Welfare analysis is a particular type of cost-benefit analysis in which costs and benefits are calculated from demand and supply curves. It is useful in examining the impact of a change in a market equilibrium in which all the costs are imposed on either buyers or sellers of a particular good or service and all the benefits accrue to either buyers or sellers. The benefit of a particular change is measured as any increase in either the consumer or producer surplus; the costs are measured as decreases in the two surpluses.

8. *Ad valorem* taxes are favored by governments because their proceeds are automatically adjusted for inflation. This is preferred by politicians as an alternative to having to go repeatedly to the voters to ask them to approve an increase in, say, a lump-sum tax.

12. Taxes and subsidies are similar in that both generally have the impact of reducing economic welfare. They are also similar in that they both tend to lead to an inefficient level of output of the taxed or subsidized good. They differ in that taxes reduce consumer and producer surplus; subsidies increase consumer and producer surplus.

14. This is an example of a price floor, and it is often referred to as a price-support program. By maintaining a price above the equilibrium level, it leads to an increase in the quantity produced and a decrease in the quantity purchased. The resulting surplus is purchased by the government and generally disposed of in some way that will not affect the demand.

Problems for Analysis:

1. In some ways, sin taxes are identical to other taxes — they drive a wedge between the buyer and seller, thereby reducing the equilibrium quantity.

   However, there are differences. Ordinarily, when a good or service is bought and used, the purchase and use affect only the buyer and seller. Therefore, the traditional welfare analysis of this transaction, which considers only the consequences to the buyer and the seller, is appropriate. However, the purchase and use of some goods produce externalities. For example, the consumption of alcohol may impose costs on third parties to the extent that consumers of alcohol are involved in more traffic accidents, and so on. The supply curve (which reflects the private costs of production) fails to include the external costs. If a sin tax is imposed, correct welfare analysis takes into account both the reduction in private costs and the reduction in costs to third parties. Therefore, a sin tax may be welfare enhancing.

Chapter 15

Questions for Review and Discussion:

2. This is an example of a positive externality. Neighbors of the person who installs the light will benefit from the increase in their safety. At the same time, this might impose negative externalities on other parties. Certain neighbors might feel that the light adds little to their safety while greatly disrupting their sleep. Potential robbers might view the light as a negative externality in that it interferes with their ability to commit thefts. If so, they might solve the "problem" by destroying the light.

4. Given the assumptions underlying the Coase theorem, it makes no difference who owns the property rights because the outcome will be the same. Suppose that party A is engaging in an activity that harms party B and that the value to A is greater than the cost to B. If A is given the property rights to continue, the amount that B is willing to pay for A to stop is less than the value to A; so the activity will be continued. If B is given the right to prevent A from engaging in the activity, the amount that A will

be willing to pay to continue the activity will be enough to induce B to sell the rights to A. In either case, the outcome is the same. Further, the efficient outcome is achieved under the two alternative assignments of property rights.

6. The Pigouvian solution makes no attempt to internalize an externality by establishing property rights in the manner of Coase. Instead, it is an attempt to tax negative externalities and subsidize positive externalities in order to artificially eliminate any difference between private and social costs. If a tax that equals the marginal external cost is imposed, a producer will be induced to take externalities into account when making production decisions.

9. Public goods are goods whose consumption is complementary rather than competitive; that is, if anyone is able to consume an additional unit of a public good, everyone else is also able to consume one more unit. Another characteristic of public goods is that it is impractical to exclude nonpayers from consuming them.

13. Assuming that Bowen-Samuelson prices are charged to a demander of a public good, there are two consequences to underrevealing one's preferences: (1) it leads to a lower level of output of the public good, and (2) it reduces the individual's tax price. Where the number of "voters" is large, the decision by any one voter to underrepresent preferences has little impact on the quantity that gets produced, but it can greatly reduce the tax price. Therefore, the advantages of reduced taxes are likely to exceed the disadvantages of receiving too little of the good, so understating one's preferences is advantageous.

15. These two demands are essentially complementary. A room that is made available during the week is available for weekend use with only a slight additional cost.

Problems for Analysis:

2. Public parks and recreational areas are generally available to the public free of charge or at a nominal admission fee. Accordingly, each potential visitor compares his marginal benefit with the price in deciding whether to visit. In doing so, the visitor rationally ignores the congestion costs that he imposes on others. The consequence may be attendance that far exceeds that which equates marginal costs and benefits.

   If the same area were operated on a for-profit basis, the owner would exercise his property rights by taking into account the externalities associated with congestion. By charging higher admission fees, he can increase the total enjoyment that visitors receive, even though there are fewer of them.

3. This argument has considerable merit. The current system of regulating airline safety has at least two flaws that could be handled by private assignment of liability:

(1) Regulations often fail to achieve given reductions in risk as cheaply as possible. For example, safety is undoubtedly improved by government restrictions that greatly limit the number of hours a pilot can fly in a given time period or that require one or more copilots on certain aircraft. However, there may be alternative actions that provide equal increases in safety but that cost less. In the absence of regulation, airlines would implement the latter in lieu of the former.

(2) There is no way of assuring that the level of safety produced by government regulation will be the optimal level. Those who make the regulations may have little incentive to balance the benefits of increased safety against the costs. Accordingly, the regulatory approach may mandate an excessively high level of safety.

Chapter 16

Questions for Review and Discussion:

2. No. That is a clear overstatement of the jobs lost because of imports. In the absence of trade, car prices would rise to $20,000 and domestic production would rise to 8 million units — not to 9 million units. Therefore, the number of jobs lost is less than 30,000.

4. How productive workers are in another country is relevant to absolute advantage, but not to comparative advantage. An ideal trading partner is one whose opportunity costs differ from ours by the greatest possible margin. This is the case if the trading partner is twice as productive in one good and 100 times as productive in a second good. It is also the case if the trading partner is one-half as productive in one good and 1/100 as productive in another.

7. This would increase the opportunity cost of producing wheat. Because the increase in capital would make labor more productive in cars, as labor is taken out of the car industry to produce an additional unit of wheat the cost in terms of cars gets higher. This would increase the maximum possible number of cars that could be produced, causing the country's graphed production-possibilities frontier to become flatter. The flatter the PPF, the lower the opportunity cost of cars (good X) and the higher the opportunity cost of wheat (good Y).

9. No. At that point, the home country's PPF is steeper than the foreign country's PPF. This means that the last car produced at home has a greater opportunity cost than the last car produced abroad. In an efficient pattern of production, the home country produces fewer cars and the foreign country produces more.

11. The increase in foreign demand would increase the equilibrium price abroad, causing the foreign *XS* to fall. This would cause the equilibrium price in the world market to rise as the number of cars imported by the United States falls.

13. If we have a capital-account surplus of $120 billion, our current-account deficit must also be $120 billion. That means that with imports of goods and services of $480 billion, our current-account exports must be $120 billion less, or $360 billion.

Problems for Analysis:

2. The notion of comparative advantage continues to make sense with more than two goods, but it is less clear. The reason is that the opportunity cost of producing one good (say, wine) can be calculated in terms of either linen or corn. In fact, a country might find that when it produces wine, its opportunity cost is higher than that of its trading partner in terms of linen but lower in terms of corn. In a case like this, to determine comparative advantage it is necessary to calculate the opportunity cost in terms of some average of the other goods.

5. The unified Germany is probably more typical (in terms of resource endowments) than either the former East Germany or the former West Germany. Because the gains from trade are largest for atypical countries, the unification of Germany will likely lead her to become less dependent on world trade.

Index

Note: Page numbers followed by n indicate footnotes.